MOSCOW
SPLENDOURS OF THE
ROMANOVS

MOSCOW
SPLENDOURS OF THE
ROMANOVS

SKIRA / GRIMALDI FORUM MONACO

Cover
One of the Kremlin Gates in Moscow
Photography circa 1890
IMAGNO/Austrian Archives
Album. Coronation of His Majesty the emperor Alexander III
St. Petersburg, 1883
© State Historical Museum, Moscow

Design
Marcello Francone

Editorial Coordination
Emma Cavazzini

Editing
Michele Abate

Layout
Paola Oldani

Translations
From French to English: Nancy Guri
Duncan Le Diascorn

Printed and bound in Italy. First edition

ISBN 978-88-572-0256-3

Distributed in North America by Rizzoli International Publications, Inc., 300 Park Avenue South, New York, NY 10010.
Distributed elsewhere in the world by Thames and Hudson Ltd., 181a High Holborn, London WC1V 7QX, United Kingdom.

www.skira.net

Credits

RUSSIA
© State Historical Museum, Moscow.
Photos: G. Sapozhnikov, M. Kravtsov, V. Boyko, E. Borisov, I. Sedenkov, A. Grachev, V. Mochugovsky.
pp. 16, 18, 19, 21, 26, 27, 34, 39, 41, 43, 44, 46, 47, 51-53, 66, 69-71, 73-75, 77, 79, 81, 84, 87, 89, 90, 91, 93- 97, 99, 101-104, 106, 109, 110, 113, 115- 120, 122, 134, 137-139, 142-143, 147, 148, 150, 152-158, 190, 228, 230, 233, 252, 261, 263
© The Link of Times Foundation
pp. 160, 162-173
© The State Museum Preserve "Tsarskoye Selo", St. Petersburg 2009
pp. 21, 36, 45, 254, 255, 256-259, 262, 265
Ekaterina and Vladimir Semenikhin collection
pp. 28, 31, 33, 274, 276, 277
Russian State Cinematographic and Photographic Archives, Moscow
pp. 23, 198, 250, 260, 261
The State historical-cultural museum-preserve "The Moscow Kremlin"
pp. 54, 57-63
The State Tretyakov Gallery, Moscow
pp. 29, 30-32, 236, 239-249

FRANCE
© Bibliothèque nationale de France
pp. 176, 177
© Boucheron
pp. 179, 181, 188, 195
© Boucheron. Photos : Mr Alain Lantz.
pp. 174, 178, 196
© Elysée Museum, Pierre Gilliard's funds, Lausanne
pp. 136, 141, 144-145, 268, 270-273
© Mellerio dits Meller
p. 194
Baccarat archives
p. 216, 217, 219-221, 223
Heritage collection, Baccarat
p. 214, 218, 220
Bibliothèque des Arts Décoratifs, Paris.
Photo: Suzanne Nagy.
p. 180
Cartier archives © Cartier
p. 199, 201, 202
Photos N. Welsh, Cartier collection © Cartier
pp. 182-184, 186, 195, 196, 200
Boissonas & Taponnier, 1912 © Cartier
p. 192
Chaumet Paris collection
pp. 185, 199, 204-206
Karin Maucotel © Paris-Musées
pp. 209-212
Van Cleef & Arpels archives
p. 189

MONACO
Prince's Palace of Monaco. Photo: Gaëtan Luci.
p. 187

Courtesy of Sotheby's Picture Library
p. 185
© Austrian Archives / CORBIS
p. 197
© La Collection / Imagno
pp. 20, 48
© Photos : Alexandre Viktorov
pp. 234, 235
© Sebastian Rosenberg, ParisBerlin>fotogroup
pp. 24-25, 124, 126-133, 224, 226, 229, 231, 232

GRIMALDI FORUM MONACO

10 Avenue Princesse Grace
MC 98000 Monaco
www.grimaldiforum.com

President
Jean-Claude Riey

General Director
Sylvie Biancheri

Director of Cultural Events
Catherine Alestchenkoff

Building Director
Guy Caruana

Director of Events
Gérard Nouveau

Administrative and Financial Director
Marc Rossi

Director of Communication
Hervé Zorgniotti

Communication Managers
Nathalie Varley
Cécile Valentin

Assistant to the Director of Cultural Events
Alfonso Ciulla

Coordination of Workshops
Laetitia de Massy

Monaco
His Excellency Mr. Jean-Paul Proust, Minister of State
Mr. Paul Masseron, Government Advisor for the Interior
Mrs Sophie Thevenoux, Government Advisor for Economy and Finance
Mr. Alexandre Orlov, the Russian Federation Ambassador to France
Mr. Claude Pallanca, the Russian Federation Honorary Consul to Monaco

Moscow
Mr. A. Avdeev, the Russian Federation Minister of Culture

EXHIBITION AND CATALOGUE

Curator

Brigitte de Montclos
Curator-in-chief of Patrimony, Honorary Curator of the Graphic Arts Department at the Carnavalet Museum

Guest curator – "Jewelry and Imperial Commands" section

Wilfried Zeisler
Graduate of the Ecole du Louvre, PhD, and Professor at the Sorbonne (Paris IV)

Authors (by order of publication):
B. de Montclos
L. Tarasenko
S. Amelekhina
N. Suetova
T. Sizova
N. Skorniakova
T. Mosjoukhina
N. Ougleva
W. Zeisler
M. Lerch
L. Iovleva
I. Bott
I. Zaitseva
D. Girardin

Editing Assistant
Céline Vacquier

Registrar
Thierry Vincent assisted by Christian Selvatico

Exhibit Design
Métaphore{s : François Payet
Assisted by Myriam Rose and Ugo Stefanini

This exhibition has been made possible through the support of:

CMB
Compagnie Monégasque de Banque
OFFICIAL PARTNER

ACKNOWLEDGMENTS

We would like to express our deepest gratitude to all those who loaned works for this show, to collectors, and to directors of public and private institutions whose generous participation has made this exhibition possible:

RUSSIA

The State Historical Museum, Moscow
Alexander Shkurko, Director
Tamara Igumnova, Vice Director, Department of International Affairs and Exhibitions

The Museum of Ceramics and the 18th Century Kuskovo Estate
Serguei Avdonine, Director
Pogocian Natalia Valerieva, Vice Director
Enikeeva Tatiana Ivanovna, Chief Curator

The State Historical and Cultural Museum-Preserve "Moscow Kremlin"
Elena Gagarina, General Director
Zelfira Tregulova, Deputy Director for Exhibitions
Maria Bogoslovskaya, Exhibitions coordinator

The State Tretyakov Gallery, Moscow
Valentin Rodionov, Director
Lidia Iovleva, Vice Director

The Link of Times Foundation
Victor Vekselberg, Founder
Vladimir Voronchenko, Chairman of the Board of Trustees

The Russian Federation State Archives, Moscow
N. Kalantarova, Director
Elena Koloskova, Head of Department exhibitions and Publications of Archival documents

The State Museum "Tsarskoye Selo", Saint-Petersburg
Olga Taratynova, Director
Iraïda Bott, Vice Director
Liudmila Kanaeva, Exhibitions coordinator

FRANCE

Maison Baccarat, Paris
Hervé Martin, General Director
Michaela Lerch, Curator of the Baccarat museums
Guillaume Gellusseau, Director of marketing and communication
Igor Baschet, Commercial director
Jean-Christophe de Monspey, Regional commercial manager

Maison Boucheron, Paris
Jean-Christophe Bedos, Chief Executive Officer

Maison Cartier, Paris
Pierre Rainero, Director of Patrimony
Nadia Cretignier, in charge of logistics for the Cartier Collection
Renée Frank, exhibitions coordinator for the Cartier Collection
Pascale Lepeu, Curator of the Cartier Collection
Betty Jais, archivist, Maison Cartier, Paris
Hélène Ribatet, exhibitions department, Cartier Collection

Maison Chaumet, Paris
Béatrice de Plinval, Curator of the Museum and of Patrimony in charge of external affairs
Mélanie Sallois, assistant to the Patrimony and to external affairs

Mellerio *dits* Meller
Olivier Mellerio, President Mellerio International
François Mellerio, President Mellerio *dits* Meller
Laurent Baty, General Director Mellerio *dits* Meller
Emilie Bérard, in charge of the Patrimony
Diane-Sophie Lanselle, press attaché in charge of communications

Van Cleef & Arpels Collection
Catherine Cariou, Director of Patrimony

Musées de la Citadelle, Villefranche-sur-mer
Madeleine Servera Boutefoy, Curator-in-Chief of the Citadelle Museums

Observatoire Océanologique de Villefranche-sur-Mer
Monsieur Mantoura, Director

Musée des Beaux-Arts, Palais Carnolès, Menton

MONACO

Hervé Irien, Secretary General of the Art Objects Commission of HSH the Prince of Monaco, Prince's Palace

SWITZERLAND

Musée de l'Elysée, Lausanne
Daniel Girardin, Curator

Private Collections:

Kenber Collection, Paris
Joseph Maouad Collection
Ekaterina & Vladimir Semenikhin Collection

The commissioners would like to thank all those who have helped us to collect the art works, and for their suggestions, their interventions and very simply, their friendship, during all the stages of the development of this project, and in particular, we would like to thank Iraïda Bott, Jean-Louis Prat, Vladimir and Ekaterina Semenikhin, Tatiana Sizova, Zelfira Tregulova.
A special mention for Tamara Igumnova who gave us her wholehearted support and whose contributions from the collections of the Moscow Historical Museum make up the very heart of our project.

In addition to the help in putting together the exhibition, the catalog editorial staff has been helped in many other ways. We would like to particularly pay homage to Ludmila Tarasenko who with the kind authorization of Tamara Igumova carried out a great deal of research for us in the Moscow Historical Museum reserves, and our thanks as well as to the specialists
S. Amelekhina, M. Bubchikova,
L. Dementieva, O. Dolganova,
L. Kornukova, G. Krouk, S. Levin,
Z. Mikhailova, N.Ougleva,
L. Petrova, L. Rudneva,
N. Perevezentzeva, A. Salnikov,
N. Skorniakova, G. Smorodinova,
E. Smirnova, N. Suetova,
N. Troepolskaya, L. Victorova.

To the Tsarskoye Selo Museum and State Reserve of St. Petersburg : Larisa Bardovskaya, Ksenia Sitnikova, Irina Zaitseva

To the National Tretyakov Gallery : Galina Churak, Nina Divova, Elena Maslova

And not forgetting : Vera Glushchenko, Alexandra Guysenova, Alexandra Kharitonova

We wish to express our deep appreciation also to all those whose names follow here. Their help has been precious to us and our most sincere thanks to them : Helena Artemeva, Olga Beloborodova, Anne Dion-Tenenbaum, Odile Emmanuelli, Sandrine Fritz, Anne Gros, Josephine Hildebrand, Barthélémy Jobert, Ekaterina Khmelnitskaïa, Jérôme Lamy, Gaëlle Naegellen, Nadège Provenzano, Katherine Purcell, Sebastian Rosenberg, Mathieu Rousset-Perrier, Ekaterina Soshalskaya, Claudine Sablier Paquet, Angela Schönberger, Xénia Sfiri, Roman Thaker, Michel Tonnelot, Christine Waidenschlager, Robert Zehil, Tatiana Zhelezneva.

Palais de Monaco

July 2009

Russia and Monaco have been linked a great many years by a deep friendship. Our shores have welcomed Russian families for more than a century now, first those coming on holiday, and then those caught in the turmoil of history. Artists have also stayed here, in quest of inspiration. It is thus "all these Russias" which we wish today to celebrate here in Monaco : those of traditions and of spiritual values which have an incontestable presence here today on our shores, but also that of artistic modernity, that special sensitivity of a many-talented people.

With the opening of the Russian season in the Principality, marked by the Centenary of the Diaghilev Ballets, the exhibition Moscow, Splendours of the Romanovs *at the Grimaldi Forum Monaco is the other major happening of the summer events, outlining a cultural and artistic twinning between the Principality and the Russian capital.*

The destiny of the Romanov family, last line of the Russian emperors, was closely linked to that of Moscow where the sovereigns were crowned over more than three centuries. Moscow, "Asiatic Rome" or "Fantastic Baghdad", as it was described by traveler-writers in the middle of the 19th century, was dotted with churches whose great power expressed itself through icons, iconostases and exceptional pieces of religious gold and silverwork, some of the most beautiful examples of which are being shown here.

Alongside these treasures of spiritual life, the Grimaldi Forum exhibition evokes the refinement and the magnificence of a whole dynasty through exceptional pieces, among which are rare pieces of jewelry coming from the Muscovite workshops which developed in the 19th century under the drive of the Imperial Court, as well as from the great Parisian firms, solicited on this side of Europe by an elite in search of luxury.

Finally, Moscow's artistic wealth is evidenced in the field of painting. The Itinerants, the Jack of Diamonds, *the* Golden Fleece*—so many groups and schools all essential for the understanding of modern art, in a city which also had its "avant-garde."*

The creation of this exhibition has been made possible thanks to the precious assistance of specialists from Moscow's National Historical Museum, guardian of the history of Russia and its capital, and thanks to the remarkable contributions from institutional and private collections: in Moscow, the Kremlin Museum, the Kuskovo Museum of Ceramics, the National Tretyakov Gallery, The Link of Times Foundation, the Ekaterina and Vladimir Semenikhin Collection and the Krasnorgorsk Archives; and in St. Petersburg, the Tsarskoye Selo Museum; the Menton Fine Arts Museum, and the Citadel of Villefranche-sur-Mer museums; in Lausanne, the Elysée Museum; and finally, in Paris, the Baccarat, Boucheron, Cartier, Chaumet, Mellerio dits Meller, and Van Cleef & Arpels firms.

As Russia revives its history, the Principality is happy to celebrate the close cultural ties which it has always held with this great country, in proposing this new exhibition in remembrance of what we are accustomed to call the Slavic soul.

H.S.H. Prince Albert II of Monaco

The State Historical Museum is the most important of the Russian national museums. Its extensive collections, unique in the whole country both by their numerical quantity and by their comprehensive nature, illustrate the history and culture of the Russian state in its entirety from the most ancient times to the present.

The Museum was founded in 1872 as the museum of the heir to the Russian throne, the czarevich Alexander Alexandrovich. Even though Moscow lost its status as capital in 1703, it remained the heart of the Russian state and depository of the historical memory of the country. The idea for the creation of a national museum accessible to all was taken by representatives of the Muscovite scientific and cultural community.

In May 1881, the Museum was granted the status of a state institution, and in 1883, at the same time as the coronation of the emperor Alexander III, the museum was opened to visitors. After May 1894, the museum was called the Russian Museum of His Imperial Majesty Alexander III. The presidents of honor of the museum were, in different years, members of the imperial family: the grand dukes Serguei Alexandrovich and Michael Alexandrovich. Thanks to them, the museum collections were enriched by donations: precious works of art, relics with historical value, and documents linked to the Romanov dynasty.

In November 1917, the Museum was given a new name—it became the State Russian Historical Museum.

The very idea of this museum, but also the way in which it was developed, in practice is a very direct reflection of the trends which dominated the époque. In fact, in the middle of the 19th century a tendency arose in Russia to seek ways of developing culture and art in finding inspiration from national traditions, and this became one of the prevailing ideas of art and culture during the time of the last Romanovs.

With its palaces and its old churches, Moscow was considered as the very personification of the Russian spirit. It was the place where important national projects conceived by the czarist government were carried out. Among these projects, the founding of the Russian Historical Museum was one of the most significant of the second half of the 19th century. In this atmosphere of both

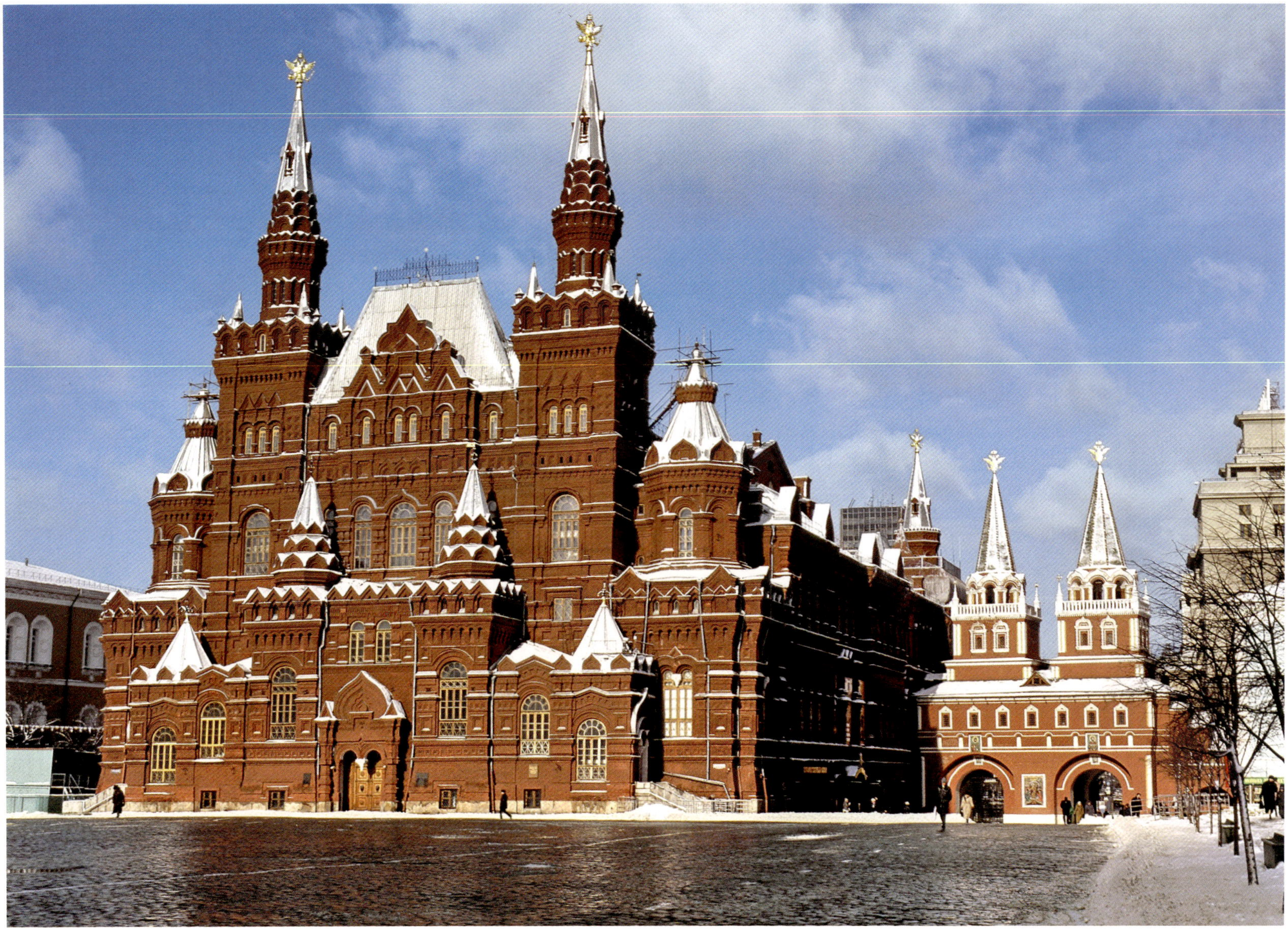

society's interest and the government's attentiveness, the museum which was created was radically innovative. A grandiose structure built in the old Russian style rose on the Red Square, becoming thereafter the very symbol of the meaning of the Russian state.

At the origins of the museum were the most eminent scholars of their time : the archeologist Count A. S. Ouvarov (first museum director), the historian I. E. Zabellin who succeeded A. S. Ouvarov as director, the paleographer and art historian V. N. Shtchepkin. The best architects, the best artists were brought together to take part in the development of the project, in the construction and layout of the museum building. A building which still illustrates today its avant-garde nature for the time regarding the technical solutions adopted, the coherence between idea and architectural forms, and the very carefully thought-out nature of innovative approaches in the presentation of the collections.

The three centuries of Russian history which took place under the aegis of the Romanovs were marked by the extent, the diversity and the dynamism of the cultural life. This period in the history of Russia is reflected in the museum collections in a very comprehensive way in terms of content and very brilliantly by the quality of the exhibited objects.

Among the works from the Historical Museum's collections which are presented in the exhibition Moscow, Splendours of the Romanovs, *many are unique in their artistic quality or their historical value.*

This exhibition is taking place at which seems to us to be a particularly appropriate moment. On the eve of the 400th anniversary of the accession to the throne of the first czar of the Romanov dynasty, this exhibition will enable a large public to open again the pages of an extremely important part of Russian history and culture, linked to the time when a great world power was developing, the Russian national character, and an artistic vision of the world which was unique, within the framework of a cultural tradition common to all of Europe.

Alexander Shkurko
Director of the State Historical Museum

CONTENTS

The catalog notices were composed by:
M. Bubchikova, L. Dementieva,
L. Kornukova, G. Kriouk, S. Levin,
Z. Michailova, N. Ougleva,
N. Perevezentseva, L. Petrova,
L. Rudvena, T. Sizova, N. Skorniakova,
E. Smirnova, G. Smorodinova, N. Suetova,
L. Tarasenko, N. Troepolskaïa, L. Victorova
of the State Historical Museum, Moscow

L. Bardovslaïa, E. Chtchvigleva,
E. Eremeeva, A. Rogatnev, I. Zaïtseva
of The State Museum Preserve "Tsarskoye Selo", St. Petersburg

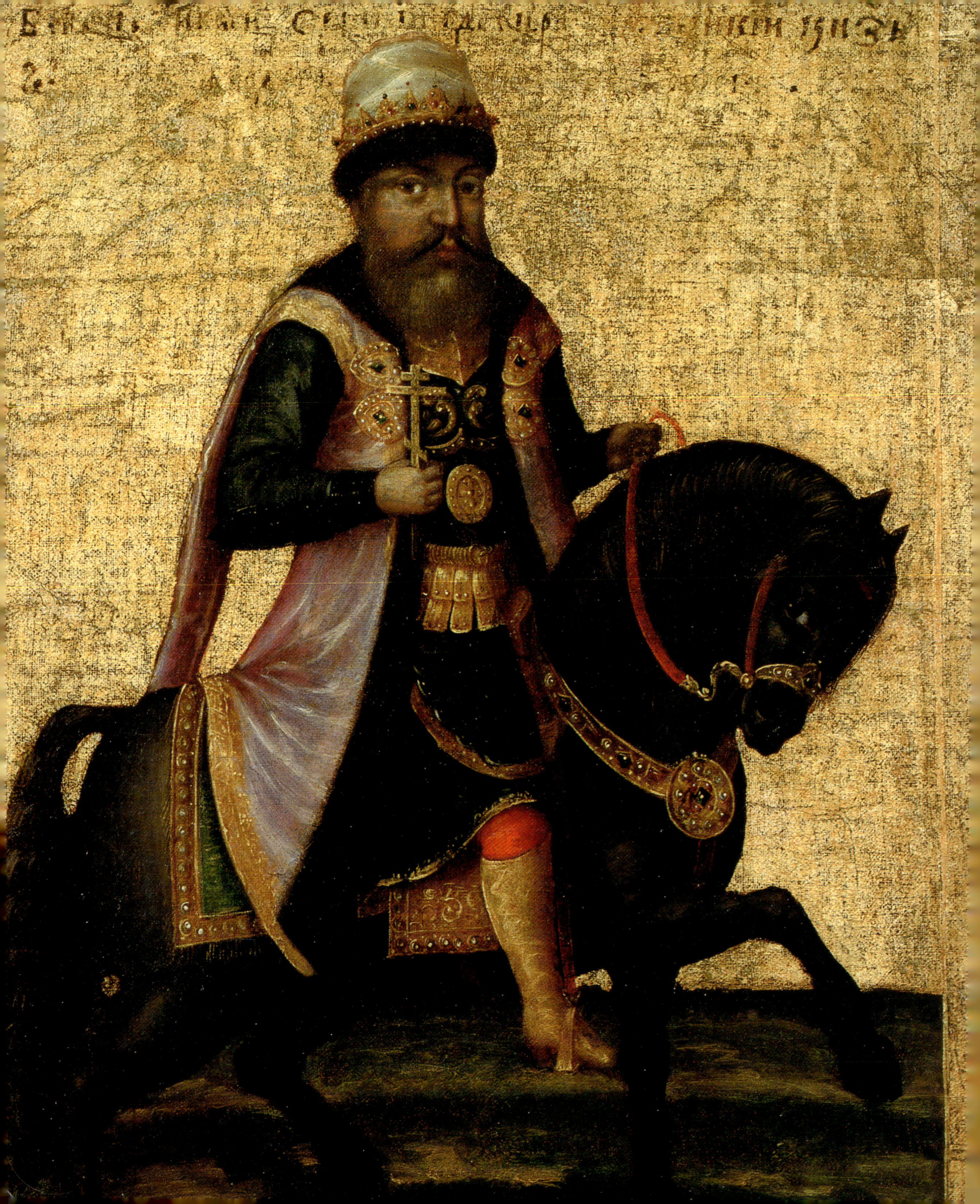

MOSCOW, CAPITAL OF THE ROMANOVS

Brigitte de Montclos

Moscow, capital of Muscovy

The first representative of the Romanov dynasty was elected in 1613 by the *Zemskii Sobor*, the assembly created by Ivan IV, called Ivan the Terrible. The mission of this equivalent of the French Estates General was to take care of specific problems, war, reforms and in particular, the election of the Czar. In this case, it was supposed to bring to an end what was called in history "the Time of Troubles", a succession of imposters, vandals and usurpers who had fought over the throne of Russia since the death of Boris Godunov, Czar elected in 1598 and whose sudden death in 1605 plunged the country into total chaos. Moscow, a city built in wood, was devastated by fire, the country was escheated, sacked, pillaged and given over to various bands. The Polish occupied Moscow hoping to acquire the throne for their sovereign Sigismond or for his son Ladislas.

1. *Anonymous* Equestrian portrait of Czar Michael Feodorovich *Second half of the 1670s, first half of the 1680s (?) The State Historical Museum, Moscow (Cat. 1)*

The Russian national alliance directed by Kuzma Minin and Prince Dmitry Pojarsky re-established an army which freed Moscow. Representatives of the clergy, of the boyars, of those who had acquired nobility, of the people of the cities and even of the peasants and all those making up the *Zemskii Sobor* chose Michael Romanov, the great-nephew of Ivan IV's first wife, as Czar (ill. 1). His young age ensured independence when confronted with the intrigues and base actions of the Court. He was sixteen. His father, Feodor, who had been forced by Boris Godunov to live in a convent under the name of Philarete, and his mother Marfa, who had endured the same destiny, had raised him in the respect of the Orthodox religion. He reigned assisted by his father who was named patriarch.

The task before him was difficult. He had to re-establish order, reform the administration, recreate the financial system, draw up a budget and sign a peace treaty with Poland and Sweden. He also had to rebuild Moscow. Unfortunately, everything had been built in wood and only in wood. Only the Kremlin fortress, a few *palaty* built by the boyars, and the churches were made of durable material, of brick. So whole districts of the city regularly disappeared because of fire.

At Michael's death in 1645, his son Alexis succeeded him. The financial balance of the country had not yet been re-established but reform of the administration was in progress with the promulgation in 1649 of the law code, the *Oulojenie*[1] which remained in effect until 1835. This code recorded the definitive attachment of the peasant to the land, in other words, serfdom.

In terms of foreign affairs, the most important event was the incorporation of the Ukraine into Russia in 1645, requested by the Ukrainians so as to escape Polish and Lithuanian control.[2] During this reign there also occurred the popular revolt in

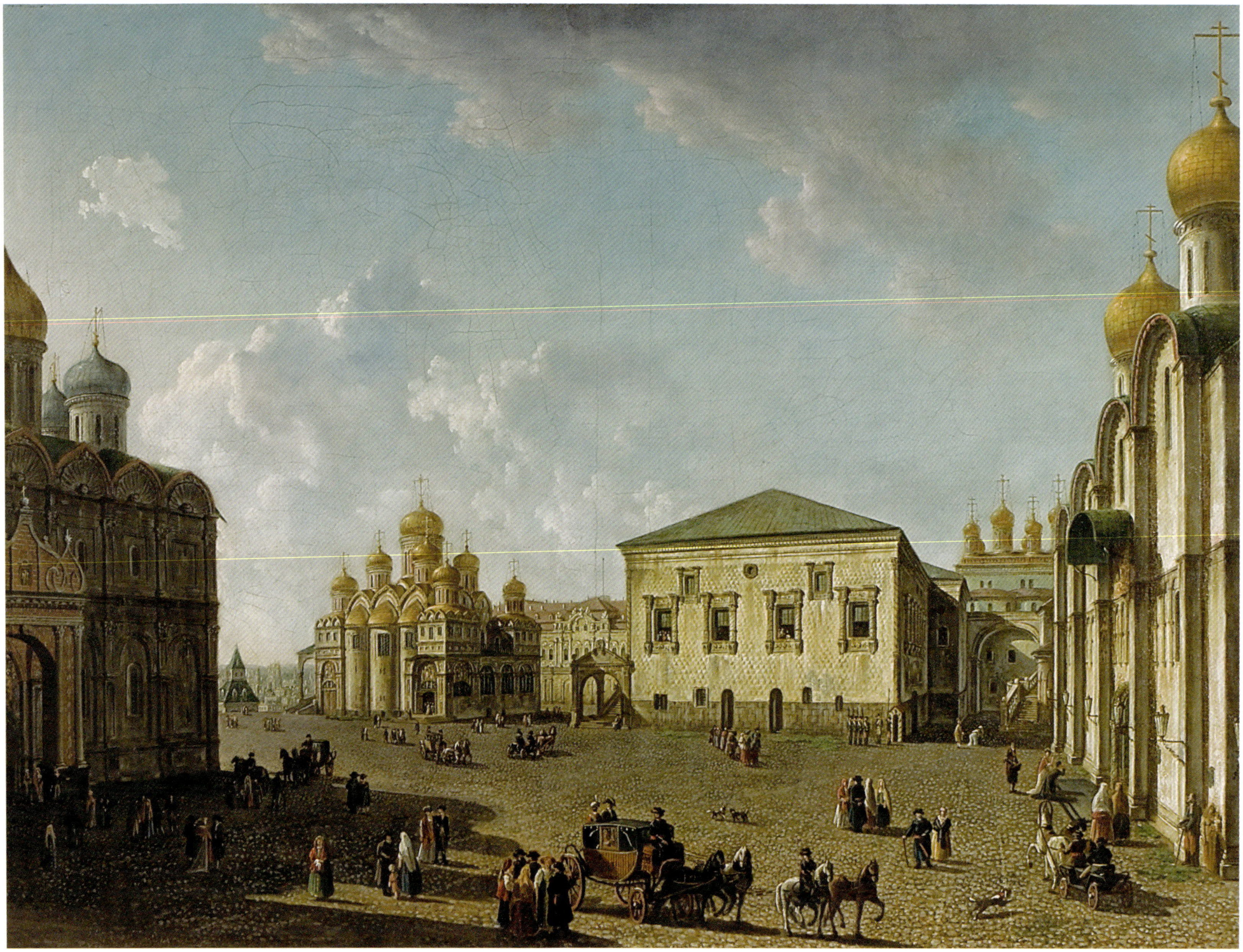

2. *F. I. Alekseev*
Moscow. View of the Square of the Cathedrals in the Kremlin
1800s
The State Historical Museum, Moscow
(Cat. 260)

3. Tankard with lid
Russia, Moscow, end of 17th-early 18th century
The State Historical Museum, Moscow
(Cat. 235)

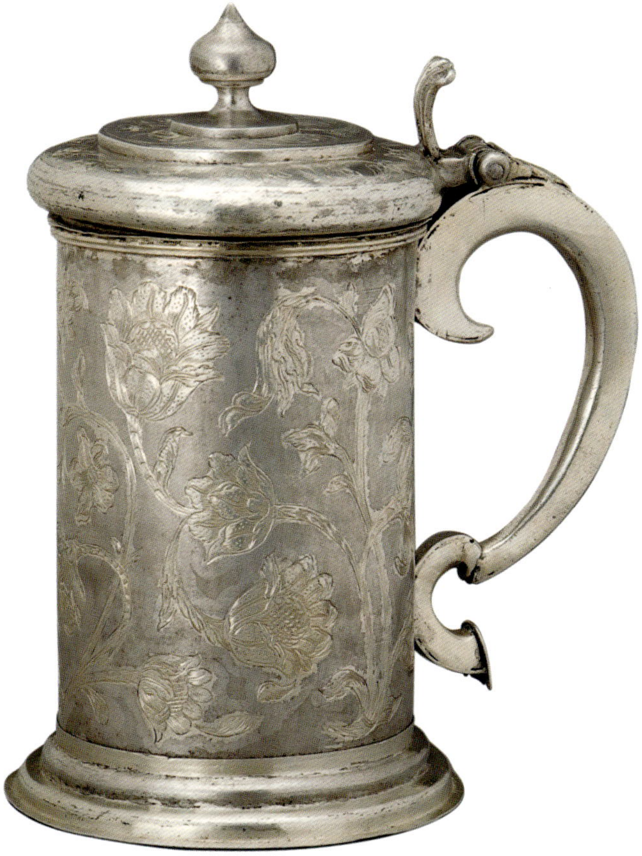

1671 led by the Cossack Steka Razin and supported by the people and the soldiers exasperated by the financial crisis. It was only brought to an end by the arrest in 1671 of the Cossack. Finally, the Schism, the *Raskol*, provoked by the patriarch Nikon's ritual and liturgical reforms which a part of the population opposed, led these *Old Believers* to go into hiding and to isolate themselves so as to avoid being massacred.[3]

The first century of the Romanovs, often pushed into the background by Peter the Great's remarkable whirlwind activity, nevertheless marks the height of architecture and traditional art and design. The new dynasty had to affirm its legitimacy at the same time as its fidelity to the past and its right to hereditary succession. Art was used as a justification whose corollary was the creation of a national style which used popular heritage and encouraged two major forms of expression: architecture (ill. 2) whose most famous examples are the *terems* in the Kremlin and the estates of Kolomensky and *Krutitsky Dvor*, and the golden age of art and design which flourished at the same time as the last of religious painting. The perfection attained by the Russian craftsmen is particularly evident in the art of *niello* work, this incrustation of black enamel on a silver base (ill. 3).

Moscow, capital of the coronation

Peter I, like his father and his grandfather, was crowned Czar in the Cathedral of the Dormition (ill. 4) in the Kremlin. All of the Romanovs without exception received the supreme anointment in that same cathedral, even if their usual residence was St. Petersburg. Moscow, the former capital, remained the coronation capital. We have detailed information about the sequence of coronation events thanks to contemporary eye-witness accounts, beginning with that of the German Jacob Stahlin. Stahlin was invited to Russia by Anna Ivanovna in 1735 for his skills with illuminations and fireworks. He spent the rest of his life there, dying in 1785 but not before having written down a precious account in Russian about the fine arts and an album dedicated to the description of Elizabeth I's crowning, illustrated by engravings.[4] We learn there that in February 1742, Elizabeth, accompanied by about 24,000 people and 19,000 horses left St. Petersburg en route for Moscow. Her absence lasted eight months. This indicates the importance of the journey and the stay in the secular capital. As for Catherine II, she prolonged the coronation rituals through innumerable festivities, thus diverting public attention from the affairs of State in order to legitimize her seizure of power.

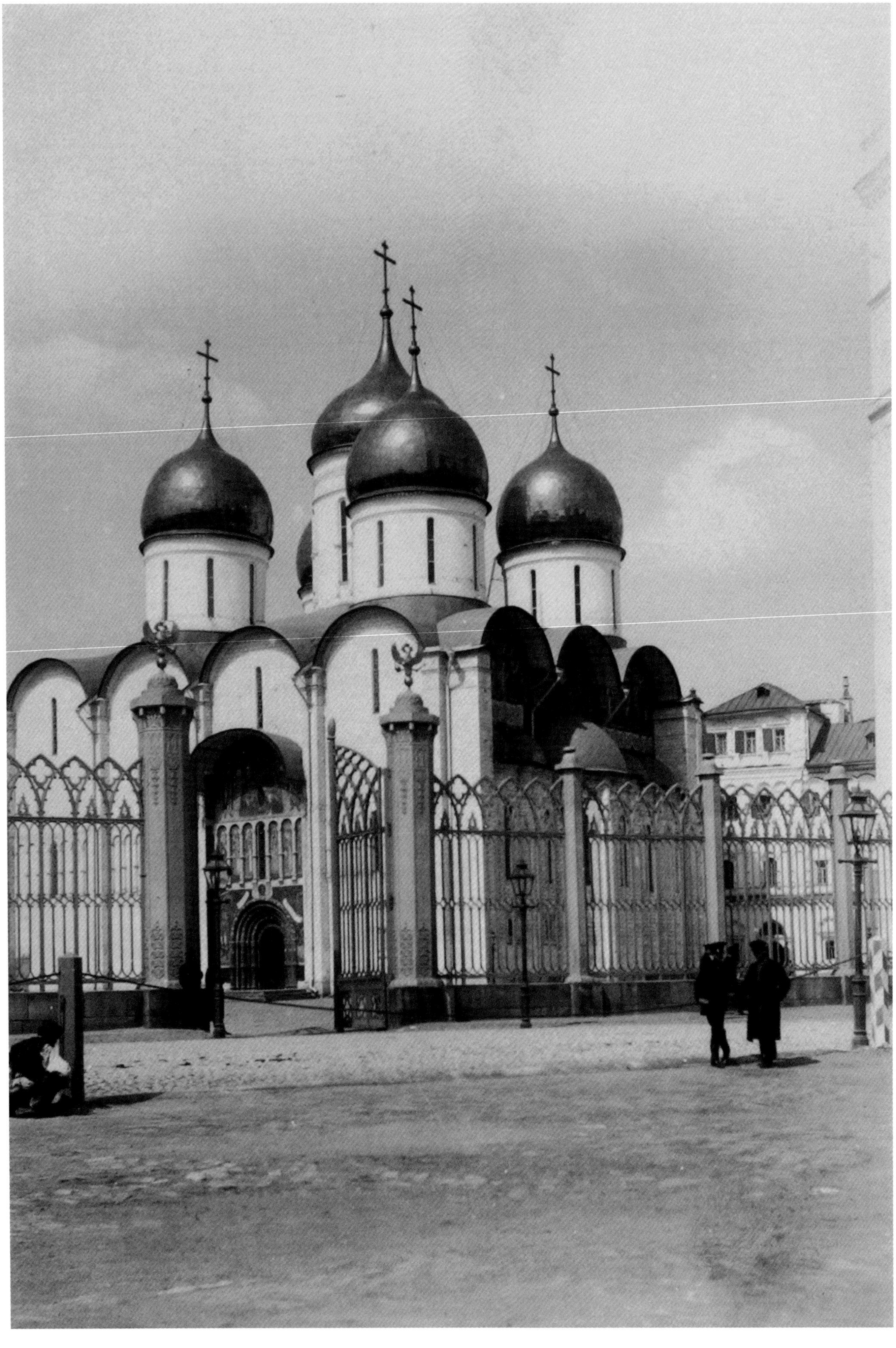

4. The Cathedral of the Dormition
Russia, Moscow, Kremlin, circa 1890
Private collection

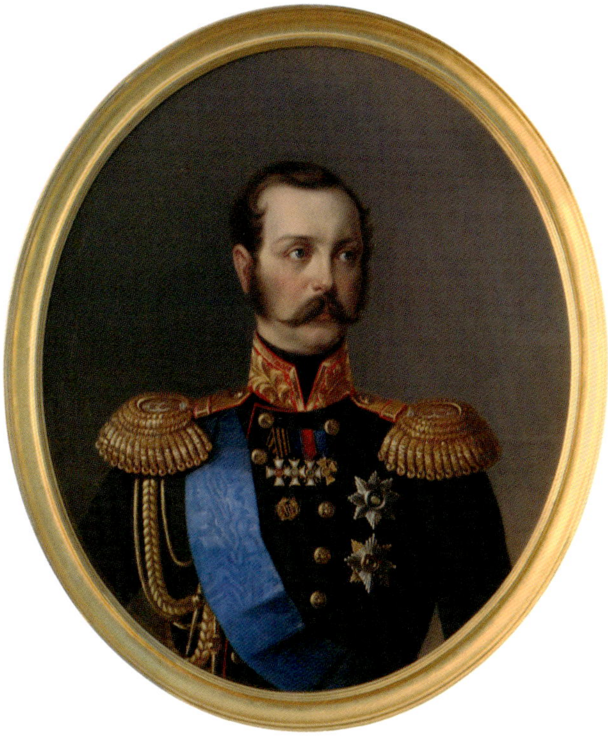

5. *Anonymous*
Portrait of the Emperor Alexander II
Russia, 1870s
The State Museum Preserve "Tsarskoye Selo," St. Petersburg
(Cat. 161)

6. *N. D. Dmitriev-Orenburgsky*
Portrait of Emperor Alexander III (1845-1894)
1896
The State Historical Museum, Moscow
(Cat. 162)

The 19th century, the century of emperors, was rich in accounts of the crowned Czar's attitude. Alexander I, dignified, was still suffering over his father's violent death.[5] Nicholas I was radiant with joy, Alexander II (ill. 5) was overwhelmed.[6] Alexander III was calm and serious but during the ceremony, after having taken the crown from the hands of the Metropolitan and placed it on his head, his face was wet with tears; in leaving the cathedral, his face was again serene, enigmatic[7] (ill. 6). As was the custom, the popular festivities continued on Khodynka Field where platforms were set up to welcome the public, who came to receive the gifts usually given. The same ceremony took place after Nicholas II's crowning but as a result of someone falling from one of the higher rows, the celebration ended in a deadly stampede for some of the people.[8]

The crowning of Nicholas II took place on May 26, 1896. He was immortalized by a photograph, an exceptional archival document which is kept today in the Krasnogorsk audiovisual federal archives center. That day was for the Czar the expression of the union between the sovereign, his church and his state, celebrated in the capital of his ancestors to whom he pledged his admiration. It was in fact in honor of Alexis Romanov that he organized the famous masked ball in 1903 where the Court, through its dress, recreated the court of Alexis (ill 7). It was also in his honor and in admi-

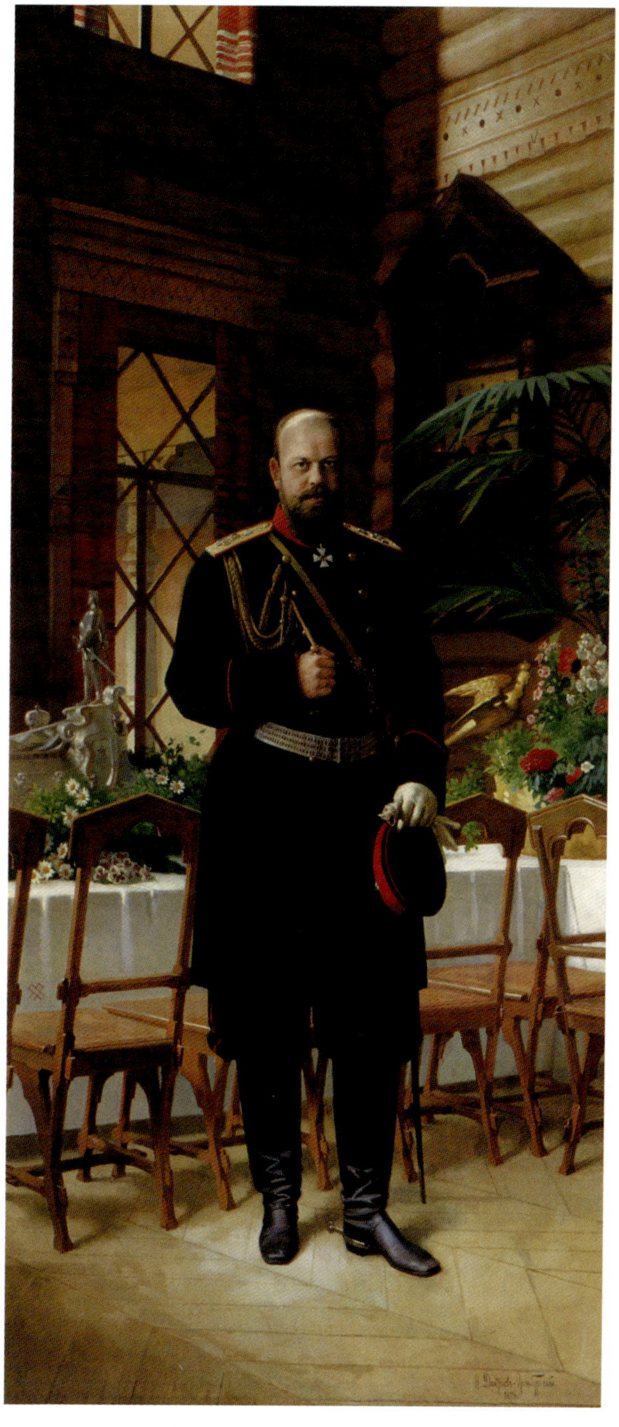

ration of Holy Russia, which he represented, that he named his son Alexis.

Moscow, a Czar's architecture

One might imagine that with the construction of St. Petersburg, there would be no more architectural expansion in the former capital. However, when Peter I returned from his long journey abroad in 1698, he was very aware of the absolute necessity to provide the city with an urbanism which up until then had been non-existent (ill. 8). The succession of *ukases* during the first ten years of the new century testify to this. After the 1699 fire which destroyed in part Kitai-gorod and Biely-gorod, and the fire of 1701 which affected the northern part of the Kremlin, it was forbidden to build in wood on the sites which had burned. In the Kremlin a "royal arsenal" was built in stone.[9] Furthermore, the well-off people were from then on obliged to build their houses in stone, the poor people using *pisé*. For the first time, a *ukase* mentions the obligation to use architects. Beginnings of city planning appear with the provision that it is forbidden to build at the back or in the middle of a courtyard, as was usual, and with the order to align the construction with the street.[10] In addition, every shipment entering the city had to bring with it three stones so as to pave the streets, which up until then were in hard earth or covered with wooden planks. In 1709 a *ukase* ordered the houses rebuilt in wood to be destroyed. Up until 1714 there was a succession of *ukases* obliging the inhabitants of the Kremlin, of Kitai-gorod and of Biely-gorod—the districts surrounding the Kremlin—to build their houses in durable materials. But starting that year, construction in hard materials was forbidden throughout the Empire because it was limited to St. Petersburg. The ban was lifted for the center of Moscow in 1718 (ill. 9). However, changes and new construction were only undertaken again when the Court returned for the coronation of Peter II, Peter the Great's grandson, in 1727. The Court stayed in Moscow that time. The Dolgoruky clan surrounded the young Czar to the point of arranging an engagement between him and Catherine Dolgoruky. The city of Munich, an old friend to Peter I who had been named governor of St. Petersburg, called for help—without upkeep it would collapse.[11] But the Czar died suddenly in 1730. The coronation of the newly elected Anna Ivanovna, Ivan's daughter (half-brother to Peter I and co-Czar until 1696) was organized by the boyars and Muscovite society, persuaded that they would regain the privileges they had lost in the immensity of St. Petersburg. But all was over when Anna went back on her promises and returned the Court to St. Petersburg. Ten years later, there was another coronation, that of Elizabeth. Attached to her father's city and respectful of what he had created—but respectful too of old Russia which everyone knew was to be found in Moscow— she received, as we have seen, a magnificent coronation. And in 1753, she asked Bartolomeo Rastrelli, her appointed architect who had designed the Winter Palace and the Smolny monastery, to build a palace to replace the southern wing of the *palaty* built in 1487 by the Italian architects of the Kremlin.[12] She also ordered the construction of a church dedicated to St. Clement-Pope-of-Rome whose name day was celebrated the day of the coup d'état, which

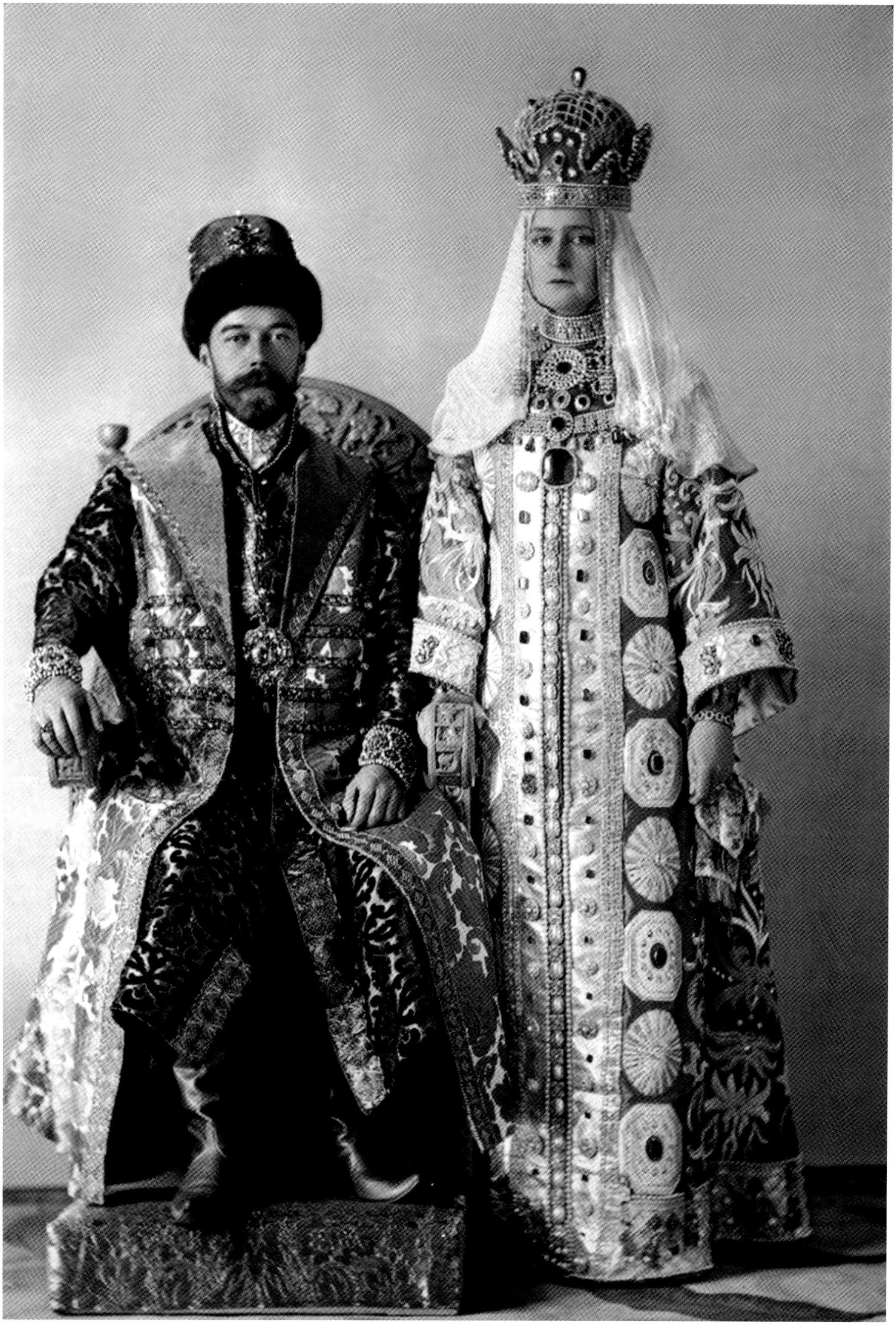

7. The Emperor Nicholas II and the Empress Alexandra Feodorovna wearing costumes of Russian czars of the 17th century
St. Petersburg, 1903
Russian State Cinematographic and Photographic Archives
(Cat. 342)

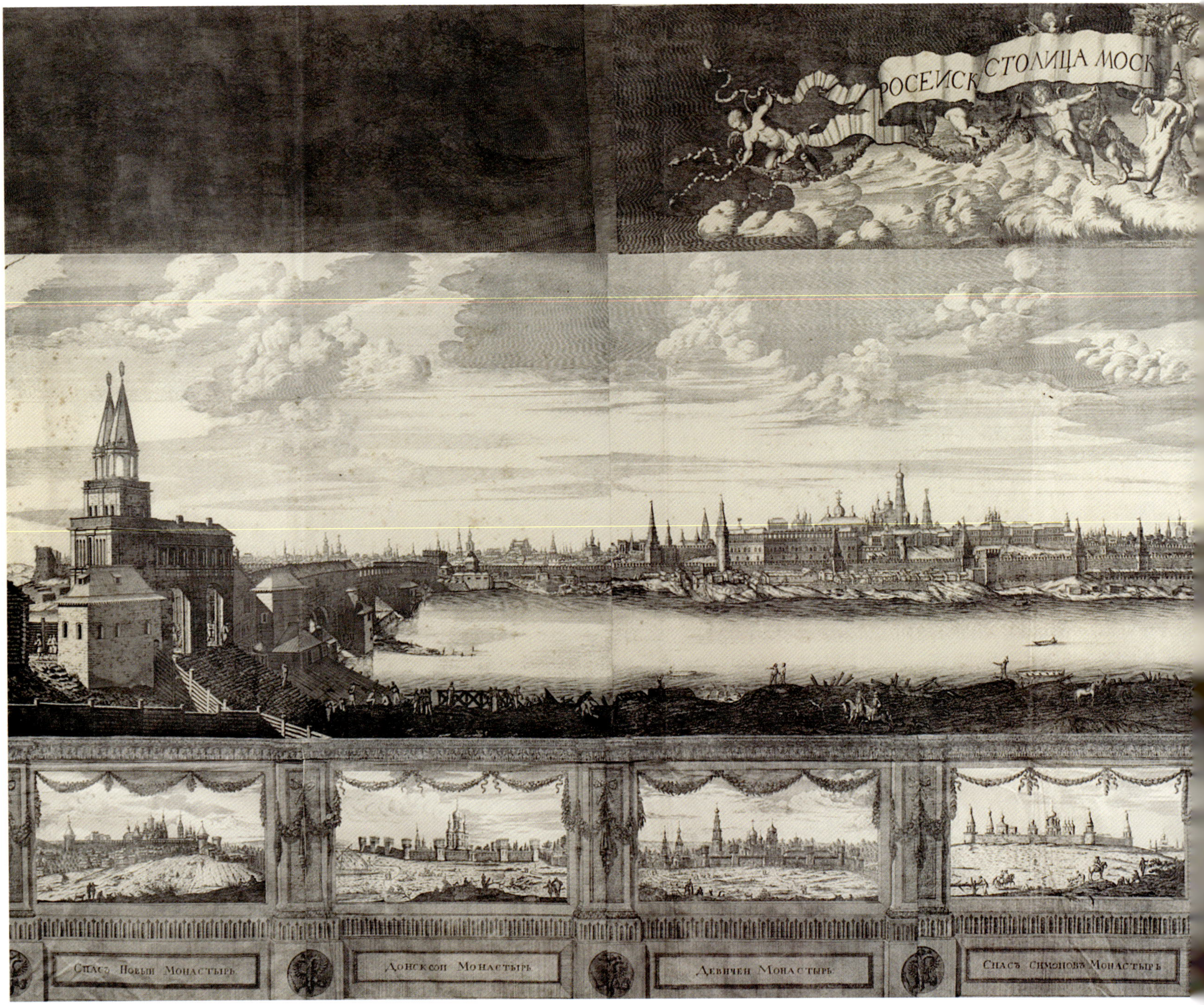

8. *P. Picart*
Moscow, capital of Russia
Beginning of the 18th century
State Ceramics Museum and 18th century Kuskovo estate
(Cat. 290)

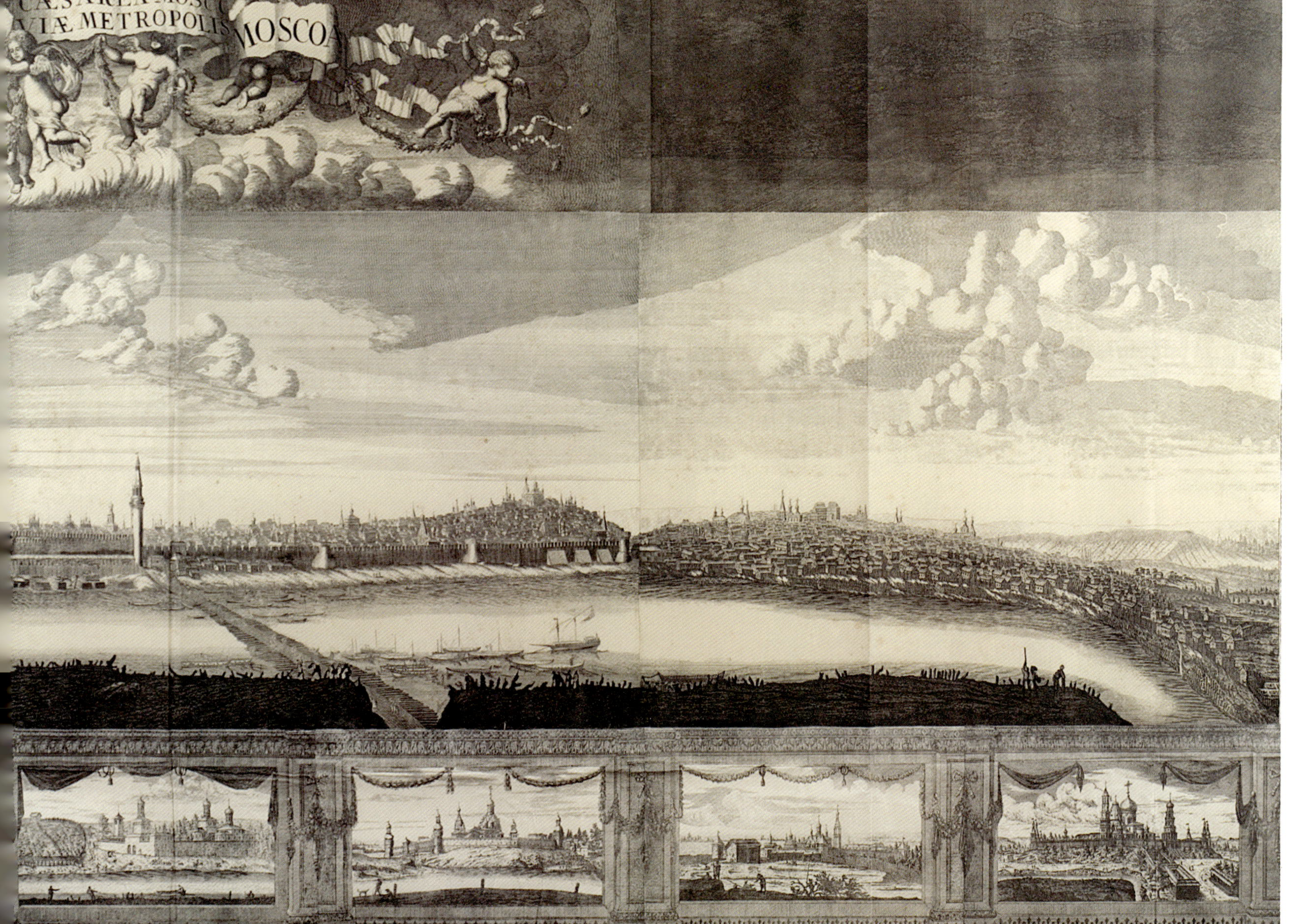

CÆSAREA MOSCO
VIÆ METROPOLIS
MOSCOA
Андреа Стратилата Монастырь
Дашловской Монастырь
Покровской Монастырь
Воскресенской Монастырь

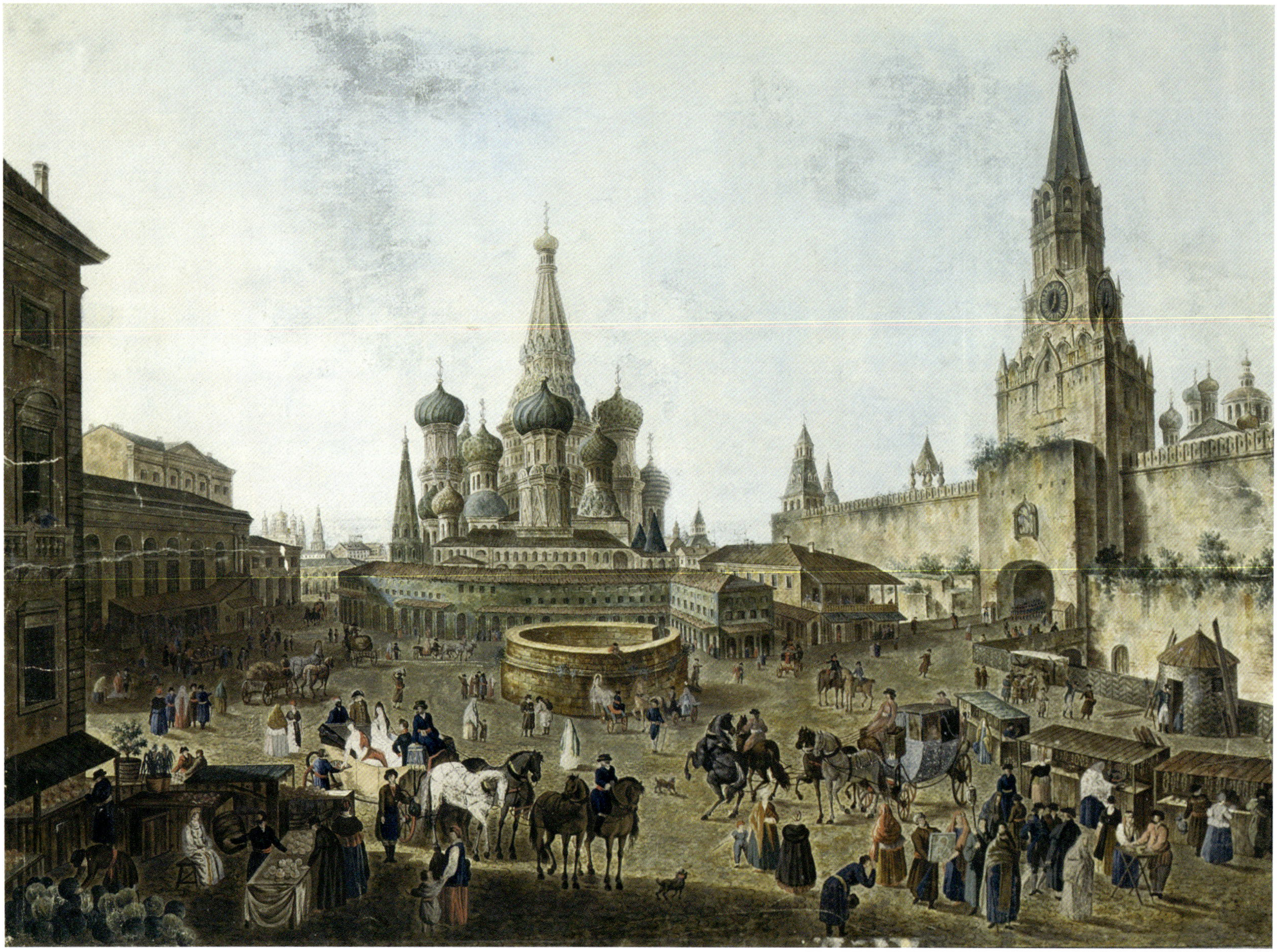

9. *F. I. Alekseev studio*
General view of the Red Square and
the Cathedral of Basil the Blessed
1880s
The State Historical Museum, Moscow
(Cat. 274)

brought her to the throne. After Elizabeth, Catherine II, who knew how to consolidate her power with the support of all Russia, and specifically with Moscow, ordered a palace from the architect Bajenov which was to replace all the buildings along the Moskva River the length of the Kremlin wall. The architect who had studied in St. Petersburg but also in Paris with Charles De Wailly, and then in Italy, was a lover of the column which he used in profusion in his gigantic project. The first stone was laid in 1773, the demolition had begun but the worksite was halted in 1775. There remains only a huge model,[13] and some drawings[14].

Catherine also ordered Bajenov to build an extraordinary palace next to Moscow, mixing Western Gothic and Russian heritage. The Tsaritsyno residence,[15] finished in 1785 was visited by the Empress who ordered its immediate destruction from fear of premonitions she believed she had there. But it was in the same spirit that she had the Petrovsky palace built by Matvey Kazakov, a relay palace which was to welcome the future Czar before his entrance into Moscow the eve of his coronation.

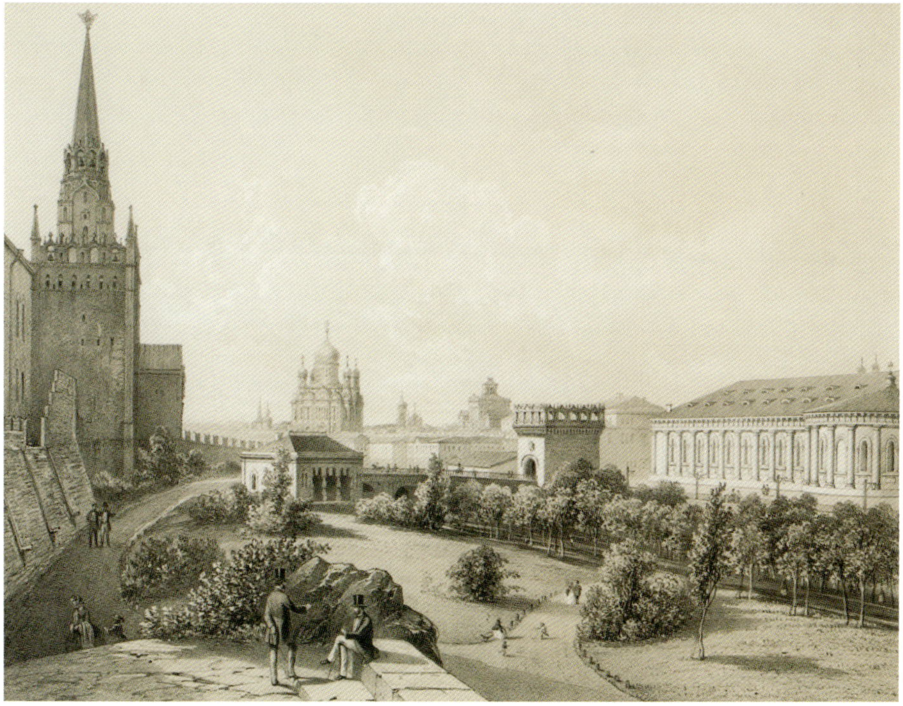

10. Ch. K. Bachelier, J. Jacottet. Based on an original by I. I. Charlemagne
The Alexander Garden. View from the Troitsky bridge toward the Church of Christ the Savior
1850s
The State Historical Museum, Moscow
(Cat. 278)

For his coronation, Paul I had Elizabeth's palace destroyed in order to build another one by Nicholas Lvov. This palace burned down in 1812. It was restored but finally replaced by the present Grand Kremlin Palace, built from 1835 to 1849 by Nicholas I's order in what is called the "Russkii style", the Russian style. The century of emperors was marked by that need to return to the heart of Russia. And if St. Petersburg glorified Alexander I in dedicating to him the high column which is in the center of the palace square, Moscow built a prestigious sanctuary, the Church of Christ the Savior, to the memory of the one who saved Russia (ill. 10). And when Alexander III offered the Michael Palace to the city of St. Petersburg in 1895 to create a museum devoted to Russian art, the National History museum had already been opened for a long time in the Red Square (in 1883) and Pavel Tretyakov's fabulous collection of ancient and modern Russian art had already belonged to the city of Moscow for three years thanks to the generous donation of the art collector.

Moscow, secular capital

This return towards Moscow and its traditional art is characteristic of this time when all of Western Europe was in quest of its national roots. In addition, the emperors were becoming less and less attached to St. Petersburg. Alexander II went often to Moscow. This is why Jules Verne begins Michael Strogoff's adventure story in the middle of a celebration given by the Czar at the new Kremlin palace: "That river was the Moskva, that city was Moscow, that fortified wall was the Kremlin, and the officer of the Chasseurs of the Guard who with

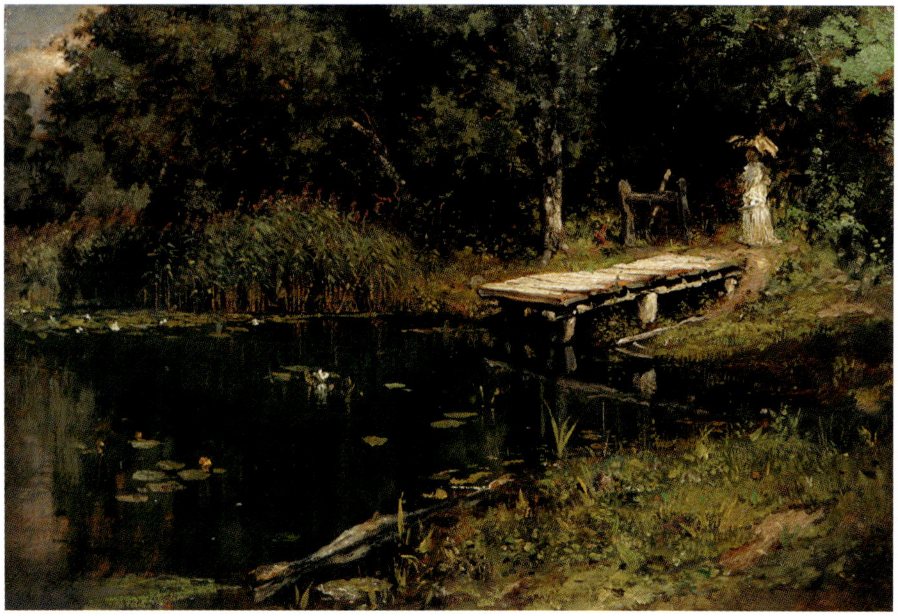

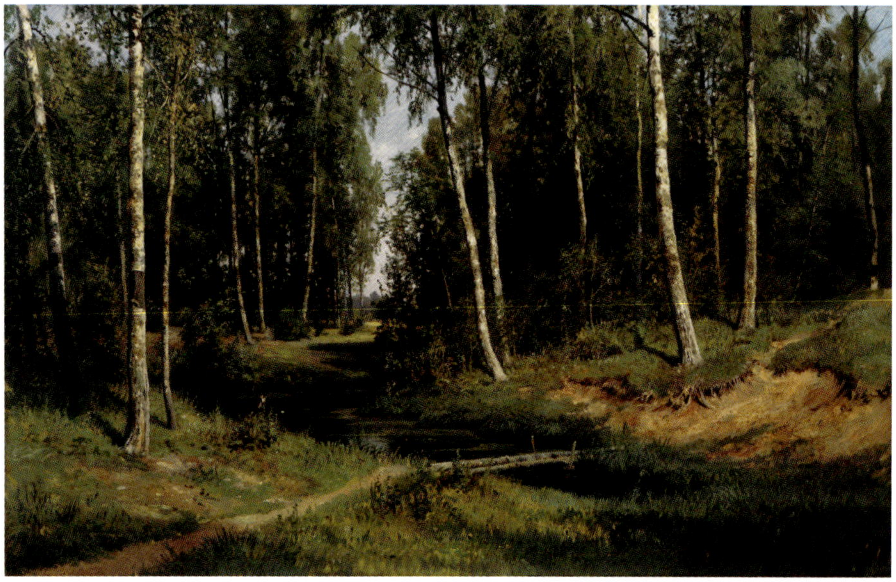

his arms crossed, his brow thoughtful, vaguely listening to the noise thrown off from the New Palace down onto the old Muscovite city, was the Czar."[16]

After his assassination which deeply moved the whole of Russia, messages arrived from around the Empire. The inhabitants of Moscow invited the new Czar to return to the capital of his ancestors where they promised him the assurance of greater safety than in the assassin city.[17] And it's true that Alexander III made his preference for Moscow very clear.

This explains why Russian historicist architecture developed significantly in the 1880s. The Muscovite church St. Basil the Blessed was the inspiration for The Church of Our Savior on Spilled Blood built at the very spot where Alexander II was assassinated in St. Petersburg. In Moscow, the National History Museum was built, which closed the north side of the Red Square, and the business galleries were built along the east side. It must be noted however that it was the picturesque character of Muscovite architecture which inspired the architects rather than the system of construction. This can be seen in the *Igumnov* house (today the French embassy), the very example of research in the best use of construction from the beginning of the 17th century. Oddly, this evocation of genuine Russian art is linked to the research of the creators of the modern Russkii, the Art Nouveau style which was to become the completion of the marriage between the return to one's roots and modernity.

Moscow, capital of new art

During that time, the great revolution in painting was in its preparation.

The Itinerant painters movement was founded in 1863 by thirteen artists who refused to treat the mythological subject imposed by the St. Petersburg Fine Arts Academy. The same year in Paris, the Salon des Refusés (Salon of the Rejected) was held. This meant that a new era in European painting was at hand. In Russia, it was a nationalist movement with its center in Moscow. The College of Moscow had taught painting and sculpture since 1843, and then, beginning in 1865, included architecture. It offered the teaching of rural landscape painting, as opposed

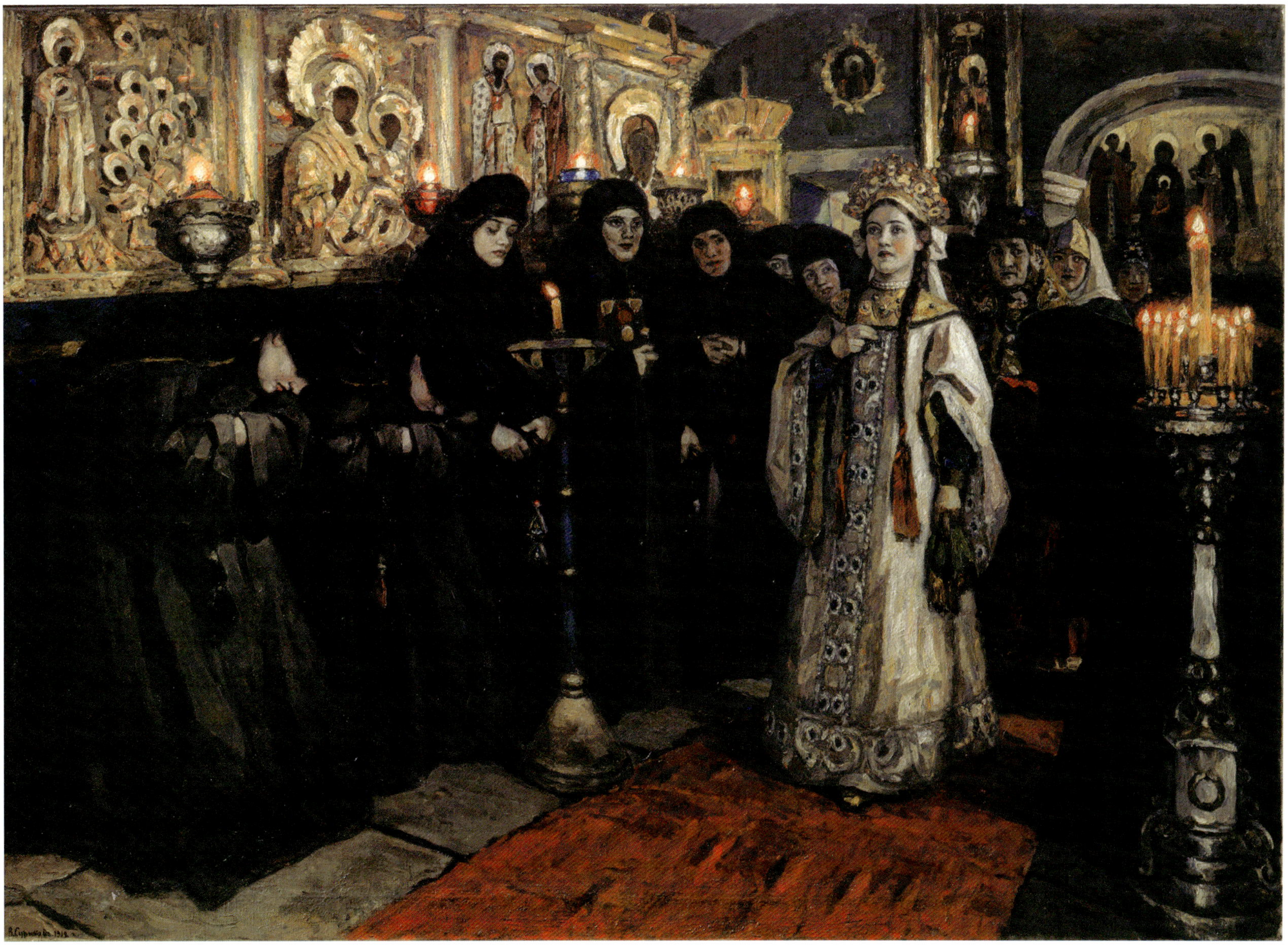

11. *V. D. Polenov*
The brushwood pond
1870
Oil on canvas
23.5 × 33.9 cm
Ekaterina and Vladimir Semenikhin Collection

12. *I. I. Chichkin*
Stream in the forest
1883
Ekaterina and Vladimir Semenikhin Collection
(Cat. 541)

13. *V. I. Surikov*
A czarina's visit to a monastery
1912
The State Tretyakov Gallery
(Cat. 549)

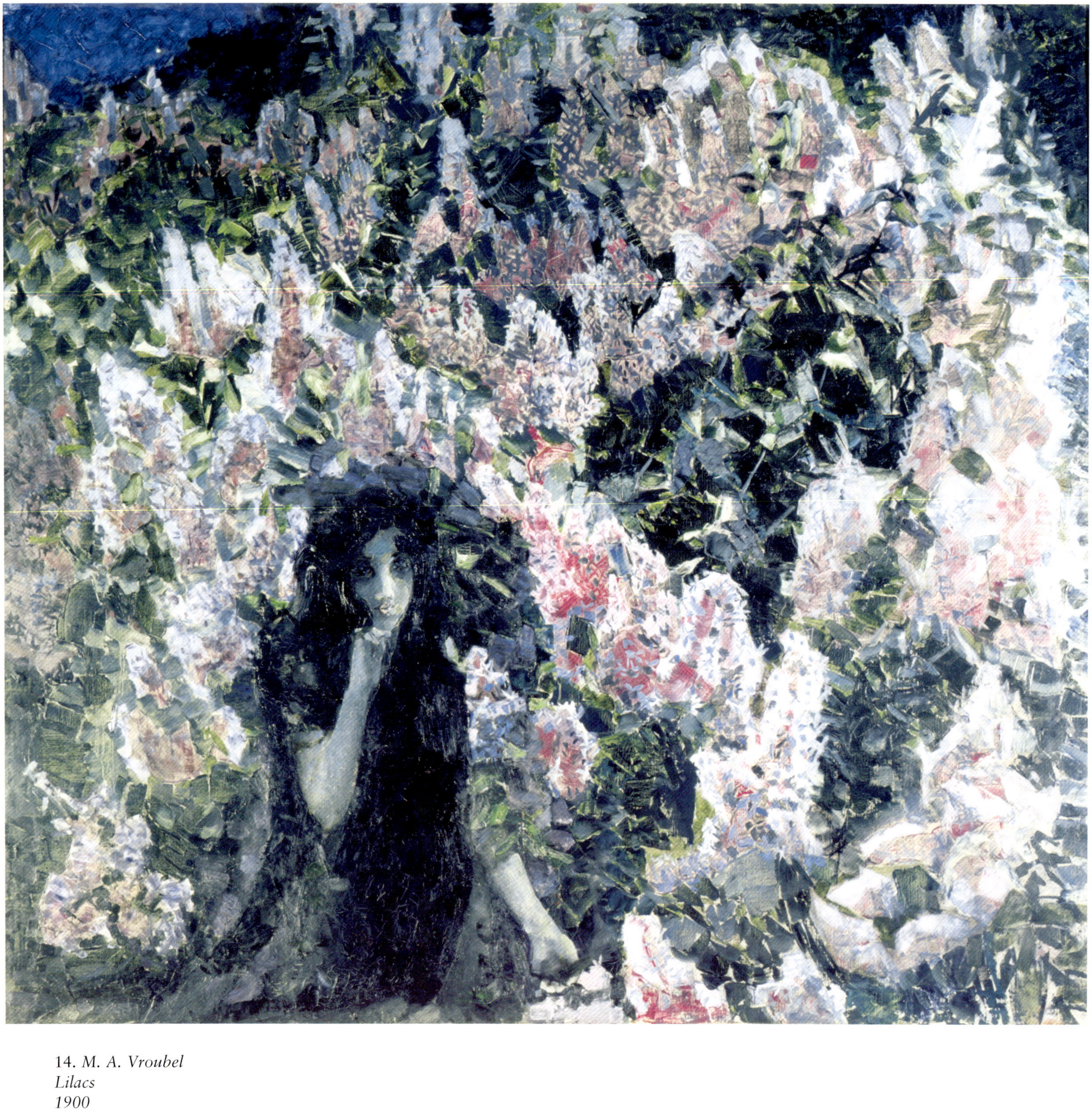

14. M. A. Vroubel
Lilacs
1900
The State Tretyakov Gallery
(Cat. 637)

15. *N. S. Gontcharova*
Thistle
1908-1910
The State Tretyakov Gallery
(Cat. 640)

to the academic teaching of St. Petersburg. The artists who went there took on the mission of explaining life by treating it in its real context and in showing it throughout the country by means of organizing "itinerant" exhibitions. The movement was backed by Muscovite art patrons such as Pavel Tretyakov, the Shchukin brothers, Ivan Morozov and the Mamontov couple. The latter welcomed the young Russian landscape painters who wished to paint their country in accordance with the descriptions given by the writers Leo Tolstoy and Ivan Turgenev to their estate of Abramtsevo: Polenov (ill. 11), Repin, Serov, Levitan, Chichkin (ill. 12), Korovin. Vasily Surikov (ill. 13), who found inspiration in Russian history and Michael Vroubel (ill. 14) who found it in fantasy joined them. Exchanges with the *Mir Iskousstva* movement created in St. Petersburg by Serge Diaghilev and the St. Petersburg artists Alexander Benois and Eugene Lanceray well illustrated the differences between styles but also showed that there was no scission between the two orientations. After *Mir Iskousstva* disappeared, the magazine *The Golden Fleece* carried on but this time from Moscow. An exceptional presentation of Matisse's work was published in this magazine.[18] The group from the *Blue Rose*, influenced by Vroubel and Borissov-Mussatov, organized its first exhibition in 1907 at Paul Kuznetsov's in Moscow and it was again *The Golden Fleece* which gave an account of its activity and which, the following year, organized a confrontation between Russian art and French art in an exhibition which included Larionov, Gontcharova (ill. 15), Braque, Matisse, Vlaminck.[19] A Russian school whose center was in Moscow developed in the years that followed. At the end of 1910, in the still famous exhibition *Jack of Diamonds*, all the artists who today have been grouped under the name of avant-garde were shown together (ill. 16). Two years later, in 1912, Larionov organized, again in Moscow, the exhibition *The Donkey's Tail,* showing the work of Larionov, Gontcharova, Malevich and

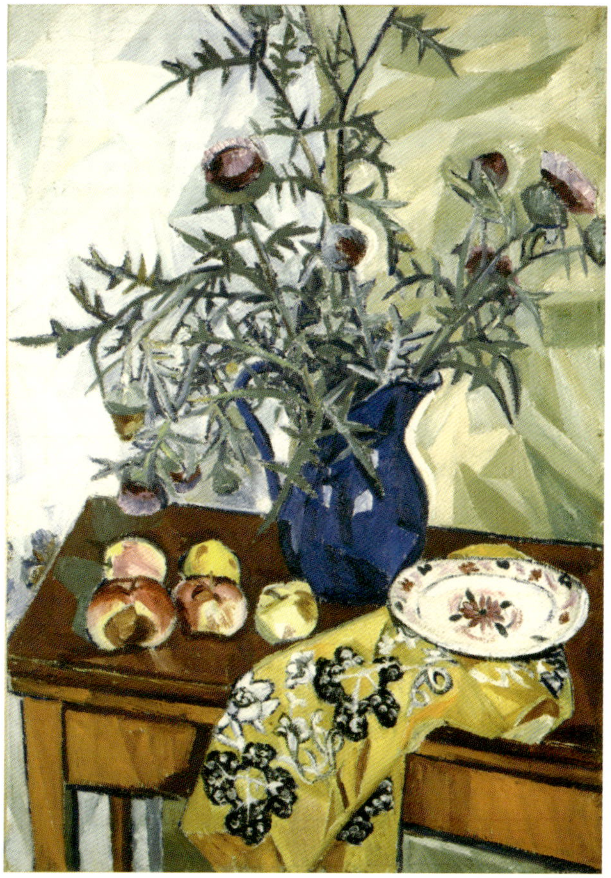

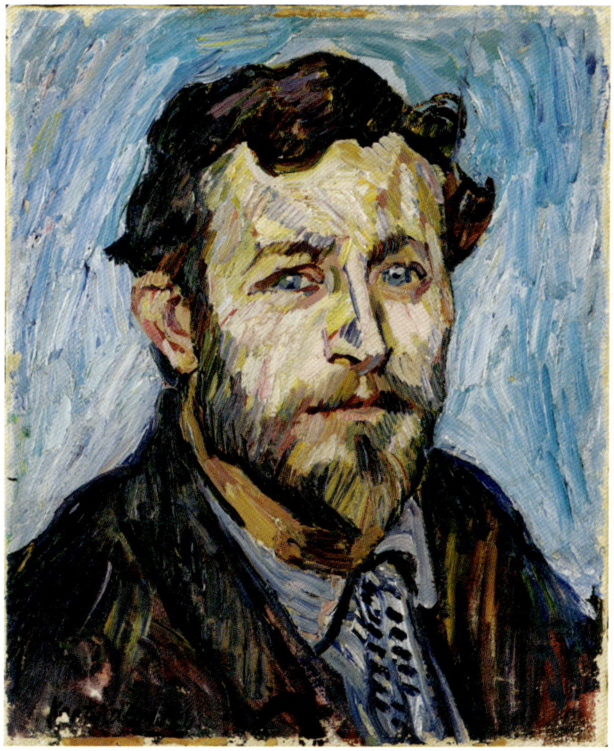

16. *M. P. Konchalovsky*
Portrait of the sculptor Galouzi
1908
Ekaterina and Vladimir Semenikhin Collection
(Cat. 643)

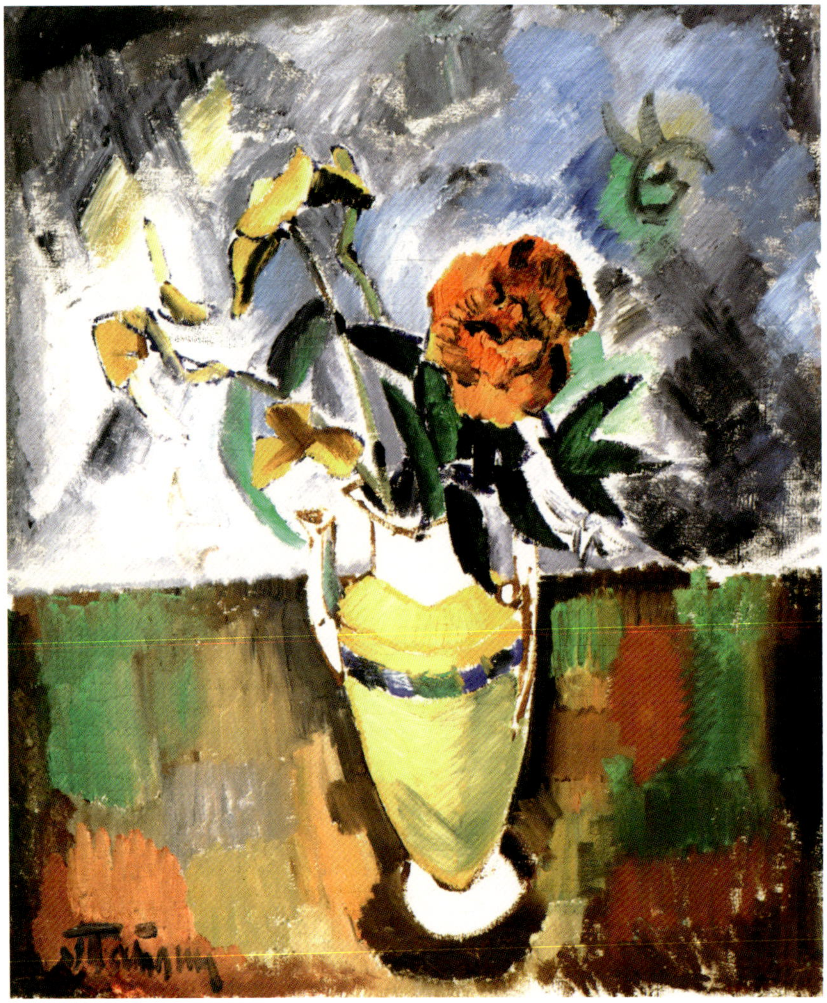

Tatlin (ill. 17), an exhibition which incited the indignation of the public, although the demonstration had intended to be the affirmation of the existence of a Russian school which was independent of all influence. Cubo-futurism, today recognized as a great movement of art renewal, was born, and born in Moscow (ill. 18) assisted by Alexander Tairov, the founder of the Kamerni theater and one of the discoverers of Alexandra Exter's talent.

The major exhibition of *Ancient Russian Painting* presented in Moscow in 1913 for the tercentennial celebration of the Romanov dynasty, revealed to the painters the purity of icon painting and the simplicity of its line, but it was at the *Café Pittoresque* created in 1917 and decorated by Tatlin, Rodchenko and Iakulov where the artists, already dizzy by the new world promised to them, were able to express themselves.

17. *V. E. Tatlin*
Still life.
Bouquet
1911-1912
The State Tretyakov Gallery
(Cat. 641)

18. *A. V. Lentulov*
Church
1916
Ekaterina and Vladimir Semenikhin Collection
(Cat. 646)

[1] The code and its evolution throughout the centuries has been analyzed in detail by Anatole Leroy-Beaulieu in *L'Empire des tsars et les Russes*, Paris 1897-1898 and by Michel Heller, *Histoire de la Russie et de son empire*, Paris 1997, pp. 334-338.
[2] M. Heller, *Histoire de la Russie et de son empire*, Paris 1997, pp. 356-359.
[3] P. Pascal, *La vie de l'archiprêtre Avvakum, écrite par lui-même*, Paris 1939.
[4] J. Stählin, *Krönungesgeschichte oder umständliche Beschreibung des solennen Einzugs (...) und Krönung Ihro kayserl. Majest der Frau Elisabeth Petrowna Kaiserin aller Russen* (...), Academy of Sciences, St. Petersburg 1745, quoted by F. D. Liechtenhan, *Elizabeth I of Russia, the other empress*, Paris 2007.
[5] Comte F. Golvkin, *The court and the reign of Paul I: portraits, souvenirs and anecdotes*, Paris 1905.
[6] A. Feodorovna Tioutcheva, *At the court of the two emperors*, Moscow 1929.
[7] S. Bensidoun, *Alexandre III, 1881-1894*, Paris 1990, pp. 55-56.
[8] M. Ferro, *Nicolas II*, Paris 1991, p. 50.
[9] A. Victorov, *Description of books, of notes and of papers of the old palais prikaz, 1613-1725*, Moscow, 1883. *Receipts and expenses and documents from the Armory Palace*, No. 986, p. 469.
[10] *Ibid.*, p. 470.
[11] P. Petrov, *History of St. Petersburg*, St. Petersburg 1885, pp. 250-267.
[12] Z. Batowski, *Architekt Rastrelli o swych pracach*, Lwow 1939, p. 53, publication of what Rastrelli wrote intended for Catherine II when the Empress eliminated him from the Court after her coronation. "I built a stone palace in the old Kremlin castle, residence of the former Czars: this building was constructed next to the big room designated as that in which the first day of the coronation would be celebrated." Rastrelli also recalled that he had built the suburban Muscovite residence of Pokrovskoye and the Perovo palace for Elizabeth.
[13] GNIMA, Shchusev Museum of Architecture, Moscow, No. R 11-26.
[14] Arsenal Library, Paris, Marquis de Paulmy, No. 729 A, B, C, D.
[15] K. I. Mineeva, *Tsaritsyno*, Moscow 1988 (in Russian).
[16] J. Verne, *Michel Strogoff, Moscou-Irkoutsk*, Paris 1875, p. 11.
[17] Sylvain Bensidoun, *op. cit.*, p. 10.
[18] *Zolotoie Rouno*, No. 6, Moscow 1909.
[19] *Zolotoie Rouno*, No. 2-3, Moscow 1909, pp. 3-30.

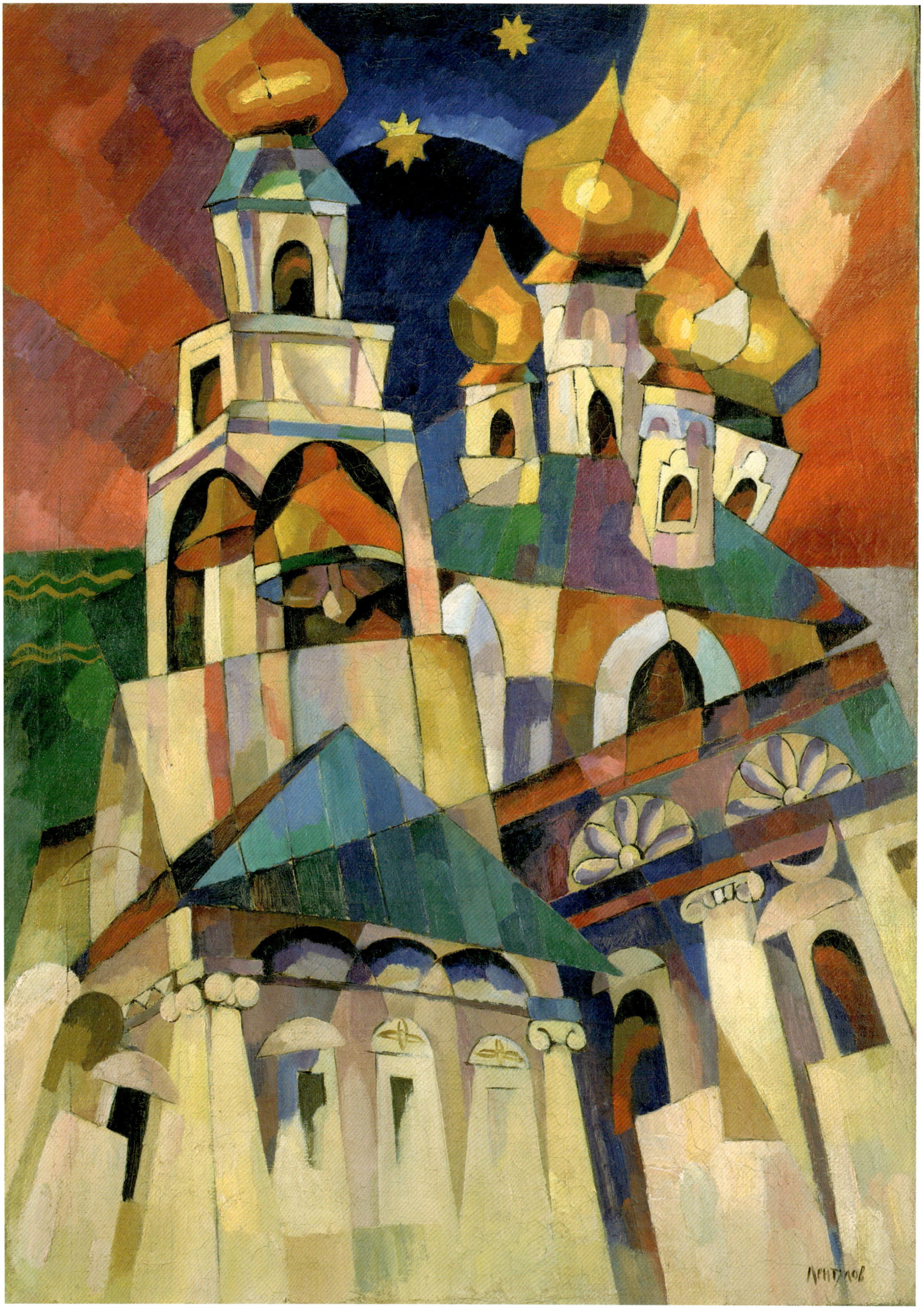
Лентулов

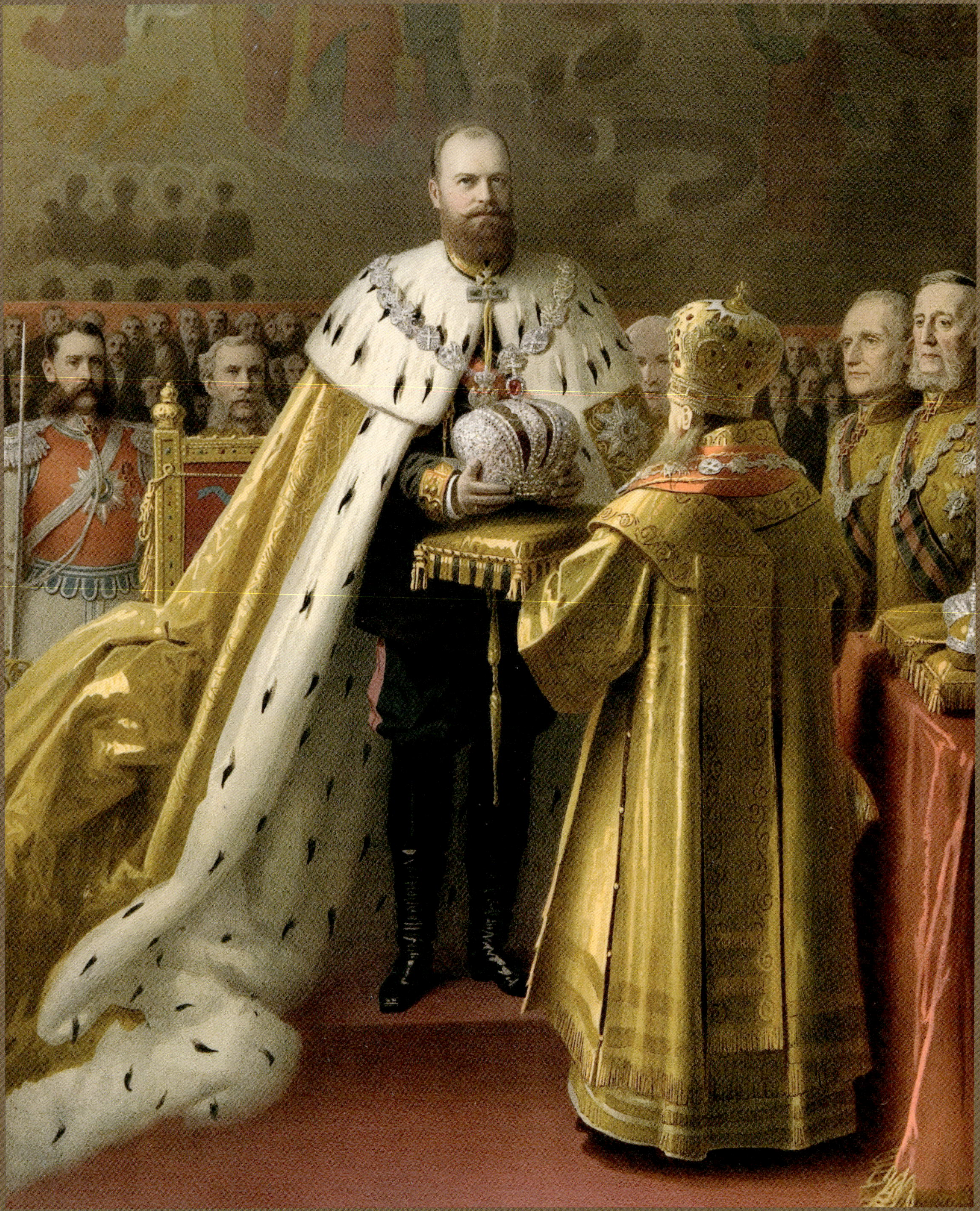

THE CORONATION OF A CZAR

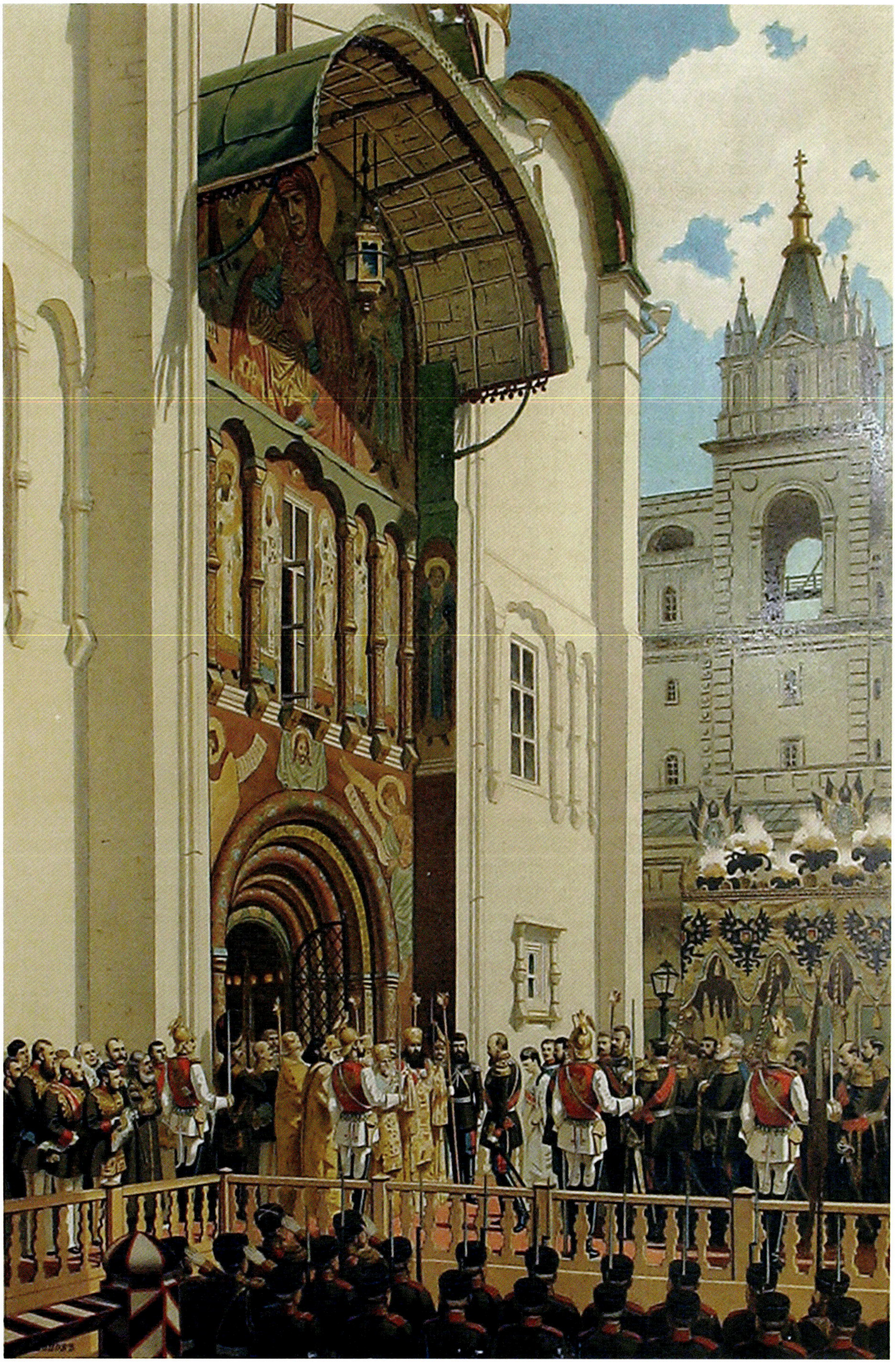

THE CORONATION TRADITIONS OF THE RUSSIAN MONARCHS

Ludmila Tarasenko

Page 34
Album of the coronation of His Majesty the Emperor Alexander III
St. Petersburg, 1883
The State Historical Museum, Moscow, GIM 70156, A-28
(Cat. 4)
Detail

1. *V. D. Polenov*
Their Majesties at the entrance of the Cathedral of the Assumption
Russia, St. Petersburg, 1883
The State Museum Preserve "Tsarskoye Selo", St. Petersburg
(Cat. 22)

After the fall of Byzantium in 1453, Russia acquired the status of the only Orthodox power to have retained its independence. This gave it an extraordinary authority in the eyes of the upholders of orthodoxy, making of it the heir and the guardian of Orthodox traditions. The marriage of the grand prince Ivan III (1440-1505) with the Byzantine princess Sophia Palaiologina (1472) granted a complementary legitimacy to the pretensions of the Russian Grand Principality to this preeminence.

The new political situation had to be explained. According to the texts of the Russian chroniclers of the time, the situation which had come about could be explained by the fact that the Greeks—who had accepted the Florentine Union in 1439—had betrayed the true faith and were thus paying for this betrayal by the fall of Byzantium, and that, at the same time they had therefore facilitated the triumph of Islam. In contrast, the grand prince of Moscow Ivan III, who had saved the Orthodox faith in its integrity, had triumphed over the Golden Hoard (1480) and furthered the triumph of Orthodoxy. As a result, Russia was justified in reclaiming the place of Byzantium in the Orthodox world, and the Russian autocrat that of the Byzantine *basileus*. Conceiving the Russian state's world historical role in such a way could of course only lead to the emergence of new ways of considering the Russian monarch and his powers.

At the end of the 15th and beginning of the 16th centuries a historiosophic theory appeared in the enlightened monarchism milieu which was later called "Moscow-Third Rome." It was based on the Biblical concept of the transfer of power (*translatio imperii*) essentially incarnated in the Book of the Prophet Daniel. In 1492 in the "Easter Exposition" by the Metropolitan Zosima, it was explicitly said that God had appointed Ivan III as the new Czar Constantine for Constantine's new city, in other words, Moscow and all of the Russian world. Another account ideologically justifying the power of the grand prince was the legend of the Monomaque regalia.[1] The later tradition which made all Russian princes descendants of the Roman Emperor Augustus also had its significance in the creation of this new ideology. All these accounts linked by the same line Vladimir Monomaque, born to a Greek queen and who had sought to reinforce the unity of Russian lands, and Ivan IV, Sophia Palaiologina's grandson who had achieved this unification of the country. In the ideas which were then being developed, the kingdom of Moscow was considered as an authentic "Third Rome" to whom a glorious future was promised as the home of the true Orthodoxy. Even more, in these texts the whole of Russian history, beginning with prince Vladimir the Saint, ap-

2. Coronation of Ivan and Peter Alexeievich
Miniature from the book of Peter Krekchin, The Life of Peter the First.
Middle of the 18th century
Manuscript: paper, watercolor, inks, cinnabar; binding: cardboard, morocco, gold
33.5 × 20 × 5 cm
The State Historical Museum, Moscow, GIM 80158 OR Bart. N°55

peared as the very particular road of the Russian people elect of God on their way toward the eschatological kingdom of Good and Light. In itself, the theory of "Moscow-Third Rome" carries an eschatological weight which is absent from the Byzantine idea of the power of the State. The Russian Czar, as the head of the last Christian kingdom, saw himself attributed a Messianic role in world history. As one of the chroniclers of the time wrote, "One and only is now the holy apostolic Eastern church, its brilliance over the surface of the earth is greater than the sun, one and only also is the great orthodox Russian Czar over all the surface of the earth, like Noah in his Ark saved from the Deluge."[2]

Thinking of Russia's worldwide role outside of the concept of "kingdom" was inconceivable for the Russian philosophers of the epoch.[3] To such an extent that the adoption of the title of Czar was the necessary expression of the Russian ecclesial and political conscience. Russia, as the heir to Greek Orthodoxy, had to have a king, a Czar, as supreme representative of world Orthodoxy.

The first sovereign under whom there was a sort of precedent to the crowning of the monarch was Ivan III who, in 1498, transmitted to his fifteen-year old grandson Dmitry in the Kremlin Cathedral of the Dormition in Moscow the crown destined to make him a grand prince.[4] The coronation ritual had been devised, inspired by the Greek example but it was not an exact copy of it.[5]

The first real crowning ceremony of a Czar took place in 1547. A royal throne and a chair for the Metropolitan had been set up on a high platform in the Cathedral of the Dormition. The regalia were placed onto a separate table, a sort of lectern: the Life-Giving Cross, Monomaque's *shapka*, the gold chain and the large necklace (*barmy*). The Metropolitan Macaire arrayed Ivan IV in these regalia and carried out the rite of unction with the Holy Chrism,[6] thus giving to the coronation a sacred nature. According to the Christian idea, with unction, the sovereign was provided with the Gifts of the Holy Spirit, with the strength and wisdom necessary to exercise the supreme power both in the domain of the affairs of the State and in those of the Church. At the same time, the Czar had taken Holy Communion which he had received in front of the altar. Then Ivan IV had visited the tombs of his ancestors in the Cathedral of the Archangel St. Michael, and had bowed down before the relics in the private chapel of the Annunciation. At the entrance of the Kremlin's three cathedrals, gold and silver coins were poured over the Czar. Having received the title of Czar in the eyes of his subjects and in his own eyes, Ivan the Terrible found himself at the same time invested with a special charisma. So there is nothing surprising in the fact that he sincerely believed his acts could not be judged by men.[7]

This crowning of a Czar, like all the ceremonies and coronations which followed, was accompanied by the ringing of bells, by a solemn meal in the Palace of Facets for high-ranking persons, by food offered to the people as well as various pardons (amnesties, annulling of debts etc.).

At the end of the 16th century, to the regalia destined for the Czar the scepter which had been given to Feodor Ivanovich during his coronation in 1584, and also the globe, also called apple, which appeared during Boris Godunov's coronation in 1598 were added. The patriarch specified the sig-

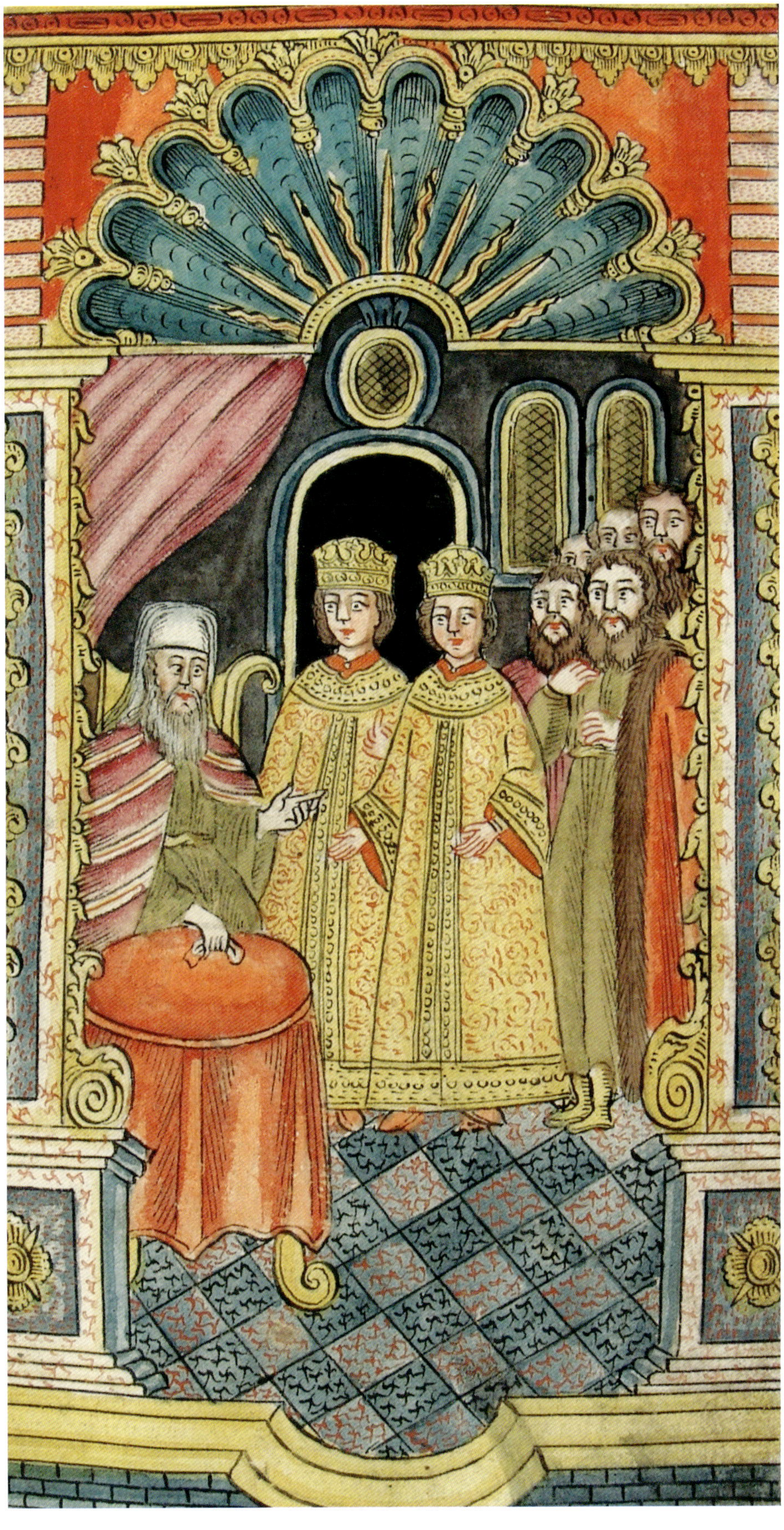

nificance and the meaning of the latter as he gave it to the sovereign he was crowning: "This apple is the sign of your kingdom; in the same way that you take this apple in your hands and hold it firmly, so firmly hold all the kingdoms which have been entrusted to you by God, in protecting them without fail from the enemies."[8] Each one of the regalia and each one of the gestures carried out during the ceremony had a symbolic significance. The royal mantle called "the purple" (*porphyra*) and the crown, insignia of the royal glory, were donned in front of the altar, symbolizing the purple and Christ's crown of thrones, reminder of the heavy weight of the royal responsibility. The union of the sovereign and the church was expressed in the profession of the Orthodox faith, the "Symbol of the Faith", equivalent to the Latin Credo, which the Czar recited out loud during the ceremony.

The organization of the coronation as it had been established under Ivan the Terrible continued practically unchanged until the end of the 17th century. There was an important innovation during the crowning of Czar Feodor Alexeievich. He was led up to receive communion on the altar itself according to Greek custom. Through this action, the Russian Czar took his place in the ecclesiastic hierarchy. The sons of Alexei Mikhailovich, Ivan Alexeievich and Peter Alexeievich were crowned Czars (ill. 2) in the same ritual in 1682. That was when the "Monomaque's shapka" was used for the last time for a coronation.

Beginning with Dmitry Ivanovich, the coronation ceremony took place at the Kremlin, in the Cathedral of the Dormition founded by the bishop of Moscow, Peter, who had transferred the Episcopal seat from Vladimir to Moscow in 1326. This action by one of the most respected Russian saints marked the beginning of the ascension of Moscow, predicted for greatness by the Metropolitan to the grand prince Ivan Kalita (1288-1340). The most sacred objects of the Russian Orthodox Church were preserved in the cathedral: relics of several saints, Russian as well as those universally recognized, and many particularly venerated icons.

Around the middle of the 16th century, the fundamental principles of the ordering of the Russian church were already in place. The high iconostasis had become the central element of the interior of the building, both in terms of significance and on the artistic level, and the way that it was organized reflected the evolution of historical knowledge and of the theological thought of Old Russia.

The coronations and anointments of the Russian autocrats took place in front of the iconostasis and the incarnate image that it displayed of the history of mankind. Icons of the Biblical kings, the prophets, the just men of the New Testament were perceived by the monarchs not as images of historical figures belonging to a distant past, but as examples of the way of serving one's people. In the Russian literature of the Middle Ages, contemporary events were always interpreted by the chroniclers and philosophers through parallels with the books of the Bible, thanks to which the timeless meaning of what had happened in the immediate reality was made clear. And so it was for the monarchs in power who, in function of their actions, were compared by their contemporaries and their descendants either to the just and wise David and Solomon, or to Constantine and Vladimir who were both said to be "Equal to the Apostles," or to Biblical tyrants without faith or law such as Nabuchodonosor, Achab and others.

Russia's great reformer, Peter I, master of absolute power and who refused any limitation on that power, suppressed the patriarchate and practically became the head of the Church. He appointed the bishops himself and in fact directed the Synod.[9] This contributed largely to the process which had begun taking place at the time of Old Russia of regarding the person of the Emperor as sacred. In the 18th century, this view of the Emperor as sacred was integrated into the mechanism of the organization of the State, and particularly of the Synod.[10] Of the anathemas pronounced during Orthodoxy Week, among the main heresies enumerated relating to dogma, the following was added during the imperial epoch, "On those who believe that the Orthodox sovereigns were not raised to the throne by a special grace of God which touched them or who do not believe that, with unction, the gifts of the Holy Spirit have descended upon them for the accomplishment of their great task, as well as on those who hatch against them rebellion and treason, may anathema be pronounced against them." In such particular circumstances, innovations also appear during the coronation ceremony.

In spite of transferring the capital from Moscow to St. Petersburg at the beginning of the 18th century, and not counting other historical events, the Cathedral of the Dormition remained the place for the coronation of Russian sovereigns. Even the great attacker of the fundaments of tradition, Peter I, considered the Cathedral of the

Dormition as the only place possible for that ceremony. Each time, at the moment of coronation, the Court was transported from St. Petersburg to Moscow, accompanied also by the representatives of foreign powers, as well as thousands of Russians pouring there in their desire to attend the decisive and solemn ceremonies for the country. During that brief lapse of time, the beating heart of Russian life moved toward what had been the first seat of power and afterwards was calm again for decades.

Beginning with Peter I's epoch, the hierarchs of the Russian church no longer had any role but that of officiator in the course of the ceremony. The innovations which Peter I introduced were the presence of heralds for the special purpose of announcing the coronation of the Emperor in advance, the institution of a special company of chevaliers-guards to accompany the course of the coronation, and the minting of medals and tokens commemorating the event. The former insignias of power were no longer in use, but they were present throughout the whole coronation on a special table in the Cathedral of the Dormition. The order of things instituted by Peter I scarcely changed after that. Firstly, he himself had not been crowned as Emperor. In a manifesto on November 15, 1723, he announced the coronation to come of his wife in these terms, "In the name of which, by the autocratic power we hold from God, for these tasks which are those of our spouse, we have decided to crown her with the imperial crown."

On May 7, 1724, Peter I gave the first example of an imperial crowning. An imperial throne (or more exactly a platform) was set up in the Cathedral of the Dormition under a canopy. There, two ancient royal thrones were set up, upon which sat the Emperor and his spouse. Peter opened the ceremony by proclaiming that he was executing

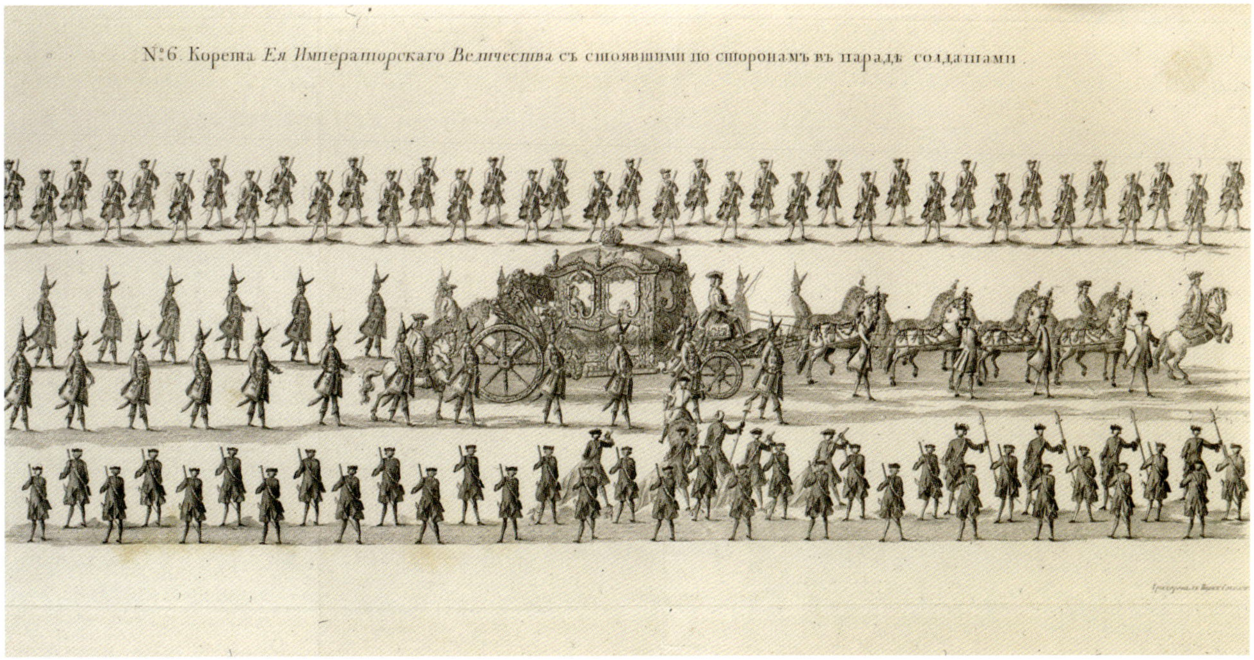

3. *I. A. Sokolov*
His Imperial Majesty's carriage
Album page
St. Petersburg, 1744
Paper, burin, etching
44.7 × 55 cm
The State Historical Museum, Moscow, GIM 70156 A-32

4. Mitre
Russia, beginning of 19th century
The State Historical Museum, Moscow
(Cat. 19)

his plan. Before the coronation, the Empress read him the Orthodox Credo which is the "Symbol of the Faith." Then the clergy gave him the insignias of power and the Emperor gave them to Catherine. At the beginning of the ceremony, Catherine, kneeling, received the unction, and after the completion of the liturgy, she took communion near the altar.

Just as for the coronation of the Czars, the people were given drink and food at the Square of the Cathedrals, while at the Palace of Facets a reception took place for high-ranking persons and notable guests. Balls and fireworks celebrated the event.

Peter II succeeded Catherine I. He was the son of the Czar Alexei who had been condemned to death. On October 10, 1727, a manifesto announced that the coronation was approaching. A triumphal arch was built for Peter's arrival to Moscow. On February 25, the coronation took place, according to the same ritual as for Catherine I. It is interesting to note that the ambassadors of foreign powers took an active part in the ceremonies. Thus, the Spanish ambassador illuminated his residence at great expense and provided food for the people the day of the coronation, just as was being done at the Kremlin. Peter's coronation was the occasion for various graces for the populace: amnesty for arrears and fines, and also lightening of sentences.

Afterwards, Anna Ivanova, the daughter of Ivan Alexeivich and who had been the Duchess of Curland succeeded to Peter's place. She was crowned on April 28, 1730 following the noticeably the same order of things. But the mantle and the crown were given to the Empress by the Archbishop.

On November 25, 1741, the daughter of Peter the Great, Elizabeth Petrovna, acceded to the imperial Russian throne. Her reign lasted almost twenty years. The solemn entrance of the Empress into Moscow took place on February 28, 1742 (ill. 3). Triumphal gates rose in four places along the way of the retinue. The Empress was welcomed in the Cathedral of the Dormition by the Archbishop of Novgorod, Ambroise, with a homily in which he spoke of the beginning of a new Russia in the history of the homeland which had suffered too long under an excessive German influence. Elizabeth Petrovna observed the coronation ritual instituted by Peter: the archpriests presented the imperial regalia to her and she put them on herself.

Illuminations, distribution of medals and tokens, balls, Italian opera, popular banquets made of these coronation ceremonies an unforgettable event. The Empress had the task of according numerous pardons. Right before the coronation, she published an edit suppressing the death penalty.

Elizabeth Petrovna's successor was her nephew Peter III but he hadn't been in power even a year when, following a coup d'état, his wife Catherine II became queen. Peter III did not receive the honors due to the crown until thirty-five years after his death when Paul I, immediately after Catherine II's death, ordered the coffin of his progenitor exhumed. He had been buried at Alexander Nevsky Lavra. Paul placed a crown on the coffin. And when the coffins of the Emperor and the Empress were being carried to their place of inhumation, the remains of the Emperor Peter III were ahead of those of the Empress.

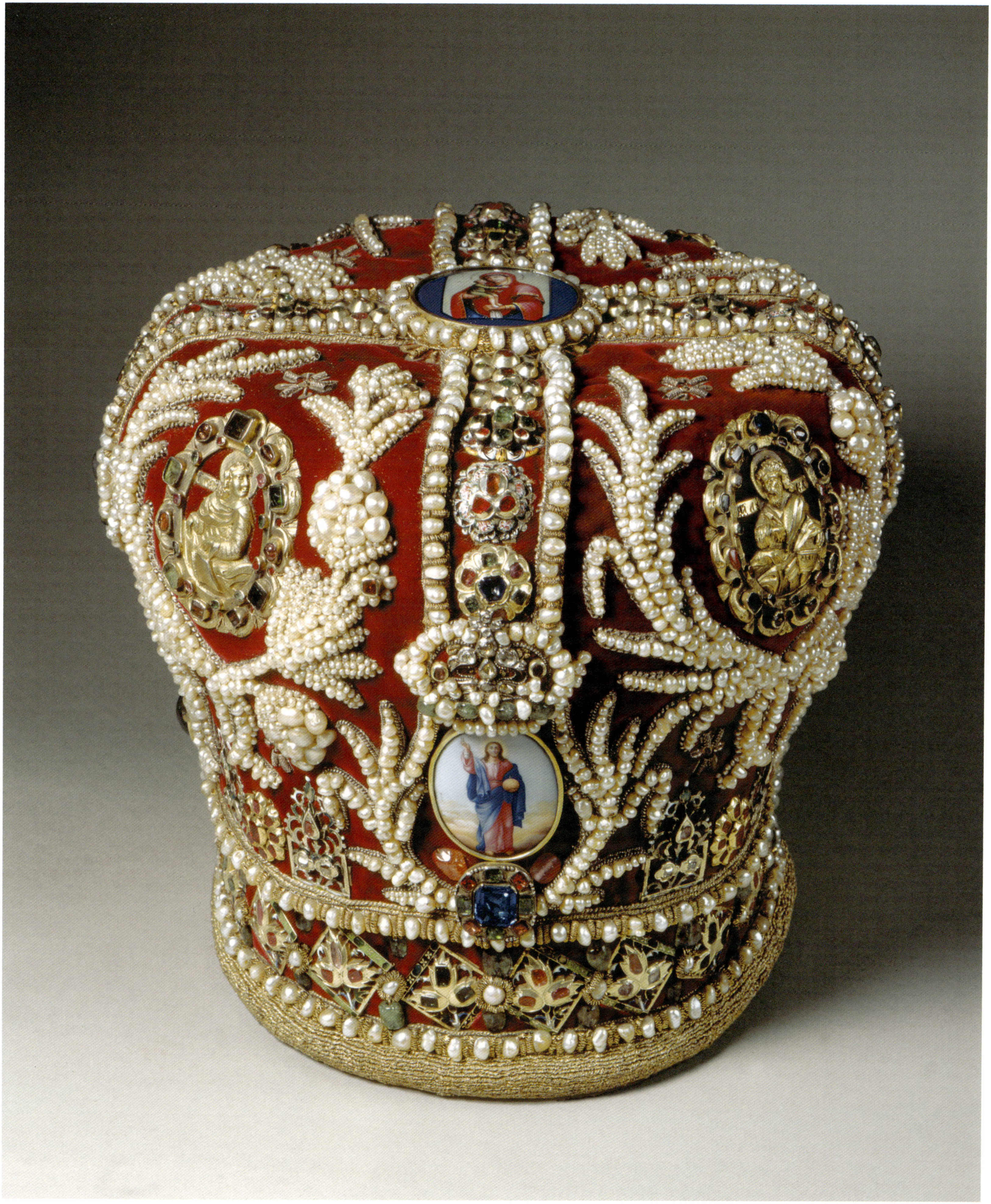

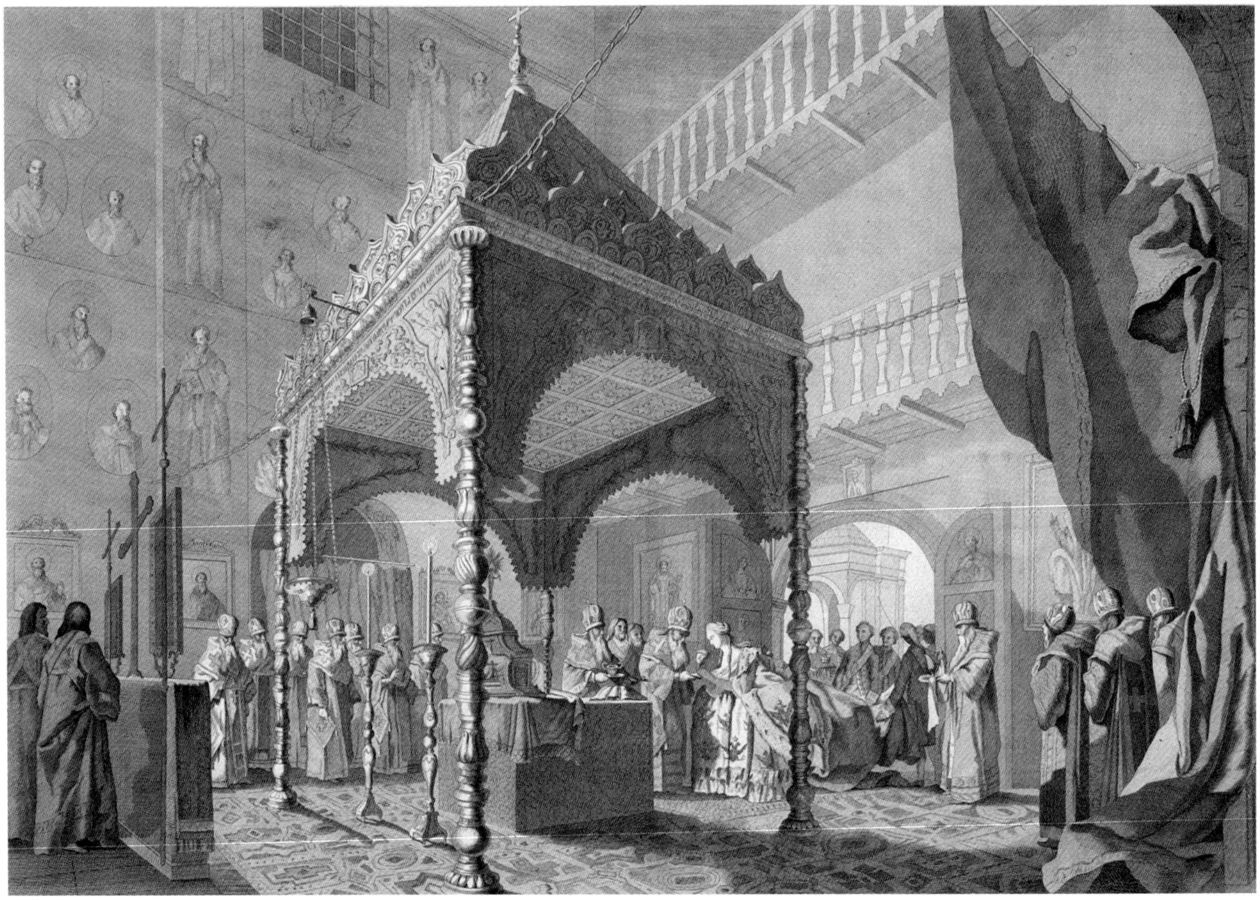

5. T. Dmitriev. Based on an original by J. L. Develly and M. I. Makhaev 1760s
Catherine II taking communion near the altar of the Cathedral of the Dormition
Taken from Drawings included in the description of Empress Catherine II's coronation.
St. Petersburg, 1857
Paper, burin
57.8 × 78.4 cm
The State Historical Museum, Moscow, GIM 70156 A-18

The Manifesto of June 28, 1762 announced Catherine II's accession to the throne, with another following closely afterwards announcing the coronation which took place September 22 (ill. 5). These ceremonies were very slightly different from the previous coronation. As had already been the case, medals were minted for this occasion representing the sovereign. The festivities for the people were particularly grandiose: special equipages distributed roast beef and bread throughout Moscow, while behind them other carts were hitched to low wagons with barrels of honey and beer. Tables were set up for the needy. The main places for the fete were the Red Square and the Lobnoe Mesto. There, tables were set up with mountains of zakusky and cakes, while wine and beer flowed freely. The Sovereign, accompanied by her retinue, circulated around Moscow, taking pleasure in contemplating the popular jubilation, all the while throwing tokens to the people. The ceremony was marked by many pardons given to the people: criminals were pardoned, those who had stolen from the public treasury, galley slaves, and still others.

Paul Petrovich was crowned April 5, 1797. He had fixed the date of the ceremony for the Sunday following Easter, and he made his solemn entrance into Moscow on Palm Sunday, thus establishing at the same time a clear parallel between the events of the coronation and the great Christian celebrations. In a way, he was placing his entrance into the former capital and Christ's entry into Jerusalem as the Messiah, King and Redeemer, on the same level, and comparing the coronation

6. *A. P. Sokolov*
Portrait of the Empress Maria Feodorovna
Russia, St. Petersburg, 1883
The State Museum Preserve "Tsarskoye Selo", St. Petersburg
(Cat. 26)

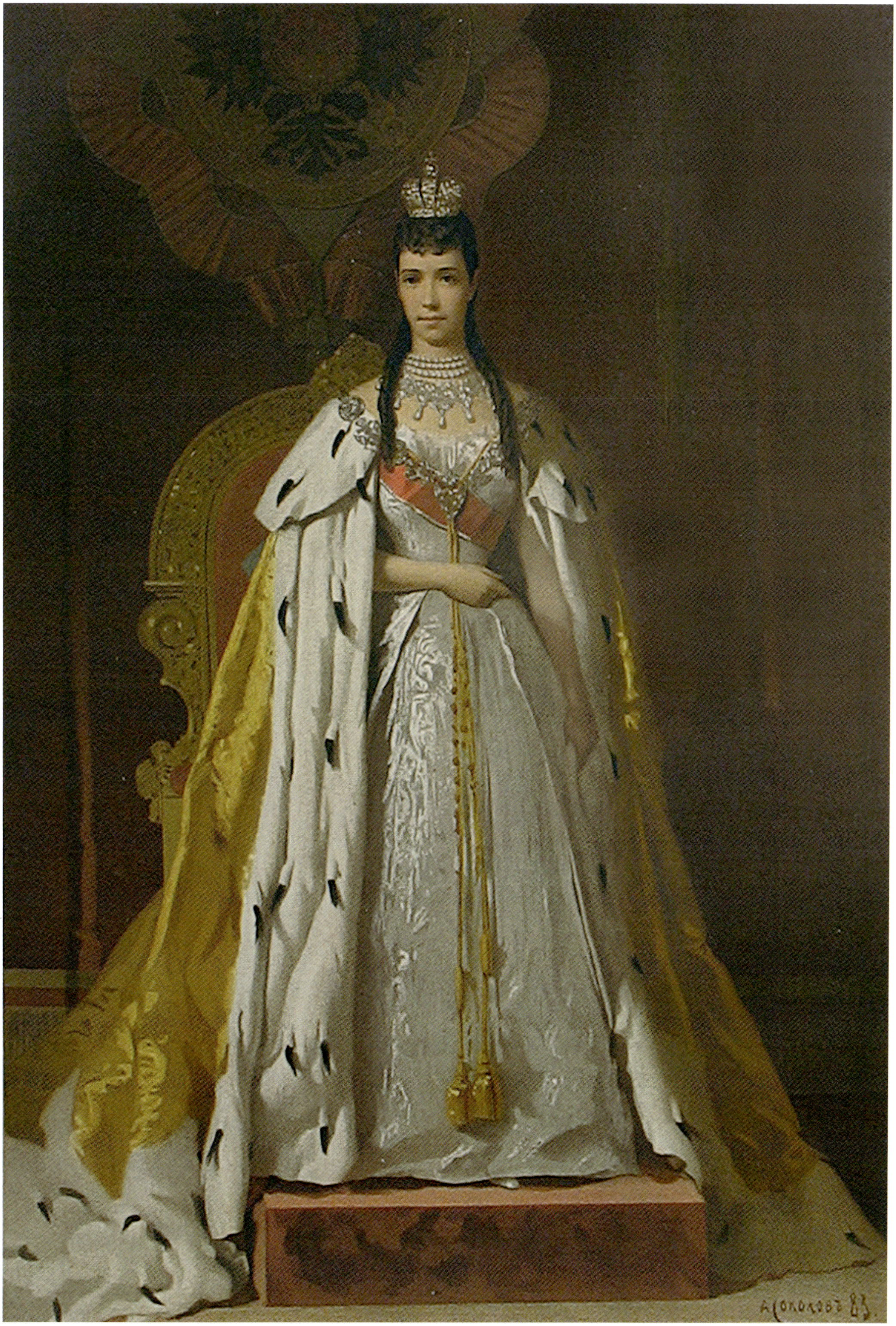

7. V. A. Courten
Coronation of the Emperor Nicholas I in the Cathedral of the Dormition
Album page
The coronation ceremonies of their majesties the Emperor Nicholas I and the Empress Alexandra.
Paris, 1828
Paper, lithography
70.5 × 54.5 cm
The State Historical Museum, Moscow, GIM 53886 A-22

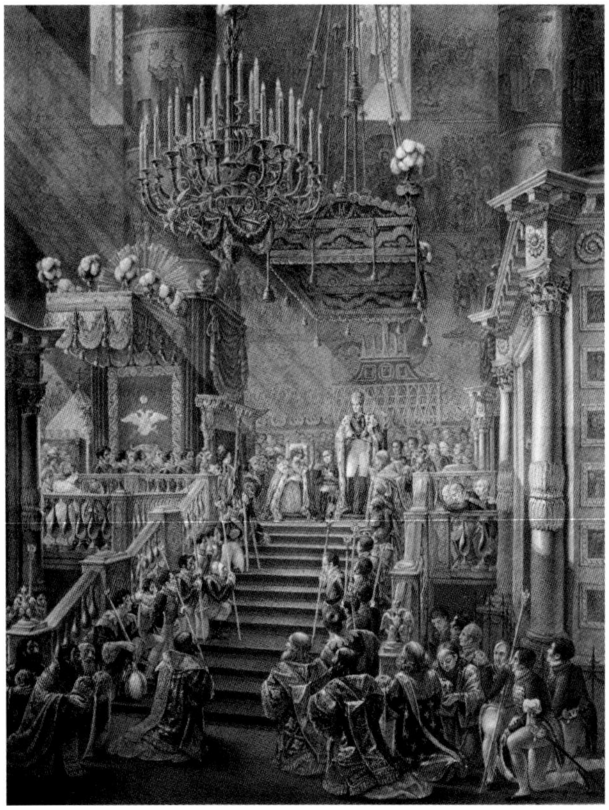

to the final glory of Christ acceding to the throne and thus redeeming humanity.[11] This time, the sequence of the coronation ceremony had its particularities. Paul I put on first the dalmatic himself and then the imperial mantle (porphyro). And it was the first time that two people were crowned at the same time. For after having received the crown, the Emperor sat down on the throne and had the Empress Maria Feodorovna come to him. She knelt before him. The Emperor took off his crown, brushed the head of his wife with it, then crowned her with a smaller crown that had immediately been given him. After that, he decorated his spouse with the Order of St. Andrew the First Called and put the imperial mantle on her. During the ceremony, Paul read the decree of the succession to the throne in which he officially declared himself to be the head of the Church. He placed this document on the main altar in a casket prepared for it and ordered it to be kept forever. It is important to note that Paul, convinced of the charismatic basis of the function of monarch as head of the Church, wished to participate in the mass accompanying the ceremony specifically in virtue of being head of the Church. Among the most significant pardons made to the people during Paul I's coronation was an edict concerning the peasants: the work of the peasants under the jurisdiction of an landowner as their master was not to exceed three days a week and it was forbidden to force the peasants to work during festival days.

All the ceremonies which followed resembled one another, with a few specific features however. The coronation of Alexander I took place September 15, 1801. For the first time, deputies from the class of nobles of the Court and the merchant class attended. The crowning of Nicholas I was marked by a touching episode: at the moment when he received the crown, the sovereign kissed his wife, thus showing the particular attachment he felt toward her. Alexander II was not immediately crowned, for he became Emperor in the middle of the Crimean War. The war ended in March 1856. On August 26, 1856, his coronation ceremony took place following the traditional order (ill. 7). Upon his entrance to the cathedral, the very pious imperial couple bowed three times in front of the Royal Gates and kissed the icons of the lower row of the iconostasis. Significant details of the ceremony: the Emperor did not allow the Metropolitans to bring him his imperial mantle, but replaced them by their sub-deacons. After having taken Holy Communion, Alexander II prayed

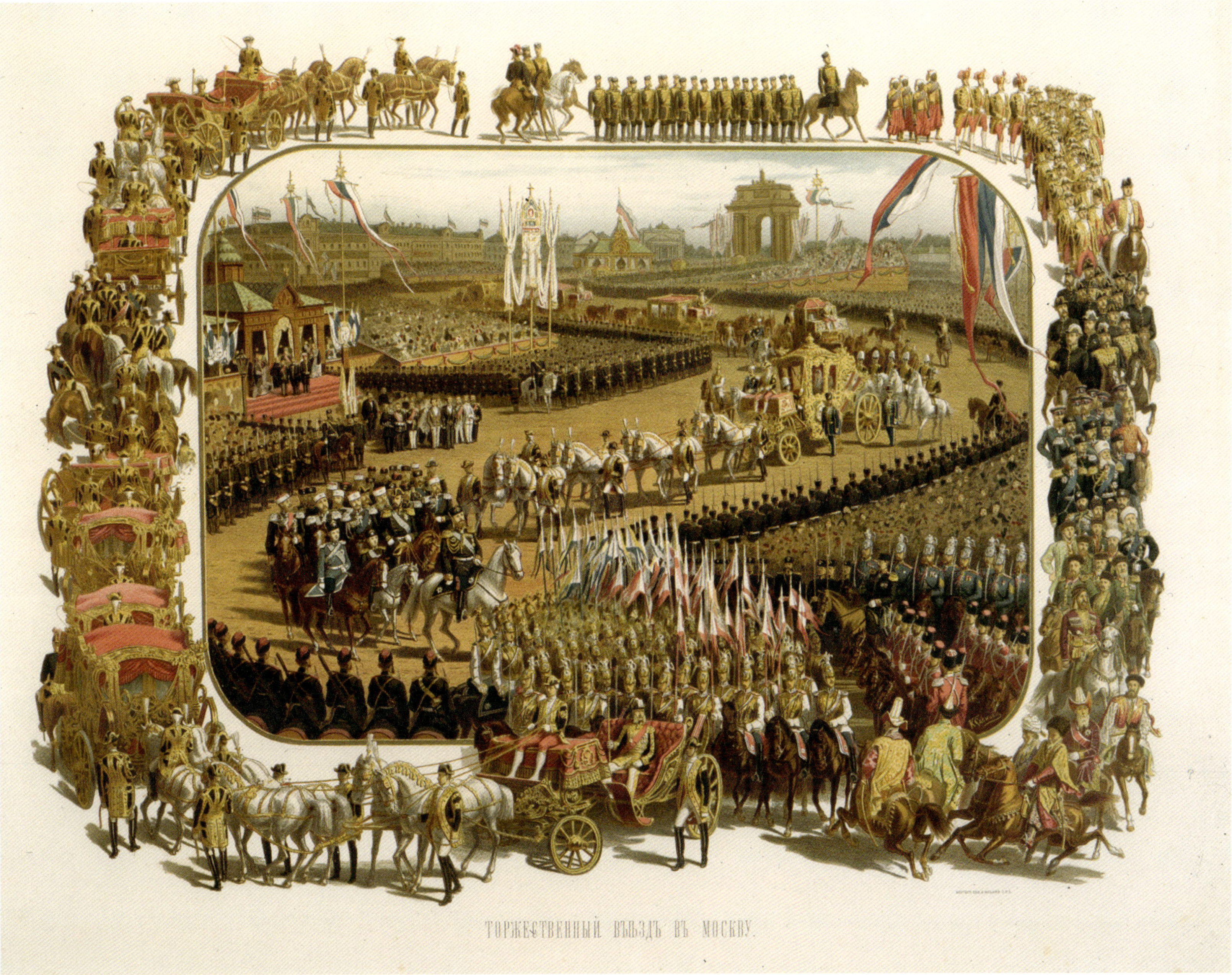

8. *K. A. Savitsky*
Solemn entrance of the Emperor
Alexander III into Moscow
Album page, The coronation of his
majesty the Emperor Alexander III.
St. Petersburg, 1883
Paper, chromolithography
67 × 53 cm
The State Historical Museum,
Moscow, GIM 70156 A-28

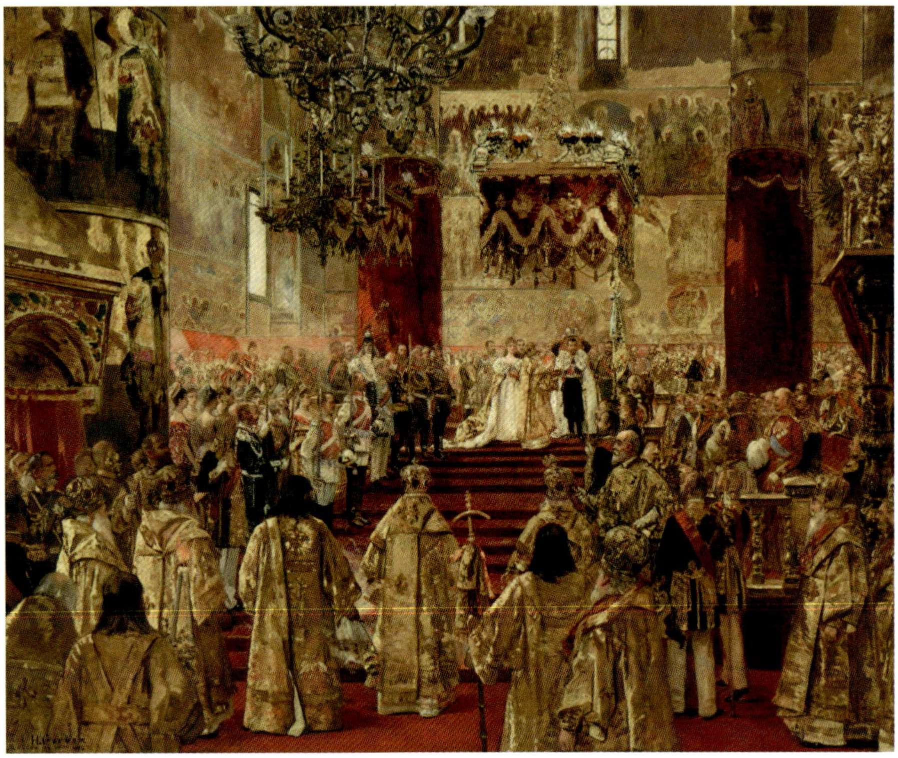

9. *H. Gervex*
The crowning of Nicholas II *(sketch)*
1896
Oil on canvas
116 × 151 cm
Paris, Orsay Museum, R. F. 1977-184

a long time, tears in his eyes. Many Decabrists who had been sent to Siberia were allowed to return, and participants in the Polish insurrection of 1831 were freed. The same year, 1856, marked the beginning of the freeing of the Russian people from serfdom, liberation ratified by the decree of February 19, 1861 which was at the origin of the Emperor being called "the Liberator" by his contemporaries.

Alexander III and his wife Maria Feodorovna (ill. 6) were crowned two years after their succession to the throne, May 15, 1883. One of the most significant moments of the ceremony was the solemn entrance of the Emperor and his spouse into Moscow which had been decorated with an exceptional majesty (ill. 8).

Finally, in 1896 the last coronation ceremony in Russia took place, that of Nicholas II and Alexandra Feodorovna (ill. 9). For the Emperor's entrance into Moscow, the official organ of the Synod, the Ecclesiastic Messenger (1896, No. 19) declared, "With the heart if not with the voice, all of Moscow and behind it all of Russia has cried, "Blessed be he who comes in the name of the Lord, the Czar and the Autocrat of Russia."[12] At the same time, the ceremony was marked by the sign of events which were considered by many contemporaries, among them certain members of the imperial family, as the portent of tragic cataclysms to come: the popular feast which had been organized without the least precaution on Khodynka Field took a dramatic turn and there were many victims.

As Father Pavel Florensky wrote, expressing the viewpoint of many of his contemporaries with royalist convictions, "...the autocracy of the Czar stems not from legal ideas, but flows from the faith, it enters into the domain of faith, and is not deduced from secular postulates which potentially take into consideration the public or state interest."[13] The phenomena of regarding the monarch as sacred which had begun in Old Russia within the context of the idea of a Moscow-Third Rome and which had incurred a few transformations during the reign of Alexei Mikhailovich, took a more specific form with Peter I. During practically the whole Synodal period, both in the sermons in the church as well as in poetic texts and others, the Emperor was often compared to God, and behind any and all events in the life of the monarch, an equivalent was made to the events of Christ's earthly life. It is very significant in this respect that during the coronation ceremony, the royal throne was compared to Mt. Tabor and, consequently, the accession to the monarch's throne was associated to the Transfiguration of Jesus Christ.

[1] The headdress in the form of a bonnet called "Monomaque shapka" is a very ancient insignia of royal power which dates from the end of the 13th -beginning of the 14th centuries. It is mentioned for the first time in Ivan Kalita's spiritual testament. According to the account which appeared in the second half of the 15th century, the "Monomaque shapka" had been transmitted to Vladimir Monomaque according to the right of blood by the Byzantine Emperor Constantine Monomaque.

[2] V. M. Jivov, B. A. Uspensky, "Czar and God, Semiotic aspects of regarding the Russian monarch as sacred," in *Languages of culture and problems of translation*, Moscow 1987, p. 55 (in Russian).

[3] M. B. Pliukhanova, *Subjects and symbols of the Moscow kingdom*, Moscow 1995, p. 7 (in Russian).

[4] For Ivan III this coronation was an important political step so as to establish the power of the descendants of his line onto the Muscovite seat. But this first sovereign to have been crowned did not however become the head of the Russian State. Two years later, he saw himself dispossessed of his right of succession.

[5] E. V. Barsov, *Ancient Russian monuments of the crowning of Czars in connection with their Greek originals*, Moscow 1883 (in Russian); V. I. Jmakin, "The coronations of the Russian Emperors and Empresses (1724-1856)" in *Russkaïa starina*, March 1883 (in Russian).

[6] The rite of unction during the coronation of Christian Emperors was practiced beginning in the 5th century. This custom was not exactly the same as the royal unction of the Hebrews (for whom it signified the elected nature) or that which accompanied the investiture for the pagans.

[7] V. M. Jivov, B. A. Uspensky, *op. cit.*, p. 56 (in Russian).

[8] E. V. Barsov, *op. cit.*; V. I. Jmakin, *op. cit.*

[9] V. M. Jivov, B. A. Uspensky, *op. cit.*, p. 93 (in Russian).

[10] *Ibid.*, p. 93.

[11] *Ibid.*, p. 108.

[12] *Ibid.*, p. 108.

[13] *Ibid.*, p. 48.

THE ICONOSTASIS

Ludmila Tarasenko

The iconostasis presents in its conspicuous fullness the history of the Building of the House of God. In its upper level the row of precursors, the patriarchs are displayed. There, one can see images of the great ancestors, from the line of the house of David which goes back to Adam and which made possible, through the Virgin Mary, the incarnation of Christ. This row of ancestors reflects how the first step of the history of the Salvation of humanity was seen, from the Creation of man to the Alliance with Moses. Under that cames the tier of the icons of the Old Testament prophets, the voice through which God had let the elected people know of their salvation to come and of the incarnation of the Messiah. Appearing most often in the center of this register (layer) is the "Virgin of the Sign", a radiant illustration of the mystery of the Incarnation. This tier shows the second step of the history of humanity, after the Alliance concluded by God with his elected people and up to the arrival on earth of the Savior.

The following register of the iconostasis, that of the Celebrations, shows the prophecies coming true: the birth of Christ and his earthly itinerary which, in saving humanity, concluded with the Crucifixion and the Resurrection. And finally the register of the *Deisis* (from the Greek word meaning prayer): an image of the Second Coming of the Messiah, this time as Judge, as Savior of the World and as the King of Kings. In the center of this row is the icon "All Powerful Savior," the Pantocrator on which Christ is represented enthroned, surrounded by celestial Forces. On both sides, as intercessors for mankind, the Saints are turning toward Christ, with the Mother of God and John the Precursor (St. John the Baptist) at their head. As the focal point of the iconostasis, the register of the Deisis incarnates the image of the Church in its eschatological aspect and reveals the accomplishment of the theme of the Building of the House of God.

On the lower level of the iconostasis, just under the step giving access to the choir, is the localtier, the one most likely to change in terms of its components. The Royal Gates are in the center, the main entrance of the iconostasis which gives access to the altar. The icons of Christ (ill. 1) and of the Virgin Mother of God take their obligatory place on either side of these Gates. The local row always includes the icons of the Russian saints and the saints common to all Orthodoxy, and a series of venerated icons. Often included are images of celestial patrons of the reigning monarch. And so, during the time of Alexei Mikhailovich, there were icons of Alexis the Man of God (ill. 2). Venerated icons of the Virgin with accounts of miracles often decorate the local registers of the iconostases (ill. 3).

1. *S. Ushakov*
The Savior "Archeiropoietos" (not done by the hand of man)
Moscow, Armory School, 1670
The State Historical Museum, Moscow
(Cat. 54)

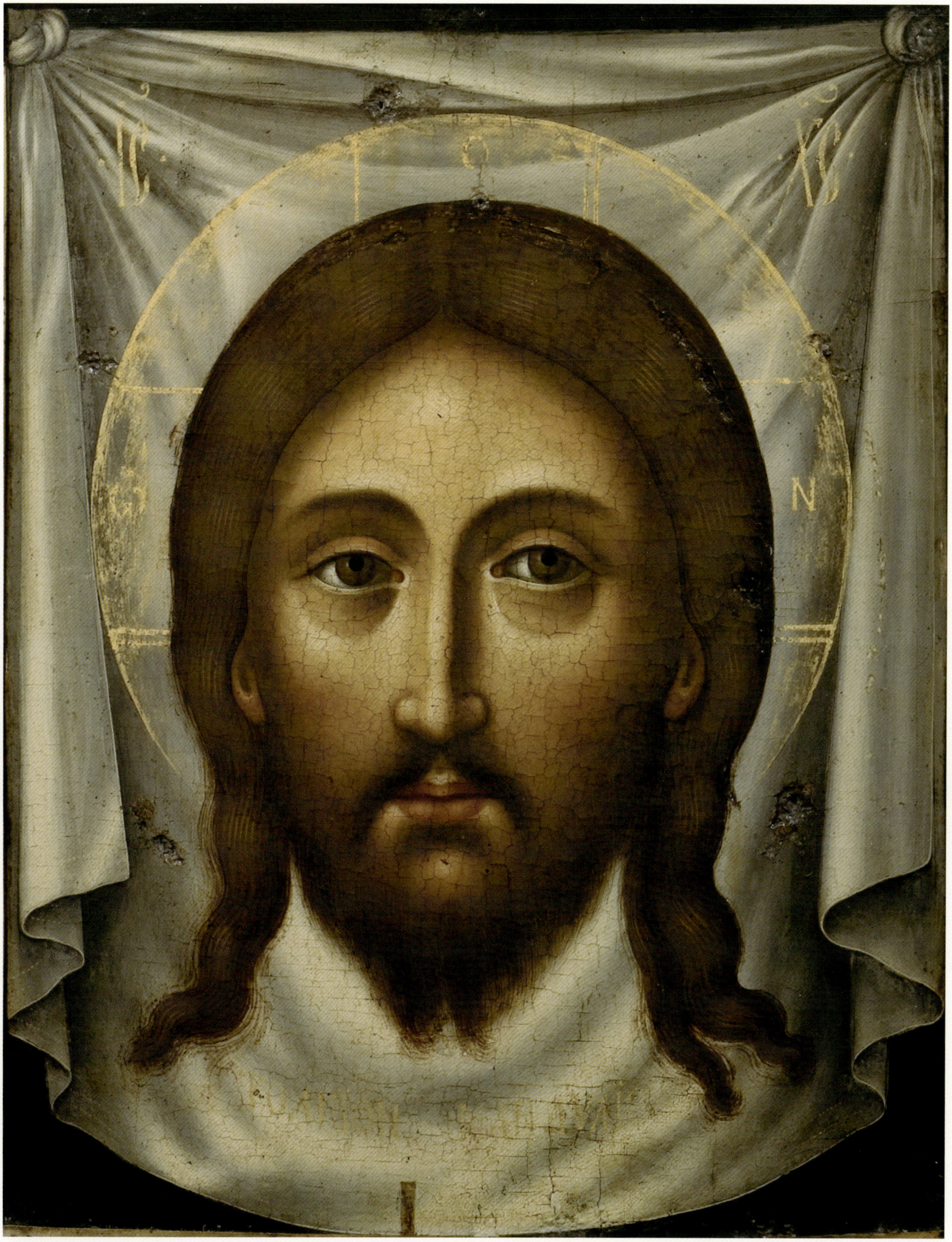

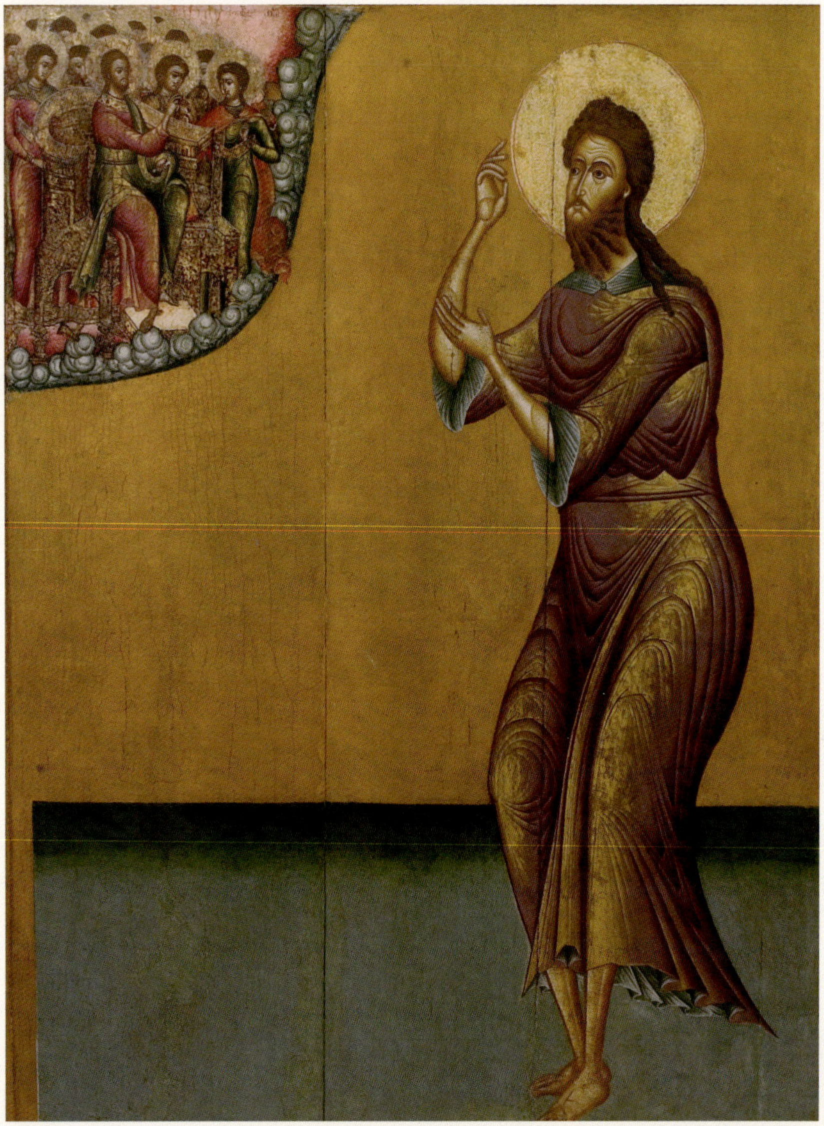

2. St. Alexius the Man of God
Moscow, circa 1650
The State Historical Museum, Moscow
(Cat. 69)

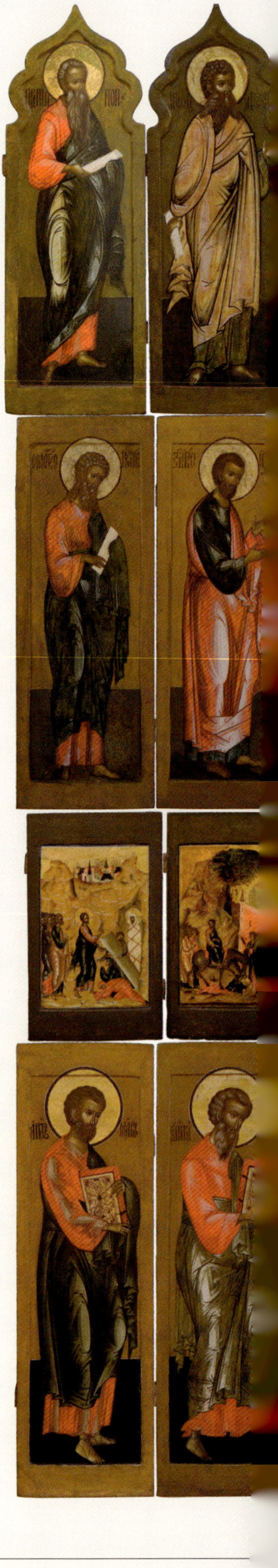

3. Iconostasis of the Trinity Church in Nikitniki
Moscow, circa 1634
(Cat. 71-115)

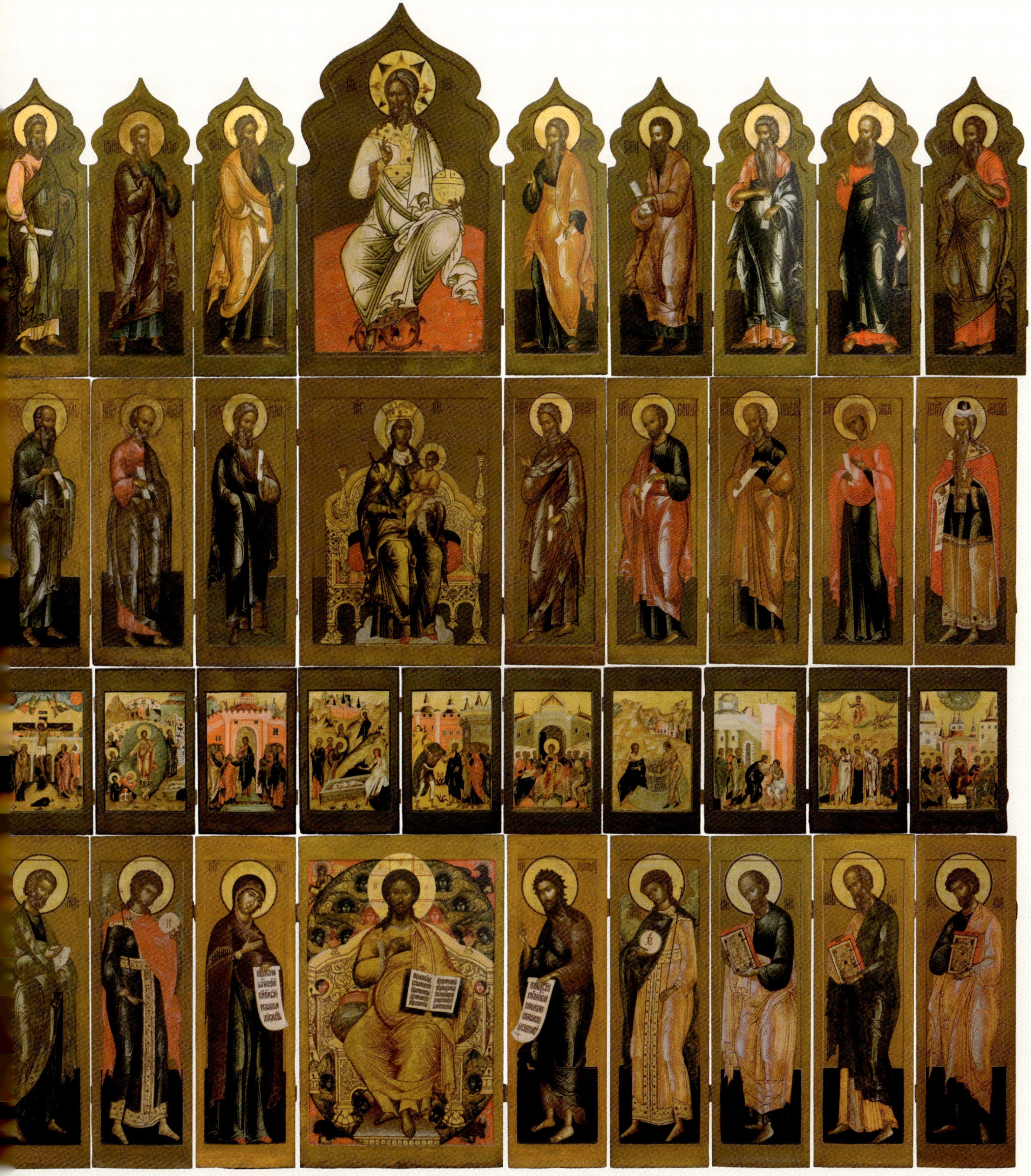

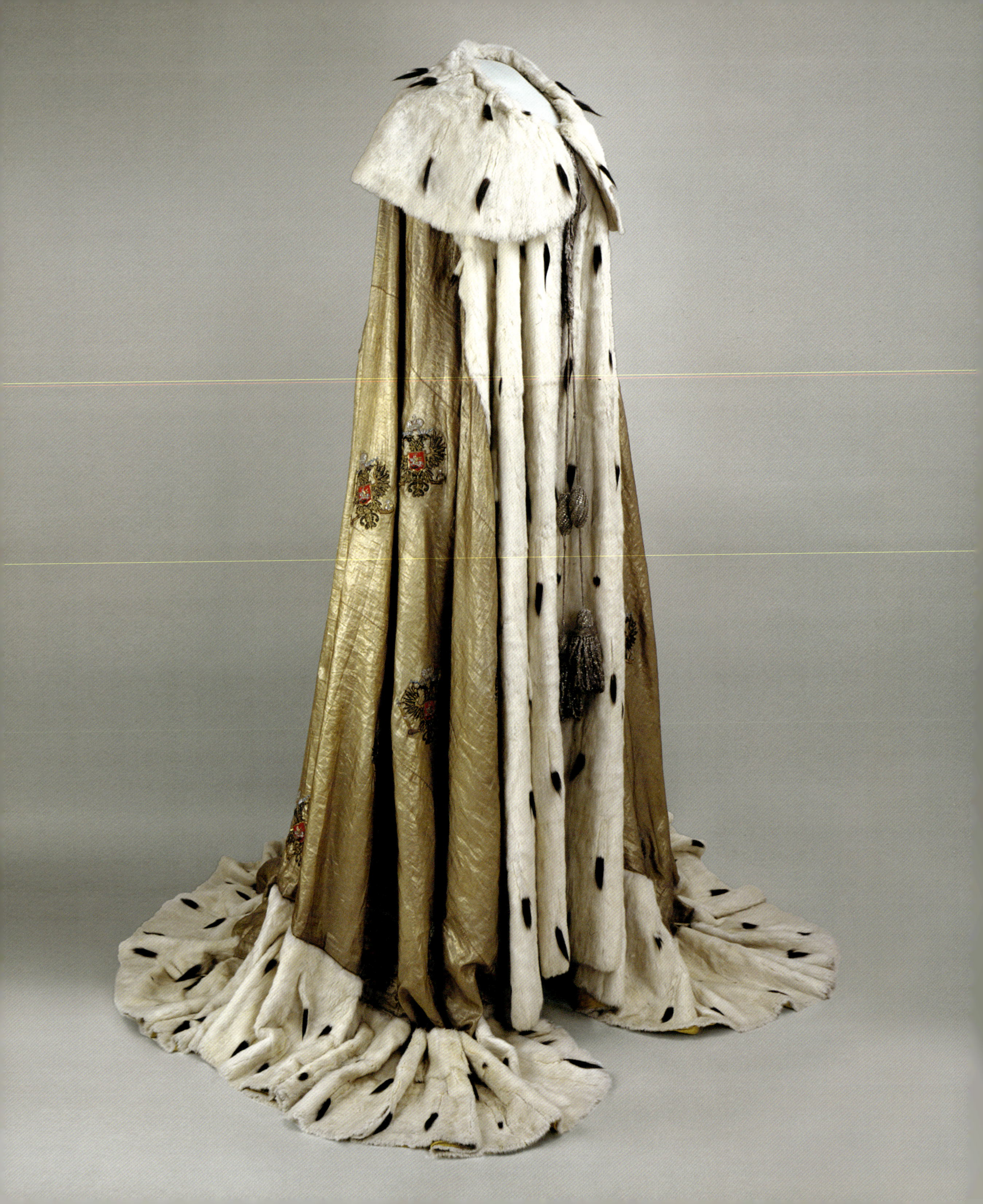

THE CORONATION FABRICS

Svetlana Amelekhina

1. Ceremonial mantle belonging to the Empress Maria Alexandrovna, spouse of the Emperor Alexander II
Russia, St. Petersburg, 1856
Moscow, Kremlin Museums
(Cat. 3)

"The coronation of the Russian sovereigns, as much by its pomp and ceremony as by the unchanging character of a very ancient organization upon which an impressive ritual developed, was for all those who participated in it a show unlike any other for its captivating beauty and its profound significance. For it was only during those few short hours that one was able to experience all at once the whole power, the whole grandeur of the Russian Empire." Thus wrote an eyewitness to the coronation of the last Czar of Russia which took place in the Kremlin in Moscow on May 26, 1896. The coronation ceremony was a great national holiday. It signified the recognition of the power of the monarch over Russia and of his consecration by the Church.

After the transfer in 1712 of the Russian capital to the city of St. Petersburg, founded by Peter I, Moscow remained the spiritual center of Russia and the place where the Russian monarchs, who from 1721 on bore the prestigious title of Emperor, were enthroned. In 1724 the first imperial coronation in the history of Russia took place. Apart from the fact that it sanctioned the sovereign's new title and settled the Godunov question of the transmission of power, its aims were above all political: the sumptuous celebrations given in the former capital of the kingdom became the occasion to demonstrate the majesty of the new empire, its wealth and its prosperity.

Developed with the personal participation of the founder of the empire, Peter the Great, the coronation ceremony brought together elements borrowed from the Byzantine ritual according to which all the Russian sovereigns, in particular the representatives of the Romanov dynasty in the 17th century, were originally crowned, and elements borrowed from the coronation rituals of the Western European sovereigns of the end of the 17th and beginning of the 18th centuries. The artistic staging of the new ceremony required a particular decorative design which was developed in 1724 with great care by the best painters and decorators and which afterwards became the reference for the ten coronations which were to follow in Russia. The preparations usually lasted a whole year, directed by the Coronation Commission which was especially created for the event, and which withdrew colossal sums from the budget. The laces and precious materials for the decoration of the palace rooms and the Kremlin churches were purchased abroad or made in the Russian workshops. As for the ermine fur used for the coronation mantles and for the canopies of the thrones, they came from Siberia.

The most eminent craftsmen worked on the creation of the coronation emblems: embroideries and

2. Ceremonial mantle belonging to the Empress Maria Alexandrovna, spouse of the Emperor Alexander II
Russia, St. Petersburg, 1856
Moscow, Kremlin Museums
(Cat. 3)
Detail

appliqués of marvelous virtuosity specially made for the coronation clothing and the mantles of the sovereigns, as well as sumptuous canopies for the decoration of the solemn procession and the places where the throne was displayed, decorative mural panels, the costumes of the heralds of arms.

Beginning in 1724, the regalia emblems of Imperial Russia's power were the following: the crown, which replaced the hereditary headdress of the Russian Czars—Constantine Monomaque's shapka—the scepter, the globe, the golden brocade mantle decorated with the coat of arms of the Russian empire and the ermine. Later to those were added, in 1730, the chain of the Great Order of the Russian empire—the Order of St. Andrew the First Called—and in 1742, the sword, the shield, the flag and the State seal, and in 1798 an imperial crown, also a chain of the Order of St. Andrew the First Called of smaller dimensions, and a mantle which was for the monarch's spouse (ills. 1 and 2). Part of the regalia was kept in Moscow, at the Armory Palace, another part was taken to St. Petersburg for the coronation. It was customary to create new crowns for every coronation but in 1762, the best goldsmiths and silversmiths and diamond cutters, directed by the jeweler Jérémie Pauzié, created a sumptuous crown for the Empress Catherine II. To make it, they selected the most beautiful precious stones of the imperial treasury: 4,896 diamonds, 75 pearls and, marvel of nature, an enormous ruby which represented the object "the most sumptuous of Europe." All the following Emperors, up through the final representative of the Romanov dynasty, Nicholas II, also wore this crown, chef-d'oeuvre of jewelry.

The veneration which surrounded these imperial emblems, as with the holiest objects, was particularly expressed during the ceremony. No one had the right to touch them except the Emperor himself and the main officiating priests. During the procession, the highest dignitaries and their assistants carried the symbols placed on golden brocade cushions created especially for this purpose. Afterwards, they were exhibited on the same cushions in the Cathedral of the Dormition, on a table, and then offered to the Emperor according to the ritual.

The new etiquette also called for new robes for the monarch being consecrated, robes which were also considered as something holy, and which the Lord's Anointed would wear this one and only time. Once the coronation ceremonies were over, the tradition called for the ceremonial robes to be transmitted to the Kremlin treasury where even today ten women's coronation dresses and seven men's outfits are still kept (ills. 3 and 4). Beginning in the 18th century, all the Russian sovereigns were crowned wearing their military uniform which had become the symbol of a supreme political superiority (ill. 5).

When the time for the coronation ceremonies approached, the whole Court left St. Petersburg for Moscow. While waiting to make its majestic entry into the former capital, the imperial family halted in the outskirts of Moscow. This was usually in the village of Vsiesviatskoye, in the Petrovsky Palace built at the end of the 18th century in the Neo-Gothic style based on a project by the architect M. Kazakov. The members of the clergy belonging to the Court welcomed the imperial couple there with the cross and with holy water, while the represen-

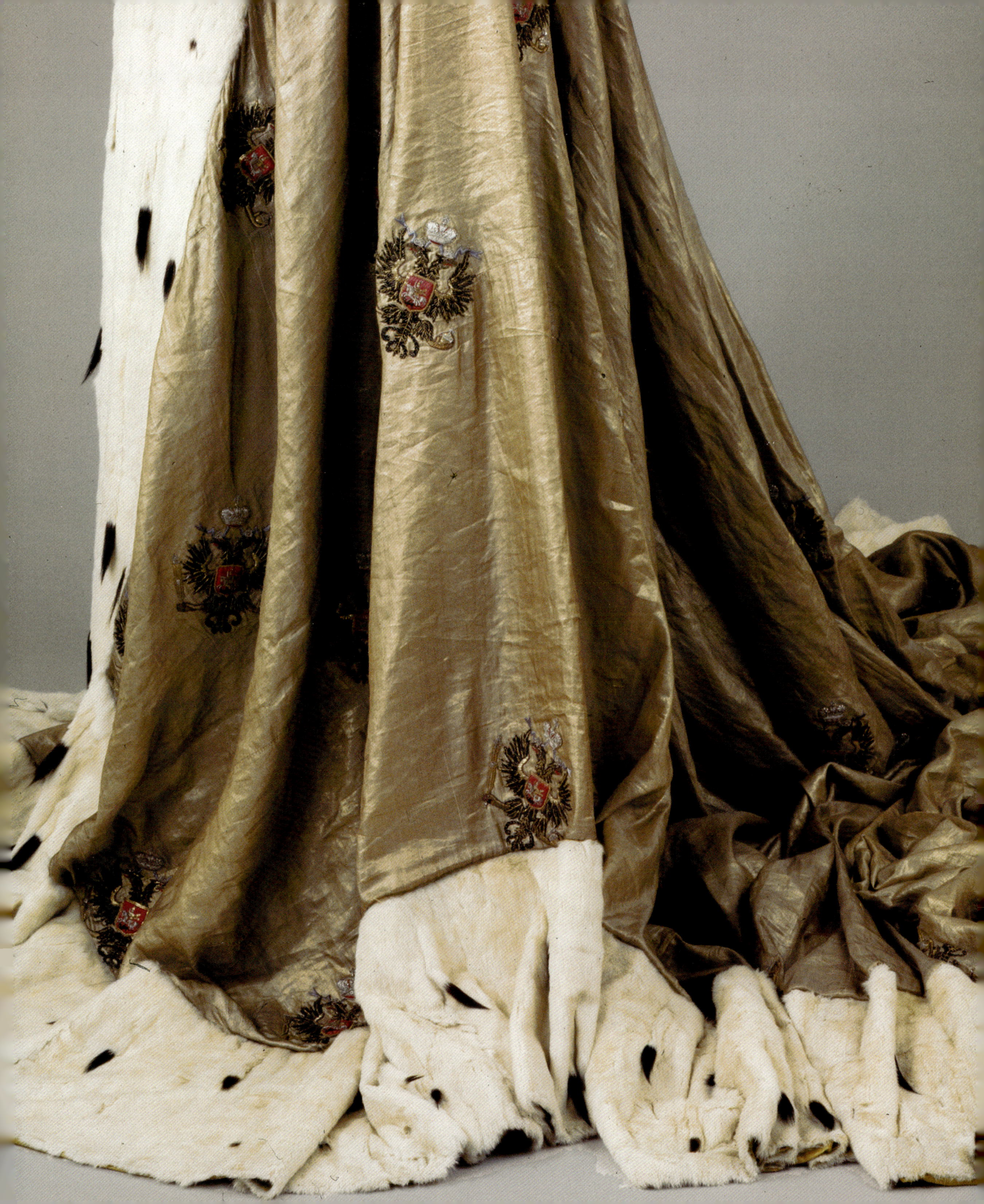

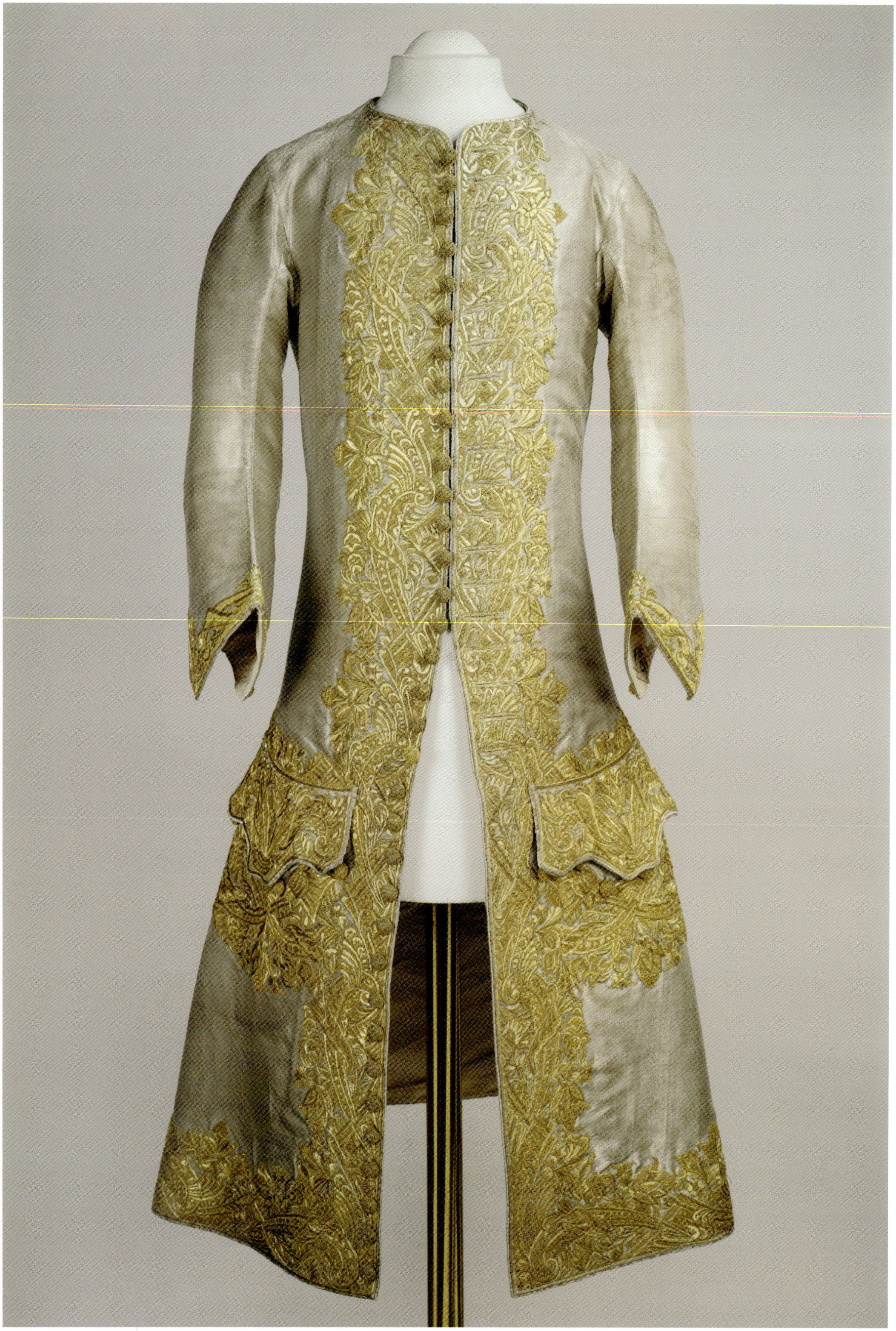

3. Doublet of the coronation dress of the Emperor Peter II
France, 1727
Moscow, Kremlin Museums
(Cat. 8)

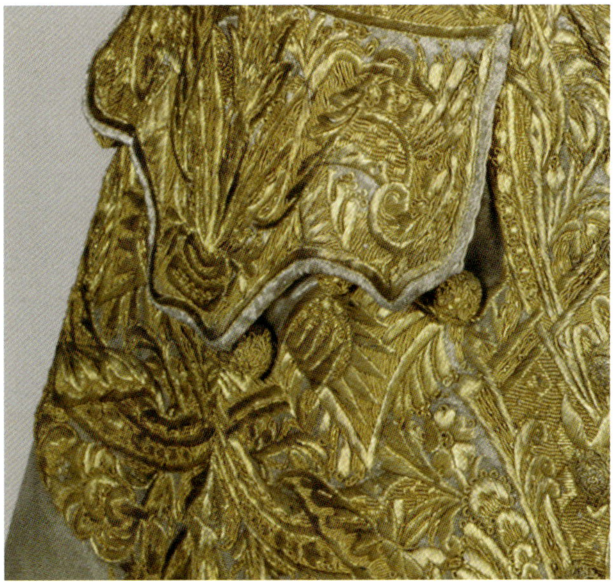

4. Doublet of the coronation dress of the Emperor Peter II
France, 1727
Moscow, Kremlin Museums
(Cat. 8)
Detail

tatives of the local authorities greeted them according to the Russian custom "with bread and salt."

The entrance into Moscow, announced by the firing of cannon, the peal of bells from the Ivan Veliky bell-tower in the Kremlin, the sound of trumpets and kettledrums, was the occasion for a grandiose procession attended by a huge crowd, including representatives of all the peoples of the huge Russian empire in a rigorously determined order which, with the exception of minor changes, remained the same until the end of the 19th century. For the coronation ceremonies, the Coronation Commission had built triumphal gates decorated with allegorical representations, paid for by the Church, the corporation of Moscow merchants and the Moscow municipality. Near the gates, the donors came to meet the monarch, with choirs performing triumphant hymns. From the innumerable Moscow churches, priests came to greet the imperial family, carrying crosses and the holy icons. Along the route of the solemn procession, all along the houses, places were set up for viewers, and above, the open windows were decked out with rugs and precious materials. The court dress, the liveries, the retinues, the harnesses, the horses—all was splendor and wealth, bearing witness to the magnificence and munificence of the Imperial Court. The different tones of the ringing bells from all the churches and cathedrals of Moscow added to the jubilation. Majestic and colorful, the procession ended at the Kremlin. There the monarch bowed before the holy objects, while a prayer offering thanks, like the Latin *Te Deum* was sung in his honor in the Cathedral of the Dormition.

The high dignitaries and the representatives of the foreign embassies were informed of the day of the coronation by the masters of ceremonies, the people instead, by the heralds on horseback, by the sound of trumpets, and kettledrums sounding on all the squares of Moscow (ills. 6, 7 and 8). The

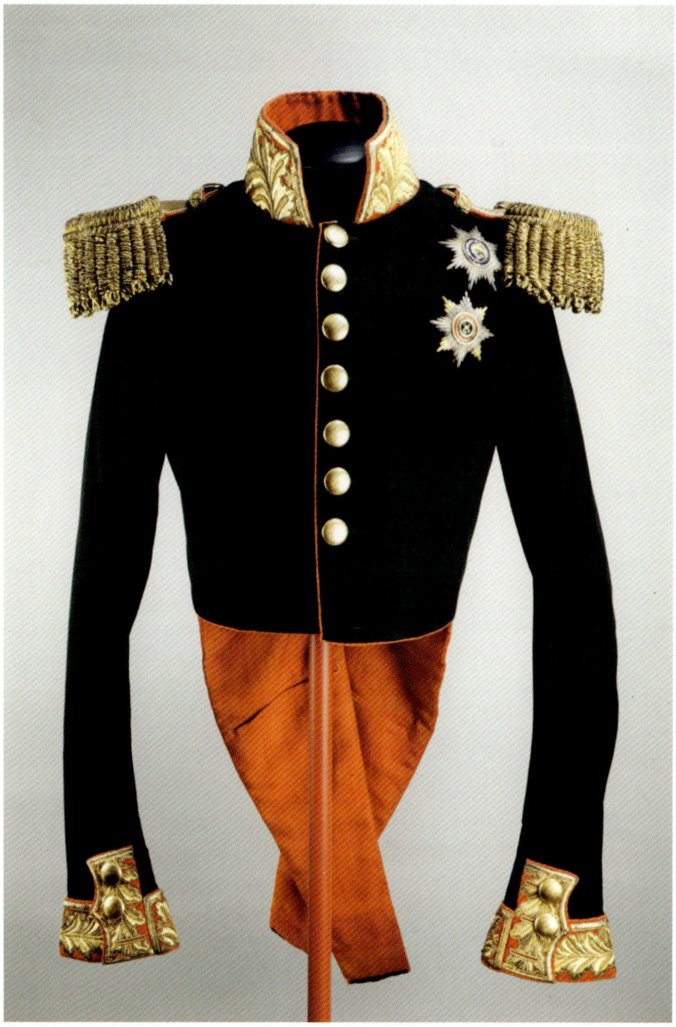

5. Emperor Nicholas I's coronation dress
Russia, 1826
Moscow, Kremlin Museums
(Cat. 7)

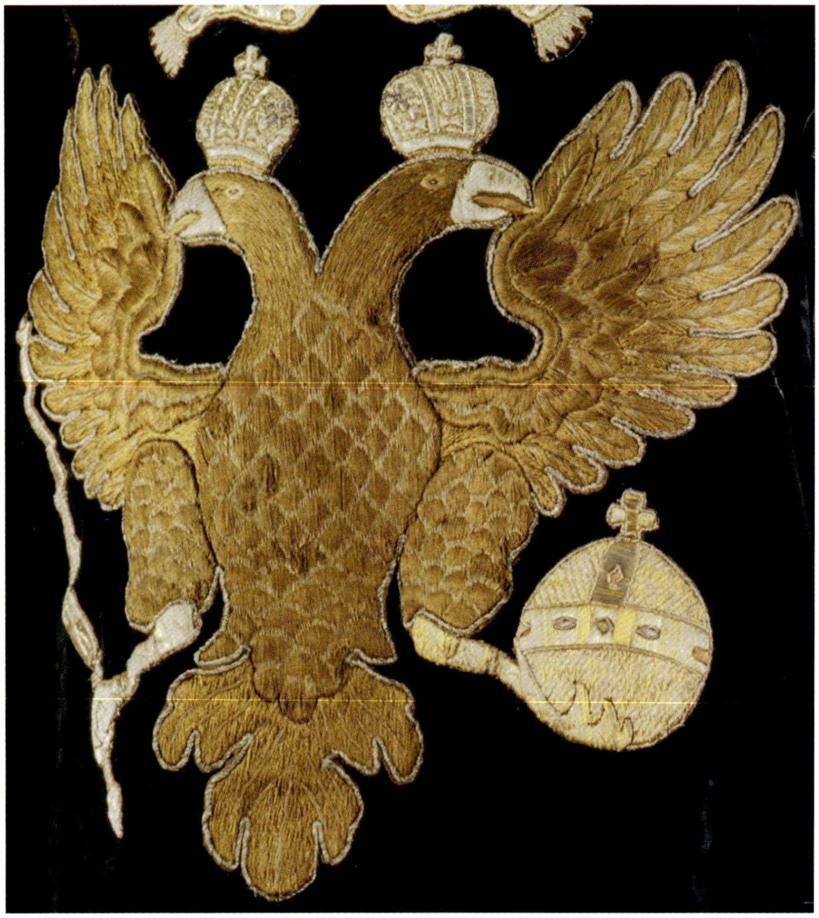

6. Tunic of a coronation herald
Russia, 18th century
Moscow, Kremlin Museums
(Cat. 5)
Detail

7. Tunic, shirt and hat
of a coronation herald
Russia, 18th century
Moscow, Kremlin Museums
(Cat. 5)

day of the coronation, canon fire announced to those who were participating in the procession to gather, a procession which was opened and closed by the mounted guard. Those taking part in the procession included the high dignitaries of the Court, high-ranking officers, generals and admirals, the representatives of the Russian nobility, Russian and foreign merchants, members of the Senate, and members of the colleges. The high dignitaries of the Empire carried the imperial emblems placed on cushions. In the middle of the procession, with a sumptuous canopy over them, proceeded the imperial couple.

The Emperor traveled along the traditional route, from the "Red Porch", in other words the Great Stairway of Honor, to the Cathedral of the Dormition, on a roadway of boards covered with a red cloth which the people were allowed to divide up afterwards as souvenirs of the coronation. As for the viewers, they were seated on high tribunes set up at the Square of the Cathedrals. During this whole time, the bells were ringing madly, the troops were presenting arms, and waving the flags to the sound of the music and the drum rolls. When the procession reached the doors of the Cathedral, all the high dignitaries of the clergy went forward to greet the Emperor. He was presented with the cross to kiss, and the pathway of His Majesty was sprinkled with holy water. The Emperor and the Empress entered the cathedral behind the clergy, went up to the holy doors of the iconostasis and, bowing there three times, kissed the holy icons. During this time, the choir was singing the "royal" psalm, "Lord, I praise goodness and justice!"

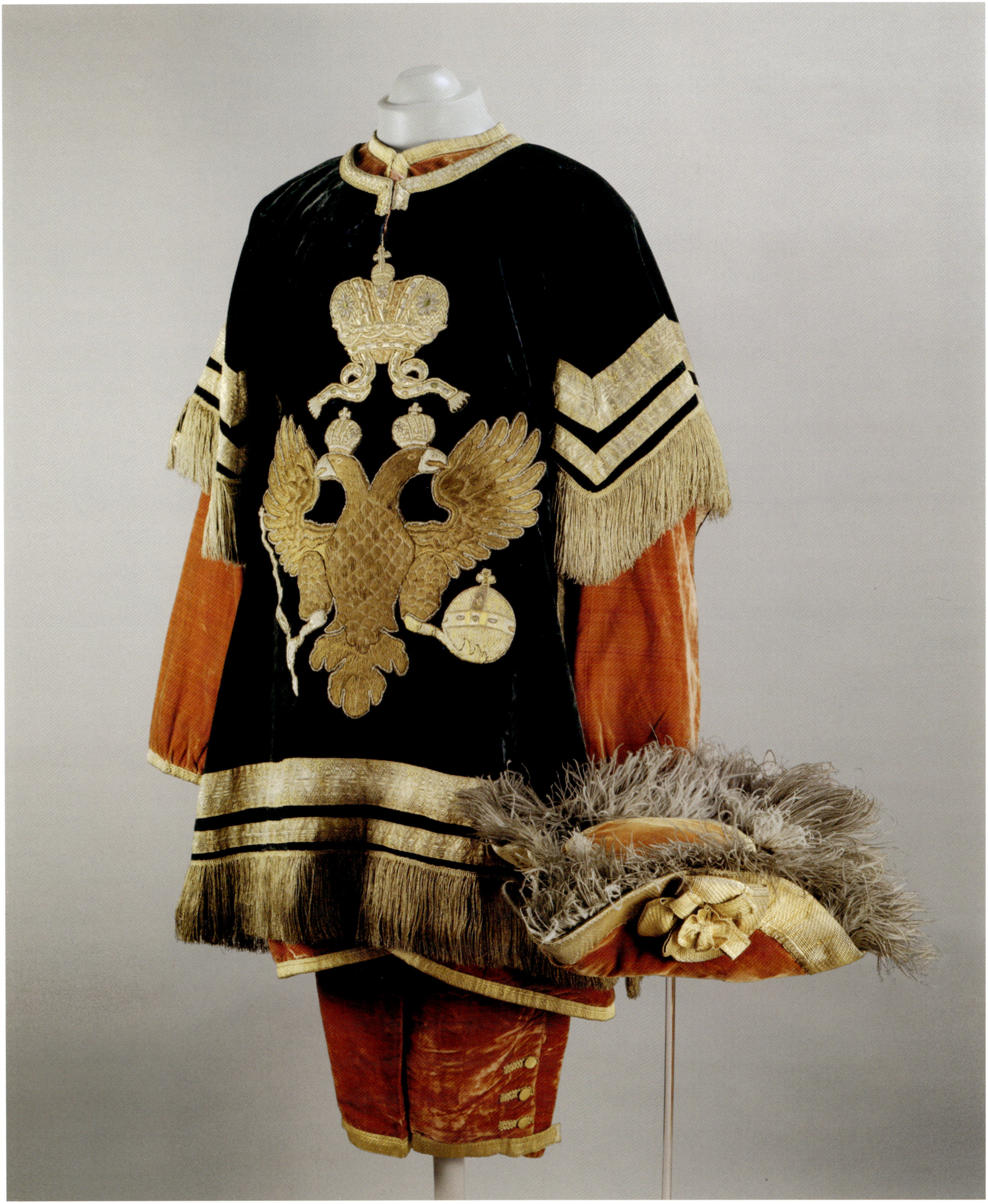

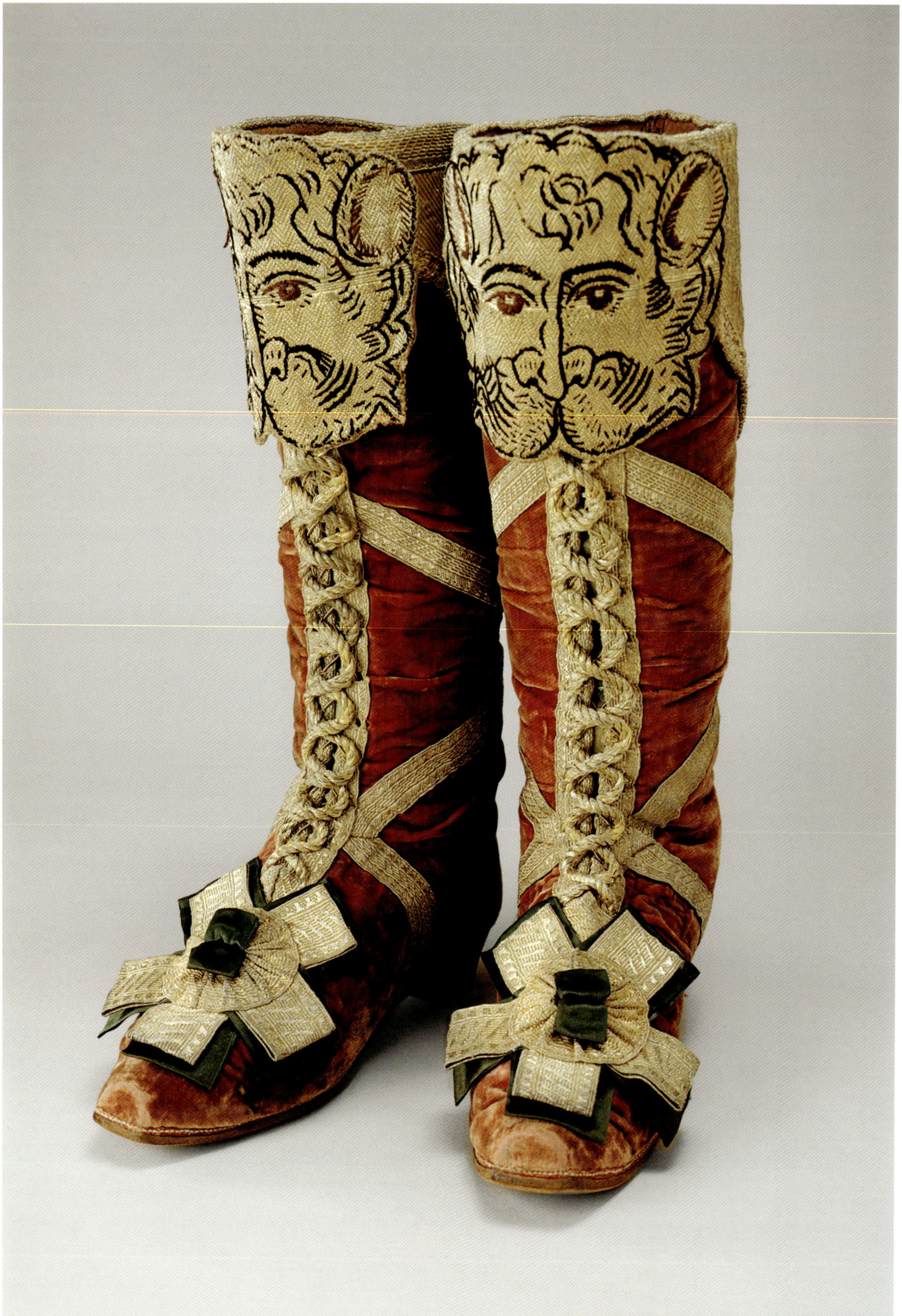

8. Boots of a coronation herald
Russia, 18th century
Moscow, Kremlin Museums
(Cat. 6)

The arrangement in the Cathedral of the Dormition was marked by a truly imperial magnificence. In the center a large platform was set up, surrounded by balustrades over which a canopy hung suspended from the vault, decorated with the embroidered coat of arms of the Russian Empire: the two-headed eagle surrounded by the coats of arms of the main provinces. The former thrones of the Czars from the 17th century were placed on this platform, specially transported there for this occasion from the Armory Palace which had acquired the status since the 18th century as the museum designated to receive the treasure of the Court; velvet cushions with the monographs of the sovereigns were attached there by golden cords (ill. 9). A table was specially set up next to the thrones to hold the regalia and was covered with a brocade tablecloth.

In the cathedral, grandstands had been built to seat the high dignitaries, with reserved seats for the ambassadors and the foreign envoys as well as for notable personalities, all of whom had received invitations to the ceremony. The men were to be dressed either in their military uniforms or in their formal attire, the women and the young girls in dresses whose style and material were rigorously defined. At the Russian Court during Catherine II's reign, by way of ceremonial dress required for the major official ceremonies, the women wore costumes in the national style whose model had been decided upon during the reign of Nicholas I in 1834. Their main particularity was the long floating sleeves, characteristic of the costume of Russian high society during the 16th and 17th centuries, as well as decorations at the front of the dress in

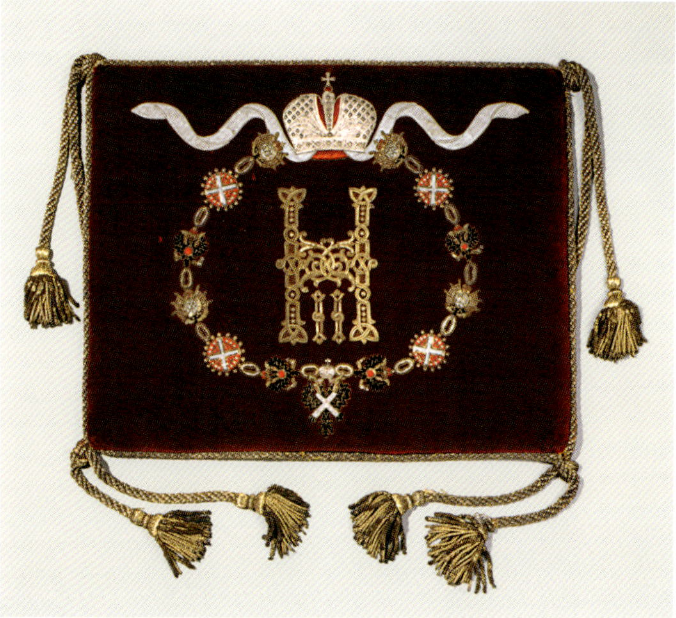

9. Cushion backing for the throne of Emperor Nicholas II
Moscow, 1896
Moscow, Kremlin Museums
(Cat. 9)

the style of the Russian *sarafan* and a large rounded headdress in the form of a *kokoshnik*, traditional elements of the Russian popular costume. All of this made the Russian Court a court unlike any other in Europe and demonstrated the union of the Czar with the people.

The actual coronation ritual began with the Emperor reciting the fundamental dogmas of the Christian faith. Then, during the reading of prayers for the monarch, the regalia, emblems of his power, were placed on him: the mantle, the chain of the Order of St. Andrew the First Called, and the crown. After that, the sovereign received the scepter and the globe from the hands of the Metropolitan, and was seated on the throne. Unlike the coronation of the Czars when the hierarchs of the Orthodox church placed "Monomaque's shapka" on the heads of the sovereigns, during Catherine I's coronation in 1724, the crown was placed on her head by her spouse, the Emperor Peter the Great. And during the succeeding coronations, the Emperor placed the crown on his head himself. Beginning with the reign of Paul I, this ritual also applied to the Empress. She knelt in front of her spouse and the Emperor, taking the crown from his head, lightly touched the head of his wife with it. Then a smaller crown was brought for the Empress.

After the handing over of the emblems of power, the praises and hymns began for the Emperor's long life, and then came the ceremony of unction and communion. At the end of the liturgy, the main presiding priest gave a sermon of congratulations. Those attending saluted the sovereigns three times and congratulated them for the happy conclusion of the coronation and the holy unction. Then the Emperor began his procession, wearing his glittering crown and clothed in the holy mantle, with, in his hand, the scepter and the globe, and accompanied by the Empress also wearing her crown and mantle. Proceeding under a canopy, they reached the Archangel St. Michel Cathedral where they bowed before the tombs of the ancestors. Then they continued on to the Annunciation Cathedral to kiss the holy icons. During this whole time, the bells were ringing and music and kettledrums sounded, as well as gun and cannon volleys. The Kremlin resonated until it shook from the cries of the jubilant people who cheered the newly crowned and anointed sovereign. Tokens of gold and silver were thrown to the people, especially minted as souvenirs of the coronation.

The procession ended at the "Red Porch" on the highest step where Nicholas I was the first of the Russian Emperors to stop after his coronation, on August 22, 1826, and, turning toward the huge crowd of people who were overrunning the Kremlin, saluted his subjects three times, once in each direction. This triple salute became a ritual carried out by the Emperor at the moment of the coronation as well as during his future visits to Moscow through-out the next century. It came to be understood as the expression of Russian national feeling and striking proof of the connection between the monarch and his people.

During the gala dinner in the Palace of Facets, the Emperor and the Empress were seated on thrones at a table placed under a canopy. According to the ceremonial ritual in effect, those taking part in the royal feast included the members of the imperial family, the high clergy, the members of the Council of State, as well as personalities from the two upper classes of society. For them the table was set with the ceremonial service and antique silverware kept in the Armory Palace. Gold medals of the coronation were given to the guests.

After the coronation ritual and for several weeks following, audiences took place at the palace during which the Emperor received congratulations and gifts from his subjects, and banquets were organized. Masked balls and theatrical performances followed one upon the other. Beginning with the coronation of Nicholas I, an unchanging part of the coronation festivities consisted of military reviews and maneuvers to demonstrate the solemn expression of the army's loyalty to the imperial dynasty.

Each time a new sovereign took the throne, the tradition was to organize festivities for the people, at the Kremlin, on the grounds of Tsaritsyno, Devitche, Sokolniky, and Khodynka. According to custom, the Emperor in person opened the festivities. A luxurious pavilion was set up in the middle of the grounds for the imperial family, with galleries for the highest ranking dignitaries and foreign guests, as well as stepped rows of seats from which the people could watch the festivities. A variety of entertainment was provided to the joy of the people: theatrical shows, swings, carousels, Russian mountains, platforms for the setting off of hot-air balloons, acrobatic and gymnastic performances. For the crowds of people who began pouring in at dawn in their festive costumes from around the whole city and the surrounding countryside, fountains of wine were set up and there were also hundreds of long tables loaded with roast beef, stuffed poultry, sheep with golden horns, and pyramids of small white loaves of bread in the shape of padlocks, the *kalatchi*.

During the solemn celebrations of the coronation, Moscow was magnificently lighted, in particular the Kremlin. All its towers were brilliantly lit and the Ivan Veliky bell-tower, topped by a crown and a cross, rose into the sky like a gigantic pillar of fire. Enthralled by the charm of it all, the people wandered through the streets, admiring this prodigious sight. The magnificent illuminations and the extraordinary fireworks which, according to tradition, marked the end of the festivities, for a time transformed the former capital into a true fairytale city.

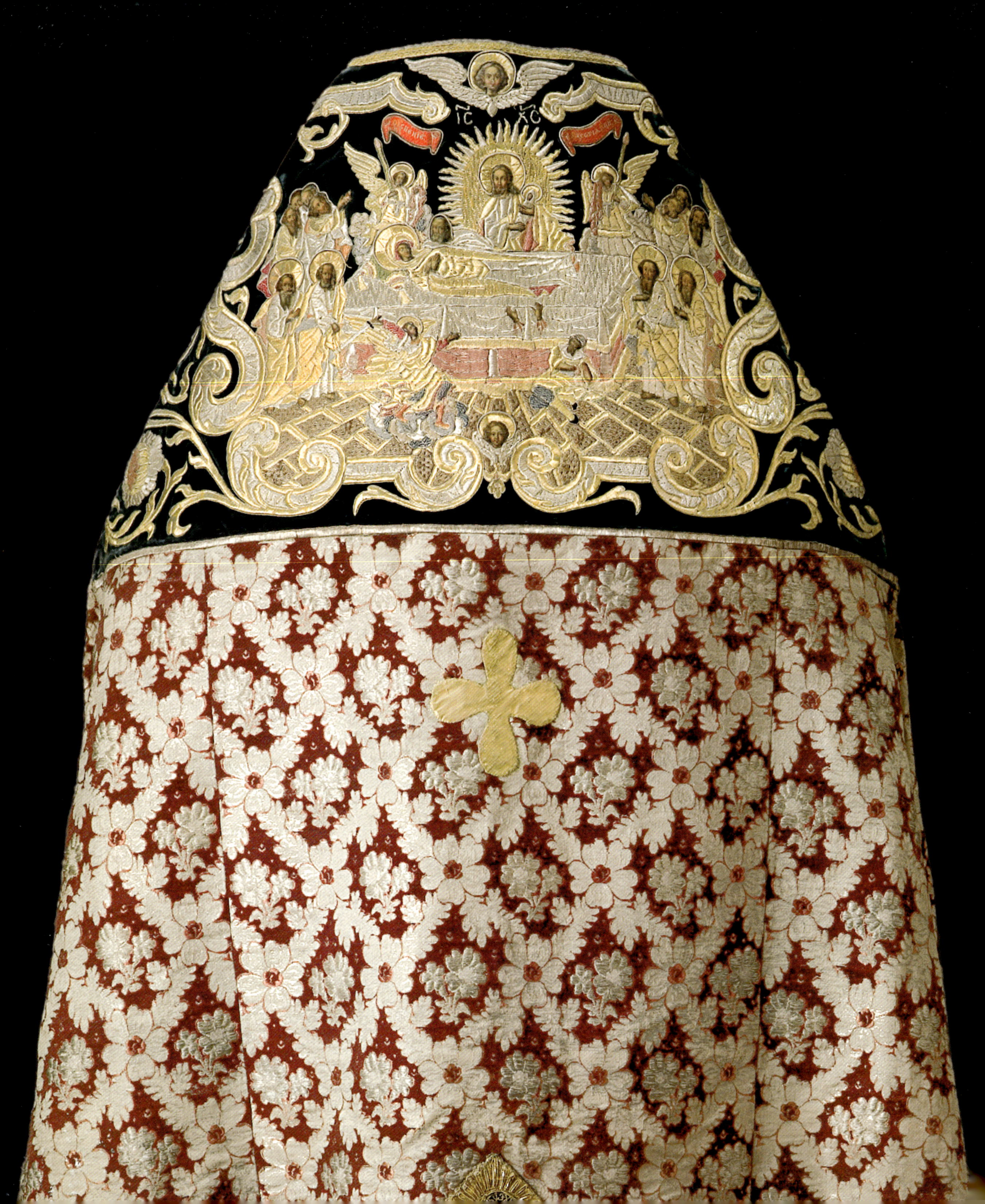
ІС ХС

THE RELIGIOUS TEXTILES

Nina Suetova

The decoration of fabric is one of the oldest art forms. Fabric was considered an essential commodity and at the same time, a material which could be transformed into work of art. In different countries, fibers of diverse origin, vegetal or animal, were used to make it.

The Russian State Historical Museum's department of fabric and costumes hosts one of the richest collections of textiles. Objects which were for liturgical use are a featured part of the collection: shrouds, small and large veils (*soudari*)[1] covering sacred vases (chalices) and patins, embroidered icons and embroidered cloth placed under the icons,[2] banners, altar frontals and also the clergy's vestments: Episcopal copes, chasubles, albs for deacons and cantors, albs for priests, diamond and rectangular shaped insignia,[3] omophores,[4] priests' stoles, deacons' stoles,[5] oversleeves (*epimanikia*) etc. Among these art works from Old Russia, the "figurative"[6] embroidery whose etymology in Russian comes from the word "figure" particularly stands out.

The adoption of Christianity as the state religion (988) brought to Old Russia a new faith with its church, its icons, and introduced these textile objects to the country, an integral part of the liturgical celebrations, and at the same time, they filled an aesthetic function in giving a solemn dimension to the interior space. Figurative embroidery, a collective creation, was very widely circulated. As well as the designer-artist who executed the design, the "foliage expert" artist who drew the decorations and the writer who composed the inscription on the piece were also often associated to the work. It was possible to lay the drawing directly onto the fabric, or to do it on paper and then recopy it onto the fabric (apparently using perforation following the contours). For the "drawn part" soot, ink, white lead, red lead and other colorants were used. But of course the most important element came from the work of the embroiderer—she was most often the one who made the choice of decorative colors and the emotional arrangement of the work.

Embroidery with a subject (figurative) was an art of the elite, in the sense that it took a lot of time (for example, the big pieces such as the shrouds and the veils could take about three years of work), and the materials were expensive.

Until the 18th century, Russia did not produce silk and brocade fabrics (although there were a few attempts to establish private businesses to make them).[7] The people were satisfied with hand-woven linen and wool fabric. For the clothes of the Czars and the *boyars*, Italian, Turkish, Persian and Chinese imported fabric was used (brocade, velvet, watered fabric, heavy-worked bro-

Chasuble (phelonion)
Russia, third quarter of 18th century
The State Historical Museum, Moscow
(Cat. 13)
Detail

cade, a mixture of silk and brocade, damask, taffetas, embossed velvet and figured velvet etc. A single fabric could be used to make ordinary vestments (men or women's) or for church decorations. It could also be used as fabric for interior décor (tablecloths, bench rugs, curtains) or as horse harnesses. There was no difference. It was only during the second half of the 18th century that a distinction began to be made between the fabrics for clothing and the fabrics for decoration and décor. At that time velvet even appeared with small motifs specially made for the male caftans. Foreign fabrics often made up part of gifts from embassies. They were expensive which is why they were appreciated and preciously preserved. The medieval guidebook the "*Domostroy*"[8] recommends taking care of even the smallest pieces of fabric either so as to be able to repair an old piece of clothing (of common use), or to add it to a new product. Even the Czarinas observed this rule.

In Old Russia, the high society women who lived a reclusive life in their *terem* devoted themselves to embroidering liturgical items. It was an area in which they could express their talents, even express their thoughts. In fact, it was believed that embroidering holy linens was an occupation which pleased God. It was customary in the churches and in the monasteries to give donations in memory of the dead—offerings—"in memory of the souls" of one's family and people close to one who had died. One also celebrated the major events in the life of the State (for example, the birth of an heir to the throne) in making donations.

In the residences of the princes and the *boyars*, in the houses of the rich merchants, the well-lighted rooms ("*svetlitsy*") were reserved for needlework and sometimes there were several dozen workers employed there. There were also similar workshops in the women's monasteries. In these homes it wasn't rare for the mistress of the home herself to take part in this work. Practically every workshop had its own "style", it's own "writing" which usually disappeared at the death of the mistress of the place. On some of the embroidered objects next to the liturgical inscriptions which were usually put along the border can be found dedicatory inscriptions (not always very correct, often with mistakes—they are distinct from the letters of the border which are clearly traced). In those inscriptions not only the donator, but sometimes the name of the main person in the workshop are mentioned, which could be Czarinas, princesses, wives of boyars, nuns and merchants' wives. The inscriptions of the donators also customarily indicated the workshop where the work was created. As of today, more than two dozen of those workshops have been cataloged. Foreigners who visited Russia invariably noted that "what the women know best to do here is how to sew and embroider with silk and with gold."

Four works of figurative embroidery from the 17th century presented in the exhibition are a spectacular example of the art of Russian embroidery. Among the objects chosen, only the embroidered linen which represents "Zosima and Savvatii" (ill. 1) has a dedicatory inscription. It clearly indicates that the embroidery was made in

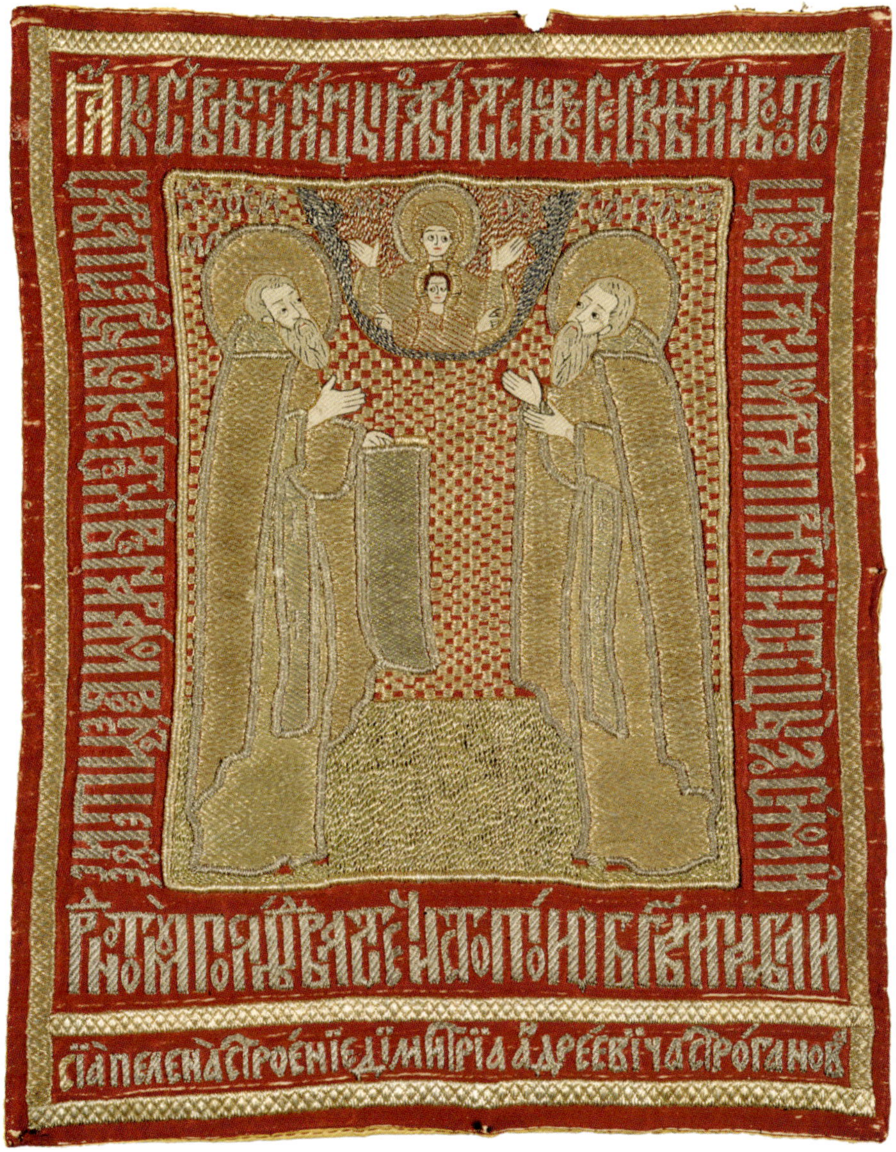

1. Liturgical linen representing
Saints Zosima and Savvatii
of Solovky
Russia, Solvytchegodsk, 1670s
The State Historical Museum, Moscow
(Cat. 132)

the workshop of Dmitry Andreievich Stroganov's second wife (1622-1670), Anna Ivanovna, whose maiden name was Zlobina (?-after 1680). After getting married (in the years 1650-1651), Anna Ivanovna directed the embroidery of the workshop for two decades, during which it reached its full bloom.[9]

The Stroganov family played a huge role in the development of the art in its most diverse forms. The beginning of their activity goes back to the 15th century. From the simple peasants that they were, they were able to rise to the rank of "merchant", and then to "notable." The latter placed them not only above simple merchants but also above the middle nobility. They had obtained exceptional authority to construct churches and monasteries. The history of the family is closely linked to the city of Solvychegodsk, favorably located along the banks of the Vytchegda river (an affluent of the northern Dvina). It was via that waterway (and further on, through the White Sea) that business with England, Holland and Scandinavia was conducted. In 1560, Joannik (Anika) Stroganov (1498-1570) undertook the construction, for his family, of the Cathedral of the Annunciation, work which was continued by his children and his grandchildren.[10]

During more than a century of existence (from the end of the 16th to the beginning of the 18th centuries), the Stroganov workshop of figurative embroidery produced several hundred pieces. Today there are about five hundred and fifty objects of this cultural patrimony in the various Russian museums.[11]

Some of the small veils ("shrouds") like *Here*

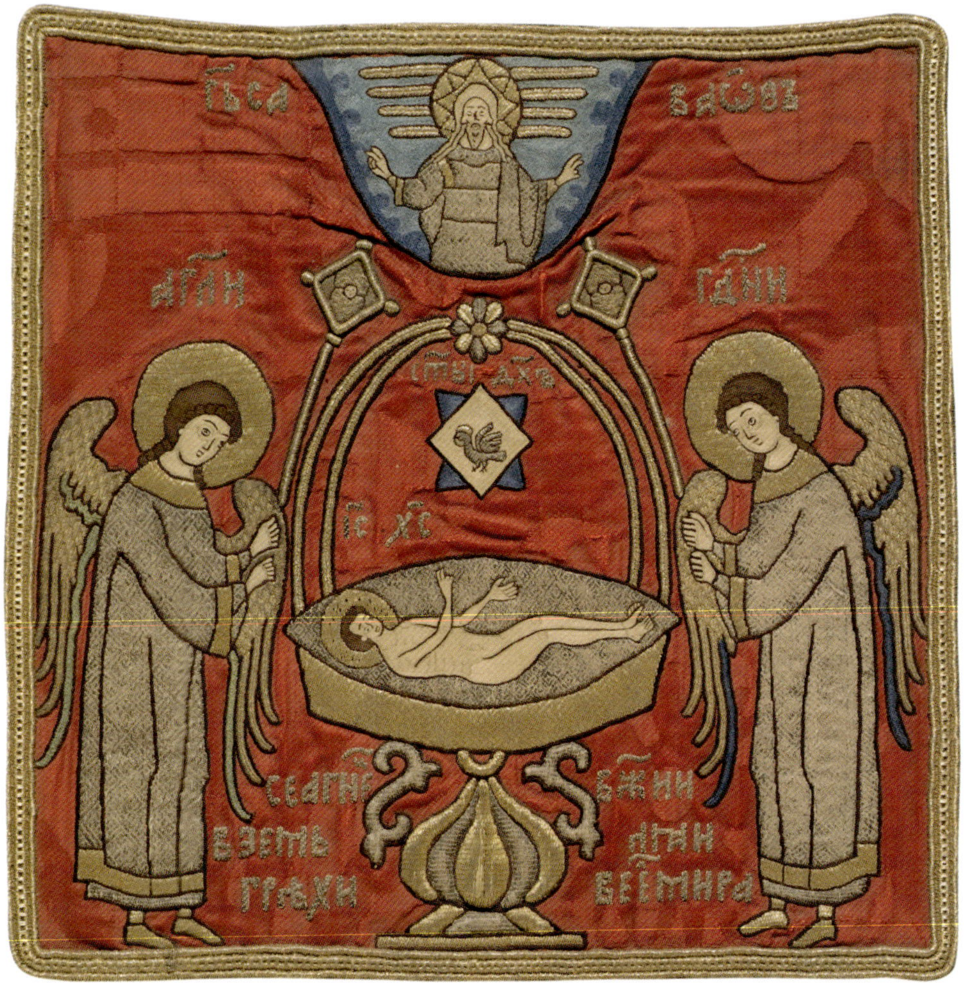

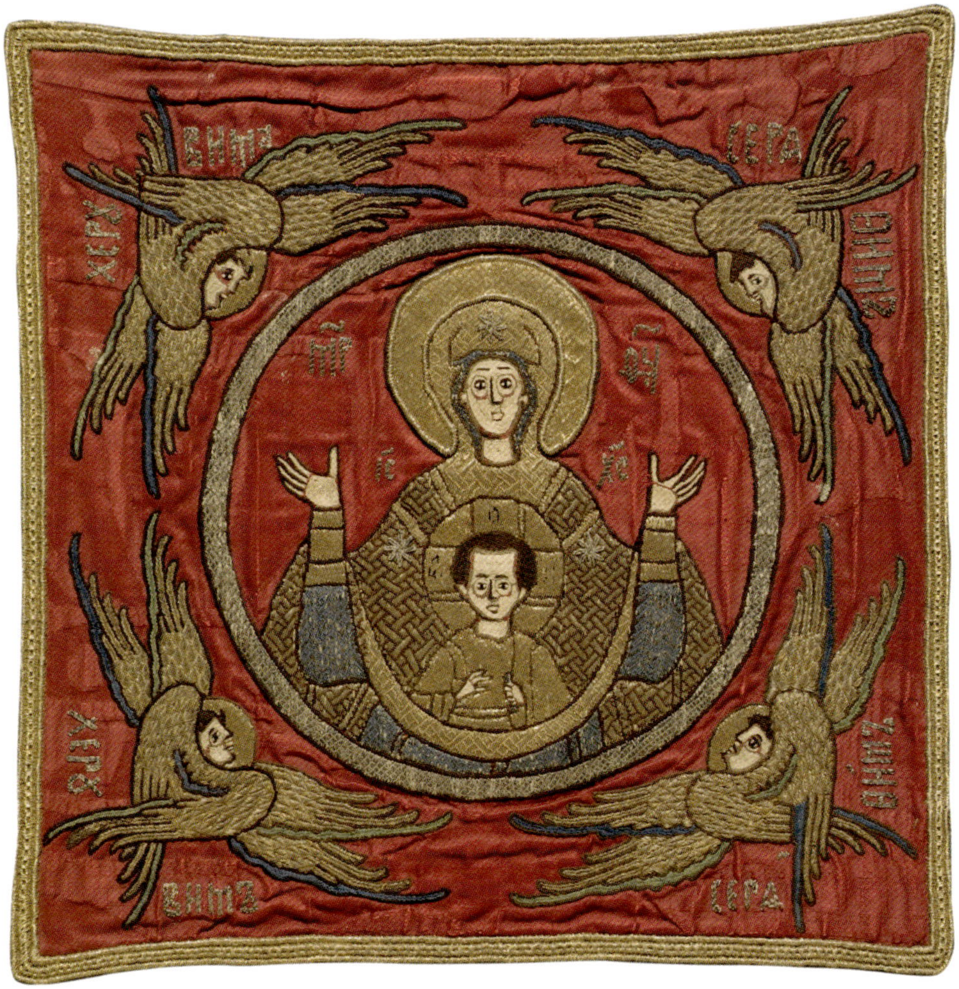

2. Paten or chalice veil (Lamb of God)
Russia, first half of the 17th century
The State Historical Museum, Moscow
(Cat. 146)

3. Paten or chalice veil (The Virgin of the Sign)
Russia, first half of the 17th century
The State Historical Museum, Moscow
(Cat. 147)

4. Liturgical linen (hanging under the icon) representing the Very Orthodox Princes Feodor, David, Constantine
Russia, second half of the 17th century
The State Historical Museum, Moscow
(Cat. 135)

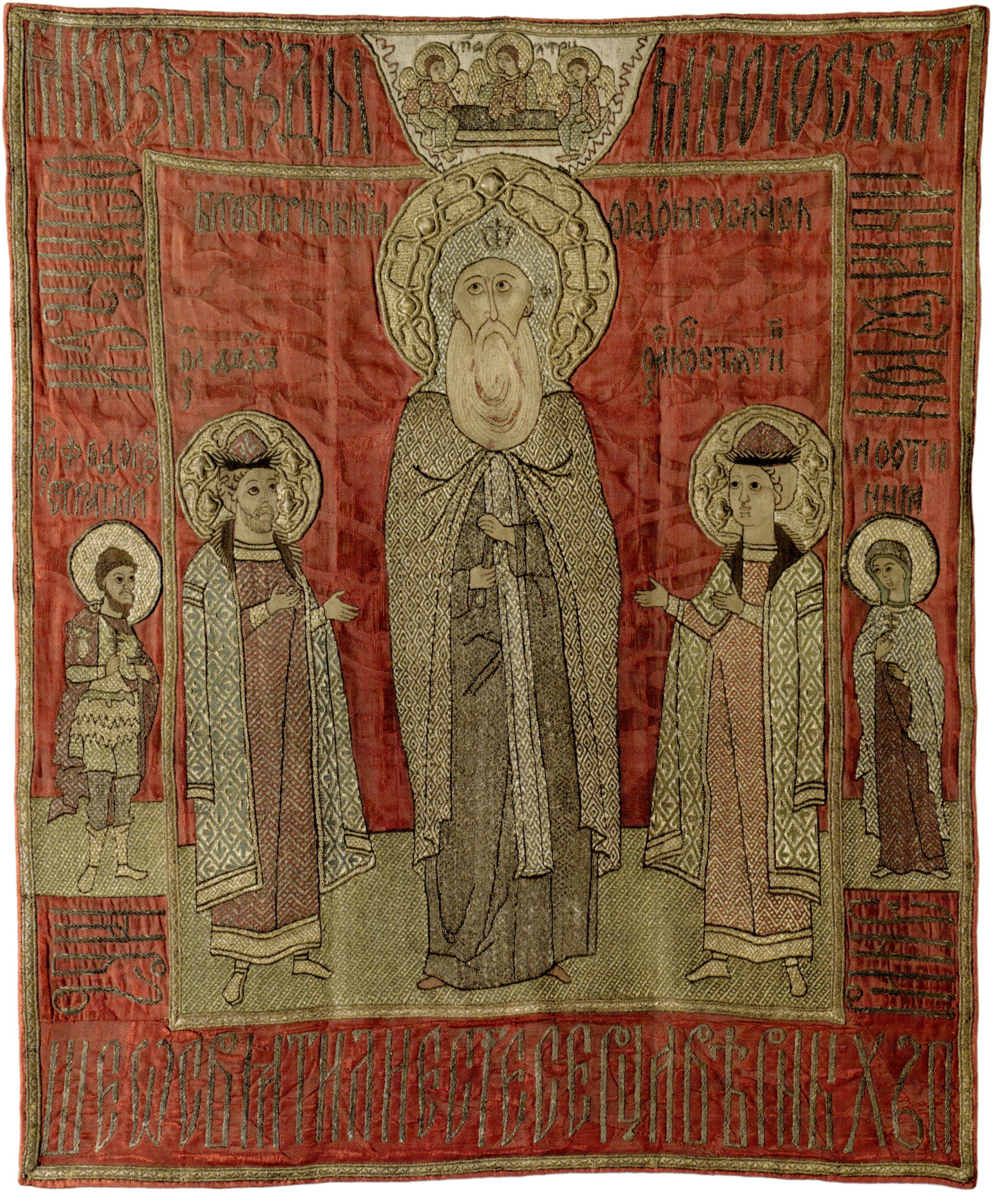

5. Paten veil (The Lamb of God)
Russia, second half of the 18th century
The State Historical Museum, Moscow
(Cat. 144)

is the Lamb (ill. 2) and *The Virgin of the Sign* (ill. 3) unfortunately have no dedicatory inscriptions but their iconography repeats those of works from the workshops of Czarina Irina Feodorovna and Dmitry Ivanovich Godunov. Later, similar iconography was used in the work of Eudoxie Lukianovna,[12] second wife of Czar Michael Feodorovich (who reigned 1613-1645). In addition, the fabric used is very close to the material which is found in the veils signed by the Tsaritsyno workshop.[13]

The veils presented in the exhibition are a striking example of how each embroiderer left the unique mark of her art on the embroidered work, independently of the fact that they were prepared in the same workshop. Although the veil *The Virgin of the Sign* forms a whole with *Here is the Lamb*, it was most likely done by another artist: the embroidery is characterized by a coarser execution of the faces.

The embroidered or figurative linen "The faithful Prince Feodor of Yaroslav and his children the saints David and Constantine" unfortunately also does not have a dedicatory inscription which is why it is impossible to determine the precise place and date of the creation of this work. (ill. 4). Nevertheless, the finesse of execution of the person's face, as well as everything preceding that step, leads one to believe that the work in question could have been embroidered in one of the famous 17th century *svetlitsy*, or possibly in the palace workshops. It is difficult to explain exactly the choice of saints which are shown on the border. If the representation of Theodore the Stratelates can be explained by a veneration for him which was shared by all the Russian faithful, on the contrary the presence of Saint Photinia most likely harks back to the veneration of a local patron saint. At any rate, the author of this piece has still not been identified. In fact, among the people, the martyred saint Photinia was worshiped as a healer of fever. Thus many sick people frequently made the vow to paint or to acquire the icon of Saint Photinia.

The saints represented on the icon cloth are historic figures. Feodor Rostislavich, nicknamed 'the Black', was the youngest son of the prince of Smolensk, Rostislav Mstislavich. In 1260, he married the daughter of Prince Vasily Vsevolodovich of Yaroslav, Marie, and began to reign at Yaroslav with his mother-in-law Xena. After the death of his wife, Feodor the Black was deposed, and his son, Michael recognized as the sovereign prince of Yaroslav. His second wife, daughter of the Khan of the Hoard, Mengu-Temir Khan (according to another version, Khan Nogay) in converting to the Christian faith received the name of Anne at her baptism. In 1292, after the death of his son Michael, Feodor was named to the throne of Yaroslav and Smolensk. He was very zealous in improving the situation and the well-being of the principality. His fame spread throughout all of Russia. Just before his death, prince Feodor received the monastic tonsure and put on the *skhima*.[14] He died September 19, 1299. The principality of Yaroslav went to David, the elder son of Feodor by his second marriage, who reigned for twenty-three years. Constantine died unmarried. All three were buried in the Cathedral of the Transfigured Christ near the monastery of Saint Savior of Yaroslav where their relics, which rest-

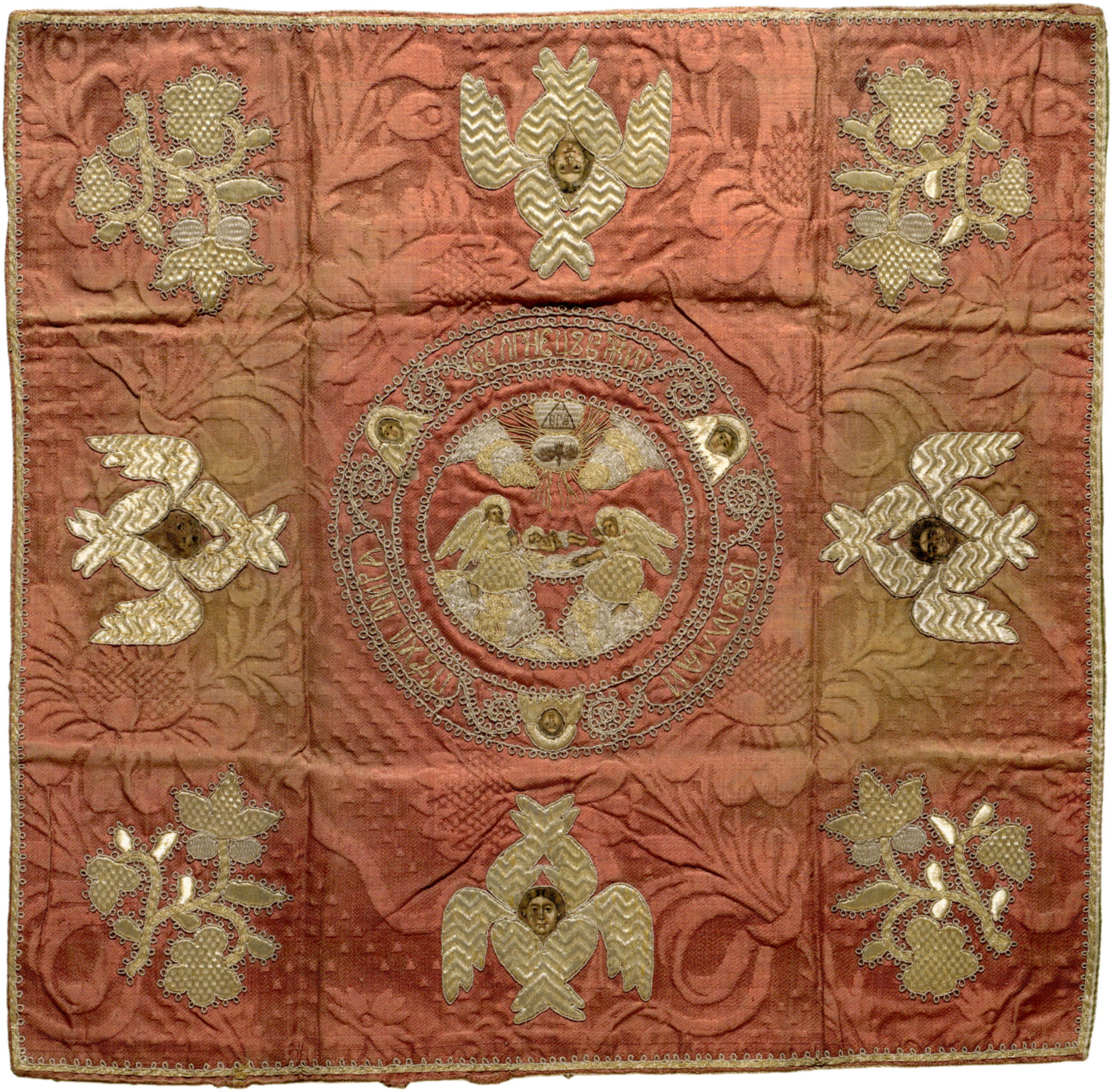

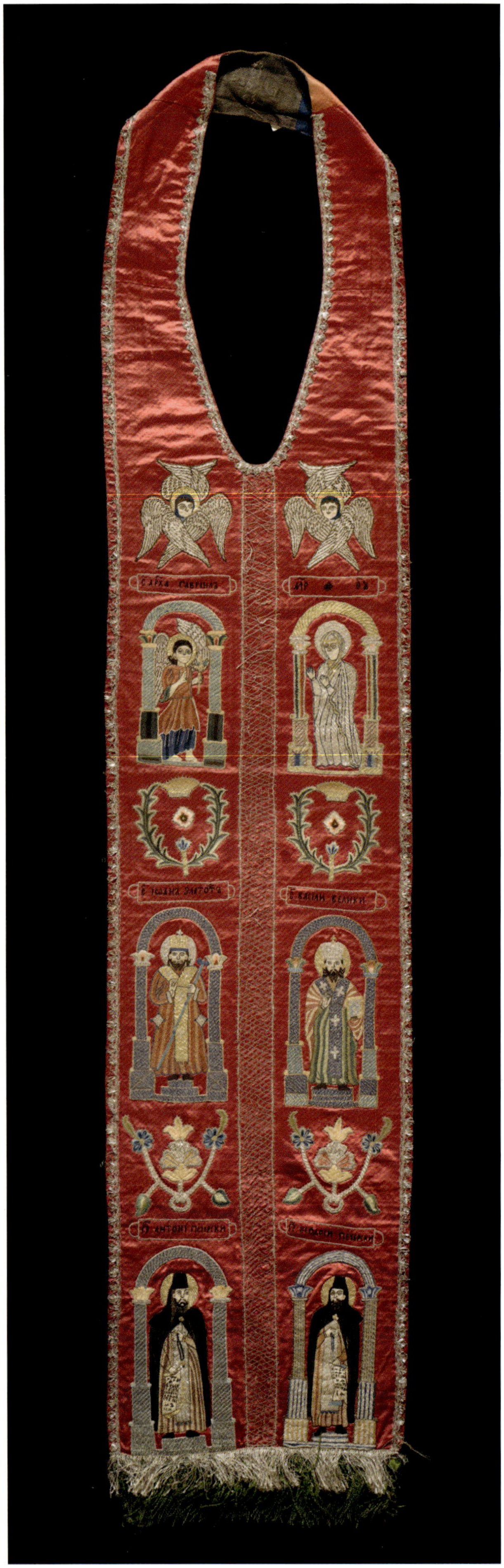

6. Stole (epitrakhelion) *Southern Russia, 18th century* *The State Historical Museum, Moscow* *(Cat. 136)*

7. Chasuble (plenonion) *Russia, late 18th century-second half of the 19th century* *The State Historical Museum, Moscow* *(Cat. 18)*

ed in the same tomb, were discovered in 1463. The chronicler, eye-witness to the events, had noted Prince Feodor's huge stature. This is also why on the linen the figure of Feodor is very significantly larger than those of David and Constantine.[15]

The ornamental motifs and the decorative subjects underwent changes over the centuries.

During the 18th century, figurative embroidery as a form of artistic expression little by little fell into decline. In place of embroidery with silk threads to make faces, the technique of using small pieces of clear fabric began to be used, drawing the features of the face using black thread. The drawing was done directly on the fabric, the pieces of cloth and paper were applied onto it and it was painted, inspired by pictorial technique (all the liturgical veils[16] in brick-colored silk fabric—ill. 5—are a vivid example of 18th century embroidery in which everything concerning the faces is painted on the fabric). There was a rejection of all the old iconographic traditions, replaced by European artistic styles: baroque, rococo and classicism.

Embroidery using gold thread, which had attained its peak in the 17th century, continued to evolve in the 18th and 19th centuries, while remaining one of the most widespread techniques to decorate different objects in fabric.

In the 18th century the form of the sacred veils changed. At first square, little by little beginning in the second third of the 18th century, they became cruciform (this was the case first for the veil which covered the chalice, and then for the others later). With the decline of figurative embroidery, the way of decorating the veils changed:

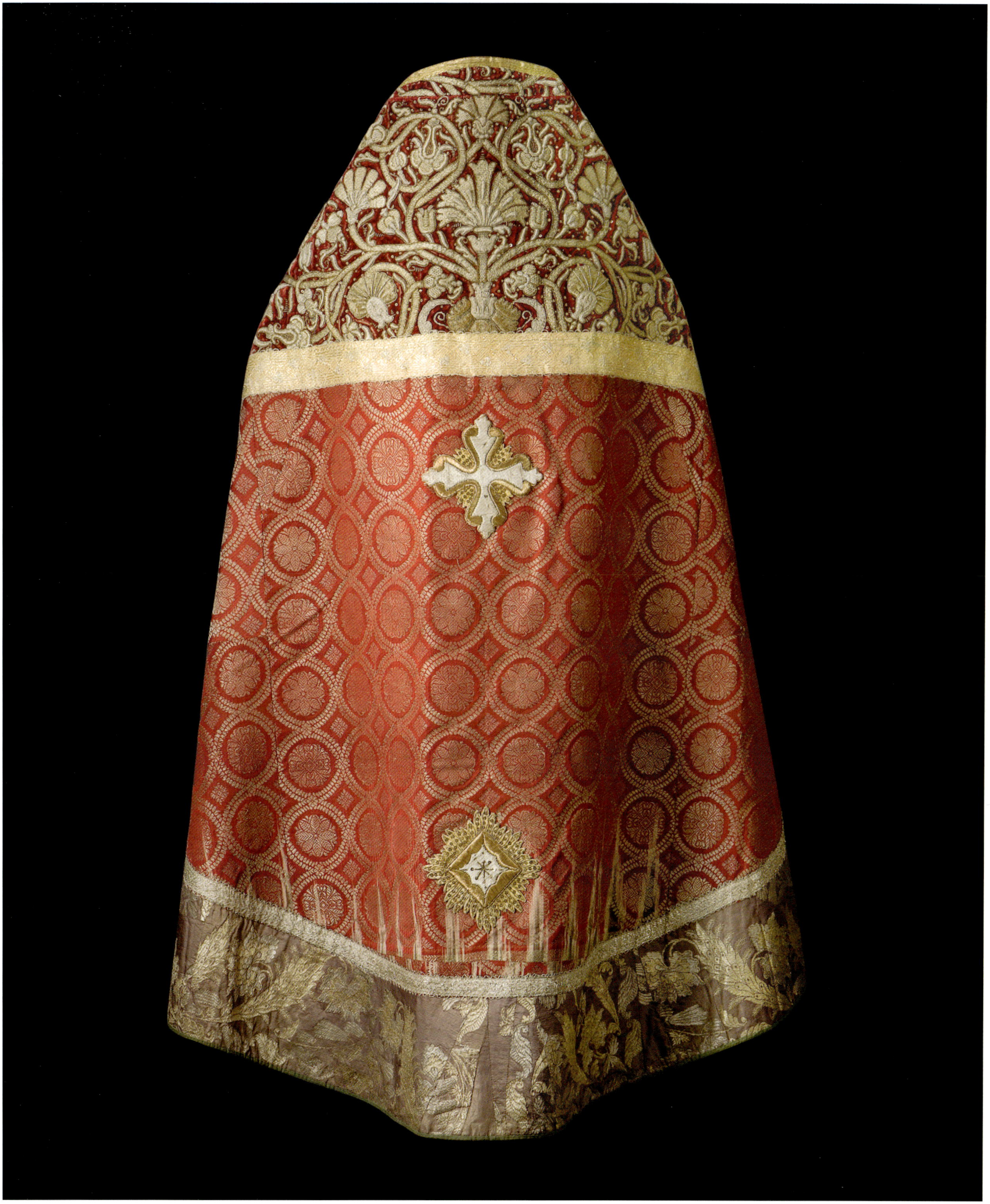

8. Chasuble (phelonion)
Russia, third quarter of 18th century
The State Historical Museum, Moscow
(Cat. 13)

in the 19th century, along with the religious subjects which we can see on the sumptuous ensemble made of red velvet with gold embroidery (which is shown in this exhibition), vegetal decorations were also used, executed using varied techniques: flat stitch or cross-stitch embroidery, pearl embroidery, crochet work etc. Sometimes there was only a cross sewn in the center (it was made with a piece of braid or with lace or trimming etc. or simply embroidered).

In the 18th century, Kiev was one of the centers for embroidery. In that city, the saint fathers of the Caves, Anthony and Theodosius, were particularly venerated. The monastery of the Kiev Caves had been founded by St. Anthony (canonized in 1133) and it was organized by St. Theodosius (canonized in 1108). It served as an example for all the other monasteries and played a huge role in the development of the Russian church. In the 18th century, the Kiev Caves Lavra (Monastery of the Caves) became a pilgrimage center for the faithful. Two veils and a *epitrakhelion*[17] of a crimson colored satin executed in the same style probably come from the workshops of the southern regions of Russia (ill. 6).

Peter I's reforms at the end of the 17th and beginning of the 18th centuries brought important changes to Russian life, including in the wearing of clothes. The nobles began to dress themselves in Western style. Russian silk manufactures appeared. But in spite of the development of the national textile industry, people continued to buy foreign fabric, still greatly appreciated. This is why during the 16th and 17th centuries, the custom became widespread to not only offer money donations to monasteries and churches but also to offer pieces of secular costumes which after being transformed were used for the liturgical services: this custom slowly disappeared in the 18th century. One of the most striking examples is Empress Anna Ivanovna's donation to the Trinity Monastery of St. Sergei. In 1730 she gave her head finery ("headdress") in silver brocade on a doubling of "white watered fabric with silver sequins", "...that she had worn in Moscow upon her accession to the Russian throne...." With this costume three archimandrite chasubles could be made: two in brocade and one in watered fabric.[18]

But it is especially curious to note that not only women's clothing, whose width made it possible to cut out whole pieces, was used to make liturgical vestments. Men's caftans[19] could also be used, as well as the badges of military orders which were taken off these caftans. And so, one of these badges of the Order of St. George of the first or second class[20] (ill. 8) was used as a custodial. It had been sewn on the brocade chasuble with the embroidered epaulette representing the *Dormition of the Mother of God* (end of the 18th century). The use of the badge of this precise order is interesting in so far as in the whole history of the existence of that high decoration, the first and the second class had been attributed to fewer than 150 people (for the first class, 23 people, for the second class, 125).

The circle of people so decorated at the end of the 18th and beginning of the 19th centuries was even fewer (among them were P. A. Rumiantsev, A. G. Orlov, P. I. Panin, G. A. Potemkin, M. I. Kutuzov etc.) It is possible that in the fu-

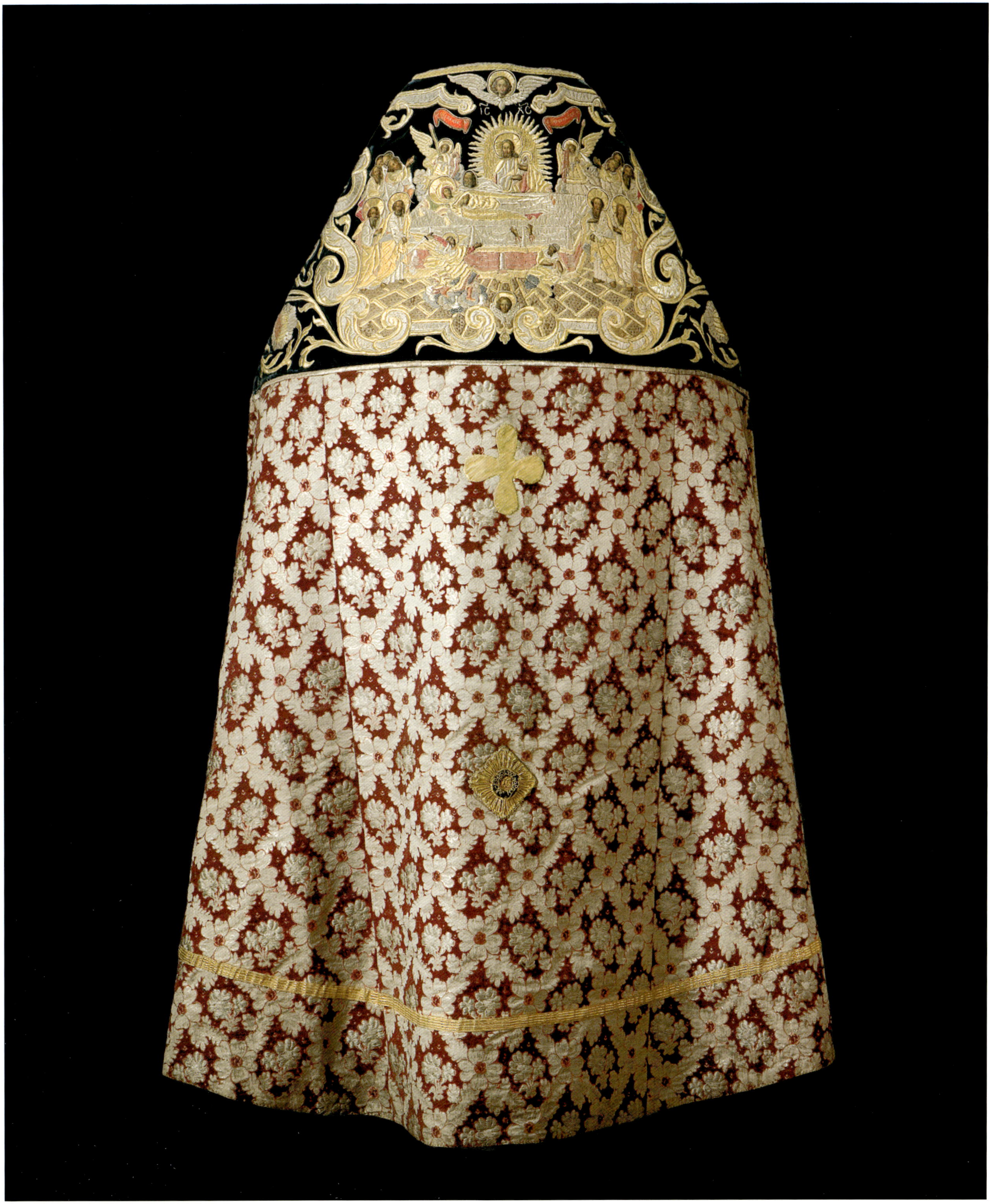

9. Chasuble (phelonion)
First quarter of 19th century
The State Historical Museum, Moscow
(Cat. 16)

ture researchers will be able to determine exactly which of them were honored by this decoration.

In fact, after their prolonged use, the woven objects inevitably became worn, and to maintain them, they were regularly repaired in the monasteries. The epaulette embroidered with pearls and gold thread was taken off the old chasubles, the borders, the cuffs, the custodials and the crosses were then sewn onto clothes made in new and contemporary fabrics. The most precious examples of decorative and figurative embroidery recuperated from the old objects could be preserved in the sacristies for many years. Pieces of liturgical vestments were used later in the redecorating or making of new pieces. We can see an example of one of these in this exhibition: the chasuble made out of a woman's veil (a silk fabric from Russian production at the end of the 18th-beginning of the 19th centuries) was completed by an embroidered epaulette from the end of the 17th century (ill. 7).

For the exhibition, we have also selected a few Orthodox clergy liturgical vestments coming from the 18th to the beginning of the 20th centuries. The liturgical vestments (commonly known as "chasubles") are divided into diaconal, sacerdotal and Episcopal vestments. The original vestment, the oldest which exists today, is a long alb with wide sleeves and a square-shaped epaulette. It was a liturgical outfit which was worn as a over-vestment by deacons and lower clerics. It was accompanied, as was customary, by oversleeves and a stole. For the priests and the bishops, the alb was worn under the other chasubles. This is why it is still called 'little cassock'.[21] (It was a little different from the alb as it had narrower sleeves at the wrists.)

The liturgical vestment which the priest wears on the outside is the *phelonion* or sacerdotal chasuble (which means in Greek "that which covers all."). In the dress of the priest, the *phelonion* is completed by the sleeves, the stole, the belt and the cross. The old *phelonions* were in the shape of a bell, in other words, the length was the same in front and in the back. So as to have the hands free during the celebration of mass, the part in front of the *phelonions* was raised and attached to buttons sewn onto the inside border of the epaulette. Later *phelonions* began to be made shorter in front, but the custom continued to raise the edge on the front and the buttoning on the inside border of the epaulette was maintained. The contemporary Russian *phelonion* is differentiated from that of the Orient by the presence of a rigid raised epaulette.

The liturgical vestments are of different colors. Progressively, every color came to correspond to particular religious celebration.

The production of brocade and velvet which began in Russia during the first decade of the 18th century very quickly attained significant success. Already in the 18th century, collections of liturgical vestments for deacons and priests existed in identical fabrics (this is the case with the *phelonion* and the alb presented in the exhibition). Russian decorative weaving followed the general evolution of European artistic styles, but in addition to the secular fabrics which, as in the past, could also be used for the Church, Specific fabrics "strewn with crosses" began to be produced

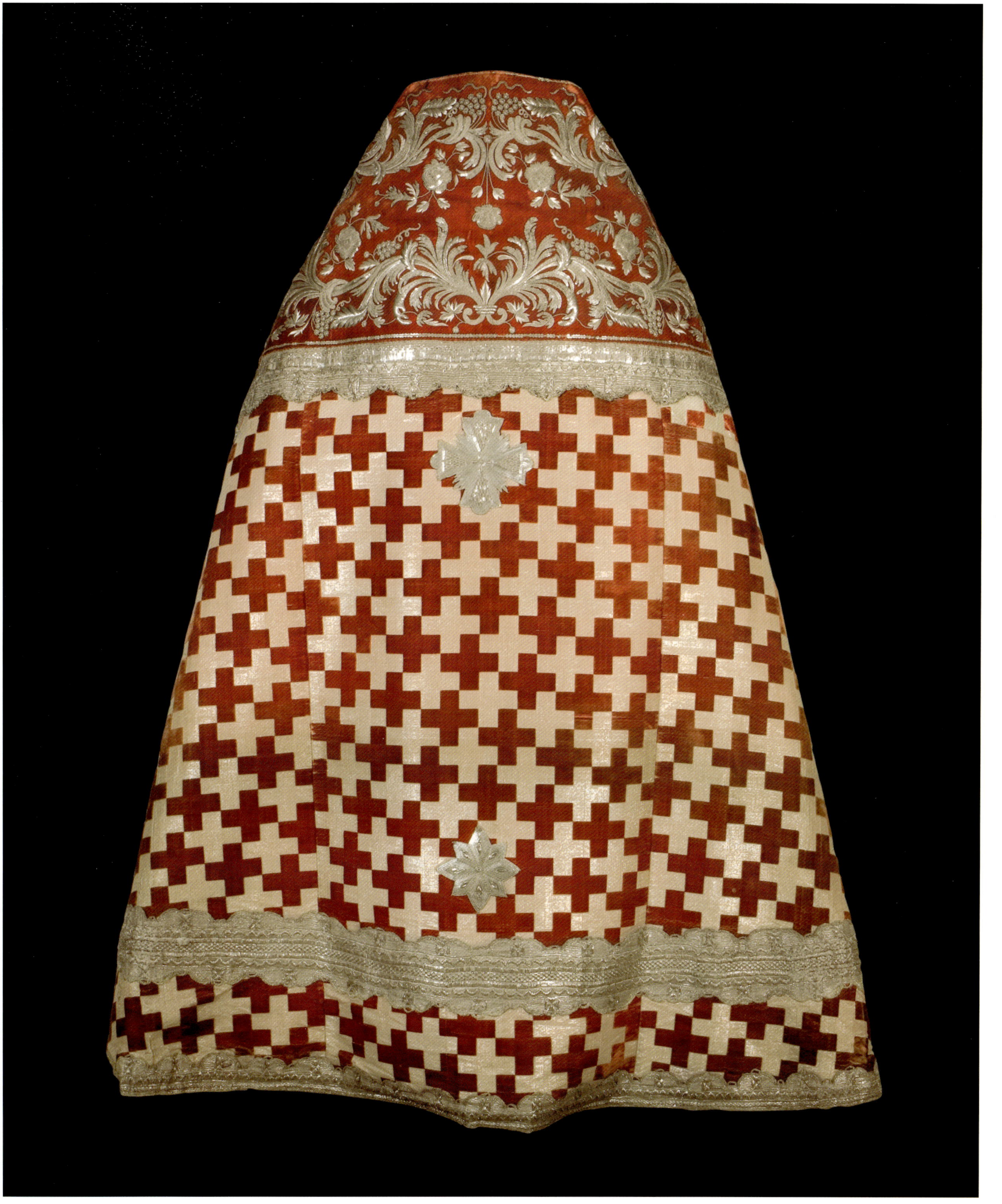

in Russia fabrics exclusively for ecclesiastic use. In Byzantium, chasubles "scattered with crosses"—the *polystauria*—were already a distinctive feature of the Episcopal function. At first in the Russian church, the right to celebrate services in *polystaurion* was reserved only to the Metropolitans. Later, it was extended to the Patriarchs, and to the Novgorod bishops. Beginning in 1768, the Emperor Paul I (1796-1801) authorized the priests who officiated in the Court churches to wear the *polystaurion*. Later, he extended this authorization to others (ill. 9).

This style of fabric was used for the first time in making the vestments of the celebrants who took part in Alexander I's coronation in 1801.

The middle of the 19th century was a period of economic growth during which time manufactures of brocade and silk fabric developed. At that time, there were mainly four Moscow workshops supplying the brocade fabric: those of P. I. Kolokolnikov, V. A. Poliakov, G. G. Sapojnikov and the Sytov Brothers.

The brocade items from the Moscow workshops and the district cities were regularly shown at all the Russian exhibitions (since 1829) and universal (since 1851) where they gained high awards. The production of fabric was enough not only to entirely satisfy the needs of the interior Russia market, but also large quantities could be exported abroad (in particular to Iran and Turkey.)

The church became the main client and user for brocade fabric.

The end of the 19th century and the beginning of the 20th century represented the last brilliant period in the history of the development of Russian brocades. It was characterized by an extraordinarily rapid rise of this unique industrial art, by an increase in the number of manufactures, of firms and commercial companies working in this field. The most important brocade producer in Russia was the firm "A. and V. Sapojnikov" which also had a store in London where Russian brocade was sold.

But it was P. I. Olovianichnikov & Sons Company of Commerce and Industry which played an unprecedented role as supplier to the Imperial Court. In spite of the absence of its own textile production until 1917, the company was very influential regarding the development of this line of industry. As a result of their extensive knowledge of traditions, the Olovianichnikovs created their own style in art and design. They were able to provide substance to the goal of renewing religious art. Most of the credit goes to Serge Ivanovich Vachkov, student at the Stroganov Institute—he created his own style, a genuine calling card for the firm.

The decorative compositions of brocade fabrics which he created during the time he worked with the Olovianichnikovs were very popular and they were taken up by diverse manufactures such as those of A. V. Golossov, G. I. Zaglodin, and the business firm of "I. Sidorin and S. Zglodin."

S. I. Vachkov was able to express in his work the "*Neo-Russian style*", the romantic national trend which had risen up around "modern art." The artist's projects, for the most part, were characterized by a return to the art of the first Christians and the Russian architecture of the 16th century, elements from which he drew his forms and his decorative motifs.

The second trend which appeared very clearly in the art of fabric in gold thread at the end of the 19th-beginning of the 20th centuries was the "Russian-Byzantine" style, characteristic of the Stroganov school. Large sumptuous decorations in gold brocade harmoniously fill the surface, covering practically all of the background. A fabric of this style decorates the lower selvage of the altar curtain with the representation of the archangel (ill. 10).

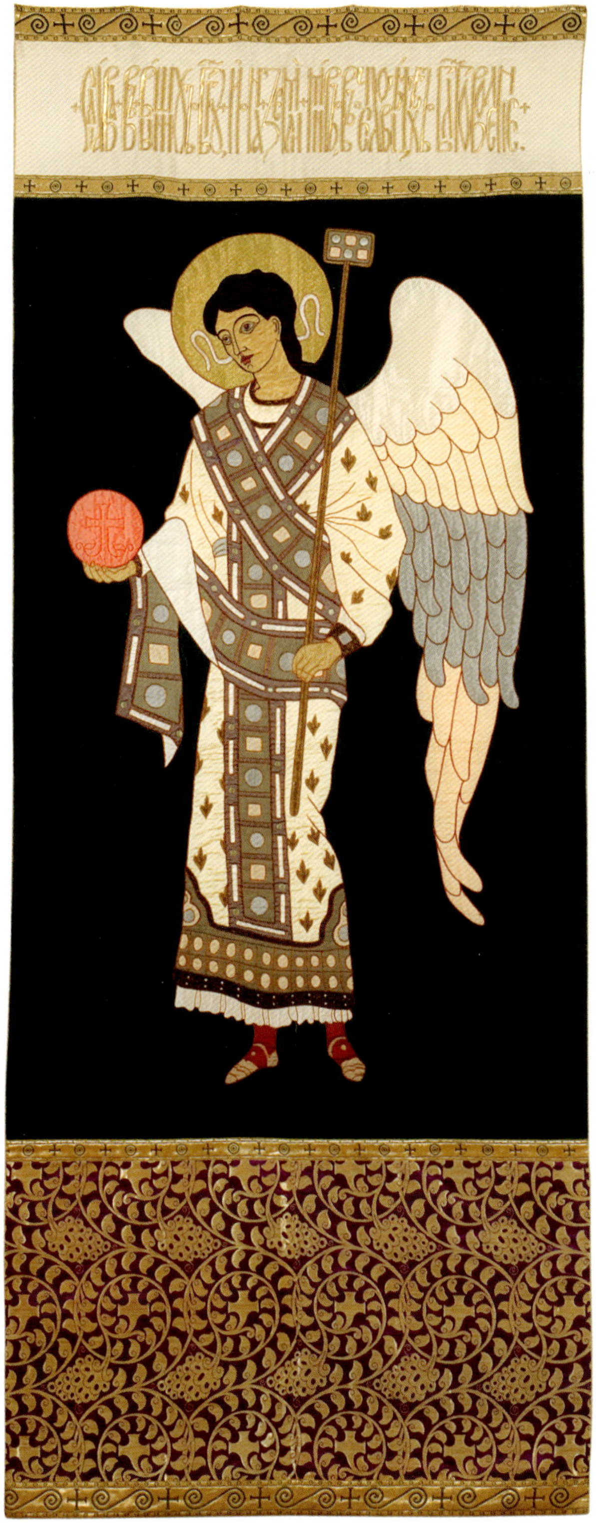

10. Altar curtain
Beginning of 20th century
The State Historical Museum, Moscow
(Cat. 139)

[1] The shroud (*soudar*) in ancient inventories is referred to as "little veil." It is almost square in shape and its sides measure about 55 cm. It rests on a paten. The shroud is the cloth which covered the head of Christ during his entombment. The representation on the shroud is linked to the liturgical function: it symbolizes the Divine essence of the Holy Donations with which the faithful receive Communion. This representation was the Cross or a composition with a "subject" (most often the embroidery was of the Crucifixion, "Here is the Lamb of God...", the Virgin of the Sign, and rarely, Christ the Savior, the Holy Trinity, the Transfiguration).

[2] These embroidered cloths often took up the subject of the icon under which it was placed; they were used as traveling icons. The piece of the fabric on which they were embroidered was not fixed and hung freely. (Translator's note)

[3] The diamond (cardboard covered with fabric and decorated with a cross), Episcopal or sacerdotal distinction, and the rectangle, first sacerdotal distinction, are derived from the Greek epigonation: the two insignias symbolize the sword of the word of God. They are worn, on the chasuble, at the height of the knee, suspended from a ribbon. (Translator's note)

[4] Large stole worn by the bishop, decorated with crosses and images. (Translator's note)

[5] Orarion or "epitrakhelion". (Translator's note)

[6] This embroidery is sometimes called "embroidery with a subject": it represents the face or the whole silhouette of the person. (Translator's note)

[7] In 1593-1594 the Western master Marco Ciponi had received the authorization to open the first establishment for the production of silk ribbons in Moscow. In 1652, a small market for velvet started up. But these businesses were only early steps. The next initiative was attempted in 1681. Paulsen (Zakhar Pavlov) obtained state subsidies to establish a velvet making factory and until 1685, he managed it at his own expense. At that date, the factory came under the control of the Treasury. Ten Russian apprentices were trained in the factory. In four years, they made 1600 *archines* (Translator's note: an *archine* was equal to 0.71 meters) of silk and mixed brocade fabric (a smooth and silky fabric) and 33 *archines* and a half of velvet. However, after Paulsen's return to his country, the production ceased. Cf. K. O. Pajitnov, *Essays on the history of the textile industry before the Revolution in Russia. he Cotton industry, hemp and linen and silk*, USSR Academy of Sciences, Moscow 1958, pp. 303-304 (in Russian).

[8] The *Domostroy* was didactic writing attributed to Bishop Sylvester (1556) in which the rules of life in the patriarchal household were laid out. (Translator's note)

[9] Cf. A. V. Silkin, *Stroganov "Figurative Embroidery"*, M. Progress-Traditsiia, 2002, pp. 9-10, 61 (in Russian).

[10] *Ibid.*, pp. 6-7.

[11] *Ibid.*, p. 129.

[12] Eudoxie Lukianovna (1608-August 18, 1645) was the daughter of an obscure noble from Mojaisk, Lukian Stepanovich Strechnev. From in 1626, she became the second wife of the first Czar of the Romanov dynasty, Michael Feodorovich. She was chosen by the Czar during the presentation ceremony of fiancées and in fact was not part of the selected fiancées but was presented as the confidante of one of them.

[13] Cf. A. Maisova, *"Figurative" Embroidery in Old Russia. Catalogue*, 2004, pp. 268-269 (in Russian); *Embroidery in Old Russia 15th-begininng of 16th centuries*, L., 1980, p. 103 (in Russian).

[14] The *skhima* is a large habit which strictly observant monks wear. It is this habit which in particular the Emperors put on at the moment of their death. This ceremony is described by Pushkin in the play *Boris Godunov*. (Translator's note)

[15] The local worship of saints began at the latest in 1468, although worship of the saints by the whole community of Russian faithful became widespread around the middle of the 16th century.

[16] During the liturgy—which was par excellence the service of the whole community of the faithful where the sacrament of the Eucharist was carried out—three veils were used: one for the paten, one for the chalice and a veil which covered the first two. The latter, usually bigger, was called the *aer*. The smaller veils, designed by the word *pokrovets*, the diminutive of *pokrov* (the veil) were called "shrouds" (*soudari*) by the first Christians. The *aer* was introduced into the celebration of the liturgy by St. Sabas the Consecrated (5th to 6th century), founder of a monastery near Jordan. During the recitation of the Credo, the celebrants waved the *aer* above the Holy Donations (the wine and the bread which symbolized the blood and the body of Christ) and by this movement produced a quivering of the air: this quivering represented the descent of the Holy Spirit onto the Holy Donations and when the "large veil" rested on them, it symbolized the funeral of Christ, at the moment when his tomb was closed. The little veil for the paten is a reminder of the shroud which went around Christ's head in the tomb. The veils first appeared in the Near East where they protected the Holy Donations from insects while the Holy Offerings were being prepared.
In Russia at the end of the 16th century, these three veils formed a set executed in the same style. The common themes (but not exclusively) for the decoration of the *aer* were, "The Entombment" (or "Christ in the Tomb") and for the little veils, "The Mother of the Sign", ("The Mother of the Incarnation"), "The Crucifixion" and "Here is the Lamb of God..." (whose subject is the Christ Child, lying on the paten, surrounded by angels with liturgical fans ("*flabella*").

[17] The *epitrakhelion* (from the Greek word "neck") is one of the liturgical vestments, attribute of the priest and the bishop. It is in the shape of a long stole around the neck, falling from the two sides over the chest. The two pieces were sewn at the front and attached by buttons. In the past, it could be made with a single piece of fabric. It was worn on the alb (little cassock) or on the cassock. It symbolized the descent of the grace of the Holy Spirit. In the image of Christ carrying the cross on his shoulders during the Passion, the priest who had received the grace to celebrate mass, carried out the sacrament of His Passion. The bishop wears the *epitrakhelion* in memory of the sacerdotal graces

which have been granted to him and which remain forever engraved within him. The priest and the bishop cannot celebrate mass without the *epitrakhelion*. In the case of the persecution of the Church, if the priest is imprisoned, the *epitrakhelion* can be replaced by any long band of fabric, or by a cord which he will have blessed before. Originally the *epitrakhelion* was the diaconal *orarion*: as the sign of the renewal of graces which take place during the sacerdotal ordination of the deacon, the second piece of the stole is brought from the back across the chest, and then the ends of the two pieces are brought together.

[18] *Dedicatory book of the Saint-Serge Trinity monastery*, ed. by B. A. Rybakov, M. Nauka, 1987, p. 32 (in Russian).

[19] In the last third of the 18th century, men wore velvet caftans richly decorated with colored silk thread embroidery (and also with gold thread, and all sorts of thin strips and sequins): the embroidery was done along the edges, on the cuffs, the sleeves, the pockets and the neck. Men's caftans were much smaller than the liturgical vestments. So it was impossible to make whole albs or chasubles out of them. This is why embroidered bands were cut from the caftans to decorate the lower part of chasubles. In the same way, women's dresses could only be used partially—only a few details from the embroidery were taken off and they were placed on the lower part or on the epaulettes of liturgical vestments.

[20] The full title of this decoration is: "Order of the Imperial war of the Saint and Victorious Meglo-martyr George". It was created by the Empress Catherine II on November 26 (December 7), 1769 to reward the officers for their actions on the battle field (it was done away with after the October Revolution). There were four degrees of decoration. The badge was given for the first and second class. Until 1854, only badges sewn onto the clothes were attributed. The badges could only be given to 148 people (23 people for the first class decoration, 125 for the second). The names of all the knights of the Order of St. George were inscribed in gold letters on marble plaques displayed on the walls of the Saint George Room in the Kremlin Palace. The officer decorated by the Order of St. George automatically received the next highest military decoration (military rank) and if he was not a nobleman, he acquired the rights of hereditary nobility. The State emphasized the exceptional high status of this war decoration.

[21] In Russian: *podriznik*.

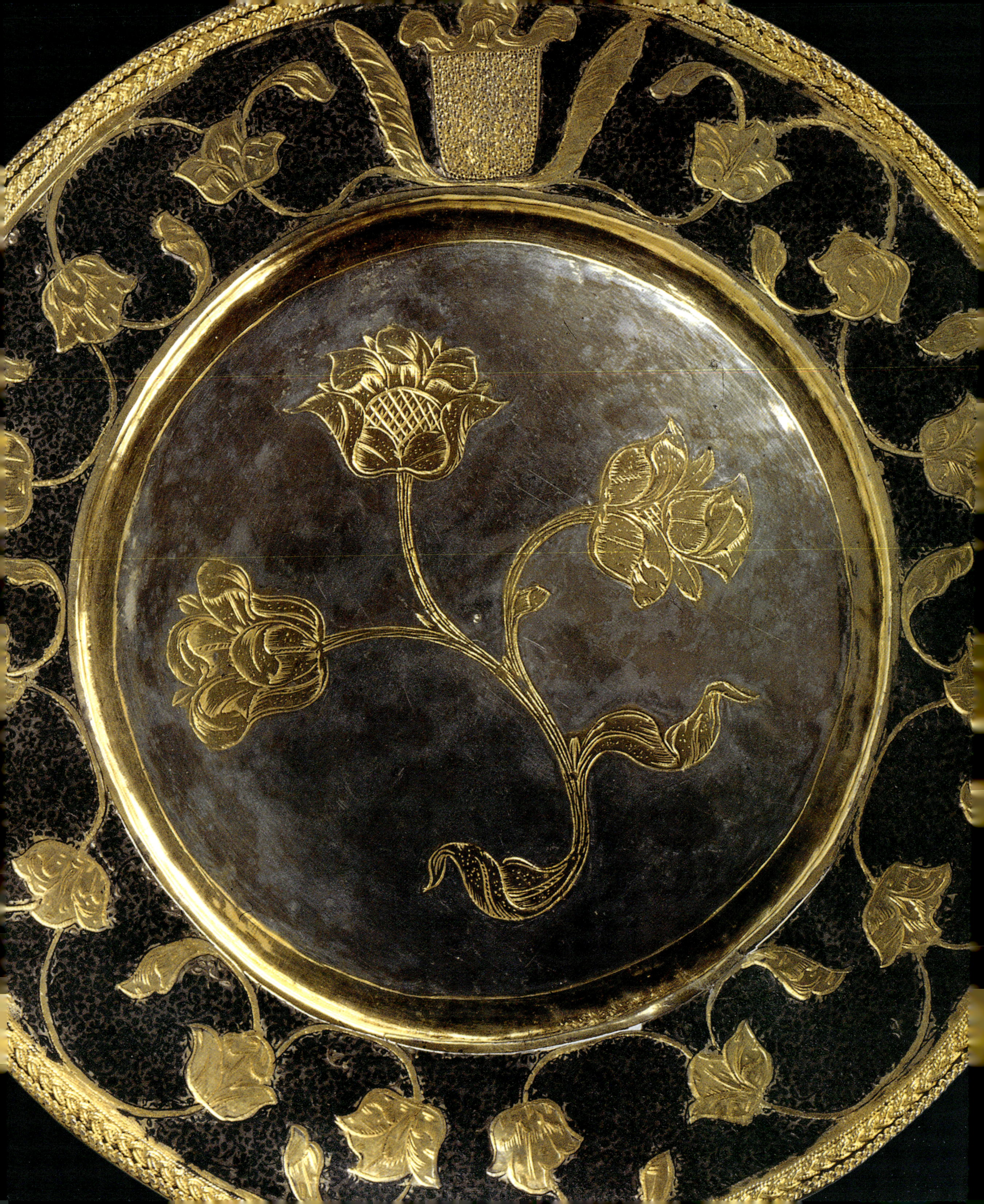

THE GOLDSMITH'S ART IN MOSCOW UNDER THE ROMANOVS REIGN: 300 YEARS OF HISTORY

Tatiana Sizova

A truly jeweled setting for Moscow and for its main square, the Red Square—this is how one might define the monumental building of the State Historical Museum which celebrated the 125th anniversary of its inauguration in 2008. The museum's collection consists of not fewer than 4.5 million indexed pieces. At the heart of the different sections in charge of the preservation of the art objects collections, the Precious Metals Department which was called at first the "Special Depot" holds the place of honor. To all effects and purposes, the department was founded in 1905, a year when the decision was taken to create a reserve especially equipped for the pieces in precious stones and metals.

The initial nucleus of the "Special Depot's" collection came from the donation by the famous businessman, entrepreneur and Muscovite art patron P. I. Shchukin who in 1905 gave more than 800 objects of Russian, European and Oriental gold and silver work to what was then the Imperial Russian Historical Museum. In 1912, the Historical Museum received another gift of a few thousand pieces of precious tableware, silver liturgical objects and valuable jewelry, all of very great quality, which Shchukin had left to the museum in his will. Throughout the 20th century, the collection was added to by donations by private persons, purchases, and deposits from various public institutions. Today, the department's collection contains about 27,000 pieces among which the productions of the Russian gold and silversmiths from the 11th to the 20th centuries occupy a unique place, recreating a picture which speaks volumes about the development of gold and silver work in fifty art centers in Russia. Its chronological scope as well as the diversity of types and forms represented, their style and their decoration, is what gives this collection its exceptional quality. The collection is also characterized by the amount and the quality of information provided by these precious objects which can be counted by the number of original historic sources: first and foremost, objects containing inscriptions about their owners which can be linked to the names of sovereigns, army leaders, famous people in the fields of art and culture or those connected with major historical events.

The Muscovite silver and gold work during the time of the Romanov dynasty belongs to the material and spiritual history of the 17th century to the beginning of the 20th. One finds in this work, sometimes directly but most often obliquely, the echo of the processes which determined the originality and richness of the cultural and historical events of this period.

The particular position of the pieces made in Moscow and their role as benchmarks are closely linked to Moscow's dominant situation, capital of

Plate
Russia, Moscow, end of 17th century
The State Historical Museum, Moscow
(Cat. 236)
Detail

1. Basin for holy water
Russia, 1672
The State Historical Museum, Moscow
(Cat. 44)

an immense Euro-Asiatic state. From the moment that it acquired its status as capital, at the end of the 15th century, it tapped the best creative forces in the country in procuring optimal conditions for the production and distribution of the most refined and costly pieces. The encounter with objects which arrived from the diverse regions of Russia and sometimes from very distant countries was a source of inspiration for Moscow craftsmen. It led them to invent new models, excited their inventive capacities and pushed them to increase their know-how. Enriched by new impressions thanks to a perfect assimilation of the traditional techniques of production, the Muscovite master craftsmen of the 17th century designed works which were characterized both by the specific national features of their time and their quality of execution. The very perspicacious ambassador of the Duke of Tuscany, Jacob Reitenfels,[1] certainly was not wrong when he wrote sometime around 1670, "The number of craftsmen of quality, formerly very few in the Moscow region, has considerably increased in our time and their know-how has been perfected to the highest degree. The Russians have achieved this thanks to a faculty of assimilation which is natural to them and to the capacities of their spirit... They welcome foreign craftsmen... invite them to come stay... and very often, in addition, they surpass them with new inventions!"

The art of 17th century gold and silver work in Moscow, evolving with the framework of a national tradition conceived as an established body of forms, stylistic modes, decorative principles and technical skills, was the expression of aesthetic ideas specific to many levels of society. For the decoration of liturgical objects, tableware and table services, the local craftsmen took inspiration from the ornamentation of ancient Russian manuscripts and miniatures from the first printed books, from Western engravings, from imported silk and velvet motifs, from the plastic repertory of popular art wood and stone sculpture.

The rapid growth in gold and silver work in Moscow in the 17th century was due to the activity of the Kremlin workshops and in particular to the existence from in the 16th century of the Kremlin Armory Palace. It was there that unique specimens of precious utensils, pieces for interior decoration, drinking implements and tableware were created for the use of the Czar, the Russian aristocracy and the high dignitaries of the Orthodox Church. Observations by contemporaries whether Russian or foreigners, frequently referred to the gold and silver objects which constituted, after icons, the main decoration of the rooms in the private part of the home, the *terem*. Used daily, the precious objects served an important function in revealing the social position of their owner, his wealth, his tastes and his habits, his fidelity to the past or his infatuation for new fashions.

The preferred gold and silversmith techniques in Moscow in the 17th century were chasing, dry point *repousse* work, engraving, gilding, *niello* work and making diverse polychrome enamels, both translucent and opaque. The brilliance and the festive character of gold and silver objects were underlined by an extended use of colored stones, semi-precious stones, pearls, amber and even pieces of glass. The opening up of 17th century Russian culture and the swiftness with which it assimilat-

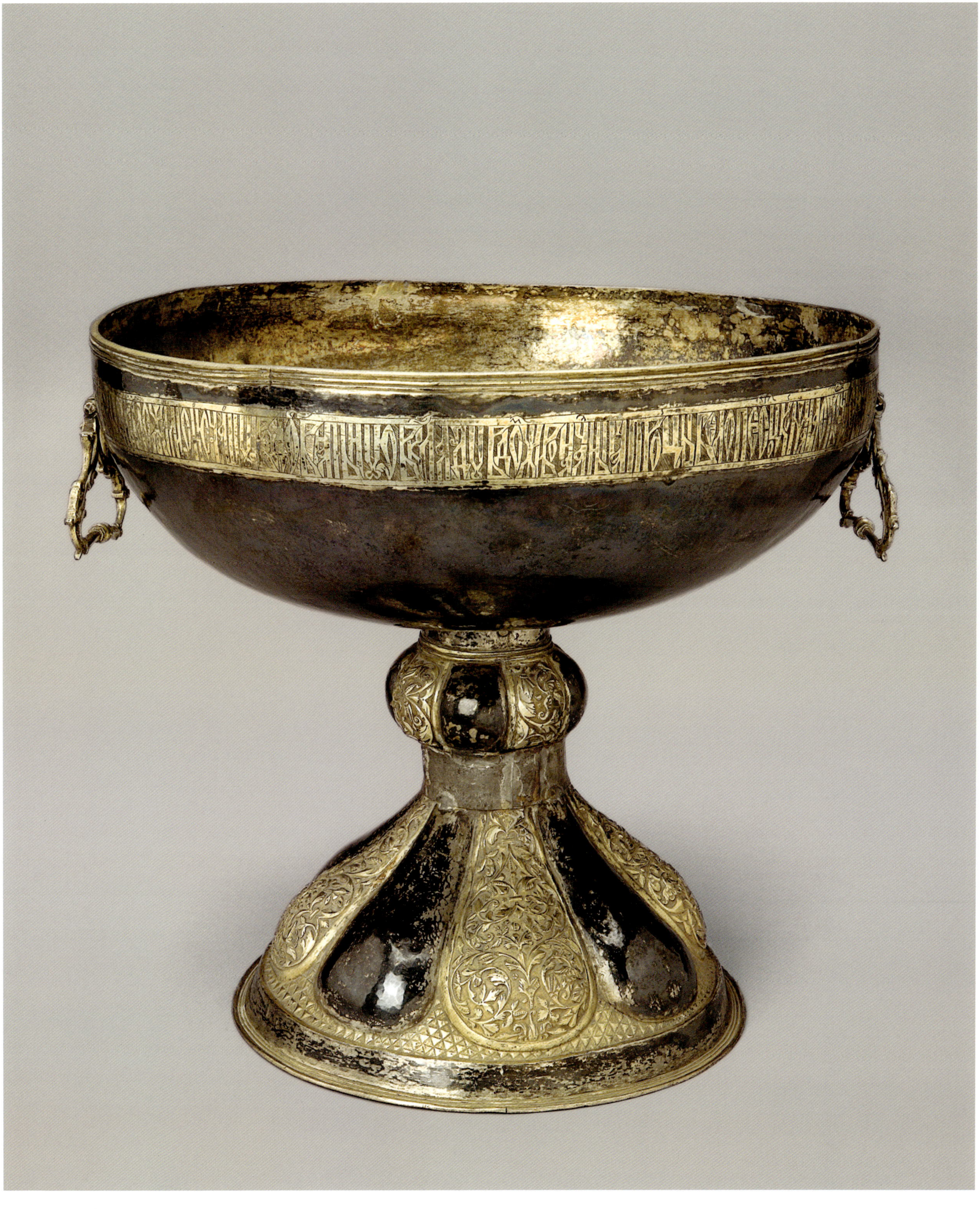

2. Tumbler (stopa)
Russia, Moscow, 1690-1691
The State Historical Museum, Moscow
(Cat. 237)

ed foreign experience explains the existence alongside the old Byzantine tradition in the art of jewelry-making in the capital, of extensive borrowing of shapes and designs from Western Europe as well as shapes and designs from the art of Oriental jewelry-making from Persia to China.

The Muscovite craftsmen perfectly mastered the traditional techniques of casting but also that of hammering, which enabled them to give form to an object from a sheet of metal. They knew how to shape by hammering tall and deep receptacles to which they gave perfect and very often complex contours, without leaving the least trace of the shaping process. In this exhibition we can see examples of pieces made for church—chalices, cup for the blessing of the water of 1672, censers from the end of the 17th to the early 18th century—as well as those made for secular use, the goblet (*stopa*) cut in facets, a tankard with fixed lid, a dish from the end of the 17th century (ill. 2).

The originality of the drinking implements for the Russian banquets struck the imagination of foreigners who had never seen anything like them, in particular and above all the precious dipper (*kovch*). The French officer Jacques Margeret who at the beginning of the 17th century was captain of the foreign body guards for the Czars Boris Godunov and the false Dmitry I, describes in his writings having seen in the royal treasury a great many gigantic "basins flanked by handles" made of silver which were used for a very popular alcoholic drink with a honey base that the participants of the banquet could draw themselves using the huge silver dippers.

This type of precious utensil which appeared for the first time in Novgorod in the 14th century was extraordinarily popular in Moscow in the 17th century. Short inscriptions of affiliation engraved on the dippers have provided information about the names of their owners. For example there is a luxurious silver dipper decorated with engraved and gilded motifs whose inscription attests to its having belonged to a Russian aristocrat, the voivod from Tobolsk, Andrey Andreyevich Golitsyn, and handed down from him to his grandson, the prince Vasily Vasilyevich Golitsyn, a high ranking diplomat who was head of the interior and foreign affairs departments for the Russian state.

For liturgical purposes, dippers in silver were used to give holy water for drinking and sometimes for taking a mixture of wine and water after communion. In very rare cases, the dippers belonging to the church were used by the highest clerical dignitaries for "benedictions" in memory of exceptional events. We know this of one of the pieces which we can see in this exhibition, the elegant benediction dipper decorated with two inlays of vivid-colored turquoise given by the metropolitan of Kazan and Sviaj Matthieu to the voivode Tomila Lugovskoy for having led the "donkey" (in Old Russia it was a horse playing the role, to which one attached big cloth ears) on which the Metropolitan was mounted during the 1630 Easter week at the moment of the procession symbolizing the entrance of Jesus Christ into Jerusalem (ill. 3).

Around the middle of the 17th century, the precious dippers made in Moscow became a sort of foreshadowing of later official decorations which

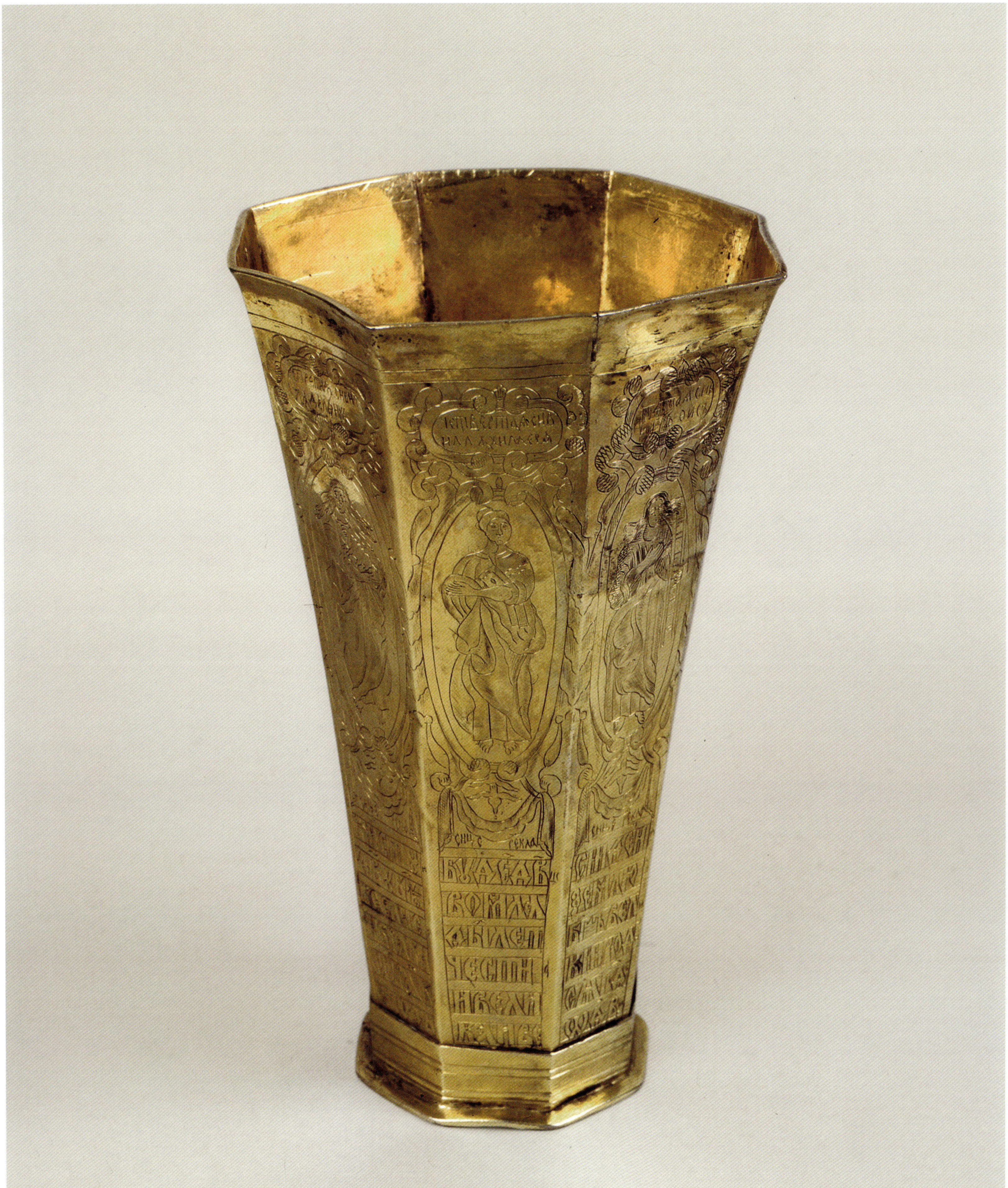

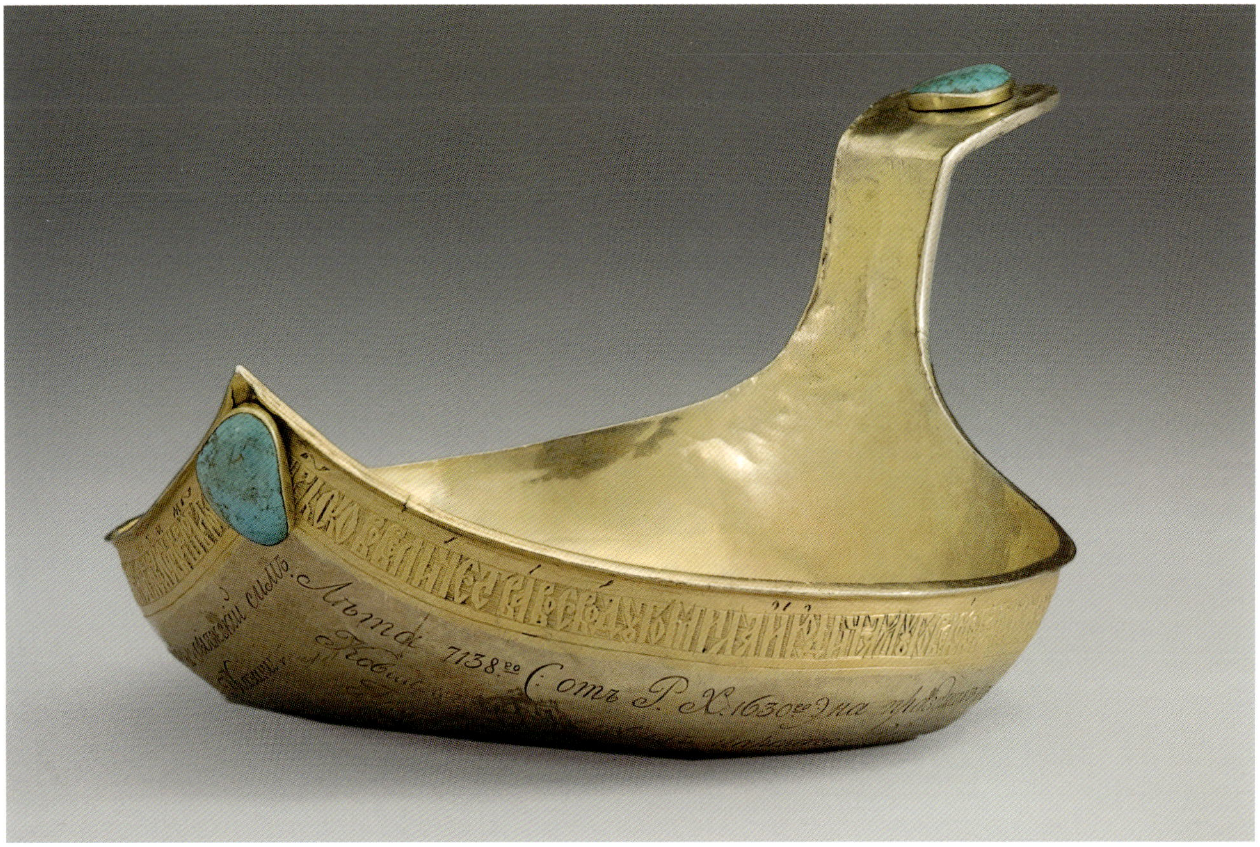

3. Ladle of honor (kovch) given to the voivod Tomila Yudich Lugovskoy by the metropolitan of Kazan and of Sviaj, Mathew
Russia, end of the 16th-early 17th century
The State Historical Museum, Moscow
(Cat. 239)

are the orders and the medals. The dippers known as "honorary ones" were decorated with hammered images, the Arms of State engraved or chased onto the background or onto the spout or handle and often had on them the image of the Czars. These dippers with their images were given by the Czars to the servants of the State, to the merchants and to the Cossack atamans for services rendered to the sovereign. This is the case of the 1693 dipper shown in this exhibition with which the young co-regents Czars, sons of Alexis I, Ivan and Peter, had "honored" Mikhail Popov for his fundraising services regarding the "alcoholic beverages profits", in other words the revenues from the sale of alcohol which was a state monopoly and an essential item of contributions to the public treasury (ill. 4).

The Muscovite master craftsmen of the 17th to the beginning of the 18th centuries possessed to perfection the art of working the precious materials in a thousand different ways and the knowhow to bring out all the characteristics of metals: they knew how to give a brilliant, mat, or grainy surface to the pieces, they handled the art of gilding on silver perfectly, covering with gold either the whole object or just certain parts of it or details. The work of the niello workers was characterized by an exceptional technical quality. They used niello (a powder especially made from a mixture of burned silver and other metals) to cover the background or for motifs and compositions engraved with deep incisions. In using various methods, they were able to vary the nuances of the niello, going from pale grey to deep black. The plate and the very original writing *necessaire* in the exhibition are perfect examples of the work of the niello masters in the capital at the end of the 17th to the early 18th century (ill. 5). The writing *necessaire* includes a three-faceted ink well in the shape of a stylized fruit and a casted tube case for a goose quill. The two pieces have been decorated with a niello background covered with a delicate vegetal motif according to a technique whose use was introduced into Russian art in the second half of the 17th century under the influence of Ottoman Empire art. The Ottoman Empire was renown for its blades decorated by this kind of niello design made up of miniscule foliated patterns with flowers and leaves. The beauty and elegance of the background was underlined by the presence of sumptuous tulip flowers freely scattered around, often executed with great realism and which can be found especially in the silverwork designs in Germany and in Holland.

Not only is the very beautiful niello covering of the icon of Nicholas the Just enhanced by traditional floral compositions but added to it are original oriental motifs, as for example, the carnation.

The processes put into practice by the Muscovite enamel workers of the 17th century were even more refined and diverse. Covering objects of silver and gold with a multicolored decoration corresponded to the inclination of the Russian people for ornamentation and brilliant colors. One can also find demonstrations of this in painting, in the decoration of wood and ceramic objects, in architecture, in the way of treating materials and embroideries. One could make a thick enamel, opaque, with vivid and contrasting colors, but one could also make it using a vitreous paste which various metallic oxides tinted and through which one could see the soft glistening of the surface of the metal which was often gilded. The Moscow enamel workers applied enamel in a number of ways: the most often onto compositions which were deeply cut (chased) and onto a filigree design. On the gold relief in the Kremlin Armory Palace, enamel was used to cover complex scenes of several figures, thus creating an impression of miniature sculptures.

In the last quarter of the 17th century, the Solvytchegodsk enamel workers who had come from the workshops of the famous Stroganov family—founders of a dynasty of barons—imported into Moscow the art of painting on enamel which they had learned from German masters. This art was quickly adopted by the capital's craftsmen, thus preparing the ground for enamel work production which was to develop in the 18th century. The exhibition presents such painted pieces: a cup, a casket with images of birds, a pectoral cross, executed in this very particular technique (ill. 6).

The end of the 17th century and first ten years of the 18th were marked by Russia developing contacts both with the countries of central and western Europe as well as with the Orient. From that period, shapes of drinking utensils and tableware begin to appear which had not been seen before, new decorative elements and ornamental motifs appeared which were most happily integrated into those more traditionally used. In addition to

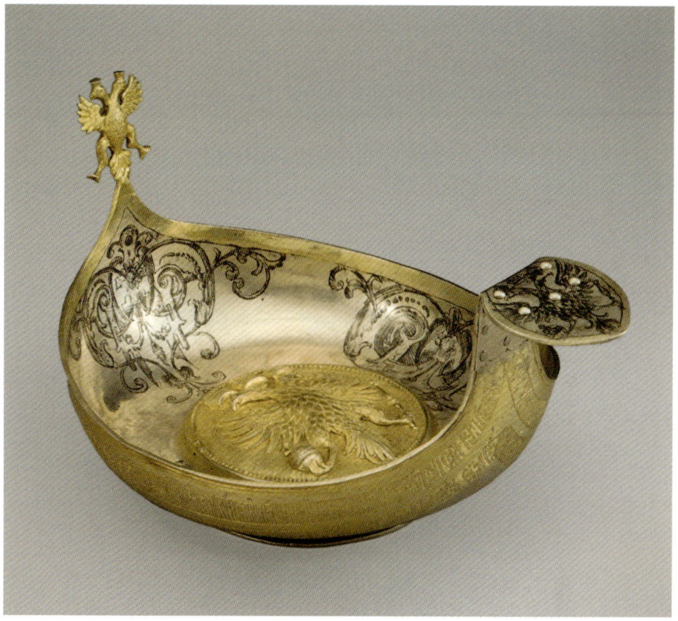

4. Ladle of honor (Kovch) given by the Czars Ivan Alexeievich and Peter Alexeievich to the elected chief Michael Popov (tax collector). *Russia, Moscow, 1693* *The State Historical Museum, Moscow* *(Cat. 240)*

subjects already assimilated composition-wise and stylistically, the artists resorted to scenes borrowed from the Bible and the Gospel which chased or engraved, were destined not only to decorate chalices, patens and asterisks, but also often objects which had no religious function.

The goal of the reforms initiated by the first Russian Emperor Peter I was to bring Russia into the circle of enlightened European states. The new measures aimed at supervising the church also transformed the way of life. The new ideas borrowed from what was happening in Europe gradually were incorporated into the art of gold and silver work, according to different periods of the 18th century. The first third of the 18th century, it was through inherent forms of the Petrovian baroque; in the middle of the 18th century it was Elizabethan rococo; and in the last half of the 18th century, it was the classicism of Catherine's time. It's important however to note that these styles virtually did not exist in their pure state in the gold and silverwork objects: ornamental elements and isolated motifs belonging to more ancient periods continued to be in use for a long time.

The appearance, in private life, of practices up until then unknown and of new manners in social life called for the creation of new objects for daily use and table service: drinking utensils and dinnerware.

If the epoch of Peter the Great profoundly changed the way of life of the upper classes of society, it did not however produce gold and silver work which was particularly remarkable from an artistic point of view. The liturgical art objects which have come down to us show a clear leaning toward traditional canons and even toward archaism. The founding of the new capital in St. Petersburg, the establishment there of the royal house, the transfer of many of the leading families, and the richest, led to a radical modification in the statute of the major artistic center which was that of Moscow. Its new role in fact became that of preserving national traditions. It is indispensable to remember once again: the art of gold and silver work of the 18th and 19th centuries was based on knowledge of the craftsmanship of the art of the epoch which preceded it. It was the 17th century which established the base on which this art took off and put into practice the technical processes which it then only had to perfect: the ornamental motifs of the new styles (rococo, classicism, empire) brought no false note regarding the earlier aesthetic concepts. The art of Muscovite gold and silverwork of the 18th and 19th centuries simply took on complementary characteristics and evolved without going through a radical revolution.

The discovery during Peter the Great's reign of rich deposits of precious metals in the Ural and in Siberia considerably increased the production of objects in gold and in silver of a very large size. We have the proof of this with some of the pieces presented in the exhibition, solid and which required a huge quantity of raw material: the covering of the Gospel engraved in 1785 (ill. 8), the tabernacle of 1788 (ill. 7), the chalice of 1795, the dish for the evening service of 1789. These pieces are decorated with painted enamel designs which show the high level of mastery of the craftsmen in the art of miniature and of engraved or molten details.

The middle of the 18th century, epoch of the

5. Plate
Russia, Moscow, end of 17th century
The State Historical Museum, Moscow
(Cat. 236)

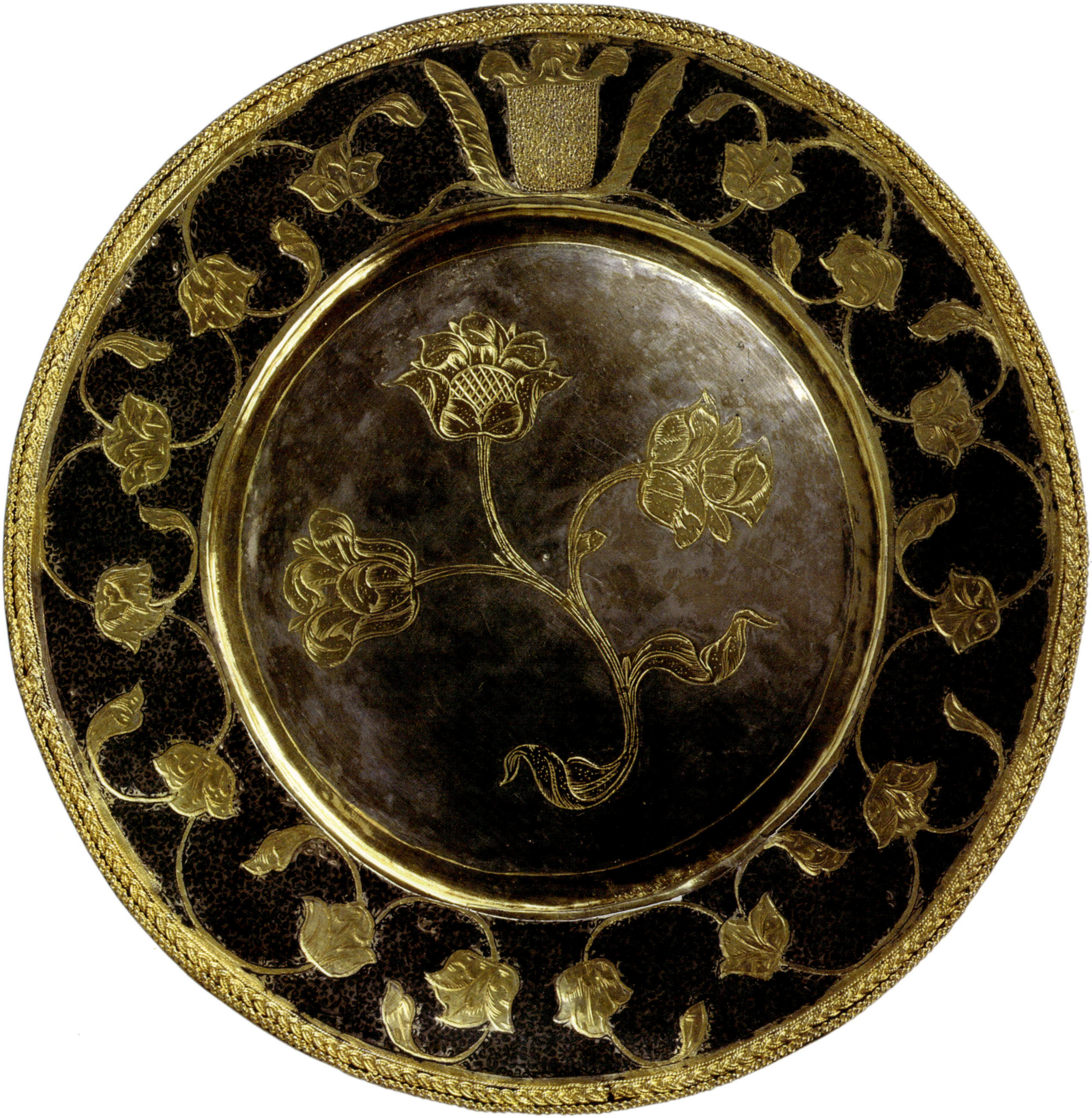

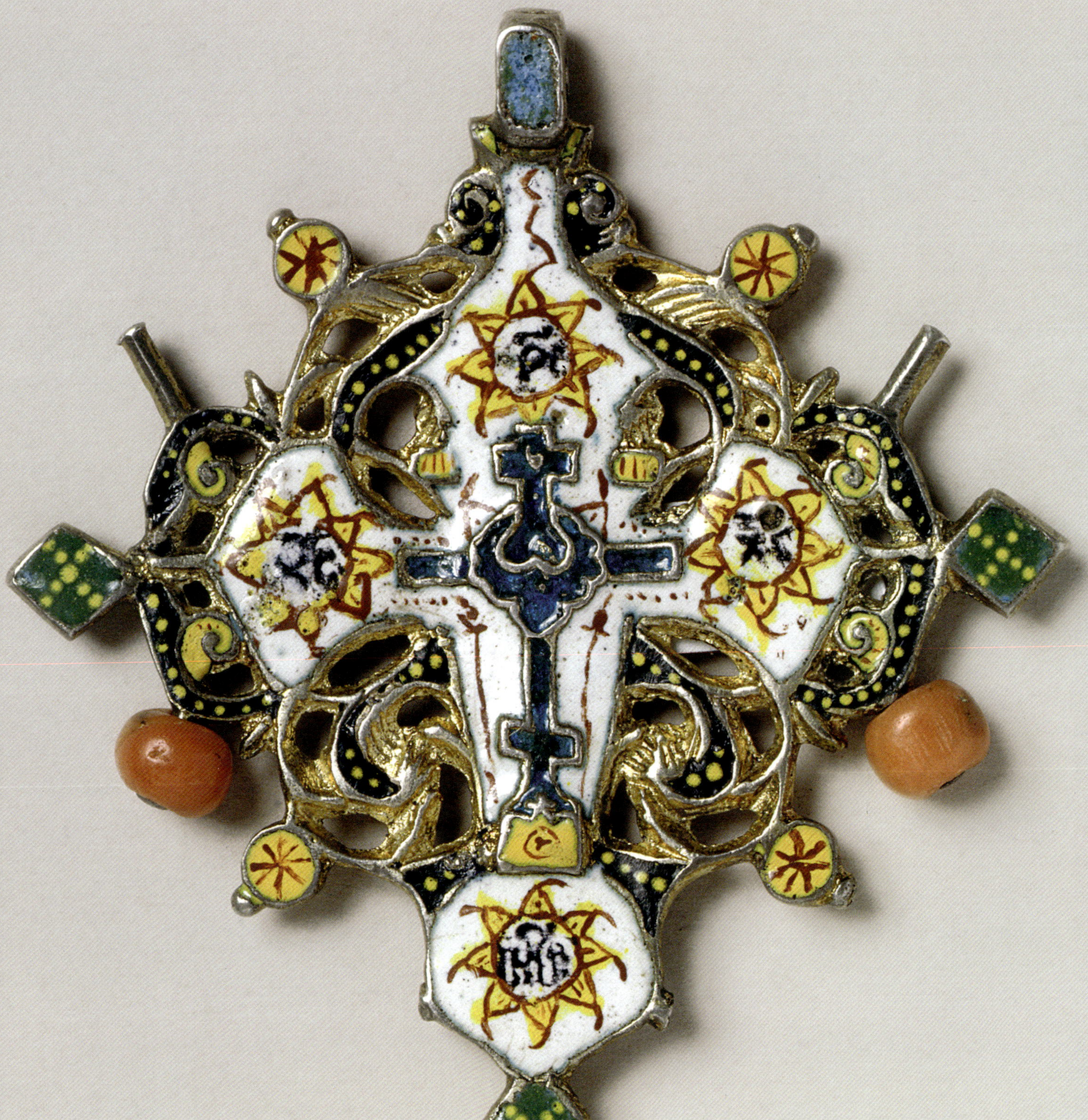

6. Pectoral cross
Russia, Solvychegodsk, second half of 17th century
The State Historical Museum, Moscow
(Cat. 50)

7. Tabernacle
Russia, Moscow, 1788
The State Historical Museum, Moscow
(Cat. 117)

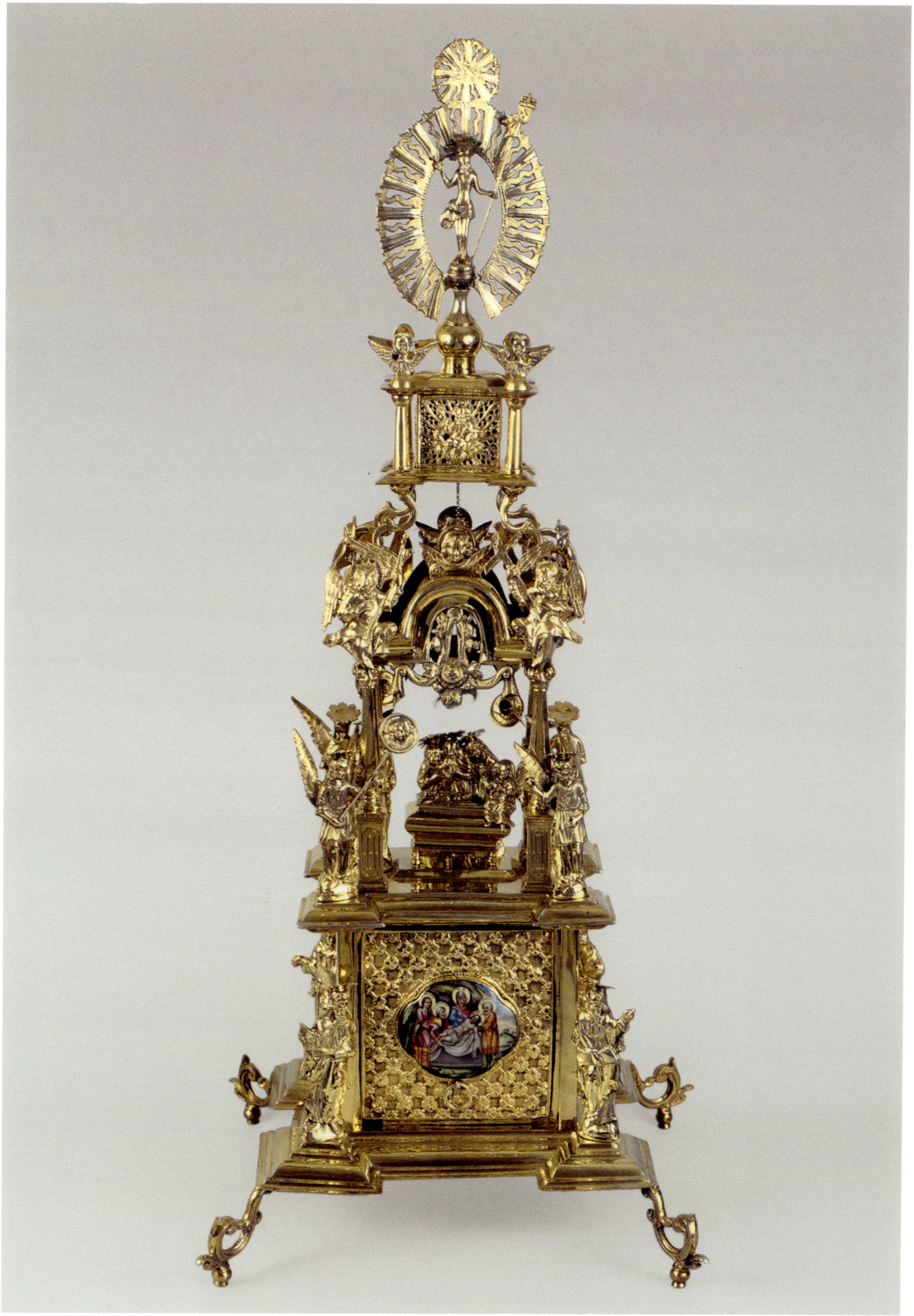

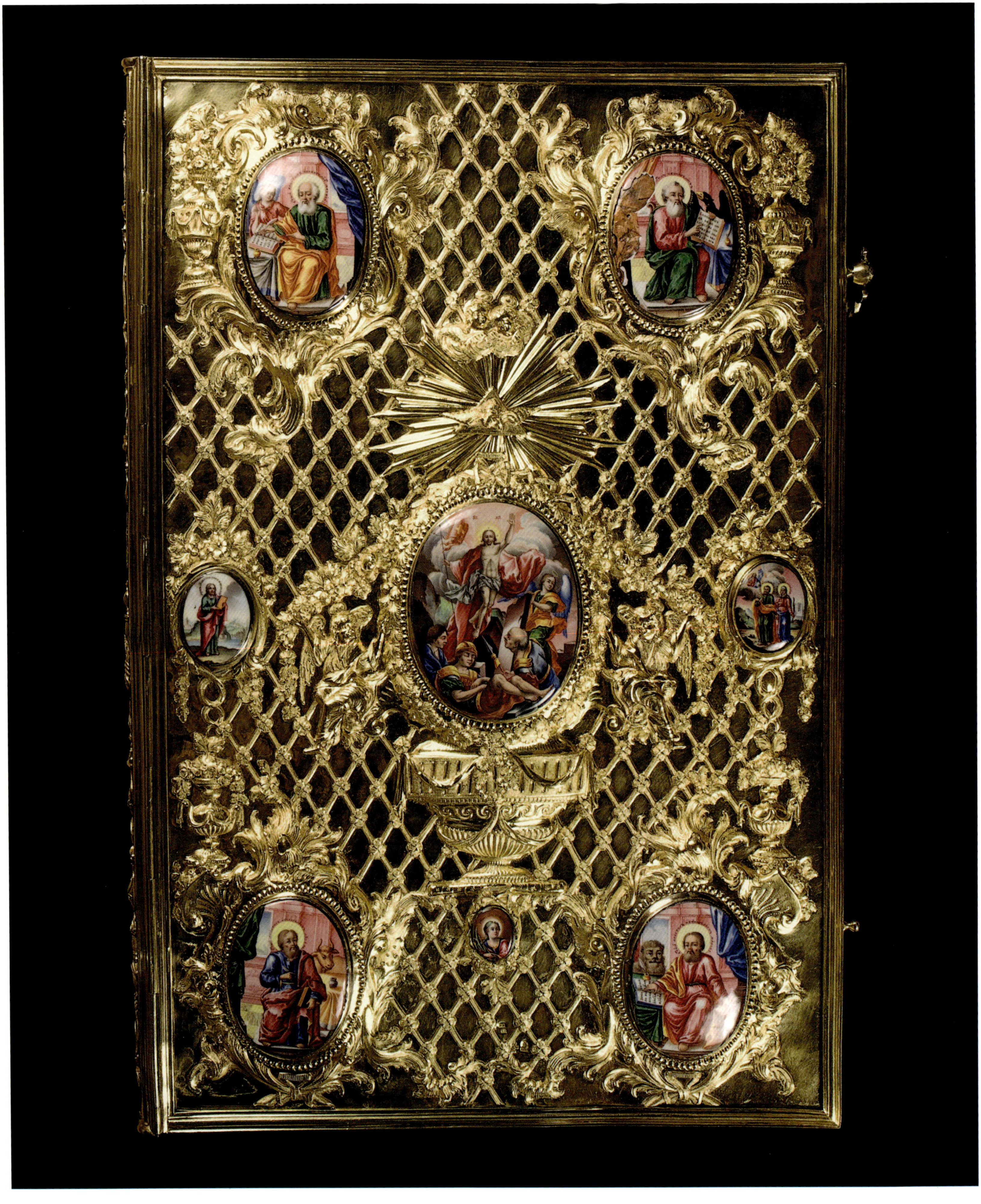

8. *Master A. I. Ratkov*
Gospel Book
Russia, Moscow, 1785
The State Historical Museum, Moscow
(Cat. 49)

9. Chalice
Russia, Moscow, 1752
The State Historical Museum, Moscow
(Cat. 118)

reign of Peter I's daughter, the Empress Elizabeth, is characterized by the co-existence of elements in Moscow's gold and silverwork belonging to late baroque, but also to the new rococo style, with the elegance of shapes and the decorative refinement unique to it. An example of the high level of the art of niello work of the era is given to us by the 1752 chalice, whose ornamentation includes a design in niello thread of great elegance, baroque cartouches with powerful emotional evocativeness encircling the images decorating the cup, and bouquets of flowers with engraved and nielloed foliated patterns, shells and palmettes decorating the different parts of the same object (ill. 9).

Beginning in the middle of the 18th century, the Muscovite craftsmen turned toward materials up until then unknown in Russia, such as ivory, which was used to create certain parts of precious utensils. Very often the ornamental motifs chosen reflected the European fashion of decorative and applied art objects in the oriental style and in the style of China and India.

Along with these innovations in Muscovite art of the 18th century, the traditional artistic processes were being perfected. First of all, that of filigree, thanks to which openwork pieces could be produced using very fine silver thread which was worked into twists. The exhibition presents some pieces worked in this very complex technique: an icon of Paphnuce of Borov in a filigreed covering with polychrome enamels dating from 1780, and also an exceptional piece from the beginning of the 19th century: the filigreed covering of an icon of St. Nicholas the Just.

In the filigreed motifs of this covering, one can

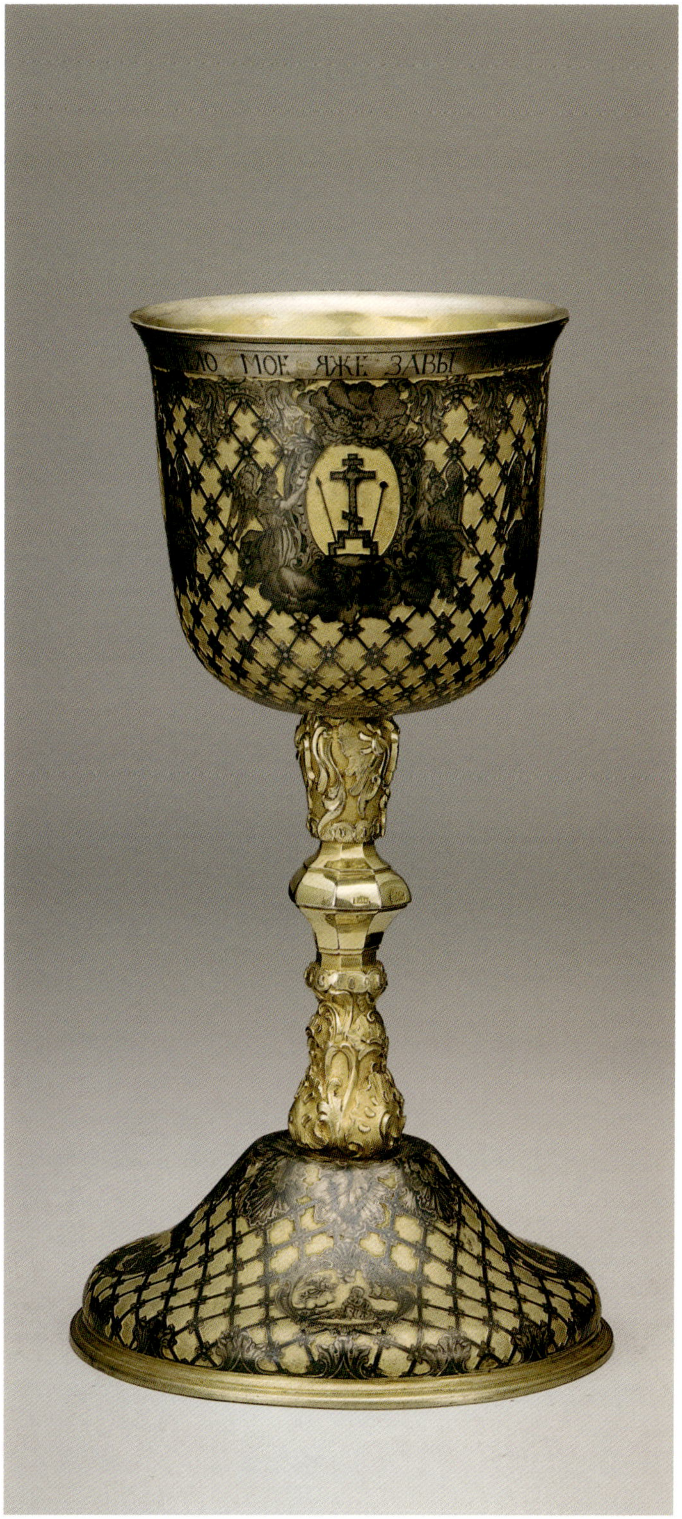

10. Panagia of honor (bishop's pectoral medallion) with a portrait in miniature in enamel of Peter I on the reverse side
Russia, Moscow, first half of 18th century
The State Historical Museum, Moscow
(Cat. 27)

clearly observe the return to the ancient Byzantine tradition—the use of a hearts motif, and of very particular shape—an entwined stem with shoots—and designs in threaded pearls all characteristics of Russian liturgical art objects.

The "brilliant" century of Catherine the Great was marked by important advances in the artistic work of precious metals. It was the epoch of the blooming of painted enamel, of an even more extended development of the art of niello work, high-relief chasing, cast iron work, engraving. The art of gold and silver work in the Russian empire of the second half of the 18th century was characterized by the refusal of blind imitation, original synthesis of new processes and secular traditions in its main centers, among which Moscow held a primary place.

In addition to the solid liturgical silverware mentioned earlier, let us not neglect the precious Episcopal medallions (*panagia*) made out of the favorite 18th century stone, the diamond cut into brilliant facets. The exhibition presents two medallions decorated in briliants. The one which has a painted portrait of the Empress Catherine I was made in St. Petersburg; the other, with a painted portrait of the Emperor Peter I also comes from the capital but it is possible that it could be Muscovite work (ill. 10). Very characteristic of this work is the way in which the visual accent of these medallions veers away from the central images which are of a religious nature, and toward their sumptuous and dazzlingly brilliant frames. The two objects were honorary gifts, as the presence of the portraits of the two most important figures of the State attests.

During Catherine the Great's era, one of the applications of gold and silver work which was greatly developed was the creation of various services: table services, tea sets, travel sets, all entirely made out of silver, often enhanced with gold, or completed by objects in glass or in porcelain. The tradition of making such services had existed in Russia since 1711 when, by a special decree of the Czar, the first silver service of 200 pieces was created. During the reign of Catherine the Great, one of the most beautiful Russian ceremonial table services ever was created. It was made in gilded silver and included about 1,500 pieces. It was a marriage gift for the illegitimate son of the Empress, the count Alexis Bobrinskoy. To give an idea of these kinds of exceptional pieces, the travel tea set belonging to the Moscow general governor the grand duke Sergei Alexandrovich is shown in the exhibition, a remarkable example of 19th century Russian silverware.

The 19th century, the "Century of Silver" for the Russian jewelers, was one which brought together the great personal know-how of the gold and silversmith artists, of the executing artist, and of a production based on using the most up to date inventions of technical progress.

All the most famous Muscovite jewelry firms, known the world over, produced pieces both for religious use and secular use. All were the guardians of national traditions while at the same time being the expression of aesthetic concepts which were current among a very diverse segments of the population. Among the oldest Muscovite firms was the P. I. Olovianichnikov manufacture of liturgical objects, supplier to the Court of His Imperi-

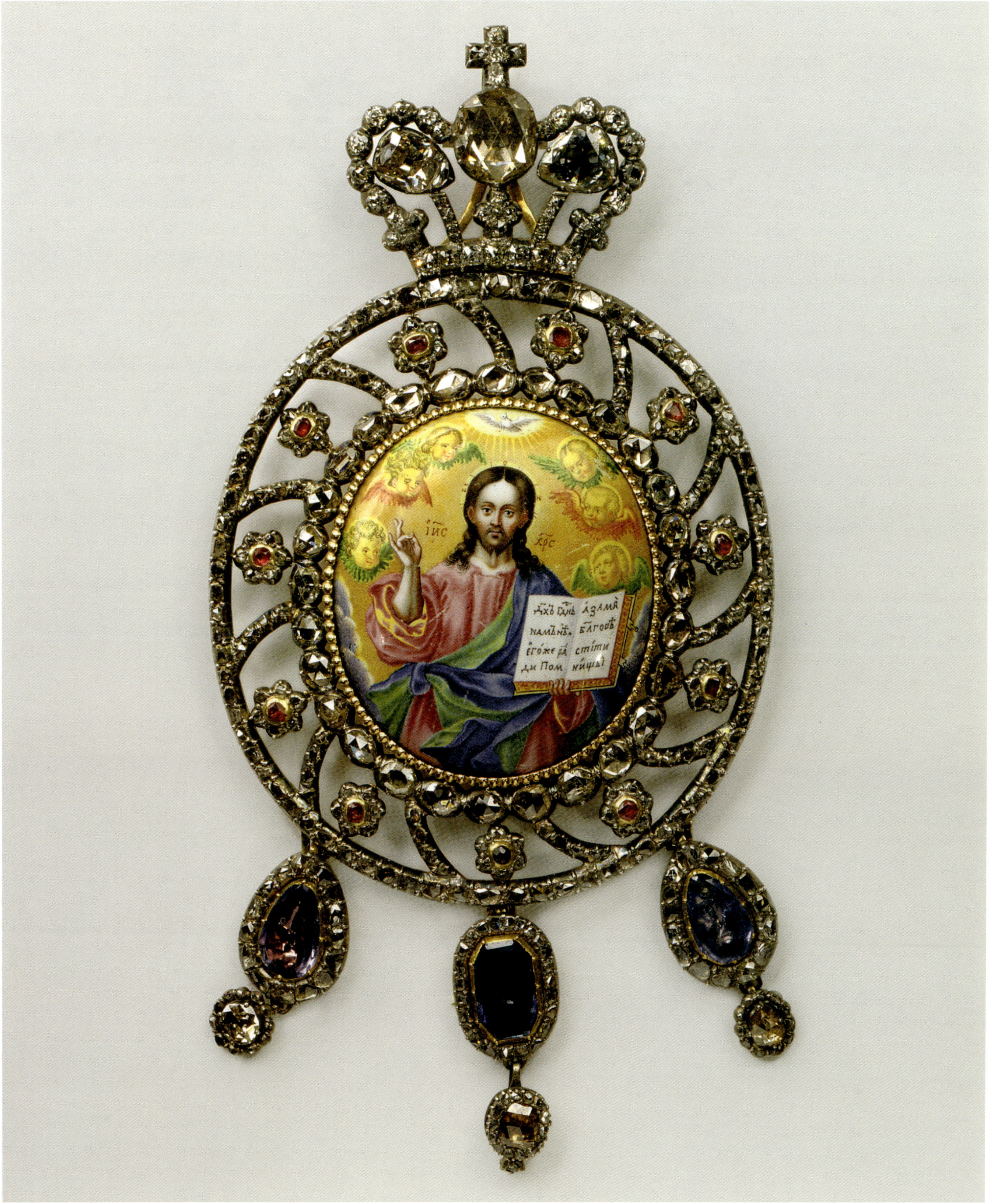

11. Mitre
Russia, Moscow, 1908-1917
The State Historical Museum, Moscow
(Cat. 34)

al Highness. The exhibition presents a mitre decorated with cloisonné enamel, and two exceptional altar crosses made by the master craftsmen of this firm (ill. 11). It was founded in 1848 and remained active until 1917. It produced all sorts of liturgical objects, as well as other objects for the home and for personal use, and also jewelry. The most remarkable particularity of this firm's production was how the person who defined the form of the objects to come—the first master, S. Vashkov—was inspired by the aesthetic of the early Christian monuments; by how the catacombs and the first century Basilicas were put together, by the symbols and allegories which were preserved in them. In going back to national traditions, the craftsmen of this firm deliberately chose ancient Russian models from the 11th to the 16th centuries in which there was a clear mix of Byzantine, Western and Oriental traditions. The firm counted among its clients the Emperor Nicholas II, the Empress Alexandra Feodorovna, their closest relatives, the representatives of the reigning families of Europe, the highest dignitaries in the hierarchy of the Orthodox church, representatives from other faiths, the flower of the Russian aristocracy and all the nobility, and finally, the rich merchants.

The P. I. Olovianichnikov firm undeniably contributed a great deal to the creation and development of the most expressive trends in 19th century Muscovite silver: the national romantic style or new Russian style.

The production of the most well-known Muscovite silver firms, suppliers to the Imperial court, who took part in the universal exhibitions and carried off awards, P. Sazikov, I. Khlebnikov, P. Ovchinnikov, was distinguished by an exquisite taste, a great artistic quality and perfect technical execution, especially for the pieces created in the spirit of the tradition of the end of the 17th century. This is an accurate reflection of the situation as it was in the middle of the 19th century, of the two main artistic schools, in Moscow and in St. Petersburg, which established the main trends of the art of Russian gold and silver work. The Petersburg artistic school was deliberately oriented toward the culture of Western Europe, a process which had been put into effect from the beginning of the 18th century. The activities of the Muscovite firms mentioned were determined by the influence of the Muscovite school which was the expression of the ideology of the new Russian style in the art of gold and silver work in Russia. This exhibition presents some remarkable works from the P. Ovchinnikov firm which was known world-wide. Among them, a solid decorative tankard mounted with an image worked in cast iron of a bust of Peter the Great, and decorated on its front by a scene in relief representing the entrance into the Kremlin of Peter the Great's army after the victorious battle of Poltava in 1709. This way of turning back to the past, to Russian history, to mythology, is very characteristic of the activity of the Muscovite gold and silver craftsmen who worked within the framework of the national tradition (ill. 12).

The Ovchinnikov manufacture also created an engraved set for a wine service, composed of a solid loving cup (*bratina*), small wine tasting cups (*charki*) a base and a serving spoon. The decoration on the whole, influenced by the aesthetic of the second half of the 17th century, relies upon

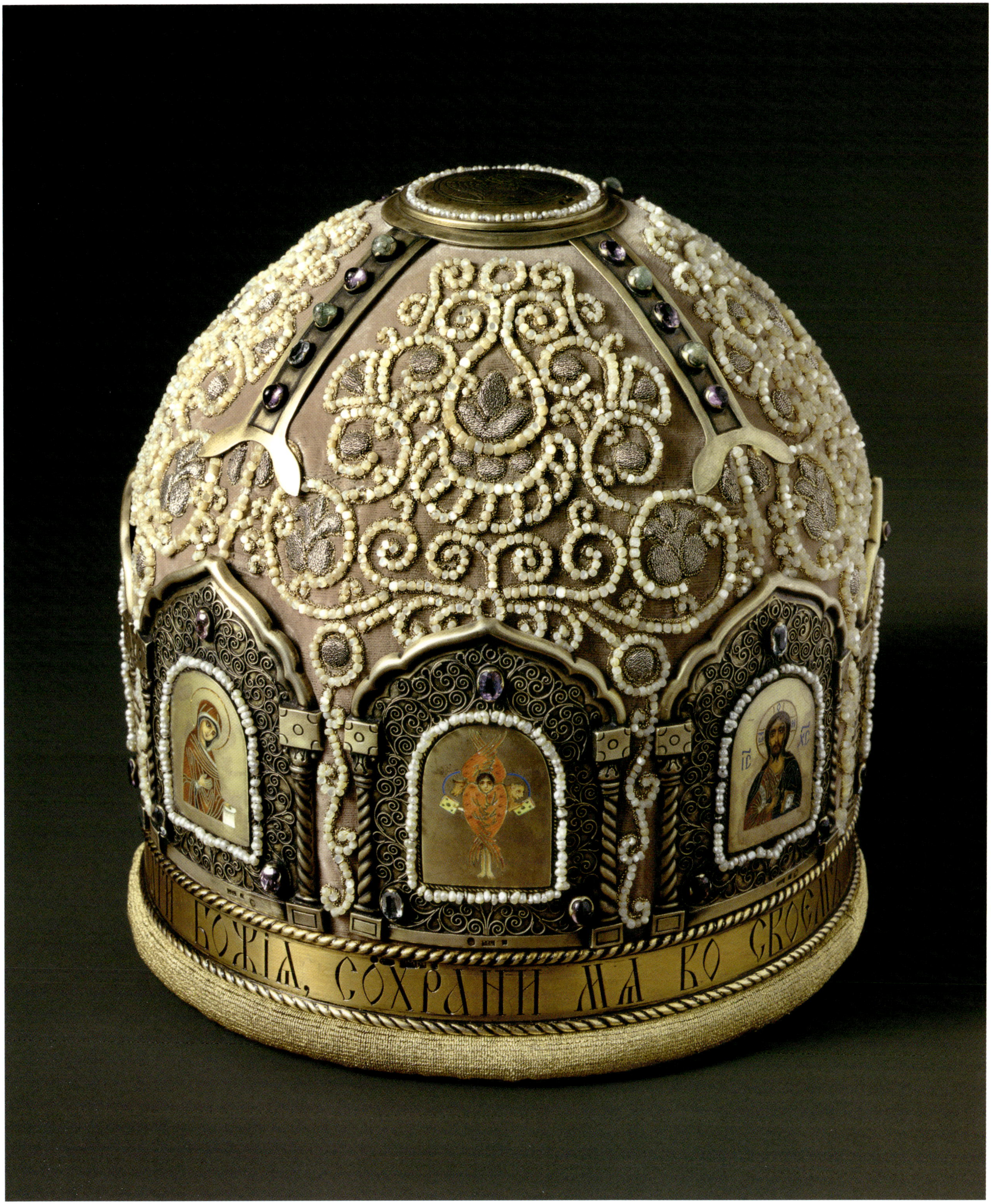
БОЖІА, СОХРАНИ МѦ ВО

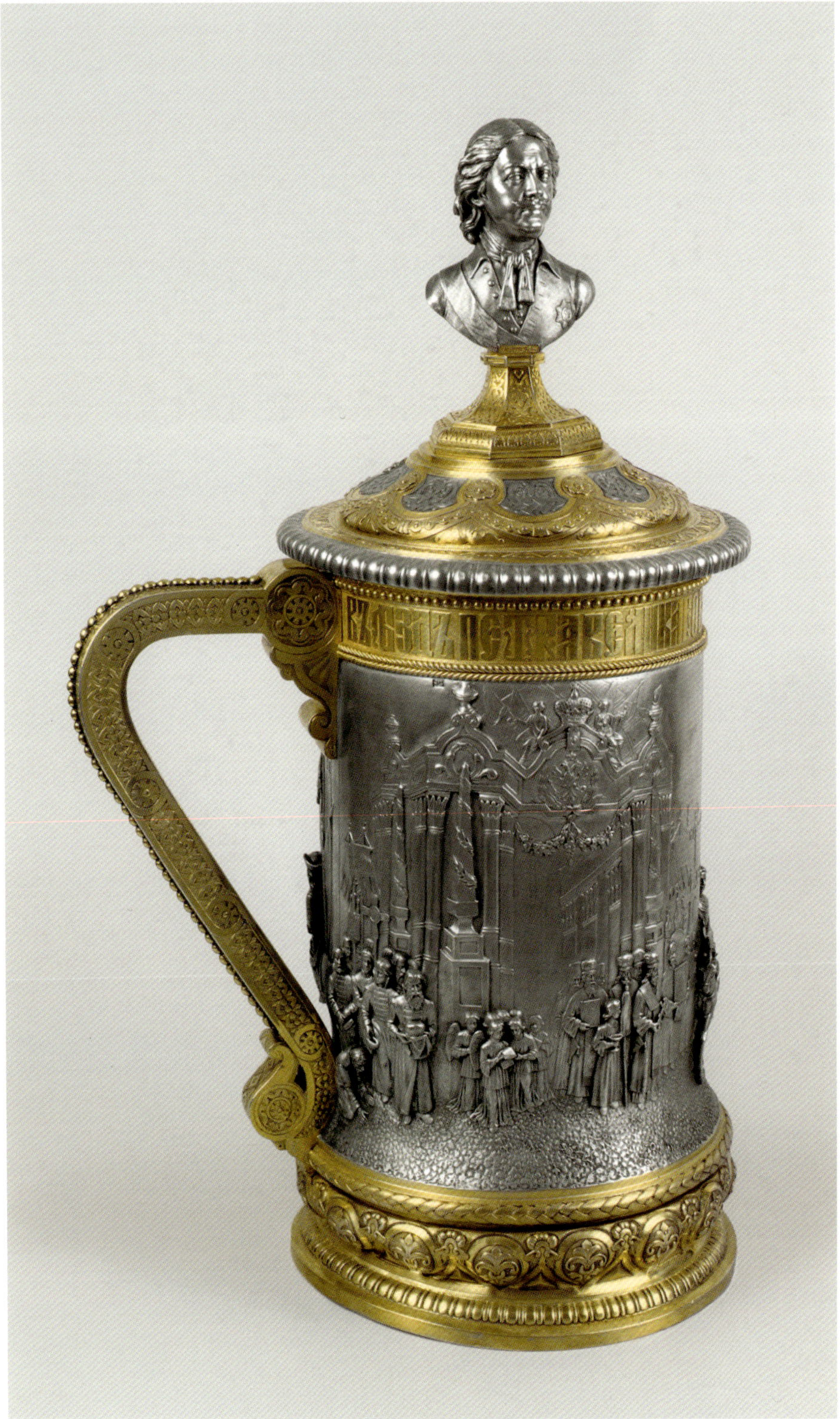

forms, motifs and the architectonic of objects from that time. In 1913, for the 300th anniversary of the House of the Romanovs, the Nijni-Novgorod nobility ordered an exceptional object from Moscow which can been seen here. It is a decorated tray with a central composition made up of several figures and of abundant designs in the style of 17th century ornamentation, enhanced by little colored stones and bright colored enamel. The execution of this work was achieved with brio by the master craftsmen of the big Muscovite firm I. Khlebnikov (ill. 13).

During the Romanov dynasty era, Moscow silverware, entirely a component of Russian culture, in accordance with the laws of artistic creation, reflected not only the history of the development and of the succession of gold and silver work styles, but also the power of the State, the talent and the distinctive features of the Russian national character.

[1] Ja. Rejenfel's, *Narrative....on the Moscow region* (Padua 1680), translated into Russian, Moscow 1905, p. 135.

12. Tankard
Russia, Moscow, 1873
The State Historical Museum, Moscow
(Cat. 486)

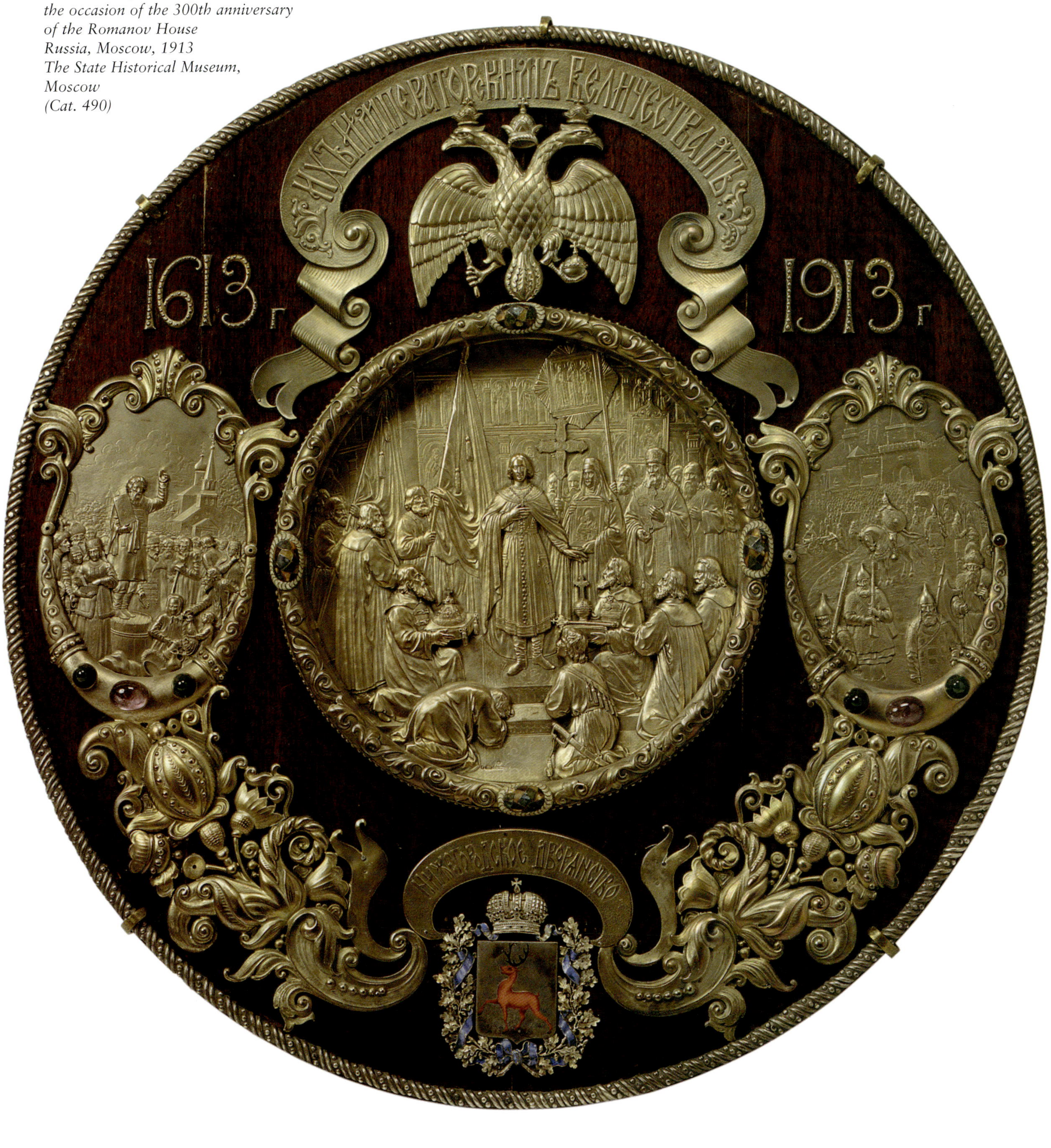

13. Decorative plate
Gift of the Nijni Novgorod nobility
to "Their Imperial Highnesses" on
the occasion of the 300th anniversary
of the Romanov House
Russia, Moscow, 1913
The State Historical Museum,
Moscow
(Cat. 490)

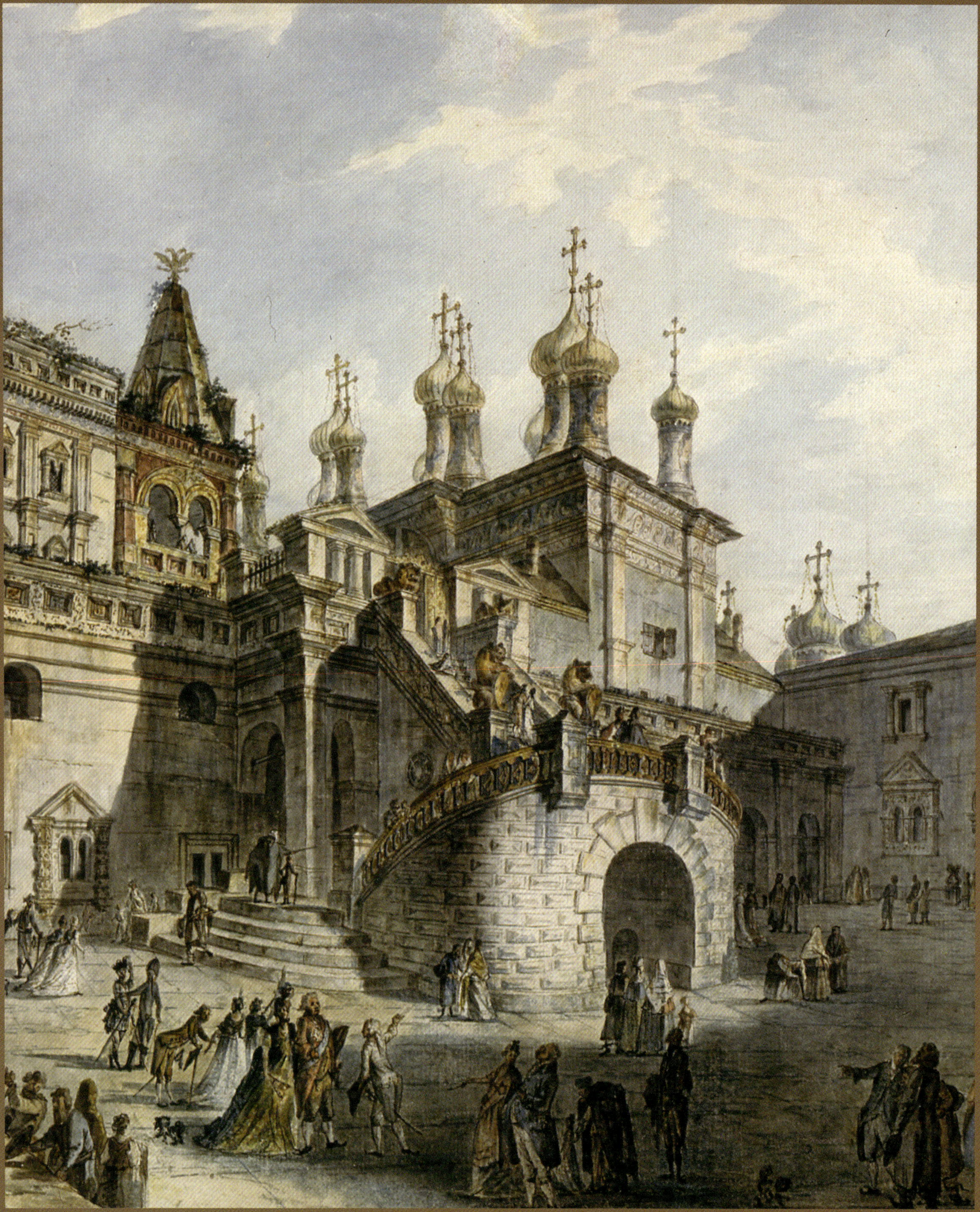

THE REPRESENTATION OF MOSCOW BEFORE AND AFTER THE FIRE OF 1812

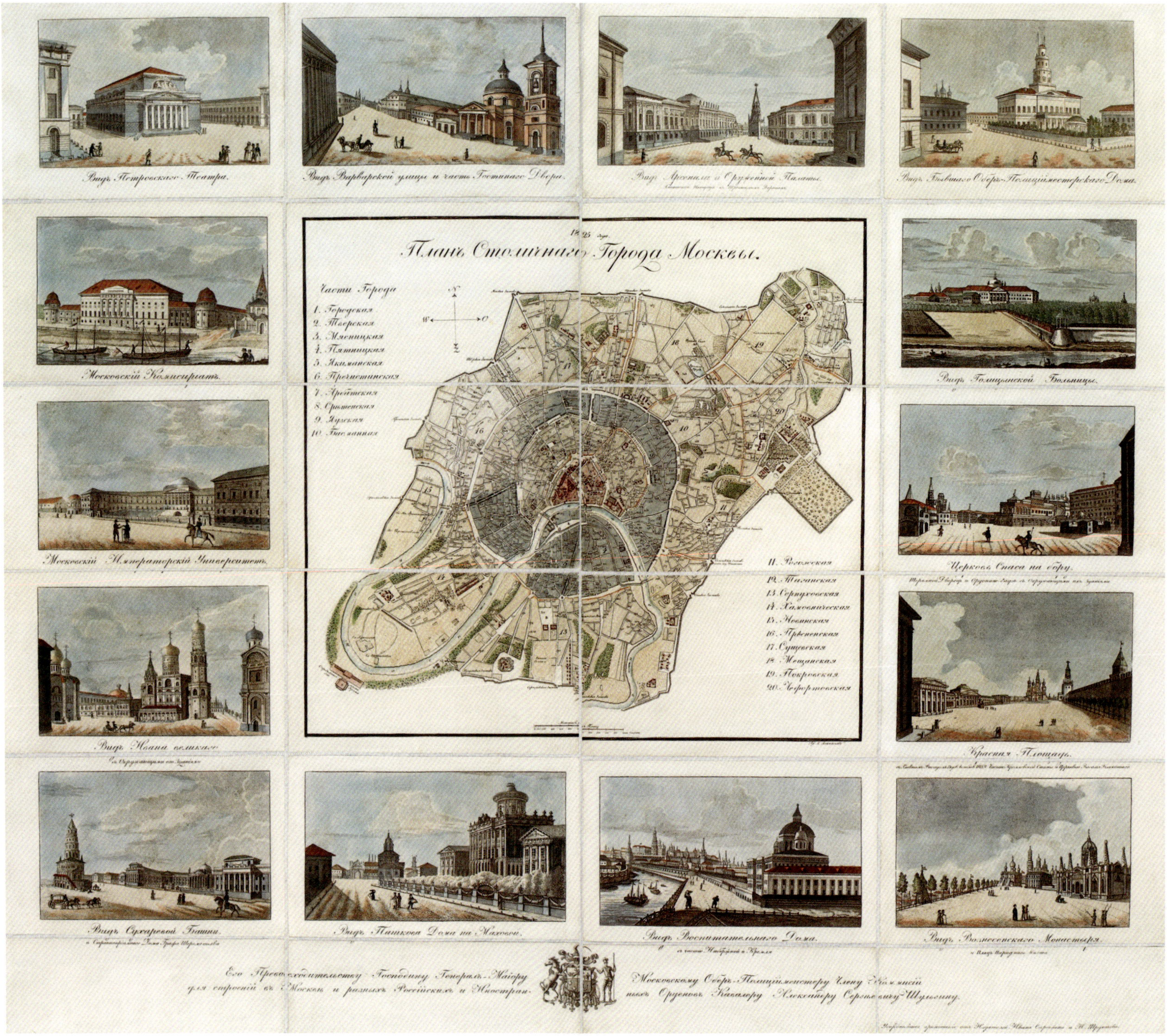
Видъ Петровскаго Театра.
Видъ Варварской улицы и часть Гостинаго Двора.
Видъ Арсенала и Оружейной Палаты.
Видъ Бывшаго Оберъ-Полицiймейстерскаго Дома.
1825 годъ.
Планъ Столичнаго Города Москвы.
Части Города
1. Городская
2. Тверская
3. Мясницкая
4. Пятницкая
5. Якиманская
6. Пречистинская
7. Арбатская
8. Срѣтенская
9. Яузская
10. Басманная
11. Рогожская
12. Таганская
13. Серпуховская
14. Хамовническая
15. Новинская
16. Пресненская
17. Сущевская
18. Мещанская
19. Покровская
20. Лефортовская
Московскій Коммисаріатъ.
Видъ Голицынской Больницы.
Московскій Императорскій Университетъ.
Церковь Спаса на бору.
Видъ Ивана великаго
Красная Площадь.
Видъ Сухаревой Башни.
Видъ Пашкова Дома на Моховой.
Видъ Воспитательнаго Дома.
съ частію Набережной и Кремля
Видъ Вознесенскаго Монастыря.
Его Превосходительству Господину Генералъ-Маіору
Московскому Оберъ-Полицiймейстеру Члену Коммисіи
для строеній въ Москвѣ и разныхъ Россійскихъ и Иностран-
ныхъ Орденовъ Кавалеру Александру Сергѣевичу Шульгину.

A VISUAL CHRONICLE OF MOSCOW
Moscow seen by F. I. Alekseev and I. H. Datsiaro

Natalia Skorniakova

Page 104
F. I. Alekseev
View of the Kremlin from Boyars Square (west side)
1800s
The State Historical Museum, Moscow
(Cat. 263)
Detail

1. *A. A. Afanassiev (?)*
Plan of Moscow illustrated with 14 views
1825
The State Historical Museum, Moscow
(Cat. 287)

For centuries Moscow functioned as a capital—the earliest written mention of Moscow goes back to 1147—as capital first of the Grand Principality of Moscow, and then of the whole Russian state, and because of this, the city played a founding role in the history of the country. It was certainly not without reason that in the Middle Ages the Westerners called all of Russia by the name of Muscovy. Moscow lost this official status with the founding of St. Petersburg along the banks of the Neva, but in the national conscience, it still remained the first capital of the throne and an extremely important national and religious center. All the Emperors and Empresses of Russia came to be crowned in Old Moscow, thus confirming their right to the throne of the Muscovite Czars. The particularly picturesque and original aspect of the city, the many monuments of ancient architecture and the particular character of daily life have always made Moscow of lively interest to artists. Thus there was a fertile ground for creation from the first half of the 18th century for a whole series of painted or engraved perspectives done by Russian and foreign artists. And so M. I. Makhaev, designer-artist and vedutisti from the Fine Arts Academy's engraving workshop, Fr. Dürfeldt, engraver, the architects Fr. Camporesi, M. F. Kazakov and G. Quarenghi, and the painter G. Delabart made names for themselves in the artistic record of the former capital of the kingdom. And yet, compared to them, F. I. Alekseev went decisively even further. The graphic series of views of the former capital which he and his students did at the beginning of the 19th century has no equal, neither in the number of monuments of Muscovite architecture that the series shows, nor in its richness and thematic variety.

F. I. Alekseev, who is considered by Russian plastic art researchers and historians to be the founder in Russia of the genre of urban landscape, was one of the first students of the St. Petersburg Fine Arts Academy which had been founded in 1757. In 1773, after having finished his studies at the academy and having received a gold medal, he was sent on an art studies program to Venice, Italy. The education that he received there prepared him for creating theater decors, but giving free rein to his own inclinations, he began to study the art of architectural landscape on his own, inspired by the works of the greatest Italian masters of perspective: Antonio Canale known as Canaletto, and B. Bellotto. He very quickly assimilated the techniques of their creations of urban landscapes and up to a certain point borrowed their way of doing them. Upon his return to St. Petersburg in 1778, Alekseev worked a lot at the Hermitage, copying paintings which by then had been collected into a museum. Commissioned by Count P. A. Zubov,

Catherine the Great's last favorite, he copied paintings of Venice by Canaletto, as well as views of Dresden, and works by Pirna de Bellotto.

Alekseev's first piece that was truly his own—views of St. Petersburg—dates from the 1790s and earned him the nickname "the Russian Canaletto." But it was his work on the former capital of white stone which truly made him famous. In 1800, Alekseev was sent to Moscow by the Fine Arts Academy on the personal order of Emperor Paul I for the purpose, as records P. P. Svinin, amateur artist, collector and the artist's first biographer, "of capturing from life views of this picturesque capital." Alekseev and two of his students, I. V. Mochkov and A. M. Kunavin spent more than a year and a half in Moscow, from October 1800 to March 1802. Clearly the old city, its original architecture, so different from the classical architecture of St. Petersburg, strongly impressed the artists. It seems that they even made a few paintings in Moscow, in particular a view of the Red Square, which were sent to St. Petersburg in 1801 to be presented to Emperor Alexander I. All the other known views of Moscow were done later, in the artist's St. Petersburg studio. These paintings consecrated Alekseev as "the first and best Russian painter of perspective" and earned him a number of private commissions, but also commissions from the Fine Arts Academy and the Imperial Court. His paintings of ancient monuments from the first capital were on view in the Imperial palaces and in the town houses of the highest dignitaries. Alekseev often repeated the same subjects which is why there are several very close variations of various views, for example, the *View of Cathedral Square at the Kremlin* or the *View of the Kremlin and the Stone Bridge* (*Kamenni most*) (ill. 2). We know that one of Alekseev's paintings—the *View of the Kremlin and the Stone Bridge*—was offered to the king of Prussia, Frederick William III in 1808. In December 1802, Alekseev received the title of professor and was admitted as one of the councilors of the Fine Arts Academy. In March 1803, he took over the class of perspective painting.

Today, Alekseev's paintings and his views of Moscow are in the most important collections of the Russian museums: the Hermitage, the Russian Museum, the Tretyakov Gallery and the Historical Museum. They have been well indexed and have been published many times in different works devoted to the history of Russian plastic art, and in catalogues. In contrast, his graphic work is much less known to the wider public.

However, in the iconography of the former capital, Alekseev's graphic work holds a very special place. His views of Moscow can rightly be considered as an iconographic encyclopedia of Moscow "before the fire." Already in 1823, V. I. Gigorovich, secretary of the Fine Arts Academy conferences, reviewed the "new works" in an article published in the *Fine Arts Review* in 1823, underlining that the painting of the Academician Alekseev "representing a view of the Kremlin from in front of the Stone Bridge (...) presents in addition a very precious interest in that it shows Moscow as it was before the enemy invasion."

The 1812 fires, in destroying nearly three-fourths of the old buildings of the white stone capital, opened a new page in Moscow's architectur-

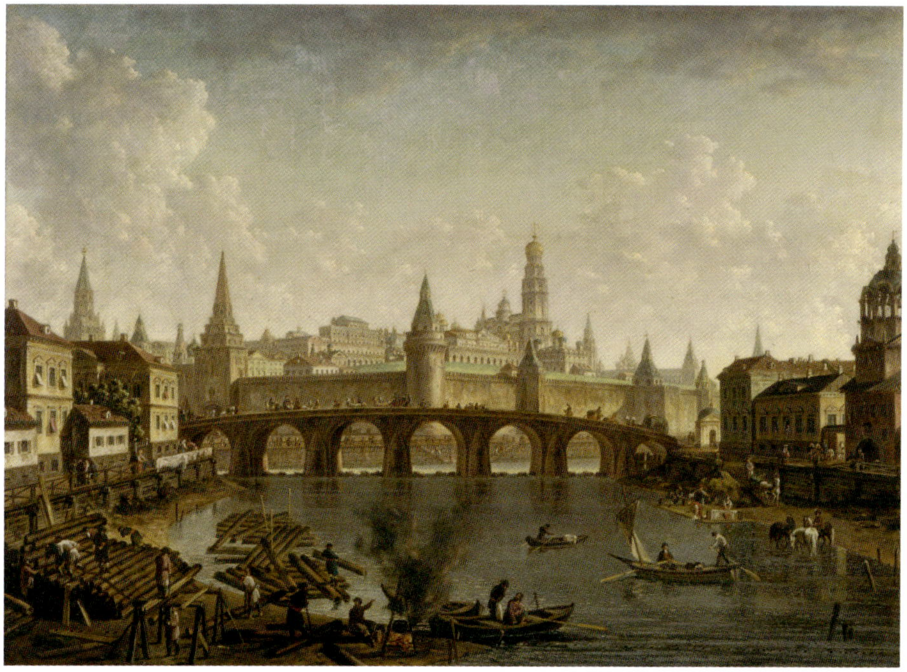

2. *F. I. Alekseev*
Moscow. View of the Kremlin and the Stone Bridge (Kamenni most)
1815
The State Historical Museum, Moscow
(Cat. 262)

al history, but much of what had in fact surprised and attracted the foreigners and even the inhabitants of St. Petersburg had disappeared forever. "It's a truly astonishing vision, this multitude of palaces, of public monuments of such beautiful architecture, of convents, churches intermingled with rustic sites and villages. This mixture of magnificence and country simplicity produces I don't know what fantastic effect which should please the traveler, always avid for originality,"[1] wrote the French artist Elizabeth Vigée-Lebrun who went to Moscow almost at the same time as Alekseev, in October 1800.

Alekseev must have also experienced similar feelings. As soon as he arrived in Moscow, he began to work on watercolor views of the city and its surroundings. The watercolors present a much larger and more varied choice of themes than his paintings do on canvas. In a way, one might consider these watercolor views as a kind of personal journal, as the detailed account of the artist's stay in the former capital of the kingdom.

In seeing them, one is struck by the wide range of the artist's center of interests. It seems that he tried to reproduce everything that was most striking and most significant in the architecture of the old city. In searching out the most interesting monuments and at the same time the most typical of the past, the artist successfully penetrated the very essence of the ordinary daily life of the capital, discovering nooks and crannies that even the most curious visitors only rarely saw. Thanks to Alekseev, we have an idea of the picturesque appearance of the Kremlin, still medieval in many aspects, or we can wander around Kitai-gorod with its ancient walls, its towers, its huge gates, we can even visit innumerable churches and monasteries, or visit well-stocked commercial galleries or more still, admire the remarkable monuments of Muscovite architecture such as the Kadachevsky Khamovny Dvor in Outer Moskva district (*Zamoskvorietchy*) (ill. 3) or the Kitai-gorod Resurrection Gate, not to mention the ancient monasteries outside of Moscow and the famous suburban Imperial residences.

To date, sixty-eight watercolors and drawings of Moscow views by F. L. Alekseev are known. Originally, they were all in the Imperial Hermitage collection in St. Petersburg. At the time they entered into the Hermitage collections, in the 19th century, specialists divided them into two groups: the First Muscovite series, and the Second Muscovite series.

The first Muscovite series includes fifty-six watercolors and two drawings and was donated to the Imperial Museum in March 1825 by his widow, soon after the artist's death.

Apparently, at the time they went into the Hermitage collection, the watercolors all received the

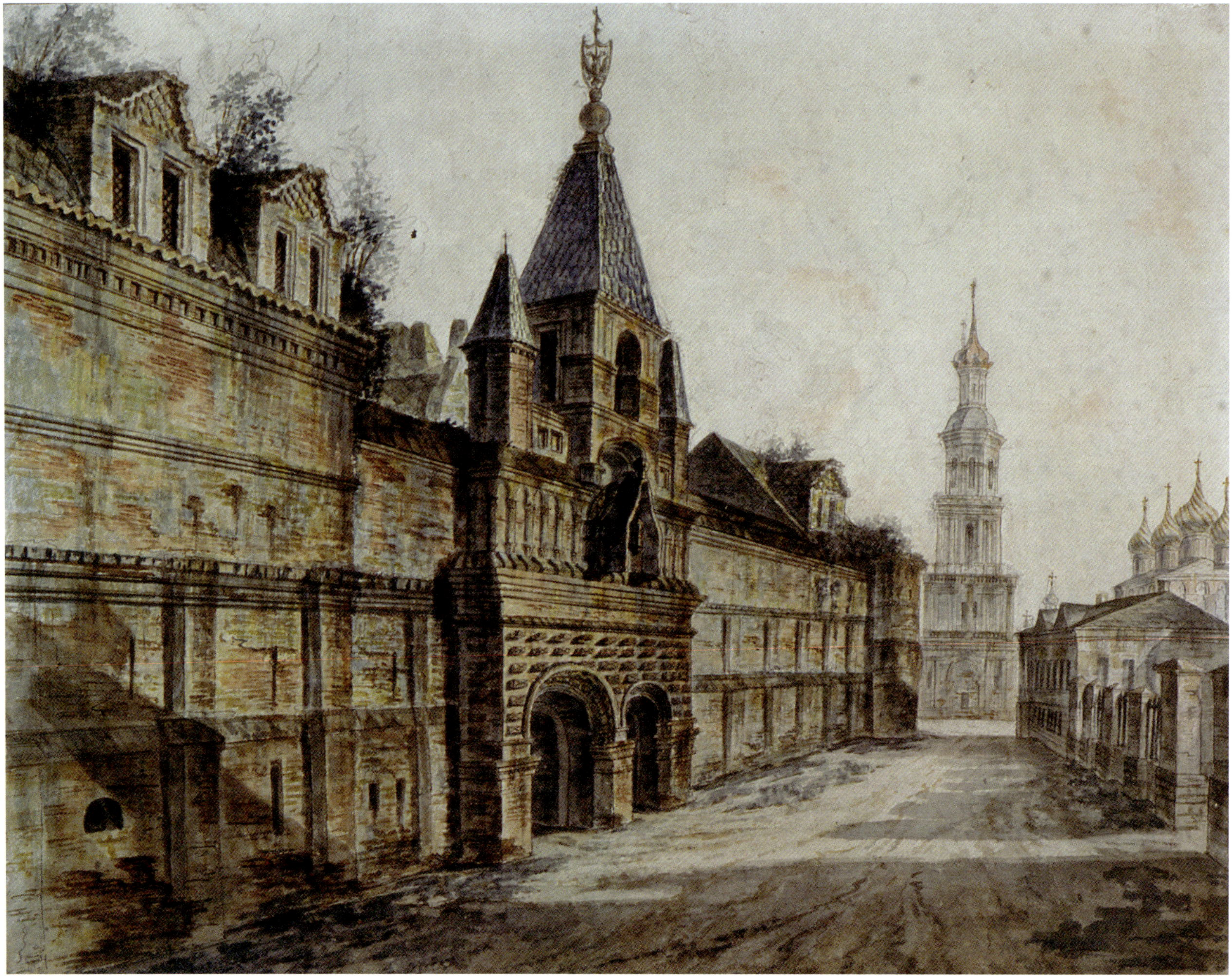

3. *F. I. Alekseev and his students*
View of the Outer Muscovy district (Zamoskvorietchy) on the Kadachevsky Khamovny Dvor and the steeple of the Church of Cosmas and Damian
1800s
The State Historical Museum, Moscow
(Cat. 272)

same treatment: they were put—glued—onto a white-colored passe-partout in Alexandrian format, and the contours of the images were underlined in black Indian ink. Then on the passe-partout, underneath the image, the following indications regarding the registration were written in ink: to the left, the order numbers based on the register book of entries into the Hermitage collections, from No. 10232 to No. 10289, and to the right, the place the documents were preserved, "Portfolio 189." (In the Hermitage, works on paper were preserved in portfolios—numbered portfolios. This is why the First series of views of Moscow is often called "Portfolio 189 Watercolors.") Underneath, in the center of the passe-partout, the name of the place shown is mentioned in pencil, according to the register list which accompanied the views of Moscow when the artist's widow gave them to the Imperial Museum.

The second Muscovite series—ten watercolors—entered the Hermitage collections a little later, likely in the 1830s-1840s. These ten watercolors have kept their original aspect: they have no passe-partout, no signature and, except for rare exceptions, no inscription. The contours of the image are underlined in black Indian ink, and below to the left, on the border, in ink and black Indian ink are the inventory numbers based on the register book of entries into the Hermitage collections which go from No. 18855 to No. 18864.

In the twenties, in virtue of a new state policy regarding the division of national museum collections, the whole series which made up the Alekseev collection was dispersed. The views of Moscow went into the collections of different Moscow and St. Petersburg museums: to the Hermitage itself, to the Institute of Languages and Russian Literature of the Academy of Science, to the A. S. Pushkin National Museum, to the A. V. Shchusev State Museum of Architectural Studies and Research, and finally to the Historical Museum where nineteen pieces by Alekseev entered the collection in January 1926 on the occasion of the exhibition, "Moscow through its images of the past."

It is usually thought that the two graphic series of views of Moscow were done in the years 1800-1802, in other words, during Alekseev's stay in Moscow with his first students. Nevertheless, it's possible that some of them were done later, in St. Petersburg, in the artist's studio after his return from Moscow, that is, in the 1800s or even 1810.

Originally, and until the beginning of the 20th century, all the views of Moscow were attributed to one and the same artist, F. I. Alekseev, since according to a tradition still in existence at the beginning of the 19th century, the work done by the students in a master's studio and under his immediate supervision were considered as works of the master himself. And even more so because they were usually not signed. Unlike with his oils on canvas, Alekseev only rarely signed his watercolors and drawings.

The first one to notice the differences in quality in the execution of the views was I. E. Grabar, in an article on Alekseev's work which was published in a 1907 issue of the magazine "Years Past." He pointed out in that article that assembled together in the voluminous portfolio preserved at the Hermitage there had been "the common work of the professor and two of his students. The differences are too great, even just in observing the work, in the single technique of execution between some of the watercolors. I haven't had the occasion to see the watercolors signed by Kunavin..." added Grabar, "but I have seen those by Mochkov and I have to say that I am strongly tempted to see the same hand in the whole series of studies in Alekseev's portfolio. Some of them are striking by the absence of elementary rules of perspective (...) while next to that there are some absolutely charming things and of a great finesse." In turn, the famous Russian specialist A. A. Fedorov-Davydov, author of a number of works on the history of the Russian landscape including a monograph devoted to "F. I. Alekseev" (Moscow, 1956), divided all the views of Moscow into four groups. In the first two, he included the work of Alekseev himself, as well as those which were corrected in his hand, in other words, "those which he finished, beginning with a sketch by his students." The third and fourth groups were made up of watercolors done autonomously by the students: Mochkov and Kunavin.

The three watercolors presented in the exhibition belong to the first group, in other words to that of the artist's original watercolors: "Boyars Square in the Kremlin," "View of Resurrection Gate and St. Nicholas and the Neglimennii Bridge," and "View of the Kremlin near Borovitskaya Gate." All three belong to the First Muscovite series (ills. 4 and 5).

These views, painted with lightness and elegance, are closely reminiscent of Alekseev's watercolors and original drawings (only four signed works are known). The clarity and transparency in the foreground is very characteristic, all in tones of warm pink-yellow which shade discontinuously into colder blue-grey tones in the background. The architectural space is always taken up by a great number of figures which suggests the atmosphere of the daily life of a big city: passers-by in various outfits, soldiers parading by, ambulant merchants, carriages and barking dogs. The figures, lightly painted and seemingly animated, present particular characteristics: elongated silhouettes, small headsand contours usually drawn with a brush. These typical figures and these little genre scenes can be found from one work to another.

The great majority of the other watercolors of the views of Moscow and its surroundings is the work of Alekseev's students. This is why when we speak of their attribution, we usually use the term, "F. I. Alekseev and his students" or "F. I. Alekseev's studio." Alekseev's first disciples, Illarion Mochkov (1778-1845) and Alexander Kunavin (1780-?) were students at the Fine Arts Academy and we know that in returning to St. Petersburg, they spent another year at Alekseev's studio before leaving him to work independently on private commissions. During their stay in Moscow, the young artists didn't then have the necessary experience in working from life and did not have enough mastery in the technique of watercolor. They imitated their professor's manner in their way of composing the architectural landscape as well as in their way of portraying the volume of the buildings. At the same time, the tonality of their watercolors was much darker, without transparency and unity. It is unfortunately impossible to determine definite attributions of one or the other of

4. *F. I. Alekseev*
View of the Kremlin: the Borovitskaya Gate, the Court Stables and the Church of the Nativity of St. John the Precursor
1800s
The State Historical Museum, Moscow
(Cat. 264)

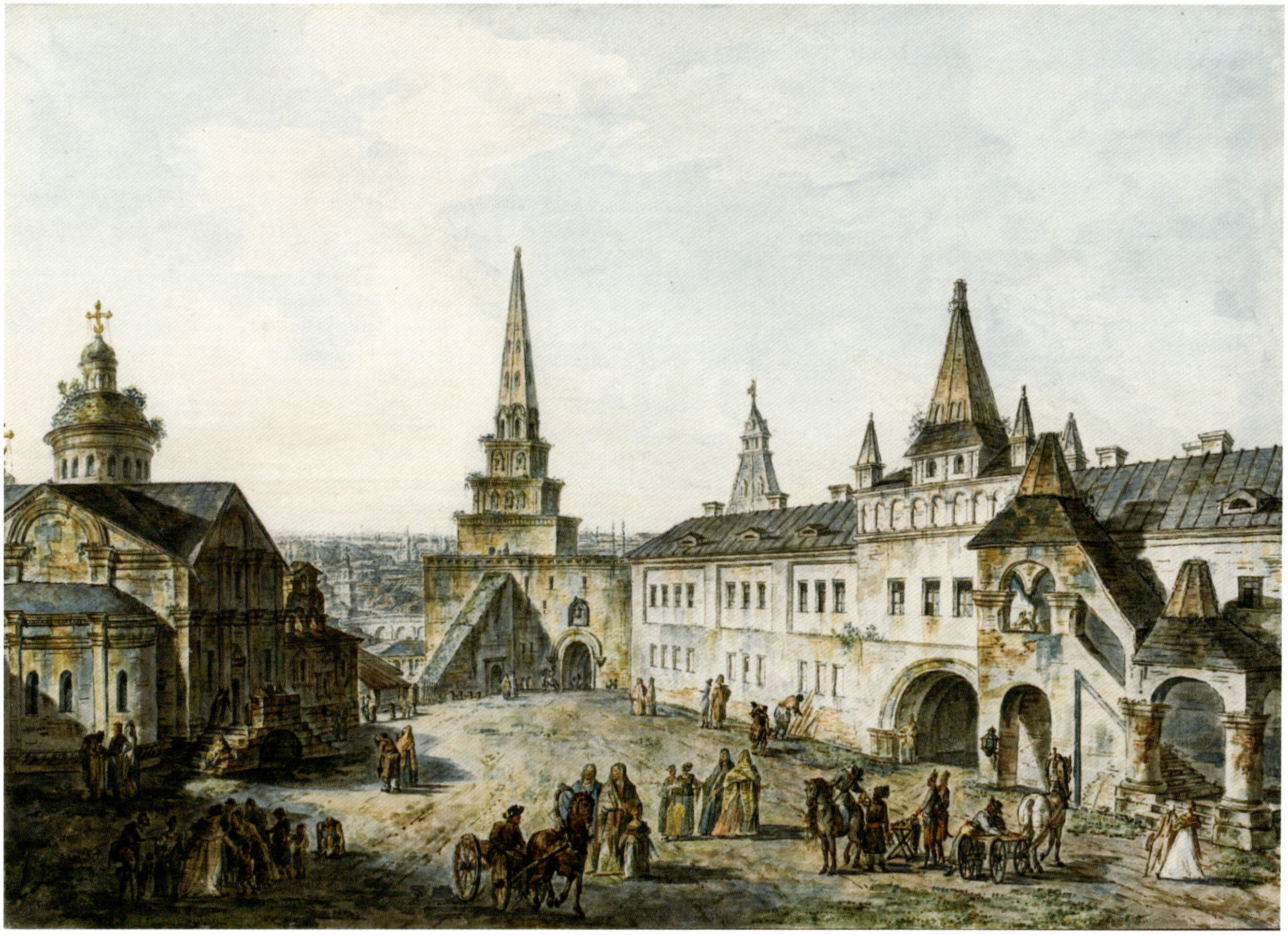

5. *F. I. Alekseev*
View of Resurrection Gate, the Grand Pharmacy, the Neglimennii Bridge and Peter's bastions
1800s
The State Historical Museum, Moscow
(Cat. 269)

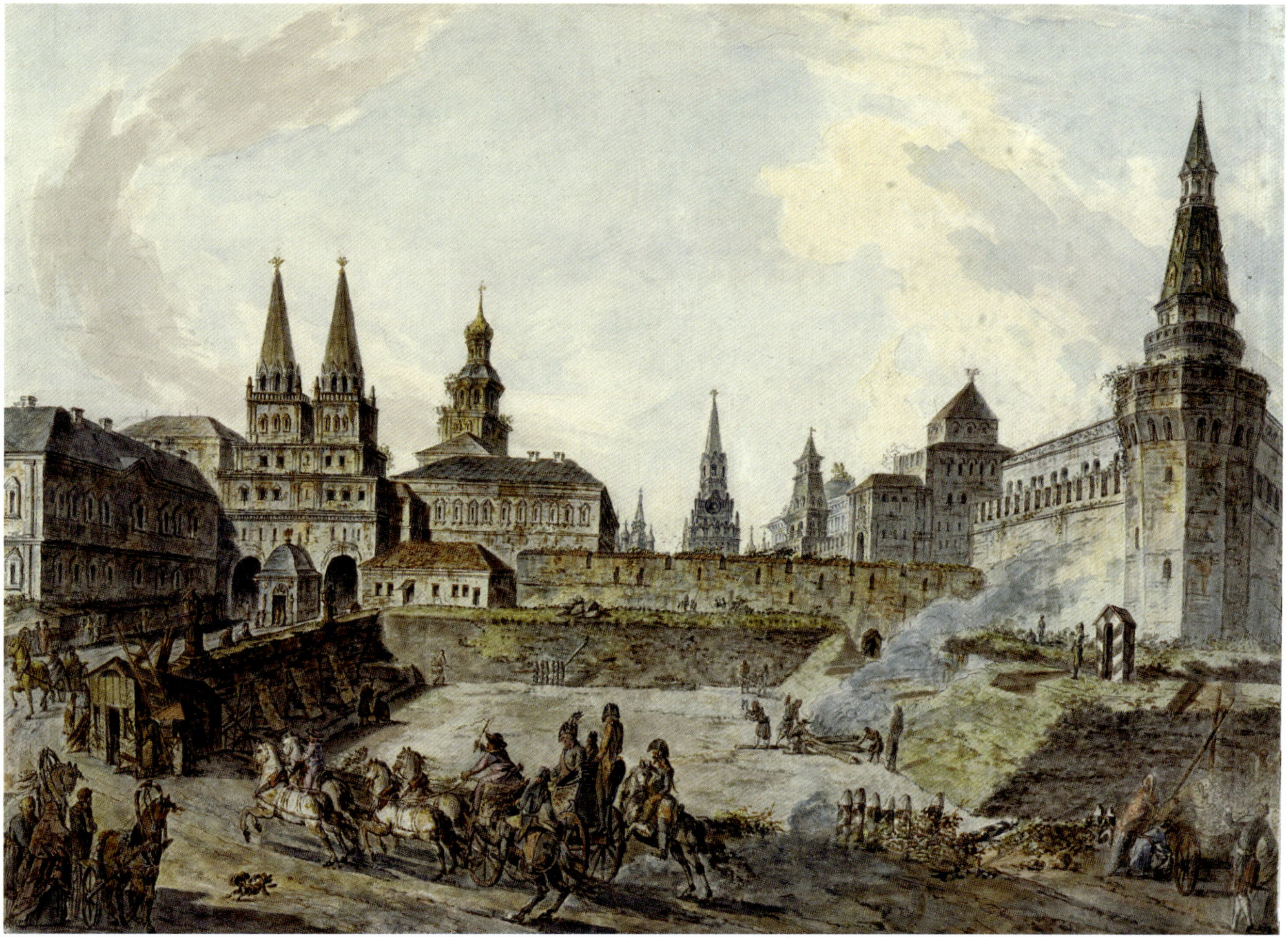

these artists to each watercolor. Even more, the stylistic analysis of each one seems to indicate that other students also participated in the realization of the views of the former capital. It is known that young artists frequented Alekseev's studio in succession over the years from May 1803 to 1815. They are the ones who undoubtedly executed the many very close variants of the most successful views, and the watercolor copies. As contemporaries reported, from the very beginning, the views of Moscow were in great demand. Thus in December 1807, the Academy Council took the decision to carry out a series of engravings of the *Views of Moscow based on the paintings of His Excellency the Councilor Alekseev.*

As has already been said above, in 1926, the Historical Museum received nineteen watercolors of the First Muscovite Series from the Hermitage. In addition to those, at different times other works linked to the name of Alekseev also came into the museum collections: oil paintings, graphic copies of oil paintings, printed reproductions of the views of Moscow, and finally, one of his rare signed drawings, *View of the Kremlin and the Stone Bridge.* A great many of these works came from the Old Moscow Museum, created in 1919, and then which was closed. This is why this little collection had as its themes the Kremlin and its immediate surroundings: the Red Square, Kitai-gorod, the banks of the Neglinnaya. The old Kremlin buildings represented in these watercolors, and which today no longer exist, have a very particular iconographic interest. Far from the famous Cathedral Square and Ivan's Square, these were family buildings under the reign of the czars Michael Feodorovich and Alexis Michaelovich (ill. 6). All these buildings—the famous Armory Gates which led to the Terems Palace, the Stables Courtyard, the Grand Palais Courtyard or the Armory Palace workshops—were demolished because of their dilapidated state soon after Alekseev left for St. Petersburg. Others, such as the Palace of Pleasures (Potechny), where in the 17th century the czar Alexis Michaelovich had set up the first Russian theater (ill. 7) or the Imperial Palace of Elizabeth Petrovna's time (ill. 8) were entirely reconstructed after the 1812 fires. Others, like the Palace of Terems and the Boyars Square (ill. 9) were integrated into the new Kremlin palace built in the middle of the 19th century based on the project by the architect C. A. Ton. All these watercolors, as an iconographic record, are of an inestimable value, enabling us to bring back to life the architectural aspect, unique in its kind, of Moscow "before the fire."

In closely observing, the watercolor landscapes done by Alekseev and his students in detail, it's impossible not to recall these lines from the article "Promenade in Moscow" by the poet C. N. Batiushkov, writing just before the Patriotic War (War of 1812) "Wouldn't you like to take a walk with me in the Kremlin? (...) It's a gigantic city, built by giants: tower against tower, wall against wall, palace against palace! A strange mixture of ancient and very new architecture, of poverty and wealth, of European ways and Oriental habits and customs! (...). Don't be surprised, my friend: Moscow is like a sign or a living painting of our country."

At the end of the War of 1812, after the series of fires which ravaged the city, more than 70% of

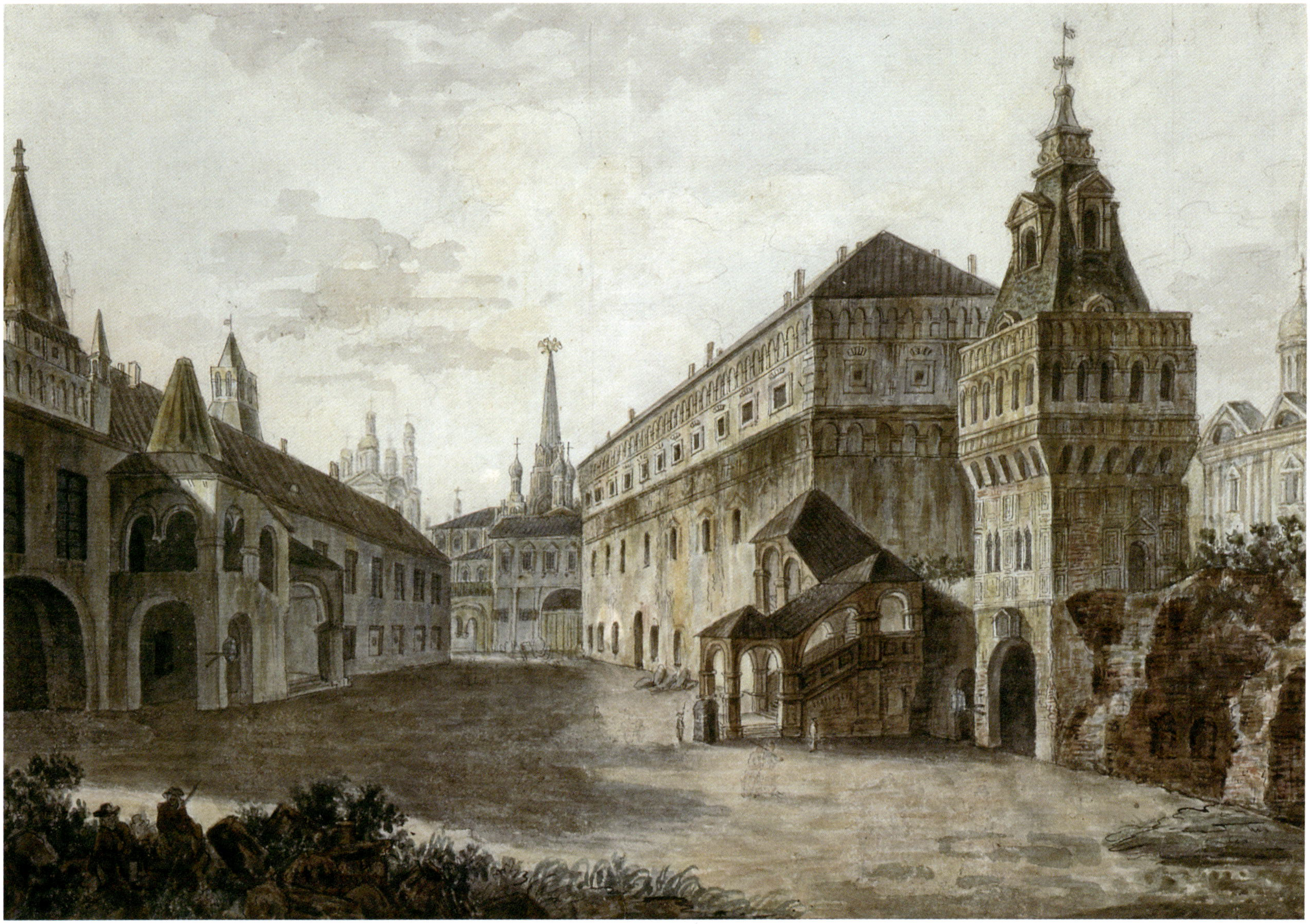

6. F. I. Alekseev and his students
View of the Kremlin on the Kremlin
Grande Palace Office, the Court
Stables and the Gate of the Armories
1800s
The State Historical Museum, Moscow
(Cat. 266)

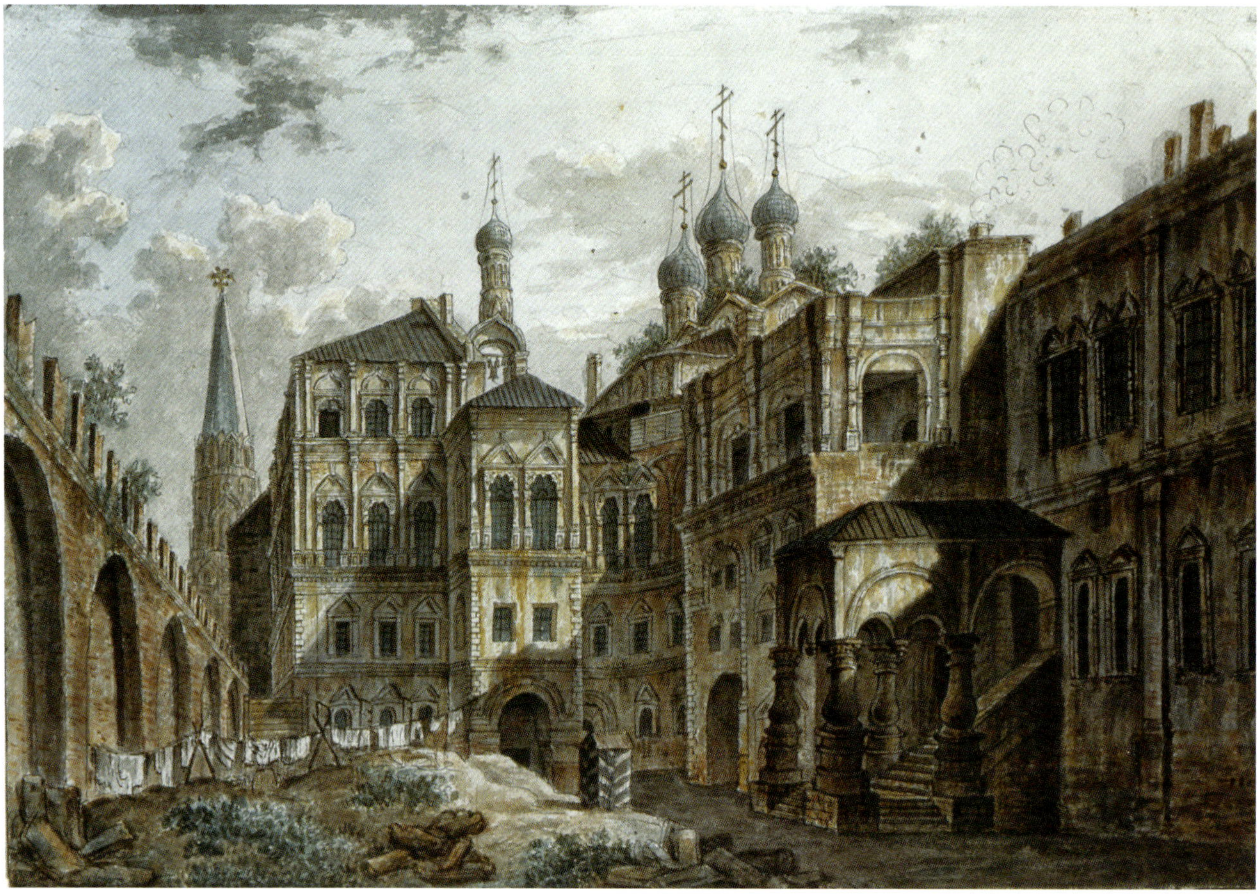

7. F. I. Alekseev and his students
View of the Kremlin on the Little Pleasures Palace from the side of the inside courtyard
1800s
The State Historical Museum, Moscow
(Cat. 267)

the residential buildings were destroyed, and the architectural aspect of the former capital was considerably changed. In 1813, a special "Commission for the Reconstruction of Moscow" was created which very quickly managed not only to restore the Kremlin and the whole of the Red Square but also to carry out the general reconstruction of the old city while preserving as much as possible the historical structure. Thus appeared new squares, new boulevards, new architectural complexes, new public buildings, and palaces for the nobility. Like the Phoenix, Moscow rose up from its ashes in the 1820s and 1830s, restored after the fires, and was represented in a series of lithographs made based on drawings by A. Cadolle and A. Durand, Ed. Gertner, published in Paris and in Munich. At that time, in Moscow itself, there was a flourishing of illustrated maps, almanacs and guides to the city on which many artists and Muscovite writers worked (ill. 1). But it was in Moscow in the middle of the 19th century, when printed views became widespread, that almost simultaneously several large lithographed series of views of the city appeared. Among them, the one published by I. H. Datsiaro over a period of ten years (from the middle of the 1840s to the middle of the 1850s) is of special interest. From its volume, from the large range of monuments it shows and from the remarkable quality of its execution, these views can only be compared to F. I. Alekseev's *Views of Moscow*.

I. H. Datsiaro (1805-1865) was Italian of origin but lived and worked in Moscow. A lithographer and publisher, he owned engraving stores

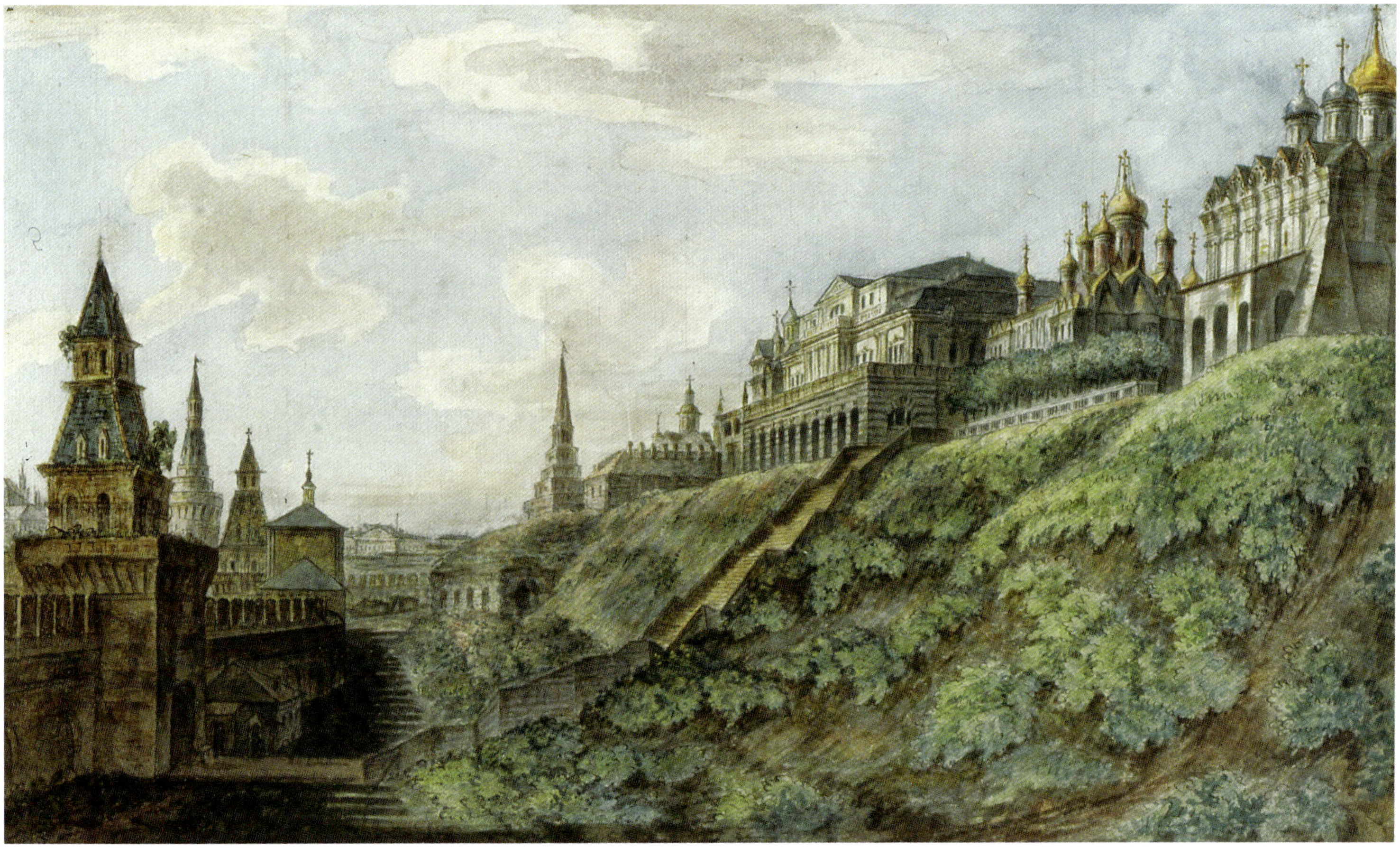

8. *F. I. Alekseev*
View in the Kremlin on the Kremlin Palace from the Podol (north side)
1800s
The State Historical Museum, Moscow
(Cat. 265)

9. *F. I. Alekseev*
View of the Kremlin from Boyars Square (west side)
1800s
The State Historical Museum, Moscow
(Cat. 263)

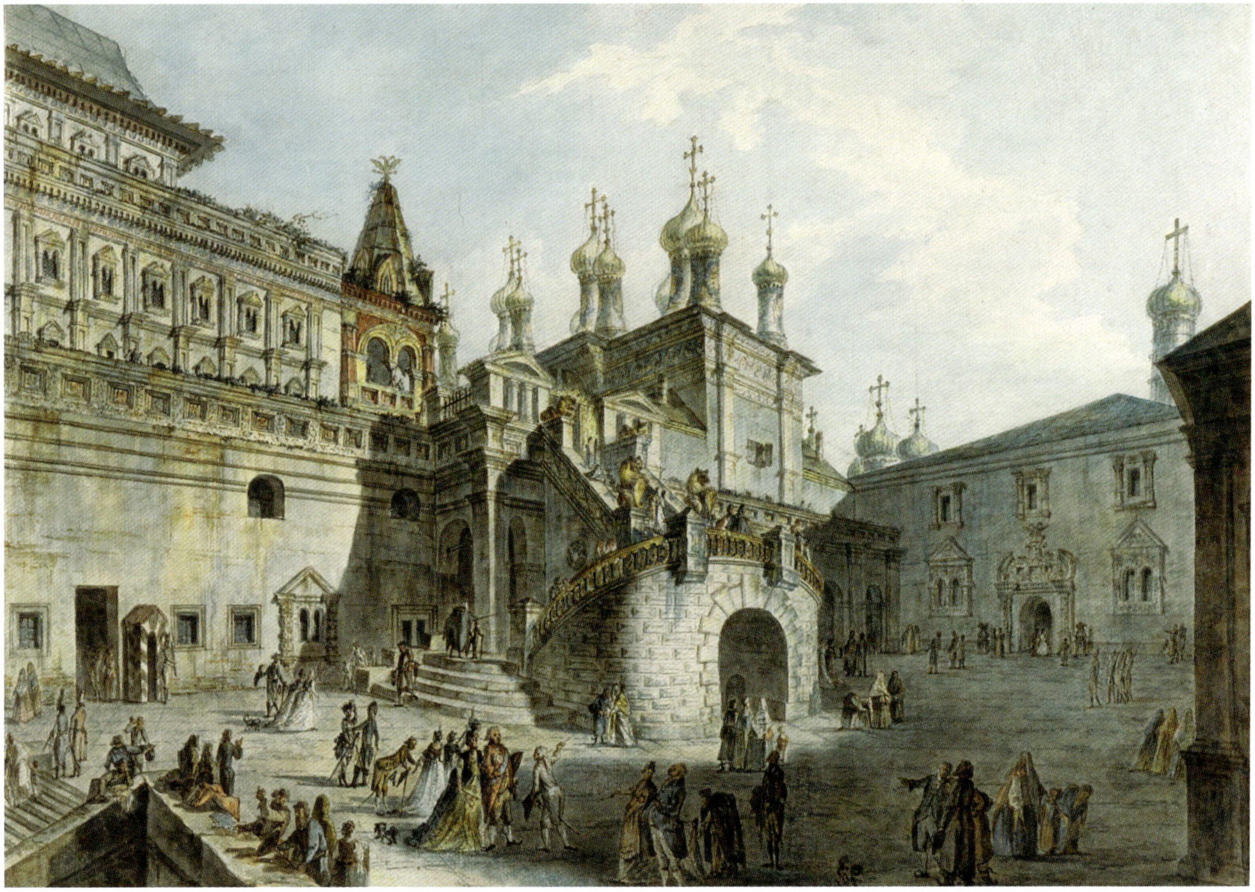

in St. Petersburg, Moscow and Paris. When the first pages of the Muscovite series began to appear, he was already well established as a publisher of several series of genre and customs scenes. *Drawings of Russian life*, *Popular Russian scenes*, *Russian Album*, and also views of St. Petersburg, based on drawings by the French artist F. Perrot, were published beginning in 1841. It should be noted that Datsiaro published views of the Northern capital, based on drawings by other artists until the middle of the 1850s.

To work on the series of views of Moscow, Datsiaro recruited a few Russian and foreign artists among those who at that time were working in Moscow. Most of them were Muscovite artists: I. E. Vivien (ill. 10), G. F. Baranovsky (ill. 11), D. S. Indeitsev, and a few others. At that time, Moscow already had its own school of architectural landscape views, linked to the activity of artistic educational institutions such as the Stroganov School of Industrial Design or the School of Painting and Sculpture or even the Palace School of Architecture, in which the study of the laws of perspective and the painting of views was accorded primary importance. It was in fact Muscovite artists who executed a great many of the drawings of the views of Moscow.

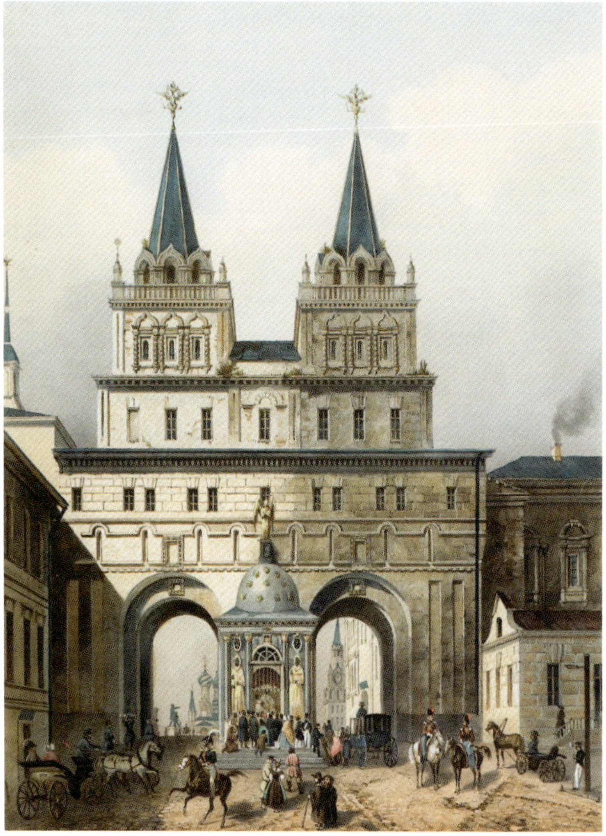

10. *Müller. Based on an original by I. E. Vivien*
The Kitai-gorod Resurrection Gates and the Chapel of the Virgin of Iberia
1840s
The State Historical Museum, Moscow
(Cat. 277)

Even more, at the beginning of the 1850s, Datsiaro published a circular panorama of the Kremlin and the Zamoskvoretchy district seen from the Tainitska Tower, based on drawings by D. S. Indeitsev. It contained ten pages of the actual panorama, and two complementary views of the engraving shops: one on Marshall's Bridge Street (*Kuznetsky most*) in Moscow and the other on the *boulevard des Italiens* in Paris. The German artist S. F. Dits who settled in Russia in the 1840s and who worked a lot on commission from Datsiaro (ill. 12), participated actively in the project of the Views of Moscow. Almost at the same time as the Views of Moscow, several views of St. Petersburg were published based on his drawings, as well as a series dedicated to Nijni-Novgorod and to the famous Makarev fair. At the beginning of the 1850s, the famous Petersburg landscape artist I. I. Charlemagne, architect by training and former student at the St. Petersburg Fine Arts Academy, was recruited to work on this series. Nine watercolors of views of Moscow, dated from the years 1853-1854 are in the collections of the State Historical Museum. Part of them were lithographed and integrated in the Datsiaro series (ill. 13). In contrast with F. I. Alekseev who predominantly worked on ancient monuments, the landscape artists of the middle of the 19th century preferred

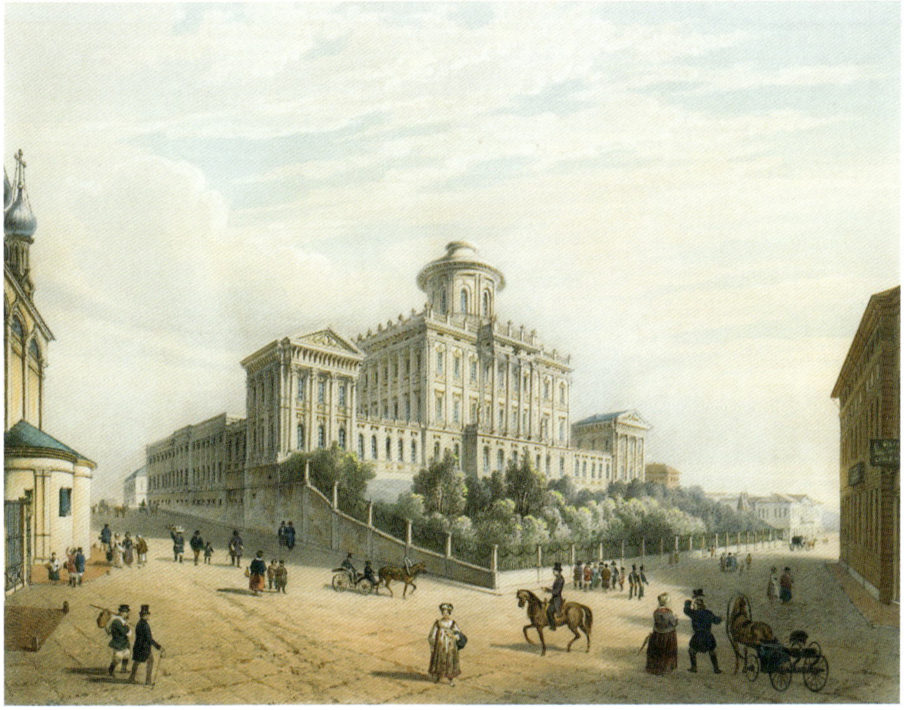

11. *L. P. Bichebois, Ch. Fichot. Based on an original by G. F. Baranovsky. Figures executed by A. Bayot* The Institute of Nobility on Mokhovaya Street *End of the 1840s* *The State Historical Museum, Moscow (Cat. 284)*

large panoramic views, painted most often from a high vantage point. Innumerable views of city streets and squares, new architectural complexes built in the 1820s such as the triumphal gates of the Tver Dam or the Tutelage Council on Solianka street were integrated into the series. They recorded with documentary precision the architectural aspect of the city and, at the same time, they introduced scenes of genre and customs into the urban landscape, in that way recreating the atmosphere of daily life in Moscow in the middle of the 19th century.

Beginning in the middle of the 1840s, Datsiaro published his complete series in Paris in P. J. Lemercier's famous studio, with the participation of a fairly steady group of French artists and lithographers with whom he maintained a fruitful collaboration for many years. It should be noted that in some cases, Datsiaro used daguerreotype views which had come out at that time as originals, or lithographs by earlier artists, such as the views of Moscow by A. Cadolle, lithographed in Paris in the years 1825-1830. In order to prepare such views for printing, the assistance of the experienced French masters was absolutely indispensable.

In some cases, French artists seemed to have corrected some of the clumsiness of the drawings but what they did especially was to add figures to these urban views. This explains why on a number of the lithographs there is the mention, "Figures done by...." Sometimes, using the same stone, several variations of the same view were printed. In general, at the top, above the image were Latin characters with the mention "Moscow" and at the bottom, below the image, the names of the artists and the lithographers and, even lower, on the border, the name of the place shown in French and in Russian. In all, forty-two views of the former capital and its surroundings were completed. They are large format lithographs, colored in the same tonality, but rather often there are also pages which have been delicately water-colored. These watercolor paintings were carried out in the lithography studio. The lithographs were sold as separate pages or in albums whose cover was printed with the title "Views of Moscow" or very simply, "Moscow." An album has been preserved in the Historical Museum's collection whose flyleaf has a dedication to the Czar's wife, Grand Duchess Maria Alexandrovna, wife to the heir of the throne, the future Alexander II. The Muscovite series was remarkably successful. To the point that Datsiaro republished it later in the form of separate pages or small sized albums—like paperback books. Nearly all the same views were shown as in the original but they also included new views some of which are rare in the iconography of Moscow, as

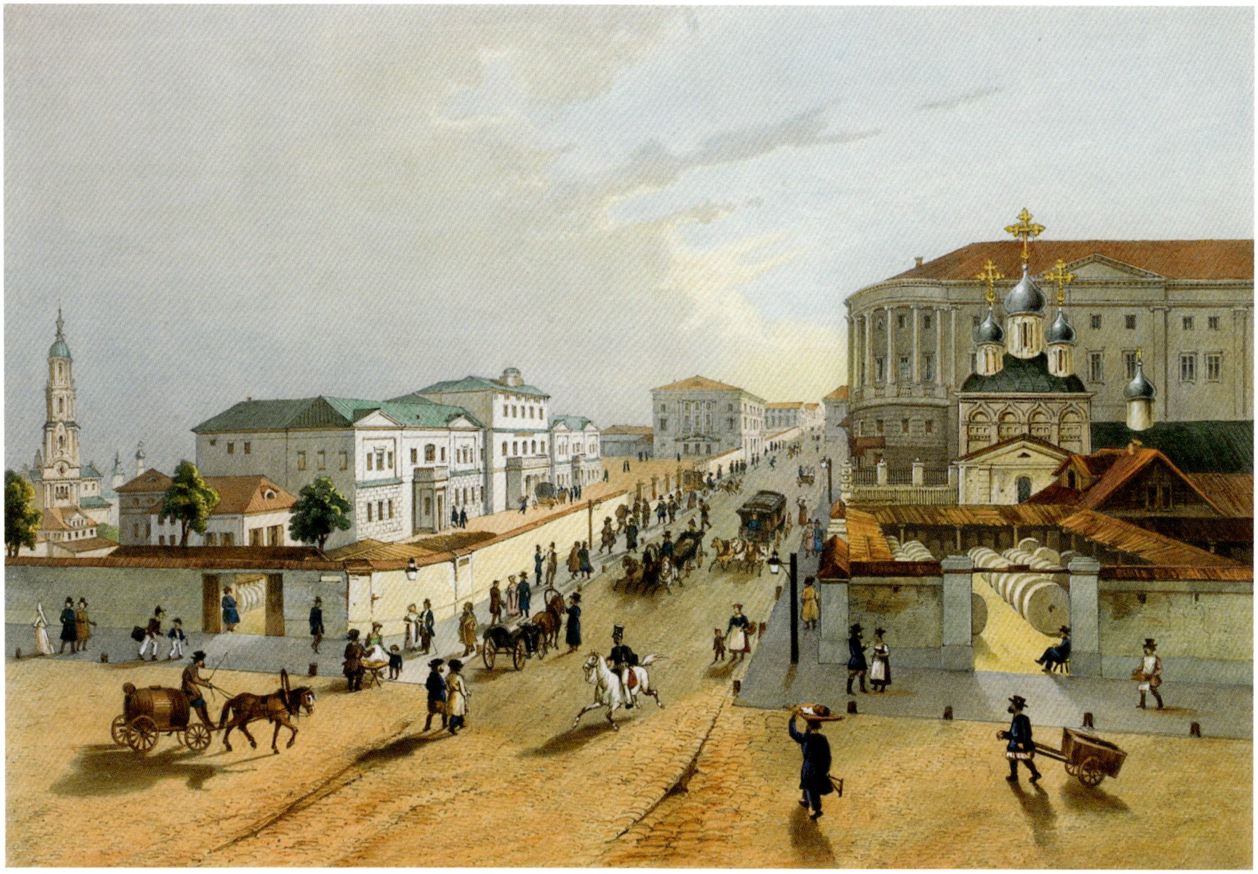

12. *Müller. Based on an original by S. Ph. Dits* Moscow Post Office on Miasnikskaya street (street of Butchers) *End of the 1840s The State Historical Museum, Moscow (Cat. 285)*

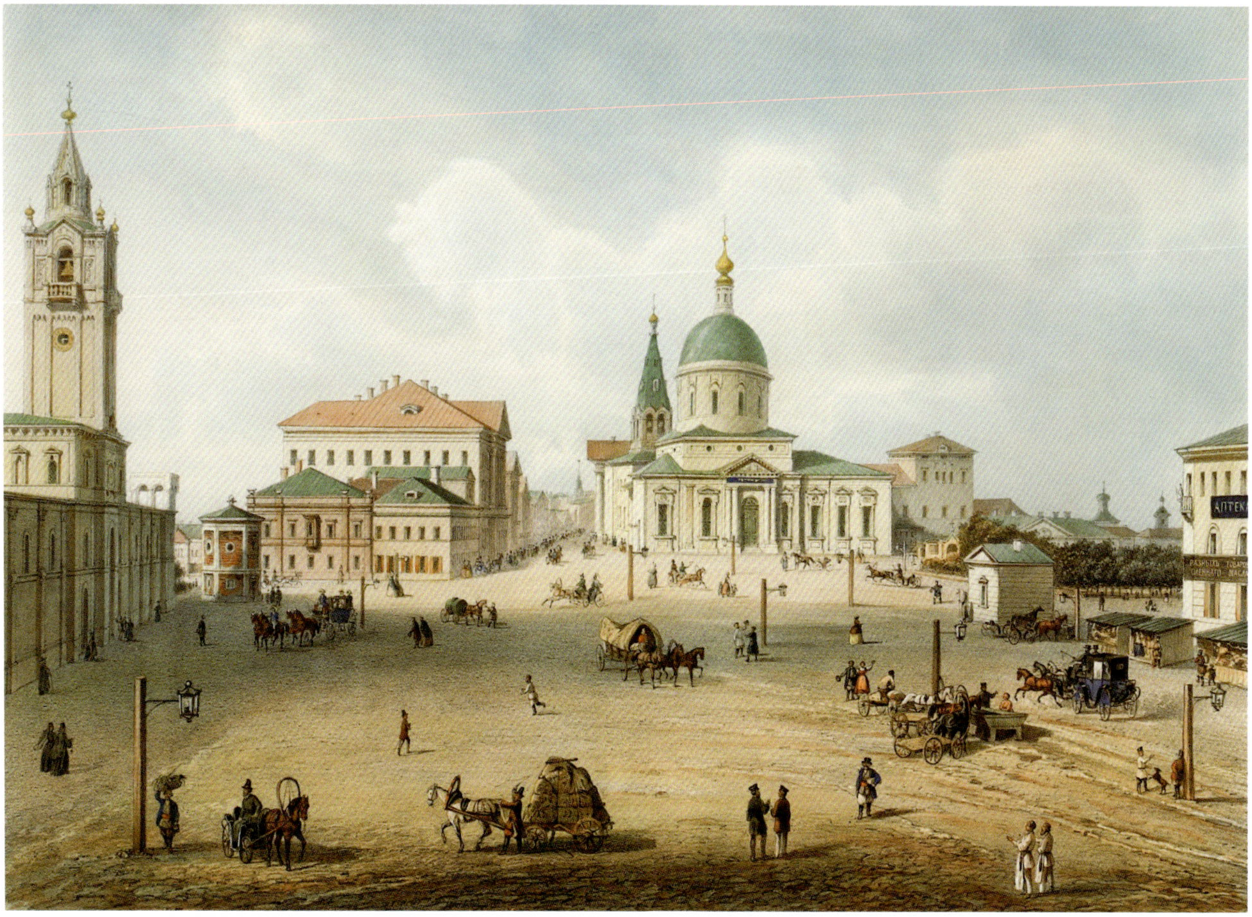

13. *Ch. K. Bachelier, J. Jacottet. Based on an original by I. I. Charlemagne. Figures executed by J. A. Duruy* Strastnaya Square (Passion Square) *Moscow, 1850s Moscou, années 1850 The State Historical Museum, Moscow (Cat. 279)*

for example the view in perspective of Tverskaya street.

The visual chronicle of Moscow which was created over several centuries is of an exceptional richness and diversity. Dozens of Russian and foreign painters, engravers, and lithographers participated in its creation. However, and this can be most definitively asserted, the two most striking facts of its history were, first, the artist F. I. Alekseev's arrival in 1800 in the former capital and, second, I. H. Datsiaro's publishing work which began in the middle of the century and lasted for many years. Thanks to them, the iconography of the city was enriched by two absolutely exceptional graphic series which recorded as completely as was possible the very colorful and diverse physiognomy of Old Moscow at different moments of its complex and dramatic history. Although the watercolors by F. I. Alekseev and his students remained practically unknown to the general public until the beginning of the 20th century, Datsiaro's lithographs were immediately published with a fairly large print run and without a doubt they significantly influenced Russian landscape lithography and the genre of urban landscape in general. It was certainly not by chance that the Muscovite editors continued for a long time to republish Datsiaro's views of the former capital of the kingdom.

[1] E. Vigée-Lebrun, *Souvenirs de Madame Louise-Elizabeth Vigée-Lebrun*, chapter IV. (Translator's note)

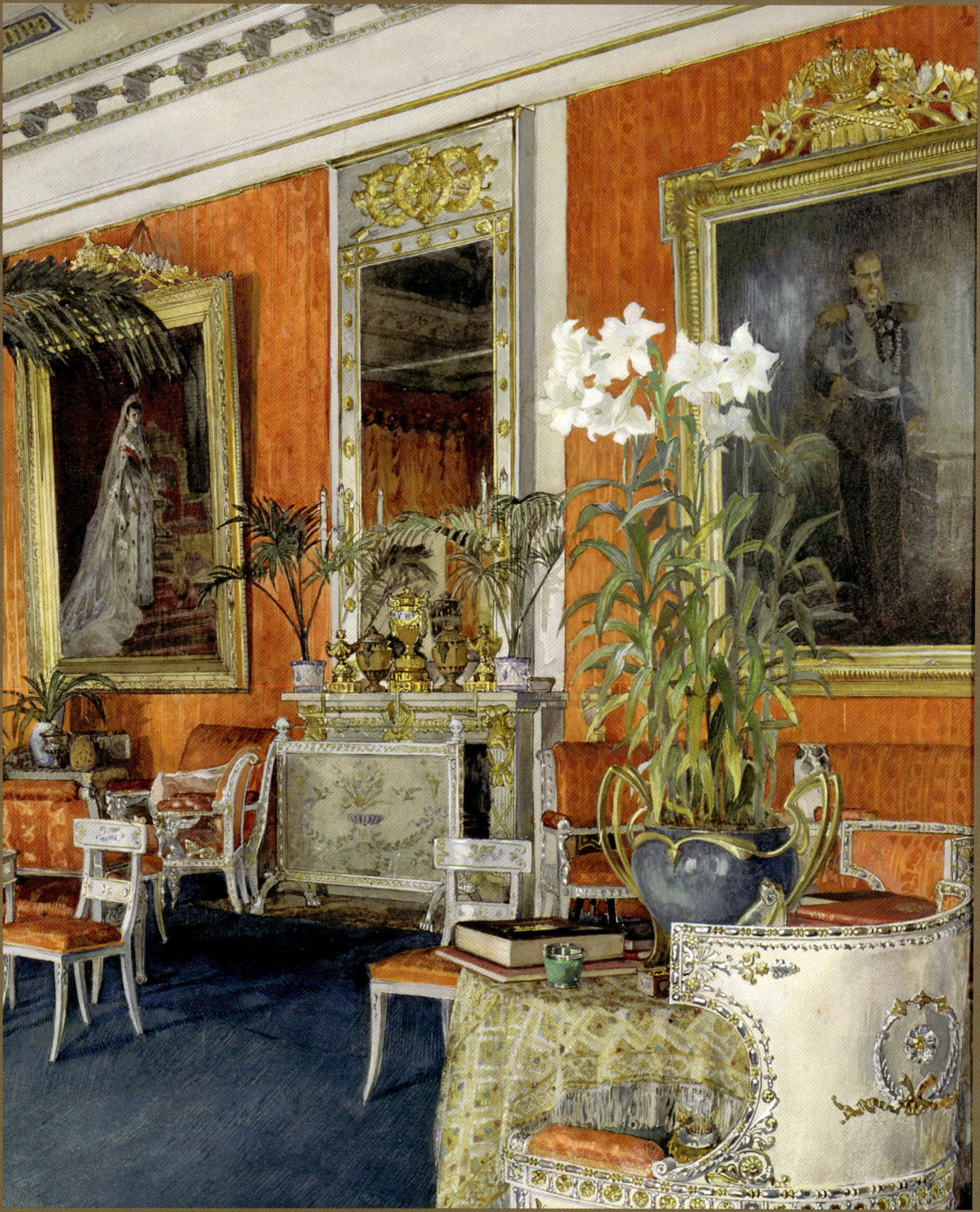

SPLENDOURS OF THE COURT LIFE

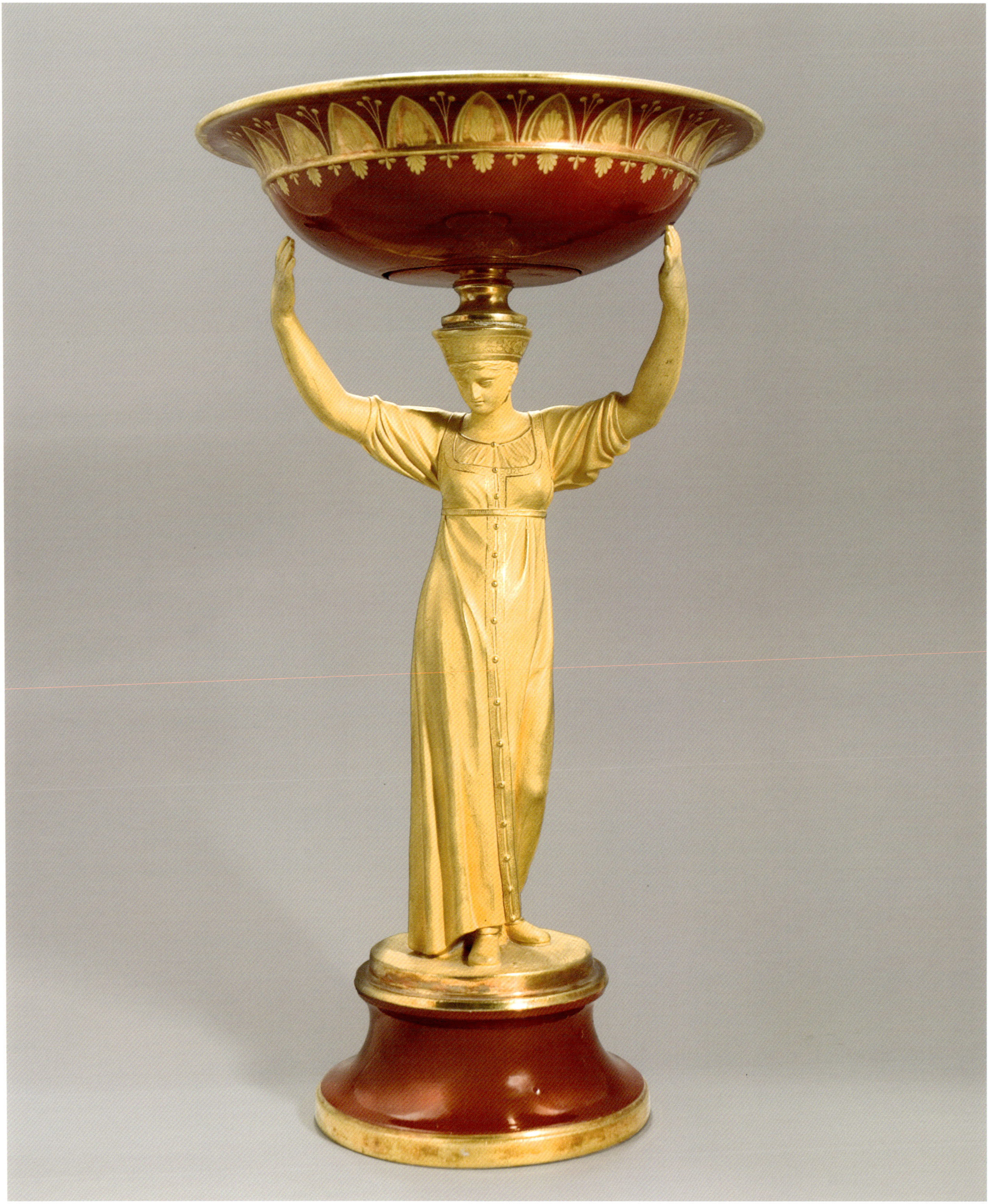

TABLE ARTS: RUSSIAN PORCELAIN AT THE END OF THE 18TH CENTURY AND FIRST HALF OF THE 19TH CENTURY

Tatiana Mosjoukhina

Page 122
A. P. Barychnikov
Red Salon with portraits of Emperor Alexander III and Empress Maria Feodorovna
1902
The State Historical Museum, Moscow
(Cat. 561)

1. Vase made on the stem of which figure a young woman peasant
Guriev table service pieces, Imperial Porcelain Manufacture, 1809-1816
State Ceramics Museum of Kuskovo
(Cat. 167)

The objects presented in this exhibition are examples of the most significant productions of Russian porcelain deriving from the collections of the State Ceramics Museum and the "18th century Kuskovo Estate" and reflect, in their way, the most diverse aspects of Russian history and culture.

In Russian history, the last third of the 18th century is traditionally called "the golden century", which well reflects the grandeur and brilliance of the epoch of Empress Catherine II's reign. Careful to appear as an enlightened sovereign, Catherine II paid great attention to the development of science and art which were to serve the glory of the Homeland. In this respect, the Porcelain Imperial Manufacture (whose initials were IFZ, *Imperatorsky farforni zavod*), founded in 1744, was certainly one of the most active. At the end of the 18th century, it was in full development, responding unfailingly to the many Court orders. Porcelain was considered as an important element, providing the Court the indispensable prestige to its etiquette and in addition endowed with the power to illustrate important governmental and political ideas.

A whole series of Manufacture productions developed the theme of a flourishing multinational power and reflected the image of the multiple concrete aspects of what was really Russia in the 18th century with its pronounced taste for the study and the discovery of new lands—lands added to the new territories won through war during the Russo-Turkish War.

The most systematic illustration of this theme appears in the sculpted series "People of Russia", created by the Manufacture in 1780-1790 under the supervision of its main sculptor, J. D. Rachette. The originality of this series, which included about sixty models, has less to do with the pleasing aspect of a very fashionable national exoticism in 18th century European porcelain subjects, but rather with a conceptual project closely linked to the historical situation. The round of figures in national costumes of all colors well illustrates the power of a huge and flourishing multinational Russia being wisely governed by the Empress Catherine the Great.

Alexander I's era, marked by Russia's victory over Napoleon and by an extraordinary national fervor (ill. 3), expressed itself with brio in the pieces produced by the Manufacture all through the first quarter of the 19th century. Its activity during this period was marked by new knowledge in perfecting technology and by recourse to talented artists and remarkable specialists from France. All this resulted in the creation of a whole series of outstanding productions, reflecting through their style and with great ex-

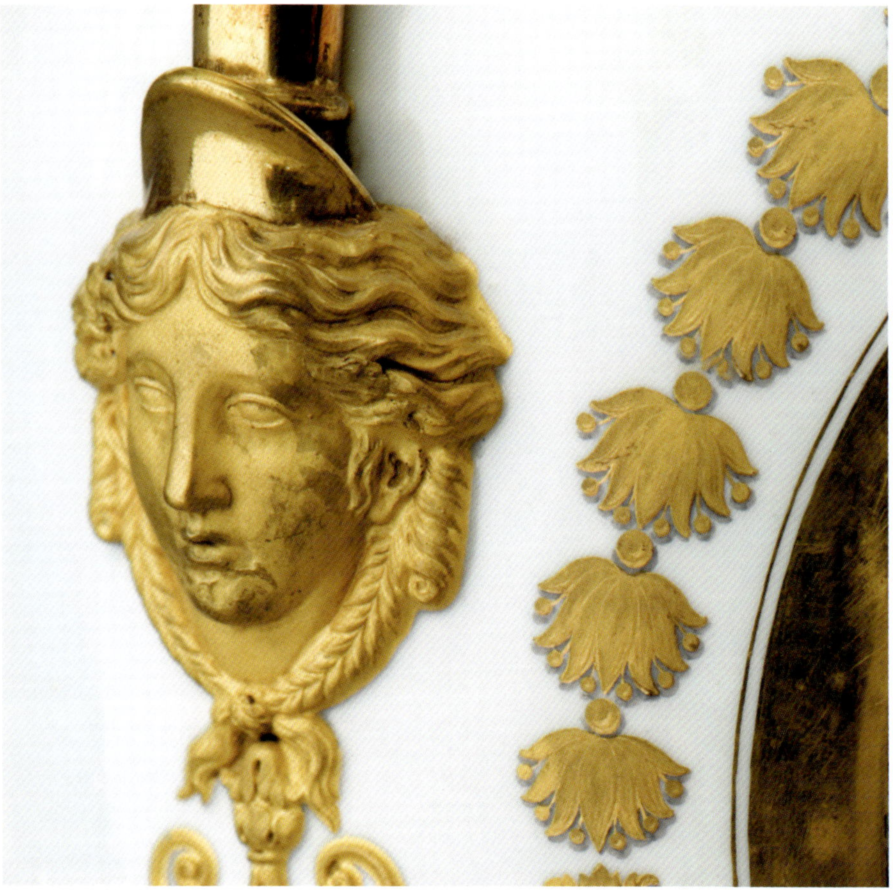

2. Guriev table service pieces
Imperial Porcelain Manufacture, 1809-1816
State Ceramics Museum of Kuskovo
(Cat. 165-170)
Detail

pressive force, an era which has left its profound trace on the history of Russia.

Consequently, the Imperial Manufacture focused primarily on the fabrication of decorative vases for the palace and on large ceremonial table services, seen as a striking illustrations of the art of the era of classicism with its emphasis on monumental ensembles for interiors. This type of production was characterized by a particularly solemn pomp and ceremony, by the beauty and harmony of forms and designs, and the originality of themes. Particularly popular in painted designs were scenes of Russia life which, indeed, was a continuity of late 18th century trends with its interest in ethnography, but which also displayed society's undisguised interest for the most diverse aspects of the life of the people.

The most famous set of Russian porcelain and also the most accomplished of the 19th century is the Guriev service which was created at that time. It was created under the supervision of the great sculptor and associate professor at the Fine Arts Academy, S. S. Pimenov, who between 1809 and 1831 headed the Manufacture sculpture workshop where he was the art director. Beginning in 1809, Pimenov and his assistants had planned the decorative project and designed the fundamental volume of the new table service which was first called "The Service representing Russian costumes" or more simply "The Russian Service" which clearly stated the basic idea. (In 1824, "The Russian Service" was called Guriev, after Count D. A. Guriev, at the time Court minister and also director of the Manufacture.) The service was finished in 1816. It was planned for fifty people and destined for the Winter Palace. Complementary pieces were added to it up to the beginning of the 20th century until the number of pieces composing it totaled 4500 (ill. 4).

Its most beautiful adornment is undeniably the multitude of dessert plates (ill. 5) whose stems are sculpted compositions of one, two or several figures. They were at the very heart of the artistic project of the whole service. With these sculpted groups of dessert vases, S. S. Pimenov brilliantly illustrated the Russian theme of the work which never before or since has found a greater or more majestic resonance. Young men and young women superbly proportioned, evoking by their gracious poses (ill. 1) ancient gods and goddesses, dressed in Russian shirts and *sarafans* which fall in harmonious folds in the classical manner, carry gracefully and lightly the bowls or openwork baskets in their arms or on their heads. The solemn nature on the whole is underlined by the combination of the matt gilding of the figures and of an earthenware base with a gilded decoration, made of stylized vegetal motifs in the ancient classical style and which are found on all the pieces of the service. The very colorful paintings on the dessert dishes and other pieces of the service form a vast panorama of Russian life. Miniatures show views of Moscow and St. Petersburg and varied scenes of the daily life of the people. One can see (ills. 6, and 7) merchants, porters and carriers, craftsmen who are selling or proposing all kinds of merchandise and objects, inhabitants of various Russian provinces and representatives of the many ethnic populations, summer games and winter games, the leisure activities of the inhabitants of the cities and of the countryside, Russian everyday customs, portraits of war heroes from the War of 1812. And so one can see represented on one of the dishes one of the participants of the conflict, the Don Cossack, Alexander Zemlianukhin (ill. 8). Sources for these paintings were engravings coming from various works: J. G. Georgi, *Descriptions of the peoples living in the State of Russia*, albums with engravings done by foreign artists who reproduced the astonishing customs and appearances of the Russians: J. B. Leprince, C. G. Geisler, J. A. Atkinson as well as the Russian E. M. Korneev.

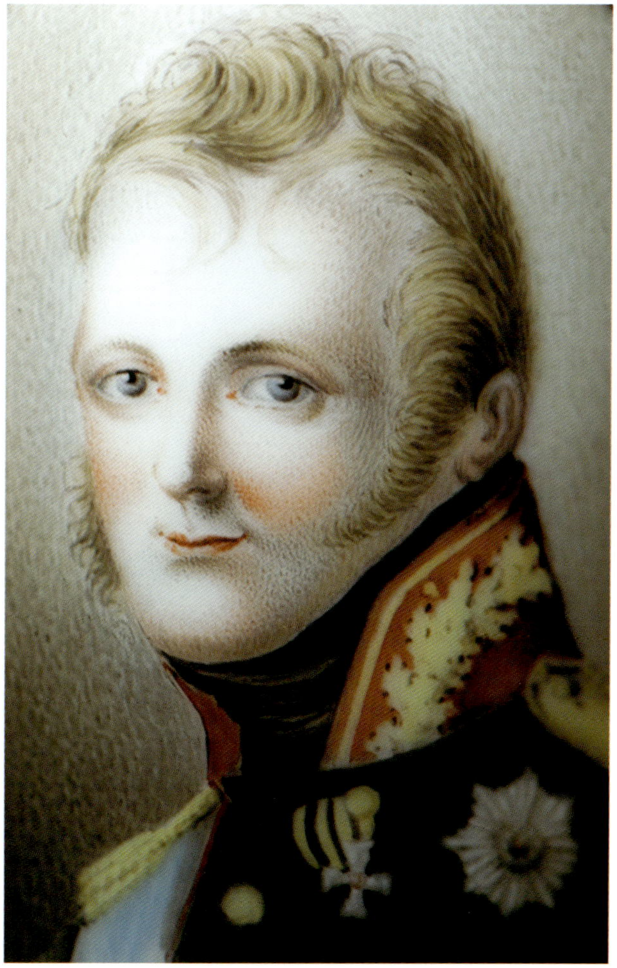

3. Cup with the portrait of the Emperor Alexander I
Gardner Manufacture, years 1810
State Ceramics Museum of Kuskovo (Cat. 218)
Detail

This subject, the representation of the most diverse aspects of Russian life which was inaugurated with such resounding success by the Imperial Manufacture, was taken up and developed in the 19th century by private porcelain factories. The Gardner Manufacture, established near Moscow, became famous in the first half of the century with a series of figures illustrating the popular models of merchants, porters and carriers, peasants, and craftsmen.

At the same time, engravings with views of the most famous monuments and buildings from the two Russian capitals (ill. 9), St. Petersburg and Moscow, enjoyed a new popularity. They were used as examples for paintings on porcelain. The most famous firms producing porcelain in the area around Moscow: the Gardner, Popov, Safronov Manufactures—produced a good number of souvenir objects with views of Moscow. Among the best are the large plates on which, according to Russian tradition, one brought the bread and the salt to one's guests of honor. Commemorative plates, decorated with the State coat of arms were made for the occasions of the most important

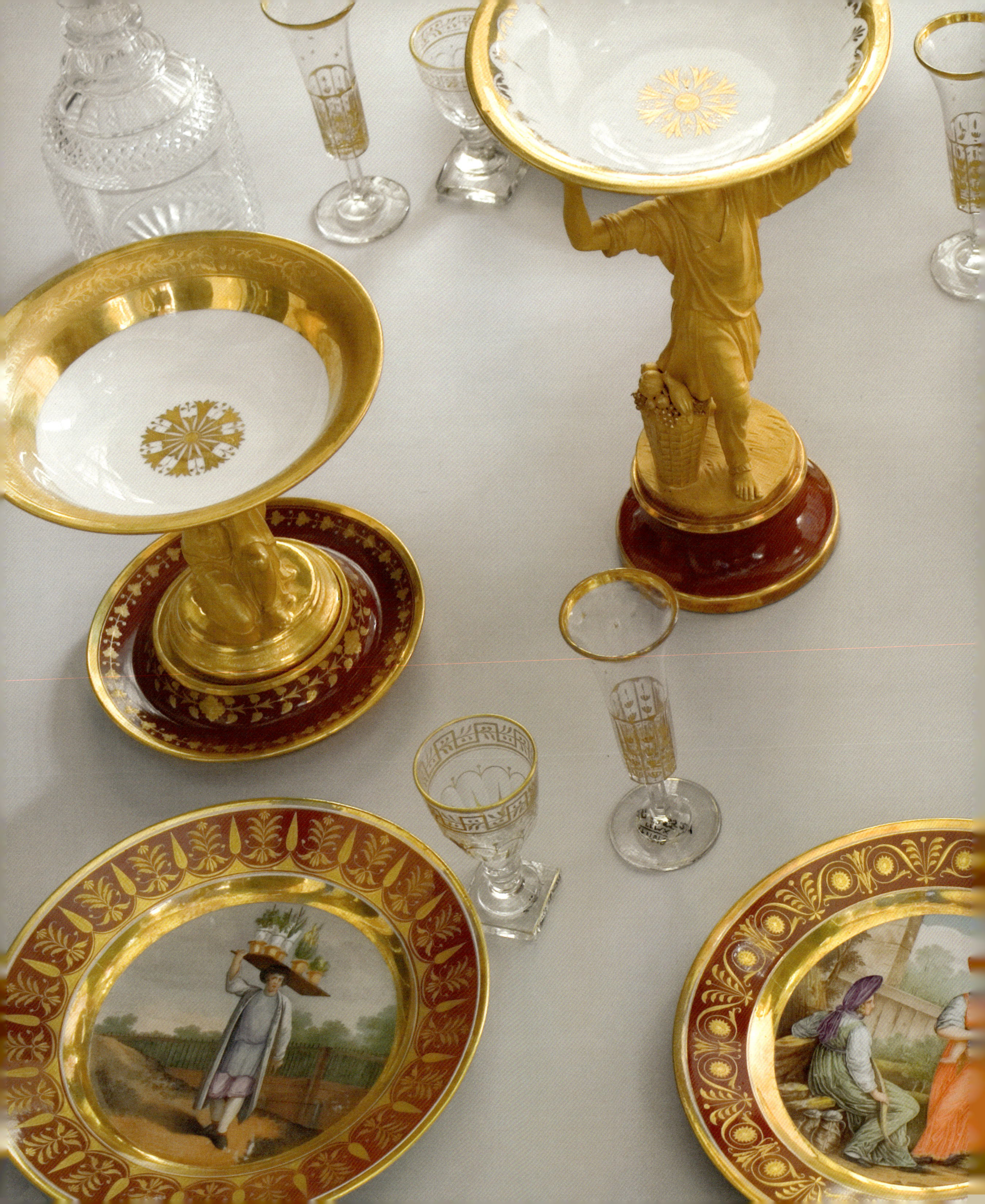

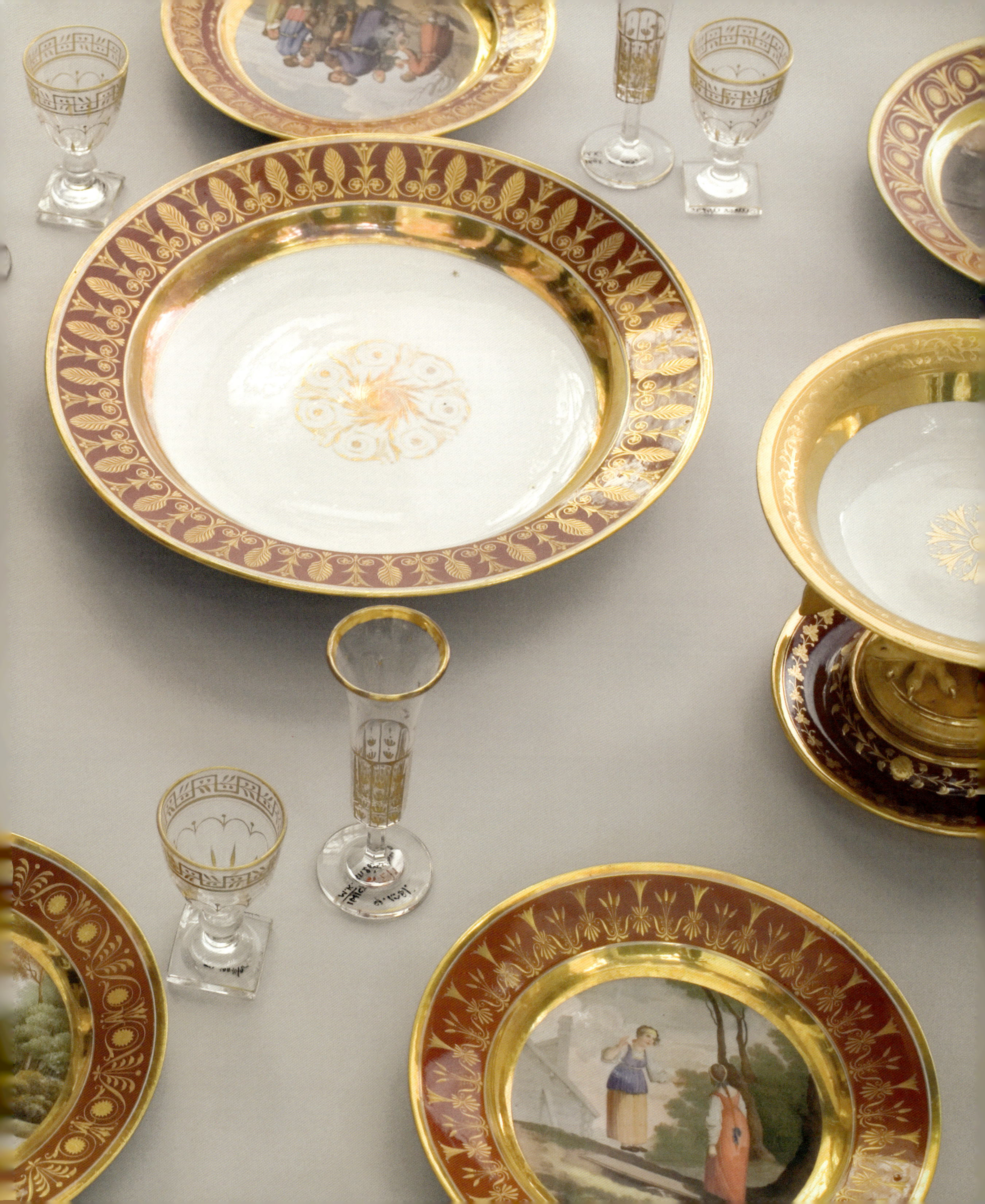

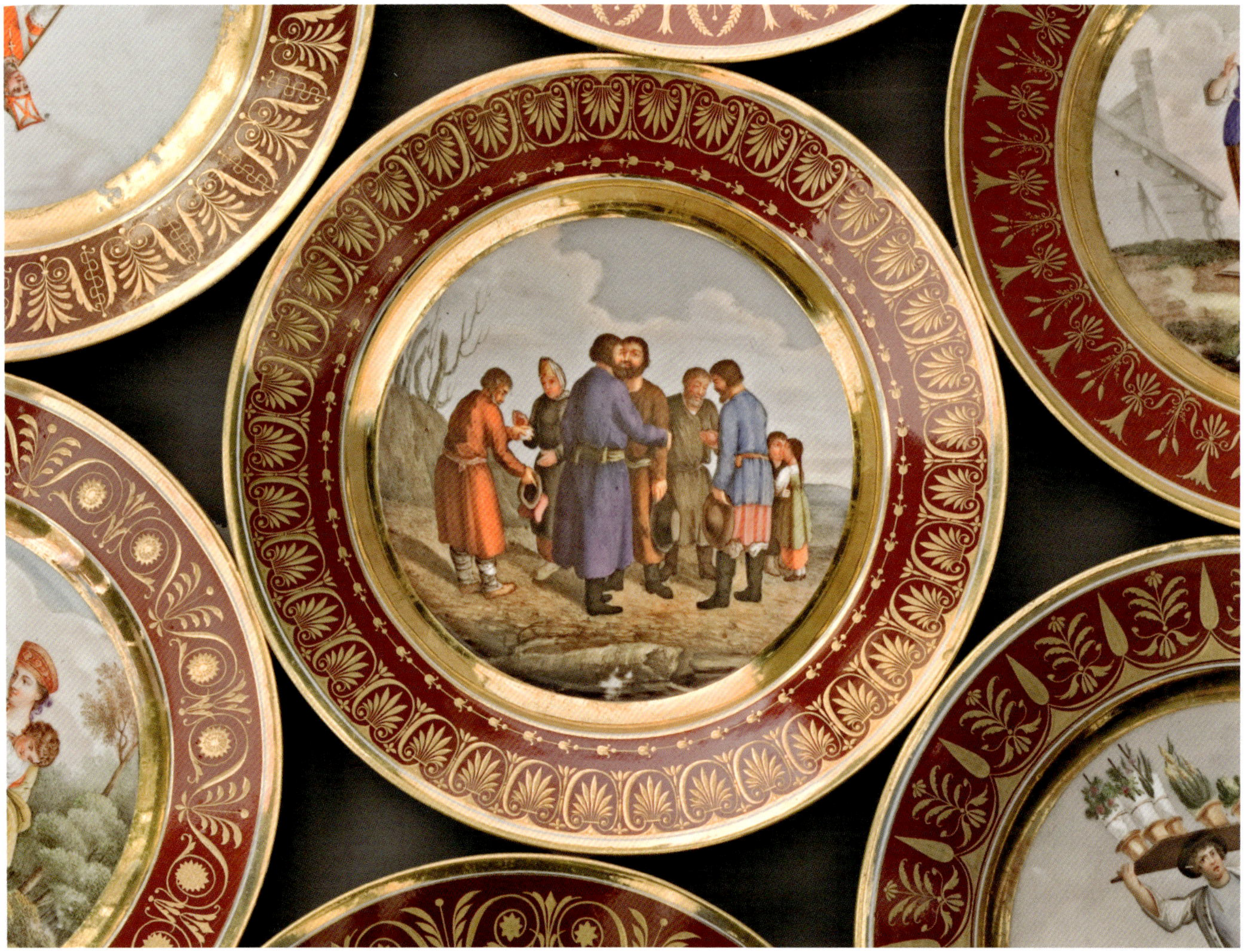

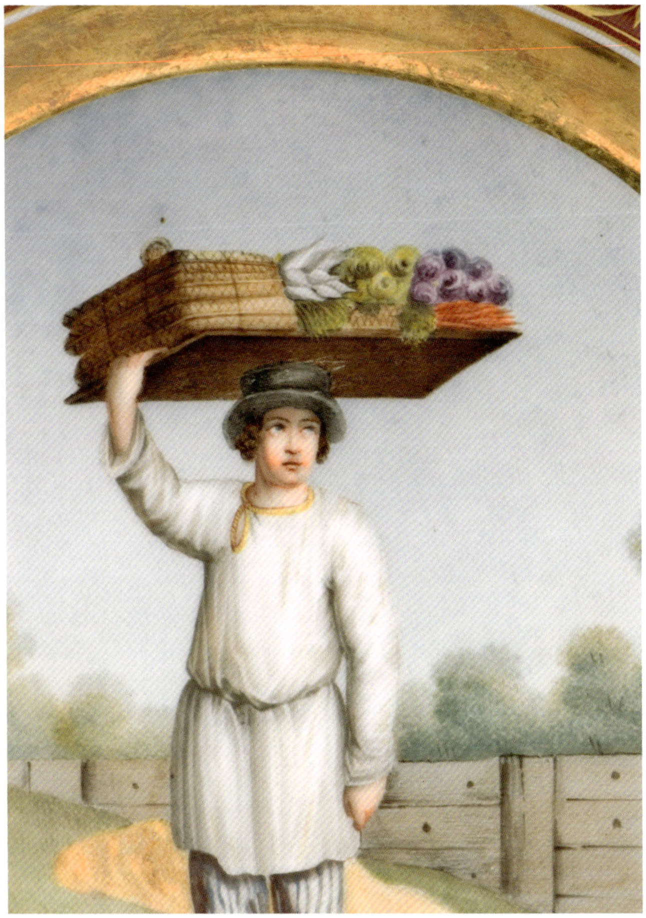

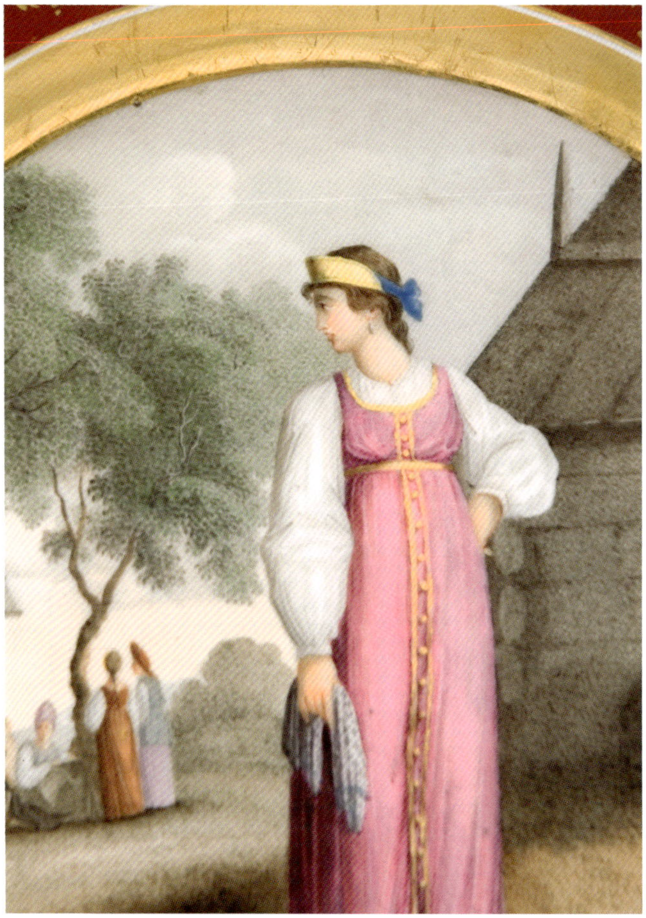

Pages 128-129
4. Guriev table service pieces
Imperial Porcelain Manufacture, 1809-1816
Glasses
Russia, first half of the 19th century
State Ceramics Museum of Kuskovo
(Cat. 165-198)

5. Small plates from the Guriev table service
In the centre: "Easter custom"
(Cat. 173)
Imperial Porcelain Manufacture, 1809-1816
State Ceramics Museum of Kuskovo
(Cat. 171-182)

6. Small plate "Fruit and vegetable seller"
Guriev table service pieces, Imperial Porcelain Manufacture, 1809-1816
State Ceramics Museum of Kuskovo
(Cat. 181)

7. Small plate "Young Countrywoman"
Guriev table service pieces, Imperial Porcelain Manufacture, 1809-1816
State Ceramics Museum of Kuskovo
(Cat. 172)

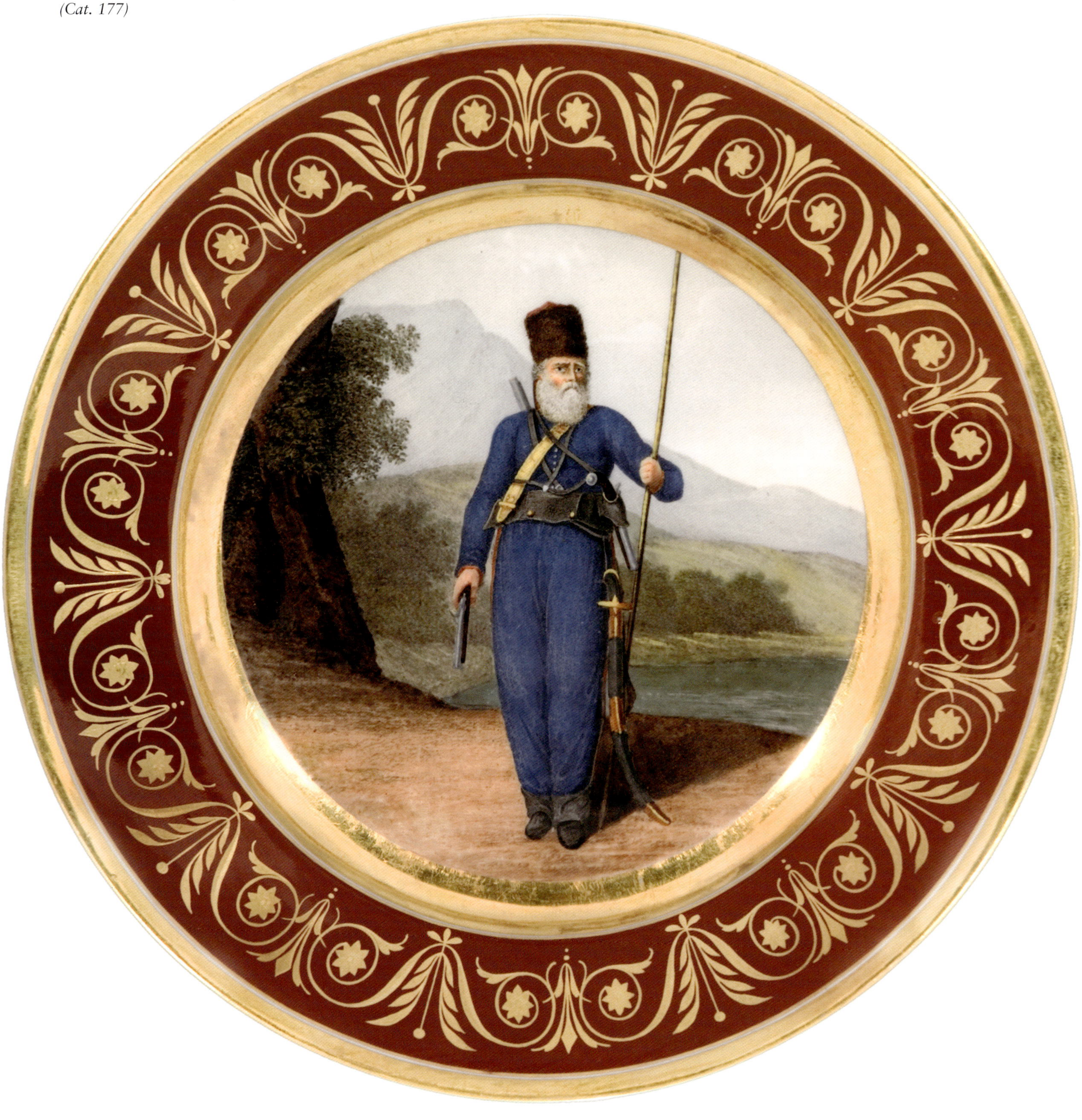

8. Plate "The Cossack Alexander Zemlianutin"
Guriev table service pieces, Imperial Porcelain Manufacture, 1809-1816
State Ceramics Museum of Kuskovo
(Cat. 177)

9. Dish with the Ivan Vekily bell
tower in the Kremkhuin
Popov Manufacture, years 1860s
State Ceramics Museum of Kuskovo
(Cat. 498)

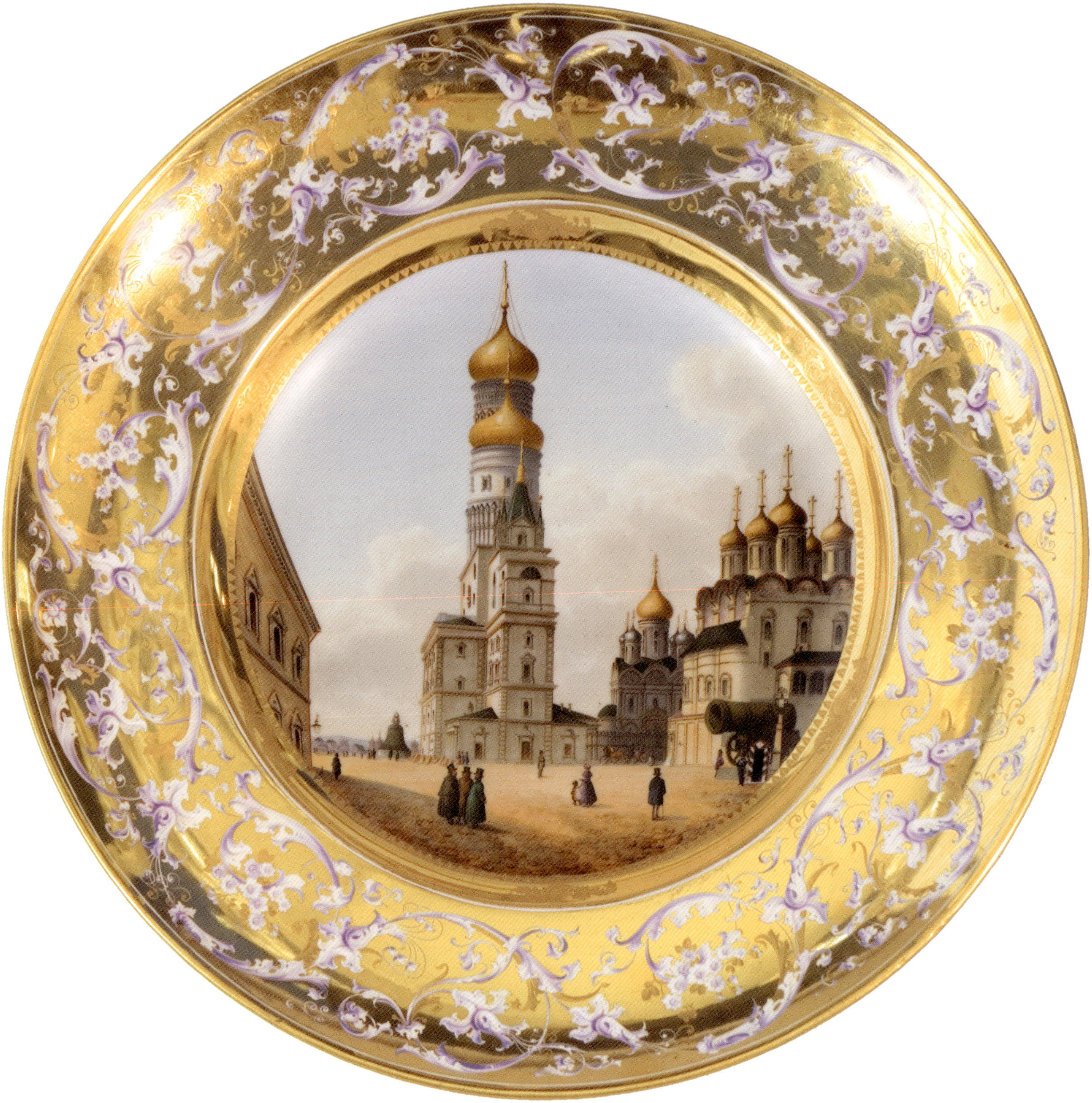

10. Cup and saucer on three stems with the portrait of the Emperor Alexander I
Gardner Manufacture, years 1810.
State Ceramics Museum of Kuskovo (Cat. 218)

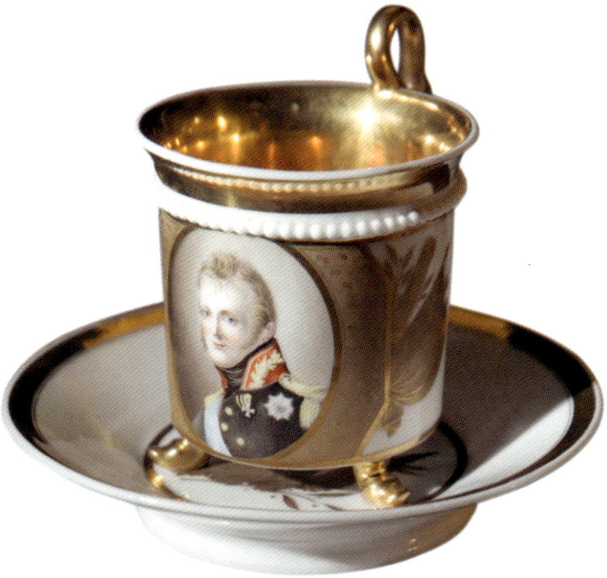

events, for example, for the coronation ceremonies which took place at the Kremlin in Moscow. Among them, special mention must be made of the plates of exceptional dimensions produced by one of the best porcelain firms in Russia: the Popov Manufacture.

Cups as gifts which had portraits of members of the Czar's family (ills. 10, 11 and 12) were especially sought after. All the country's major manufactures produced them. The exhibition shows pieces from the Imperial Manufacture, the Batenin Manufacture and still others, from around the Moscow area.

These porcelain objects in which are reflected the most diverse events of the life of the State, scenes of Russian daily life as well as portraits of the reigning families, monuments of the past dear to the hearts of all the inhabitants of Russia in the former capital Moscow, will enable visitors to the exhibition to become more acquainted with the history of Russia, and help them, as it were, to immerge themselves into the Russian way of life of the 19th century.

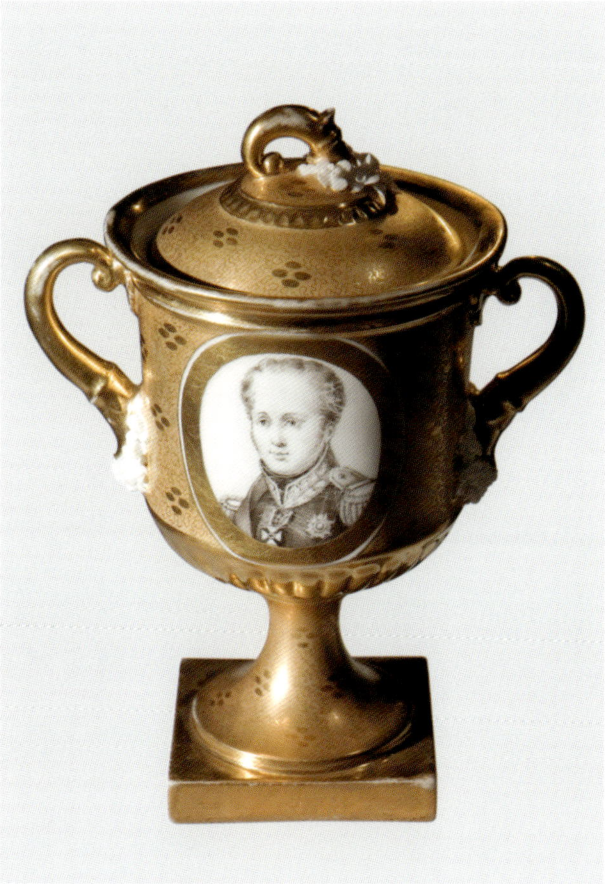

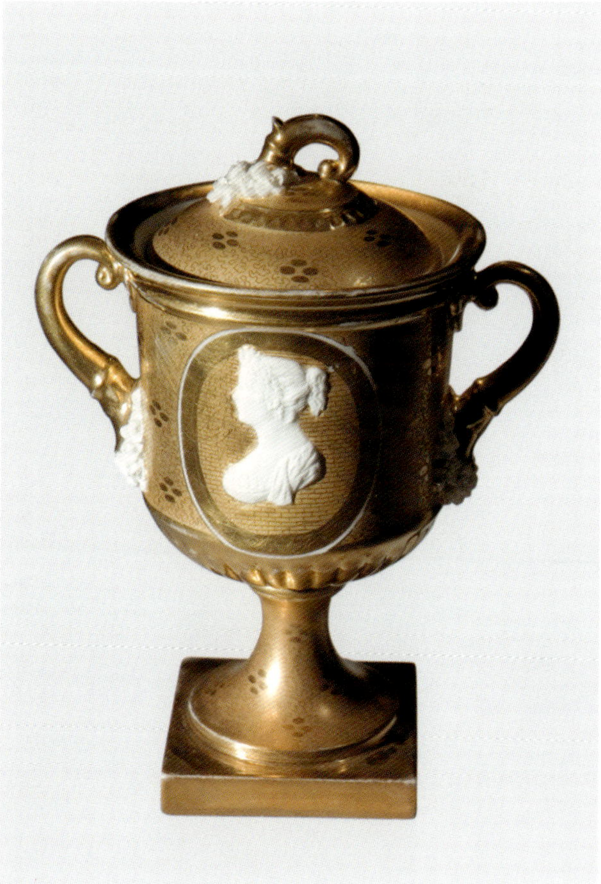

11 and 12. Small vase with lid with the portraits of the Emperor Alexander I, and the Empress Elisabeth Alexeievna (front and back)
Imperial Porcelain Manufacture, 1st quarter of the 19th century
State Ceramics Museum of Kuskovo (Cat. 216)

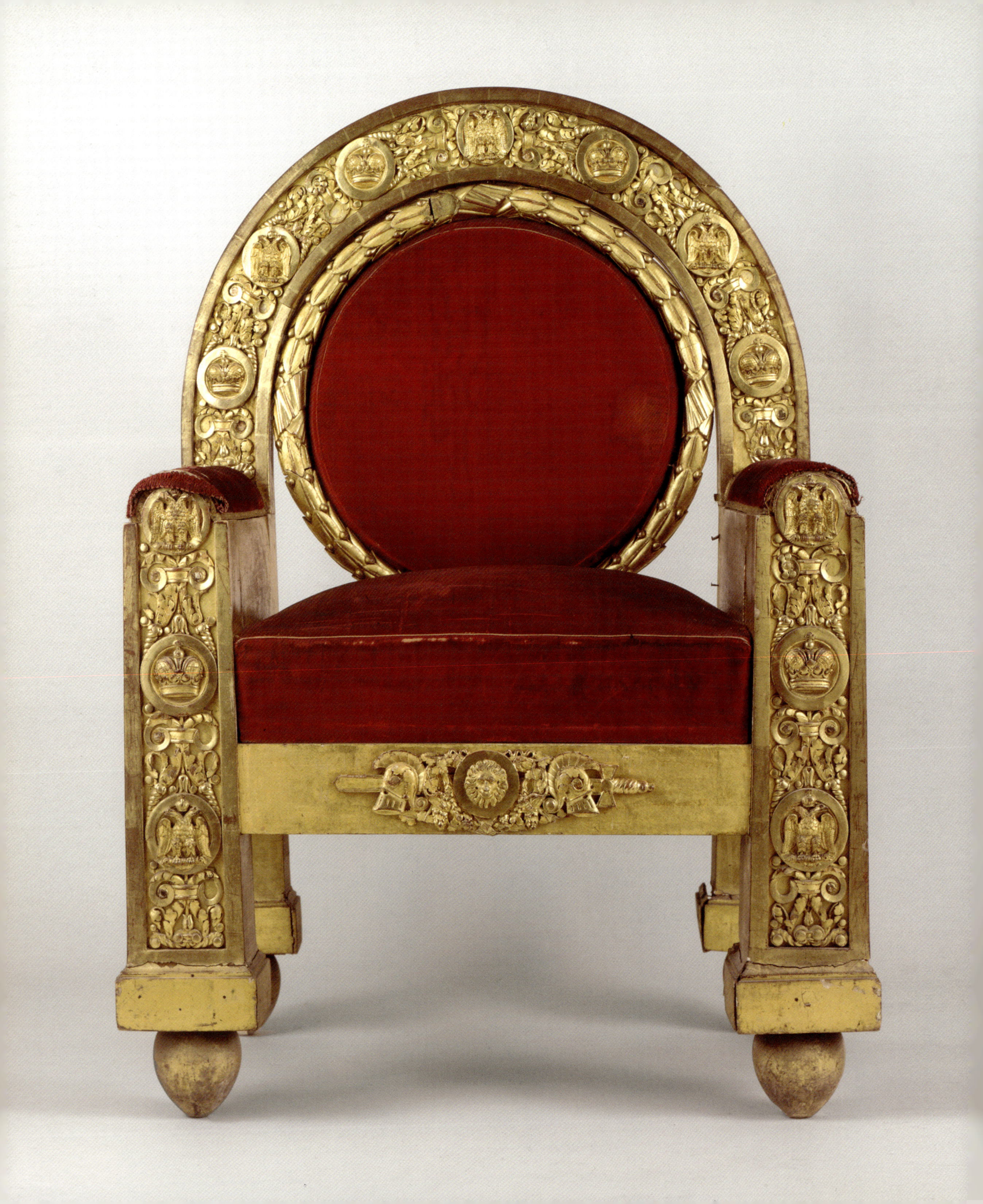

HISTORY OF RUSSIAN FURNITURE

Natalia Ougleva

The art of Russian furniture is a unique source of information, for upon it is superimposed the history and culture of the Russian people. The history of this art now extends back more than four hundred years. For periods in the past, our knowledge of objects which furnished interior spaces is based exclusively on written sources, representations in icons, on coins etc. The oldest pieces preserved to date go back to the 16th century. There are just a few such items in museum collections, and as such they constitute artifacts of great rarity.

The State Historical Museum is the only museum in the world whose collection of furniture reflects all the phases of this form of applied decorative art. It has an exceptional collection of pieces from the 16th century to the middle of the 20th century. Among these pieces, the place of honor goes to a 16th century armchair covered in leather whose architectonics reflect the medieval canons of furniture building. Medieval traditions are present in all the furnishings and in the configuration of habitable space, and both in the residences of the upper levels of Russian society, as well as in those of the lower levels from the 16th to the 17th century. The main principle is expressed in the structural link between the furniture and the walls of the house, excluding the table, benches and chests. Benches were placed along the perimeter of the dwelling, often decorated with cornices—they were built into the walls, the only supports being frontal ones. The place of honor was made up of a little table where icons were displayed. In front stood a table with its bench. The benches sometimes had folding backs and particular care was given to their decoration. They were decorated with sculptures and often painted in various colors. In the same way, the tables were decorated with sculptures, paintings and polychrome and the table trays were covered with decorative compositions which took the place of tablecloths and imitated worked fabrics. The armchairs were the privilege of the Czars and the boyars, or they were reserved for liturgical use—they looked like thrones. The tradition of this kind of organization of domestic interior space, with built-in furniture, proved so lasting that it was maintained by the people until the middle of the 20th century.

The beginning of Peter I's reign (1682-1725) saw radical transformations in interior decoration, resulting from global changes in the Russian way of life. In Russia, an interior style was spontaneously created during this period. Objects conceived in a single decorative tonality appeared in furnishings, produced by European and Russian masters. Traditional banquettes, benches, and chests progressively gave way to armchairs, chairs, sofas, beds and to wardrobes in new shapes. These

1. Emperor Alexander I's throne
Russia, first quarter of the 19th century
The State Historical Museum, Moscow
(Cat. 211)

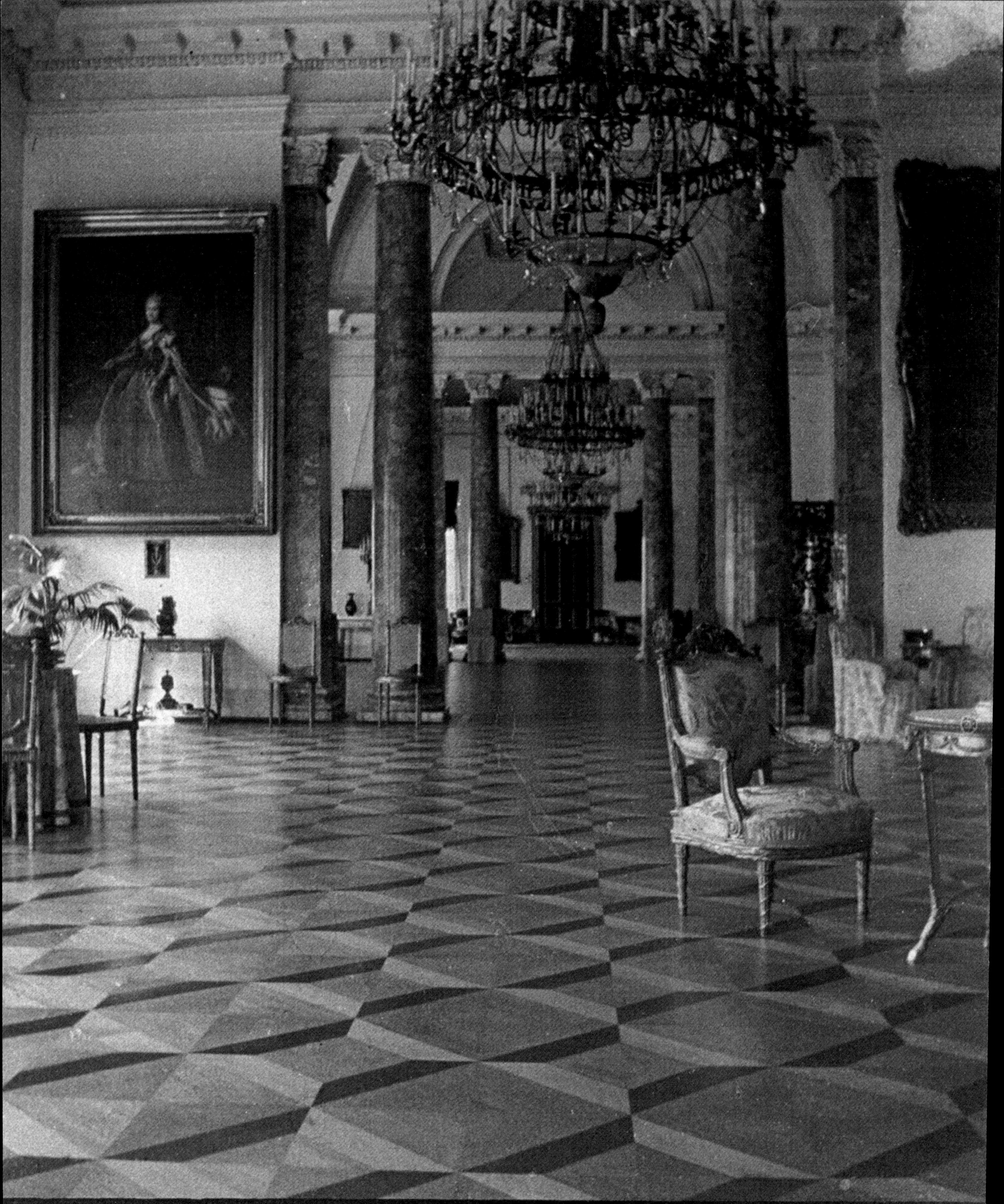

2. *P. Gilliard*
Portrait room and Hemicycle room, Alexander Palace
Tsarskoye Selo, Russia, 1913
22 × 22 cm
Elysée Museum, Lausanne, call number AH XI/1

3. *A. P. Barychnikov*
Inside view of the chamber of the Grand Duke Sergei Alexandrovich
Moscow, 1902
The State Historical Museum, Moscow
(Cat. 558)

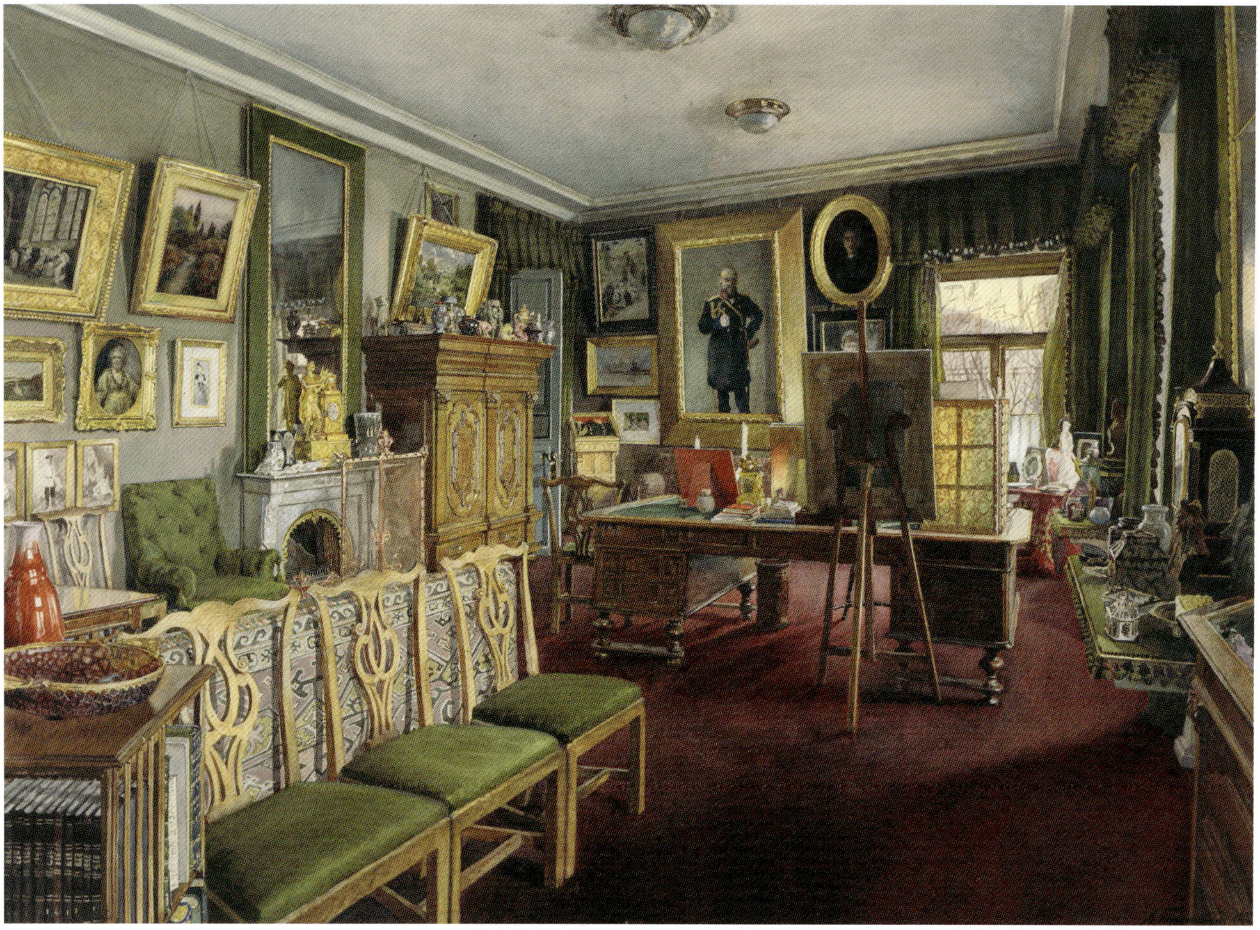

elements were characterized by their comfort and their special decoration. At the same time, mirrors became widespread in dwellings: they were used not only to reflect the images of people but they also had a decorative function.

The baroque during Empress Elizabeth Petrovna's reign (1741-1761), Peter I's daughter, took over from Petrovian baroque. Its qualitative difference took the form of the elaboration of an interior space integrated into an architectural whole, in the spatial interdependence between the object and the style of the environment. The baroque palaces built based on projects by F. B. Rastrelli, S. I. Tchevakinsky, D. V. Oukhtomsky introduced an interior decoration in which gilded sculptures, mirrors and bright lighting accessories were widely used. To make the furniture and to plan the interior design of the palatial residences, St. Petersburg masters were called upon but also master craftsmen who had designed monasteries and estates, as well as Moscow sculptors experienced in the sculpture of iconostasis gilded at several levels. It was at this time also that, influenced by French fashion, rococo furniture which had been introduced for European use by the court of Louis XV began to be used in Russian palaces alongside

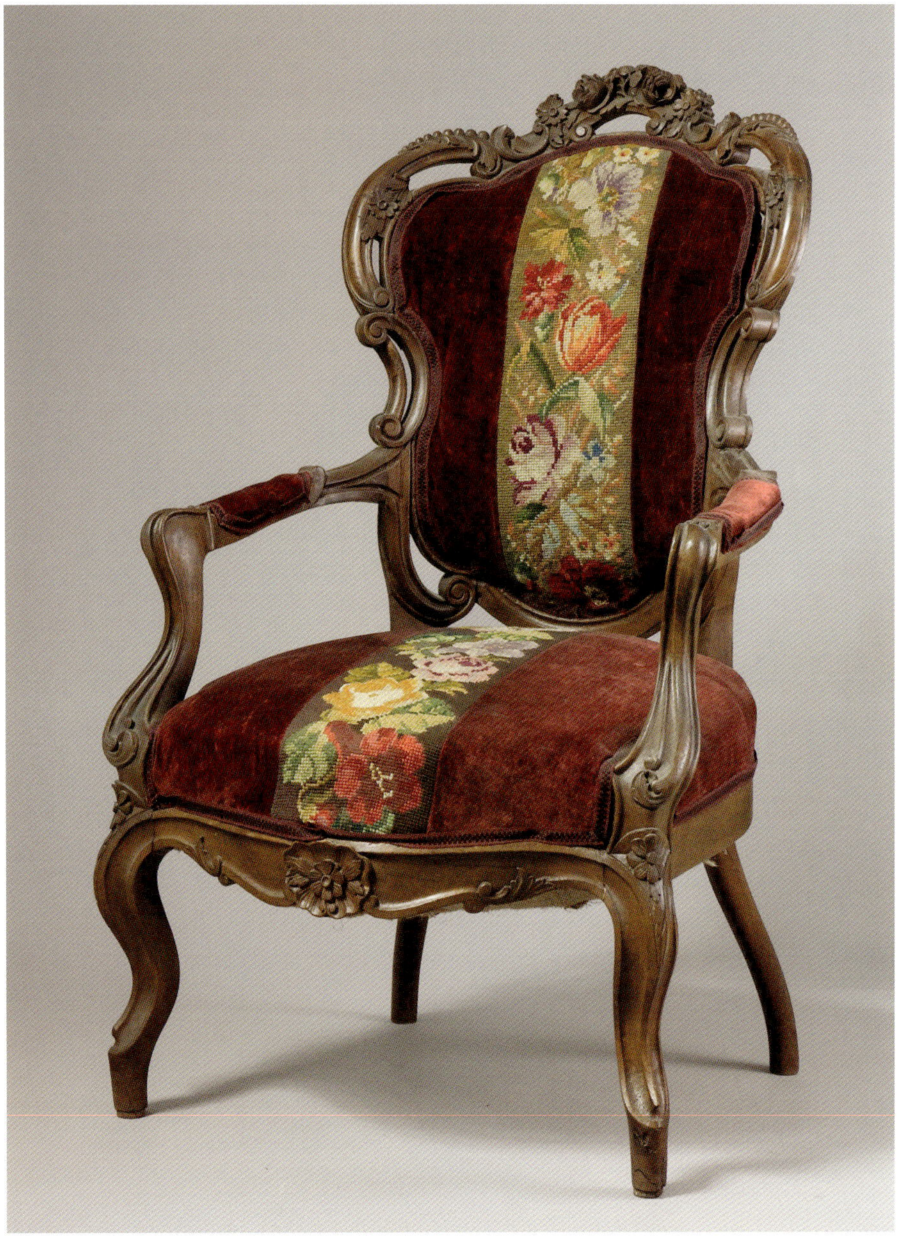

4. Drawing Room Armchair
Russia, Tula government, second third of 19th century
The State Historical Museum, Moscow
(Cat. 214)

the baroque objects. If during Elizabeth's reign, French influence spread into the reception room of the palace, English furniture was nevertheless used to furnish the living quarters. Quality English furniture in rococo style is closely linked to the name of T. Chippendale—his furniture was imported into Russia in large lots. To make furniture, Russian cabinet makers used not only the real models but also referred to the album representing the furniture projects of master craftsmen, published by Chippendale in 1754.

Around 1780, during the reign of the Empress Catherine II (1762-1796), the baroque and rococo styles were replaced by classicism which resurrected the traditions of ancient Greece and Rome. From Moscow to St. Petersburg, an intense activity took place with the goal of reconstructing old buildings and raising new ones which incarnated the principles of the style of the time. The job of the main architects—M. F. Kazakov, V. I. Bajenov, Ch. Cameron, G. Quarenghi, I. E. Starov—was first of all to prepare an architectural project and second, to design the interior spaces, including the furnishings. In their drawings, the famous Russian architects took up the traditions of the original models, all the while however developing a brilliant creative style. Louis XVI's pompous style had a fundamental influence in the development of Russian classicism, as did the austere pure forms of the English architect Robert Adam. His collection of interior decorating projects and furniture-making published in 1776 contributed to the popularizing of the English interpretation of classicism.

"Paul I's furniture" is an emblematic phenomena in the history of the art of Russian furniture. Under this label not only all the furniture made during the period of the Emperor Paul I's reign (1796-1801) is included, but also the interior decoration of the palaces of Pavlovsk and Gatchina. Louis XVI Court style continued to be widely used in the ceremonial rooms, filling them with gilded sculpted furniture produced by Russian masters and by two famous French cabinet-makers, the Jacob brothers. But in spite of the strong French influence, the Russian architects cre-

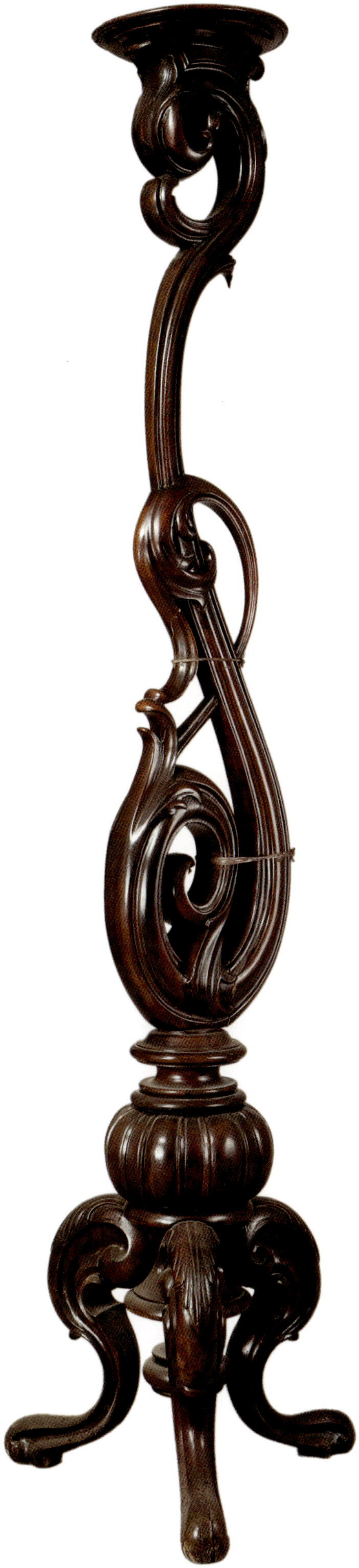

5. Torch Holder
Russia, St. Petersburg, middle of 19th century
The State Historical Museum, Moscow
(Cat. 215)

ated an independent furniture art, with unique pieces, in turning back to the monuments of ancient Greece and Rome. While still following the general trend of European fashion, the Russian masters endeavored to produce furniture with rational forms, more comfortable and democratic in use. This led to research in the field of the graphic structure of legible contours, and in the use of the natural structure of wood for decorative ends. In addition to mahogany, the Russian cabinetmakers at the end of the 18th century used poplar and Karelian birch for the veneer which possessed the textures of voluted veins in contrast to a light background. Such objects, marked by a rational simplicity of form combined with light wood veneer, are classified in the category "Paul's furniture" even if the production survived a decade after the Emperor who had given it his name.

The supremacy of the empire style is linked to the period of Alexander I's reign (1801-1835), considered as the Golden Age of the art of Russian furniture. Eminent architects such as A. N. Voronikhin, A. D. Zakharov, K. I. Rossi, G. Quarenghi, Thomas de Thomon, O. I. Bovet, V. P. Stassov and others worked to create new architectural complexes after the victory in the Patriotic War (War of 1812). Nothing could better correspond to the image of the power of the Russian Empire than the ideological idea of the empire style. It was realized in the art of Russian furniture.

One of the most evocative examples of the representation of Russian furniture in all its magnificence is Emperor Alexander I's throne (ill. 1) which is in the State Historical Museum collection.

6. *P. Gilliard*
Serghievskaya dacha
Peterhof, Russia, 1905
22 × 22 cm
Elysée Museum, Lausanne, call number AH XI/88

It was probably made based on a project of the great Russian architect Auguste de Montferrand for one of the Senate rooms in Moscow in the first quarter of the 19th century. Its composition is distinguished by the monumental character of the form in which can be found echoes of productions of ancient Rome. The combination of red velvet with an over-abundance of gilded and sculpted decorative ornaments using the attributes of war—the representation of eagles—is an artistic process unique to the famous architect. Emperor Alexander I's throne is reminiscent of Napoleon's. It was designed by Napoleon's architects, Ch. Percier and P. Fontaine in the studio where August de Montferrand developed his own aesthetic ideas. It is possible that the Russian architect turned toward the legacy of his masters and that he used this form known for its stylization in which he symbolically expressed the idea of the country's power, the authority of the Emperor, and the victory of the Russian armies in the Patriotic War (War of 1812).

The 19th century could be called the century of "retrospectivism" in the sense that there was a comeback of styles from earlier periods with a new significance, their reinterpretation and their assimilation in the Russian homeland. Alongside the renewal of Gothic artistic inheritance, the development of the second rococo style played a huge role in the art of Russian furniture. It began in the 1830s and by the middle of the 1840s had widely spread into Russian homes.

Alongside gilded furniture in the Louis XV style, the pieces made from the essence of dark woods, in particular walnut, and the upholstered furniture whose structure was almost entirely hidden by padding, became very widespread. Unlike the originals , the examples from the 19th century were distinguished by a great diversity of shapes, as can be seen especially for the chairs. In addition to the armchairs and chairs in fantastic shapes and diverse contours, it became customary to have round or several-sided ottomans for the center of a room, as well as chaises longues in rococo style, duchesses with footrests, a variation of the confidante sofa—a piece of furniture which unites in a single element both sofa and armchairs—and that which was named "a block", a sort of rounded or several-sided divan, placed in the middle of the room, with a raised platform in the middle for the placing of flowers.

The exhibition presents an armchair and a torch holder (which is reminiscent of an occasional table), done in sculpted walnut (ills. 4 and 5)—they come from the State Historical Museum collection. These pieces are representative of the art of Russian furniture during the period of second rococo. In the artistic treatment of the torch holder, one can clearly see the stylistic features which echo the main note of the decoration. In fact, the torch holder has been perceived at first as a decorative work of sculpture, in which the dynamic of the elastic line of the tight volute which rises toward the top is held back by the functional part of the element. Second, it is perceived as an object of common use. The design of the armchair is built on a rhythmic dynamic of equal curves, placed symmetrically on other side of the central vertical. The accent of the internal equilibrium of the decoration is furnished by an ornamental band of hand-

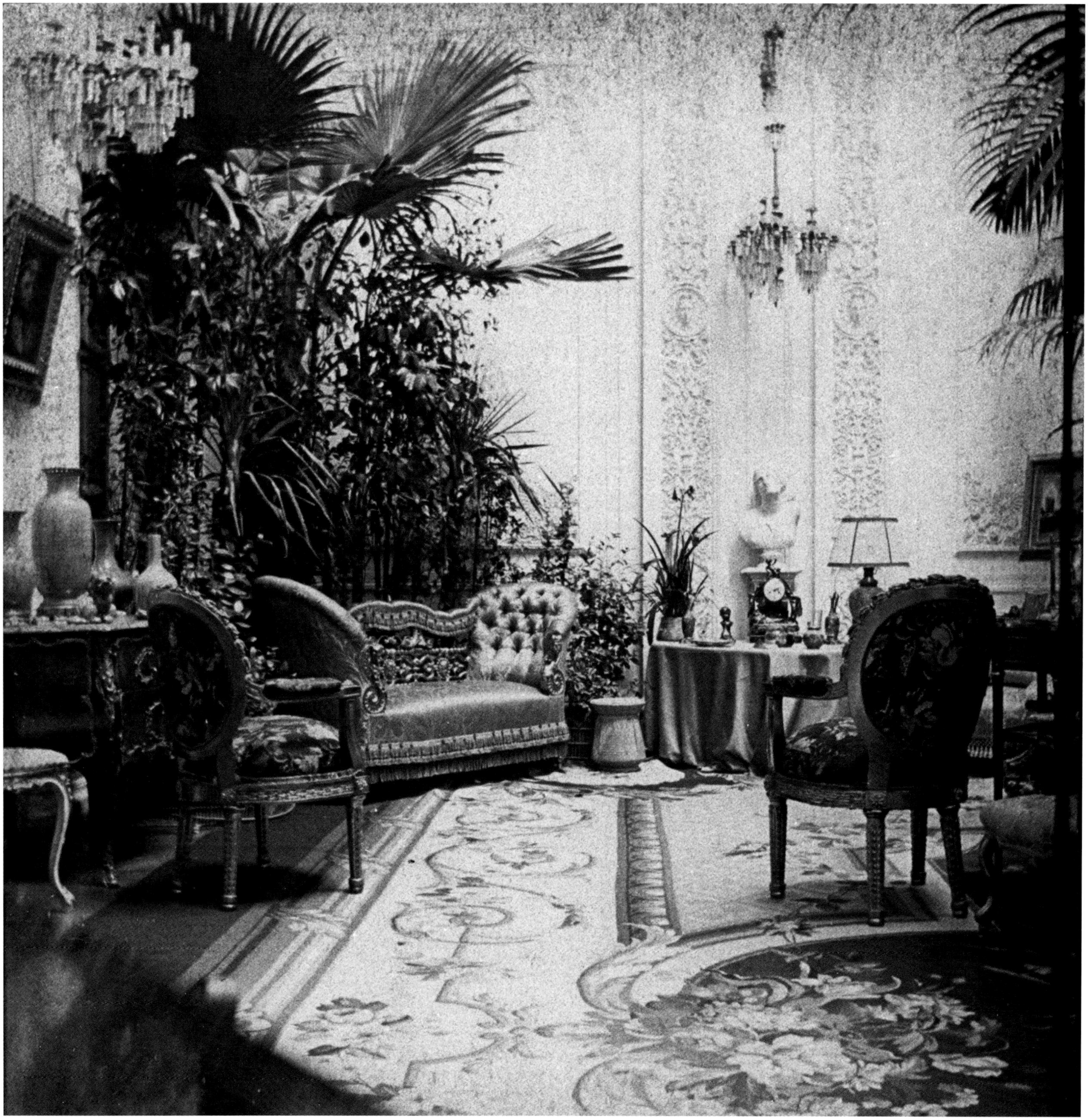

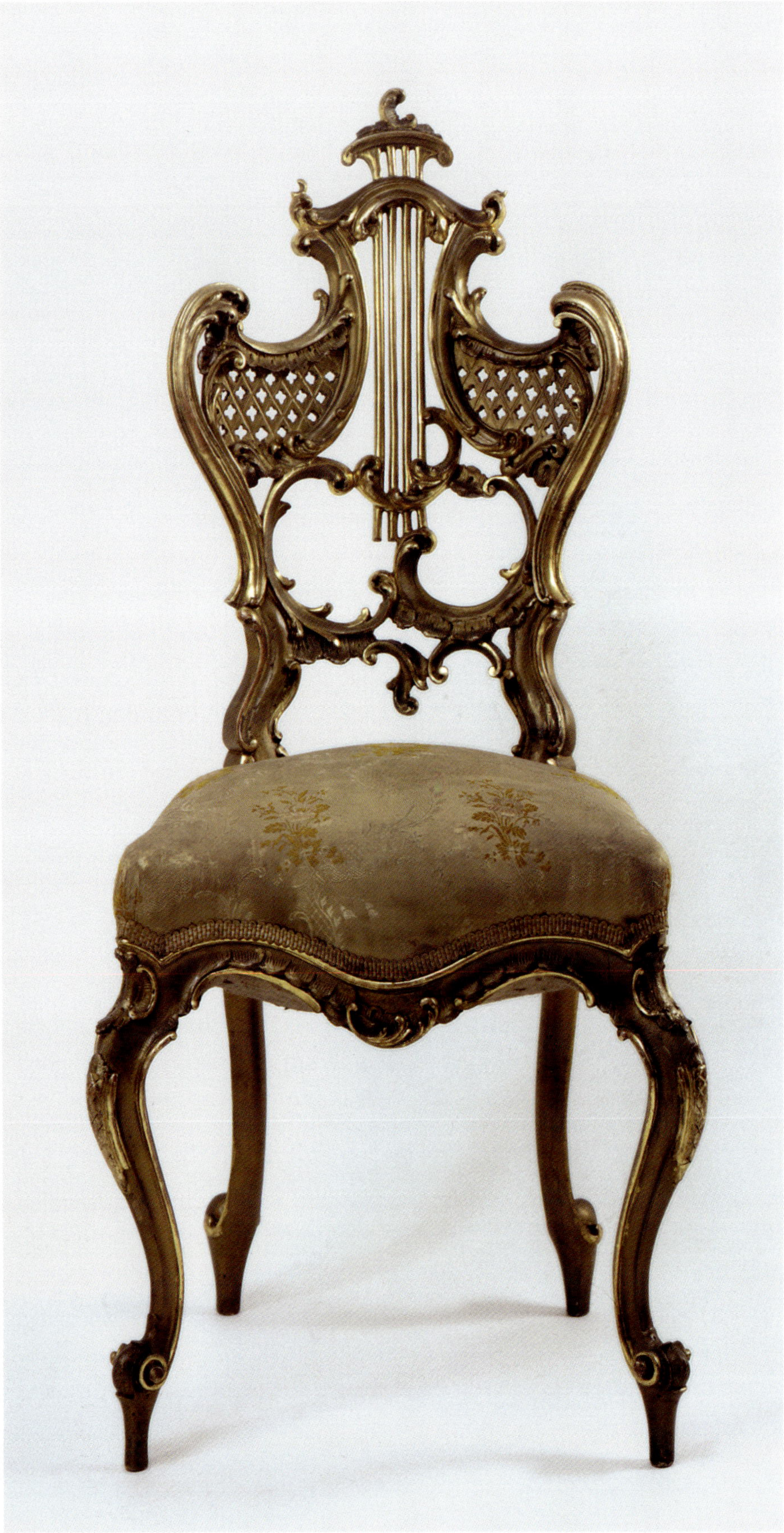

made embroidery which destabilizes the organic rococo structure. In fact, the armchair and all the furniture of the drawing room of which this piece is a part were made in the middle of the 19th century and were part of the furnishings of the home of the general of the Tula government. In 1870, this furniture was sold to a merchant and transported to Yaroslav where its decorative composition was completed by embroidery of the latest fashion.

The gilded chair (ill. 7) which was part of a drawing room furniture set is also a piece in the rococo style—it comes from the State Historical Museum collection. It goes back to the third period of the renaissance of this artistic trend, to the end of the 19th-beginning of the 20th century. The manner of treatment shows a great freedom in the interpretation of already known forms in opting for an elegant sculpted composition in the decoration at the back. The use of gilt in an innovative spirit to reinforce decorative expression is illustrated here by two surface techniques: matt and glossy.

The stylization of baroque forms is an aesthetic trend which was current in the framework of "retrospectivism" in the second half of the 19th century. This is the case with an element of the "silver drawing room" group presented in the exhibition, which comes from the State Historical Museum—it illustrates the principles of composition unique to this artistic phenomena. Here the rocaille lines of the contour of objects are combined with neo-classical supports. However, the element of the decoration—a sculpted representation of a reclining putto—finds its prototype in the "negresco"

7. Drawing room chair
Russia, St. Petersburg (?), end of 19th- beginning of 20th centuries
The State Historical Museum, Moscow
(Cat. 471)

8. Chair from the "Silver Drawing Room" set
Moscow, last quarter of 19th century
The State Historical Museum, Moscow
(Cat. 569)

9. Small table from the "Silver Drawing Room" set
Moscow, last quarter of the 19th century
The State Historical Museum, Moscow
(Cat. 568)

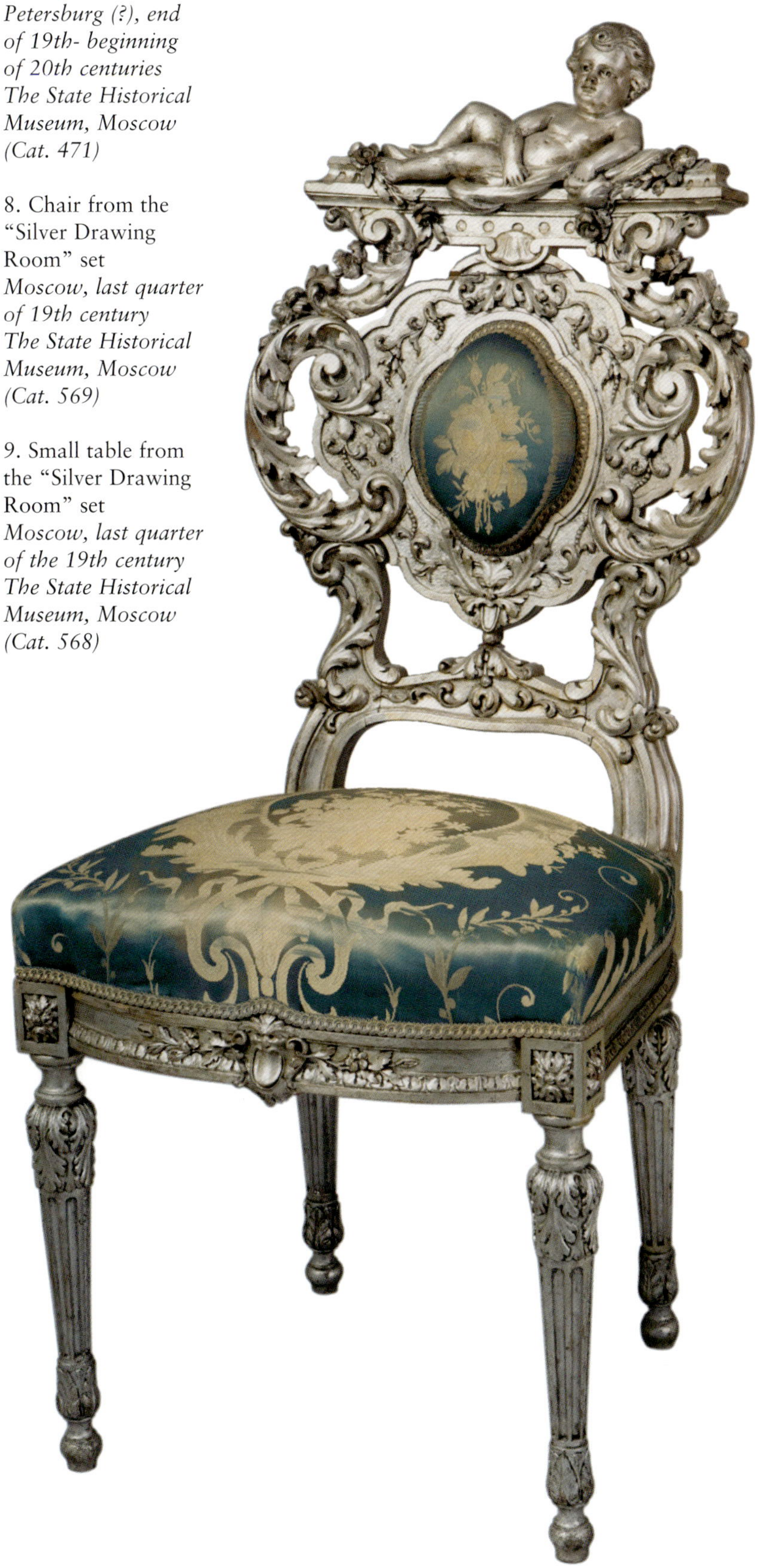

armchair by Andrea Brustolone, made in Italy during the baroque period. The "silver drawing room" (ills. 8 and 9) was probably produced in the Schmitt manufacture of Muscovite furniture—he made expensive and fashionable furniture which was distinguished by the high quality of its production.

The future and the evolution of national romanticism in the art of furniture refers to the period of "retrospectivism." The notion of national style, which takes its source from the second half of the 18th century, developed very clearly in the second half of the 19th century and beginning of the 20th. Here, the whole range of currents of aesthetic thought is represented: from the copying of the monuments of Old Russia and the borrow-

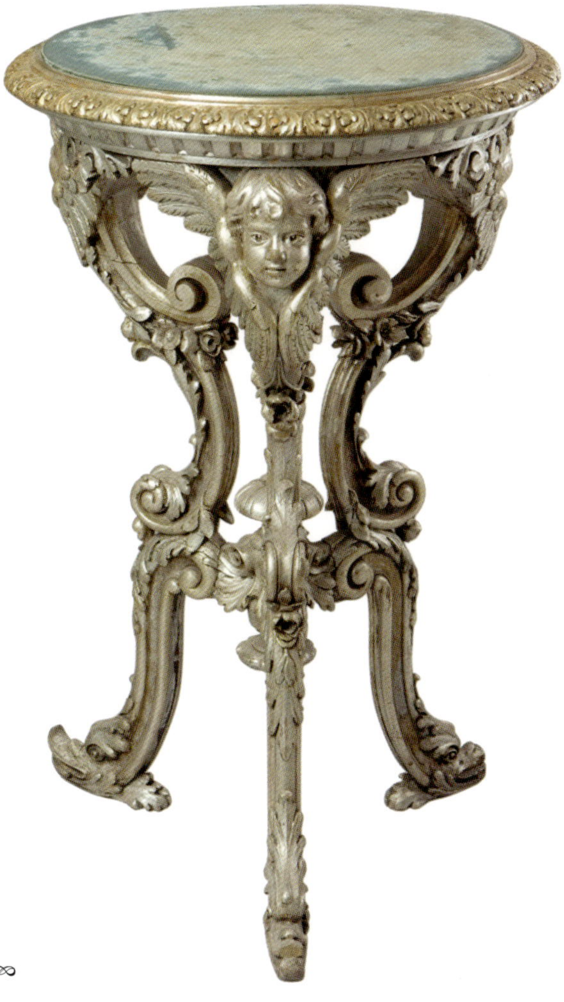

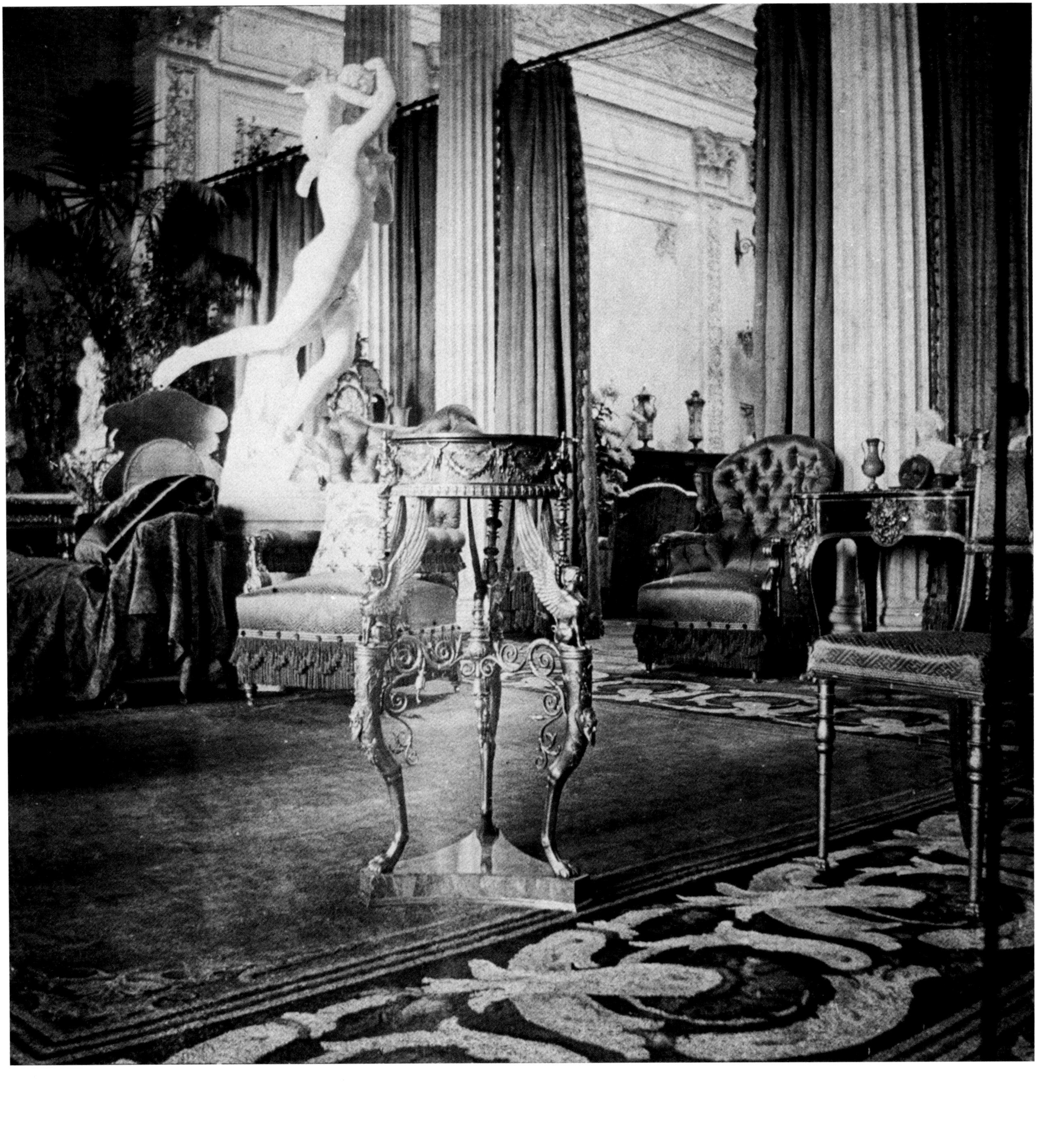

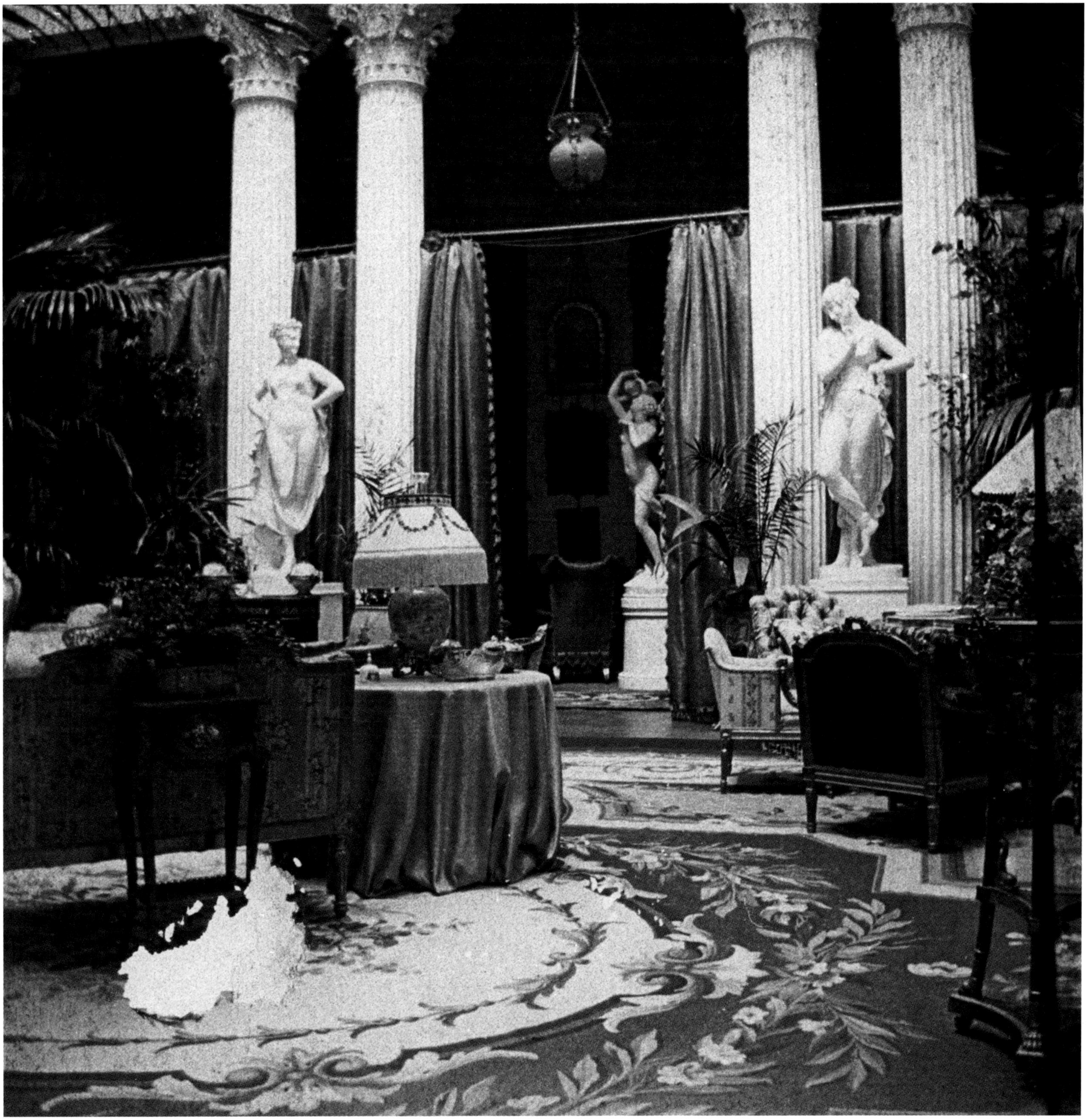

Pages 144-145
10. *P. Gilliard*
Serghievskaya dacha
Peterhof, Russia, 1905
22 × 22 cm
Elysée Museum, Lausanne, call number AH XI/56

11. *P. Gilliard*
Serghievskaya dacha
Peterhof, Russia, 1905
22 × 22 cm
Elysée Museum, Lausanne, call number AH XI/40

12. Chair
Russia, second half of 19th century
The State Historical Museum, Moscow
(Cat. 241)

ings from Western European Middle Ages art to original artistic creations which resulted in a philosophical interpretation unique to Russia. Among the well-known artists who developed designs of furniture in the Russian style N. F. Nabokov, I. A. Monighetti, V. P. Choutov (who, in 1870, created the famous armchair "The bow, the axe, the gauntlets") and V. M. and A. M. Vanetsov can all be mentioned. Also included among them was E. D. Polenova who directed the Abramtsevo furniture workshop and whose work was honored with a gold medal in 1900 during the Paris Universal Exhibition. The pieces which came from the Talachkino furniture workshop were also honored at the same exhibition: their creators were M. K. Tenichev, S. V. Maliutin, A. P. Zinoviev, N. K. Roerich and V. V. Beketov. Later, furniture in the Russian style was very sought after not only in Russia but also in Europe.

The chair presented in the exhibition (ill. 12) with the bronze Cheremetiev family coat of arms on the back is an example of the Russian style from the second half of the 19th century—it comes from the State Historical Museum. It was inspired by the stylized decorative ornamentation of Old Russia with its syncretic composition made of tracery in the Celtic style, enriched by Byzantine stylistic. The impression communicated of the whole is of an extraordinary sumptuousness and of a striking archaic decoration. Centered on the family arms, which make up the semantic center of the composition of the design on the back, the idea is to perpetuate and exhibit the history of the Chermetiev dynasty, relatives to the Romanovs, and who were the first in Russia to receive the title of count from Peter the Great.

The furniture in "modern style" appeared in Russia at the beginning of the 20th century and spread first to the interiors of the palaces and townhouses of the court aristocracy and of the business elite. The benchmarks of this style were the Empress Alexandra Feodorovna's "Maple Salon" and Nicholas II's ceremonial chamber in the Alexander palace. Their design was carried out based on the project of the Court architect R. F. Melzer. Not less important in this new artistic trend were the pieces created by the architect F. O. Chekhtel. He designed a series of buildings with furnishings for their interior space, among which the famous Muscovite townhouses of S. P. Riabuchinsky and A. I. Derojinsky. As in European art, in Russian "modern art" two main currents existed: the French "floral style" and the "modern constructivist."

The development of modern art and of the Russian style was interrupted by the First World War. Then the Revolution and the changes in Russia's political organization brought modifications to later evolution in general and to the art of furniture in particular.

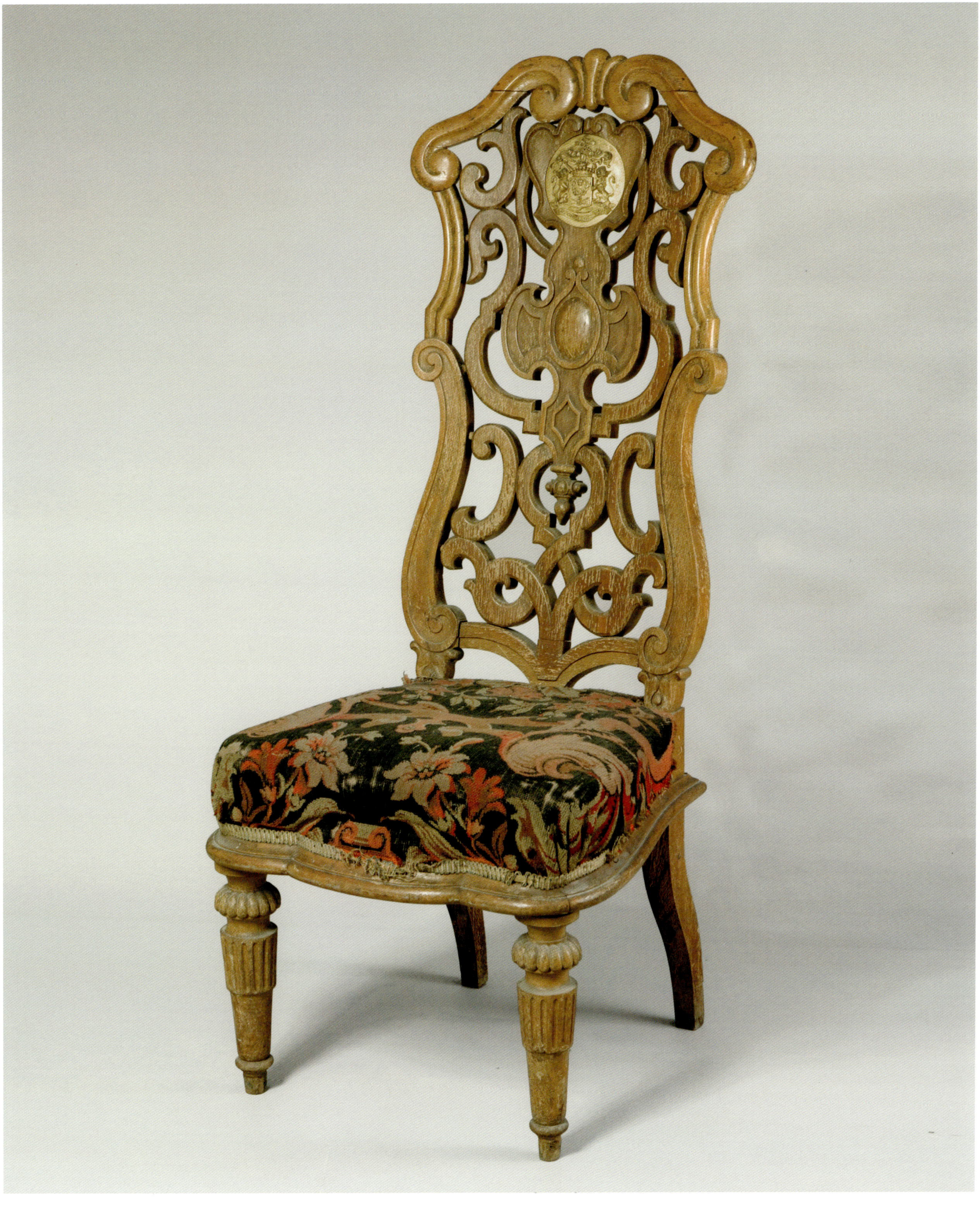

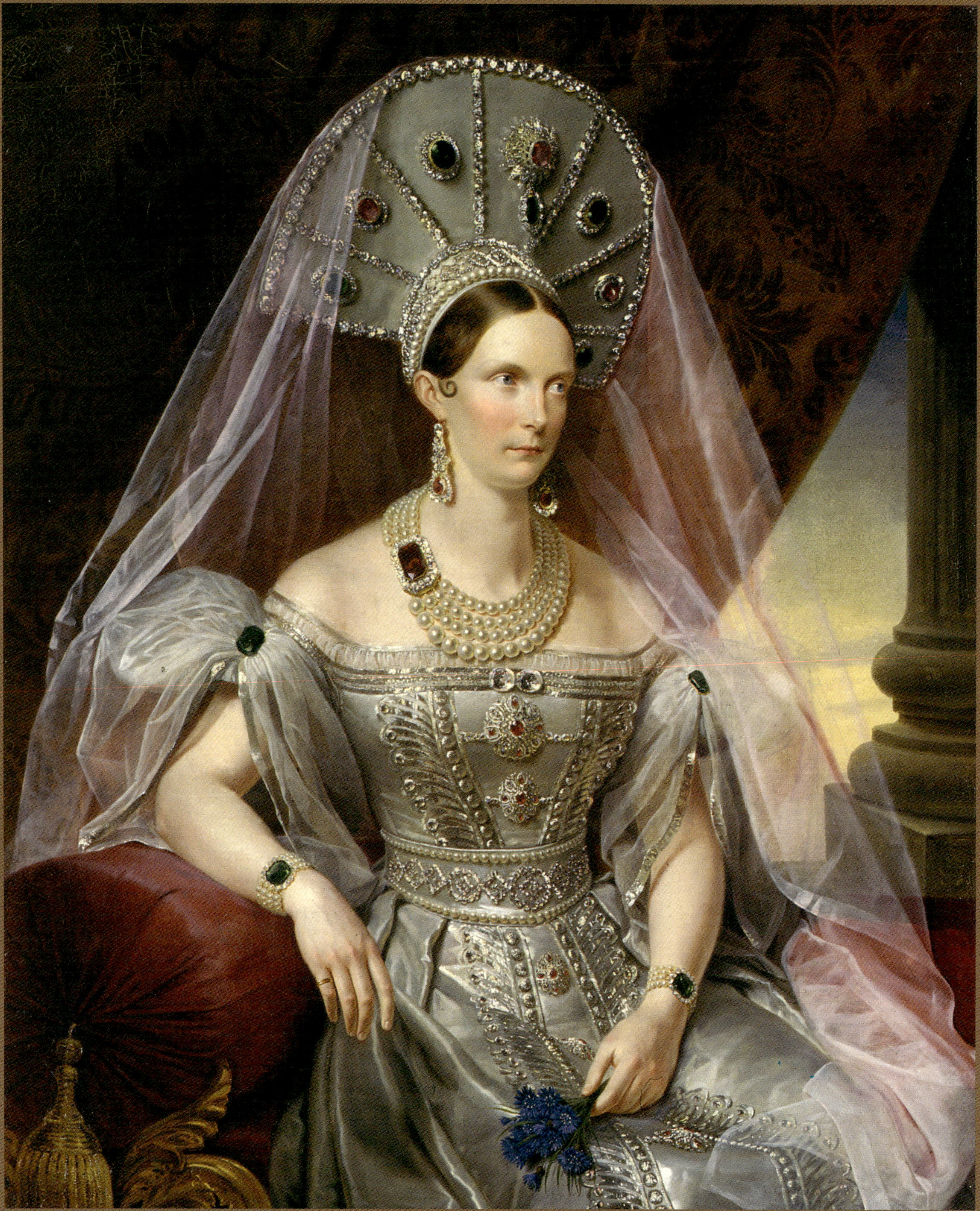

RUSSIAN JEWELRY
& IMPERIALS
COMMANDS

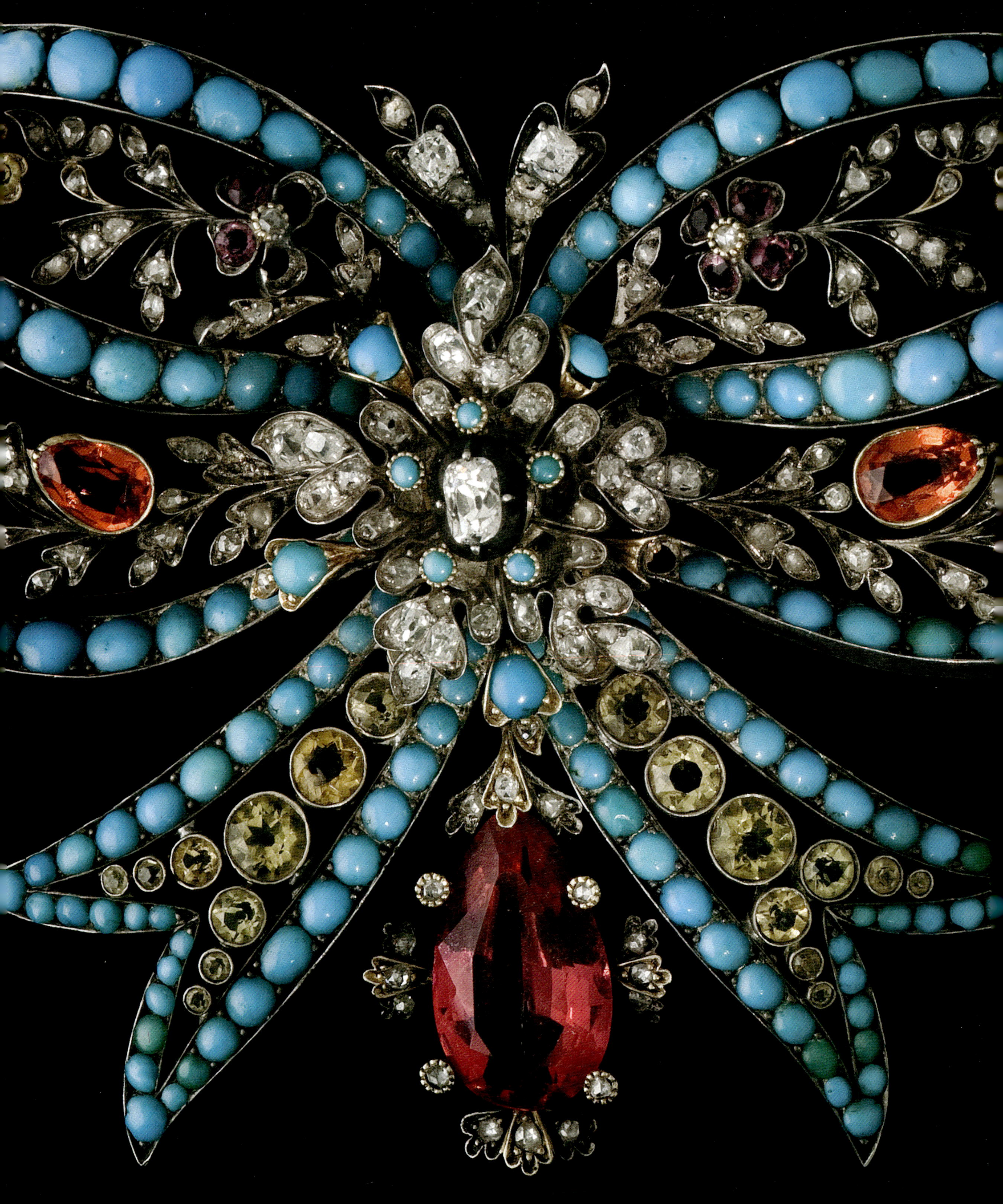

RUSSIAN JEWELRY FROM THE 18TH TO THE BEGINNING OF THE 20TH CENTURY

Tatiana Sizova

Page 148
F. Krüger
Portrait of the Empress Alexandra Feodorovna (1798-1860)
Russia, Saint-Petersburg, after 1836
The State Historical Museum, Moscow
(Cat. 159)

Brooch
Middle of 19th century
The State Historical Museum, Moscow
(Cat. 304)
Detail

As always and as everywhere in the world, the art of gold- and silverwork in Russia is indissolubly linked to man's eternal desire to make himself attractive, to have his external appearance and his spiritual world exist in harmony.

Considered as a special branch of gold- and silverwork but also as an important constitutive element of clothing, jewelry provides us with information on a certain number of features particular to aesthetic conceptions of the Russian society from the 18th to the beginning of the 20th century.

The national costume as it developed in the 17th century in Old Russia revealed no clearly expressed social differences. The type of clothing worn was above all determined by practical considerations and by profoundly deep-rooted traditions. The many images that one can see in the icons, on frescos, not to mention miniatures, are reasonably reliable sources illustrating the history of Russian clothing. Contrary to European fashion at the same time, the clothing of the Russians, both for men and women and whether it was daily wear or festive clothing, was characterized by the simplicity of the cut which entirely covered the body leaving nothing uncovered. The peasant's clothing and the Czarina's, cut in the same fashion, differed only in the material in which it was sewn.

The ornaments were in large measure an integral part of the dress. First of all there were a multitude of precious buttons of a great variety of sizes (from the small pearl to the pigeon egg), as well as all sorts of ornaments sewn with gold and silver, including precious stones, pearls, enamels, and which were attached to the collar, to the sleeves, to the bottom of the outfit and to the headdresses.

The favorite jewels of the men and women of the 17th century were the pendant earrings and the chains made of precious metals to which one attached a great variety of objects: it could as well be a ceremonial pectoral cross with painted enamel and precious stones, as a travel flask. Particularly popular were rings of all sorts which were often made based on examples borrowed from Western Europe or from the Orient and were decorated with round polished uncut precious stones or had engraved images on them, used as seal-rings.

The reforms that Peter I put into place at the beginning of the 18th century radically and quickly transformed the Russian way of life, especially for the dominant class. It was specifically during Peter's epoch that Russia saw itself provided with an essential and unique reference for its future development: Europe. The onset of new behavior in private life and new forms of social life

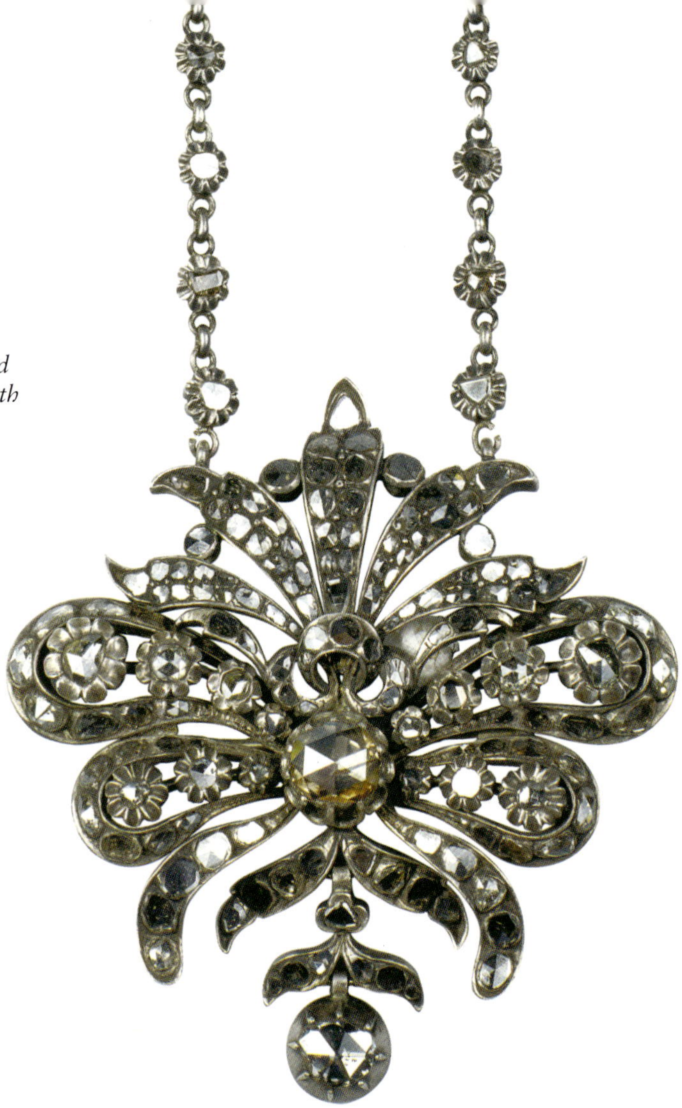

1. Pendant brooch
Russia, second half of the 18th century
The State Historical Museum, Moscow
(Cat. 295)

resulted in the need to create objects for personal use which up until then Russia had known little about, to create other kinds of jewelry to complete outfits which had never been seen before, having been inspired by European fashion. Bracelets richly decorated with enamel appeared, sprig-like brooches to be pinned to the bodice, special jewelry in complicated shapes to put in one's hair. The bare neck required heavy pendant necklaces in the shape of knots on small chains (ill. 1).

The main feature of this sort of ornament consisted of large diamonds inserted into deep cavities which deprived them of a part of their original brilliance. The appearance of the first stone cutting workshops during the reign of Peter I where stonecutters were skillful in enhancing the natural beauty of colored stones was linked among other things to the new fashions, the desire to brighten up one's clothing by very colorful and sparkling accessories.

The Imperial Court and, in its wake the Russian aristocracy and all the nobility, began to dress in clothing that was most often imported, ordering their jewelry from gold- and silversmiths who had been invited to come work in the country or from craftsmen of foreign origin (most often Finnish and Swedish) who had become, by the force of historical events, subjects of the Russian empire. These artists, who had not been subject to the constraints of the aesthetic tradition determining the way of making shapes and types of Russian jewelry, elaborated evocative pieces of quality in the late Baroque style and in the early Rococo style with that gracious allure and ornamental refinement which are unique to it. It often happened for example that gold earrings decorated with precious stones made in the first third of the 18th century but based on a model which had been popular originally in the 17th century, would take on such a complex form and design that they could be considered as illustrating a perfectly new type of women's jewelry. Solid, with many pendants, colored stones and pearls, the jewelry of this epoch nonetheless harkens back to Oriental motifs (Turks and Persians; ill. 2).

The second half of the 18th century was one of the pinnacles of the art of Russian gold and silver work. The pieces from these decades reflect a keen interest for the sparkling of diamonds which,

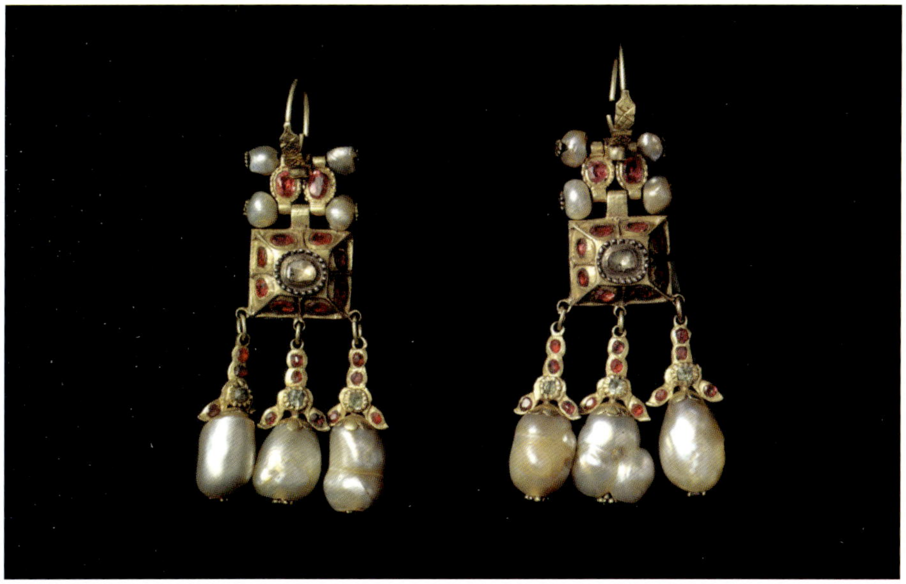

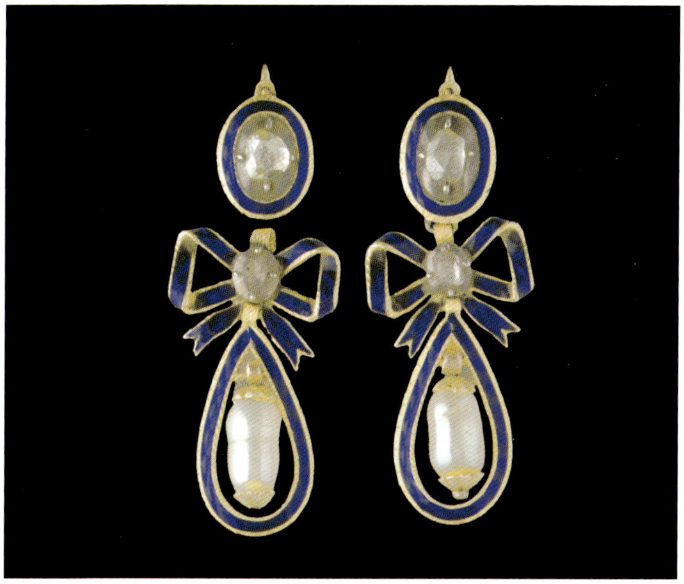

2. Pair of earrings
Russia, 18th century
The State Historical Museum, Moscow
(Cat. 297)

3. Pair of earrings
Western Europe, end of 18th-first quarter of 19th centuries
The State Historical Museum, Moscow
(Cat. 305)

4. Comb
France, Paris, 1798-1809
The State Historical Museum, Moscow
(Cat. 299)

to prevent their changing color, were mounted in silver and which were used to make earrings, bracelets and brooches.

The array of semi-precious stones used to create jewelry was greatly enlarged in the 19th century. Polychrome enamels were abundantly used, and jewelry makers turned toward materials as evocative as amber and ivory. At the beginning of the century, a value was set on restraint and elegance of form, which corresponded perfectly to the Empire style. The knotted earrings, in gold with diamonds, dark blue enamel and oval pearls arranged vertically according to a technique called "tongues", in other words, the jewels strung onto a stem, the bottom half of which was fixed, gives a good idea of the nature of the jewelry of that epoch (ill. 3).

The reference, for the gold and silversmiths and jewelers of the capital, were the precious jewels made in France, very widespread at Court. The Parisian comb from the beginning of the 19th century can only incite our admiration by the art with which it was made, the refinement with which mosaics and river pearls have been associated (ill. 4). Such objects served as examples for putting into effect a similar production in the Moscow and St. Petersburg workshops.

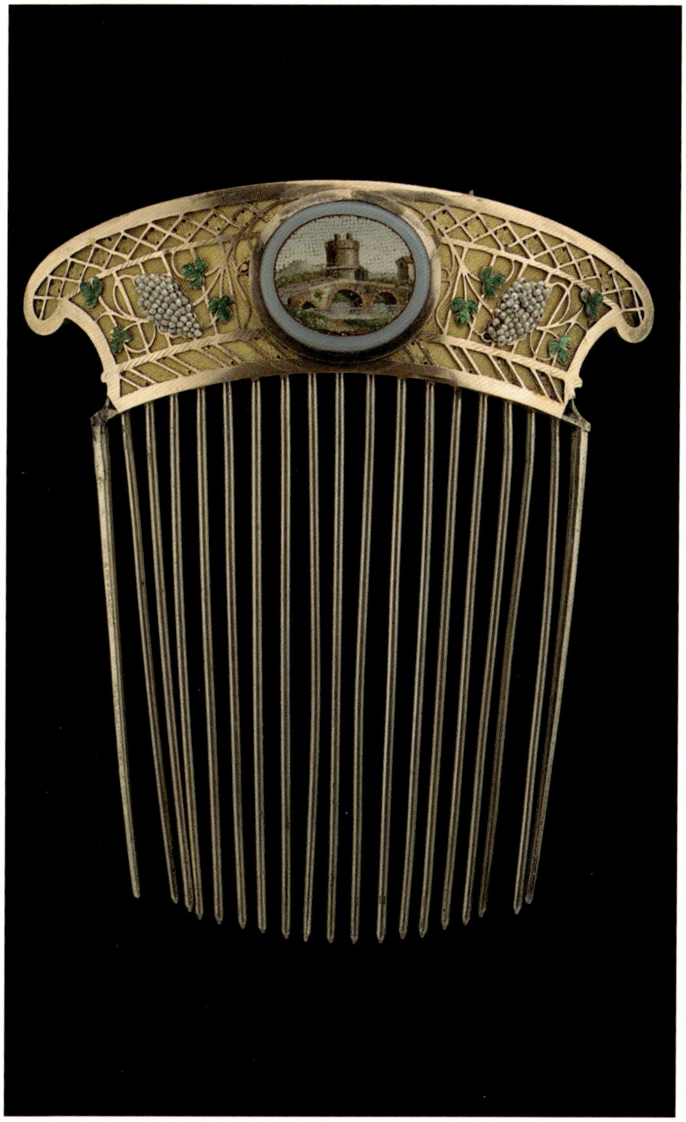

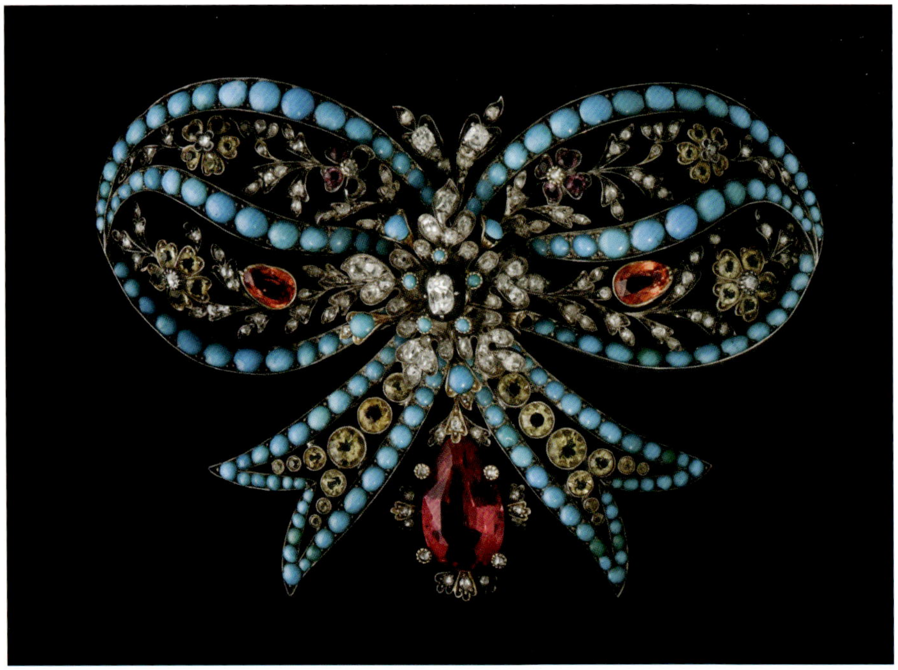

5. Brooch
Middle of 19th century
The State Historical Museum, Moscow
(Cat. 304)

6. Bracelet
Russia, middle of the 19th century
The State Historical Museum, Moscow
(Cat. 296)

7. *I. D. Tchitchelev (?)*
Cuff bracelet
Russia, Moscow, 1860s
The State Historical Museum, Moscow
(Cat. 301)

The 19th century is famous for the diversity of its styles, styles which in the field of the creation of jewelry co-existed throughout the entire century. The knotted brooch with a pendant (ill. 5) reveals an obvious recourse to the 18th century style with its exacerbated decorative tendency, its taste for associating turquoise, diamonds and precious stones in red tones. Turquoise, diamonds and rubies mounted in gold decorated the handle of the cane having belonged, if one can believe the legend, to the Empress Catherine II. It is possible that such objects inspired the 19th century masters in the conception of their masterpieces. By the originality of its appearance, its brilliant association with deep blue, red and green precious stones, the solid bracelet made of stones from the Ural in saturated colors and with its bands of dull black enamel (ill. 6) is tremendously impressive. One can see similar pieces of jewelry in the many portraits of Russian beauties of the mid-19th century.

In the 1860s, one of the best Moscow goldsmiths, I. D. Chichelev, made a wrist bracelet in a class of its own: a model of taste, of refinement and of technical perfection. The pieces made by this master enjoyed extraordinary popularity and his contemporaries held him in great esteem. I. D. Chichelev's jewelry workshop, founded in 1815, and which continued to be active until 1916, was one of the most famous of the former capital. His gold jewels with diamonds, precious stones, pearls and enamel were considered worthy of the highest awards during exhibitions in London, Paris, Vienna, Philadelphia, Moscow and St. Petersburg. As a reward for his particularly remarkable successes, the goldsmith received the title of appointed supplier to the Imperial Court of Russia. He was also the appointed supplier to

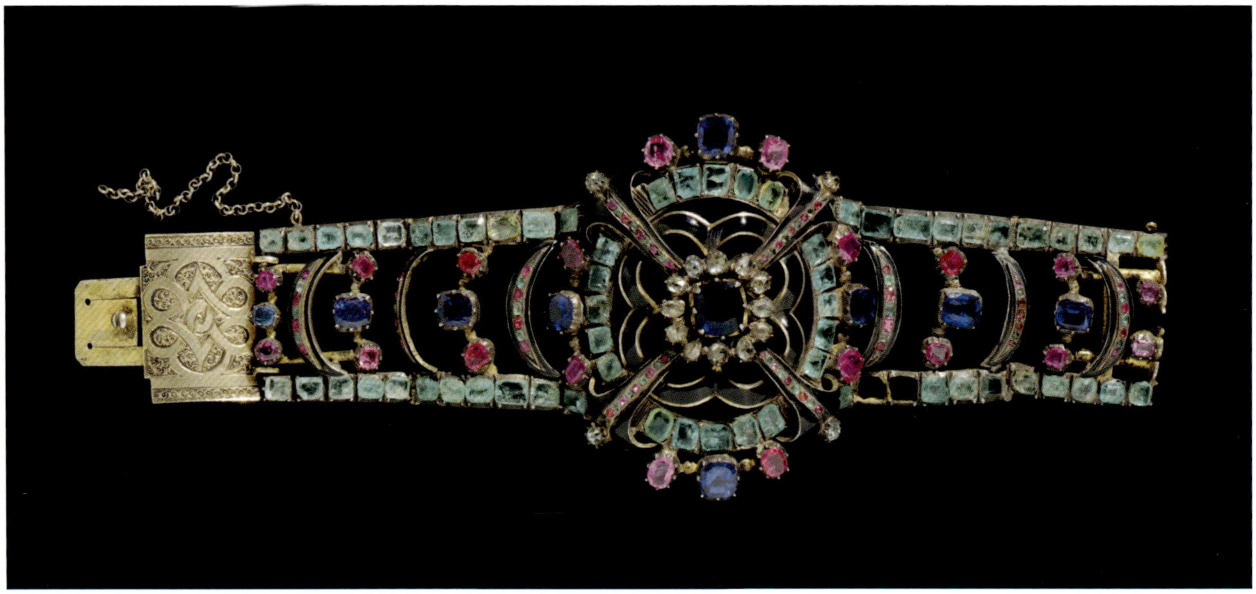

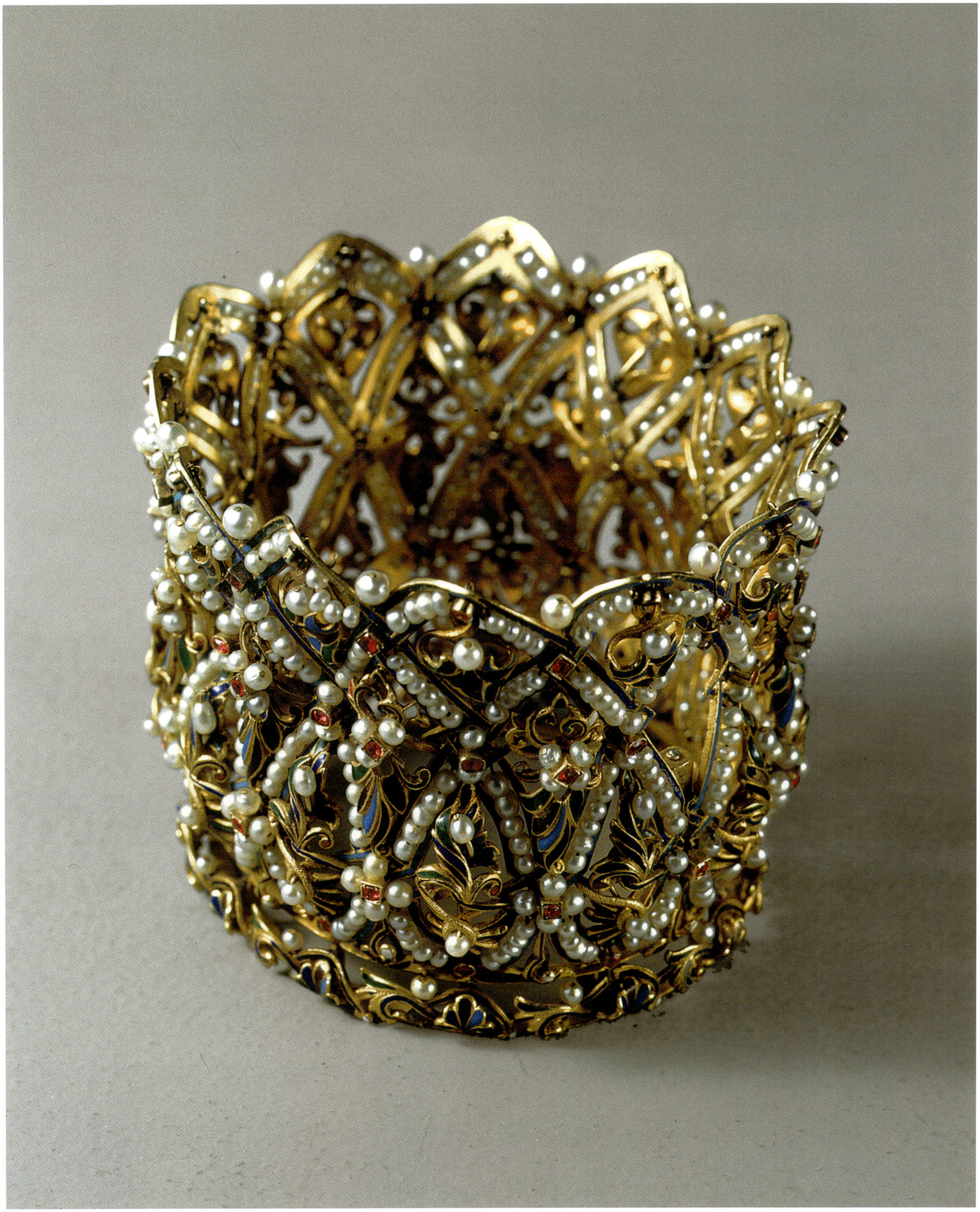

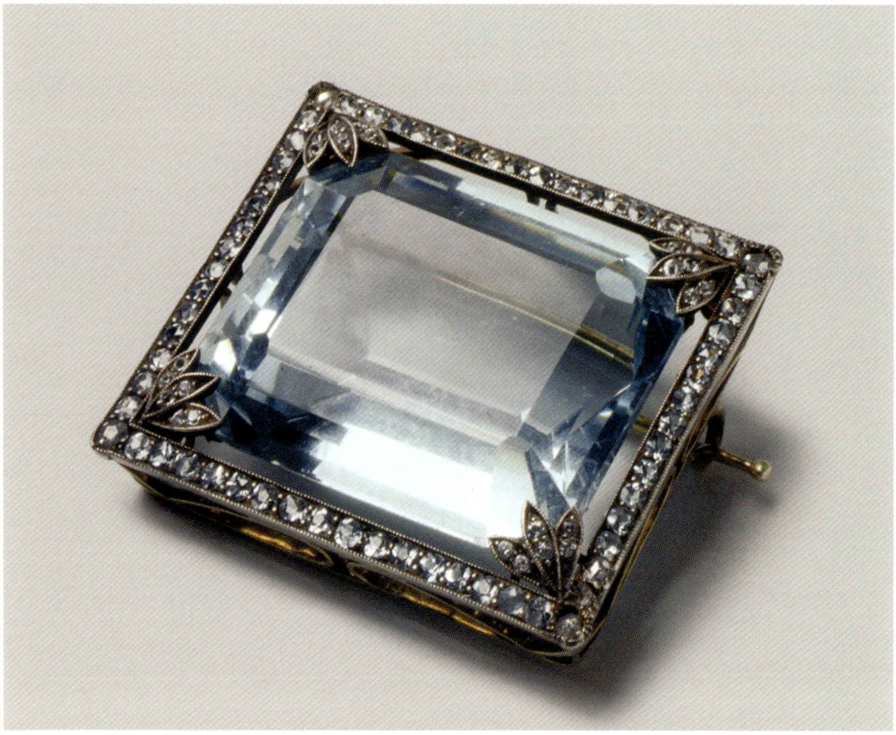

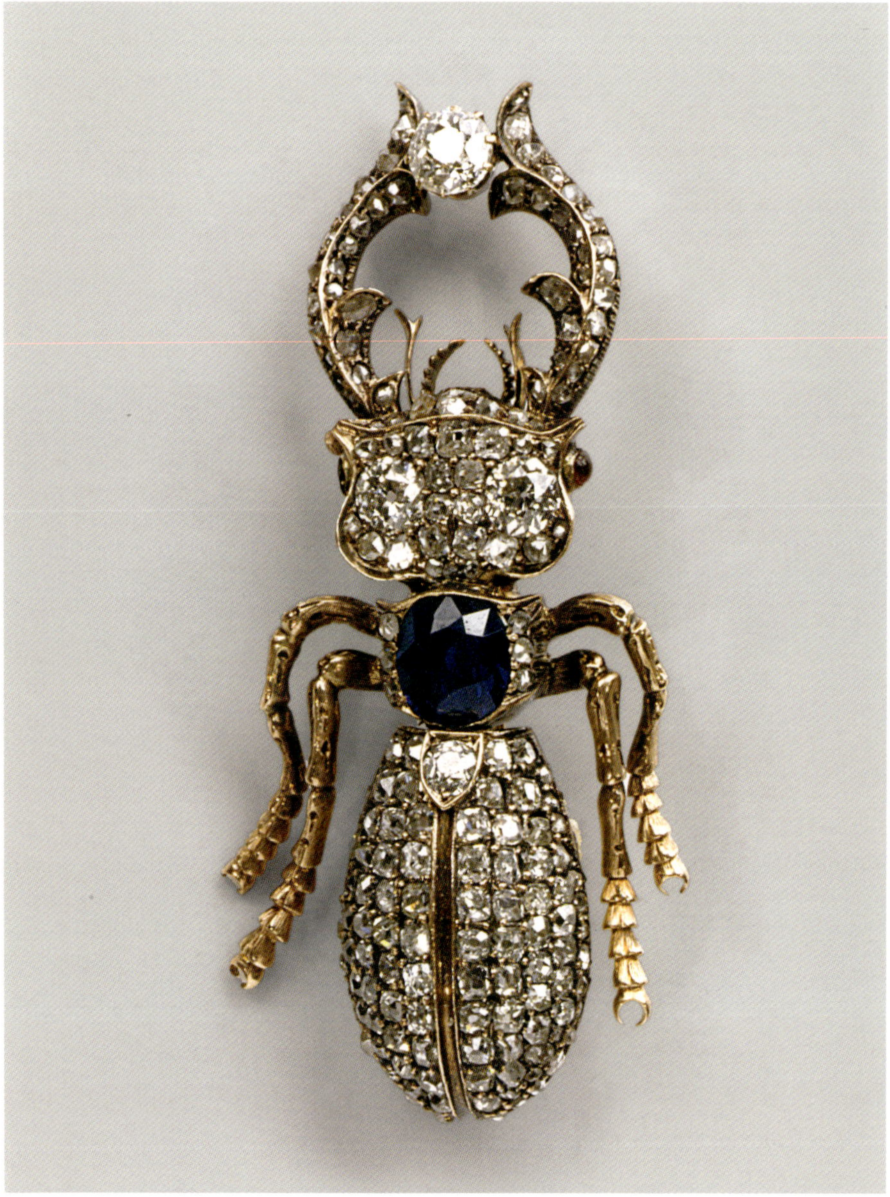

the King of Italy Victor-Emmanuel and to the Emperor of Austria Franz-Josef. Unfortunately, the works of this brilliant and unequalled goldsmith are extremely rare, even in the greatest museums. In Moscow, the only jewels possessing the master's stamp which have been preserved are in the collection of the precious metals department of the State Historical Museum (in addition to the cuff bracelet, the collection also has a brooch-medallion.) The bracelet was apparently one of the elements of a costume, part of which consisted of a blouse in what is called the "Russian style" with large floating sleeves held tight by two bracelets forming a pair which were perhaps shown for the first time at the 1882 exhibition in Moscow (ill. 7).

The jewelry made by the most famous firms supplying the Imperial Court, such as "Sazikov", "Khlebnikov", "Ovchinnikov", "Fabergé", "Bolin" and others, was not just in great demand within the country. Orders arrived from abroad. At the same time, pieces by French or English creators could also be found in the shops belonging to those same firms and were also popular with Russian purchasers. Thus the French-made pendant brooch, in the shape of a woman-butterfly was sold by a shop belonging to the Fabergé firm, as bears witness the mark appearing on the packaging (ill. 11).

The jewelry of the second half of the 19th century and beginning of the 20th well illustrates the stylistic complexity of the epoch and the rapidly changing tastes and fashions. As is the case for the other forms of applied art, the jewelry created at this time reflects the inclination of the artists for new original shapes and designs. What is strik-

8. *Carl Fabergé.*
Workmaster:
Albert Holmström
Brooch
Russia, St. Petersburg, 1908-1917
The State Historical Museum, Moscow
(Cat. 293)

9. *Master Goldsmith: Henri Lassas*
"Scarab" brooch
Russia, St. Petersburg, last quarter of 19th century
The State Historical Museum, Moscow
(Cat. 300)

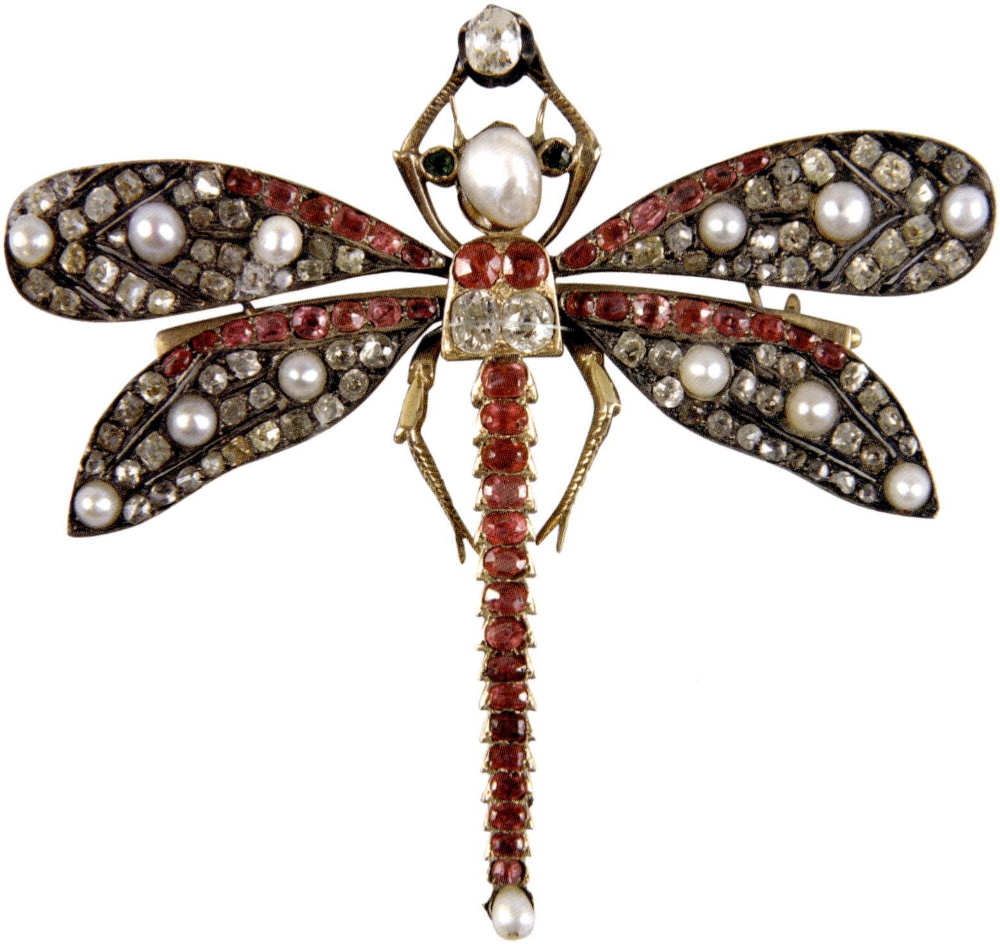

10. "Dragonfly" brooch
Russia, Moscow, 1899-1908
The State Historical Museum, Moscow
(Cat. 302)

ing is how they include new and original decorated motifs in traditional types of pendants, necklaces and bracelets. "Modern" art showed a growing interest for the world of nature: plants, animals and insects. The brooch in the form of a beetle created in St. Petersburg in the last quarter of the 19th century by Henri Lassas (ill. 9) and the brooch in the form of a dragonfly which is the work of Vasily Agafonov's Moscow workshop at the beginning of the 20th century (ill. 10) made with gold, diamonds, rubies, emeralds, pearls and sapphires, reflects the extremely high level of the technical possibilities of the russian goldsmith-jewelers, the finesse of their taste and the mastery of their art. These productions are in every way equal to the work of the most celebrated gold and silversmiths in Western Europe.

The work of the master craftsmen of the firm of Carl Fabergé, known all around the world, reached the pinnacle of the art of gold and silver work. Its productions were distinguished by the richness of their forms, the diversity of the materials used and the virtuosity of their execution. They had their own style, an absolutely unique

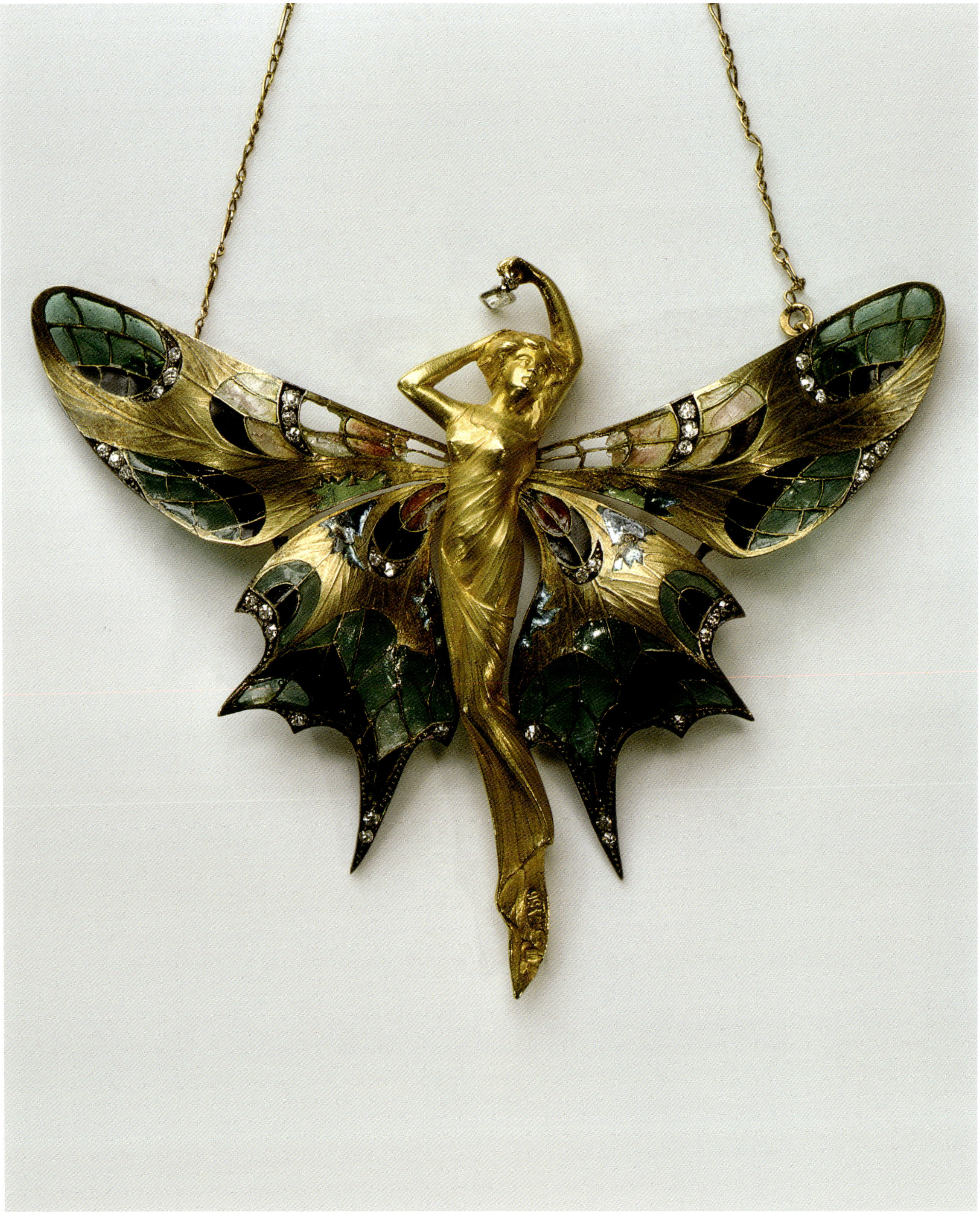

11. G. *Lafitte*
"Butterfly"
pendant
France, Paris, 1904
The State Historical Museum, Moscow
(Cat. 402)

style which has entered into the history of world art under the name of "Fabergé style." Although they enjoyed the possibility of using the most sought-out and most sumptuous precious stones, the master craftsmen at Fabergé often preferred to work with stones from the Ural: chrysolith, chrysoprase, alexandrite, garnets, and aqua-marine. The beautifully cut pale blue aqua-marine skillfully fixed to a rectangular mount with some discreet embellishments decorated with diamonds constitutes a brilliant demonstration of the extraordinary know-how of the master craftsmen of the Fabergé firm who created this masterpiece (ill. 8).

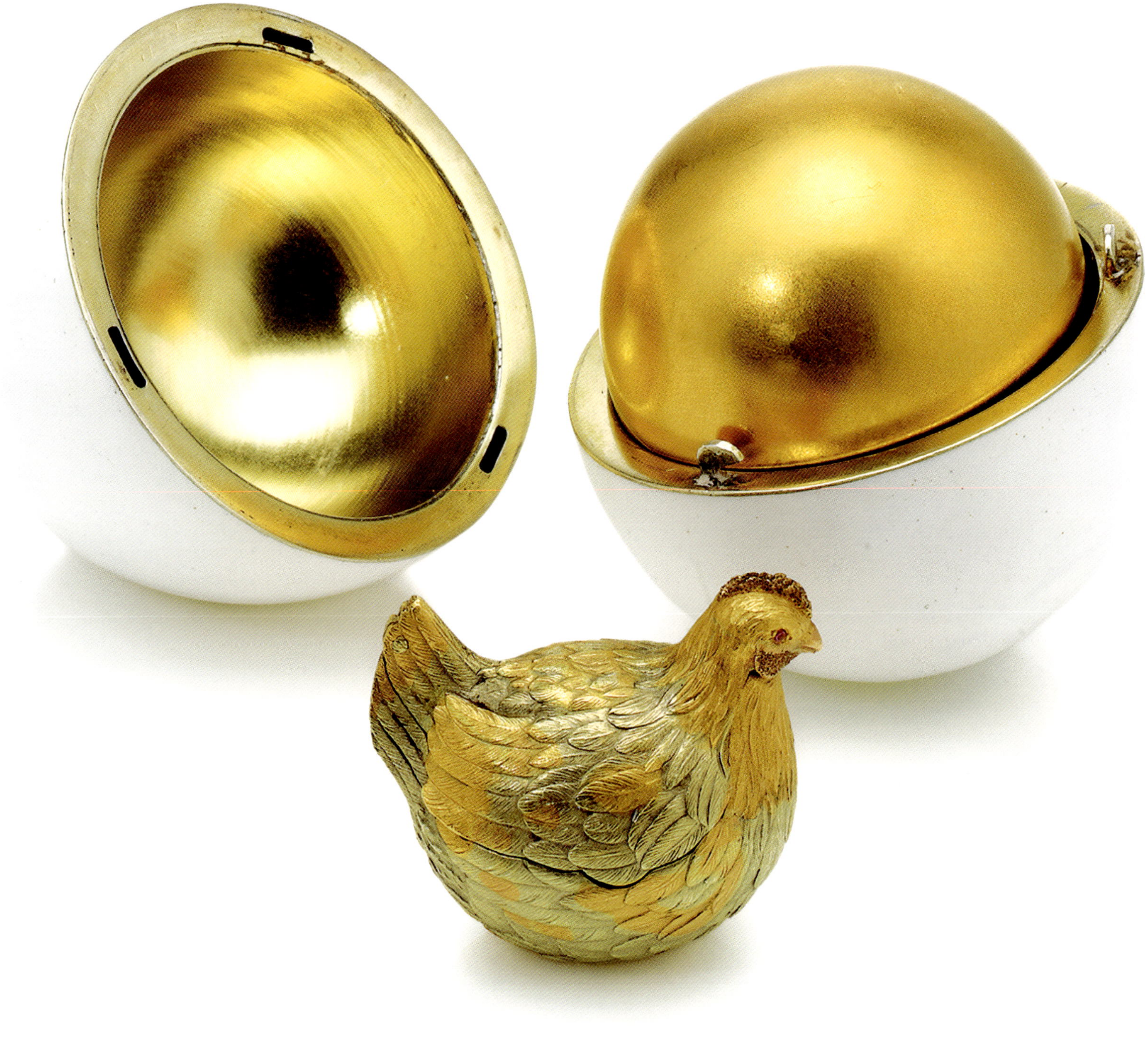

FABERGÉ, OFFICIAL COURT'S SUPPLIER

Brigitte de Montclos

From the time Gustav Fabergé opened a jewelry and diamond business in St. Petersburg until his son Carl was driven into exile by the Russian revolution, 76 years passed, during which the Fabergé firm had conquered an international reputation resulting from its unparalleled production.

In the middle of the 18th century, a category of privileged gold and silversmiths appeared in St. Petersburg: the Court suppliers who benefited from a direct order from the Czar or from his cabinet. The privilege became de facto institutionalized at the beginning of the 19th century—by 1840 it had been embodied by the right to use the symbol of the two-headed eagle next to the master's hallmark. This privilege was obviously greatly sought after. At this time, the majority of gold and silversmiths were of German origin or nationality. There had been a total of more than three hundred German names listed in the profession since the founding of the city.

1. *Carl Fabergé Workmaster: Erik Kollin (?)* Hen Egg (First Imperial Egg) *1885 Gift from the Emperor Alexander III to his wife Maria Feodorovna The Link of Times Foundation (Cat. 417)*

Bolshaya Morskaya

In the 1840s and 1850s, the opening of a jewelry and diamond business on the ground floor of a building on the Bolshaya Morskaya by a certain Gustav Faberg or Faberger, a Russian from the Baltic provinces originally come from Germany, was nothing out of the ordinary. The building had just been constructed by P. Jako, the first architect to organize small shops in Western style on the ground floor of new houses, with large rectangular shop windows. The location choice was excellent. It was the equivalent of Paris's Faubourg St. Honoré street, a district which was both residential and a luxurious shopping area, a street which linked the Nevsky Prospect to St. Isaac Square. According to oral tradition, Gustav Fabergé set up his establishment in 1842 although it is only first mentioned in the Russian archives in 1849. At any rate we know that Gustav Fabergé was born in 1814 in Pernau (Pirnü) in Estonia, and was of Russian nationality as Estonia belonged to the Empire. He was the son of Pierre Fabergé who was first mentioned in 1800 as being in that city.

The French origin of the Fabergé family is known. They were inhabitants of Picardy converted to Protestantism after the revocation of the Edict of Nantes in 1685. They left France under the name of Favri or Fabri, settled in Schwedt-on-Oder, next to Stettin under the name of Fabrier or Fabriger. The destination of their journey was St. Petersburg. Gustav worked with the jeweler André-Ferdinand Spiegel and with Johann-Wilhelm Keibel, president of the Guild of Foreigners, before opening his own shop.

He married Charlotte Jungstedt, of Northern origin. They had a son on May 30, 1846, baptized

2. *Carl Fabergé*
Workmaster: Erik Kollin
Scythian-style Bracelet
The Link of Times Foundation (Cat. 416)

3. *Carl Fabergé*
Workmaster: Henrik Wigström
Wild Pansy Sprig
The Link of Times Foundation (Cat. 454)

in the Protestant church of St. Petersburg and named Peter-Carl but who would always be known to the Russians as Carl Gustavovich.

The years of training

Carl Gustavovich's education was well taken care of, first at St. Anne's school, and then at the St. Petersburg German Lycée. His first technical training took place most naturally with the goldsmith Peter Hiskias Pendin, his father's partner. But in 1860 when Gustav decided to retire to Dresden and to leave the management of the store to his associate V. A. Tsayontchkovsky, his associate (whose workshop was just in front), Carl was only fourteen, and so he went with his father. In Dresden, he was well trained with the *Grünes Gewölbe* (Green Vault). One of the most famous royal treasures of Europe could be seen there, created especially at the beginning of the 18th century by J. M. Dinglinger who was the goldsmith for the Elector of Saxony Augustus II the Strong.

Carl Gustavovich then traveled within Europe, to the jeweler Friedmann in Frankfurt-on-the-Main where he also studied economy, and then to Italy and to France. He returned to St. Petersburg in 1870 and at the age of 24, took over the management of the Fabergé firm. It was prosperous enough that he was able to give up the first location and set up a bigger store on the other side of the street, at 16, Bolshaya Morskaya, next door to V. A. Tsayontchkovsky's workshop which was at number 18.

In 1842 he married Augusta Julia Jacobs, daughter of the inspector of imperial furniture workshops. They had four sons: Eugene, born in 1878, Agathon in 1876, Alexander in 1877, and Nicholas in 1884.

In the ten years which followed, with Carl taking over management of the business, the traditional enterprise would be transformed into a workshop of creation.

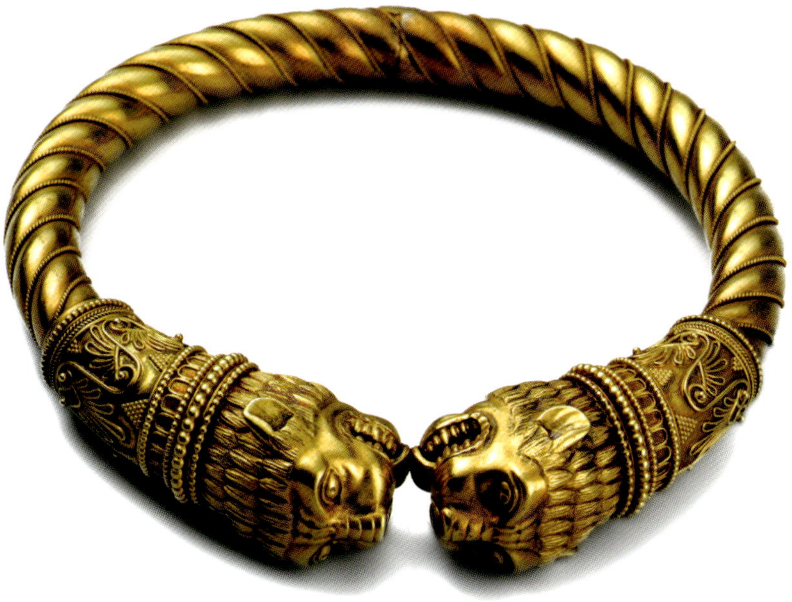

The rise to fame

The artistic invention of his young brother Agathon, who had come from Dresden to join him in the eighties, provided the creative impetus, while Carl's spirit of organization, linked to international culture, led to the rapid growth in production. In 1882, he participated for the first time in a Pan-Russian exhibition, the one in Moscow whose opening had been delayed because of Alexander II's assassination. It was one of the most important events of this sort with four thousand participants exhibiting. Fabergé received a gold medal. An article in the catalogue cited his remarkable copies of Greek jewels which had recently been discovered in excavations in Kerch, Crimea.

But Carl wanted more, he wanted the ulti-

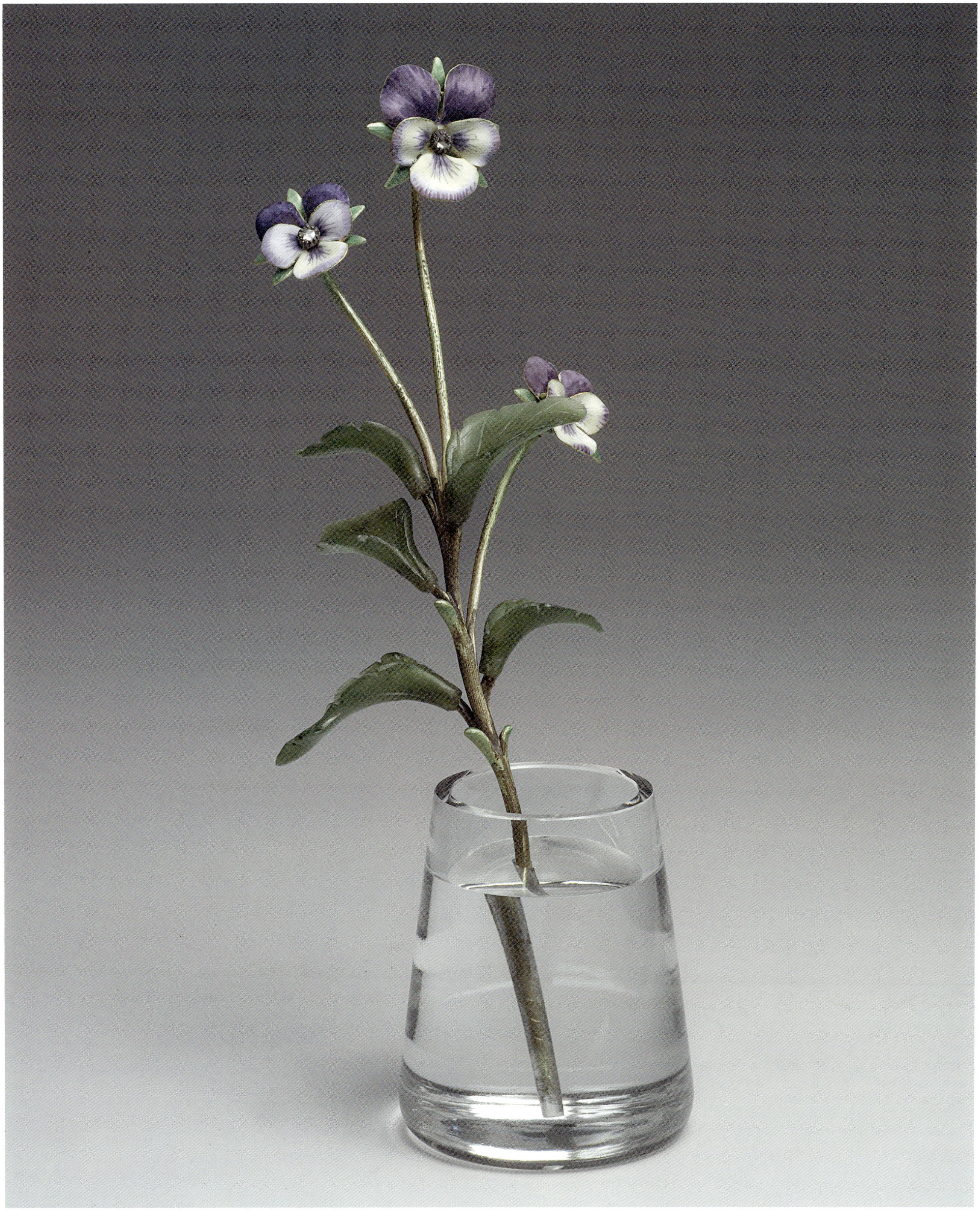

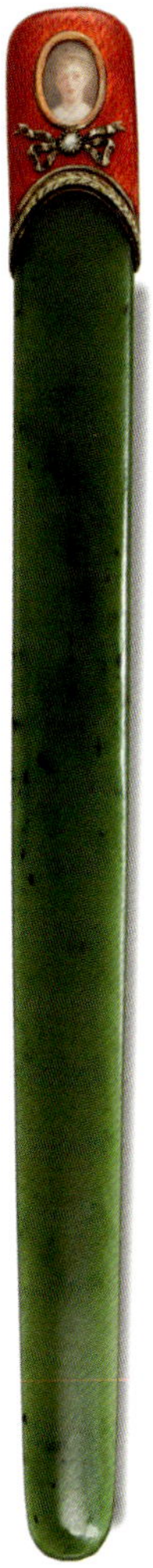

4. *Carl Fabergé*
Grand Duchess Olga Paper Knife
The Link of Times Foundation (Cat. 445)

mate privilege which his Russian competitors had already received, Ovchinnikov, Khlebnikof, Sazikov: the certificate of Court supplier. He had himself presented by his master Julius Butz and his name appeared in the account books of the Czar's cabinet in 1883. On April 16, 1885, he received a payment and the right to stamp the objects he produced with the imperial emblem. The same year, he created the first Easter egg which Alexander III gave to his wife Maria Feodorovna. The tradition of imperial eggs which would make his name was born. After these first successes, Carl took part in the major international exhibitions: in 1885 in Nuremberg, in 1896 in Nijni-Novgorod, in 1897 in Stockholm, in 1900 in Paris where he received the Legion of Honor and the title of "Master." Already, he was the recipient of many honors. In 1890 he was named expert to the Czar's cabinet, and in 1892 he received the Order of St. Anne, 3rd class.

He founded subsidiary companies: in Moscow in 1887 with Allan Bowe and his brothers Arthur and Charles as associates; in Odessa in 1890, and in Kiev in 1905. In 1903, Arthur Bowe established

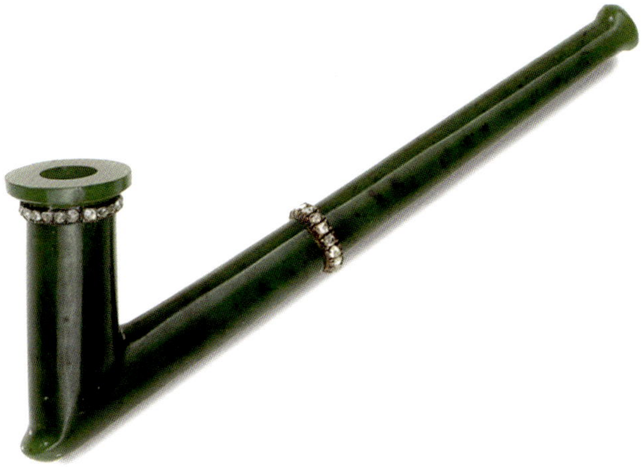

5. *Carl Fabergé*
Pipe Cigarette Holder
The Link of Times Foundation (Cat. 442)

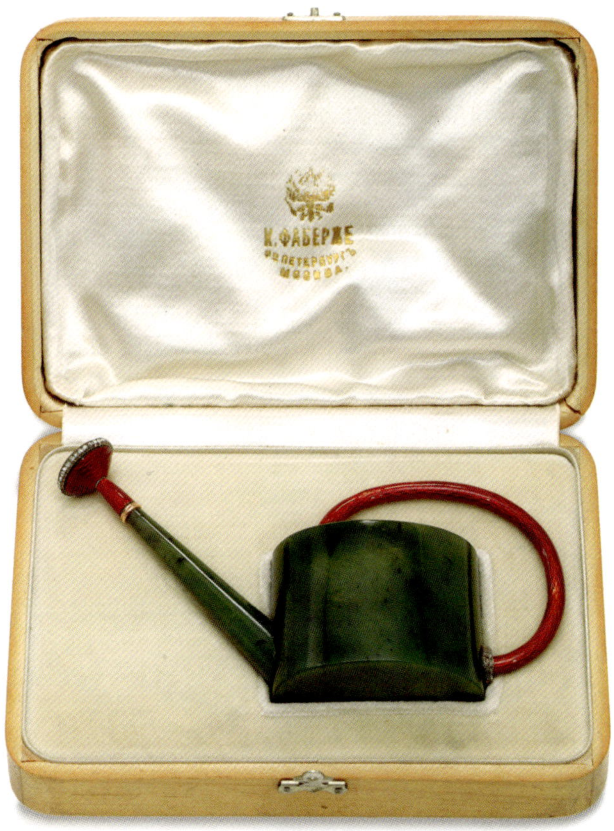

a contact office in London in the Berners Hotel. This was followed in 1906 by the opening of a store managed by Nicholas Fabergé, Carl's youngest son, and by H. C. Bainbridge at 48 Dover Street. It was the only foreign subsidiary.

A family business, the changing of the guard

During this time, Gustav, Carl's father, died in Dresden at the age of 79. His brother Agathon also died in St. Petersburg in 1895 at the age of 33. Carl began to involve his sons more and more in the business: In 1894, his eldest son Eugene became his main assistant, in 1906, Alexander took over the management of the Moscow subsidiary and Nicholas that of London. Agathon, like his uncle, was the artist of the family. He designed, and he had a particular skill for evaluating stones.

The success of the Fabergé firm meant a need

6. *Carl Fabergé*
A miniature
watering can,
in fitted case
The Link
of Times
Foundation
(Cat. 453)

7. *Carl Fabergé*
Miniature
bonbonnière
in the form of
a Louis XVI-
style armchair,
in case
The Link of
Times
Foundation
(Cat. 451)

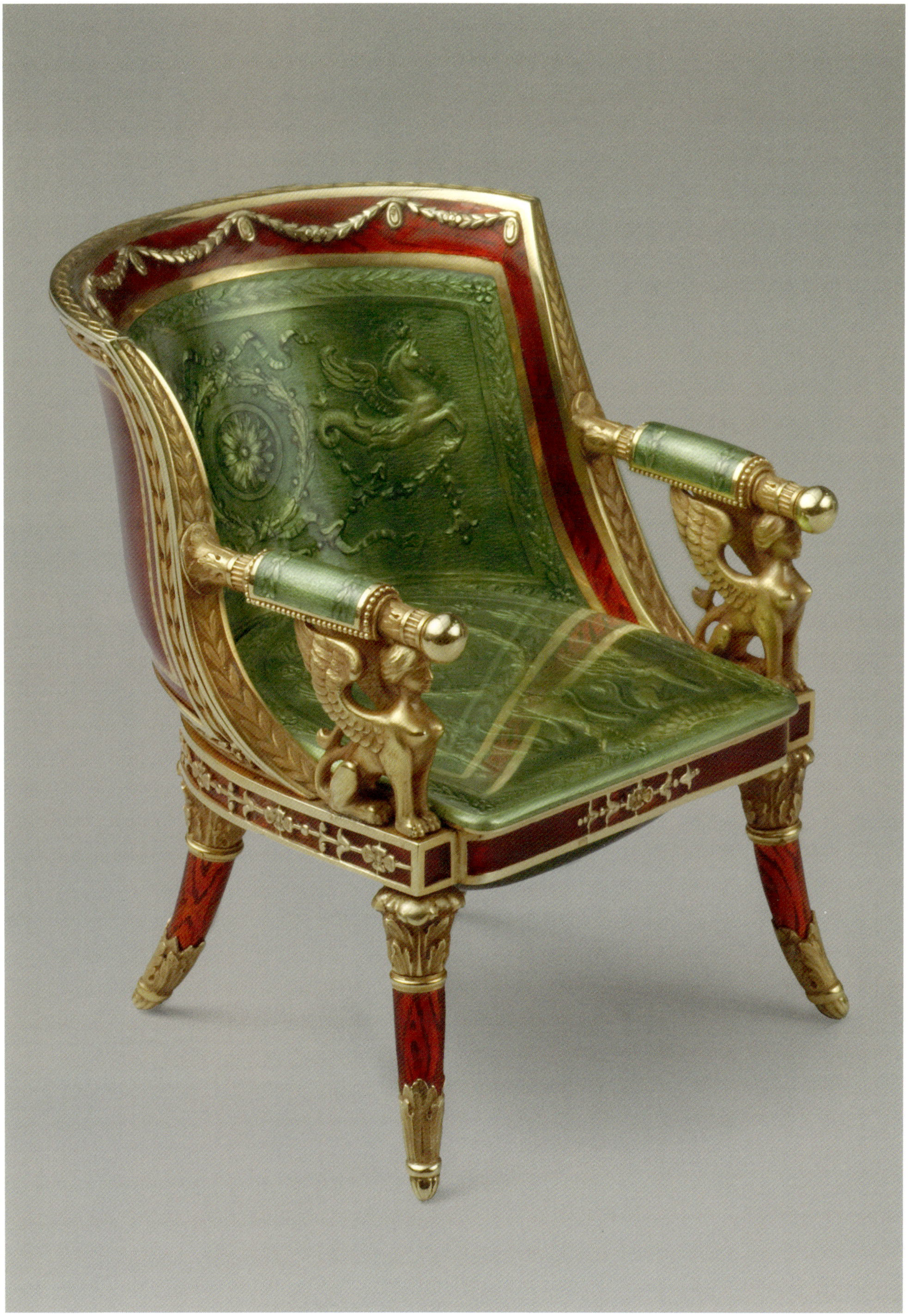

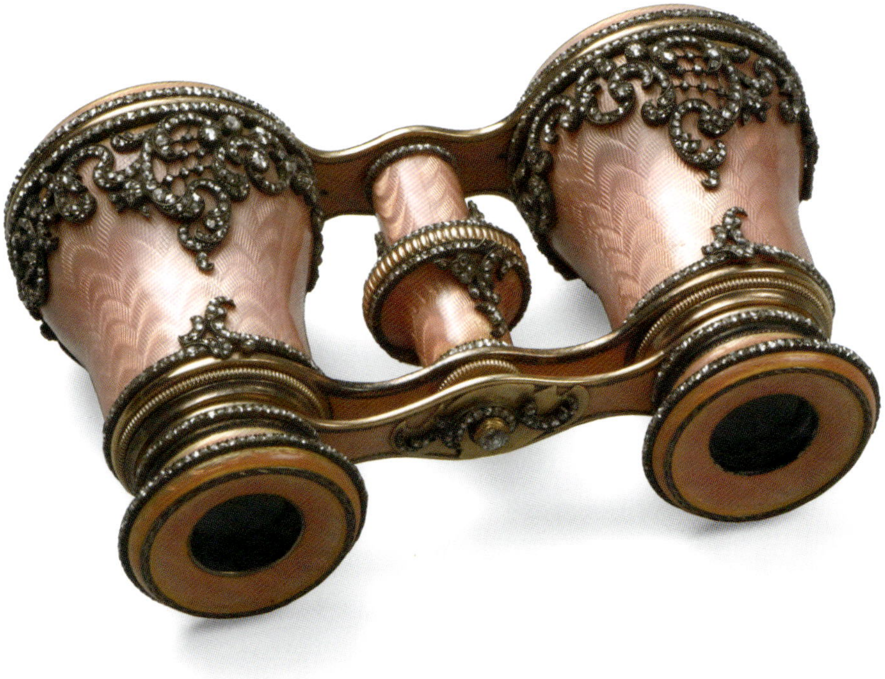

8. *Carl Fabergé Workmaster: Michael Perkhin*
A pair of opera glasses
The Link of Times Foundation (Cat. 448)

9. *Carl Fabergé*
Nobel Necklace / Bracelet
The Link of Times Foundation (Cat. 447)

for larger premises. Carl bought the building at 24 Bolshaya Morskaya for a million rubles. He had the house entirely renovated by the architect Karl Schmidt so as to be able to house all the firm's activities: workshops, store, apartment, library and offices. He moved his company into the new premises in 1900. For the first time, all the workshop foremen were together under the same roof.

The first master gold and silversmiths were beginning to pass away, but their succession was assured. The Swiss François Birbaum succeeded Carl's younger brother Agathon as artistic director. Enrik Kollin, who had been one of the first master shop foremen, died in 1901. The technical director Michael Perkhin died in 1903 and was succeeded by Henrik Wigstrom. Then one of the jewelry workshop foremen August Holmström died, replaced by his son Albert. In 1909, the main jewelry workshop foreman Alfred Thielemann died, in 1915 it was August Hollming, in 1916, Julius Rappoport, the silversmith. As can be seen, most often the workshops remained in the same families which ensured the perenniality of the work.

The international reputation

The Empress Maria Feodorovna, wife of the Czar Alexander III, was sister to Queen Alexandra, wife of Edward VII, King of England. They were the daughters of Christian IX of Sweden. So it's not surprising that Fabergé products circulated around Europe. However, the relationship which Carl built with the King of Siam and the Maharajah of the Indies was entirely due to his own personal reputation. In the United States, where today there are perhaps the greatest concentration of Fabergé objects, it was Julia Grant, granddaughter of the President of the United States who introduced the Fabergé fashion. She had married Prince Cantacuzene, lived part of the time in St. Pe-

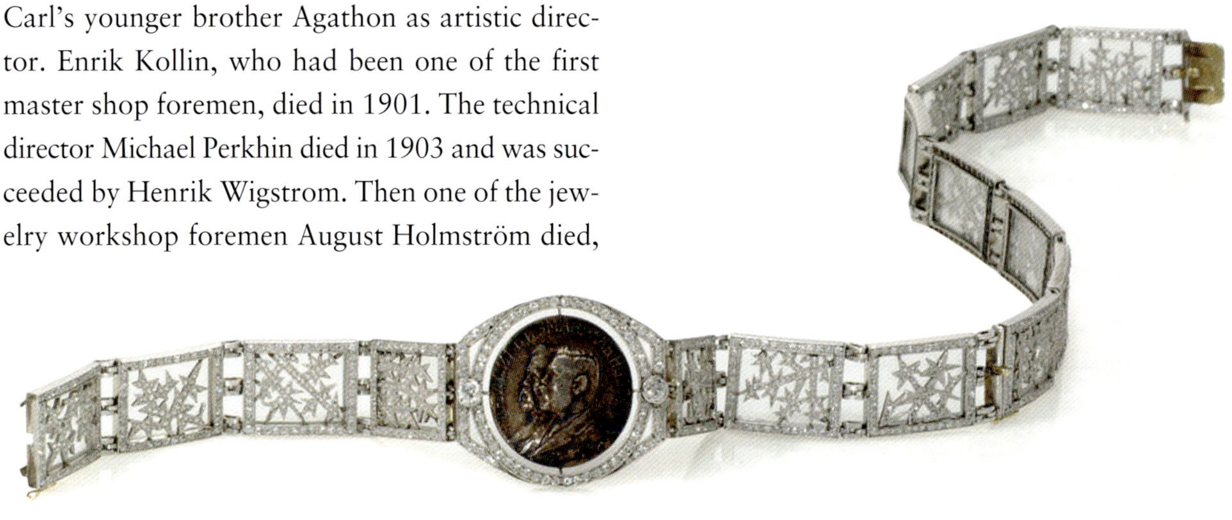

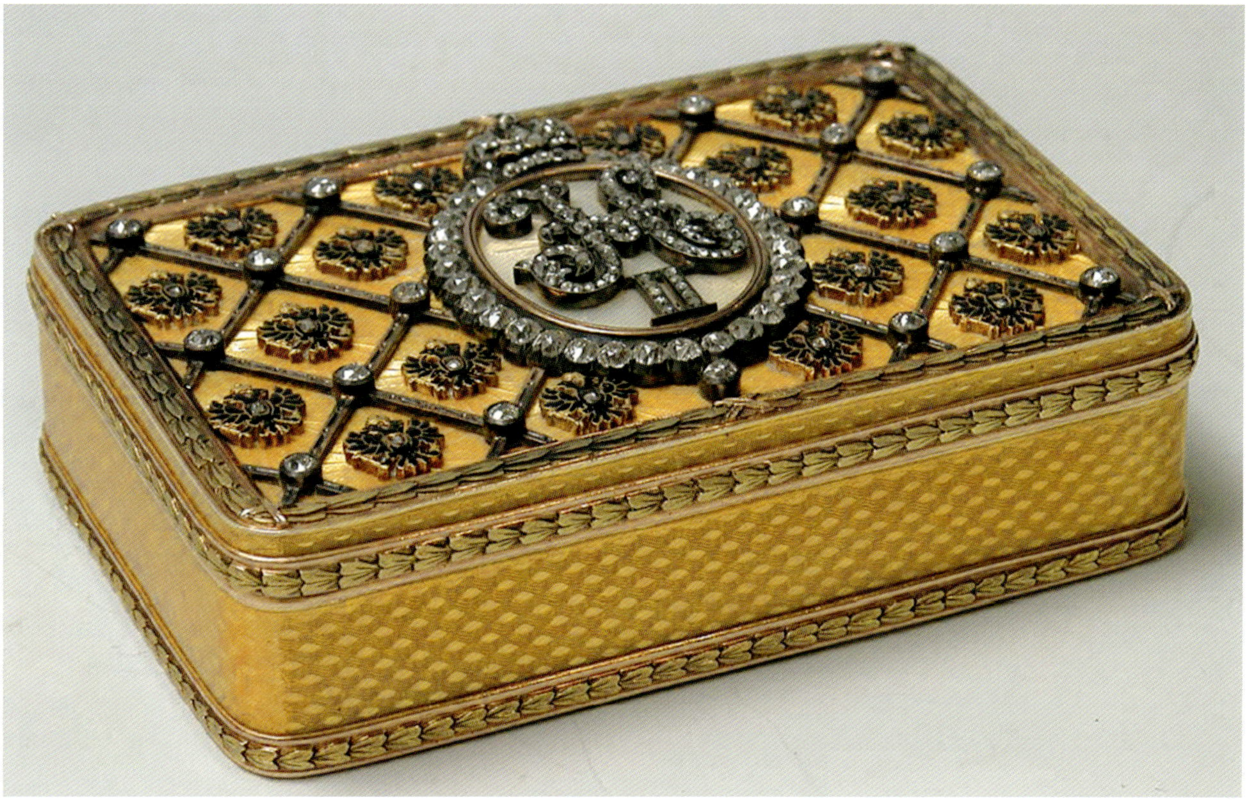

10. *Carl Fabergé*
Workmaster:
August
Holmström
Coronation Box
Saint-Petersburg,
1896
The Link of
Times
Foundation
(Cat. 438)

tersburg, frequented the Fabergé firm and spread the news about it to her friends the Walters in Baltimore. This was the beginning of the Walters Art Gallery and a major Fabergé collection.

Other clients, in addition to the reigning families in Europe, included Prince Yussupov, the counts Stroganov who had ordered the Kerch replicas, the Nobel brothers who had been educated in St. Petersburg, the gold mine magnate Kelch, and the rubber manufacturer Neuscheller. They all belonged to the highest level of European society.

The final years

In 1915, the London subsidiary was closed as Russian capital had to be sent back from abroad because of the war. In 1916, the Fabergé firm was transformed into an anonymous society with a capital of 3 million rubles in sixty actions, the majority of which belonged to Carl. In 1917, the St. Petersburg firm was managed by a "committee of employees of C. Fabergé Society." Soon afterwards, the Moscow subsidiary closed. By 1918, everything was over.

Carl managed to flee from St. Petersburg in September under the protection of the British embassy, making the opposite journey to that of his ancestors. He crossed through Germany and arrived ill in Wiesbaden in May 1920. Mrs. Fabergé left Russia with Eugene in December 1918 under extremely difficult conditions. After a long journey, she arrived in Lausanne and went to get her husband in Wiesbaden. Eugene, who had remained in Stockholm, joined them there. They took Carl to Lausanne where he died in September 1920 and was cremated. Mrs. Fabergé died in Cannes in 1925 and was buried in the Protestant cemetery there. In 1929, Eugene transferred his father's remains to Cannes, placing them in his mother's tomb and covering the whole grave with a Swedish black porphyry stone onto which he had engraved the names of his parents, with their dates of birth and death.

The legend

The Fabergé firm existed for seventy six years. In forty of those years, the jewelry house had become an international business. As we know, Carl Fabergé was the inventor of the novelty object, this combination of an art object, a jewel and a useful object. But his personal genius resided in fact on two very simple principles: culture and organization. Culture, meaning not only the product of education which his father wished him to have—both a general education and technical training—but also the prodigious assimilation of all the cultures he had encountered in Europe. A surprise-egg for example; what is it but a *matriochka*, one of those Russian wooden nesting dolls one of which fits into the other. The first Imperial egg was of white enameled gold. You opened it, there was the golden yolk. You opened the yolk, there was a hen. You opened the hen, there was a holy crown. When you opened the crown, there was a ruby egg. Based on examples he found, Fabergé was able to discover and individualise originality everywhere.

The organization was based first on a careful selection of associates, on the best gold and silversmiths, the best designers; and then, on the principle of division of work: before beginning the manufacturing of any new piece, he held a meeting of consultation with all the workshop foremen enabling each one to define his position in the manufacturing line; and finally, on an ability to direct as well as having a true business strategy. This strategy depended upon talent to provoke demand. How could the Russians' attention be directed to the small animal sculptures in hard stone which local craftsmen had always made in wood? By presenting these exotic objects in London and then receiving the royal order to create the Sandringham Farm in miniature. The Russian infatuation for them followed.

The Fabergé epoch, now seen as the last hurrah of the Russian empire, was one of those brilliant leading companies which were prominent at the turn of the century in Europe. Its abrupt end avoided the slow decline to which the 20th century would have inevitably led.

Famous pieces coming from the Russian collections appeared on the international market, European and American, all during the 20th century. The biggest collection of Imperial eggs and objects from the Fabergé firm were collected together by the American billionaire Malcolm Forbes. His descendents decided to put them on sale in February 2004 at Sotheby's. This is when the Russian businessman Victor Vekselberg decided to acquire the totality of them even before the sale began—a first for Sotheby's—so as to prevent the dispersion of this rare collection of nine Imperial eggs and almost 190 objects. And so these masterpieces of an inestimable historical and cultural value returned to Russia where they have already been shown to the public. Several exhibitions of the Fabergé collection have been organized in Russia and abroad, as for example in Moscow, Ekaterinburg, St. Petersburg, Berlin, Brussels and Zurich.

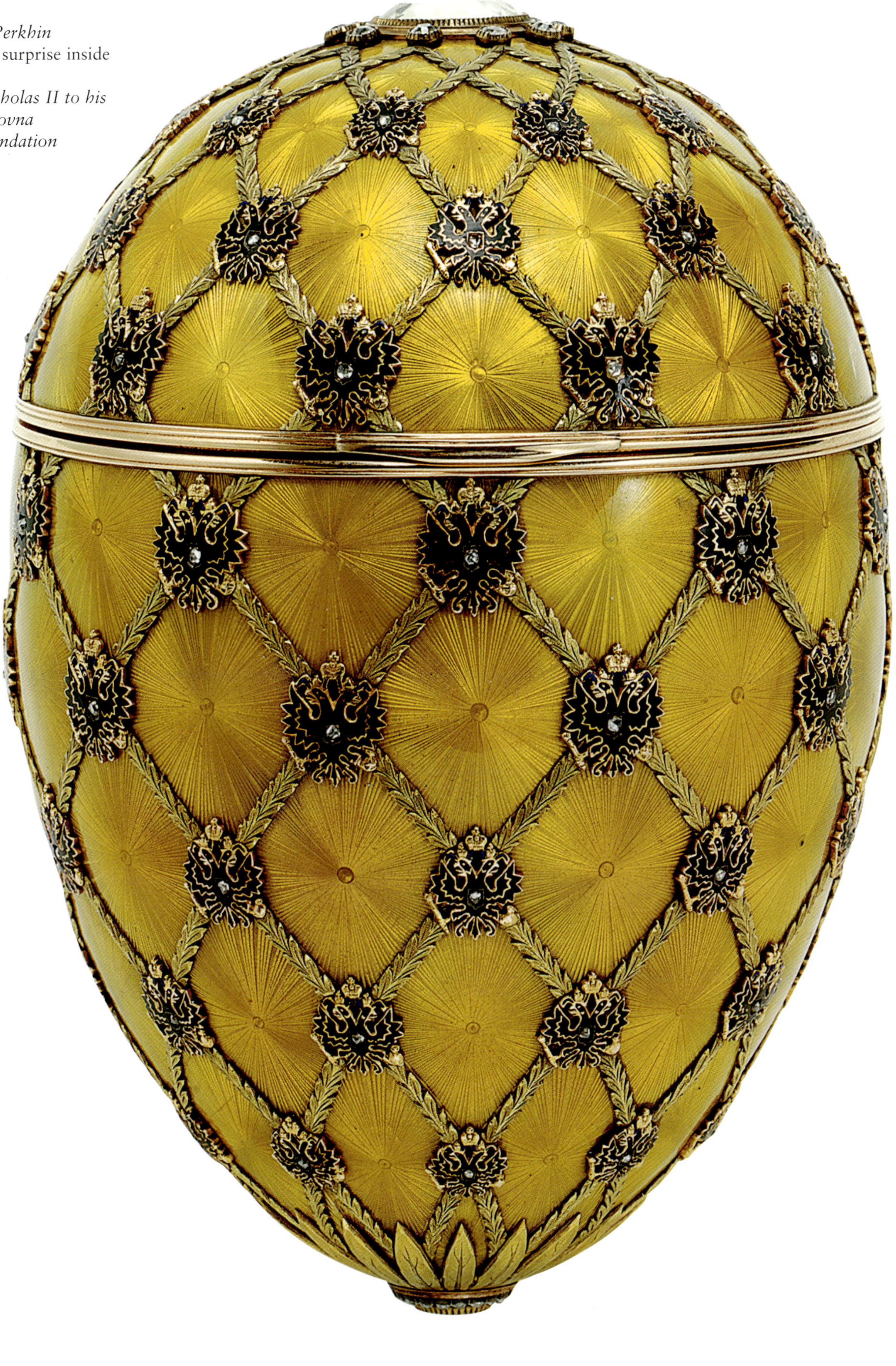

11. *Carl Fabergé.*
Workmaster: Michael Perkhin
Coronation Egg with a surprise inside
St. Petersburg, 1897
Gift from Emperor Nicholas II to his wife Alexandra Feodorovna
The Link of Times Foundation
(Cat. 470)

12. *Carl Fabergé.*
Workmaster: Michael Perkhin
Lilies of the Valley Egg
St. Petersburg, 1898
Gift from the Emperor Nicholas II to his wife Alexandra Feodorovna
The Link of Times Foundation
(Cat. 412)

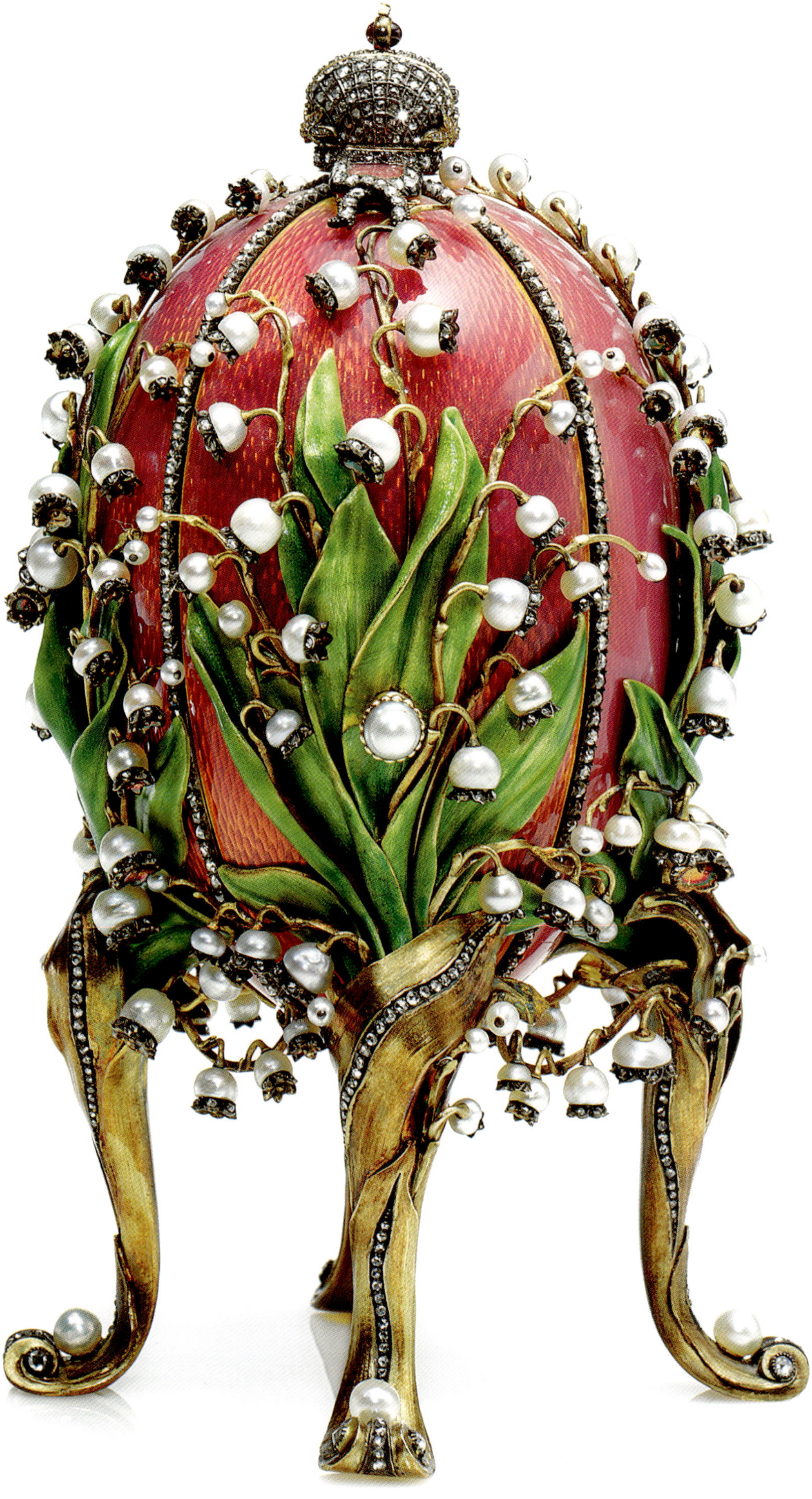

13. *Carl Fabergé.*
Workmaster: Henrik Wigström
Fifteenth Anniversary Egg, with stand
St. Petersburg, 1911
Gift from the Emperor Nicholas II
to his wife Alexandra Feodorovna
The Link of Times Foundation
(Cat. 413)

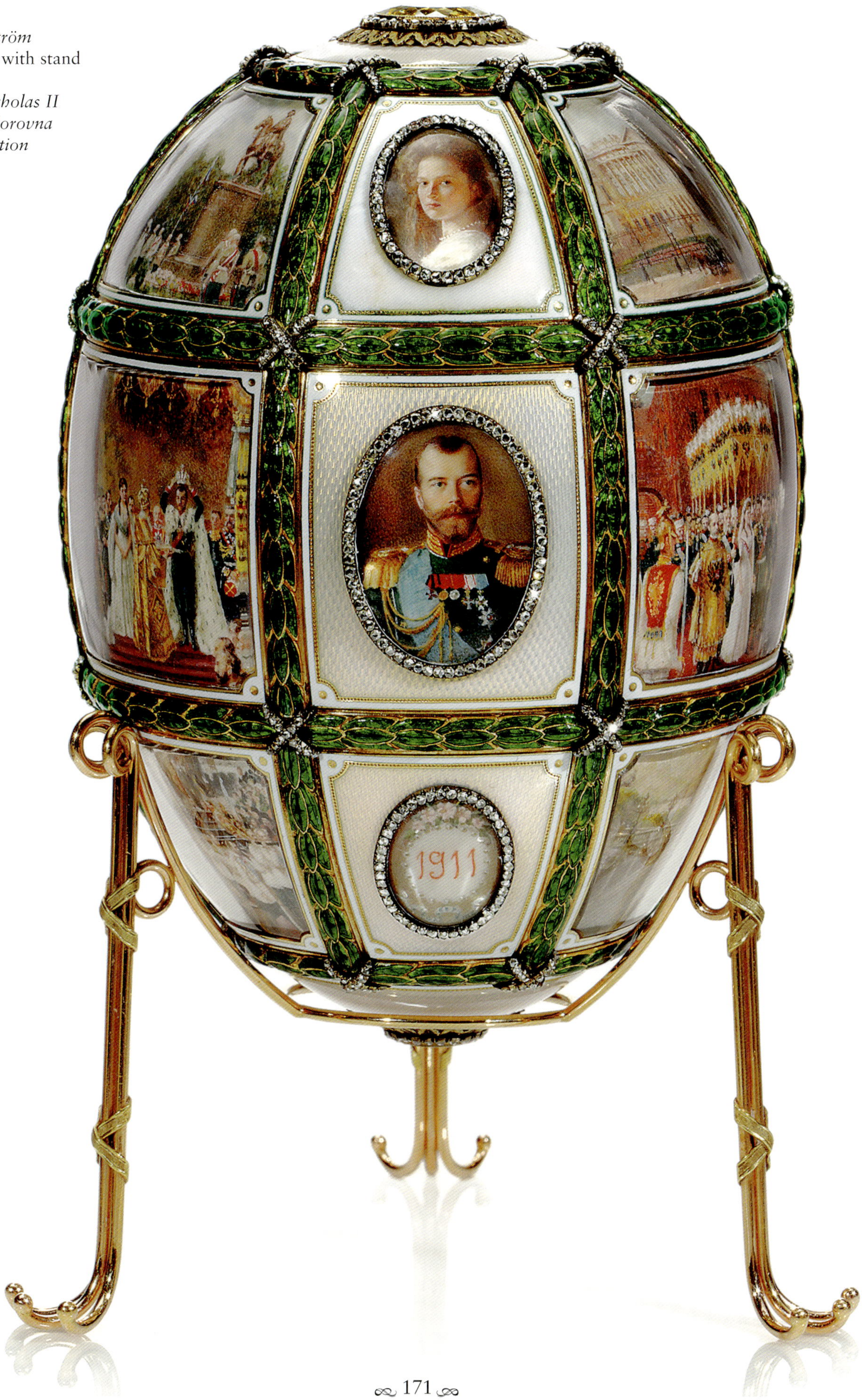

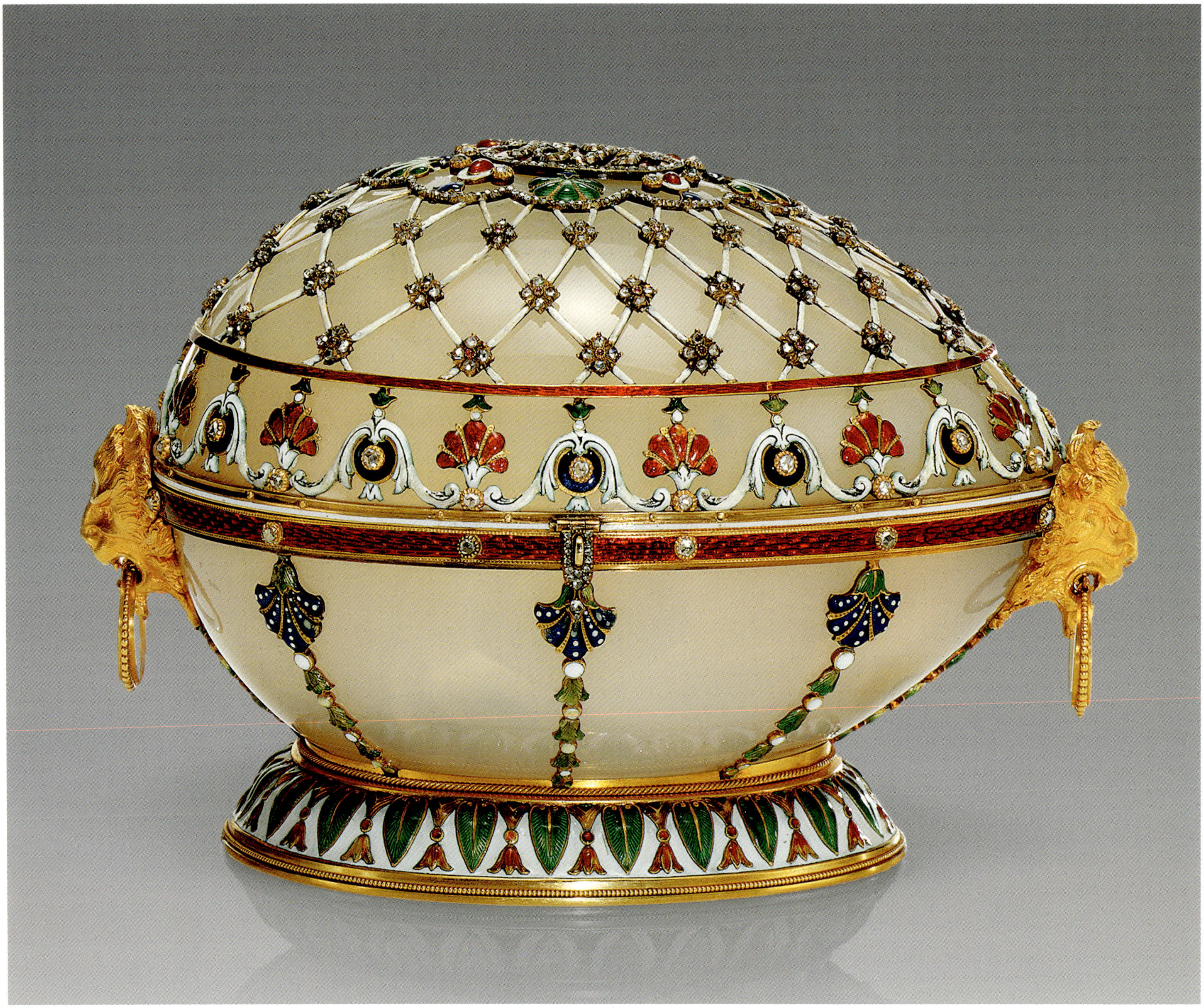

14. *Carl Fabergé.*
Workmaster: Michael Perkhin
Renaissance Egg
St. Petersburg, 1894
Gift from the Emperor Alexander III
to his wife Maria Feodorovna
The Link of Times Foundation
(Cat. 414)

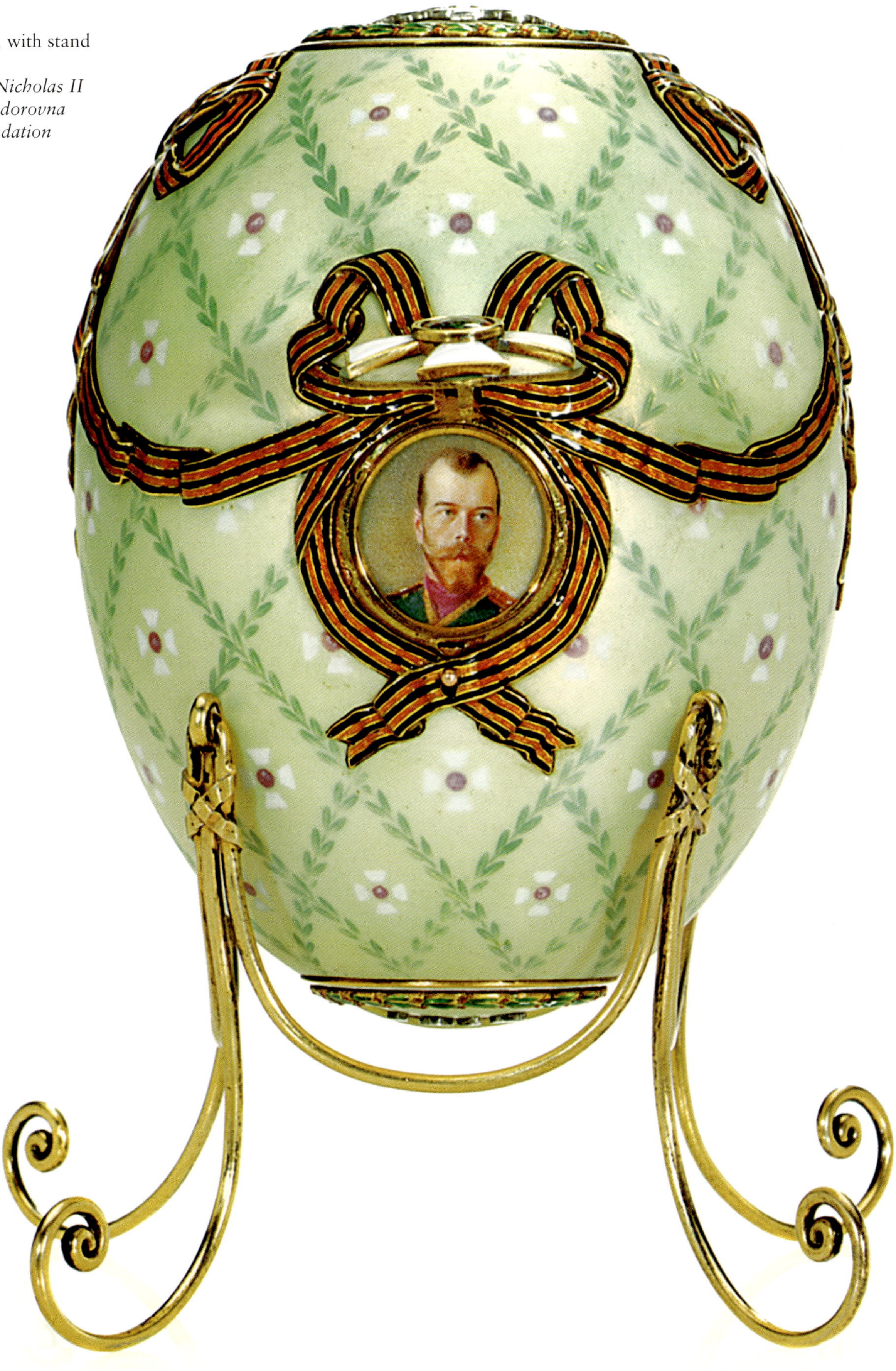

15. *Carl Fabergé*
Cross of St. George Egg, with stand
1916
Gift from the Emperor Nicholas II
to his mother Maria Feodorovna
The Link of Times Foundation
(Cat. 415)

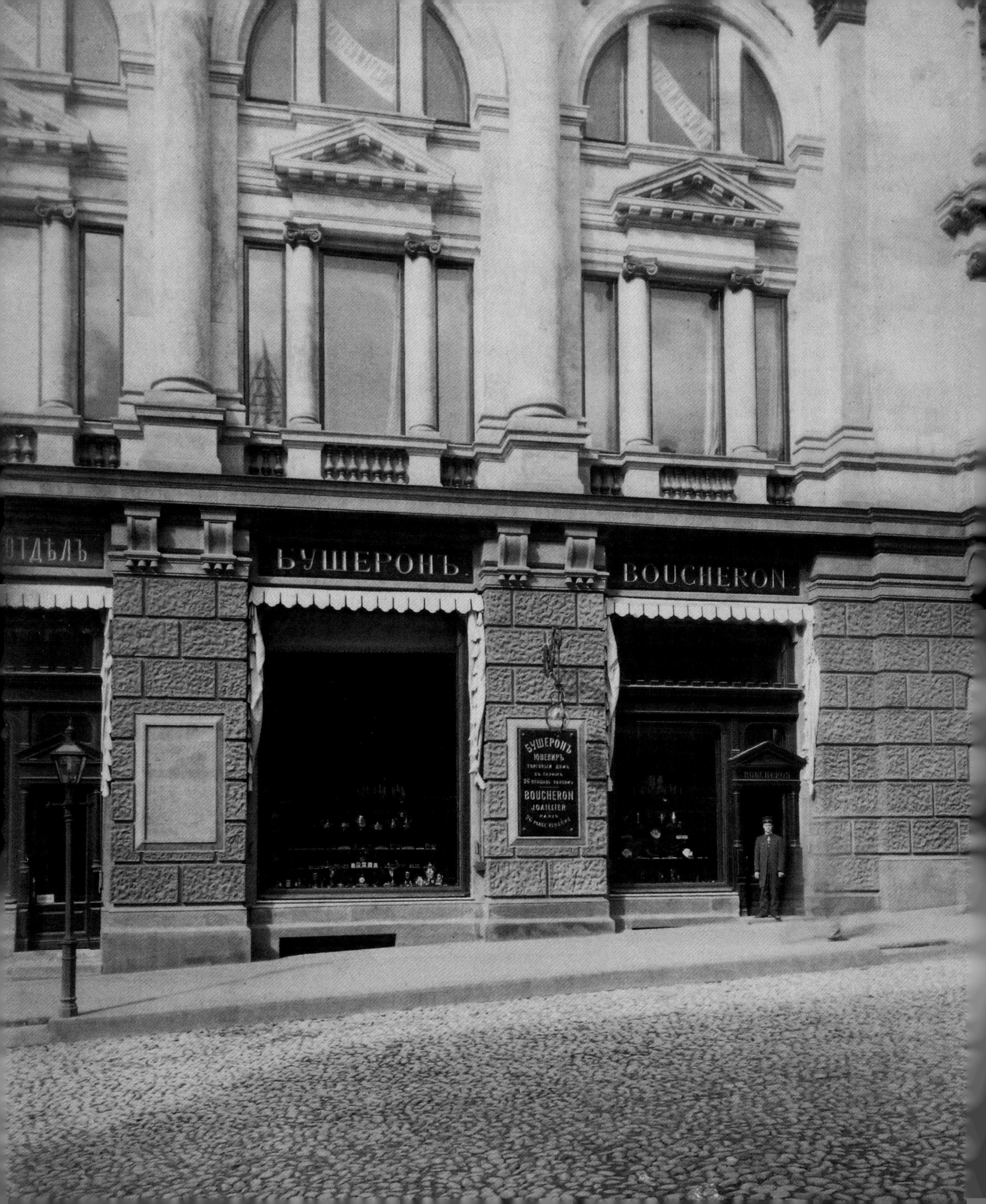

ОТДѢЛЪ
БУШЕРОНЪ
BOUCHERON
БУШЕРОНЪ
ЮВЕЛИРЪ
BOUCHERON
JOAILLIER
PARIS
BOUCHERON

MOSCOW, A "FAR EAST" FOR THE FRENCH ART INDUSTRIES

Wilfried Zeisler

The Western model imposed on the Court by Peter the Great had led to the development of cosmopolitan society from the 18th century, which loved all things French, as evidenced in particular by the purchase and orders of pieces of art. Even in Moscow, a city traditionally turned toward its Slavic past, these objects were available.

During the 19th century, the opening of Russia and its economic development, symbolized through the construction of several railway lines linking the Empire to great European capitals, facilitated the introduction of French art and luxury industries to St. Petersburg, as well as Moscow.

The Muscovite shop windows, reflections of French creation

In 1913, Emile Haumant in his work *La culture française en russie (1700-1900)*[1] recorded what Alexander Turgenev said about the French culture of the Russian princes: "Who among them hardly knows where his own village is, but he knows everything about the Versailles de Saint-Simon; suggest that he learn about Russia and he will answer you that he's too busy, he's reading Faublas.[2] His homeland is Marshall's Bridge street and his paradise is Paris."[3]

Marshall's Bridge Street remains today the Muscovite equivalent of *la rue de la Paix* and *la place Vendôme* together. It is *the* luxury destination with its many fashion shops and novelties such as the ancestral "*A la ville de Lyon*" or Charov & Cie—"*Latest fashions from Paris*" whose names bear witness to the origin of the models and the products.[4]

There were also the Russian equivalent of the Parisian luxury shops on Marshall's Bridge Street, such as Giroux or the Crystal Stairway, heirs to the notions merchants of the *Ancien Régime* and which participated in the evolution of taste. Thus at the beginning of the 20th century Christolfe gold and silver work could be found at Eugene and Alexis Flegontov's who ran one of these stores. The French manufacture had expanded its presence in Moscow since the 1860s and in particular maintained a business relationship with Luccacini, a jeweler established on Marshall's Bridge Street, in the Salodownikov passageway.

In fact, as Tatiana Muntian emphasizes, Marshall's Bridge Street could have been nicknamed the "street paved with diamonds"[5] given the concentration of gold and silversmiths, jewelers and jewelry stores, most of them suppliers to the court: Ivan Khlebnikov, Pavel Ovchinnikov, Ch. Bock, Bolin and Lombardo, not to mention Fabergé, who opened a branch in 1887.[6] Then the Boucheron firm followed and set up a branch there too.

In addition to their own creations, some of the Russian gold and silversmiths proposed imported

1. Outside façade of the Boucheron store in Moscow (opened in 1897)
Boucheron archives
(Cat. 323)

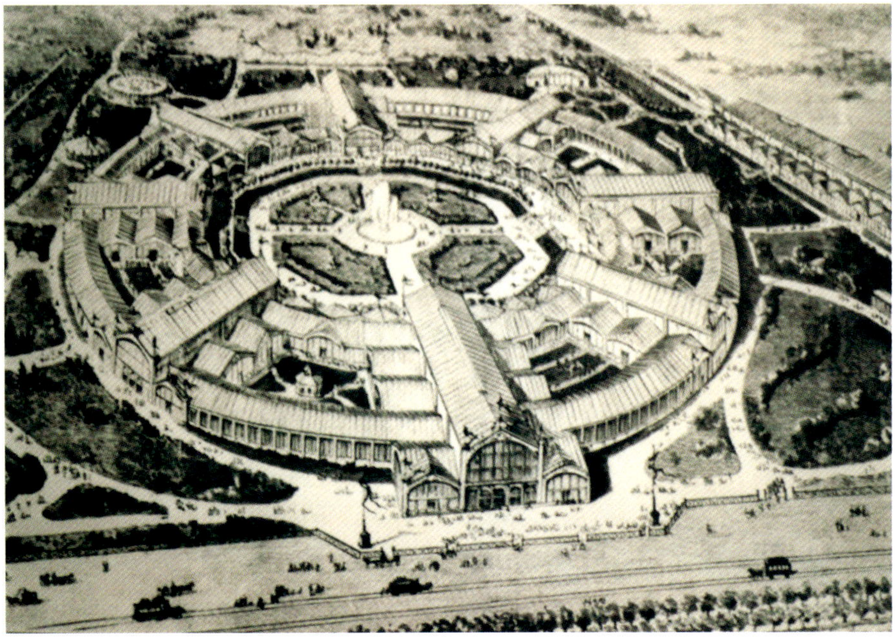

2. General view of the French exhibition in Moscow, 1891 *(Cat. 330)*

pieces from France to their clients such as Baccarat crystal[7] which were used to make bowls and mounted pieces in silver, very popular in Russia. Among these Muscovite and St. Petersburg gold and silversmiths who were clients of Baccarat—Gratchev, Ivanov, Khlebnikov, Kuriukov, Kuznetsov, Morozov, Nemirov, Ovchinnikov, Prokhorov, Tchuksanov and Wladimirov—the famous Fabergé firm must be mentioned. Some of the mounted vases which Fabergé sold also came from the Tiffany and Emile Gallé[8] workshops. Their work was greatly appreciated by the Russian clientele and largely imitated by local glassmakers.[9]

These various merchants or Russian creators were supplied directly by the French manufactures or by their representatives who traveled around the Empire. As early as 1882, Georges Delavigne was named by the Boucheron firm to investigate the Russian market. Like the brothers Falize, Pierre Cartier went personally to Russia, to St. Petersburg and Moscow in 1904-05 where exhibition-sales were regularly organized. The businessman Désiré Sarda was then Cartier's representative in Russia.[10] As for Chaumet, he hired Mr. Farein, who established contacts with the Muscovite clientele.[11]

Finally, the presence of an agency of the Crédit Lyonnais Bank[12] on Marshall's Bridge Street resumes in itself the economic importance of Russia for France at that time. This context encouraged the establishment of close links between the French republic and the Russian monarchy which was contemplating the establishment of a new union, the future Franco-Russian Alliance, aimed at redefining the fragile European equilibrium shaken since the founding of the Reich in 1871. These arguments were at the origin of a French commercial exhibition held in Moscow, organized "in the name of industrial and commercial interest, in the name of patriotism."[13]

Triumph of jewelry at the French exhibition in Moscow in 1891

After the success of the 1889 Universal Exhibition, the project of a new exhibition in Russia was backed by several politicians favorable to the Franco-Russian rapprochement, such as Emile Flourens, former foreign affairs minister, or by several craftsmen maintaining friendly relations with Russia, such as Fauré-Lepage, G. Boin, and Boucheron.

Moscow appeared to be the perfect location—its city was by then a great industrial center at the crossroads of the main commercial routes and with an aristocratic clientele used to French tastes, as well as a new class of rich industrialists and businessmen.

The Emperor Alexander III who needed "to be agreeable to France and to its ambassador"[14] approved the project and had it adopted by an *ukase* promulgated on April 25, 1890. The Russian government placed several buildings which

3. *Th. Bourdier*
Imperial egg offered to Maria Feodorovna during the French exhibition in Moscow in 1891
(Cat. 334)

had been built for the Pan-Russian exhibition on the Khodinka Field at the disposal of the exhibitors (ill. 2).

The event included almost two hundred French entrepreneurs and creators, divided into nine groups.[15] The 18th class was that of the jewelers and there too, some of the greatest names were side by side: Louis Aucoc fils, Frédéric Boucheron, Th. Bourdier, L. Coulon et Cie, Jacta Fils, Vever…

New firms could be found alongside old and famous ones.

Louis Aucoc Fils for example was the descendant of a very old firm which had worked for Russia during the 19th century, and Jacta's father had been named appointed supplier to the Court of Russia in 1865. Jacta junior enjoyed great success at the exhibition, especially with his accessories which were popular in Russia such as his canes and cane knobs in engraved repoussé gold, rock crystal, nacre and jasper.

The creations presented were thus adapted to the tastes of the clientele whom they were intended to attract.

Boucheron chose to present among various jewels, art objects and gold and silverwork pieces, "a jewel for the occasion, a portrait of the Emperor Alexander III surrounded by rubies".[16] Indeed, the ruby dominated the jewelry of this famous Parisian firm.

Léon Coulon, Boucheron's former associate, exhibited a diadem *kokoshnik* inspired by traditional Russian headdresses which attracted the attention of the Empress Maria Feodorovna. However, Coulon was also known, as were other exhibitors, for works which reflected the Parisian jewelry trends. The *fin de siècle* variations of style were illustrated in his showcases by a pocket mirror in gold in the "Louis XV style", style which spread through-out Russia in the form of a third rococo, or by a "Renaissance style" damascened steel brooch.

Vever also presented numerous art objects in eclectic styles: the chivalrous Middle Ages: *Basse Taille* enamels; Renaissance style with a molded silver frame based on an example by Louis Bottée and decorated with an enameled portrait of Vittoria Colonna,[17] of a chest decorated with ancient cameos;[18] Oriental enchantment with a table lamp decorated in plaques of gold pierced with translucent enamels[19] and Japanese evocation with a spray of daisies in gold in a bronze Japanese vase.

In Moscow, the most zealous of the Parisian

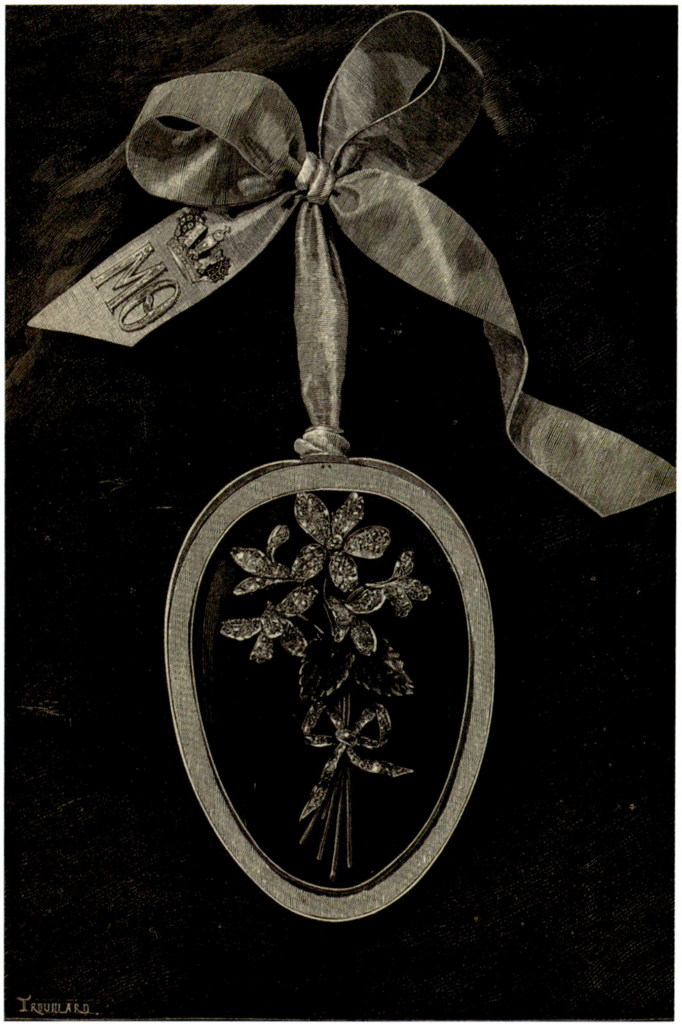

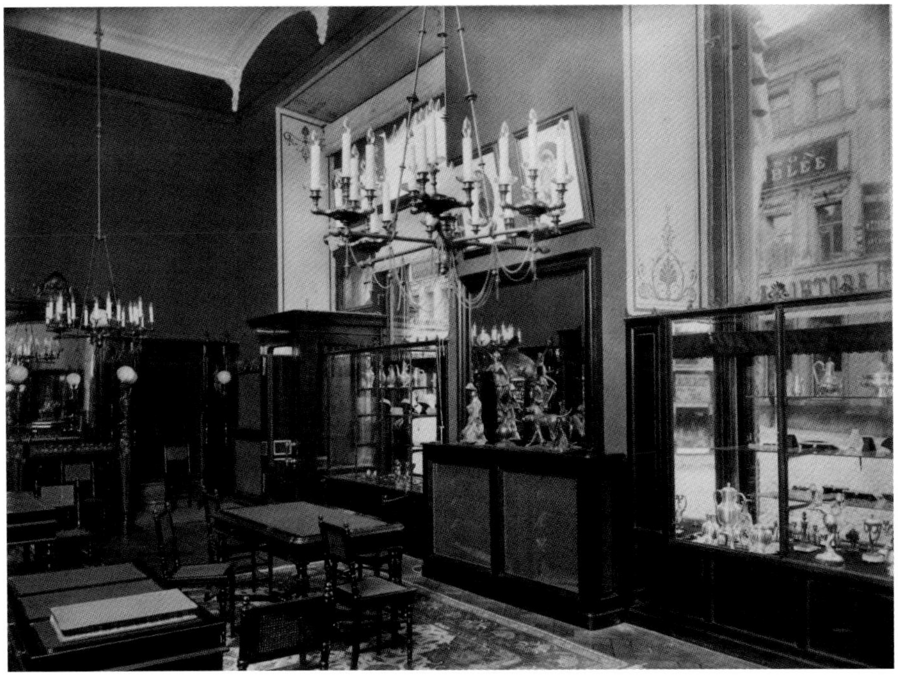

4. Inside of the Boucheron store in Moscow (opened in 1897)
Boucheron archives
(Cat. 324)

5. *Boucheron, Menu*
Round watch and knot brooch
1898
Boucheron Collection
(Cat. 326)

masters was the jeweler Bourdier. Not content to just present pieces of jewelry and art objects,[20] he offered an imperial egg (ill. 3) to the Empress Maria Feodorovna.

Created for the occasion, this egg in silver was suspended by a pink enamel bow decorated with the Empress's monogram. It was covered with a "Limoges" enamel, decorated with "Boucher style" cupids in blue-turquoise monochrome,[21] and contained a surprise: a flower-shaped brooch of violets. This item was inspired by eggs in wood, stone, porcelain, crystal and precious metal which were given for the Russian Easter holidays following the exceptional Imperial models by Fabergé.[22] Beyond its formal aspect, it is stylistically in the "rococo" taste of the Empress, characteristic of many of her purchases. This egg is also the reflection of an aesthetic inheritance unique to the elite French jewelry makers if one considers the egg form of the Fontenay perfume burner presented at the 1878 Universal Exhibition,[23] formal foreshadowing of the Bourdier night lamp presented in 1889 (ill. 6) and perhaps even of the first Fabergé eggs.

Aimed at pleasing her, this gift is one of the rare ones accepted by the Empress during her visit to the exhibition. The public law specialist Philippe Deschamps didn't hesitate to consider it "as a token of France's friendship for Russia."[24] As such, Bourdier's egg was reproduced in the press, the Emperor thanked the jeweler with a present, and, the height of success, the Empress honored him in taking a bracelet from him, "the prettiest item in the display case".[25] In 1898 came the ultimate consecration, he received the title of appointed supplier to the Russian Court.[26]

Maria Feodorovna, known for her taste for jewelry, acquired several pieces at the stands in the exhibition. Having admired the creations by Coulon she bought "two small roses in fine stones"[27] from him while at Louis Aucoc's she took a cameo brooch in moonstone set with diamonds and sapphires.[28] Alexander III, attracted by the enameled objects presented by Vever, chose one[29] and other members of the Imperial family bought him a bracelet decorated in diamonds, a candy dish and some buttons. In fact, the Grand Duke Serge, governor of Moscow, and his wife visited the exhibition several times with the Grand Duke and Duchess Wladimir.

The first event of the future Franco-Russian alliance was taking place—the French squadron led by Admiral Alfred-Abel Gervais was anchored at Cronstadt, from July 23 to August 7, 1891—and so the success of the exhibition was above all promotional. It was a manifesto of French and Russian political intentions, such as when the French Embassy chargé d'affaires, Count de Vauvineux, offered fans to Maria Feodorovna, Xenia Alexandrovna, and Elizabeth Feodorovna.[30] It bore witness to the Imperial Family's taste when this fam-

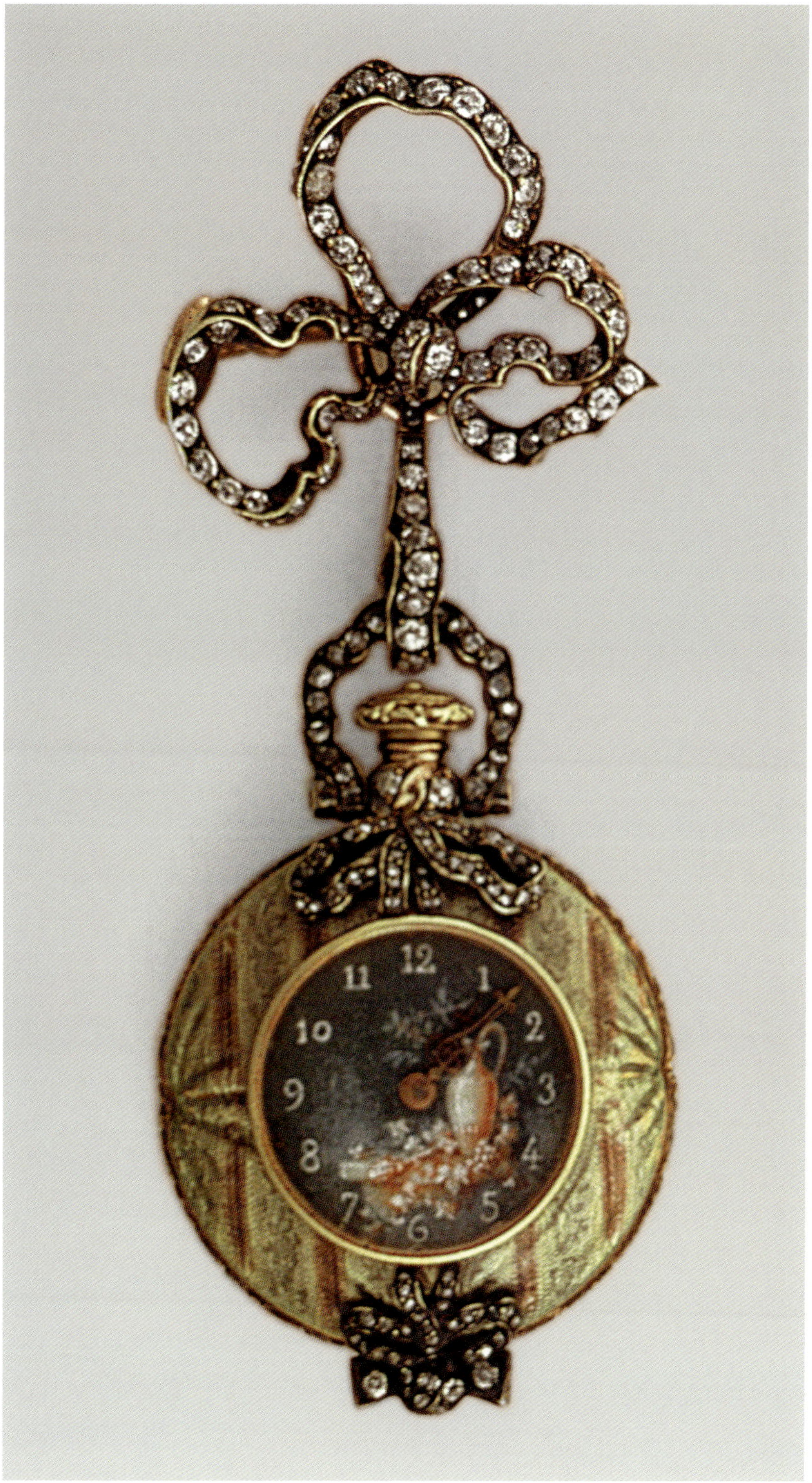

ily, through its purchases announced in the press and underlined by official reports, expressed its friendship for France.

Reinforced by this experience, several firms then developed their business dealings with Russia.

Boucheron's Muscovite adventure, and Cartier's Russian exhibitions

Boucheron, which from its beginnings had a large Russian clientele, had progressively invested in the Russian market since the 1880s. In 1897-1898, the firm decided to open its Muscovite shop on Marshall's Bridge Street (ills. 1 and 4) which was managed by Georges Delavigne and his two sons. In the old photographs of the inside of the establishment one can get a glimpse of jewelry and a lot of gold and silverwork, small fashionable items and designed pieces, all the diversity of the firm's creations.

There are two account books preserved in the archives concerning the activity of the Muscovite subsidiary.

From 1901 to 1906, the members of the Imperial family and the greatest names of the aristocracy are mentioned, such as the Empress mother Maria Feodorovna, the Grand Duke Serge and his wife, the Grand Duchess Elizabeth, the Yussupovs, all of whom are also recorded in the account books of the Paris store.

After that, the Imperial family disappears from the Muscovite books and appears less and less in Paris as well. In contrast, the clients from the industrial bourgeoisie—the Kelch, the gold magnates; the Kharitonenko, the sugar kings; the Riaouchininsky family; the Morozov family—are more and more present.

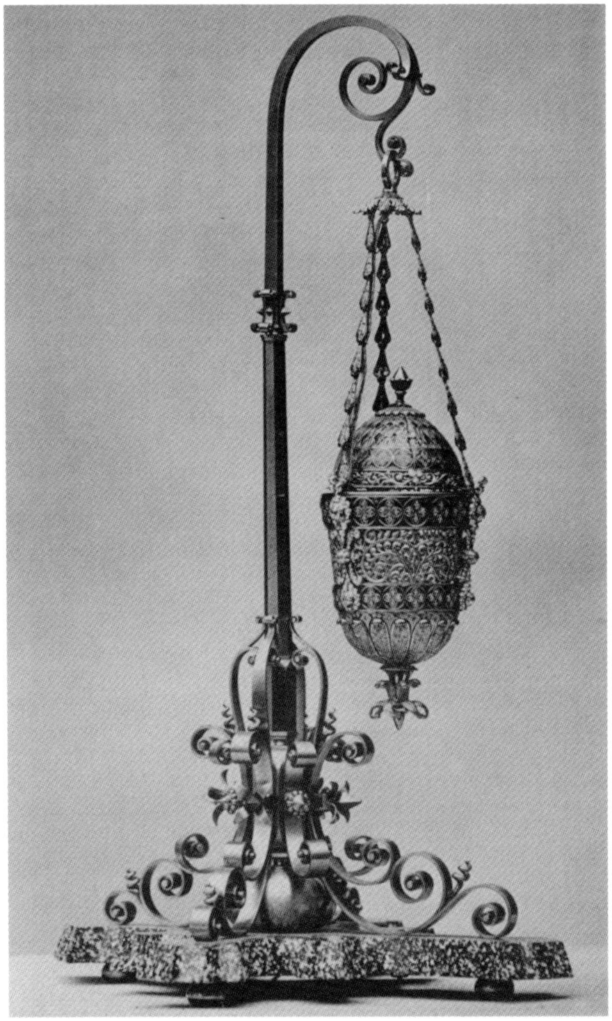

6. Object apparently presented by Bourdier during the Moscow French exhibition in 1891
Taken from Victor Champier, "Les industries d'art à l'Exposition Universelle de 1889 et de 1900," Revue des arts décoratifs, *Paris 1902.*

7. *Boucheron, J. A. Martel*
Large vase with chrysanthemums
Circa 1905
Mould of Russian importation
Boucheron Collection
(Cat. 329)

The existence of a Muscovite store facilitated participation in the large commercial exhibitions organized in St. Petersburg: the Franco-Russian exhibtion of 1899 at which were present Aucoc, Falize or Froment-Meurice; several French creators such as Aucoc, Chaumet, Falize and Keller[31] were also present at the international exhibition organized in 1901 by the St. Petersburg Society for the Encouragement of Art, and also at the international exhibition of historical costumes of 1902.

To publicize the Boucheron firm, Delavigne multiplied his trips: he went to Baku, to Tiflis, Odessa and Kiev. In 1911, Delavigne and his son Henri traveled throughout the south of Russia. They were carrying 500,000 francs worth of merchandise with them. On March 11, 1911, they were assassinated and robbed on a train on the return journey. The tragedy led to the closing of the Muscovite store.

In 1911, Alexander Alexandrovich Tillander (1870-1943), goldsmith and jeweler of Finnish origin, settled in St. Petersburg, took over the inventory of the store and became Boucheron's official representative in St. Petersburg (26 Nevsky Prospect). The last recorded sale is on November 8, 1917. The change in regime and the takeover by the Bolsheviks led to the closing of the store which ceased all business in Russia, as did Tillander. Today, several objects preserved in Russia, bearing a stamp of Russian importation or the inscription "Paris-Moscow" bear witness to their presence on the territory of the Empire (ills. 5 and 7).

Like Boucheron, the Cartier firm also developed its links with Russia. After having received the title of appointed supplier to the Court in 1907,[32] the firm regularly organized exhibition-sales.

In 1908, Paul Cheyrouze, associate of Louis Cartier, and his assistant Desbaines were en route for St. Petersburg[33] where they met Désiré Sarda. Cartier enjoyed the support of the Grand Duchess Wladimir, one of his major clients, who rented a residence for him for two months. It was located at 28 Palace Quay, in one of the dependencies of the neighboring Wladimir palace (no. 26). The installations in the palace was finished on December 9 and the name "Cartier" was displayed in front of the Neva, just two steps from the Winter Palace.

During his stay, Paul Cheyrouze delivered diverse objects to the Empress Maria Feodorovna, living in the Gatchina palace.[34] Prince Orlov and the

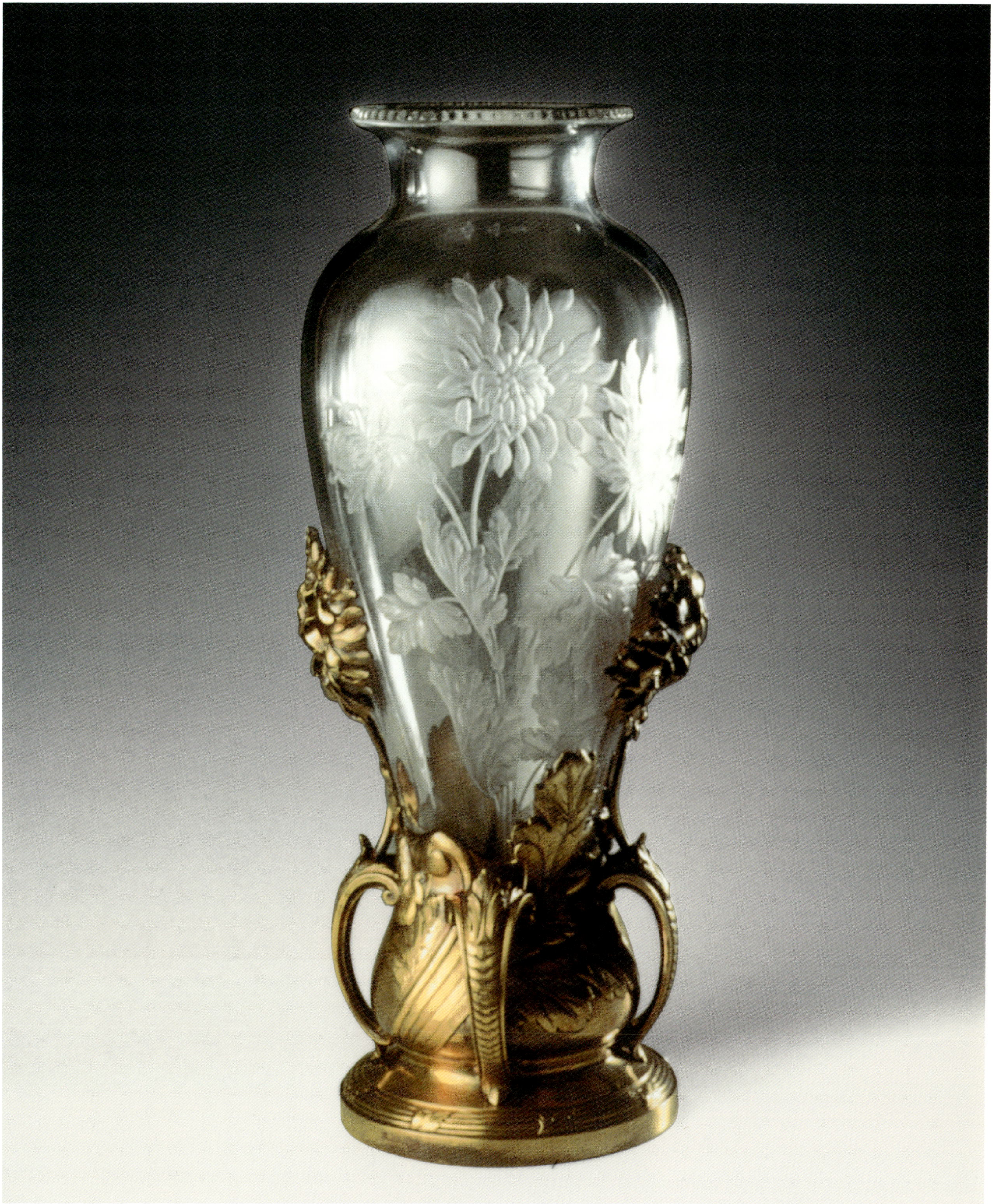

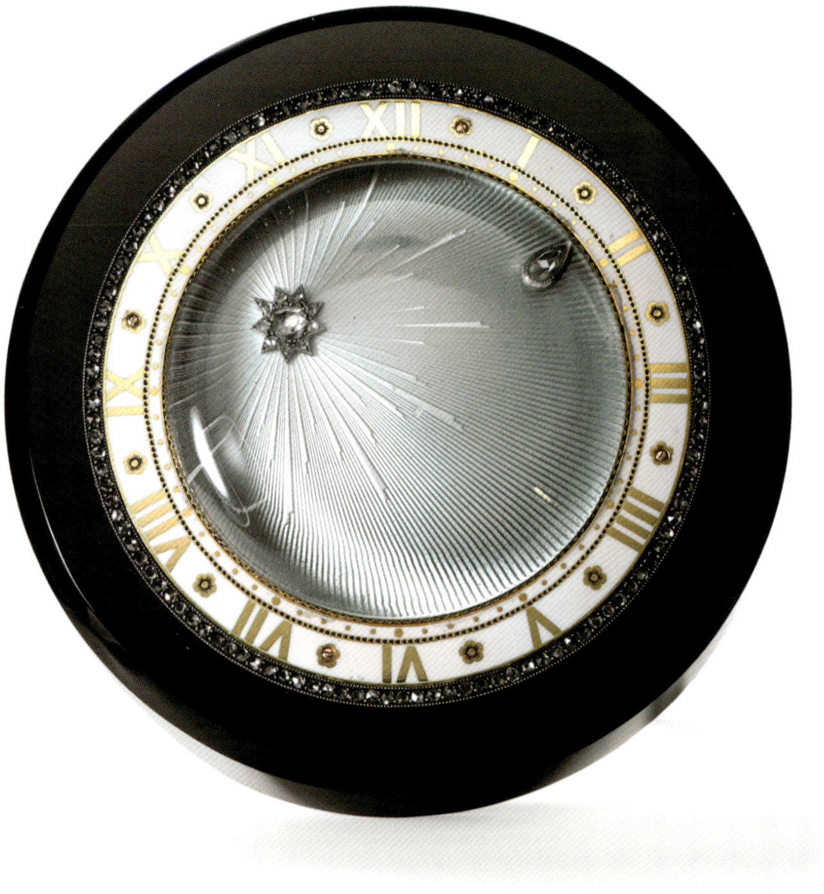

8. Comet Clock
Cartier Paris,
1918
The Cartier
Collection
(Cat. 381)

Grand Duchess Wladimir facilitated Paul Cheyrouze's introduction with the Emperor and the Imperial couple chose a few pieces of jewelry in an audience at Tsarskoye Selo in 1908.[35]

Paul Cheyrouze was then invited to participate in the charity sale organized at the Circle of Nobility by the Grand Duchess Wladimir. The appeal was a success but the accounts remained in debit.

While maintaining Sarda, the firm's representative, in the country, Cartier temporarily drew back from opening a subsidiary in Russia, preferring to organize this type of exhibition twice a year, most often organized at the Europe Hotel in St. Petersburg. Cartier personally took the trip from Paris in 1910, accompanied by his designer Charles Jacqueau (1885-1968). The difficulty in going through customs did not prevent them from participating in the Grand Duchess Wladimir's[36] charity sale where they presented dozens of precious stones, including thirteen diadems—one of them was in the form of a *kokoshnik*—and many clocks and watches. Louis Cartier took advantage of his stay to visit the collections of the Hermitage Museum where he was able to perfect his knowledge of the Russian collections and of the taste of the Imperial family. It was in drawing inspiration from the same jewels that Fabergé had gained the confidence of the whole Imperial family in the 1880s, whose taste he perpetuated while at the same time flattering it.

Louis Cartier, Charles Jacqueau and Léon Farinès, his salesman, next went to Moscow and Kiev. In Moscow, settling at the National Hotel, Cartier made contact with the collector Ivan Morozov, an important art enthusiast and one of the wealthy elite of the city. Moscow, heart of Russia, was thus one of the goals of the greatest French creators, first among them, the gold and silversmiths, and jewelers, who went directly to their clients to attract them, bringing new sources of inspiration to the Russian firms.

Moscow-Paris: forms and influences

When the Parisian gold and silversmiths and jewelers made *bratina*—brotherhood cups—or night lamps strangely resembling the little lamps which are suspended from icons, or when several of the pieces of jewelry exhibited in 1891 took the form of *kokoshnik* diadems, or of an Easter egg, they were showing their knowledge of the Russian forms and styles, revealed in France because of the presence of Russian creations in the French market or because of the collaboration of masters settled in Russia.

9. Powder box
Cartier Paris, 1911
The Cartier Collection
(Cat. 394)

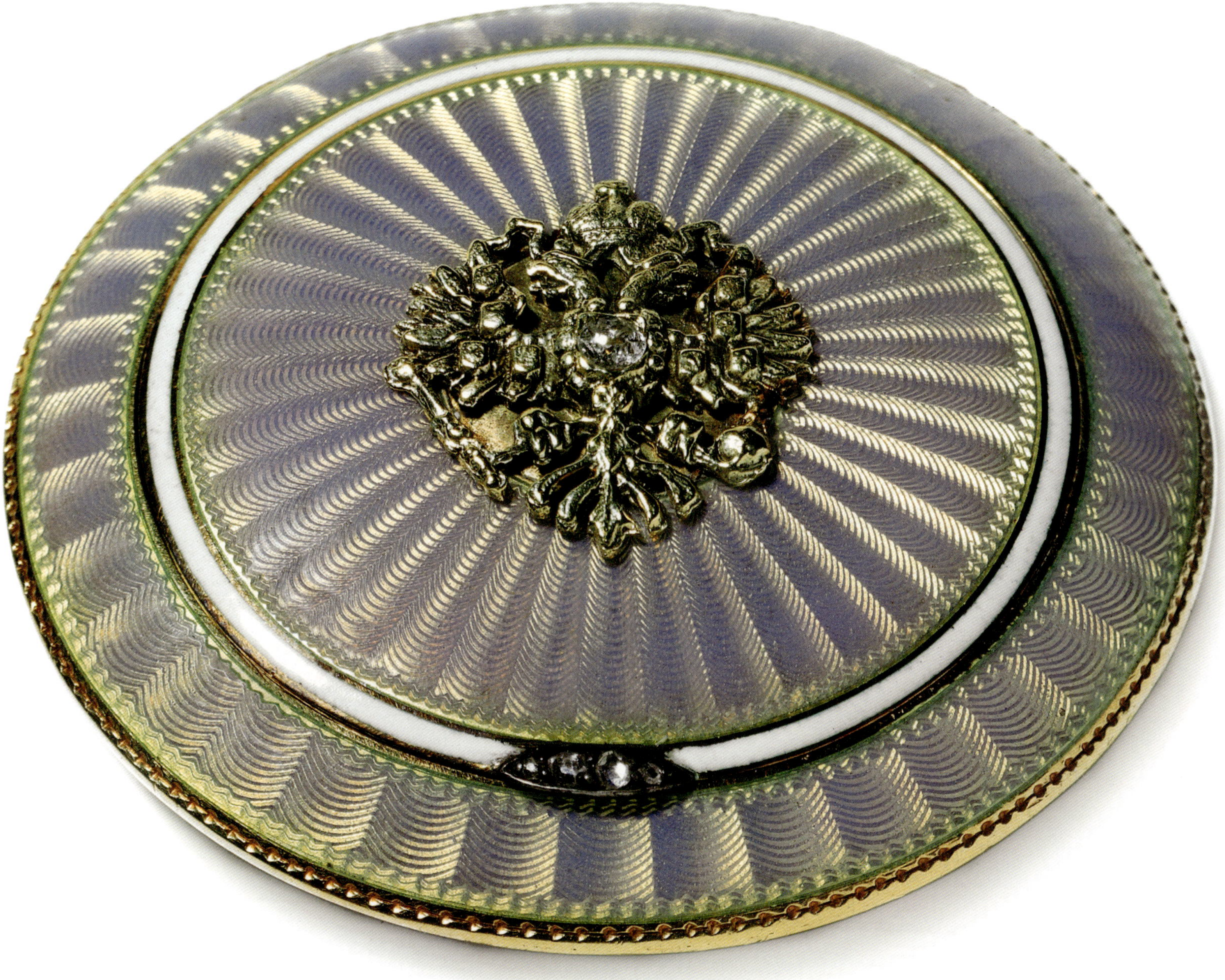

10. Desk Clock with Strut
Cartier Paris, 1914
The Cartier Collection
(Cat. 385)

11. Desk Clock with Strut
Cartier Paris, 1912
The Cartier Collection
(Cat. 383)

Russian gold and silversmiths, jewelers at the Paris universal exhibitions 1867-1900.

The French universal exhibitions, fabulous moments of exchanges and face to face meetings, included a large Russian section beginning in 1867. This exhibition grouped all the assembled production techniques with other countries into distinct groups, these groups themselves divided into classes. Thus gold and silverwork was separated from the jewelry group, even if the workshops were sometimes gathered together under the management of the same firm. As in France, many Russian creators such as Khlebnikov and Fabergé proposed gold and silver work, fashion accessories, and jewelry to their clients.

Among the number of Russian gold and silversmiths present at the 1867 exhibition were Basil Semenov and Ovchinnikov. The goldsmith I. Sazikov's showcase, considered as "the richest and most complete" displayed several objects with Russian subjects and Russian Byzantine style for the pleasure of the public. In 1867, only the Muscovite jewelers were represented by creations "of a very pronounced and very interesting national style"[37] bearing witness to a very high quality know-how "proverbial in Russian jewelry"[38] and illustrated by the work of Tchitchelev which was inspired by the richness and the polychrome of traditional Russian parure. The Russian exhibition was not limited to these very typical examples. Fulda Fils, one of the most famous Moscow jewelers, incarnated Western jewelry trends in Russia with pieces of jewelry in the form of butterflies or with her wide bracelets with naturalist decoration.[39] This dichotomy unique to Russian cre-

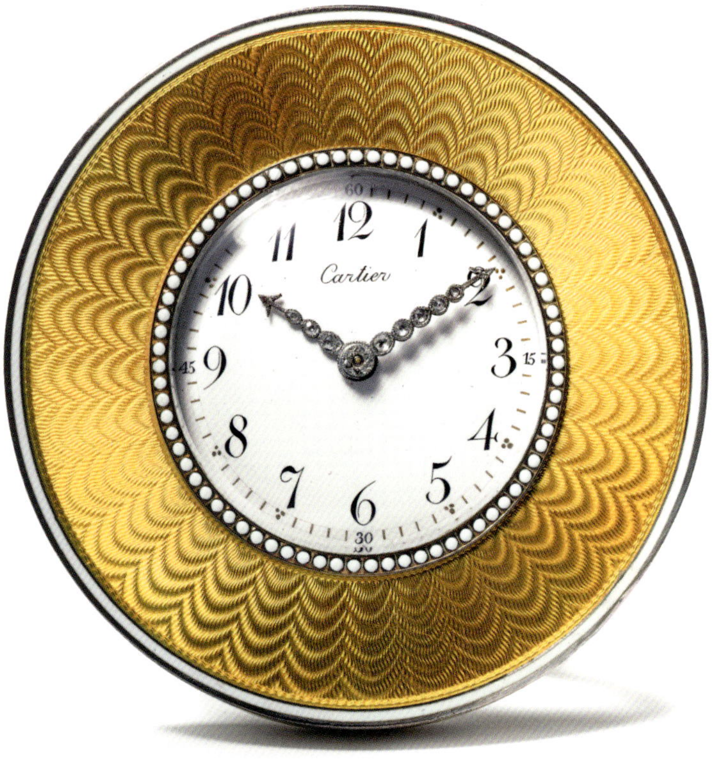

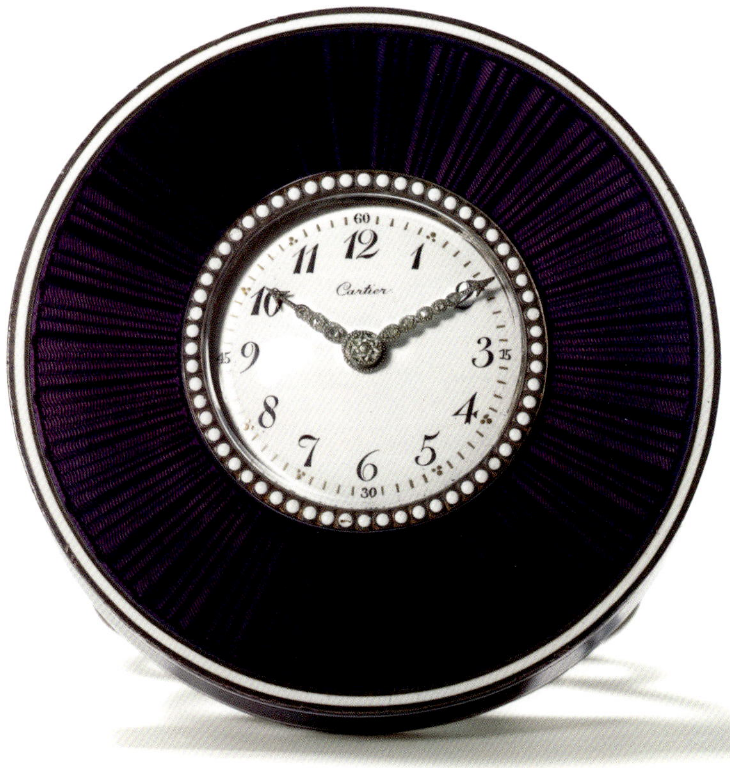

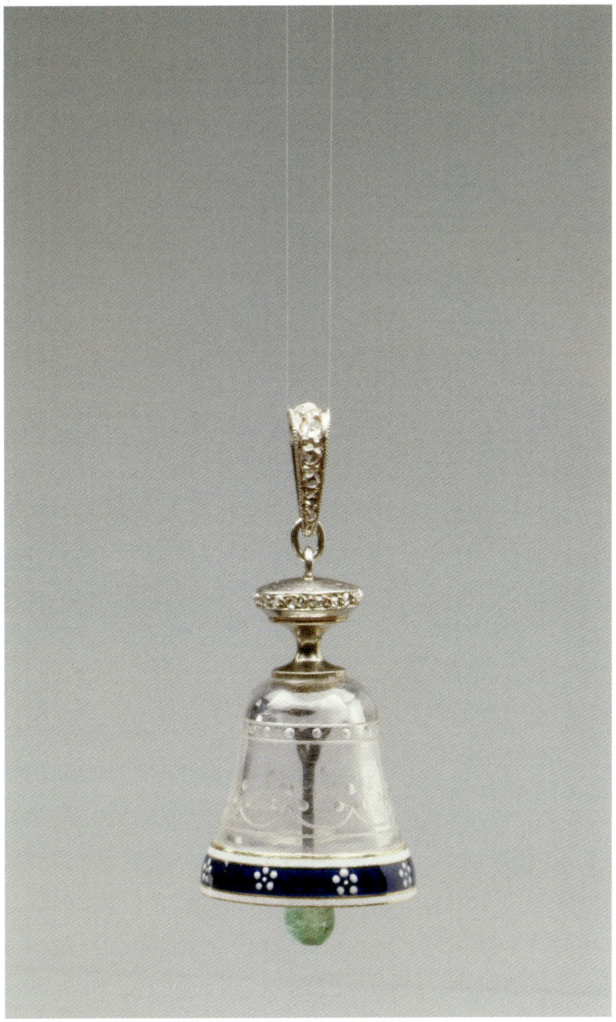

12. *Joseph Chaumet*
Chain with small bell pendant
Paris, circa 1911
Chaumet collection, Paris
(Cat. 401)

13. *Carl Fabergé.*
Workmaster: M. Perkhin
Case
St. Petersburg 1899-1908
Joseph Maouad, private collector
(Cat. 386)

ation was particularly obvious at the 1878 Paris Universal Exhibition, where the national style triumphed again in the showcases of Sazikov, Khlebnikov, and Ovchinnikov or in the luxury jewelry.[40]

In 1889, the Russian participation, although remarkable, was less important because it came from private initiative. The Russian government had not wanted to be officially associated with the event which the French Republic had chosen to link to the centenary of the 1789 Revolution.

The main goldsmiths were Ovchinnikov and Khlebnikov who received a gold medal for their enamel and in particular for the quality of their cloisonné-a-jour enamels, a genuine technical prowess comparable to those exhibited by Boucheron who excelled in that complex art. If jewelry was brilliantly absent in 1880, it enjoyed great success at the 1900 Exhibition: "It is work pushed to the extreme limit of perfection, it's the transformation of a jewel into a genuine work of art." This opinion concerning the Fabergé display cases was more nuanced when it had to do with the St. Petersburg Koechli firm or the Bock firm.[41]

As for gold and silverwork, along with Ovchinnikov and the Gratchev Brothers from St. Petersburg, Fabergé, a member of the jury, also attracted a great deal of attention even if his *"pieces are related more to the art of jewelry making.*[42] The Imperial loans such as the *Memory of Azov* egg[43], the *Lily of the Valley* egg,[44] the *Pansies* egg[45] were greatly admired by the public. In the span of about forty years, Russian gold and silverwork and jewelry had become known in France and served as examples for the creation of works destined for this market. At the turn of the century, with more and more intense Franco-Russian exchanges, certain forms and techniques became progressively mastered both by the French and by the Russians.

Reciprocity of the sources of inspiration

Although the declining eclecticism of an exacerbated neo-Louis XV "third rococo" reigned in arts and design which led sometimes to the sinuous

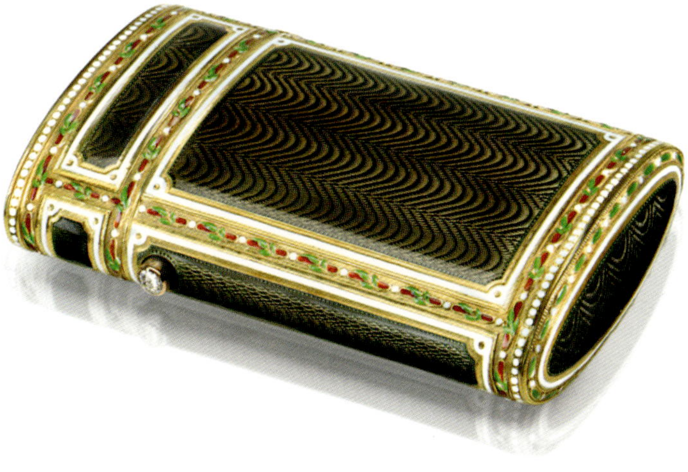

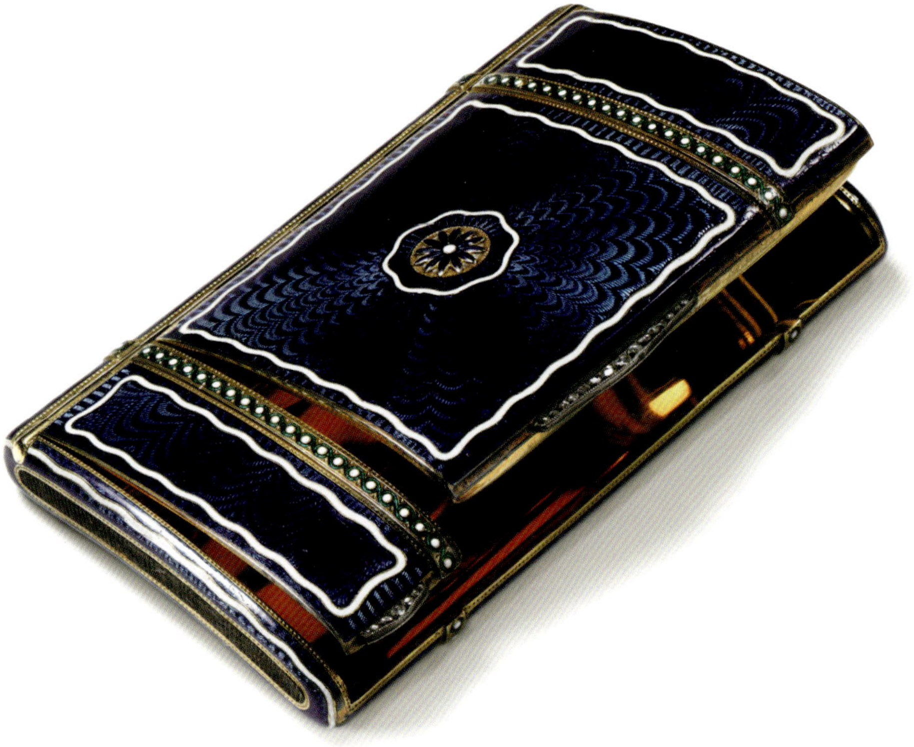

14. Cigarette case
Cartier Paris, 1907
The Cartier Collection
(Cat. 374)

15. *Carl Fabergé; Workmaster: M. Perkhin*
Small blue snake clock
1887
Present of the Emperor Alexander III to his bride Maria Feodorovna
Prince's Palace, Monaco
(Cat. 403)

and naturalist lines of an ephemeral Art Nouveau, the beginnings of a new style showed itself through the resurgence of neoclassical forms of the late 18th century. This taste, described as Louis XVI-1900 expressed itself both on the formal level—straight lines, geometric designs inspired from the ancient past—as well as on the technical level—gold of different colors, miniatures and enamels.

This communion of style practiced by the greatest Russian and French firms was furthered by their international existence as a result of their having opened branches around the world (St. Petersburg, Moscow, Paris, London, New York) and by sharing the same sources of inspiration.

Regarding historical styles, the examples were drawn from the examples of the past which were found in drawings, engravings and objects preserved by collectors, libraries and museums of the French and Russian nations, or from collections of the jewelry makers' creations departments. Even as the contemporary works exported to Russia were also a source of inspiration, so too did the Russian collections of art and design, in particular those of the Stieglitz museum or the Imperial Hermitage, provide the Russian creators with excellent ancient and modern examples, exactly as Paris did with its Louvre or Decorative Arts museum.

In addition, many craftsmen and Russian masters were formed *à l'Européene*, such as Peter Carl Fabergé who took his European "tour" with Julius Butts, son of the St. Petersburg jeweler. From Florence to Paris to Dresden, he gathered together an inexhaustible repertory of examples which he exploited in his production. Restoring and assessing the old Imperial collections, the Fabergé firm then developed its knowledge of techniques and styles.

The Imperial eggs which made the firm's reputation are excellent examples. By their form, they recall several creations from the French 18th century. For example, the first egg given by Alexander III to his wife in 1885 was inspired by the egg that the Emperor discovered in the Royal Danish Collections.[46] In the same way, the *Blue Serpent* egg given in 1887[47] repeats the composition of an ovoid clock by Jean-André Lepaute dated around 1785 (ill. 15).[48] As for the *Renaissance* egg in 1894[49] in agate enhanced with decorations in enameled gold, it is the interpretation of a jewel created by Le Roy and preserved in the "Green Vault" in Dresden.

Inspired by the old French models, the Russian eggs led a number of French jewelers to produce this sort of object. The Bourdier egg presented in 1891 (ill. 3) is one of the most accomplished with that of Cartier dated 1906. In a "Louis XVI-1900" style, it hides, like the imperial eggs, a surprise inside the structure: a portrait of the Czarevich.[50] At the beginning of the 20th century, the

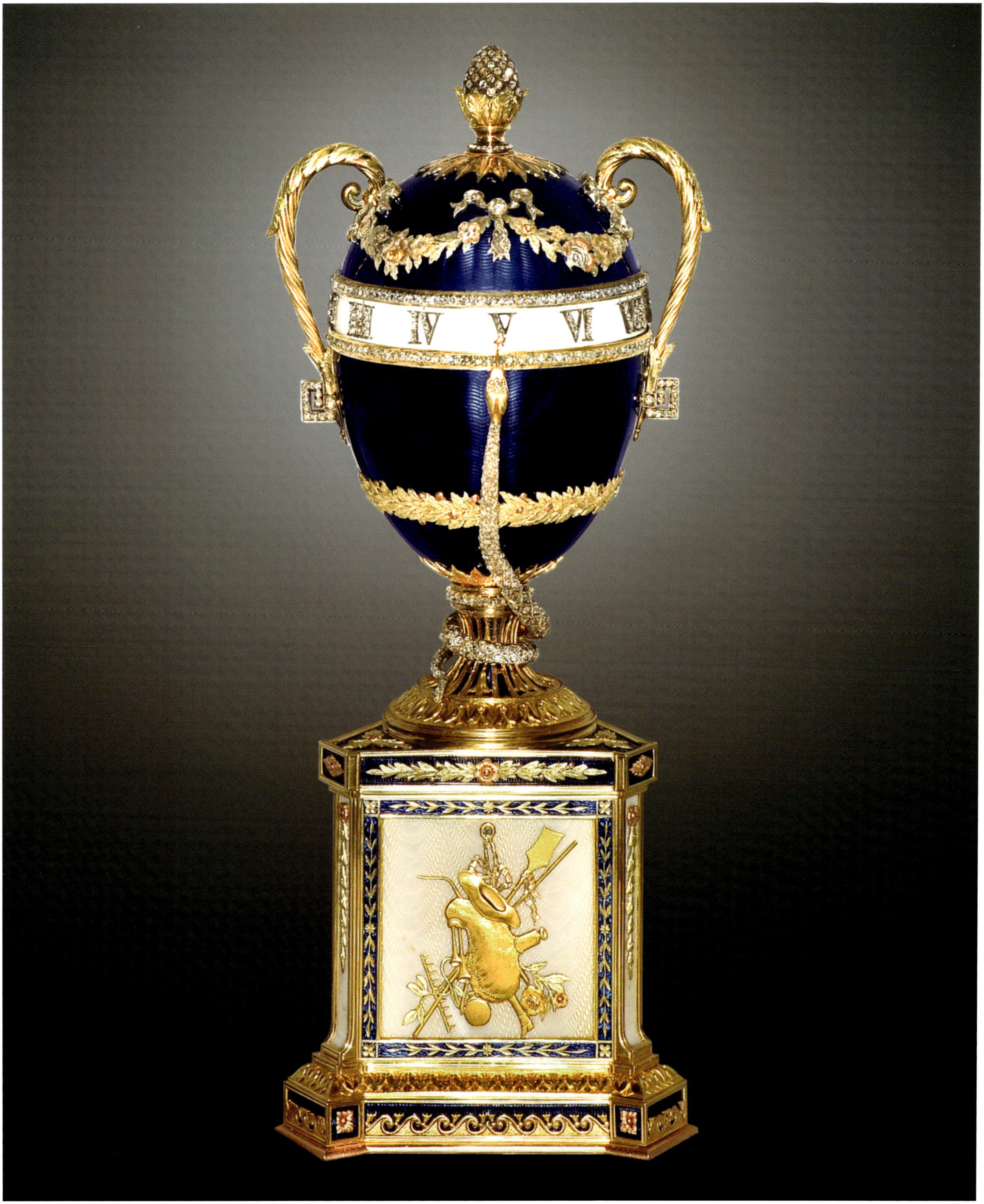

16. *Boucheron*
Paper knife and page marker
Boucheron Collection
(Cat. 391)

17. *Bolin (?)*
Mary of Serbia's diadem
Circa 1880
Van Cleef & Arpels Collection
(Cat. 294)

ovoid form was used by Cartier or Chaumet for the concept of clocks or little Easter eggs which the firms regularly presented to its Russian clientele.[51]

Among the creations by Fabergé and its French and Russian competitors, a diverse number of accessories, from the fan to the cane handle, to clocks, frames, boxes and cases, formed a body of work of similar inspiration. Produced in the first years of the 20th century, these pieces were characterized by the use of different enamel techniques. Applied onto simple forms, large guilloche surfaces were covered with translucent and polychrome enamels with radiant effects, or undulated with great refinement.

One such a case was made by Fabergé (ill. 13), another by Cartier (ill. 14) or other Paris firms. It should not be forgotten that Pierre Cartier profited from his stay in Russia in 1904-05 to develop commercial ties with the St. Petersburg and Muscovite craftsmen. Extending all the way to Russia, the practice of subcontracting was a way of offering one's clientele the best of the production. Thus Cartier called on certain Russian enamellers such as Yahr of Moscow from whom he also bought boxes and small items. These importations also concerned lapidary art work,[52] carried out based on examples furnished by Cartier or coming directly from the Russian workshops represented by various craftsmen such as the Muscovite Svietchnikov, Karl Woeffel from St. Petersburg, Denissov-Uralsky, supplier to Fabergé, and finally the goldsmith Ovchinnikov. However Cartier did not neglect the French workshops, such as those of Varangoz, Fréville, and César.[53] This taste for decorative stones also included the use of nephrite.

At the end of the 19th century, Fabergé popularized the use of nephrite to make frames, cases and other accessories. At the same time, this stone was also used by Cartier and Boucheron (ill. 16). Around 1900, resorting to foreign creators was also characteristic of one of Fabergé's major Russian competitors, the Bolin firm, which had been founded back in the 18th century. The history of this dynasty of gold and silversmiths and jewelers is relatively complex and was divided between several branches working in St. Petersburg and Moscow.[54]

The *kokoshnik* diadem of cabochon emeralds[55] which is attributed to Bolin (ill. 17) shows the importance of the traditional forms imposed by the splendors of the Court beginning with the reign of Nicholas I. In contrast, the diadems ordered under the reign of Nicholas II were very international in form, appropriate for an imperial family which was linked to all the dynasties of Europe.

This trend was well illustrated by the diadem of diamond and emerald knots which the Empress Alexandra ordered from Bolin around 1900. The Sovereign wore it with the elegance which characterized her for her portrait made in 1907 by the painter Nikolai K. Bodarevsky in the Alexander Palace[56]. A comparable *1900-classicism* character-

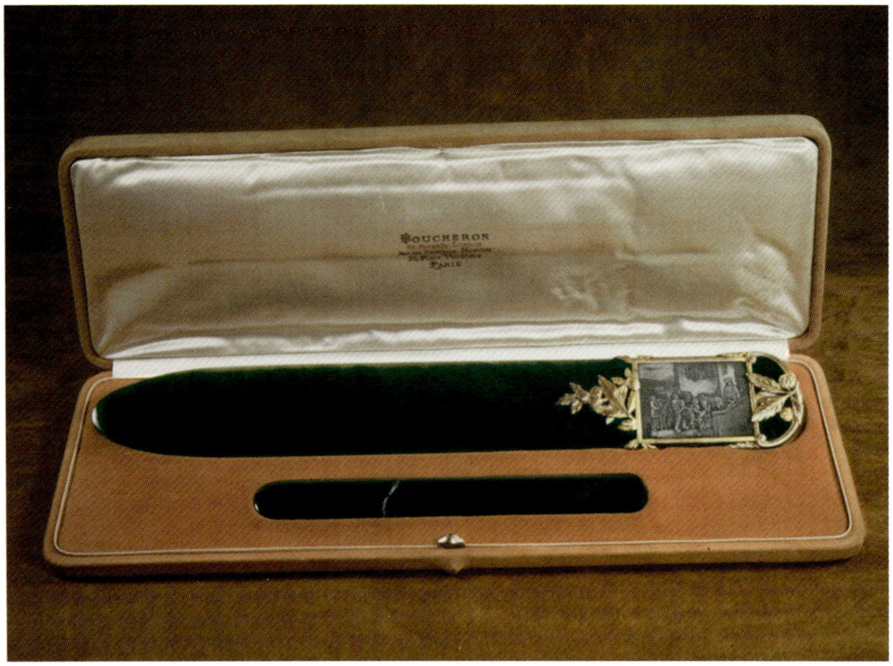

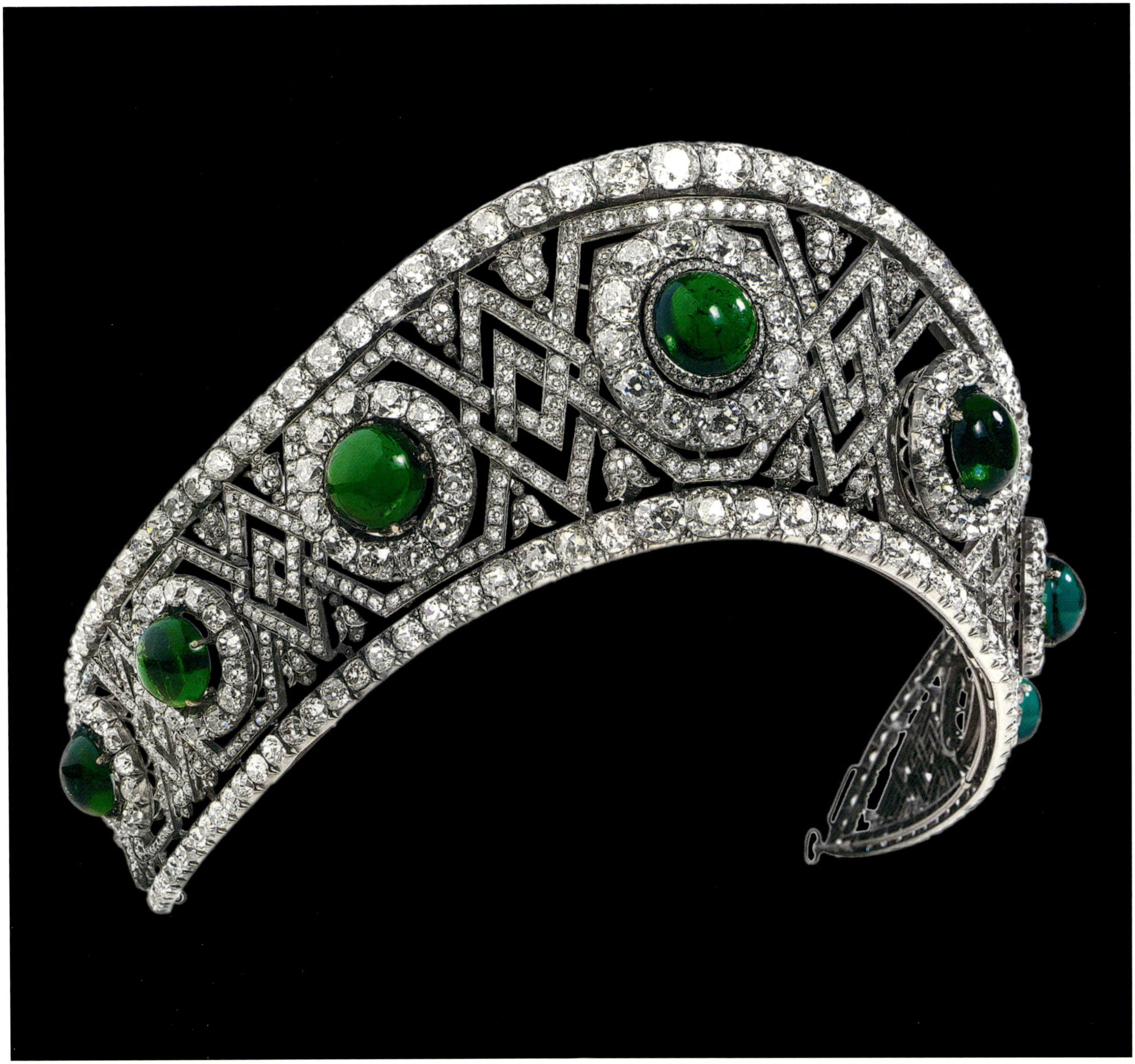

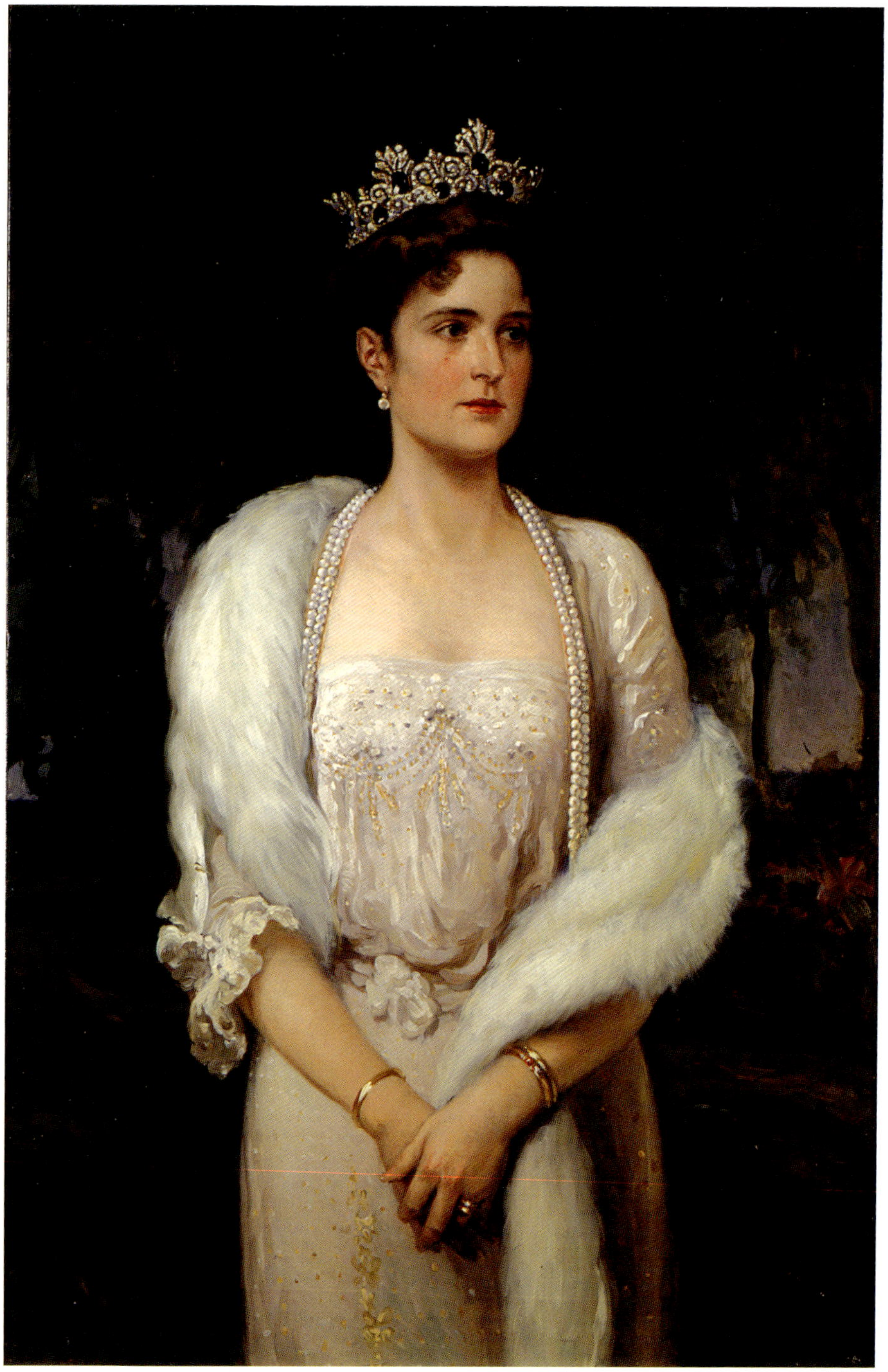

18. *A. V. Makovsky*
Portrait of the Empress Alexandra Feodorovna (1872-1918)
1914
The State Historical Museum, Moscow
(Cat. 164)

ized the diadem with palmettes and diamond and sapphire volutes ordered of Koechli and which the Empress is wearing in a portrait painted in 1914 by A. V. Makovsky (ill. 18).[57]

For a part of his production, Bolin also adopted a moderate Art Nouveau style. These new sources of inspiration are in particular due to the activity of Wilhelm A. Bolin (1861-1934). Trained in France, he used examples furnished by renown artists in the French art and luxury industries in his Muscovite workshops, artists such as Auguste Moreau, Joseph Chéret, and Paul Liénard. The first two, sculptors and decorators, promoted the introduction of the sculpted human figure in decorative arts. Moreau, who belonged to a dynasty of sculptors, also created models for the French gold and silversmiths A. Boulenger et Cie, and Ed. Tétard. As for Chéret, brother of the famous painter and poster designer, he worked with many French and foreign craftsmen and firms touching on all the techniques: the crystal making Baccarat, the gold and silversmith Christofle, the ceramist Théodore Deck, the Sèvres manufacture, the bronze smith E. Soleau. Considered as an "*heir of Clodion*", Chéret created models on which figures in movement, smiling women, and laughing cupids, are one with the object.[58] But the introduction of modern French style was especially accomplished through the drawings by Paul-Gabriel Liénard, sculptor and jeweler, whose rare creations are masterpieces of the spirit of Art Nouveau.[59]

The circulation of examples of inspiration and of artists led to a resemblance between certain Russian and French creations at the turn of the century.

[1] E. Haumant, *La culture française en Russie*, Paris 1913
[2] *Les amours du chevalier de Faublas*, one of literature's big successes in the years 1780 to 1790 by Jean-Baptiste Louvet de Couvray.
[3] E. Haumant, *op. cit.*, p. 259.
[4] O. Policarpova, T. Troitskaya, "La mode parisienne et son influence à Moscou," in exhibition cat., *Souvenirs moscovites 1860-1930*, Musée Galliera, Paris 1999-2000, p. 37.
[5] *Fabergé, joaillier des Romanov*, exhibition cat., ING Cultural Espace, Brussels 2005-2006, p. 133.
[6] See Brigitte de Montclos's article, pp. 161-173.
[7] See Mme. Michaela Lerch's article, pp. 215-223.
[8] M. Lopato, *Gold and silversmiths and jewelers of ancient St. Petersburg*, Hermitage, St. Petersburg 2006, p. 194, (in Russian).
[9] See T. I. Sizova's article, pp. 149-159.
[10] H. Nadelhoffer, *Cartier*, Edition du Regard, Paris 1984, p. 115.
[11] D. Scarisbrick, "Russland und Chaumet 1900 bis 1917," in exhibition cat., *Fabergé-Cartier. Rivalen am Zarenhof*, Kunsthalle der Hypo-Kulturstiftung, Munich 2003-2004, p. 119.
[12] R. Nougaret, *The French bank, the Crédit Lyonnais, in Russia 1878-1920*, Paris 1922, (in Russian).
[13] *La nouvelle Revue*, April 1, 1891, p. 9.
[14] *Ibid.*
[15] L. Plarr, *La France à Moscou-exposition de 1891*, De Soye et Fils, Paris 1891, pp. 237-241.
[16] J. Balmont, "Une visite à l'exposition de Moscou", in *Revue des arts décoratifs*, July-August 1891, p. 35.
[17] Musée des Arts décoratifs, Paris, inv. 24488.
[18] Likely the chest preserved at the Museum of Decorative Arts, Paris.
[19] Likely the night lamp preserved at the Museum of Decorative Arts, Paris (inv. 24481).
[20] He exhibited notably a table lamp which was likely presented at the 1889 Paris Universal Exhibition.
[21] Hermitage Museum, St. Petersburg, inv. ЭPO 8804. The egg was kept at the Gatchina palace, one of the favorite residences of the Empress, and was undoubtedly transferred into the Hermitage collections at the time of the Revolution.
[22] See Brigitte de Montclos's article, pp. 161-173.
[23] Orsay Museum, inv. OAO 264.
[24] Ph. Deschampe, *Le livre d'or de l'alliance franco-russe*, Leroux Editeur, Paris 1898, p. 5.
[25] L. Plarr, *op. cit.*, p. 222.
[26] V. V. Skurlov, A. N. Ivanov, *Suppliers to the Imperial Court*, St. Petersburg 2002, p. 12, (in Russian).
[27] J. Balmont, *op. cit.*, p. 31.
[28] L. Plarr, *op. cit.*, pp. 221-222.
[29] The major Turgan factories, *Mémorial de l'exposition française de Moscou, 1891*, book offered to His Majesty the Emperor Alexander III by the major French firms, *Administration des grandes usines*, L. Berger and Cie Editeur, Paris, p. 314.
[30] *Journal de l'exposition française à Moscou en 1891*, No. 5, May 26, 1891, p. 4.
[31] Regarding the business dealings maintained by the Keller firm, appointed supplier to the Russian Court beginning in 1900, see W. Zeisler, "French Art Nouveau in Russia and the Imperial purchases from the Keller firm" in *At the turn of the century, art during the "Modern" epoch*, Hermitage Museum, St. Petersburg 2006, pp. 137-143, (in Russian).
[32] V. V. Skurlov, A. N. Ivanov, *op. cit.*, p. 21.
[33] H. Nadelhoffer, *op. cit.*, p. 113.
[34] G. von Habsburg, "Cartier in Russland," in *Fabergé-Cartier. Rivalen am Zarenhof*, *op. cit.*, p. 83.
[35] *Fabergé-Cartier. Rivalen am Zarenhof*, *op. cit.*, p. 438.
[36] H. Nadelhoffer, *op. cit.*, p. 118; G. von Habsburg, *op. cit.*, p. 86.
[37] *1867 Universal Exhibition in Paris. Reports of the International Jury*, Paul Dupont administrative printing press, Paris 1868 (13 vol.) gr. IV, cl. 36, p. 422.
[38] *Ibid.*, p. 430.
[39] Fr. Ducuing, *L'exposition universelle de 1867 illustrée*, Dentu, Paris 1867, 2 vol.
[40] *1878 Universal Exhibition – International Jury Report*, 1890-1893, gr. IV, cl. 39, p. 18.
[41] 1900 International Universal Exhibition in Paris—International Jury Report—Group XV, Class 95, Paris, Imprimerie Nationale, 1902-1906, p. 371.
[42] *Ibid.*, cl. 94, p. 330.
[43] Armory Palace, Kremlin, Moscow, Inv. MP 645 ½.
[44] See Brigitte de Montclos's article, pp. 161-173.
[45] Private Collection.
[46] *Fabergé, joaillier des Romanov*, *op. cit.*, pp. 35-38.
[47] See Brigitte de Montclos's article, pp. 161-173.
[48] "Artistic Luxury: Fabergé, Tiffany, Lalique," exhibition cat., The Cleveland Museum of Art, 2008-2009, pp. 176-177.
[49] See Mme. Brigitte de Montclos's article in this catalogue, pp. 161-173.
[50] J. Rudoe, *Cartier 1900-1939*, Somogy, Paris 1997.
[51] H. Nadelhoffer, *op. cit.*, 1984, pp. 115, 120.
[52] *Fabergé-Cartier. Rivalen am Zarenhof*,, *op. cit.*, pp. 441-448.
[53] G. von Habsburg, *op. cit.*, p. 78.
[54] About Bolin, see M. Ribbing, T. Muntjan, V. Skurlov, L. Zavadskaja, *Smychen & Silver för tsarer, drottningar och andra/W. A. Bolin 200* A R, Västeras, 1996.
[55] Van Cleef & Arpels Collection, Paris. For more on the history of the Tiara, see Munn, Geoffrey C., Tiaras—*A History of Splendour,* Paris, Antique Collector's Club, 2001, pl. 246.
[56] Tsarskoye Selo Palace Museum, inv. 635 X
[57] Moscow Historical Museum, inv. ГИМ 65858 / ИИ 3962.
[58] On Chéret, see among others J. Hargrove, "Gustave-Joseph Chéret's Day," in *Cleveland Studies in the History of Art*, vol. 8, 2003, pp. 215-221.
[59] M. Ribbing and *alii*, *op. cit.*, p 78. A bowl decorated with a swan produced in the Bolin Muscovite workshops illustrates most likely Liénard's influence. Hessische Hausstiftung, Kronberg, inv. WO s 8076. Cf. exhibition cat., *Russland 1900*, Mathidenhöhe, Darmstadt, 2008-2009 ill. p. 229.

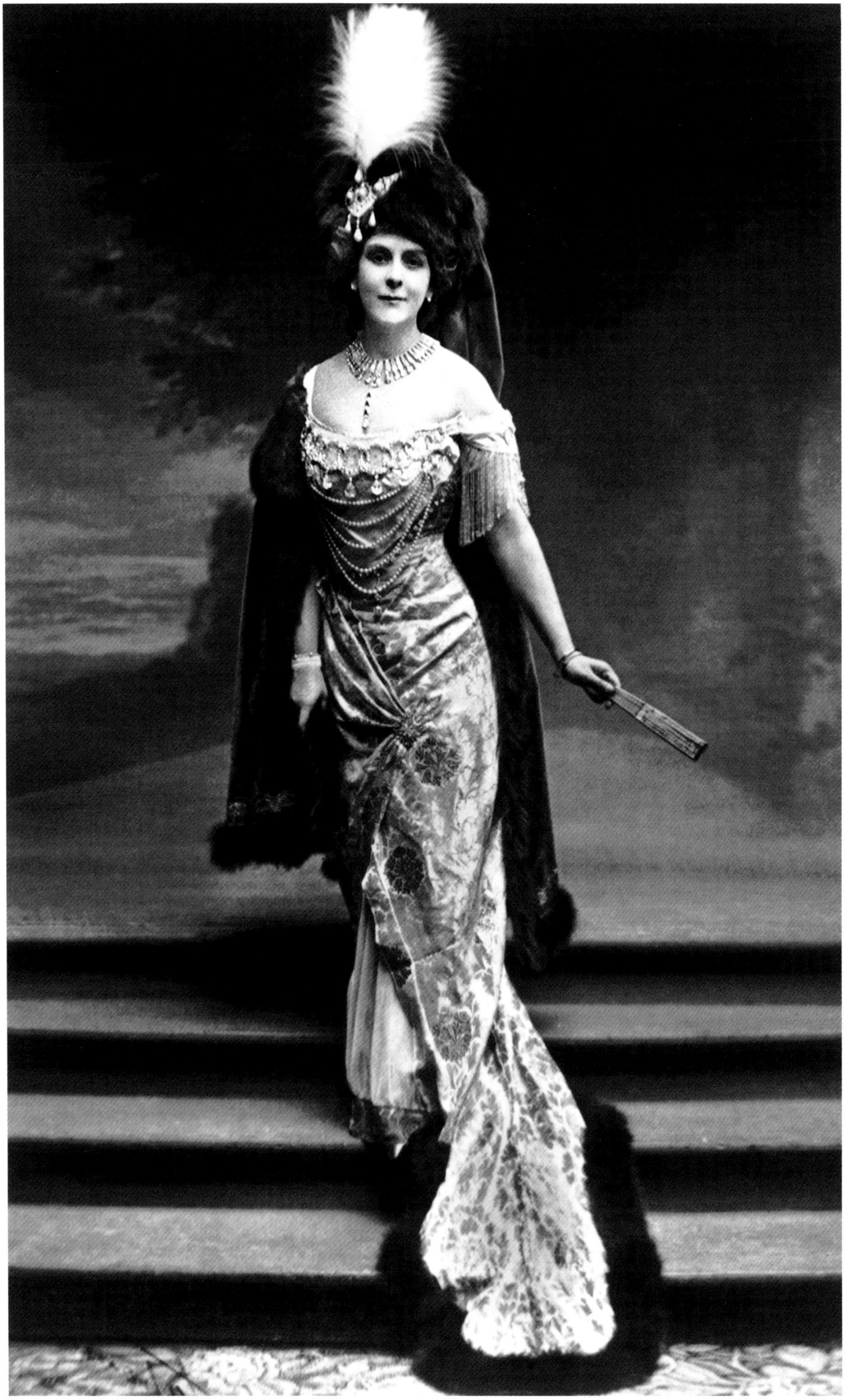

FROM MOSCOW TO PARIS: RUSSIAN CLIENTS AND COMMANDS IN FRANCE

Wilfried Zeisler

At Alexander II's accession, Russians began to increasingly frequent both Paris as well as the Riviera. This presence was favorable for purchases and the jewelry firms encountered their first Russian clients: on August 29, 1859, prince Gortchakov at the Boucheron firm, and in 1860, count Soltykov at Cartier. The old firms such as Fossin (the future Chaumet) or Mellerio dits Meller renewed their contacts with these Russians, most of whom were nobles. In 1867 for example, count Demidov acquired a "marabout feather with knots of brilliants" at Mellerio's. Its memory is evoked by a similar creation preserved in a private collection (ill. 2).

The Russian colony, whether permanent or seasonal, reached its peak during the Third Republic with the Franco-Russian Alliance. This clientele, from the Court to the upper classes, evolved but nearly always went to the best French creators who were famous from international events and were established in the districts where the Russians lived.

1. *Boissonas and Taponnier*
The Princess Olga Paley, Countess Hohenfelsen, wife of the Grand Duke Paul
1912
Cartier archives, Paris
(Cat. 365)

The Grand Dukes' Third Republic

In Imperial Russia, the title grand duke which is translated rather by 'Grand Prince', is borne by the Emperor's sons and grandsons who have the right to the title of His Royal Highness. At the age of twenty, every Grand Duke becomes financially independent. In 1867, the Grand Duke Wladimir, Alexander II's son, thus was granted an annual income of 142,850. 14 silver rubles and 600,000 rubles for the construction of his palace.[1]

This fortune often was completed by revenues coming from their residences and especially coming from the various official duties which the Grand Dukes held concurrently from highest state level. Their considerable financial means enabled them, with a reduced suite and more relaxed etiquette, to travel abroad more freely than the Emperor.

In Paris, these Romanovs were sometimes lodged at the Embassy, rue de Grenelle, or in the best hotels which stood in the heart of the Parisian luxury districts. Sometimes even, as the grand duke Alexis or the grand duke Paul, these clients owned their own pied-à-terre.

The purchases they effected were very diverse: art, antiques, furniture, bronzes, fashion items and art objects. Jewelry and accessories were particularly popular for they had a ceremonial usage, very developed at the Court. They were also the worldly image of a sought-after Parisian fashion. From the diadem to the simple ring, the array of feminine finery was appreciated. Nor was masculine elegance neglected, and these Russians also selected "coat hanger" brooches, tie pins and sliding rings, boutonniere pins, rings, shirt buttons or cuff links. These ob-

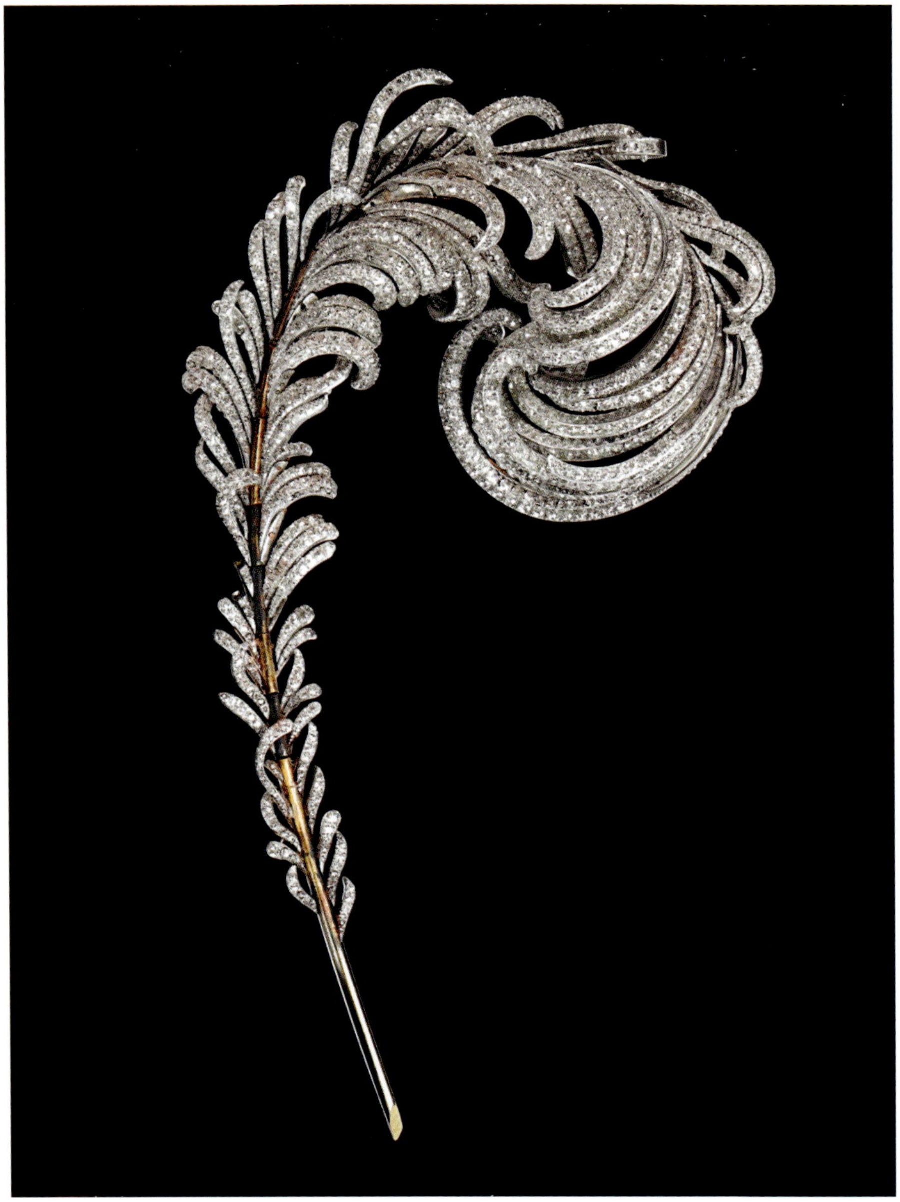

2. *Attributed to Mellerio dits Meller*
Jointed feather
Circa 1870
Mellerio dits Meller collection
(Cat. 317)

jects were also ones that Russian clients were happy to repair for a few francs: pins to be straightened, stones or pearls to be reinserted, gilding or enameling to be redone and especially long pearl necklaces to be restrung.

This clientele also chose small precious objects in Paris, indispensable for daily luxury and which reflected the customs of the *Belle Epoque*: canes and cane handles, watches, salt-cellars, fans, hand-mirrors, cigarette lighters, cigarette holders, cigar cutters, playing card cases, pencil cases, blotters, paper cutters, book dust jackets, theater binoculars, thimbles, thermometers, whistles, rattles, and various cases.

Sometimes the purchase was worthy of the image of splendor one still had of the Imperial court. For these jewelry orders, the precious stones were often furnished, sometimes recuperated from old jewelry.

Among the some twenty "little courts" formed by the grand dukes and grand duchesses and their suites, a few were notable for their orders and purchases of jewels in France—these were the Czarevichs Alexander and then Nicholas, and also Alexander III's brothers.

During a trip he took to Paris, the Grand Duke Alexander Alexandrovich (the future Alexander III) acquired several pieces of jewelry from the Boucheron firm on February 7, 1876. While his mother, the Empress Maria Alexandrovna was satisfied with four pairs of cuff links, the Czarevich spent 12,600 francs for a rose-enameled watch decorated with his monogram, a Rosaline chatelaine decorated with diamonds and a large diamond fern. The watch was for him and the fern was certainly for his wife, the Grand Duchess Maria Feodorovna. The same loving care was shown in the acquisition of a crown by the Grand Duke Nicholas Alexandrovich (the future Nicholas II) in 1894. The Czarevich, embarked upon the imperial yacht Polar Star and went to visit his young fiancée in England where he stayed from June 8 to July 12. At Windsor, the Grand Duke gave an engagement gift "a ring mounted with a pink pearl, a necklace of large pearls, pink also, a bracelet shaped like a chain with an enormous emerald, and a brooch decorated with sapphires and dia-

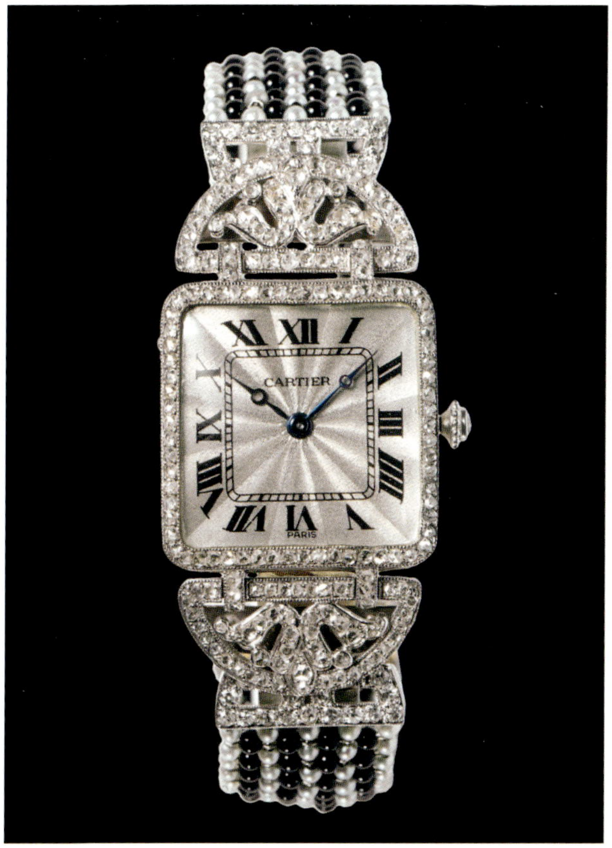

3. Acanthus-pattern Wristwatch
Cartier Paris, 1912
The Cartier Collection
(Cat. 316)

monds”,[2] completed by a string of pearls by Fabergé estimated at 250,000 gold rubles, a gift from the Emperor.

This event was the occasion for the French jewelers to present their creations. In his journal, Nicholas II mentions these contacts several times: Monday, June 27, he admires with Alix the jewelry of one of the four creators whose cards he had received,[3] a little later, on July 5, he buys a piece of jewelry from each of the two jewelers who had shown their creations in his room.[4] One of them was François Aubert, one of Frédéric Boucheron’s assistants, who was received by the Czarevich on July 17 and the jewel chosen by the young fiancés was a “small floweret crown of brilliants and pearls” (27,500 francs) (ill. 5). The little crown was regularly worn by the Empress and it can be seen in many of her photographic portraits (ill. 7). Its destiny remains unknown: it did not appear in the sale of some of the crown jewels organized by Christie’s in London on March 16, 1927. As a personal piece of jewelry, this small crown was perhaps among the jewelry and precious objects taken by the Imperial family into its exile in Siberia.[5]

The second French jeweler encountered in London was perhaps Vever, whose name appeared that year in the Emperor’s cabinet accounts.[6] It could also be Lalique, who around 1893-1895 executed a jeweled fan with the imperial coat of arms.[7]

Once he became Emperor, Nicholas II, wanting to mark his interest for France and its art, sometimes acquired pieces which were presented to him by Boucheron, Cartier, or Lalique during their “Russian expeditions.” Rare, these purchases could not be compared to those, more regular, of the grand dukes, in particular his uncles when they were in France.

The Grand Duke Wladimir, Alexander III’s younger brother, was passionate about history, art

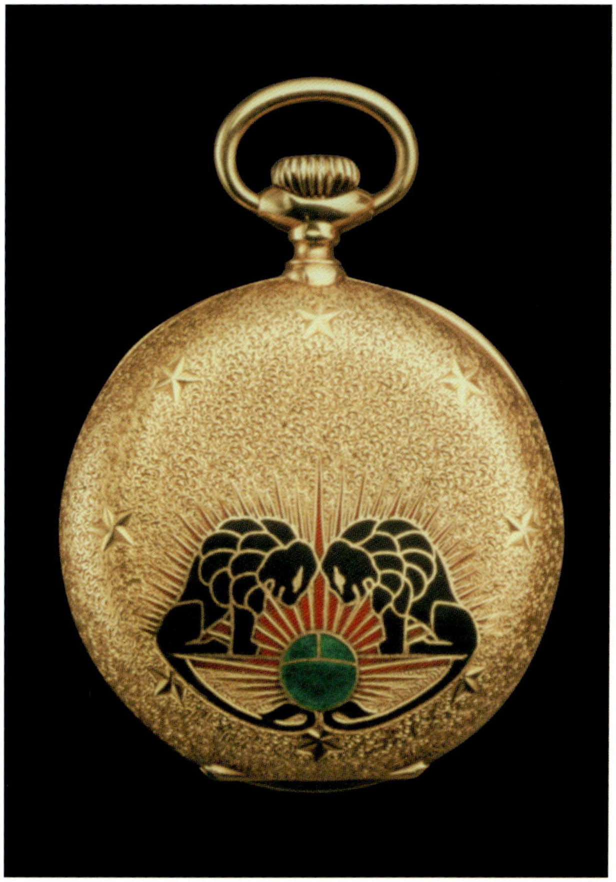

4. *Boucheron*
Waistcoat pocket watch
1908
Boucheron Collection
(Cat. 327)

5. Small crown decorated with eighteen pearls, diamonds and rose-cut diamonds, No. 12286
Purchase by the future Nicholas II in 1894
Boucheron archives
(Cat. 340)

6. Cigarette case
Cartier Paris, 1912
The Cartier Collection
(Cat. 396)

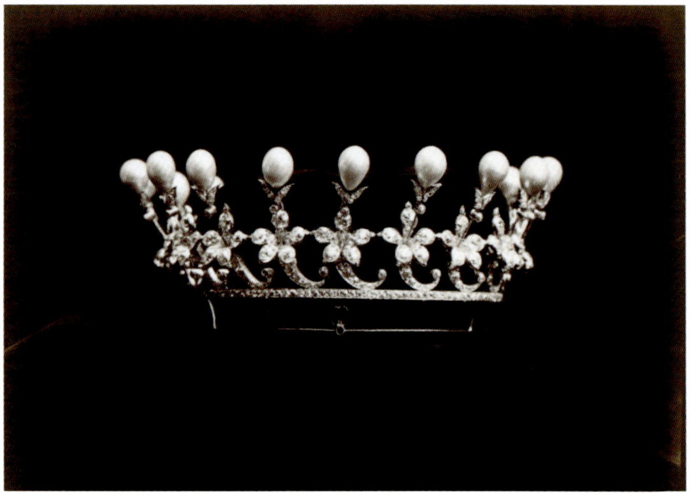

and dance. He was one of Serge Diaghilev's rare backers.[8] In 1874, he married Maria Pavlovna (ill. 8), sister to the Grand Duke Friedrich Franz III of Mecklemburg-Schwerin. She was one of the most important women figures of the Russian Court.[9] The grand ducal couple began traveling regularly to Europe, and stayed twice a year in France, according to the Grand Duke Alexander.[10] During these trips, the grand duchess took her jewelry case with her which she exhibited during receptions given her by Parisian high society.

And so in 1882, she left St. Petersburg with twenty-four pieces of jewelry including several from Tiffany's.[11] The Parisian branch of the New York firm in fact obtained the title of appointed supplier to the Court in 1882. Far from being satisfied with these jewels, the Grand Duchess immediately began completing her jewelry sets. In January 1883, she spent 2,700 francs at Tiffany's[12] and appeared along with the Grand Duke in the Boucheron firm's account books, firm the couple had frequented faithfully since 1880.

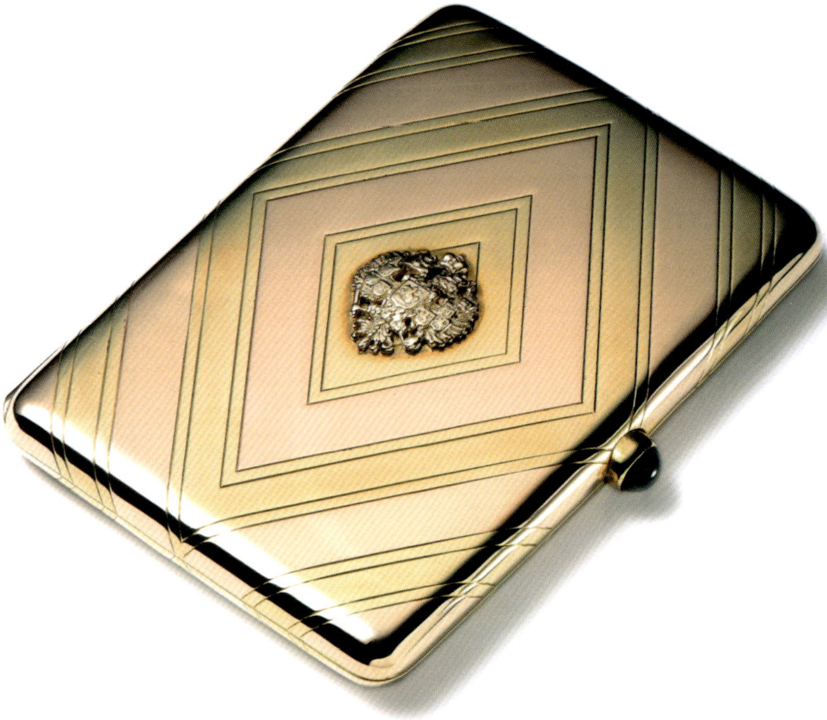

The Grand Duchess is again mentioned in 1891, and in 1893. Two days before New Year's Eve, the Grand Duke spent 65,000 francs for "two earrings" made up of two white pearls, one of 95 and a half grains and the other of 108 grains. This purchase shows the largely widespread taste in high society for pearls. In 1895, the Grand duchess bought a diamond sliding ring for 1,900 francs, and then with her two sons, the Grand dukes Boris and Cyril, she was mentioned for the last time in 1897.

Although the grand duchess Wladimir frequented the jewelers such as Boucheron or Tiffany, her tastes changed around 1900 and, like the Grand dukes Alexis, Paul and Serge, she appreciated Lalique's modern creations.[13]

At the same time, on July 28, 1899, Maria Pavlovna gave her first order to Chaumet who created a "waterfall" diadem (75 carat diamonds)[14] for 60,000 francs (ill. 9). During the ball given at the Winter Palace in 1903, the Grand Duchess, dressed in 17th century Russian fashion, wore an impressive *kokoshnik* set with precious stones and pierced with three openings so that three waterfalls of diamonds appeared in the diadem.

The Grand Duchess, who at the beginning of the 20th century was a faithful client of Chaumet, in 1914 promised a place for his next charity sale.[15] In doing so, she showed the interest she had for

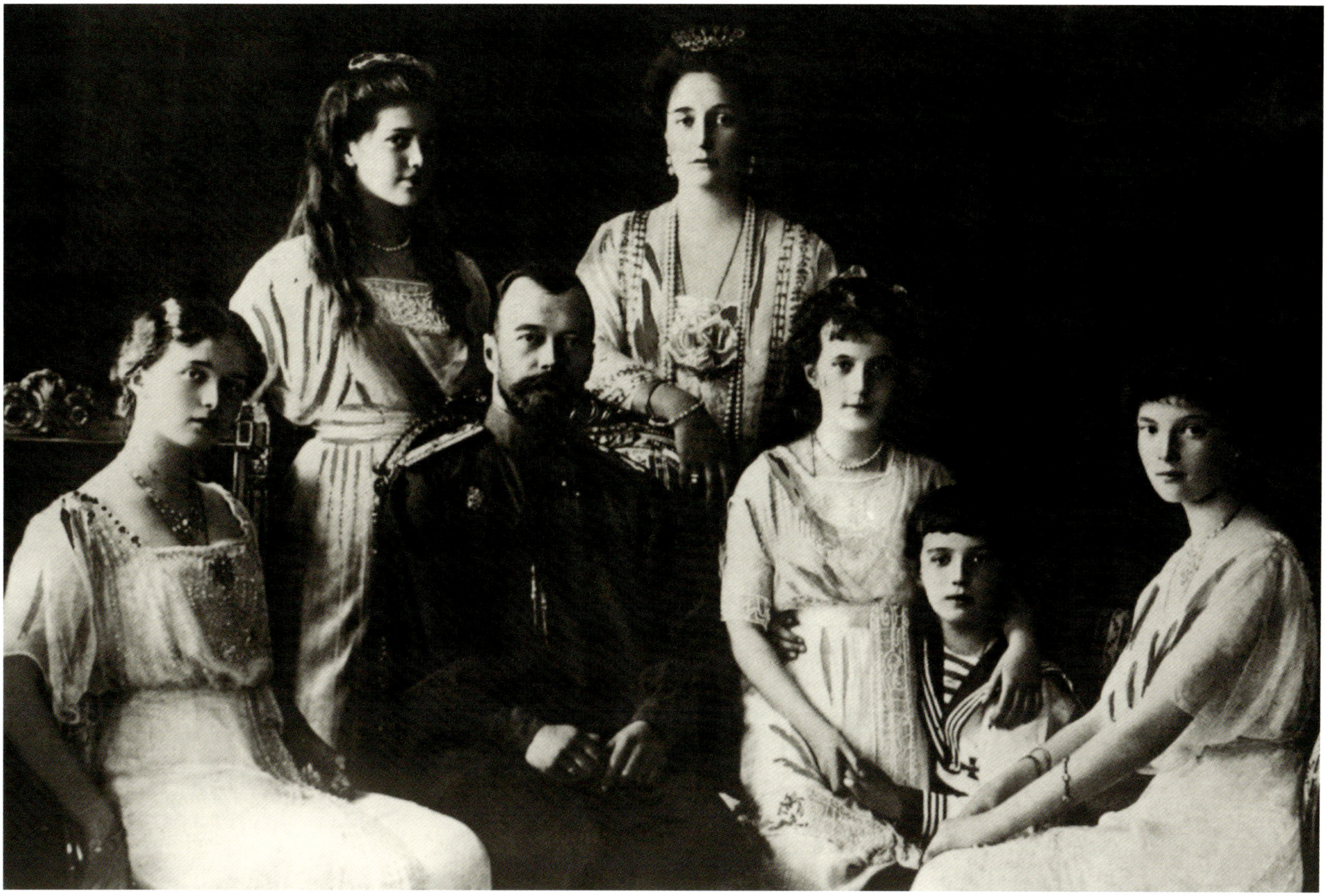

7. Czar Nicholas II and his family
Circa 1910
(Cat. 341)

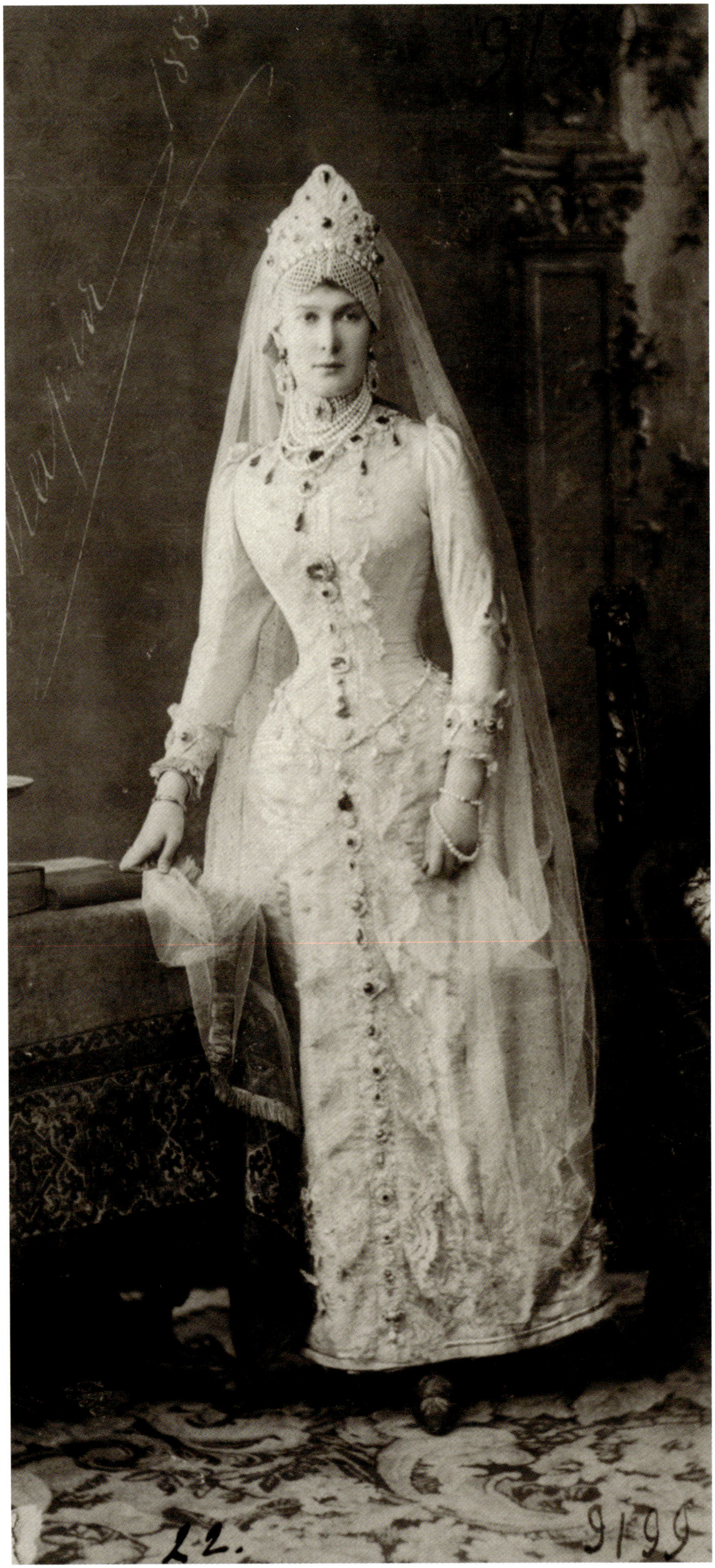

several French jewelers, among them Cartier, who she backed during his St. Petersburg exhibition in the winter of 1908.

At the beginning of the century, Maria Pavlovna made her first order, asking Cartier for the creation of a choker in pearls decorated with two eagles in Russian diamonds which she furnished[16] (ill. 10). In the Wladimir archives in St. Petersburg, a letter from 1902 addressed to the Grand duchess staying at the Continental Hotel in Paris mentions the dismantling of jewelry given to Cartier for "the execution of necklace plates."[17] In 1908, the Grand Duchess had a diadem composed around some "Beauharnais rubies",[18] no doubt the piece of jewelry mentioned in a sheaf of documents which Cartier sent to her at the Continental Hotel on June 2.[19] It was also in using old jewelry pieces that in 1909 the Grand Duchess ordered a diadem in the form of a *kokoshnik* in sapphires and diamonds,[20] arranged around a central cushion-shaped 137.20 carat sapphire and six cabochon sapphires of 102.16 carats placed in a setting of round diamonds. Louis Cartier took personal charge of sending the piece of jewelry to Russia in March and received the compliments of the Grand Duchess.[21] For Christmas, 1909, the Grand Duchess wanted a bodice front "very worthy of the great sapphire diadem" according to the very words of the jeweler who furnished a 162-carat sapphire to decorate the center. The list of jewelry furnished by the Great Duchess for the realization of this work as well as the project designed for the bodice front have been preserved.[22] This commission, worth 175,000 francs, also included the modification of a dog collar whose diamonds, worth

8. *Photographer C. Bergamasco*
The grand duchess Maria Pavlovna
St. Petersburg, 1883
Russian State Cinematographic and Photographic Archives
(Cat. 354)

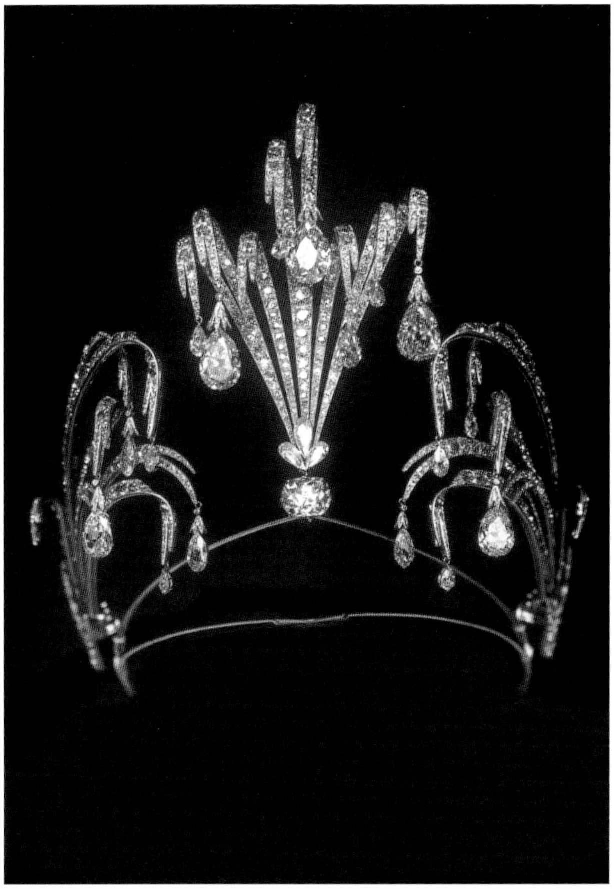

9. Diadem called "the waterfall" which belonged to Grand Duchess Wladimir
1899
Chaumet collection, Paris
(Cat. 357)

10. Dog collar in pearls and diamonds with two plates on which figures the motif of the imperial eagle
Order by Grand Duchess Wladimir, Paris, 1900
Cartier archives, Paris
(Cat. 351)

75,000 francs, had been furnished by the Grand Duchess.

Far from being exhaustive, this enumeration bears witness to the collection of jewels amassed by the Grand Duchess which were completed by her orders made in Russia with the jewelers Bolin, Butts, or Fabergé, main suppliers to the Court.

If Grand Duke Alexis or Grand Duke Serge also appreciated French jewelry, within the heart of the Imperial family only the princess Paley, qualified as "*Juwelenfanatikerin*" by Géza von Hapsburg[23] could rival the expenses of the Grand-Duchess Wladimir. Born Olga V. Karnovich and divorced from General Pistolkors, officer of the Grand Duke Paul and youngest of Nicholas II's uncles, she became the second wife of the Grand Duke in 1902. The morganic marriage of the future princess Paley, named Countess of Hohenfelsen in 1904, did not please the Empress, and Paul was sent into exile, first of all to the south of France and then to Paris, where he bought the former Yussupov residence. Reinstated into favor at the beginning of the 1910s, the Grand Duke Paul and princess Paley returned to St. Petersburg.

The couple appreciated antique art, in particular from the French 18th century, and frequented the Parisian gold and silversmiths and jewelers such as André Aucoc, the Keller brothers, Boucheron, Chaumet or Lalique and Tiffany-Paris. The Grand Duke[24] was a regular client of Cartier. Between 1902 and 1903, he purchased two necklaces, one with nine drop diamonds; a long bodice front; and a diadem of meanders certainly for his wife, just as devoted to the jeweler.[25]

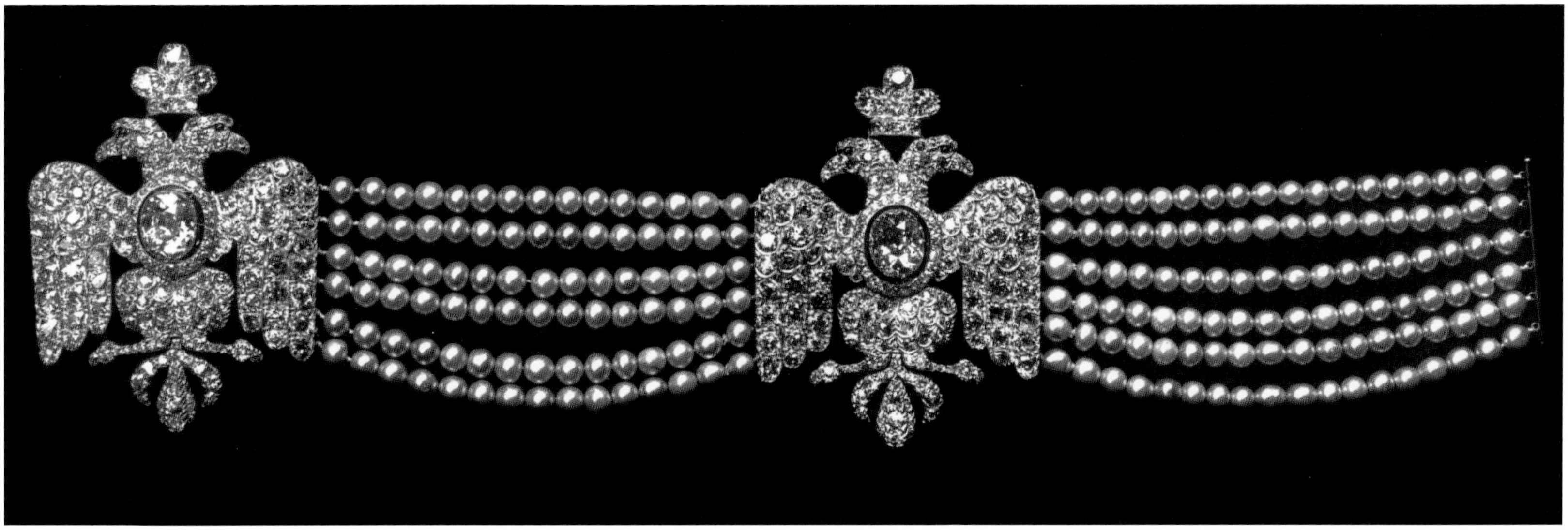

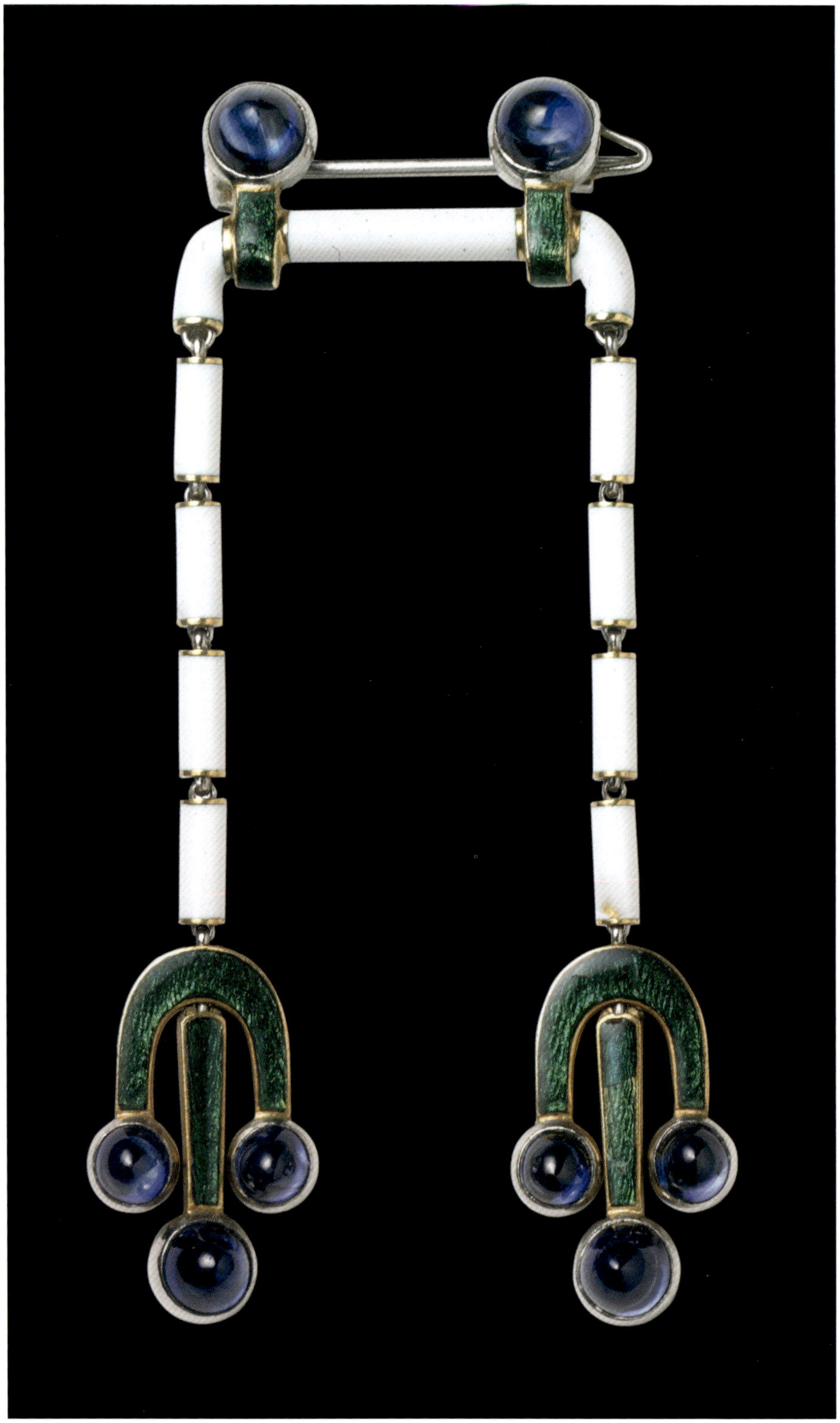

On January 22, 1908, the Grand Duke Paul spent 420,000 francs for a diadem made up of seven pear-shaped diamonds, and on April 13, 100,000 francs for another diadem in sapphires and diamonds.[26] The first of these jewels was for the Countess of Hohenfelsen (ill. 12),[27] the second, undoubtedly for his daughter, the grand duchess Maria who married Prince William of Sweden on April 20, 1908.

The same year Cartier created for the Countess of Hohenfelsen a bodice front in diamonds and pearls, three of which were pendants (ill. 14).[28] This piece of jewelry could be used in different ways, as illustrates a photo by Boissonas & Taponnier taken at the Yturbe reception in 1912 (ill. 1). Princess Paley, dressed in a "Slav" costume created by the famous fashion designer Worth, wore her bodice front as a hat brooch and her intertwined diadem as a bodice ornament.[29]

Thus in her finery, the Princess encountered the members of the Imperial family in Paris who, in St. Petersburg, closed their doors to her. This situation attracted the attention of personalities of the Parisian world. Boni de Castellane, close to the Wladimirs, recalls, "I was attending an evening at the Russian embassy where all the grand dukes were present. Among others, the princess Paley was there, then Countess of Hohenfelsen, morganic wife of the great duke Paul, who was wearing royal jewelry: the Great Duchess Wladimir took offense and gave her the evil eye."[30]

In Paris as in Moscow, the jewelers and jewelry makers weren't only dependant upon imperial orders but were equally solicited by a diverse wealthy elite.

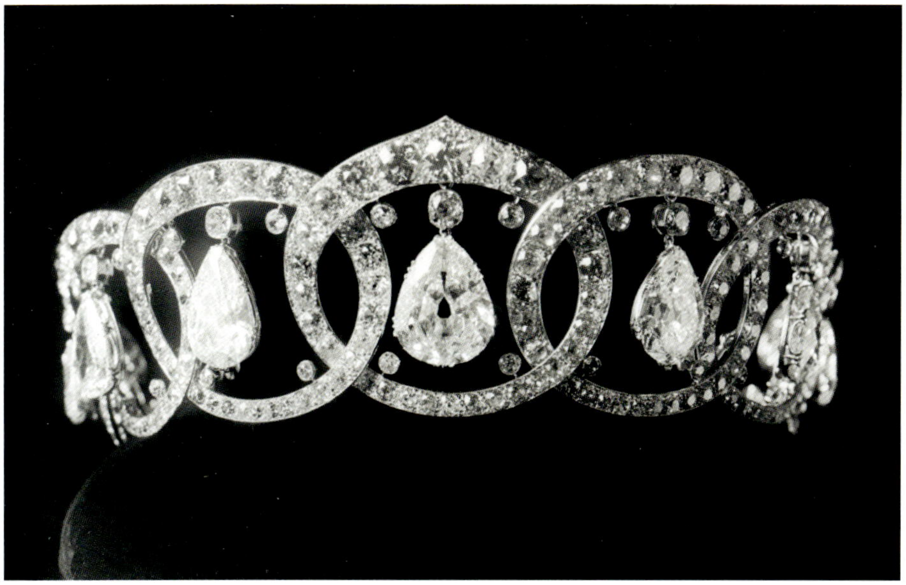

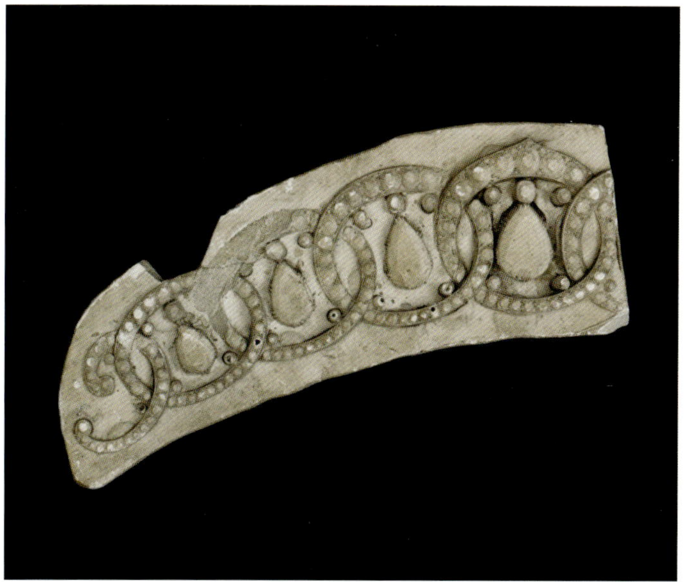

11. Brooch
Cartier Paris, 1913
Sold to the Countess of Hohenfelsen
The Cartier Collection
(Cat. 366)

12. Diadem in diamonds with a motif of entwined rings
Order by Countess Hohenfelsen, Paris, 1911
Cartier archives, Paris
(Cat. 364)

13. Partial plaster cast of the diadem which belonged to the Countess Hohenfelsen
Paris, Picq workshop, 1911
Cartier archives, Paris
(Cat. 367)

One of these was Alexander Polovtsov. Married to the only daughter of the baron Alexander Stieglitz, he inherited an immense fortune. His position and his brilliant career—he was senator and member of the State Council—made him a close acquaintance of the Imperial family. Faithful client of French luxury products, he also frequented the Parisian art market to complete the collections of the Stieglitz Museum-School. This museum of decorative arts which trained Russian craftsmen and industrial draughtsmen had been founded by his father-in-law.[31] Polovtsov and his daughters, the princess Obolensky and the countess Bobrinsky were clients of Boucheron between 1876 and 1894, and two purchases effected in 1887 are particularly evocative of his taste.

On October 18, he acquired two antique pieces of jewelry: "two large pendants made of 28 brilliants set in claws, plus five small brilliants at each end" which came from the Empress Eugenie's large diadem with pendants sold in separate lots with the French crown jewels. Boucheron bought several elements from them and the two pendants for which Polovtsov paid 168,000 francs are undoubtedly the two pieces sold to Boucheron for 141,000 francs.[32] A few days later, on October 29, Polovtsov ordered a "large diadem with three knots of brilliants and rubies" made up of 209 diamonds (168 carats) and 14 rubies (37 carats; ill. 13). In classical form, the diadem with a value of 191,211 francs is a detachable model: the knots can form elements of independent sets. In 1909, this headdress along with other jewelry was in the sale of a part of the Polovtsov collection after his death.

Member of the new Russian elite, Varvara Petrovna Kelch, like Polovtsov, frequented Boucheron both in Paris and in Moscow—she was at that time one of the jeweler's biggest clients

Settled in Moscow, she was the heir to a family whose fortune came from the Siberia gold mines and the maritime and railway transportation companies. She married Nicholas F. Kelch, and then his brother Alexander F, from the St. Petersburg nobility. Varvara Kelch left Russia at the beginning of the 20th century to settle in Paris.

She appreciated Boucheron's pearls and jewelry and her expenses were extravagant. Thus on July 23, 1898, a necklace of large pearls cost her 540,000 francs. In order to renew her jewelry sets, she regularly gave back or sold her earlier purchases and orders to her jeweler. Several drawings of jewelry that was made in 1906 and 1912

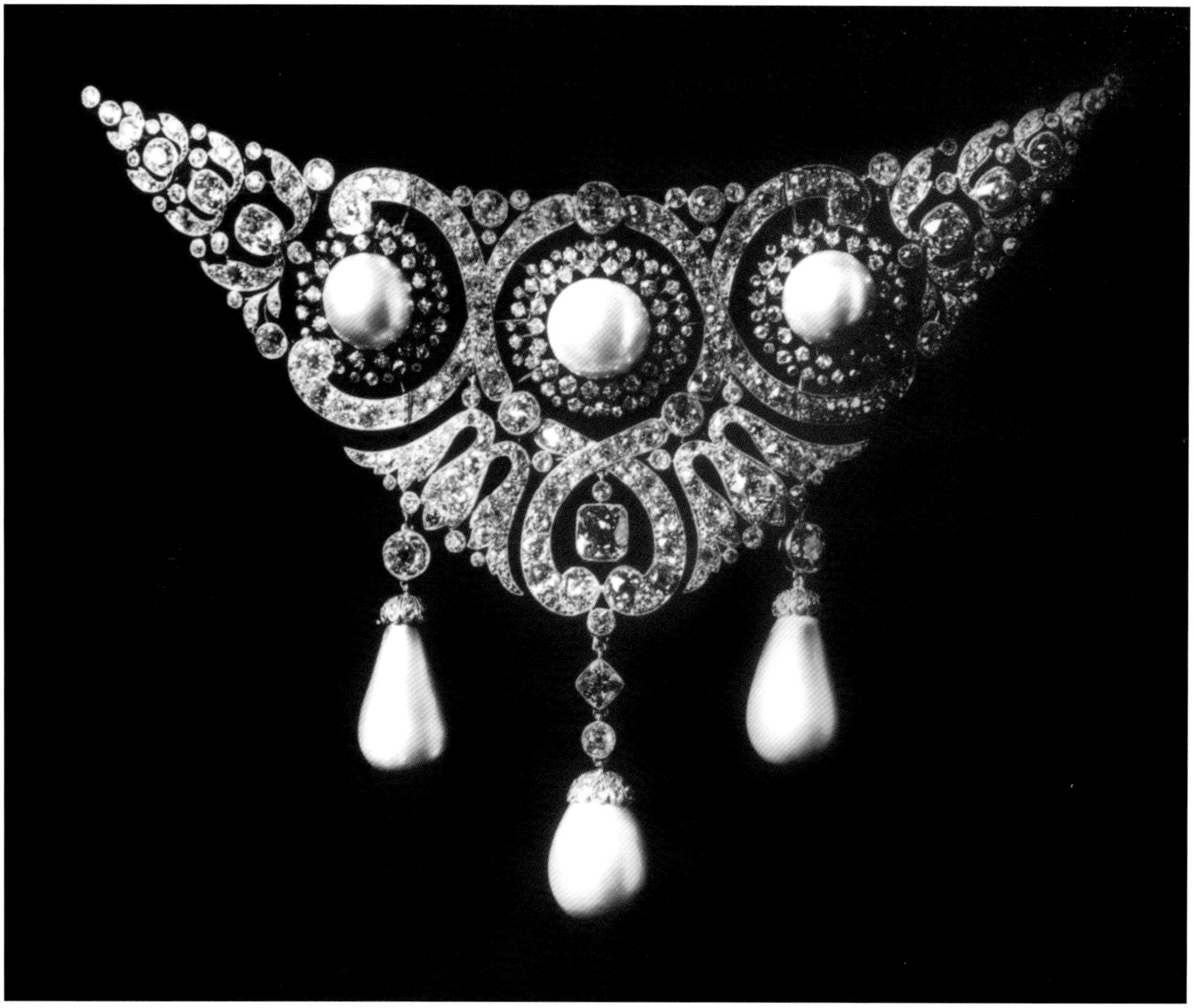

14. Bodice front in pearls and diamonds
Order by Countess Hohenfelsen, Paris, 1908
Cartier archives, Paris
(Cat. 363)

illustrate the wealth of her jewelry collection in diamonds, emeralds and rubies. Varvara Kelch was also one of the rare Russians to obtain Fabergé eggs from her husband which were every bit the equal of the mannered style of the imperial examples.

Thus an incredible collection of French jewelry was created in Russia. Assembled by the Imperial family, the Court or the financial elite, most of it was dispersed following the Revolution. Among the connoisseurs, the Yussupov family held a predominate place. The family also ordered an "imperial" egg from Fabergé and this collection which is partly French and which was begun in the 18th century, merits special study.

The Yussupov French jewelry collection, 1856-1914

The Yussupovs, descendants of a princely family whose origins are lost in the history of the Golden Hoard, enter into the history of art with Prince Nicholas Borissovich (1751-1831). An enlightened connoisseur, he developed an interest in European styles during several journeys abroad and created one of the biggest collections of art works in Russia. In 1811, the collection was transferred to Moscow where the Prince displayed it in his residence, Arkhangelskoye, then nicknamed the "Muscovite Versailles."[33] His only son, the prince Boris Nicholaievich (1794-1849) divided the collection between Moscow and St. Petersburg, collection which continued to grow until the Revolution.

Starting in 1793, after the marriage of the prince with one Catherine II's favorite ladies-in-waiting, Tatiana V. Englehardt (1769-1841), niece of the munificent Potemkin, this collection was enriched by jewels and precious objects. The princess Tatiana, who "especially had a passionate love of jewelry"[34] brought the *Polar Star* and the famous *Pelegrina* into the collections. The former, a cushion-shaped 41.28 carat diamond, had belonged to Joseph Bonaparte.[35] As for the Pelegrina, one of the most famous pearls in the world, it had been a part of the Spanish royal collections, and until 1792 a part of the French royal collections. It appeared on the Muscovite market in the 19th century and quickly became a part of the Yussupov collection. A legendary piece of jewelry, it was said to have been the pendant of the pearl dissolved by Cleopatra in a glass of vinegar so as to impress Mark Antony. And indeed this scene is the subject of one of the masterpieces of the Yussupov collection: *Cleopatra's Banquet* by Tiepolo.[36]

Exceptional stones and pearls, such sums up the Yussupov taste, were reproduced by the following generations who also went to Paris for their purchases. Prince Boris's young widow, the princess Zenaide Ivanovna (1809-1893), her son the prince Nicholas Borissovich the young (1827-1891), and his wife, the princess Tatiana Alexandrovna (1828-1879) divided their time between Russia and the Second Empire France. Princess Zenaide Ivanovna settled in Paris around 1855 and built a hotel, park for Princes, at Boulogne-sur-Seine. It was certainly at Napoleon III's Court where she met Charles Chauveau (1828-1889) whom she married May 7, 1861. The princess, Countess of Chauveau, was sometimes mentioned in the account books of the jewelers Boucheron and Mellerio *dits* Meller.

Zenaide's son, married abroad, was embassy attaché in Paris where he resided from 1856 to 1858. There his collections and his expenses had already aroused amazement. "He has the most beautiful diamonds in the world, family diamonds and those he's purchased, several of which have a historical genealogy..."[37]

In Paris, the Prince acquired a great number of decors and furnishings for his palace which was being renovated. But it was especially in the domain of jewelry that he added to his collection, particularly from the jeweler Mellerio *dits* Meller. In February 1857, he purchased an "Acerado diamond" for 82,300 francs, placing an order for a square appliqué in diamonds. He also chose an "Emerald Scarab Egyptian bracelet" for 1,125 francs. The same year, a set made up of a necklace and a bodice front is listed on the princess Yussupov's account. The whole item, costing 70,000 francs, was decorated with 81 emeralds including 38 cabochons and several hundred diamonds.

These pieces of jewelry were catologed in the inventory of the Yussupov family jewels dated April 4, 1887. It describes only the jewelry caskets received by the daughters of the prince Nicholas Borissovich, Zenaide Nicholaievna (1861-1939) and Tatiana Nicholaievna (1866-1888).[38] Classified by type of object, this inventory records at least six diadems, fifteen necklaces and sets, eleven pairs of earrings, forty-nine brooches, clasps, Sevigne or pins, twenty-three bracelets, five medallions, seven solitaries,

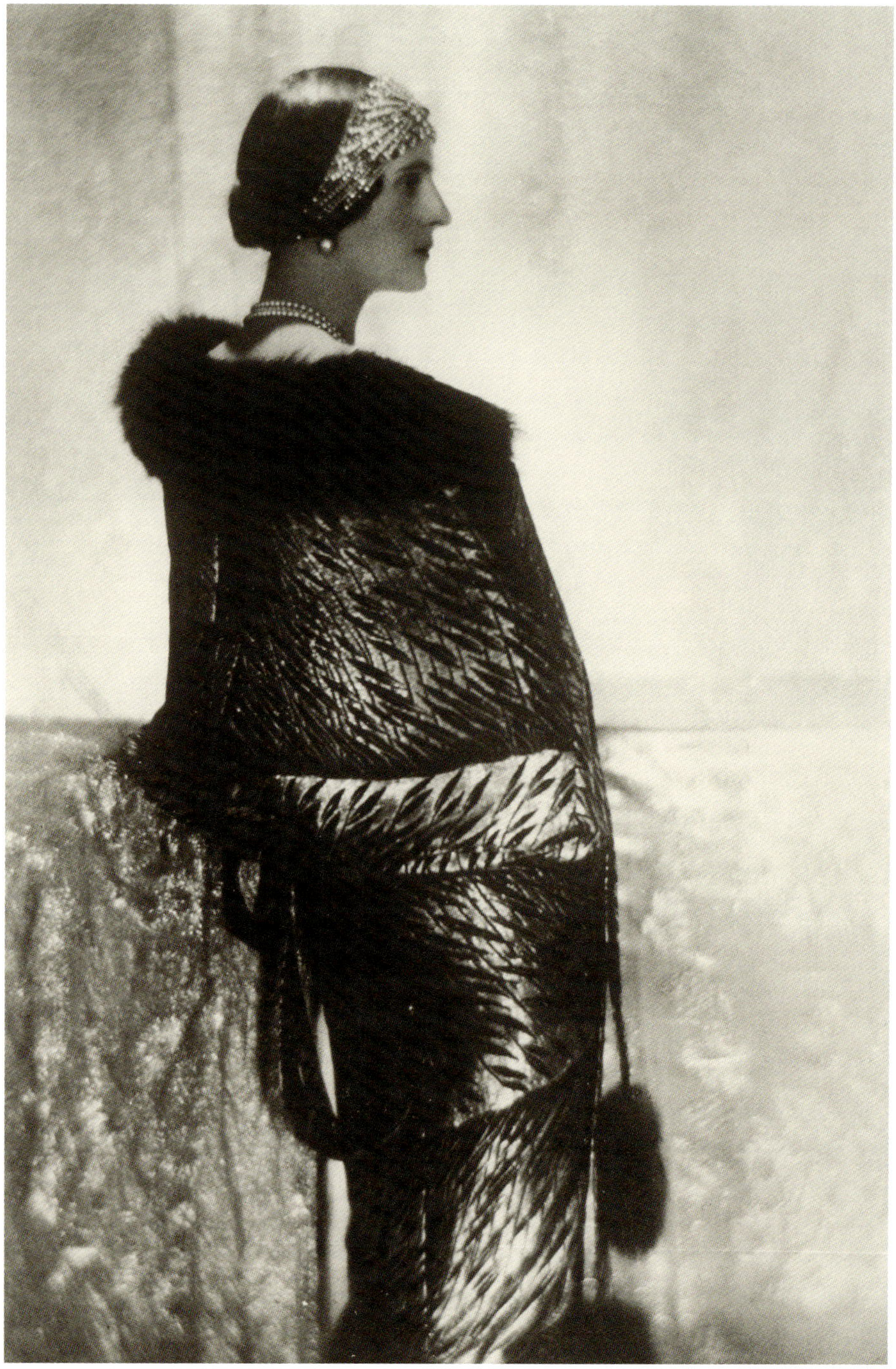

15. Portrait of Princess Felix Yussupov
Chaumet collection, Paris (Cat. 315)

all purchases made at Mellerio *dits* Meller. In looking through this list, one sees the number of purchases and orders recorded as "bought in Paris." The oldest Parisian acquisitions went back to 1856 with a turquoise and diamond necklace. 1957 was an extravagant year for in addition to the Mellerio pieces indexed, in the French capital the Yussupovs selected a Greek diadem in diamonds, a set in diamonds, a pearl and diamond necklace as well as a large 25-carat ruby, the "Bengal fire." In 1858, a gold brooch set with emeralds, rubies and diamonds; and a turquoise and diamond set were added to the inventory. In 1867, perhaps for the Universal Exhibition, the document reports the acquisition of a necklace with five gold medallions and different precious and ornamental stones.

The following generation remained faithful to the Mellerio firm. On June 15, 1887, the spouse of the princess Zenaide Nicholaievna, the count Felix Sumarokov-Elston (1856-1928) bought "three sapphire briolettes with diamond calottes and topped by a brilliant" costing 26,000 francs.

1887 was also the year of the sale of the French crown jewels. The Regent and the Napoleon Pearl, an egg-shaped pearl of 337 grains set on a diadem belonging to the Empress Marie-Louise, made by Nitot in 1811, and then placed into a bodice ornament by Lemonnier in 1853 was purchased for the princess at 176,000 francs. It was inventoried in 1887 with other pieces of jewelry coming from the Empress Eugenie.

Under the Third Republic, the Yussupovs also turned toward other Parisian creators. They bought pearls in 1887 from the jeweler Dumoret and in 1892 from Paul Hamelin, a jeweler-jewelry-maker established at 23, rue de la Paix. Princess Zenaide and prince Felix were clients of the Boucheron firm in 1893 and 1894. In particular the Prince had a diamond star made from a diadem he furnished, and ordered several pieces of jewelry including a "large bodice front with six knots of brilliants for hanging three large pear brilliants and a large steel brilliant." (19,218 francs).

16. Three views of Princess Yussupov's diadem with its motif of écus comptés
Original gelatin-coated silver print on mat paper
Photo shoot February 18, 1914
Chaumet Collection, Paris

The family also appeared in Boucheron firm's Muscovite account books, and the Paris jewelry firm present in the homeland was favorable to purchases. During the first years of the 20th century, the Yussupovs were very interested in all the aspects of Cartier production: jewelry making, clock-making,[39] lapidary art.[40]

These treasures collected over several generations were the pride of the princess Zenaide Yussupov who only wore them on rare occasions but which were exhibited during large receptions. Prince Felix wrote in his *Memoirs* about the sets exhibited in the Princess's room, displayed for observation by the guests who were fascinated by the brilliance of these marvels.[41] He recorded the memories of the Infanta Eulalia, aunt to the king of Spain, who was received in Moscow. "Of all the celebrations given me in my honor, the one by the princess Yussupov particularly impressed me. (...) she lived in incredible luxury, in a place of unequaled magnificence (...). Luxury, the magnificent, splendid and ostentatious luxury of Russian life, there reached its highest point, combined with the purest French elegance. At that reception, the mistress of the house wore a Court dress all sewn with brilliants and immaculate orient pearls. Tall, with admirable timeless beauty, she was wearing the kokoshnik, decorated with gigantic pearls and enormous brilliants, a jewel which takes the place of our diadem at court and just alone represented a fortune of precious stones. A dazzling display of fantastic jewels from the Orient and the Occident completed the display. Pearl necklaces, bracelets in solid gold with Byzantine motifs, pendants in pearls and turquoises, rings which glittered sending out fires of all colors gave the princess Yussupov the aspect of an empress of the Lower Empire."[42]

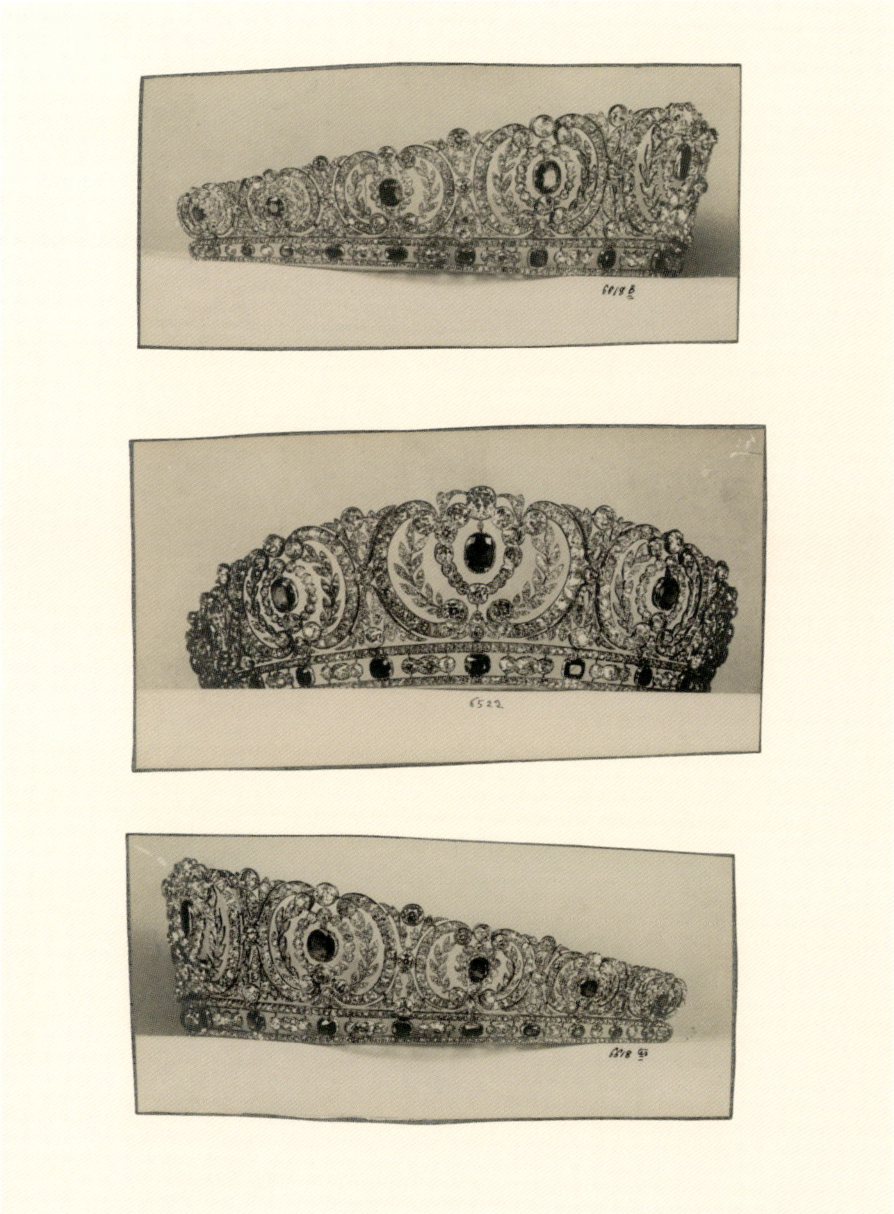

In 1914, the marriage of the young prince Felix F. Yussupov (1887-1967) with the princess Irina Alexandrovna Romanov (1895-1970), niece to Nicholas II (ill. 15), was the occasion to create a wedding basket. In January, Cartier sold the Prince a diadem worth 31,655 francs. The style, called Renaissance style, created in 1911 based on drawings by Charles Jacqueau, was made up of rock crystal sticks set under a gallery of round diamonds[43]

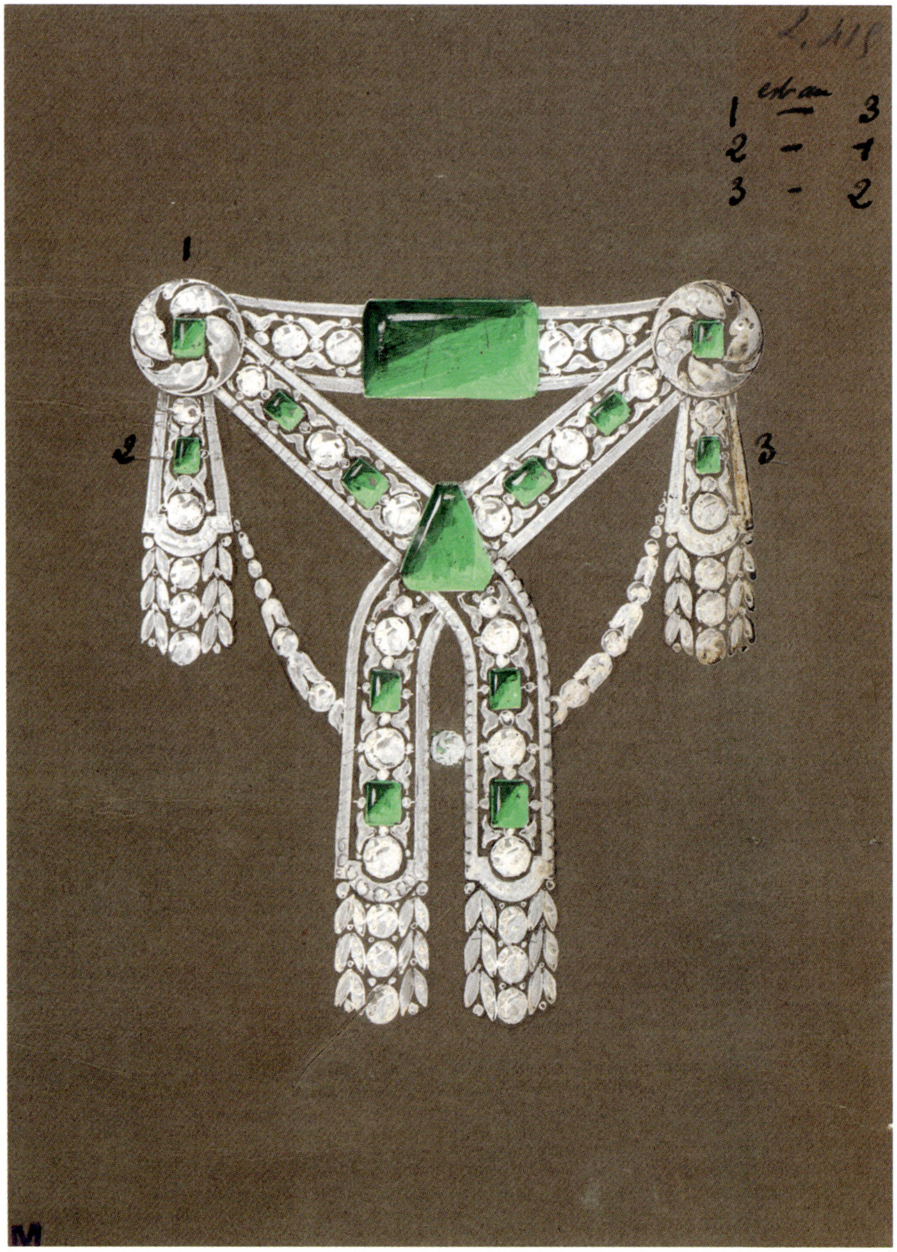

17. Drawing for a bodice front in garlands of emeralds and diamonds, from a collection of drawings for jewelry for Princess Felix Yussupov's wedding presents
Watercolor and gouache on paper
Joseph Chaumet, 1914
Chamet collection, Paris
(Cat. 311 à 314)

and apparently was worn by the Princess the day of her wedding.[44] The Chaumet firm which had already worked for the family during the Second Empire also was involved in the order of the wedding basket.[45] Chaumet met the royal couple in Paris. The couple gave him their jewelry sets so as to "modernize them."[46] The whole remodeled group included a headband in diamonds and rubies with *écus comptés*, a narrow headband open-worked in diamonds with in the center, a quadrangular emerald, a "rising sun" egret with the "Polar Star", a sun diadem jointed with diamonds, a large sapphire and diamond chain, another in rubies and diamonds, a jewelry set in diamonds and emeralds based on the famous Marie-Antoinette's "*Queen's necklace*" in the center of which Chaumet placed a 14-carat emerald, a bodice front in diamonds and rubies, a dog collar in diamonds and pearls (ills. 16 and 17).[47]

Most of these pieces of jewelry remained in Russia during the Revolution, with the exception of the jewelry that the princesses Zenaide and Irina were in the habit of carrying with them.[48] The former were mostly destroyed or dismantled and have disappeared. The latter enabled the Yussupov family to survive in exile and some of the pieces, passed from owner to owner, appear from time to time on the art market.

[1] Information furnished by Mme. Ekaterina Khmelnitskaia. As for the grand duchesses, daughters and granddaughters of the Emperor, they received a million rubles as dowry.
[2] R. K. Massie, *Nicolas and Alexandra*, Paris, Stock, 1969, p. 54. This information, cited without any source, has been repeated by most biographers.
[3] Nicholas II, *Journal intime*, Payot, Paris 1925, p. 69.
[4] Nicholas II, *op. cit.*, 1925, p. 76.
[5] W. Clarke, *The lost fortune of the Tsars*, St. Martin's Press, New York 1994, pp. 72, 153.
[6] *The Brilliant Fabergé Epoch*, exhibition cat., St. Petersburg, Paris, Moscow, Catherine's Grand Palais, Tsarskoye Selo, 1992, p. 229, (in Russian).
[7] *René Lalique Bijoux d'exception 1890-1912*, Luxemburg Museum, Paris 2007, No. 43, p. 66, Ill. p. 45, Lalique firm, Paris, inv. 6.1.001.
[8] Alexander of Russia, *Einst war ich ein Grossfürst,* Leipzig, Paul List Verlag, 1932, p. 141.
[9] *Von Mecklenburg nach Russland – Maria Pawlowna – ein Leben am Ende einer Epoche*, exhibition cat., Schwerin Chateau, Schwerin 2001, p. 19.
[10] Alexander of Russia, *op. cit.*, 1932, p. 140.
[11] Russian National Archives, St. Petersburg (RGIA), f. 528, op. 1, d 341.
[12] *Ibid.*, pp. 342-343.
[13] W. Zeisler, "Grand Duchess Maria Pavlovna and Grand Duke Vladimir: Enthusiasts of Artistic Luxury," in *Artistic Luxury. Fabergé, Tiffany, Lalique*, exhibition cat., Cleveland, 2008-2009, pp. 188-195.
[14] D. Scarisbrick, *Chaumet, joaillier depuis 1780*, Alain de Gourcuff, Paris 1995, p. 195, ill. 56, p. 197; A. von Solodkov, "Grossfürstin Wladimir und ihre Passion für Schmuck und Pretiosen," in exhibition cat., *Fabergé-Cartier. Rivalen am Zarenhof*, Munich 2003-2004, p. 112 and ill. 4, p. 111. See also H. Nadelhoffer, *Cartier*, Paris 1984, p. 70, pl. 59 et pl. 79 and G. C. Munn, *Tiaras. A History of Slendour*, Antique Collectors' Club, Paris 2001, ill. 289, p. 319 who attributes this object to Cartier.
[15] D. Scarisbrick, *op. cit.*, p. 341.
[16] H. Nadelhoffer, *op. cit.*, p. 50; A. von Solodkoff, *op. cit.*, p. 114.
[17] RGIA, f. 528, op. 1, d. 952, l. 9.
[18] H. Nadelhoffer, *op. cit.*, p. 117
[19] RGIA, f. 528, op. 1, d. 952, l. 1-3.
[20] F. Chaille, *La Collection Cartier—Joaillerie*, Flammarion, Paris 2004, ill. p. 58. On the destiny of the diadem, see G. C. Munn, *op. cit.*, p. 308.
[21] H. Nadelhoffer, *op. cit.*, 1984, p. 50; Solodkoff, *op. cit.*, 2003-2004, p. 114.
[22] RGIA, f. 528, op. 1, d. 952, l. 4, 5 et 7.
[23] G. von Hapsburg, "Cartier in Russland,"in *Fabergé-Cartier..., cit.*, p. 83.
[24] Between 1903 and 1904 he acquired twenty-nine objects, and then another sixty-nine articles up until 1906. *Ibid.*
[25] She acquired forty-four objects between 1903 and 1906, then between 1908 and 1914, twenty-three pieces, among them three necklaces. *Ibid.*
[26] H. Nadelhoffer, *op. cit.*, 1984, p. 114.
[27] G. C. Munn, *op. cit.*, 2001, ill. 276, p. 305.
[28] J. Rudoe, *Cartier 1900-1939*, Somogy, Paris 1997, ill. pp. 47, 49.
[29] The central diamond weighed 27 carats and the seven other stones 121.42 carats. Cf. H. Nadelhoffer, *op. cit.*, pl. 61 and p. 78.
[30] Boni de Castellane, *Mémoires*, Perrin, Paris 1986, pp. 334-335.
[31] O. Neverov, *Grandes Collections de la Russie Impériale,* Flammarion, Paris 2004, pp. 147-153.
[32] B. Morel, *Les joyaux de la couronne de France*, Albin Michel, Paris 1988, p. 381.
[33] O. Neverov, *op. cit.*, 2004, pp. 89-103.
[34] F. Yussupoff, *Memoirs*, V&O, Paris 1990.
[35] H. Nadelhoffer, *op. cit.*, 1984, p. 286.
[36] Painting still in the collection at Arkhangelskoye.
[37] *The Artist*, March 28, 1858, 13th issue, p. 215.
[38] Hermitage National Museum Archives, St. Petersburg (AGE), f. 1, op. 5 (part I), d. 32-34.
[39] AGE, f. 1, op. 5 (part 2), d. 268, l. 162.
[40] *Fabergé-Cartier. Rivalen am Zarenhof*, *op. cit.*, p. 447.
[41] F. Yussupoff, *op. cit.*, 1990.
[42] *Idem*, p. 36.
[43] G. C. Munn, *op. cit.*, ill. 281, pp. 309-310.
[44] F. Yussupoff, *op. cit.*
[45] D. Scarisbrick, *op. cit.*, p. 141.
[46] F. Yussupoff, *op. cit.*
[47] *Idem*, ill. 16, 18, 64, pp. 166, 173, 175, 201, and Scarisbrick, *op. cit.*, 2003-2004, pp. 120, 123.
[48] F. Yussupoff, *op. cit.*

THE POSY-HOLDER IN RUSSIA

Wilfried Zeisler

The definition of the posy-holder[1] has been unclear for a long time. In France, the term appeared around 1860 in the Littré Dictionary, "a sort of *parure* which is used to carry bouquets (...) little flower vase."

The posy-holder as its name indicates allows one to carry one or several flowers kept in a receptacle vase, arranged in different ways. Held by the hand or attached to clothing, the accessory was often prolonged by a handle. Posy-holders, made of diverse styles and materials, were often incorporated with accessories: small additional elements such as mirrors, dance programs, and sometimes even by a base.

The posy-holder originated in Francc—and was not the naming of these objects abroad often *à la française*? It's called *bukethalter* in Germany, *buketthallare* in Sweden and in particular, *portbuke* in Russia.

In the Russian empire where French taste and fashion were always appreciated and sought after, the success of this accessory, whose usage spread through-out France during the reign of Louis XIV, was assured.

At the Court, adding flowers made of precious materials, such as stems in gold or silver and petals in stones or pearls, to one's clothing or headdress was considered fashionable. In 1797, during Paul I's coronation, the grand duchess heir Elizabeth added a natural rose to her precious stones "bouquet", thus setting off a new fashion indeed, that of posy-holders. The Russian Diamond Fund has preserved a rare posy-holder brooch of the 1760s originating from the crown jewels. It is a sort of an enameled gold and silver bottle, decorated with a ribbon and knot of diamonds.

In the 19th century, the custom of wearing flowers stimulated creativity, and new types of posy-holders made their appearance. The object was no longer limited to a simple conic receptacle, it included a handle and various ways of attaching it. The oldest pieces date from the Victorian era, a period during which the use of the posy-holder became widespread. The object was widely circulated over the course of the century, thanks to mechanical innovations. Designs in series produced by stamping enabled manufacturers to make fashionable posy-holders inspired by more luxurious examples which were made by the great jewelers. From Paris to St. Petersburg, the posy-holder was a new accessory for the elegant woman.

In 1835, on an engraving in *Modes de Paris*, two dancers are talking to each other, one of them, seated on a sofa, holds in her right hand flowers placed into a posy-holder in the shape of a horn of plenty. This object, so the legend goes, came from a jeweler specialized in this kind of production, "Monsieur Bourguignon passage de l'Opéra."[2]

At the same time, Queen Victoria acquired her first posy-holders and in Russia, its use spread throughout the imperial family starting with the reign of Nicholas I.

In 1841, a bill addressed to Prince Wolkonsky, Court minister, recorded the purchase of a "silver and enamel posy-holder" from the Nicholls and Plinche firm in St. Petersburg.[3]

The imperial example was followed by the nobility, and the society portraits which convey

1. Posy-holder
Russia, 1850-1856
Kenber Collection, Paris
(Cat. 406)

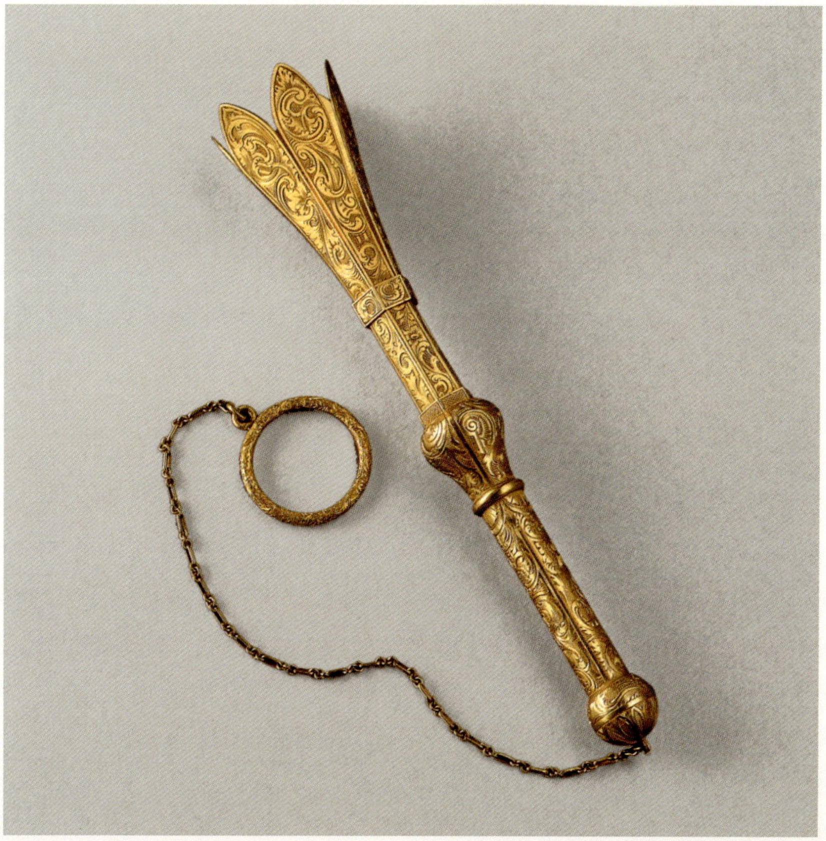

the position of the model by the quality of her clothing and *parures* sometimes illustrated the posy-holder fashion. In 1848, the painter Gavril Yakovlev (1819-1862) thus represented Yulia Teliakovskaya, wife of an engineering officer, in a white dress. On her arms she was wearing bracelets in romantic style, and in her hands she was holding a gilded posy-holder filled with flowers.[4]

During Alexander II's reign, the posy-holder continued to be an appreciated accessory, as bears witness one of the posy-holders from the Kenber collection (ill. 1). Made in finely-engraved gold with rococo motifs, it belonged to the princess Varvara Gagarin (1835-1893), wife of the baron Otto de Plessen (1816-1897), Danish plenipotentiary minister to Russia.[5] She wore it to Moscow during the coronation ceremonies of 1856.

The posy-holder, in the image of its cousin in the family of accessories, the fan, often became a souvenir object which commemorated an encounter or an event. In France, with the pomp and ceremony of the Second Empire, the posy-holder gift became very popular. During a ball given in 1853, the Senate gave Empress Eugenie a precious gold and silver posy-holder.[6]

Its style, in the fashion of the time, recalled the creations of the famous Froment-Meurice who delivered eleven posy-holders to the city of Paris on the occasion of the Imperial Prince's baptism in 1856.[7]

In 1863 for the marriage of Princess Alexandra of Denmark to the future Edward VII, Maharajah Duleep Singh gave her a fan, along with a posy-holder in gold, crystal, diamonds, emeralds, and rubies made by London & Ryder.[8] In the same way, several posy-holders were distributed to guests at the wedding of the Duke of Aosta and the princess Marie Laetitia Bonaparte in Paris in 1888.[9] In 1906, for the marriage of the king of Spain, Alphonse XIII, his wife, the princess Victoria Eugenie of Battenberg, received a precious posy-holder from the famous jeweler Masriera, offered by a committee of Catalan monarchists.[10]

This spirit of commemoration led to the creation of a posy-holder conceived by the Russian goldsmith Ovchinnikov for the grand duchess Elizabeth Feodorovna on the occasion of the jubilee for the Preobrajensky[11] regiment, as well as to the creation of an Irish model by West & Son offered to Queen Victoria by the Royal Irish Yacht Club on April 3, 1900.[12]

Alongside these commemorative creations, the posy-holder

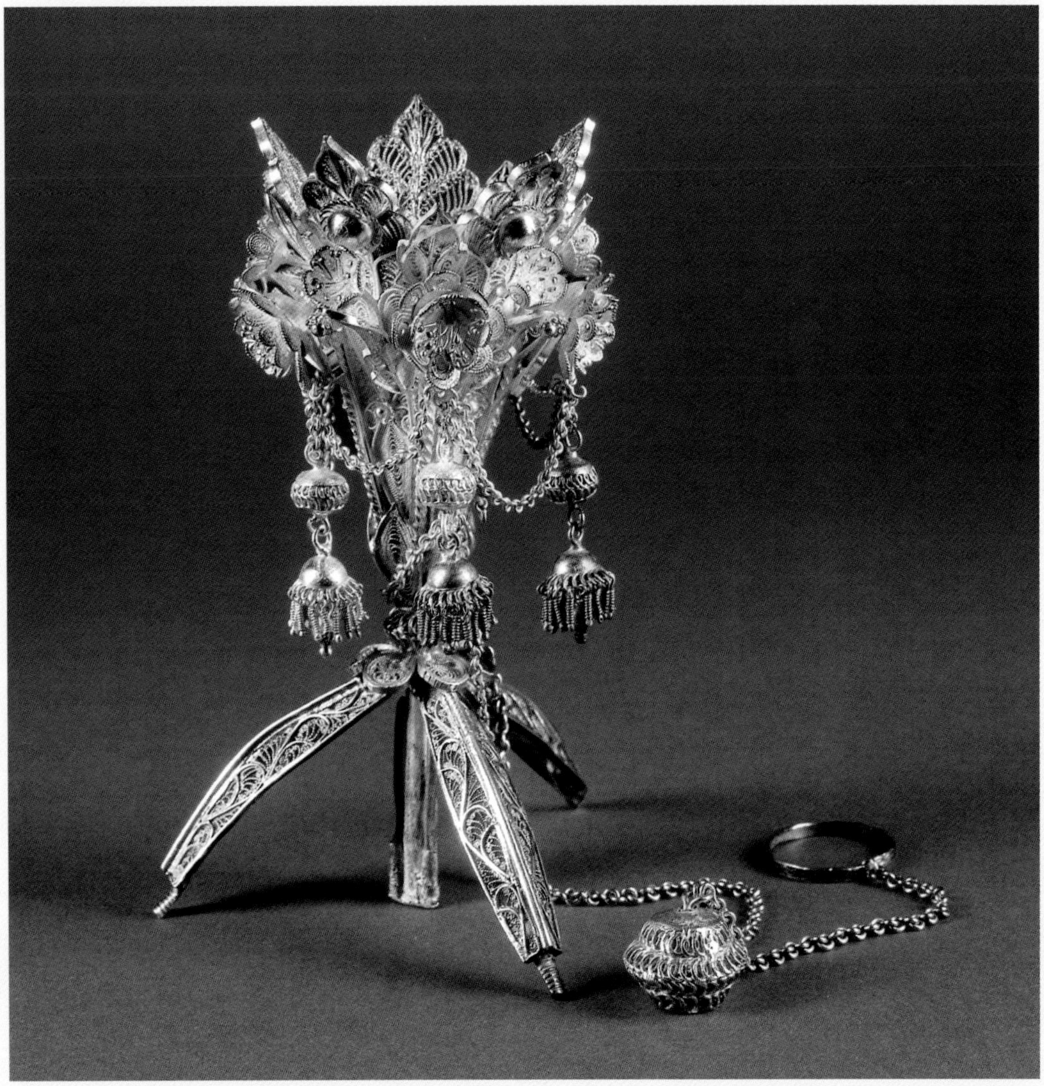

2. Three-branched posy-holder
Russia, 1870-1880
Kenber Collection, Paris
(Cat. 408)

3. Three-branched posy-holder
Russia, 1900-1910
Kenber Collection, Paris
(Cat. 411)

continued to be popular. Its diverse production went on until the end of the century.
In October 1874 for example, the jeweler Boucheron responded to a request from the Duke of Praslin who wanted the creation of "a branch with leaves in rose-cut diamonds and diamonds so as to be able to fix a real flower and to hold a small watch." Classed into the categories "brooches" or "diverse", the different posy-holders mentioned in the firm's stock book are of many different shapes and styles. They are with a "snake motif", "a knot", "ornament", or "butterfly" and for the most part, made of gold, diamonds and precious stones.[13]
In Russia, the posy-holders were produced in the capital, at Moscow, and in the provinces. Thus posy-holders were made as far away as in the province of Kostroma by the gold and silversmith Ivan Zinoviev Manilov, active in Aleevo, in the *volost* of Sidorovskoye (ill. 4) in the Caucasus, or in other regions where posy-holders were made in silver filigree (ill. 2).
The most important families of the Russian aristocracy had them, as indicates an inventory beginning in 1887 taken at the Yussupov Palace in St. Petersburg, in which is mentioned a posy-holder in gilded metal, openwork, decorated with flowers, and with a nacre handle.[14] As for the Empress Maria Feodorovna and her daughter the grand duchess Olga Alexandrovna, they kept a collection of thirty-nine posy-holders.[15]
All of them were in the Gatchina Palace, favorite residence of the Emperor Alexander III, and then of his widow. The old inventories and documents record that the Empress kept many precious objects there: jewelry, eggs, vases etc... The most important of them were evacuated during World War I. However, the posy-holders were still there in 1925[16] and eventually became a part of the collection of the Museum of Historical Costumes organized from the imperial collections.
In a funnel shape, with a vegetal style or evoking the cone of a rolled napkin, they were mostly decorated with polychrome enamels, especially "in the

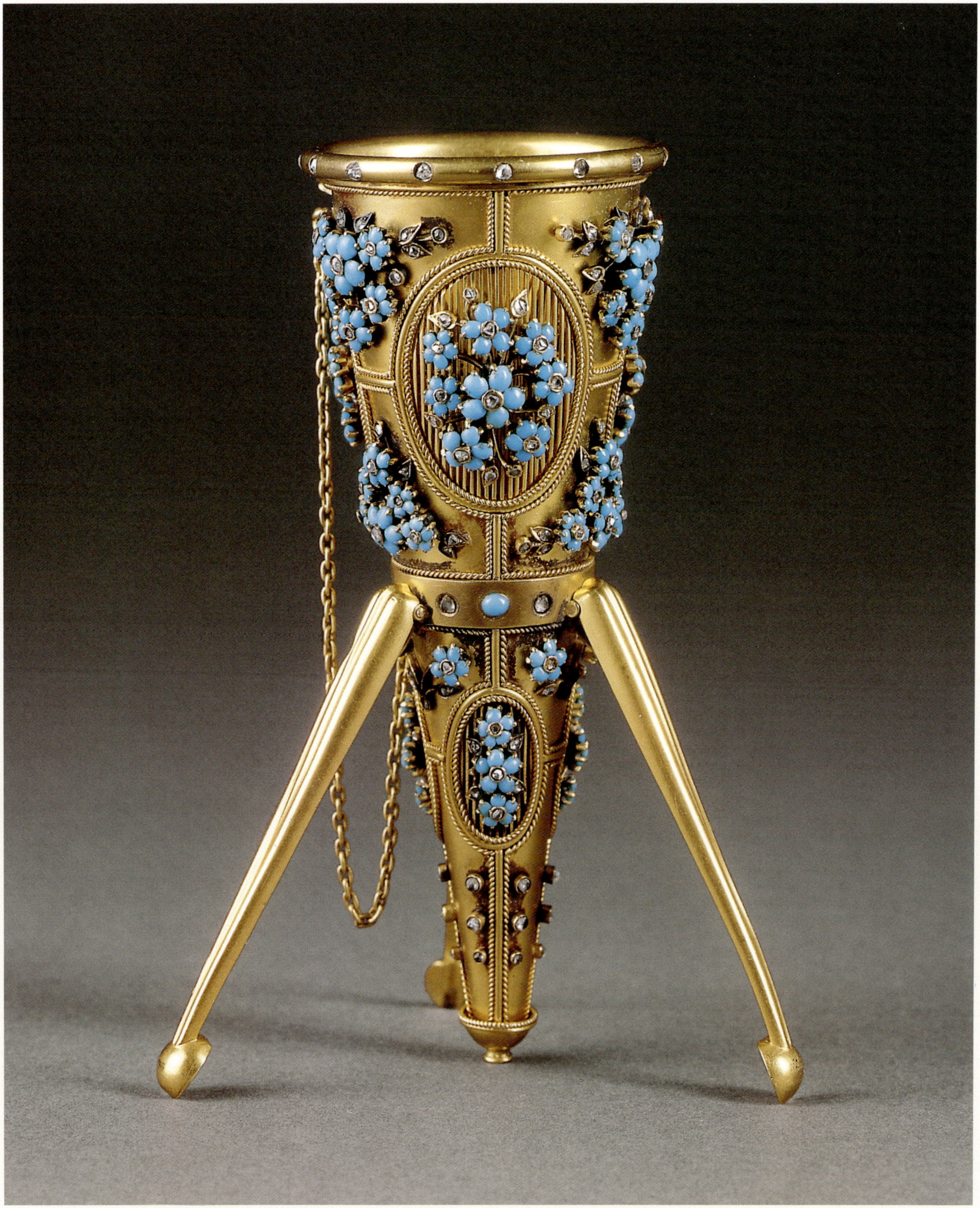

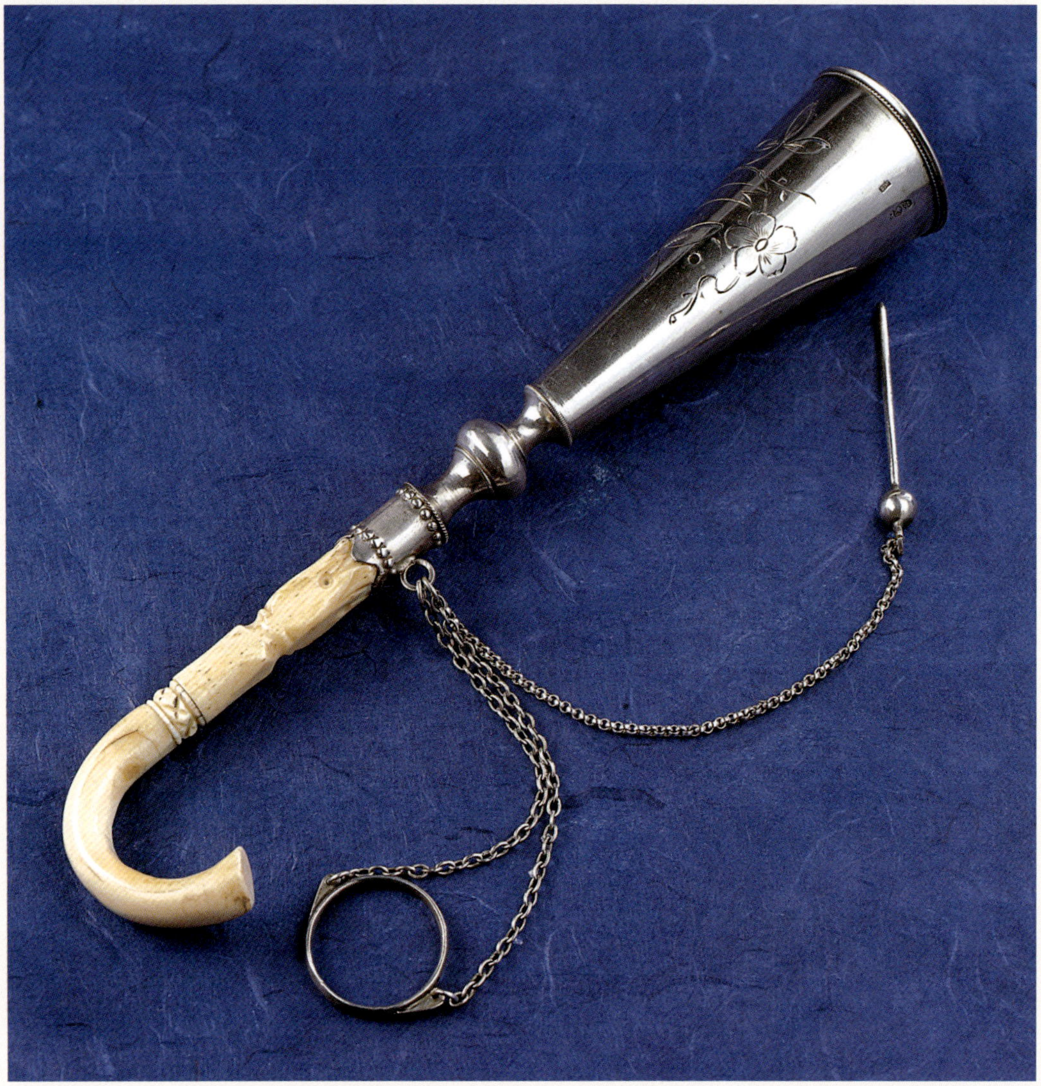

4. *I. Z. Manilov*
Posy-holder
Russia, Kostroma, Aleevo, 1899-1905
Kenber Collection, Paris
(Cat. 410)

Russian style", bearing witness to a production of a national nature transplanting itself onto the eclectic 19th century taste, illustrated by posy-holders with Renaissance motifs or rocaille style. Gilded or in silver, they were often lengthened by a handle. Some of them were decorated with an imperial crown or the monogram of the Empress. Several examples are dated 1888 and have the name of the city or institution on them, such as "Vladikavkaz 1888" or "Second boys gymnasium of Tiflis 1888." They are evidence of the gifts received by the Empress during a visit of the Imperial Family to the Caucasus at Vladikavkaz, Batum, Tiflis and Baku in the autumn of 1888.[17]
Only one posy-holder includes the name of its author: the goldsmith from Moscow, Ovchinnikov.
At the time of the "Silver Century", the Russian equivalent to the *Belle Epoque*, the mannered style of accessories continued to be in vogue. In 1899, the Muscovite catalog for the Fabergé firm offered two examples of posy-holders in engraved oxidized silver, one for eighty-five rubles, the other for a hundred. In the shape of a cone, these pieces are with a base and include a needle fix-bouquet (ill. 3). The most expensive one is enriched with petals at the level of the belt. In 1904, the catalogue of the famous Muscovite firm Khlebnikov mentions among the objects "to offer as gifts", posy-holders from twenty to a hundred rubles. In 1910, the accessory was still appreciated by the cosmopolitan Russian clientele, for Mme. Muravieff asked the Odiot firm in Paris to engrave a monogram on "six English posy-holders."[18]
Definitively relegated to the category of the useless and futile during the twenties, the posy-holder disappeared from the catalogues of the jewelers and from the jewelry boxes of their clients.
In Russia, although the collection which was at Gatchina has disappeared, many posy-holders are still preserved in the museums. After the Revolution, they were collected as patrimonial objects

of a sociological nature. As such, some of them entered into the Leningrad Museum of Ethnography before being redistributed into diverse Russian institutions. In that first collection, they illustrated one of the aspects of former life, the accessory of an outdated and obsolete way of life in the eyes of the new authorities. Today, the Hermitage Museum collections include several posy-holders including a very beautiful example from the 1860s in nacre and porcelain from the St. Petersburg Imperial Manufacture,[19] and several filigree pieces imported from the Far East.[20] The Pavlovsk Palace-Museum also has some in its collection as does the State Historical Museum in Moscow where is a beautiful group of at least seven posy-holders of diverse styles and materials.[21] The Kenber collection, which was created more than fifteen years ago, has gathered together more than a hundred and thirty posy-holders in France, five examples of which show the success this discreet companion of floral jewelry sets enjoyed in Imperial Russia.

[1] On posy-holders, see especially B. Kenber and W. Zeisler, "Els porta-bouquets," in exhibition cat., *Porte-bouquets Insolites joies de la colleccio Kenber*, Frédéric Marés, Barcelona 2008, pp. 21-44 (pp. 364-378 in English); "Che cos'è un porte-bouquet?," in exhibition cat., *Fiori freschi*, Mario Praz Museum, Rome 2007; "Porte-bouquets," in exhibition cat., *Passions d'un collectionneur*, Carcassonne, Fine Arts Museum, Carcassonne 2006; "Qu'est-ce qu'un porte-bouquet," in exhibition cat., *Porte-bouquets*, Cognaq-Jay Museum, Paris 2005, pp. 15-26.

[2] F. Falluel, "Porte-bouquets, mode et société", in *Porte-bouquets*, *op. cit.*, pp. 45-46.

[3] Russian National Archives, St. Petersburg (RGIA), f. 468, op. 1 (part 1), d. 401 (1841), l. 222.

[4] Hermitage Museum, St. Petersburg, Inv. 2644.

[5] During the reigns of Nicholas I (1825-1855) and Alexander II (1855-1881).

[6] *Dix siècles de joaillerie française*, exhibition cat., Louvre Museum, Paris 1962, No. 133, p. 108.

[7] Paris Archives (PA), VK3/77, document dated September 19, 1856. On this occasion Froment-Meurice delivered "sixty-six gold decorations for the women of the municipal corps and eleven posy-holders…".

[8] These two gifts have not been found but several old reproductions show the posy-holder.

[9] An example in silver decorated with the arms of Savoy and of the Bonapartes is preserved in the Museo Napoleonico in Rome. Inv. MN 473, *Fiori freschi*, *op. cit.*, p. 6, ill. 2.

[10] Kenber Collection, Cf. *Porte-bouquets Insolites joies de la colleccio Kenber*, *op. cit.*, No. 130, p. 237.

[11] The posy-holder, incomplete, is preserved at the Moscow Historical Museum (Inv. OK 7030). My thanks to Mme. Galina Smorodinova, curator of the museum, for her assistance and welcome.

[12] Kenber Collection. Cf. *Porte-bouquets Insolites joies de la colleccio Kenber*, *op. cit.*, No. 129, p. 236.

[13] Information provided by Mme. Sablier Paquet, Patrimony Dept., Boucheron, Paris.

[14] Hermitage National Museum Archives, St. Petersburg (AGE), f. 1, op. 5, d. 37, l. 373, No. 9204.

[15] Some are however indicated as pairs.

[16] Gatchina Palace Archives, inventory of the silver for the year 1920, Inv. 1271, No. 249 to 287. The collection is found in the inventory of precious objects of 1925 (Inv. 1270). For the complete list see *Porte-bouquets*, , *op. cit.*, pp. 214-215. We would especially like to thank Mme. Helena Artemeva, curator at the palace for her welcome and her precious assistance.

[17] L. V. Bardovskaya, "Journey of Alexander III and Maria Feodorovna in the Caucasus in 1888," in exhibition cat., *Alexander III and Maria Feodorovna*, Manege Exhibition room, St. Petersburg 2006, pp. 101-107 (in Russian).

[18] Odiot Archives. I would especially like to thank Mme. Joski and Monsieur de la Morinière from the Odiot firm in Paris for their assistance and welcome.

[19] Inv. Э РФ 4740. My thanks in particular to Mme. Ekaterina S. Khmelnitskaïa who pointed out and showed me this piece of artwork.

[20] Inv. Э 9818 and Э О 5036

[21] Inv. OK 7030; OK 19360; OK 17303; OK 19360; OK 4589; OK 5739.

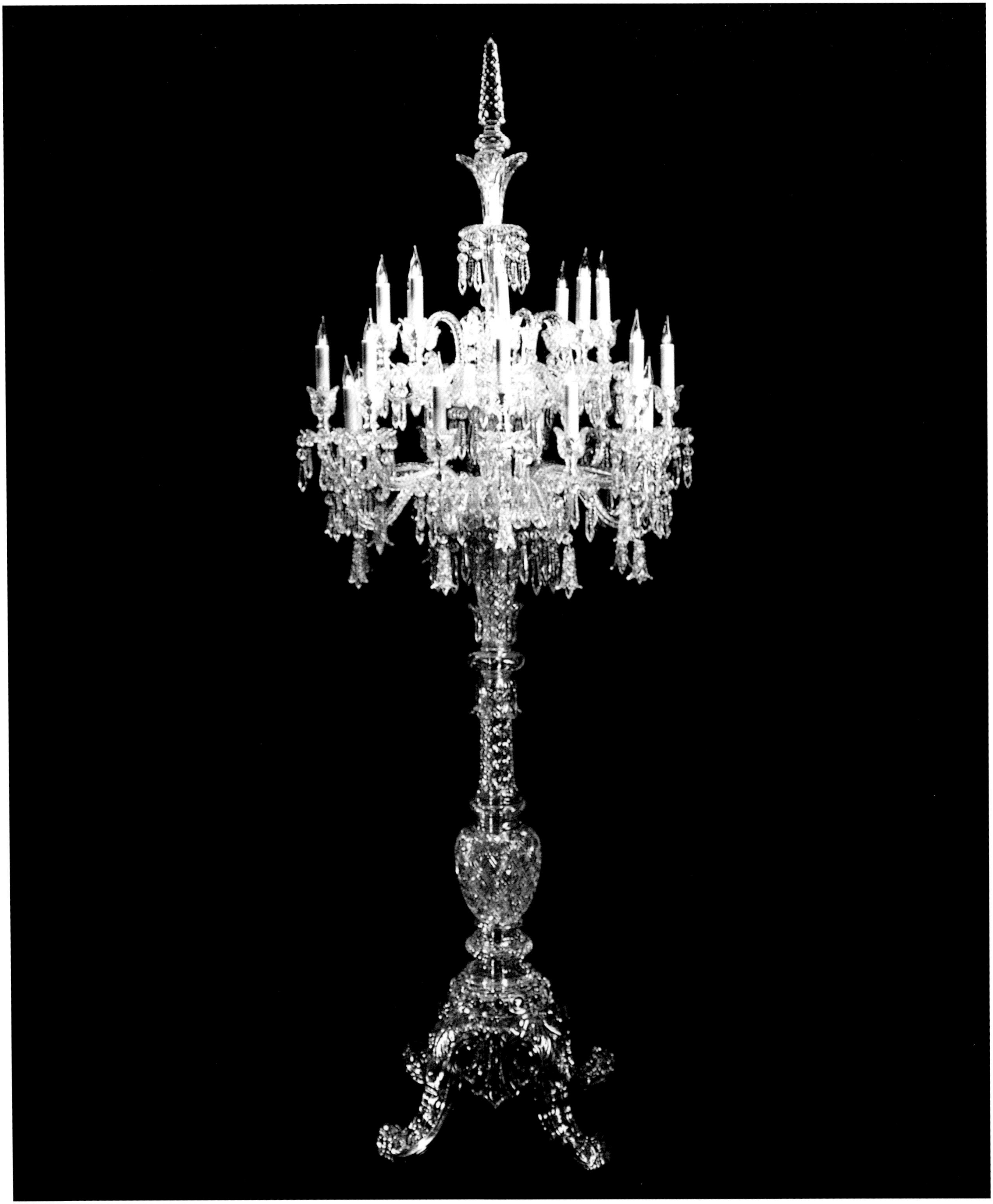

BACCARAT AND RUSSIA

Michaela Lerch

Baccarat was founded in 1764, when King Louis XV authorized the Bishop of Metz to establish a glassworks in Baccarat. Aimé-Gabriel d'Artigues converted its production to crystal in 1816, and it has borne the name of the little Lorraine village ever since. Baccarat, where the glasshouse was originally established, is located on the slopes of the Vosges along the Meurthe river banks, about fifty kilometers from the city of Nancy. Within a few years it became the most important crystalworks in France and soon one of the most prestigious in the world. Orders from sovereigns and important personalities worldwide multiplied, echoing the precedent of King Louis XVIII's first prestigious commission.

The awards won by Baccarat during the universal exhibitions (1867, 1878, 1889, 1900) only added to its prestige, prestige backed by an exceptional know-how. As early as 1830, Baccarat sent out its traveling salesmen, the "globe-trotters," to conquer the world and so perpetuate the image of a cosmopolitan art of living in the great French tradition. Beginning in the 1860s, the Russian market started to open up to Baccarat.

1. Candelabrum known as "the Czarina's candelabrum" 1867 *Heritage collection, Baccarat (Cat. 248)*

Baccarat and Russia is, first of all, the story of a privileged relationship between the prestigious crystal manufacturer and the Court of the Czars.

During his stay in France, Alexander III had admired the most dazzling Baccarat masterpieces presented at the 1867 Universal Exhibition in Paris: a monumental fountain seven meters high, immense chandeliers, a pair of vases engraved by Jean-Baptiste Simon, many polychrome glazed vases and other marvels of more delicate craftsmanship such as wheel-engraved stemware services. On this occasion, a table, a crystal fountain and a 2.15 meter high candelabrum bearing 24 lights (the "CD 225"), created for display at the exhibition, were named in honor of the Czarina Maria Alexandrovna. Little by little, the imperial homes such as the Gatchina palace—one of Alexander III and Maria Feodorovna's favorite residences—began to be decorated with Baccarat crystal pieces.

In 1896 the Czar Nicholas II and the Czarina Alexandra, by way of honeymoon following the coronation festivities, undertook a European tour which took them to Germany, Denmark, England and finally to Paris. This visit had above all a diplomatic goal: to strengthen the fragile Franco-Russian Alliance signed two years before in 1894. But beyond that, Nicholas II was struck by the flamboyant welcome given by the Parisians who acclaimed the royal couple as they traveled along the great boulevards. It was during this trip that the Czar became acquainted with Baccarat, thus reviving his grandfather's passion.

The Czar had finally found who would be able to meet his demands: the Baccarat master glassmak-

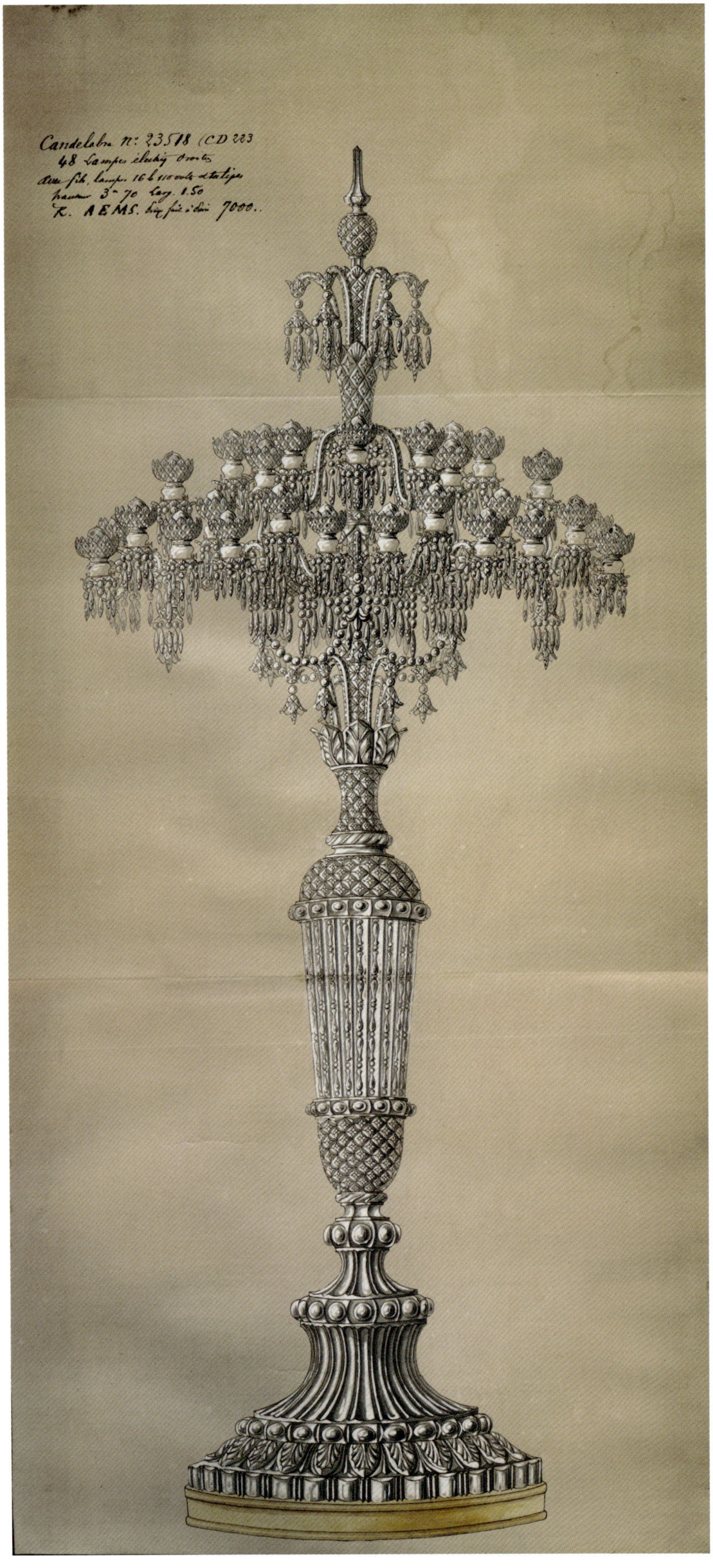

ers and their exceptional know-how. These requirements expressed not only the personal taste of Nicholas II but also the sovereign's desire to show the world the modernity of his empire, through the technical feats and innovations achieved by the crystalworks.

Consequently, some of the candelabra were modified so as to be electrified, thanks to the creation of special moulds to make hollow arms. This was the case of the famous "CD 225", known as "the Czarina's candelabrum", and the "CD 223" known as the "Czar's candelabrum", a 3.85 meters high lighting fixture of 79 lights. The piece known as "the Czar's candelabrum" is a variation of the "CD 223", a 48-candle piece originally presented at the Universal Exhibition of 1878, and electrified around 1897 into a 48-light version (ills. 1-4).

For the palaces of St. Petersburg and Moscow, Baccarat created standing crystal fountains—also called "the Czarina's"—, monumental chandeliers illuminated by 140, 160 and up to 190 candles, and other splendid pieces. A new glass design was created for the table of Nicholas II. Made of cased crystal, featuring a very tall stem and an overall rich-cut pattern, the "Czar's service" was created in six different shades. The princes of his retinue and some aristocrats imitated him, ordering these sets characterized by an elaborately carved design of "diamond points", palmettes and festooned stems. Today, this "Czar's service" is still featured on the catalogue and the object of prestigious commissions (ills. 5 and 6).

In fact, besides the Czars themselves, other members of the Russian imperial family were illus-

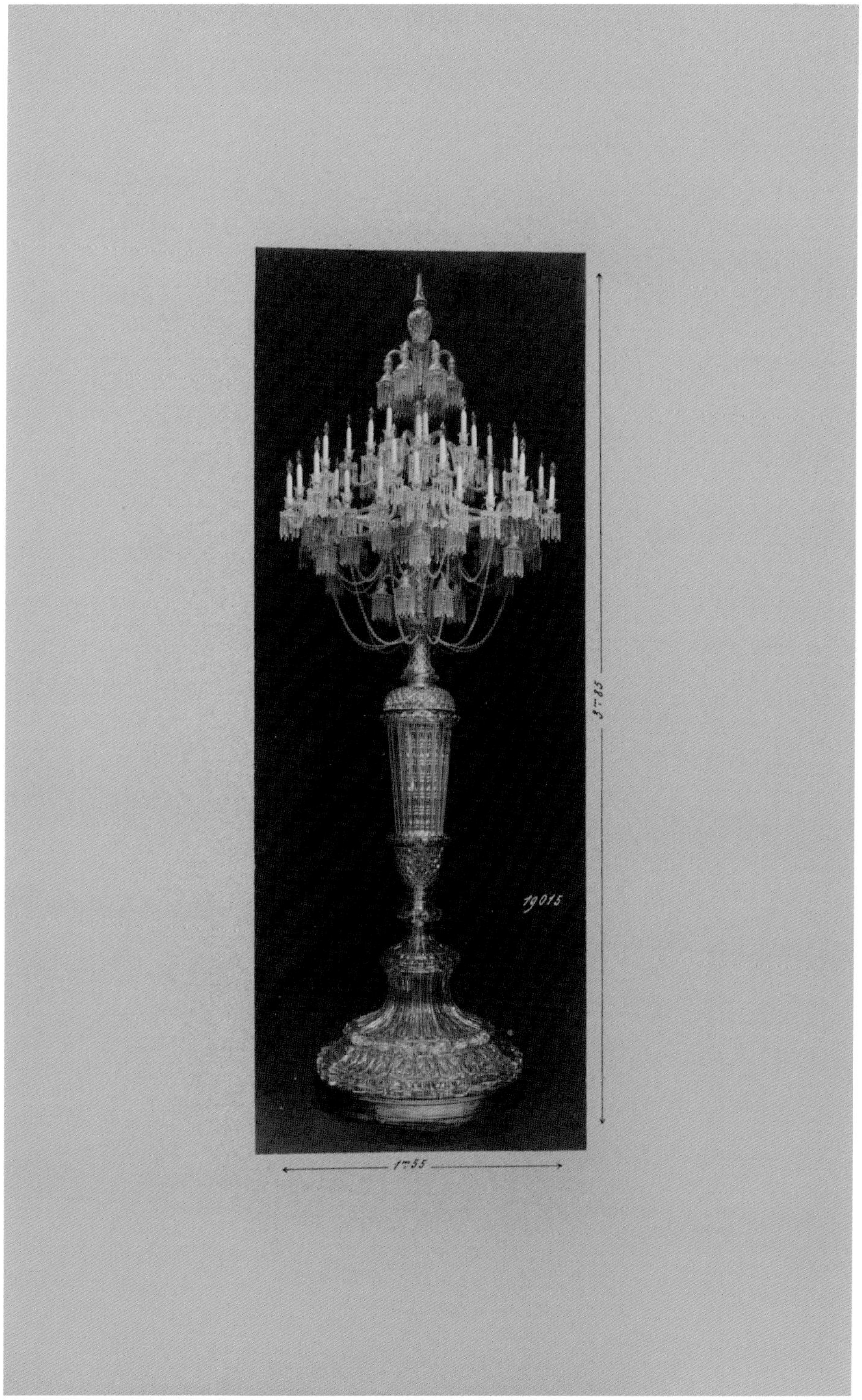

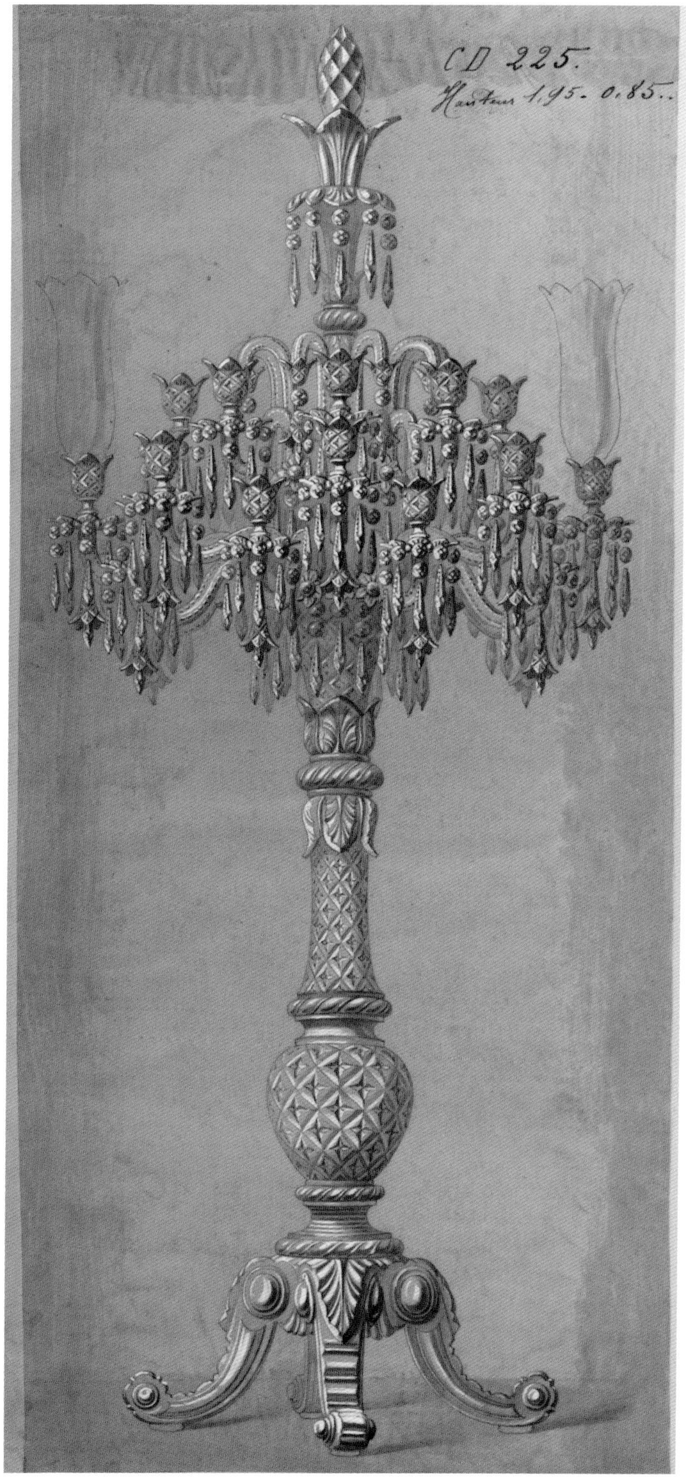

2. Drawing of the "CD 223",
a 48-electric light candelabrum
circa 1897
Baccarat Archives
(Cat. 258)

3. Candelabrum known as "the Czar's candelabrum"
1909
Black and white photographic print with watercolour highlights
Volume 1909 Nancy Exhibition,
Baccarat Archives

4. Drawing of the "CD 225"
a 24-electric light candelabrum
circa 1897
Baccarat Archives
(Cat. 258)

5. "Czar's stemware"
1909
Heritage collection, Baccarat
(Cat. 249-252)

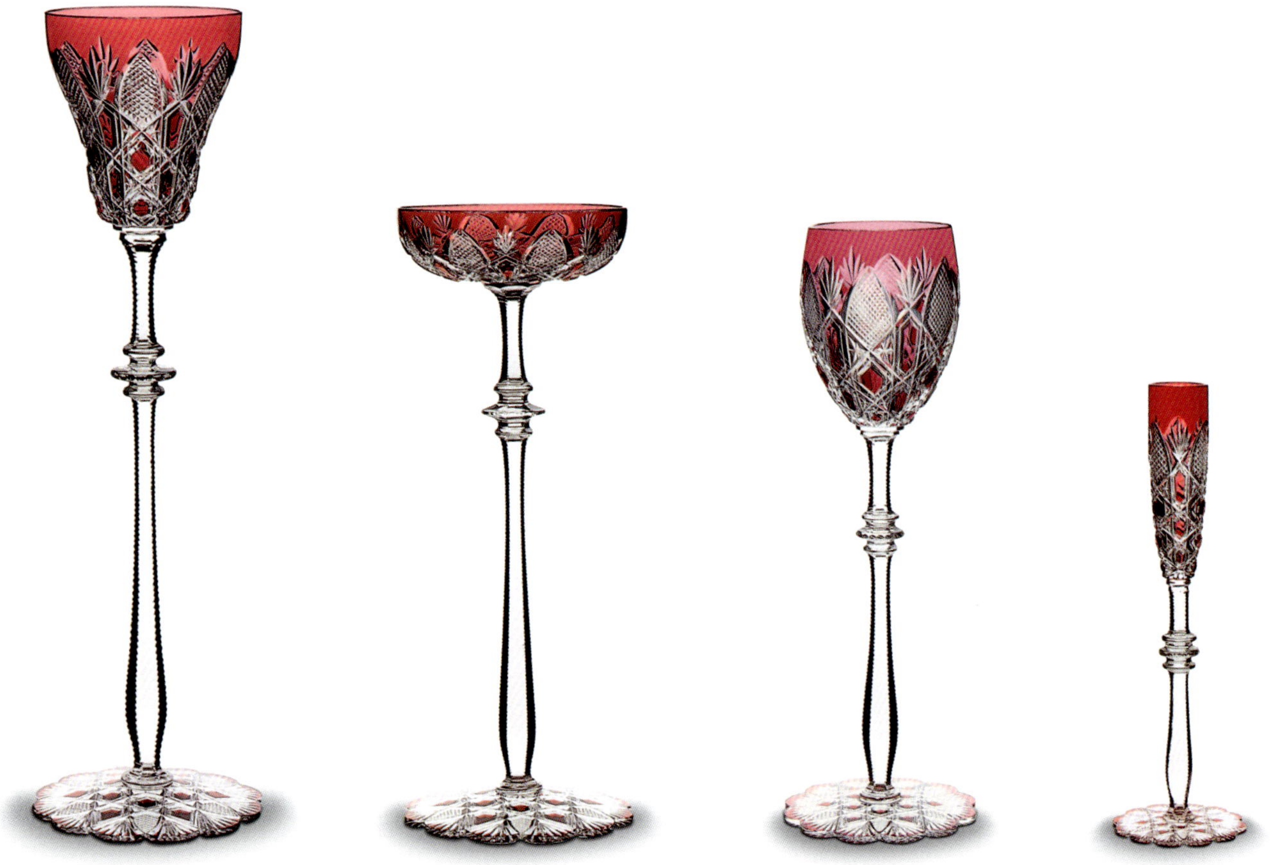

trious patrons of the factory: the Grand Dukes Vladimir and Alexis, great connoisseurs of French luxury goods and of Baccarat in particular and whose prodigality was legendary, the Grand Duke George Alexandrovich, Nicholas II's brother, and the Grand Duke Dmitry Pavlovich, first cousin to Nicholas II. In June 1914, the Grand Duke Pavlovich ordered the T service introduced at the 1878 Universal Exhibition, enhanced with his monogram topped by a crown. For the record, the latter is said to have designed the Chanel No. 5 perfume bottle (ills. 7 and 8).

The great aristocratic families and personalities included also the prince Paul Pavlovich Demidoff, the prince Orloff, the princess Tereotchenko as well as Ivan Abramovich Morosoff. The latter, member of one of the most illustrious merchant families in Russia, liked to play host to high society in his Muscovite town house. He organized gala dinners and receptions, enabling his guests to admire the impressive collection of paintings he had acquired during his trips to Europe, particularly in Paris where he zealously frequented exhibitions, salons and art dealers. He placed several orders between 1890 and 1914 to decorate the tables of his palace with Baccarat emblazoned glasses, vases, mounted centerpieces and decorative objects. As early as 1900, he acquired electric ceiling lights (ills. 9 and 10).

The order books also included many names

of goldsmiths and silversmiths such as the famous houses Fabergé and Christofle, but also Gratchev, Khlebnikov, Kurliukuv etc. who were regular clients of Baccarat crystal. They enhanced them through their mountings while complying with the latest Russian fashion: imposing centerpieces with gilded bronze mountings adorned with chimera and sphinxes, vases, pitchers and decanters mounted with precious metals, table accessories (salt cellars, mustard pots, oil and vinegar sets etc.) and also candle holders, chandeliers, toilet sets, decorative objects (ill. 11).[1]

Some clients who went frequently to France and in particular to Paris—one of their favorite destinations—preferred to place their orders directly with the factory or with the director of the Paris Depot, on the rue de Paradis. They also could place orders via middlemen and traveling salesmen such as Mr. Bénit and Mr. Pichon, or with retailers such as Marcerou.

In addition, Baccarat had a representative in Russia, Mr. Hermanovitz, an important figure who could boast contacts at the Imperial Court. He stayed in the best Moscow hotels where commercial agents from the main cities would visit him. He carried a few samples with him but most of all he had a richly illustrated catalogue with explanations in Russian, which even featured the "water

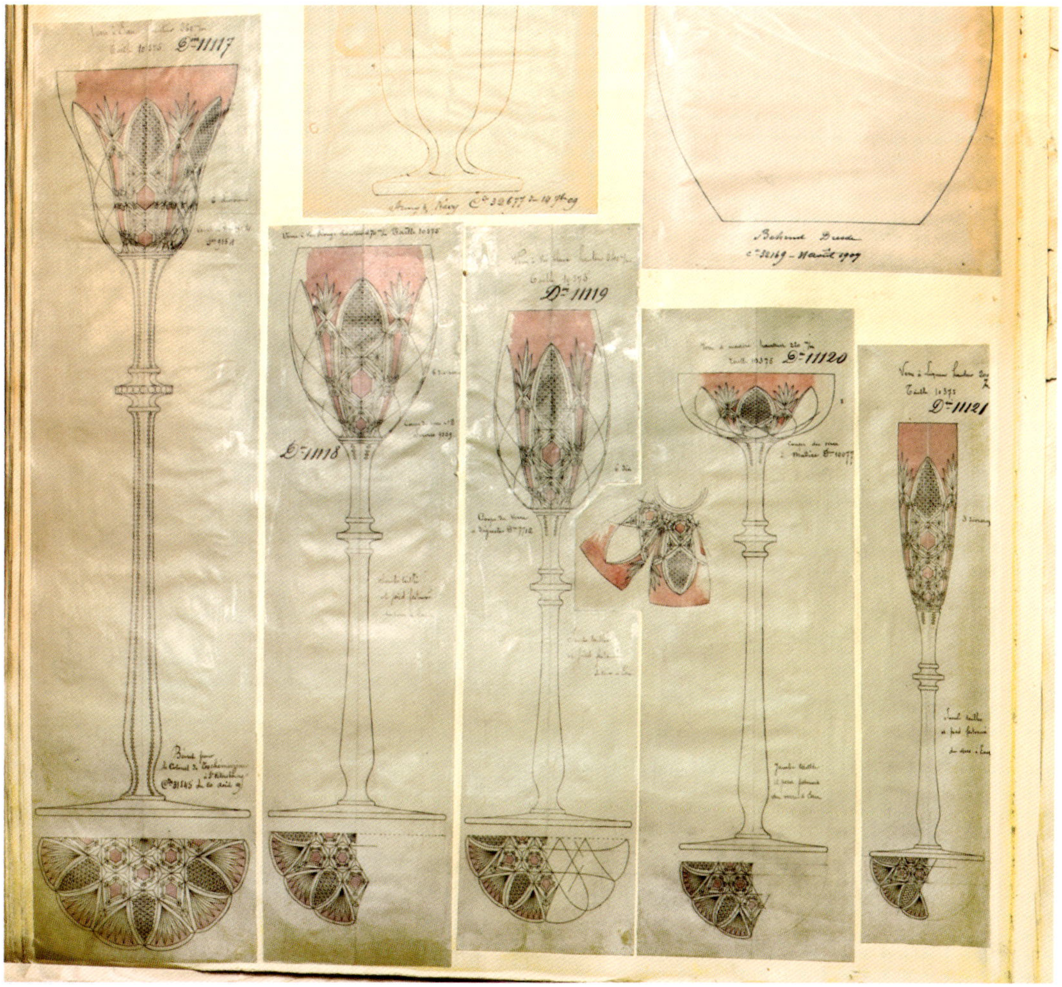

6. Design for the "Czar's stemware"
Beginning of the 20th century
Heritage collection, Baccarat
(Cat. 253)

7. Glass created for the Grand Duke Vladimir Alexandrovich
1870
Heritage collection, Baccarat (Cat. 255)

8. Drawing of a glass created for the Grand Duke Dmitri Pavlovich
1914
Ink highlighted with watercolor on tracing paper glued onto squared paper
Inscription: "Order 43353, June 12, 1914, His Imperial Highness the Grand Duke Dmitri Pavlovich. Glass No. 2, T Service"
Armorial bearings volume, Baccarat Archives

9. Glass from the G Service intended for Mr. Morosoff
1878
Heritage collection, Baccarat (Cat. 256)

10. Drawing of the G Service water glass
Pencil, Indian ink and ink wash highlights on paper glued into a volume
Volume "A-S glasses service" from the 1878 Paris Universal Exhibition

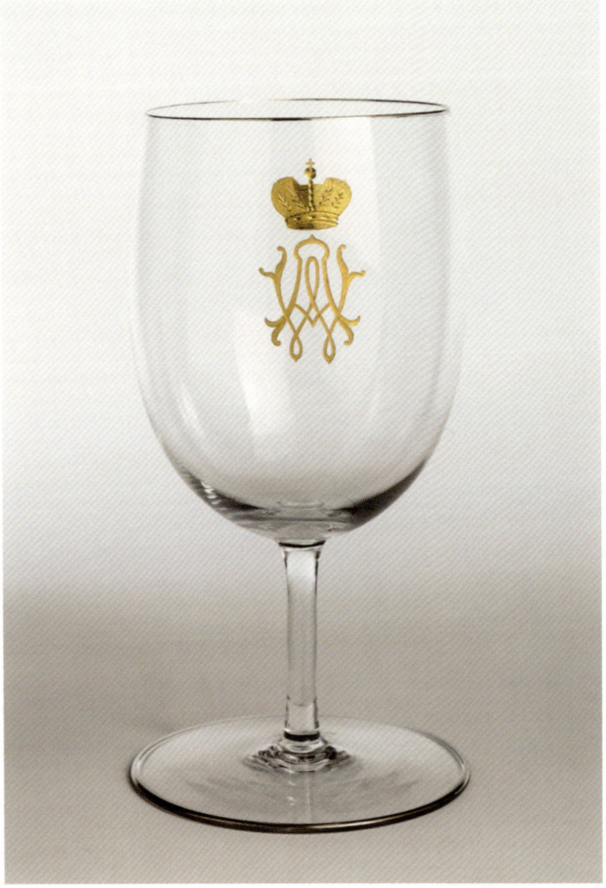

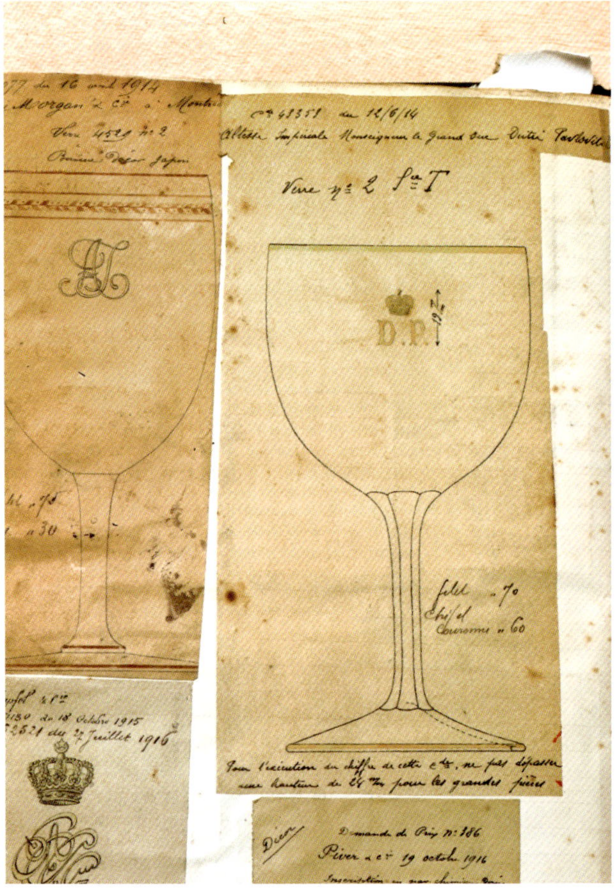

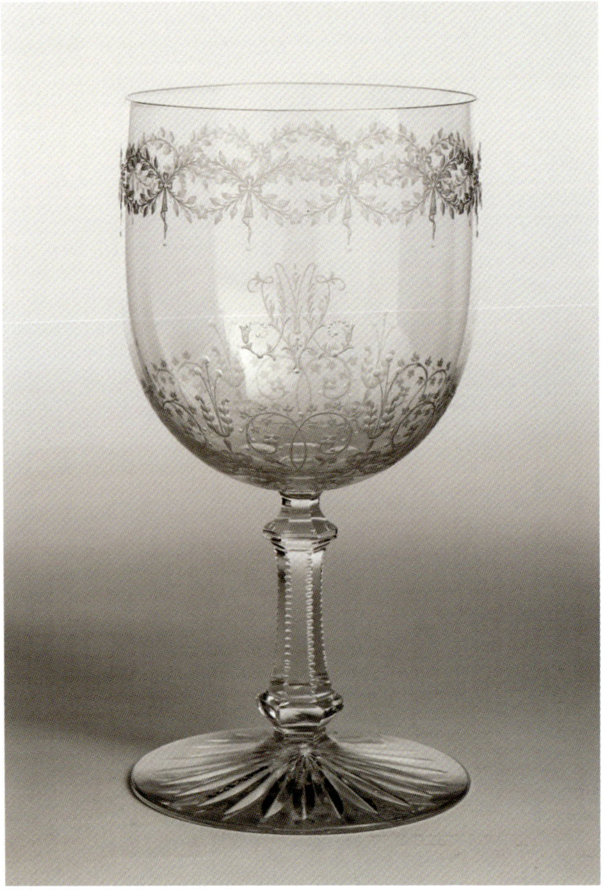

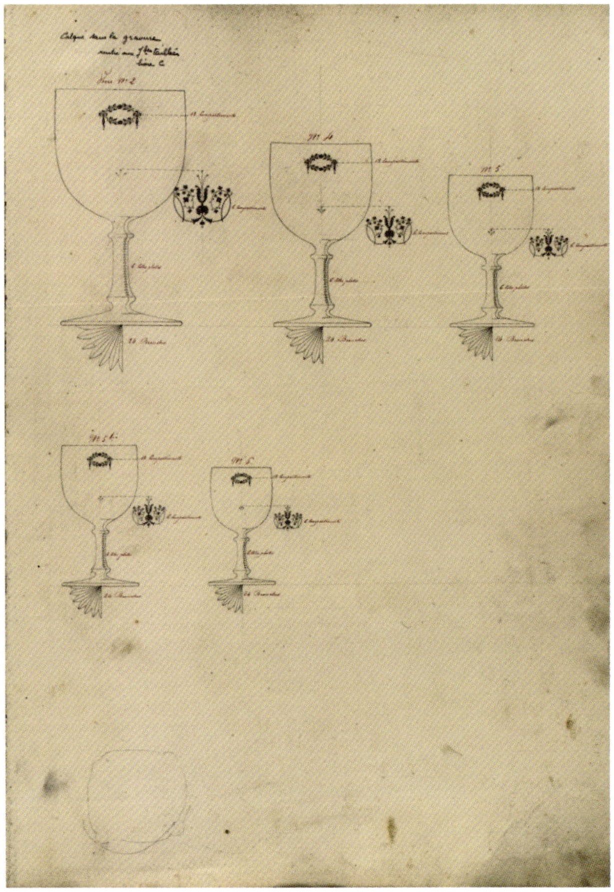

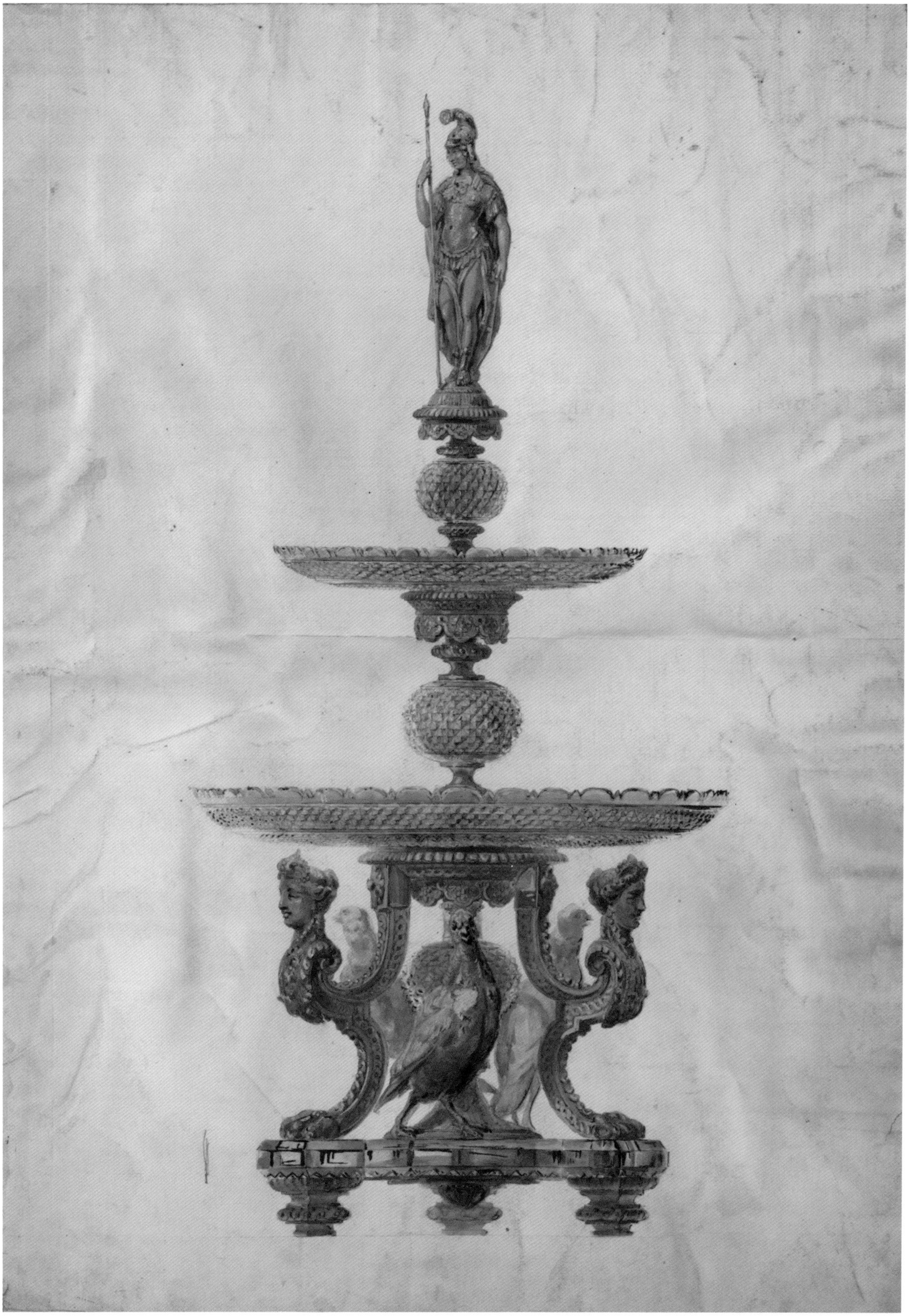

11. Drawing of a centrepiece with gilded bronze mounting created for the 1867 *Paris Universal Exhibition Gouache, ink wash and pencil on paper glued onto paper Volume No. 3 of the 1867 Paris Universal Exhibition, Baccarat Archives*

glass" services and toilet sets, displaying a "Russian" design. Each client knew that what he ordered would be exactly like the picture. His business prospered and it was said that he didn't hesitate to offer mink coats to his most important female clients (ill. 12).

At the beginning of the 20th century, the Russian market represented a great part of the Glassworks exportations. A large number of workers, sometimes as many as one thousand, were exclusively engaged in processing such orders. Of the three furnaces operated at the manufactory in the 1900s, one was entirely dedicated to filling the famous Russian "special orders" and was named "the Russian furnace."

These dream cargos were sent by sea. The wreck of one of the ships taking the Baltic route which linked the ports of the North Sea to St. Petersburg—the Kursk cargo ship which had sunk off of Antwerp the night of August 26, 1912—was discovered in 1999 by Belgian explorers. Within its hold was a treasure of several thousand pieces of Baccarat still intact, among which were several stemware services (including the Colbert model with its rich-cut pattern) and crystal candle rings indicating the presence of huge chandeliers or candelabra which were being transported in the form of individual components.

In addition to sets of glasses, other Baccarat crystal objects *a priori* destined for a longer life decorated the imperial residences, the Gatchina palace for example—candlesticks, vases, toilet sets, table decorations and lamps. But the wars and the post-revolutionary dispersion of the imperial furnishings have left only too few and rare remaining examples.

The Baccarat archives preserves their traces: the order books, merchant books, collections of initials and armorial bearings, plans and patterns specify the names of its numerous Russian clients such as Wladimiroff, Korniloff, Kurhukoff, Tscherepennikoff, Tchuksanoff, Pioshoroff, Prokofieff, Aleschef, Nemiroff Kolotkin, Orbeloff, Froloff, Schtcherbakoff, Kustionoff, Kusnezoff, Kobylin, Kobbe and the Hermitage Society.

The Baccarat Heritage collection counts a few specimen glasses embellished with the monograms of its clients. They were used as models to create emblazoned services and to fill complementary orders.

These jewels of the Heritage collections are on display to the public in the Baccarat Museum of Paris, among which the stunning piece known as the "Czar Nicholas II's candelabrum"—one of the two devoutly preserved by the firm—and the sumptuous "Czar's stemware" in its red-overlay cased crystal version.

[1] In volume No. 3 of the 1867 Paris Universal Exhibition there is also the mention of an order for cut and pierced bowls to be mounted as a table centrepiece for the Hermitage Society in Moscow.

XI

ОБЩІЯ ЗАМѢЧАНІЯ

I. — Всѣ наши издѣлія снабжены наклейкой, ярлыкомъ или штемпелемъ, рисунокъ котораго помѣщаемъ рядомъ.

II. — Въ прейсъ-курантѣ указаны цѣны за товары на нашемъ складѣ. Упаковка для отправки ставится въ счетъ покупателя.

III. — Мы не отвѣчаемъ за повреждение товаровъ въ дорогѣ отъ какой-бы причины оно не произошло. По прибытіи товара покупатель можетъ, если найдетъ достаточныя основанія, искать убытки съ лица взявшаго перевозку.

IV. — Во избѣжаніе недоразумѣній просимъ покупателя при составленіи заказа весьма точно обозначать: названіе выбраннаго предмета; номера по порядку и по серіямъ; величину предмета.

V. — Мы даемъ въ настоящемъ прейсъ-курантѣ изображеніе части метра, чтобы покупатель имѣлъ возможность точно опредѣдить величину заказываемаго предмета.

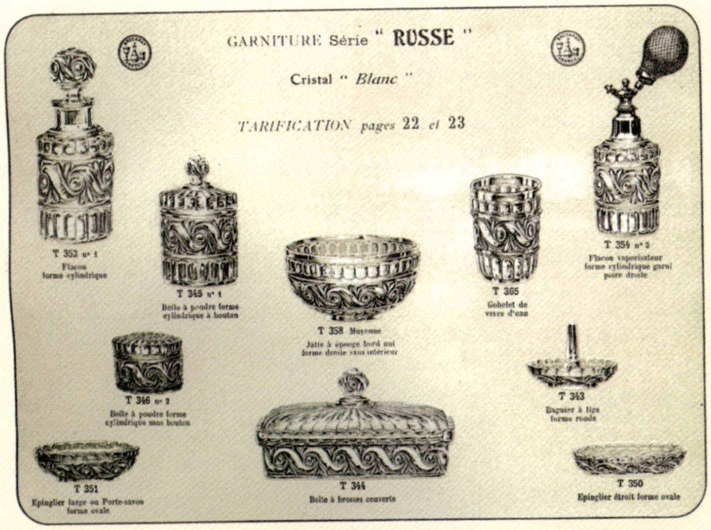

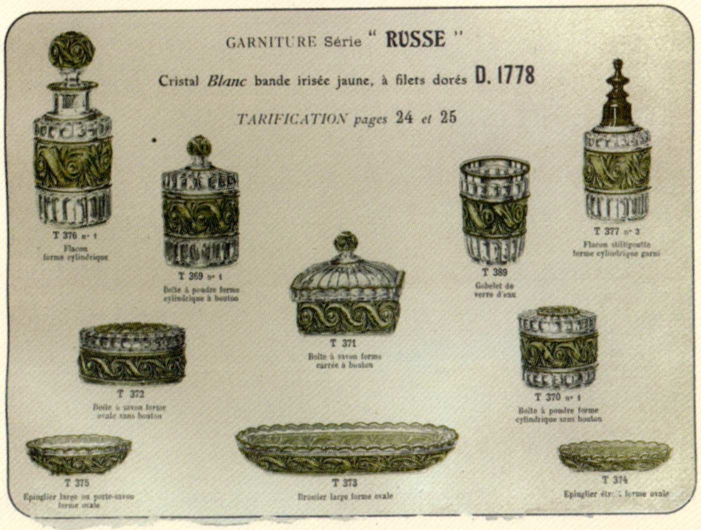

Consultez Observations générales en tête de l'Album — 13 — Les articles sont reproduits au quart de leur grandeur naturelle

12 and 13. Pages of a commercial catalogue, "General Observations" in Russian, and "Molded Toiletries, Russian series"
1903-1904
Baccarat commercial catalogue, Baccarat Archives

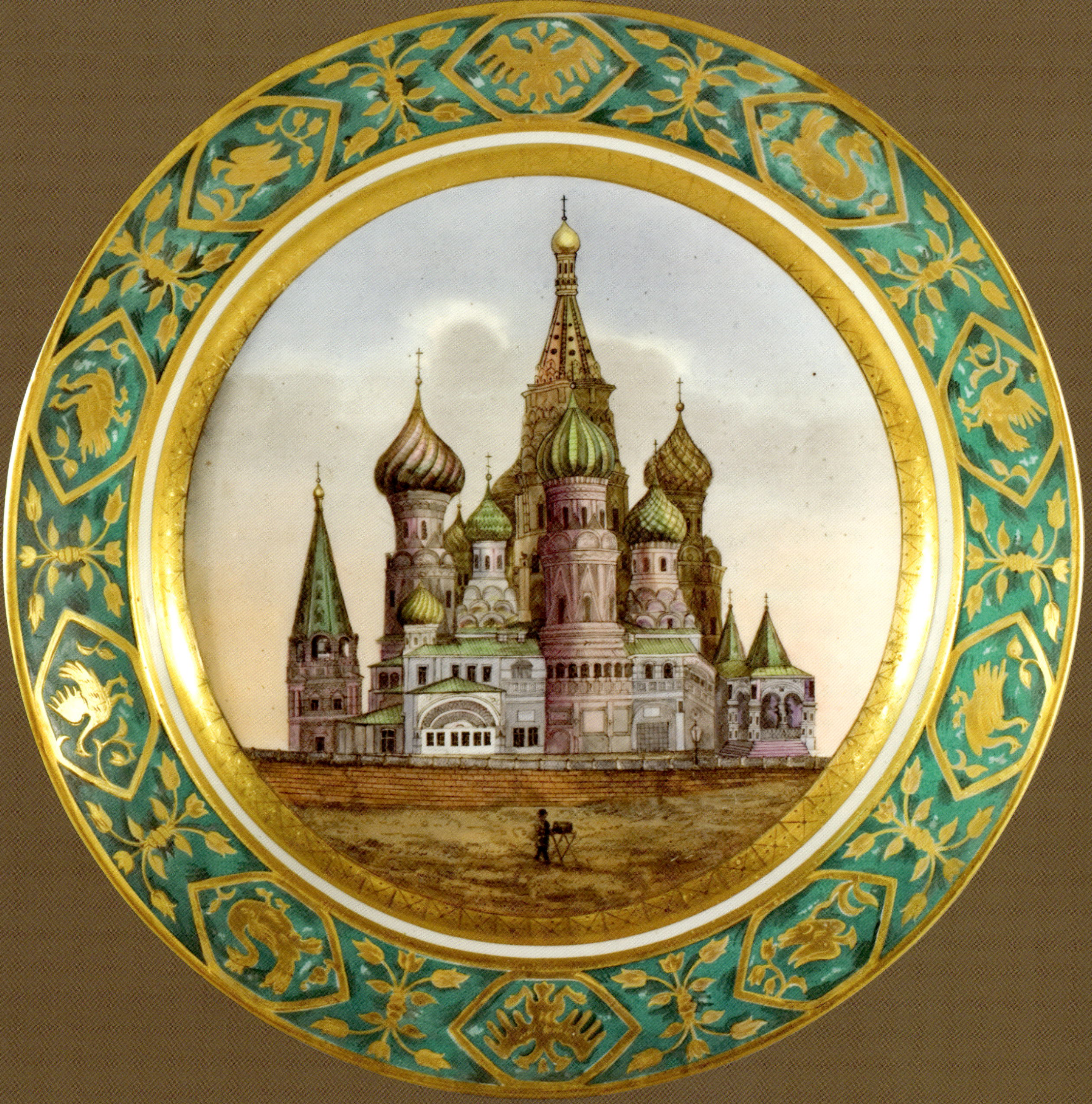

A NEW GLANCE ON RUSSIA

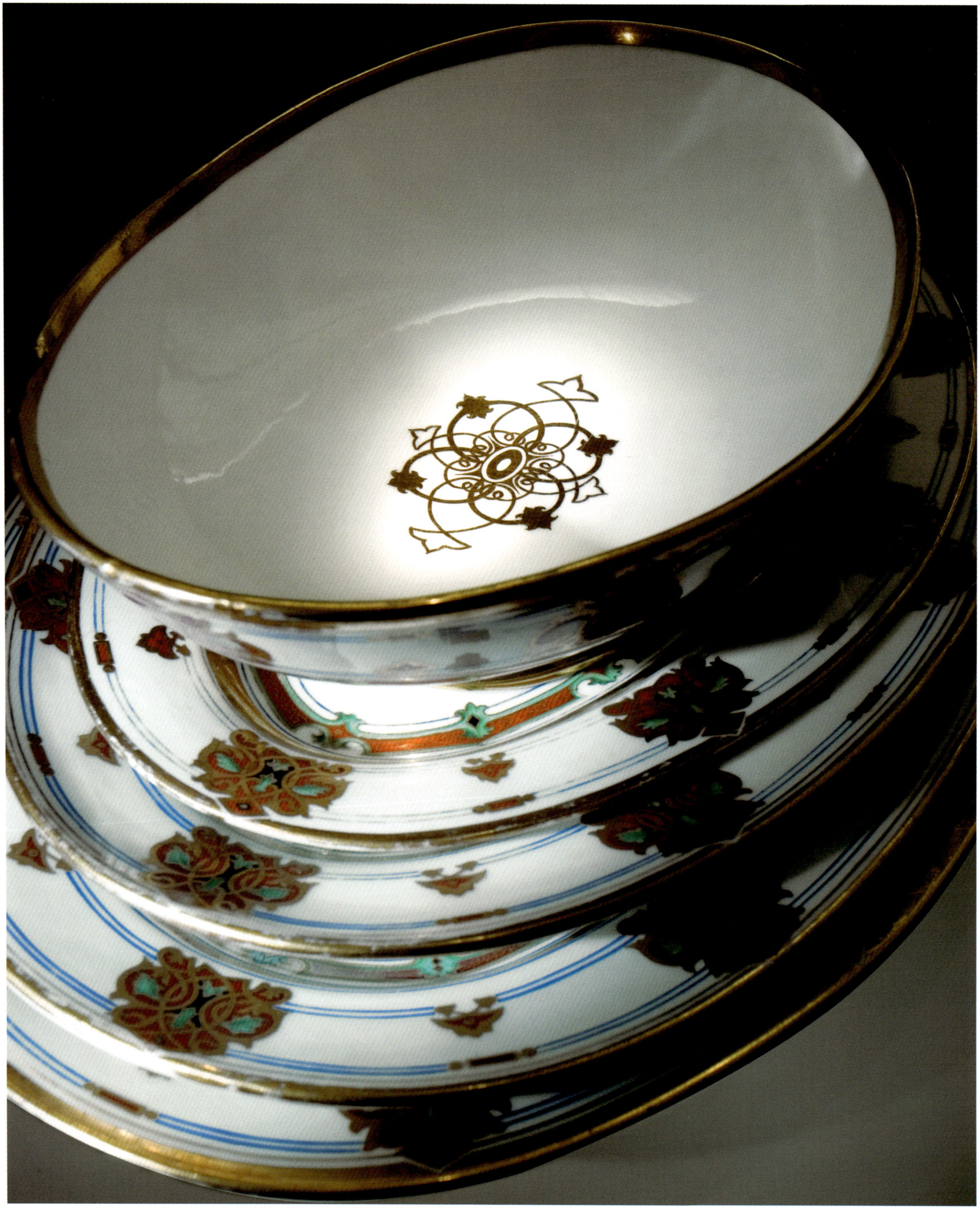

RUSSKII STYLE, THE RUSSIAN STYLE

Brigitte de Montclos

Page 224
Round plate with green edging and with view St. Basil the Blessed Church in Moscow
Gardner Manufacture, 1850s-1860s
State Ceramics Museum of Kuskovo
(Cat. 497)

1. Pieces of Great Duke Constantine Nicholaevich's ceremonial service
Based on F. G. Solntsev's project.
Imperial Porcelain Manufacture, 1848
State Ceramics Museum of Kuskovo
(Cat. 522-537)

From the end of the 18th century, a new appreciation of Gothic art appeared throughout Europe, as evidenced by the quest for a national art deriving from the medieval epoch. This trend, appearing early in England, crossed country borders. Catherine II of Russia filled her parks with Gothic gates and had the Petrovsky palace, built in Moscow (1775-1782), peppered with very Russian remembrances of the past such as bulging columns or bay window casings (ill. 2). The nature of this evocation of Russian patrimony calling on a national tradition, in spite of a rationalist organization of construction, is eminently political. It was necessary to show the State's attachment to the country's historic power. This is why at the same time, and also in Moscow, the Empress gave the order to the architect Vasily Bajenov to build the imperial residence of Tsaritsyno, a complex grouping of several buildings in which were mingled Russian and Western traditions and the use of the antique column. But when Catherine visited the residence in 1785, although it had practically been finished, she ordered it to be destroyed. The architect was linked by Free-Masonry to her son, the grand duke Paul and to anti-establishment members of the opposition. Matvey Kazakov succeeded the disgraced Bajenov and built a different set of buildings in which the presence of Russian patrimony was more pronounced. Nicholas I, Catherine the Great's grandson, drew from the same sources in building and decorating his "cottage" of Peterhof.

However, it was particularly around the 1830s that the real return to traditions developed with the need to get rid of the influences of that intrusive West imported by Peter the Great, as well as by his successors including Alexander I, under whose reign cities were covered with columns. With Nicholas I's accession to the throne, the Slavophiles took over and advocated the return to national sources. The Czar supported them for a long time because their principles reinforced his policies based on the famous dogma "Orthodoxy, autocracy, patriotism" coined in 1833 by Sergei Ouvarov, minister of education.

The Slavophiles drew from the repertory of tradition what constituted their act of faith in a Russia purified of all Western influences, where natural harmony would lead to unity and peace. This ideology was developed mainly in the Muscovite salons, made up of the great land owners, less concerned than those of St. Petersburg about the absolute necessity of following Western fashion whether intellectual or physical, and closer to the world of the countryside. Even as German romanticism was in reaction to the French example at the end of the 18th century, so did this trend express itself by creations imbued with mysticism which

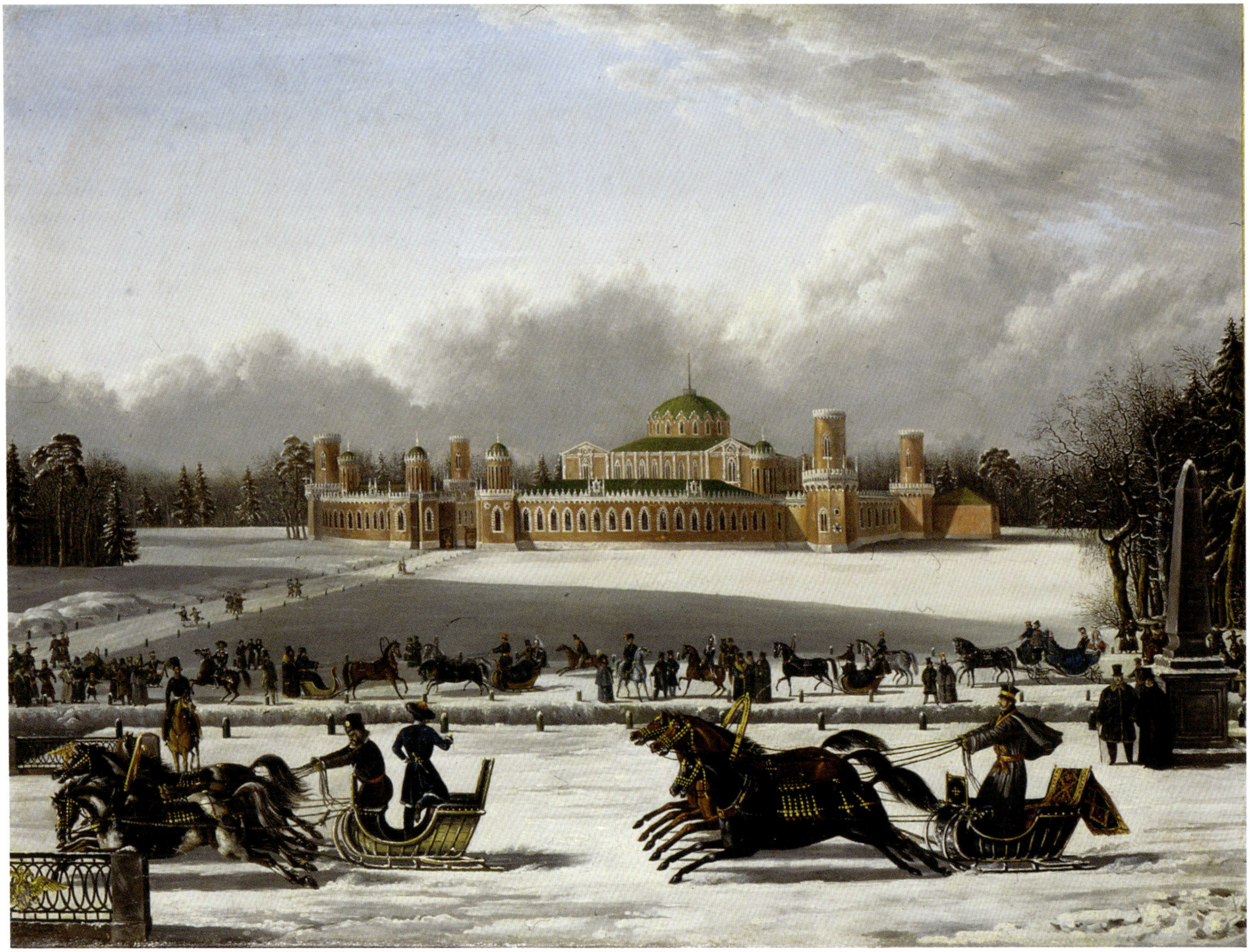

2. *Prince A. A. Golitsyn*
Sleigh race on the St. Petersburg roadway near the Petrovsky Palace
1848
The State Historical Museum, Moscow
(Cat. 291)

harkened back to national traditions and legends as well as to architectural and decorative styles of Old Russia. But in contrast to French romanticism which returned to medieval sources in order to free itself of the shackles of classicist rules and which was therefore synonymous with liberty, the Slavophiles went back to ancient sources to resuscitate a national structure devoid of liberty and openness but on which a form of art could be based freed of Western influence. The result of a growing awareness of a culture which is unique to itself, Russian art discovered its own personality. It was helped in that by the consciousness of Russian history: the last volume of *History of the Russian State* by Karamzin appeared in 1926.

Decorative art benefited from this new historical knowledge for it now drew its repertory from reputedly sure sources. The views of old cities, in particular those of Moscow, rebuilt as new after the fire of 1812 (ill. 3) constitute a rich itemization. It is true that the restoration of the Kremlin buildings, begun as soon as the clearing away of the burned parts permitted it, was very much supported by Nicholas I. The Emperor was well aware of

3. Round plate with green edging and with a view of the Kremlin from the other side of the Moskva river
Gardner Manufacture, second half of 19th century
State Ceramics Museum of Kuskovo (Cat. 496)

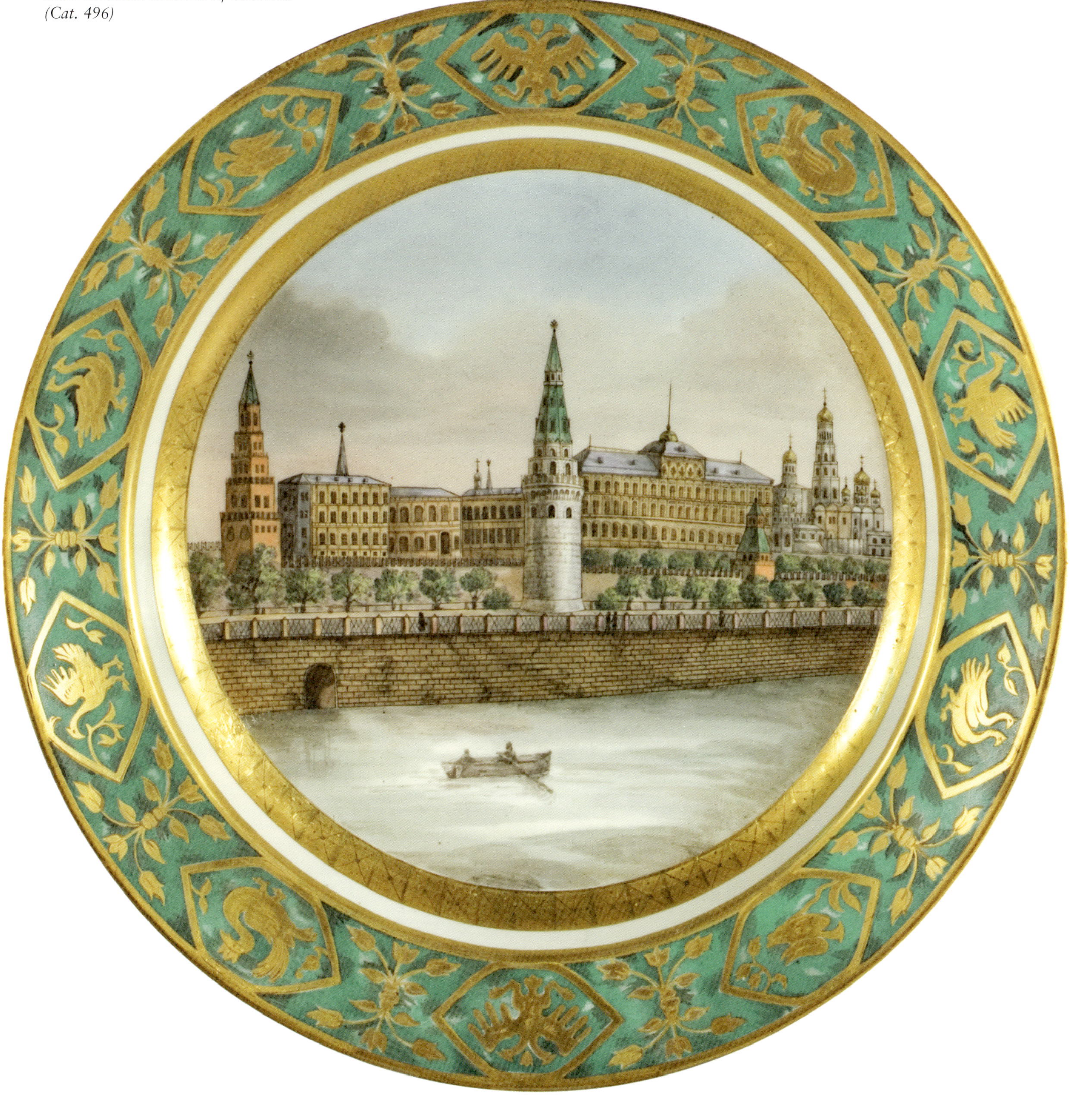

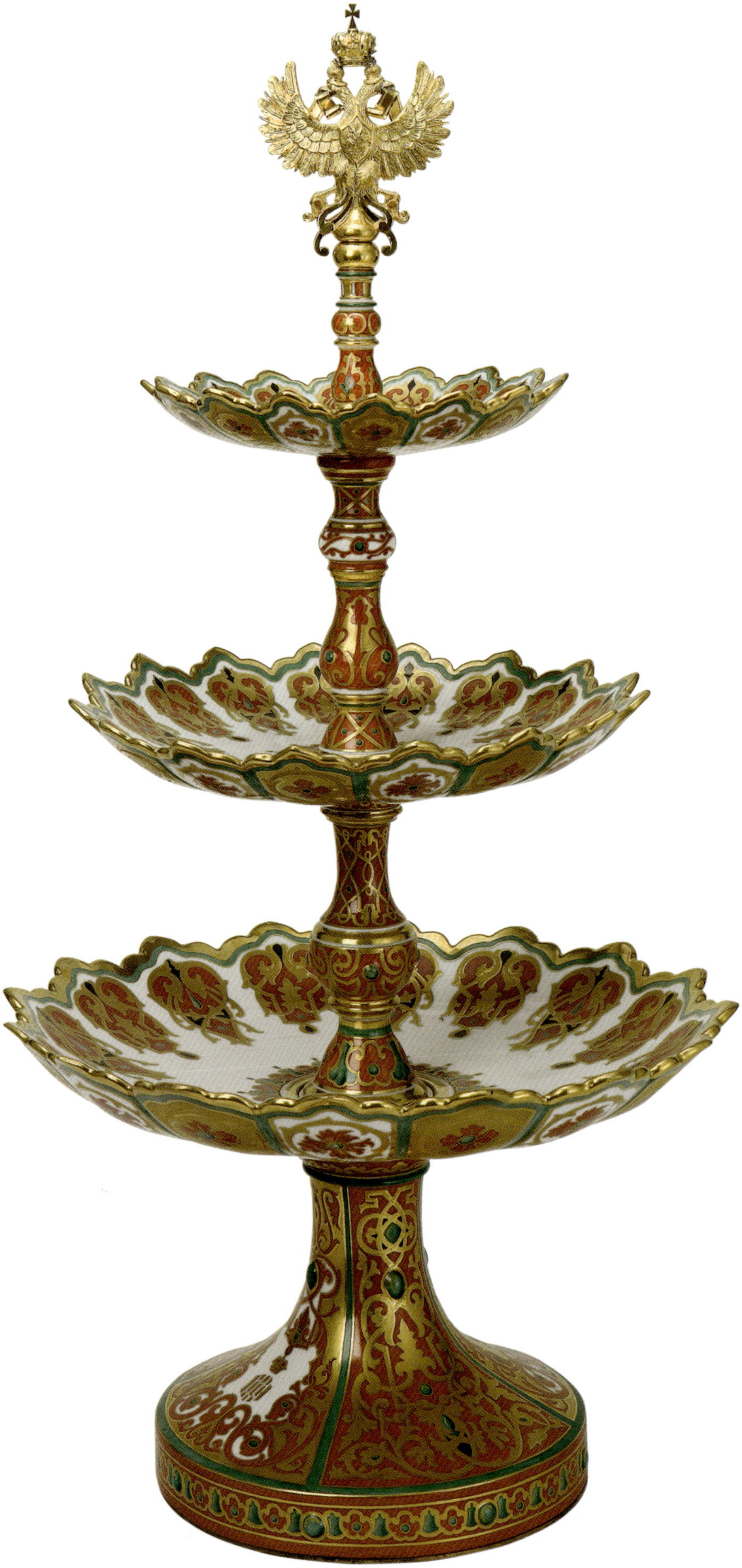

4. Display stand with three shelves
Piece belonging to the grand duke Constantine Nicholaevich's porcelain service
St. Petersburg, Imperial Porcelain Manufacture, 1848-1852
The State Historical Museum, Moscow
(Cat. 517)

5. Tall-stemmed cup belonging to a dessert service
Pieces of Great Duke Constantine Nicholaevich's ceremonial service
Based on F. G. Solntsev's project.
Imperial Porcelain Manufacture, 1848
State Ceramics Museum of Kuskovo
(Cat. 520)

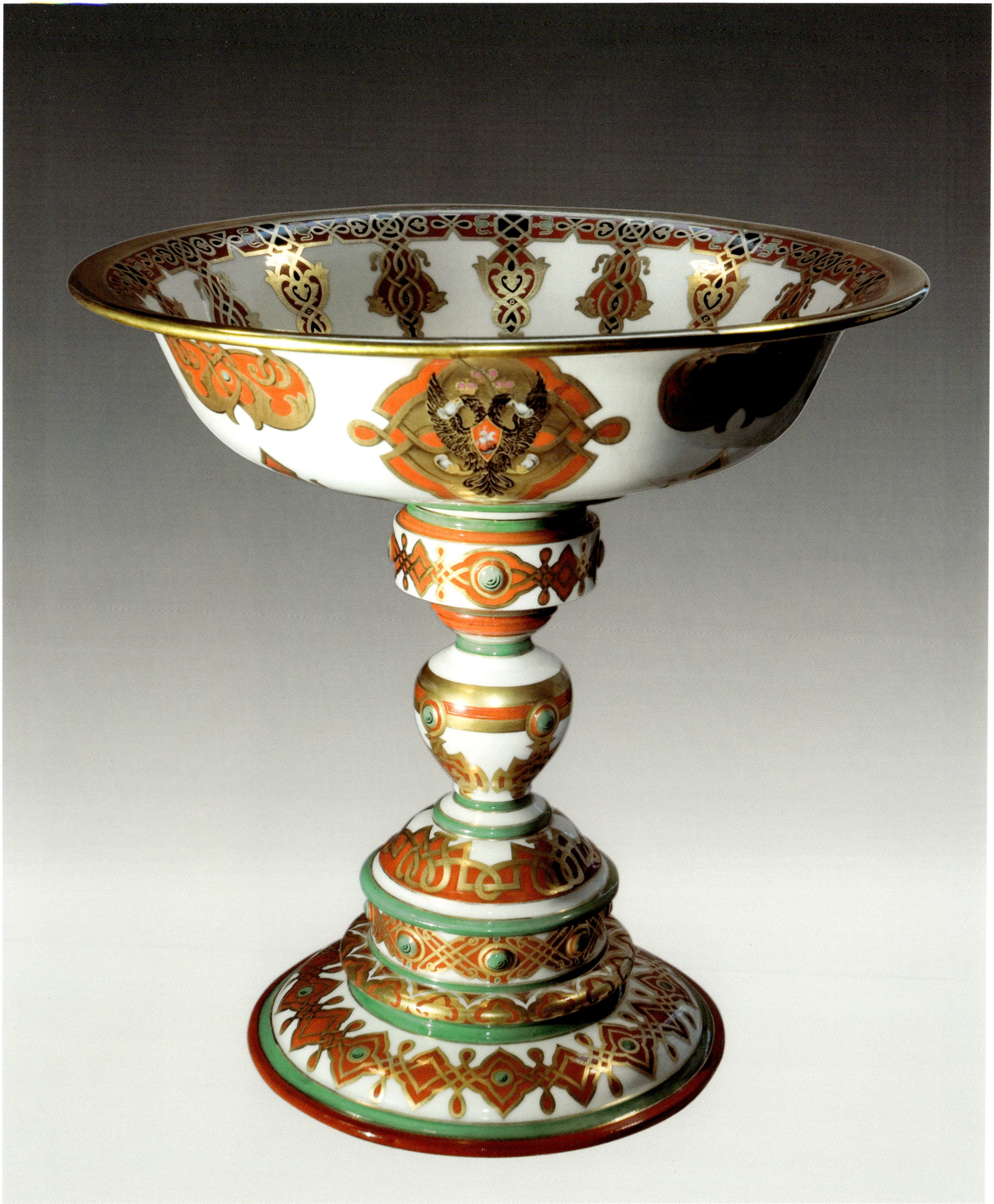

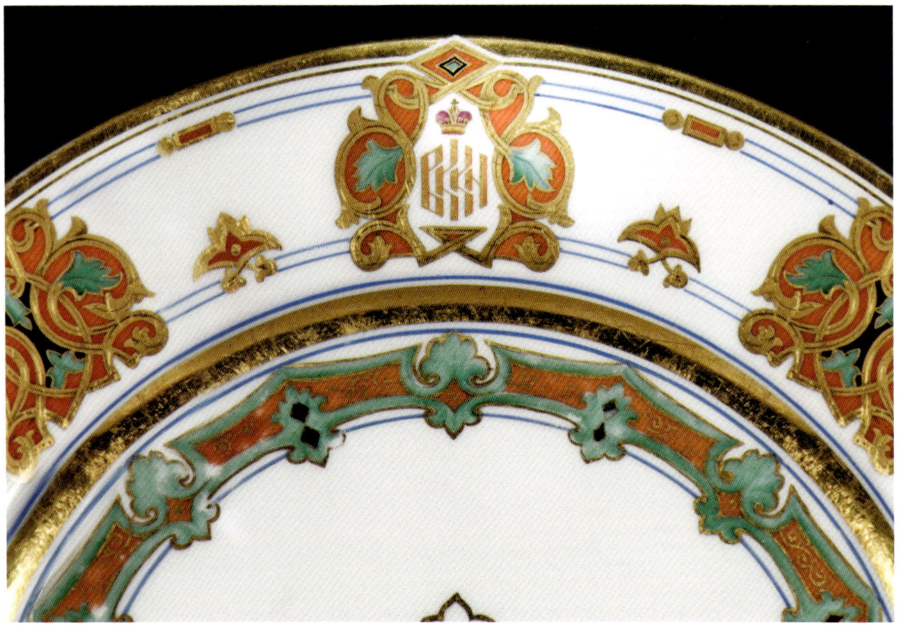

6. Plates from the Great Duke Constantine Nicholaevich's ceremonial service
Based on F. G. Solntsev's project.
Imperial Porcelain Manufacture, 1848
State Ceramics Museum of Kuskovo
(Cat. 526 to 537)
Detail

the importance of this monument in the history of the Romanovs and starting in 1830 undertook the restoration of the palace of *terems*, the palace of the Czar. Michael Feodorovich Romanov's apartments, decorated in the 17th century by the great icon painter Simon Ushakov, were entirely repainted according to the spirit of the 19th century which created tracery of greenery and colored plants founded on the principle of historical origin. In particular, Nicholas I gave the order to Constantine Ton to build the Grand Palace, built from 1838 to 1849, in the Russkii style which was based on characteristics of Russian medieval architecture to which were associated foreign elements but which had been for a long while assimilated. The same architect built the Armory Palace from 1844 to 1851, heir to the Royal Arsenal, formerly where armament was made but also the main headquarters for precious metal work. It was to be used to store the precious clothing and objects of the czars and patriarchs preserved now as relics.

The Russkii style had a long future ahead of it, for the successors of Nicholas I—Alexander II, as well as Alexander III and Nicholas II—were all to favor this direction. Nicholas I's young son,

7. Ink Pot
Russia, Moscow, 1899-1907
The State Historical Museum, Moscow
(Cat. 488)

Constantine Nicholaevich, received a porcelain service in 1847 decorated with very colorful vegetal tracery which responded to the décor themes used in the palace rooms of the *terems* (ills. 1, 4, 5 and 6). Alexander II, his heir, encouraged the Pan-Russian exhibitions organized according to the French example of the first Products of Industry exhibitions. Their purpose was to promote industrialization of the immense country which was Russia and were presented in Moscow, St. Petersburg, and Nijni-Novgorod. One of the most important of them, delayed following the assassination of Alexander II, took place in Moscow in 1882 and four thousand exhibitors participated. Art and design were given a prominent place there.

There was an exceptional renaissance of cloisonné enamel due to the Ovchtchinikov firm, founded in Moscow in 1853. Its work was presented at the Philadelphia international exhibition in 1876, and won awards at the 1882 Pan-Russian exhibition. The Khlebnikov firm, founded in St. Petersburg in 1867, set up in Moscow in 1871 and of course presented its production. And it was the first time that Carl Fabergé participated in a Pan-Russian exhibition. There he received a gold medal which was to be an important reference for becoming a Court supplier.

This return to popular origins was backed by two patrons, Savva Mamontov in Abramtsevo, near Moscow, and the princess Tenisheva in Talashkino, near Smolensk. The iconographic research which they encouraged enabled artists to revive the repertory of mythical animals, swastikas and siren-birds. Russian history is illustrated by small sculptures, the *bogatyrs* scrutinizing the horizon according to the

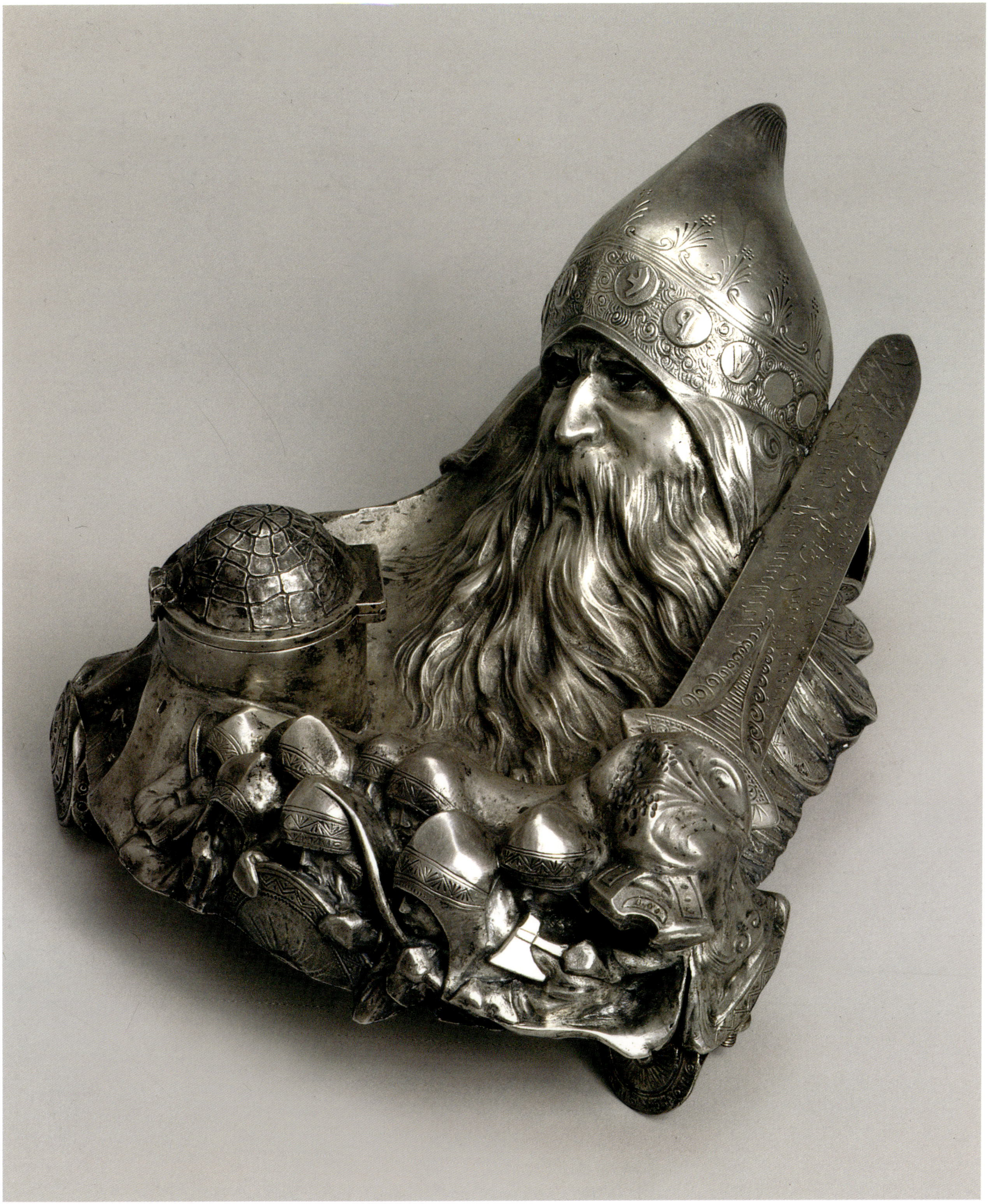

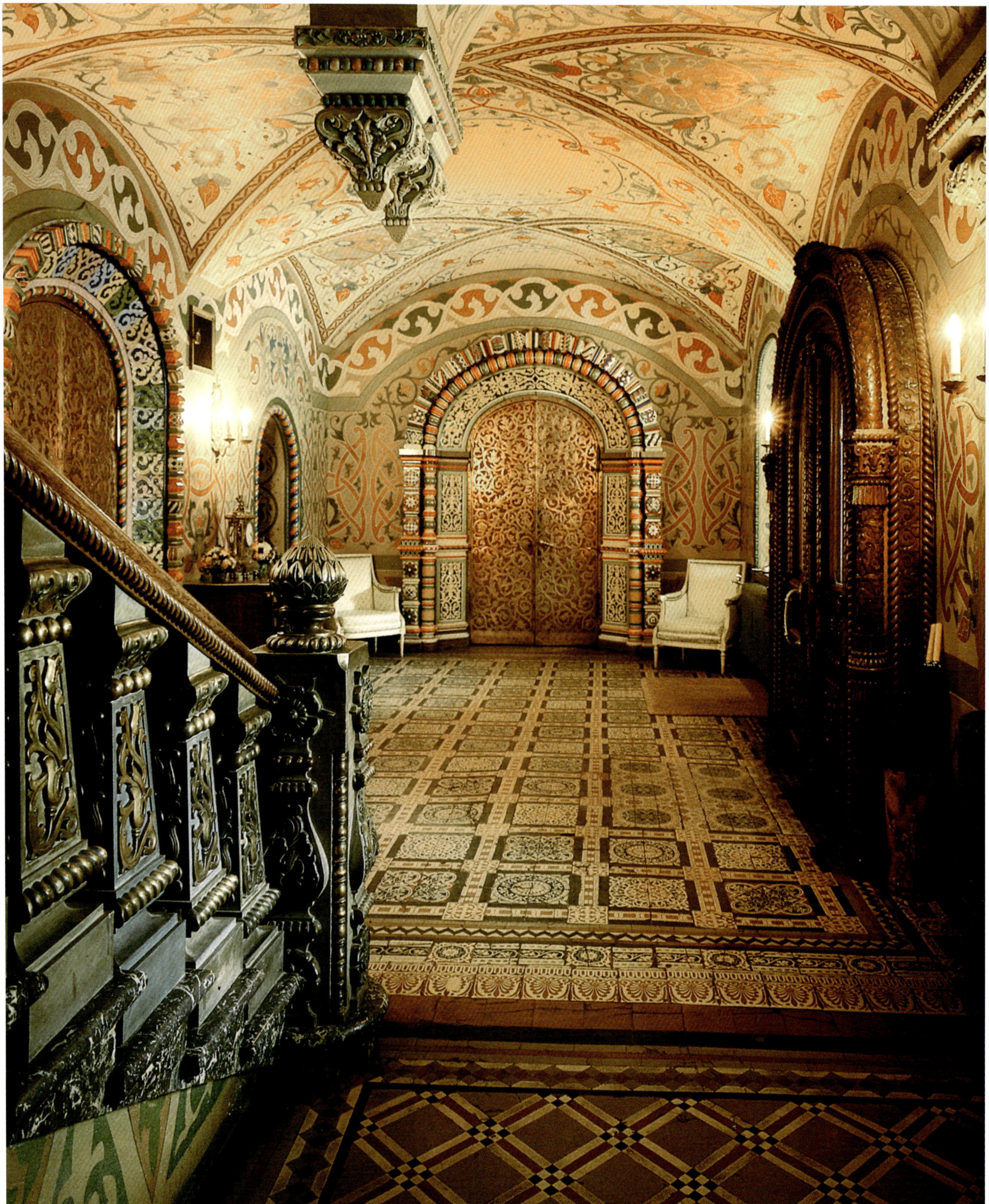

8. Entrance of the Igumnov House
Taken from The Igumnov House, residence of the French Ambassador to Moscow, *Friends of the Igumnov House, 1993*

example given by Victor Vanetsov in his famous painting. One can find them in silver relief (ill. 7), and in designs of various services.

The painters also discovered a majestic spirit in the revelation of Russia's history. The popular tales of oral tradition were rich in inspiration for Victor Vanetsov; history-motivated scenes of complex and deeply moving compositions inspired Vasily Surikov and Ilia Repin; and legends were inexhaustible for Nicholas Roerich.

It was perhaps in the field of architecture where this return to sources was most visible. The economic development of the capital took place in the second half of the 19th century and so there was a need for new buildings which were all constructed according to the Russkii style principles: the City *Duma* (formerly the Lenin Museum), the Gum department store, the National Museum of History, Three Station Square, and, at the end of the century, a genuine little masterpiece, the Igumnov house, today the French Embassy.

The architect Nicholas Pazleev was commissioned by Nicholas Igumnov to build the house which was completed in 1893. It was built according to 17th century Russian examples—the Yussupov *palatys* in Moscow are an example. In them are to be found the big bulbous balusters supporting the weight of small bell towers, steps with bulging columns and polychrome ceramics (ills. 8 and 9). The entrance, the stairway and the antechamber upstairs were given a unique décor in its genre, particularly representative of the "Russian style."

9. Igumnov House, façade on the Iakimanka Bolchaya
Taken from The Igumnov house, residence of the French ambassador to Moscow, *Friends of the Igumnov House, 1993*

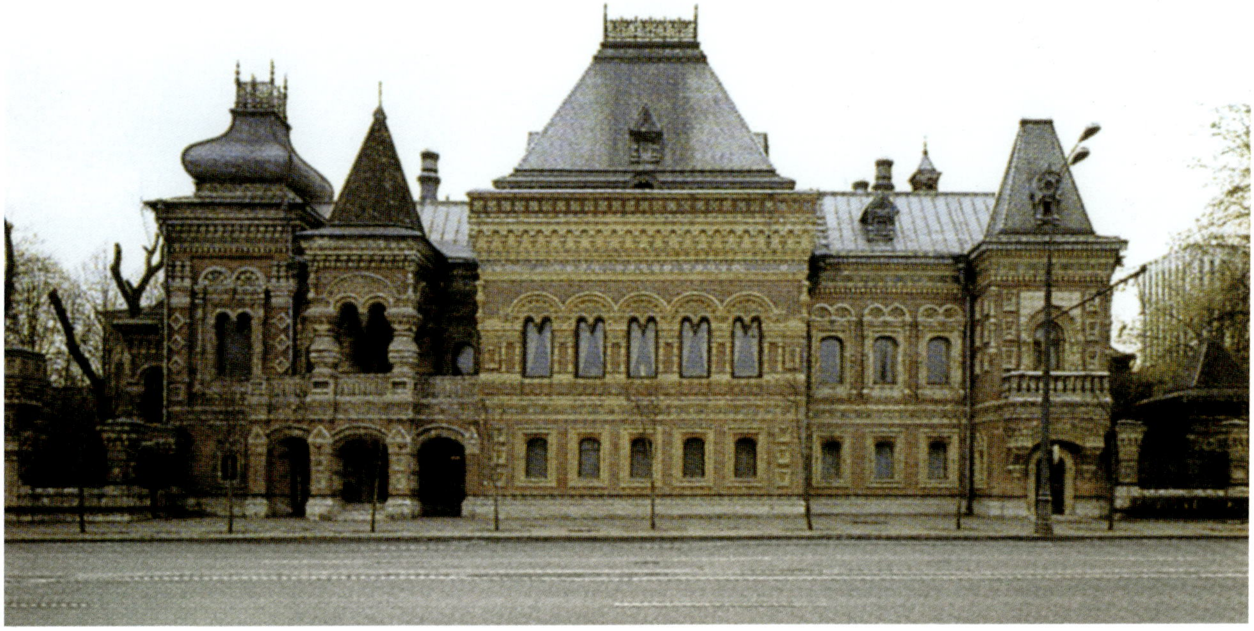

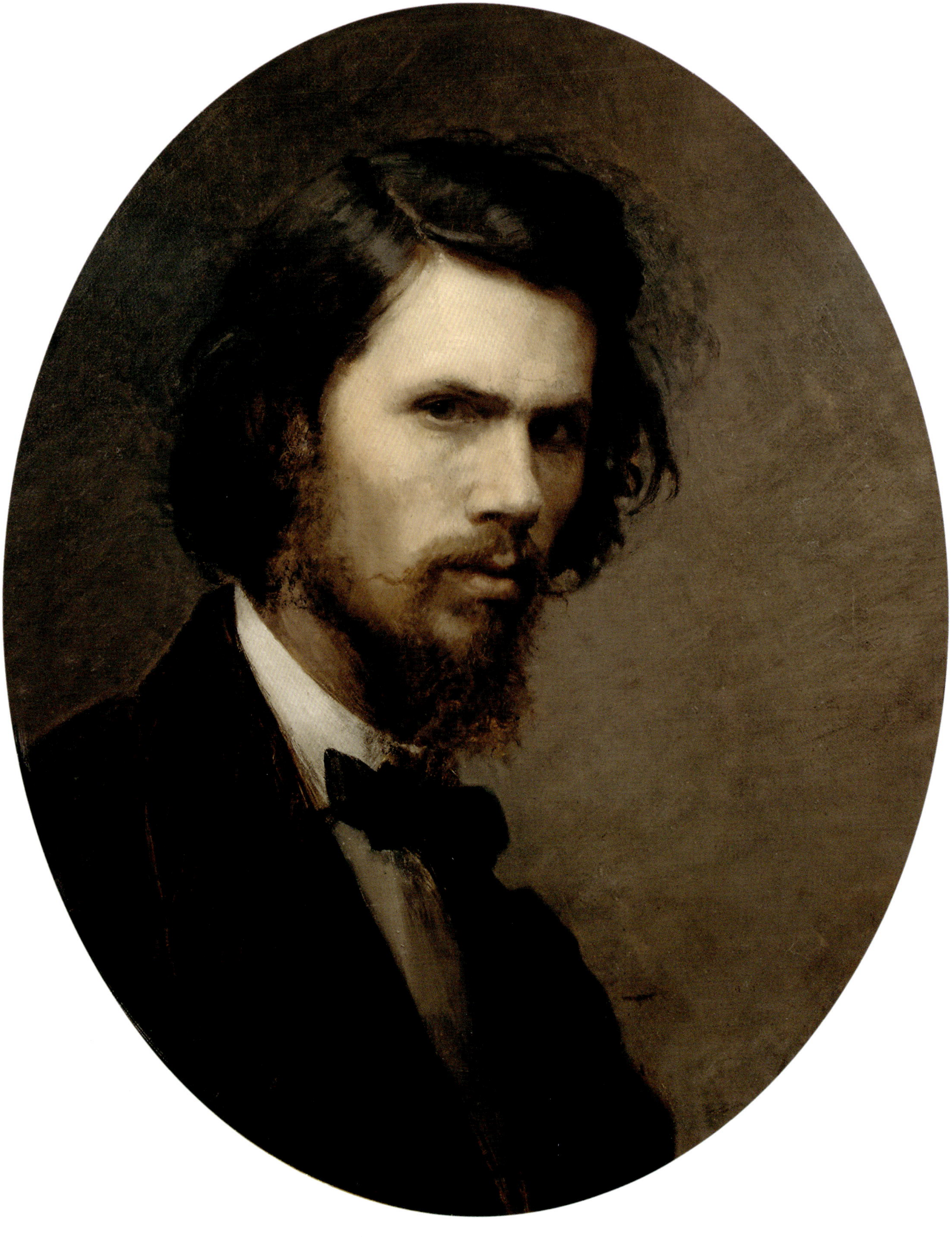

FROM PEREDVIJNIKI TO THE AVANT-GARDE

Lidia Iovleva

Major changes took place in Russian art in the middle of the 19th century, and then again at the beginning of the 20th, as was also the case, given a time lapse of fifteen or twenty years, throughout Europe. The crises of the kingdoms, the revolutionary movements of the 1840s and early 1850s, the Republican slogans, and the necessity to democratize social and political life in one way or another, eventually reached far away Russia. Until then, it had remained not only an unshakeable bastion of czarism in its extreme autocratic form, but also a country in which more than half of the population, in other words the peasantry, were under the yoke of a serfdom which was scarcely different from feudal slavery even if it was tempered by very old patriarchal traditions. It's not at all surprising then that the trend toward realism taking place around Europe toward a rapprochement of art and reality (which could be observed in the 19th century in France, for example), was welcomed enthusiastically by young Russian artists and, even more, that it colored the background canvas of Russia with a clearly-expressed character of social criticism. In Russian society during the years 1850-1860, the "mentors" had been writers (literature has always had a great social importance in Russia), literary critics, journalists, and especially those who were called "the commoners", in other words children from the diverse classes, land owners, provincial civil servants, priests and peasants. Having come to the capital (either St. Petersburg or Moscow) for their studies in the universities, they continued to maintain strong ties with the places where they had grown up, thus forming a powerfully democratic current, leading sometimes even to a very strongly revolutionary one.

Serfdom was abolished by a *ukase* of the Emperor Alexander II the Liberator on February 19 1861 but the questions of society, the social theme, long remained determinant for literature, poetry, painting and even Russian music. "The judge is now the mujik," wrote the young Ilia Repin in 1872 while he was working on a painting *The Haulers of the Volga* (Russian State Museum, St. Petersburg), "and this is why we must reproduce what interests him."[1]

The main protest of the young artists in the 1860s and early 1870s was primarily directed against the unbearable weight and routine nature of the academic rules which hindered the freedom of creation, and this even though most of the Russian painters received their training, often very excellent, at the St. Petersburg Fine Arts Academy. But it was nonetheless precisely with the Academy that the first serious conflict of the young reformers took place. In the fall of 1863, fourteen students graduating from the Academy, all four-

1. *I. N. Kramskoy*
Kramskoy self-portrait
1867
Oil on canvas
52.7 × 44 cm
The State Tretyakov Gallery, inv. 645

2. *I. E. Repin*
Leon Tolstoy resting in a forest
1891
The State Tretyakov Gallery
(Cat. 548)

teen of whom were in competition for the Grand Gold Medal, addressed a request to the head of the Academy to allow each of the painters to freely choose the subject of his competition work (to obtain their diplomas). This request which appears perfectly natural and totally innocent was categorically rejected by the Academy which saw in it the demonstration of a detestable revolutionary spirit which had already poisoned social life in Europe and which was penetrating more and more into Russia's social and cultural life.

Winning this academic competition promised considerable advantages for the artists, such as a very desirable trip as a scholarship student to blessed Italy, or to France, country to which the Russian cultural world turned more and more for inspiration. In response to this refusal of a free choice for their subject, the young "rebels of the 60s promotion" withdrew from the competition, and in protest, quit the Russian Fine Arts Academy and organized the first independent artist's association: the St. Petersburg Artel of Artists whose project was to mutually ensure the free creative activity of its members. The head of Artel, the one who was at the origin of its creation as well as of the "revolt of the fourteen," was Ivan Kramskoy (1837-1887; ill. 1), a recognized ideologist of Russian realism in the second half of the 19th century.

The St. Petersburg Artel of Artists was mostly a gathering of a circle of painters and sculptors from the city who were all motivated by the interest they had in realism, but similar movements were taking place in the other cities of Russia as well, especially in Moscow where the center of current artistic life and its revival was the Moscow School of Painting and Sculpture (which later became the School of Painting, Sculpture and Architecture) and its young students and professors, Vasily Perov (1834-1882), Alexei Savrassov (1830-1897), Illarion Prianichnikov (1840-1894) and others still. Along with St. Petersburg, it was this school which led the movement of Russian art toward realism, a rather naïve realism at the beginning, but which became more acute and more of a protest movement, denouncing social evil and injustice, and accompanied by a profound compassion for "the man of little" as well as for the "humiliated and the insulted ones" (Fyodor Dostoyevsky). In the front ranks of this powerful movement toward "the truth of life" was great Russian literature, which in the 1870s included not only Alexander Pushkin and Nicholas Gogol, but also Fyodor Dostoyevsky, Leon Tolstoy (ill. 2), Ivan Turgenev, Nicholas Nekrassov and many others who certainly today are the pride of Russia but also the jewels of whole world culture.

At the beginning of the 1870s, new trends in Russian art had been so affirmed that they had forcefully invaded the creation not only of the "elders" of the sixties, Vasily Perov, Ivan Kramskoy (ill. 3), Alexei Savrassov, Vladimir Makovsky (ill. 4), Alexei Korzukhin, but also the generation of the realist painters who came after them: Ilia Repin, Vasily Surikov (cf. p. 29), Victor Vasnetsov, Vasily Polenov (cf. p. 28), Arkhip Kuindji (ill. 5). Created in 1870 on the initiative of the "elders" and with the complete support of the "young", a new association for creation replaced the ephemer-

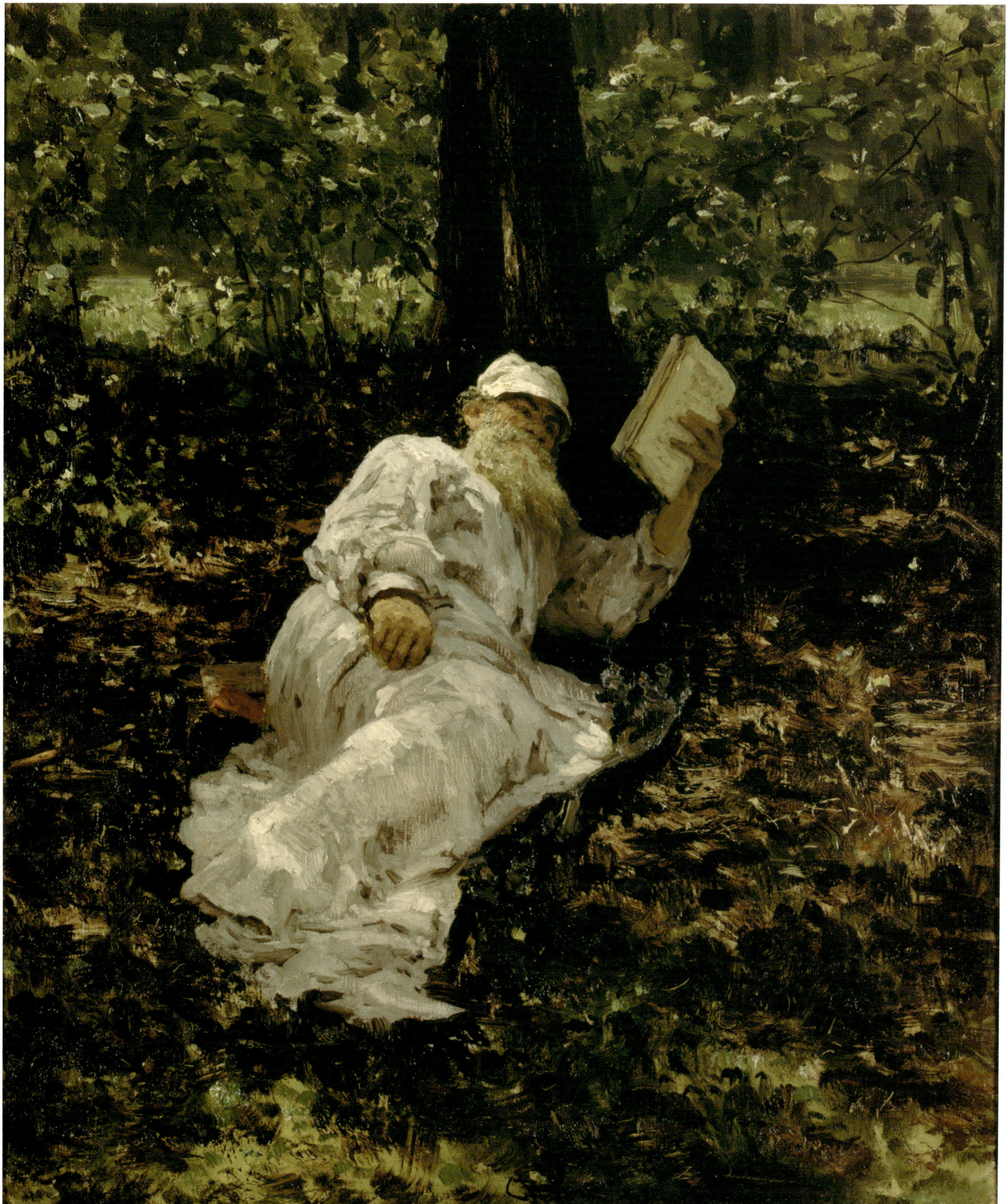

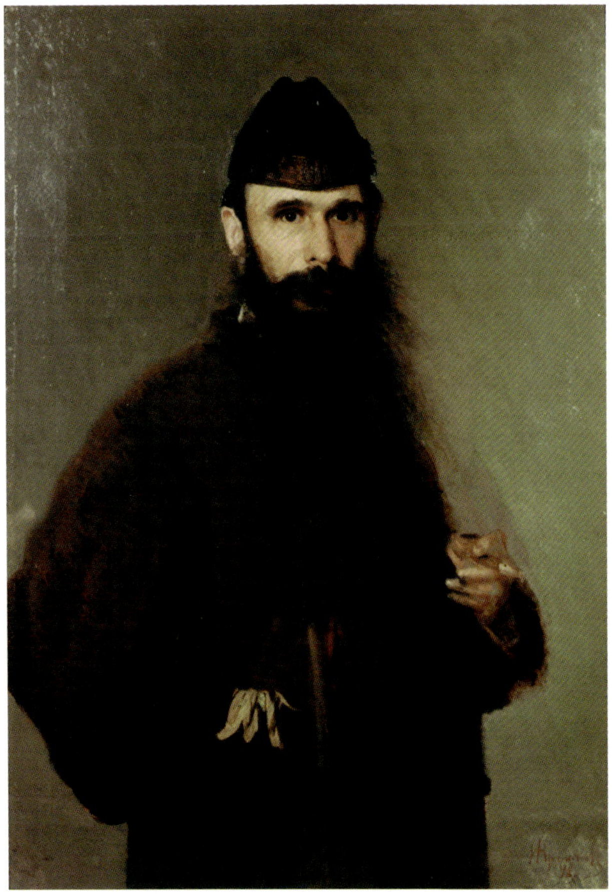

3. *I. N. Kramskoy*
Portrait of the painter Alexander Dmitrievich Litovtchenko
1878
The State Tretyakov Gallery
(Cat. 543)

al Artel of Artists. It was called the Society of Itinerant Artistic Exhibitions (which continued to exist until 1923), and appeared as the logical incarnation of the artists' communal efforts to bring art closer to reality, the art of the people and of society. Such an idea was most strikingly displayed in the project of organizing itinerant exhibitions during which the purpose was less to sell the paintings than to show them to a wide and varied public, a "classless" public.

The influence of the "Itinerants", as members of the Society began to be called, was enormous in the years 1870-1880, having an impact not only on Russian society but also on the formation of aesthetic tastes, on how art was seen, and even on political passions. It was during these years that the major works of Russian realism were created, those that today hang on the walls of the Tretyakov gallery in Moscow and in the Russian museum in St. Petersburg, some of which are presented here in this exhibition, *Moscow, Splendour of the Romanovs*.

From a stylistic point of view, compared with their realist predecessors of the 1860s, the realism of the Itinerants had become more forceful and assured: the paintings were considerably bigger, the elaboration of subjects was polished, the space of the canvas had become more extended, a whole crowd could easily be included there, like a real landscape with its far-away horizons. In place of naïve effects of shadow and light, there was the desire to recreate the real light of fresh air and the atmosphere of the outdoors. The Russian artists approached the theme of color and began to observe the painting of the French impressionists. "We must absolutely go toward light, colors, air," wrote the leader of the Itinerants, Ivan Kramskoy in 1874—"but how to do this without losing along the way the most precious quality for a painter, his heart?!"[2]

This latter remark by the famous artist who inspired the younger artists to "not lose along the way the most precious quality for a painter, his heart" exactly defines the essence of Russian realism of the years 1860-1870: the artist must not lose his "heart", in other words, he must not forget the content, the meaning and the finality of art.

But in all the epochs, art lives from the quest for meaning, direction, impressions etc. susceptible to renew creation, and the Russian artists were no exception to this rule. Beginning at the end of the 1860s, they practically stopped going toward the "Mecca" which up until then had been Italy, and turned toward Paris, and then toward Munich, and elsewhere.

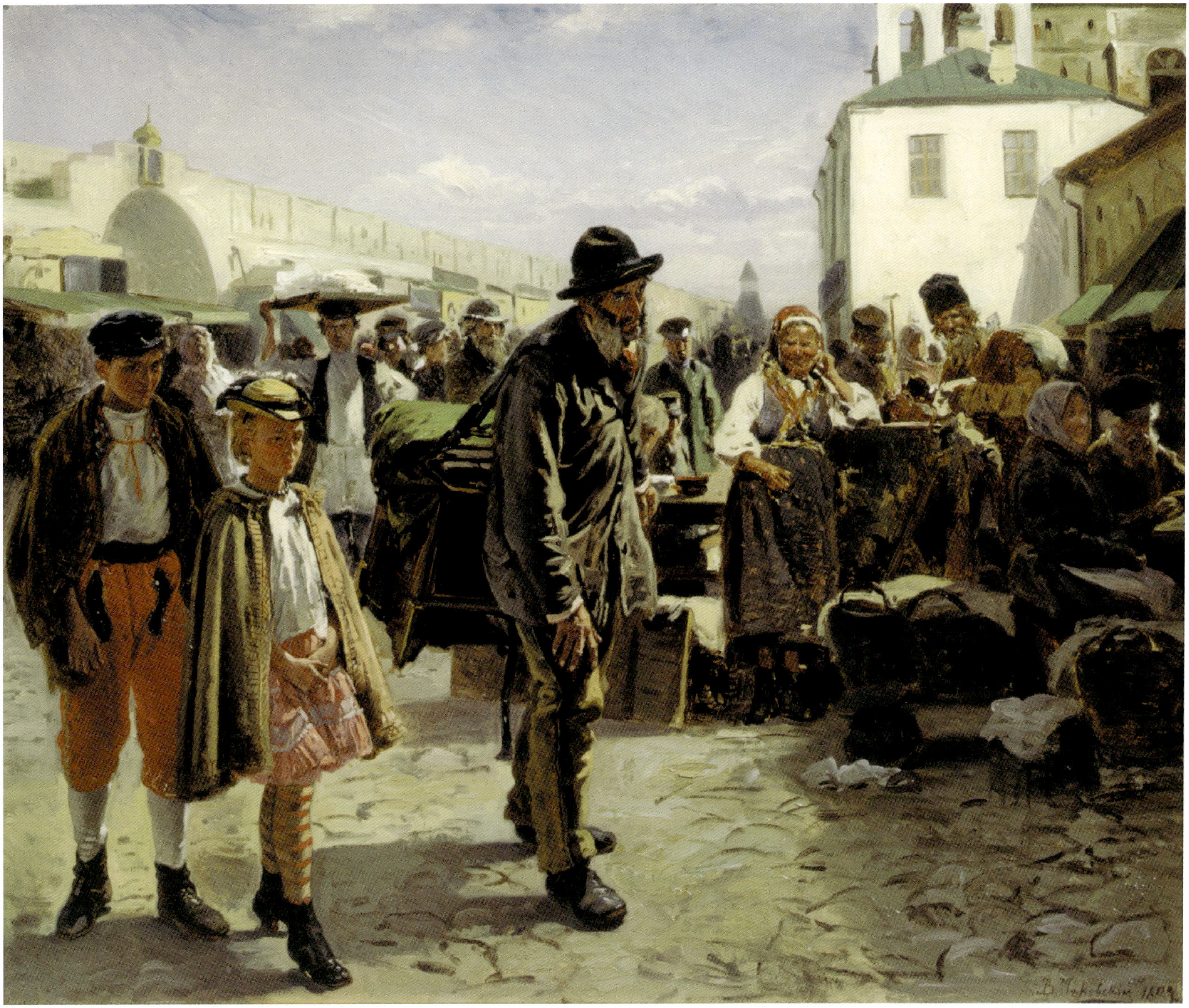

4. *V. E. Makovsky*
Barrel organ player
1879
The State Tretyakov Gallery
(Cat. 546)

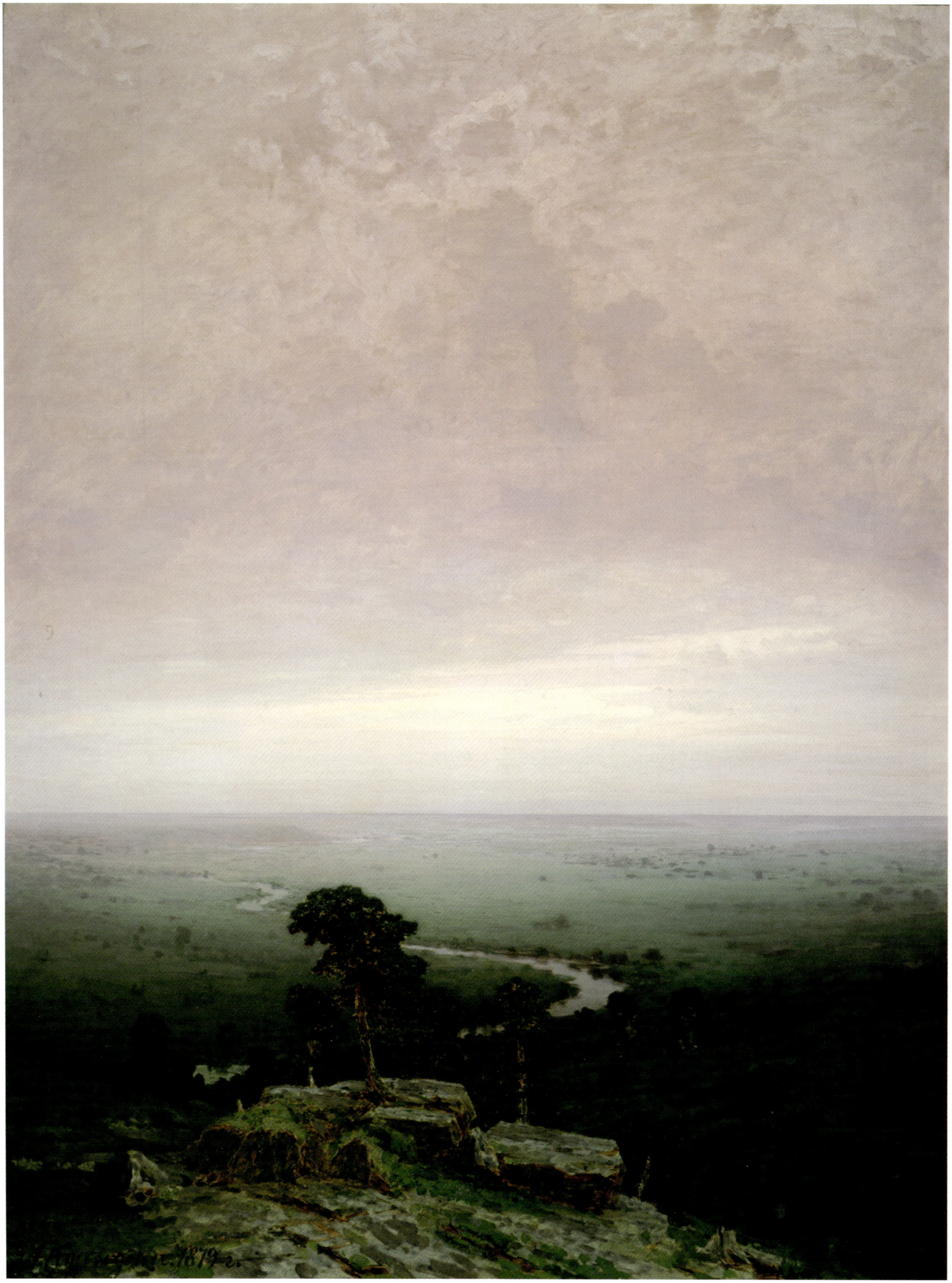

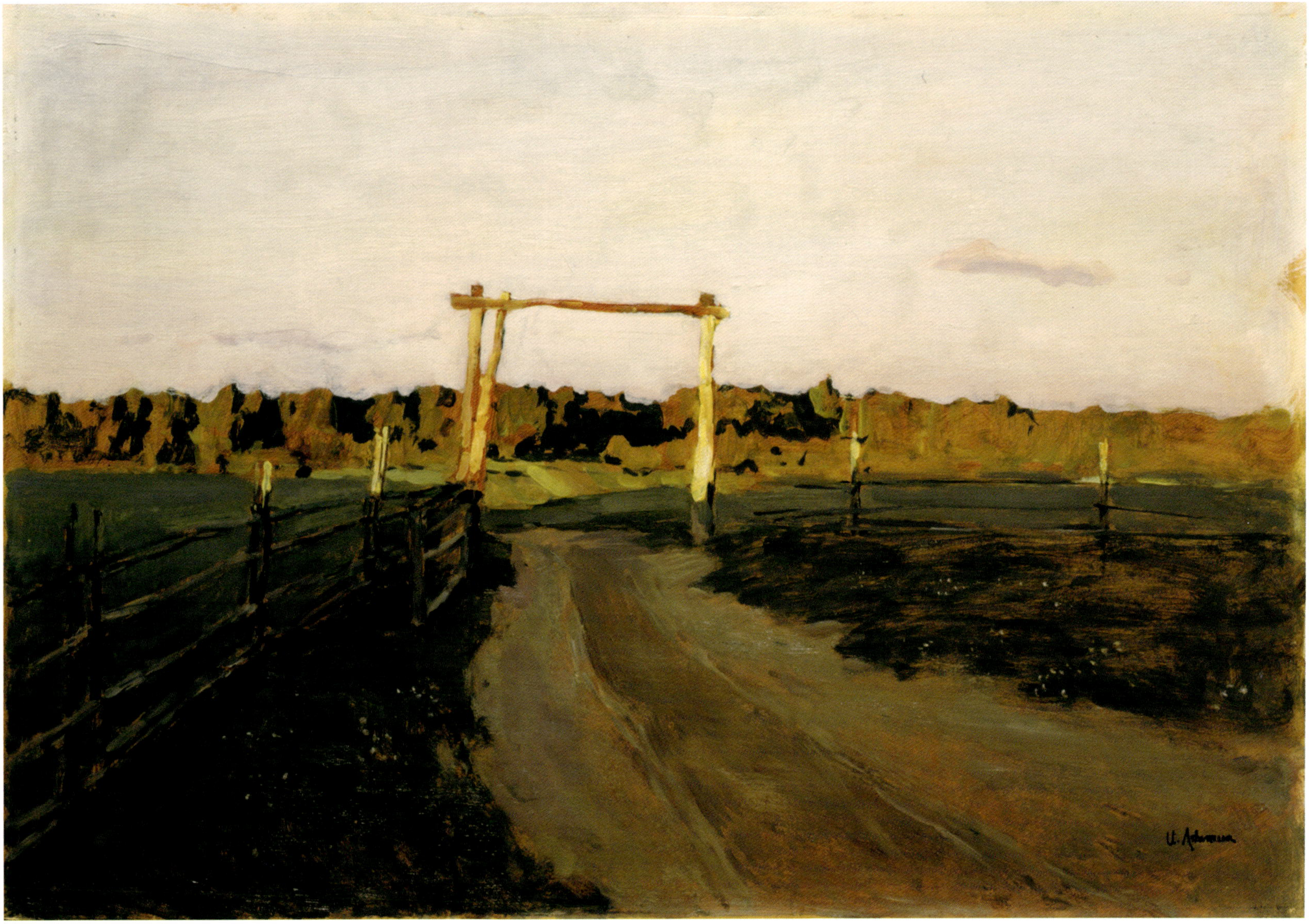

5. A. I. Kuindji
In the North
1879
The State Tretyakov Gallery
(Cat. 544)

6. I. I. Levitan
A summer evening
1900
The State Tretyakov Gallery
(Cat. 545)

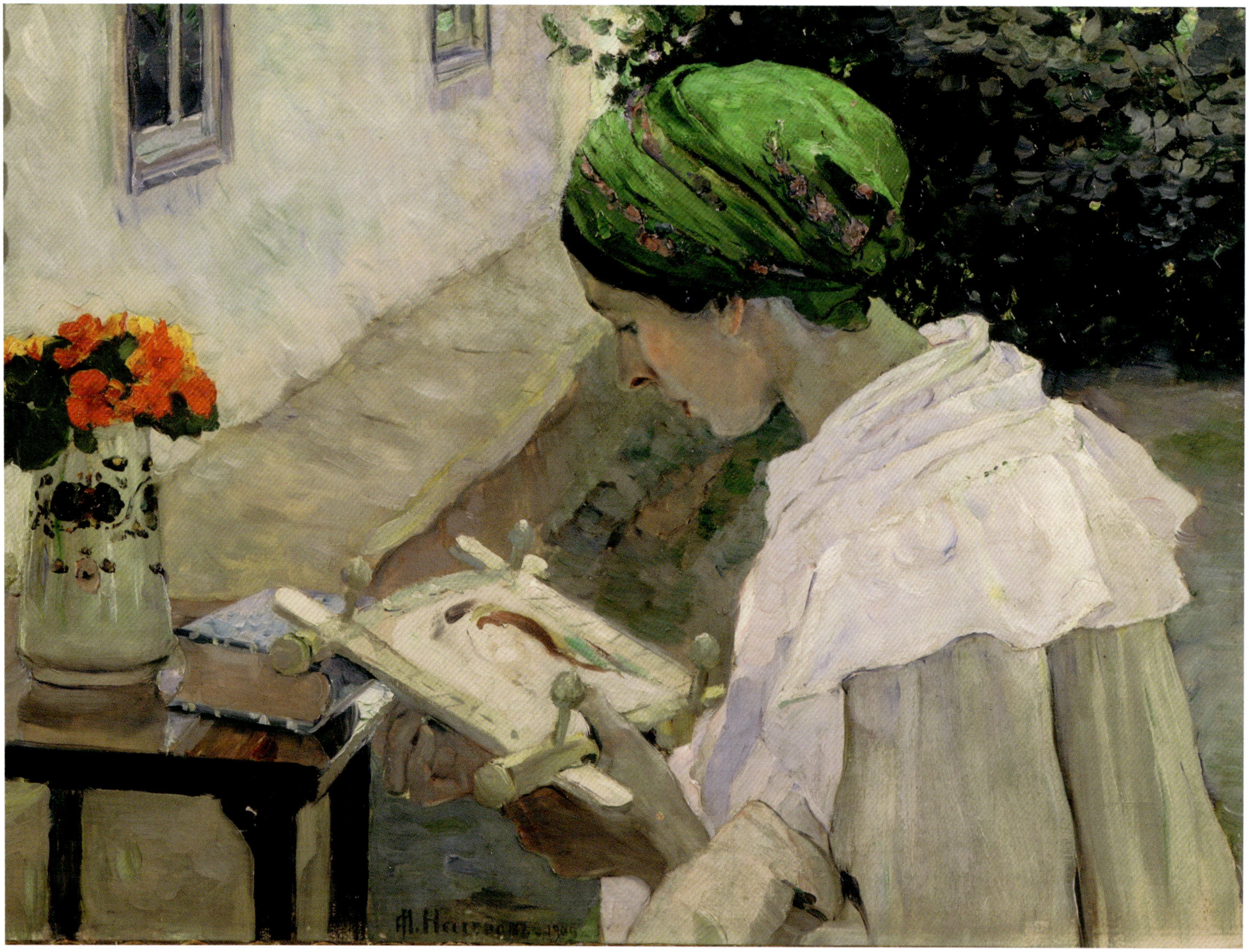

7. *M. V. Nesterov*
Portrait of Ekaterina Petrovna Nesterova embroidering
1909
The State Tretyakov Gallery
(Cat. 639)

At first, the Russians were particularly attracted by the art of the French open-air painters and the masters of the Barbizon school. The Russian realists were the closest in spirit to those pictorial modalities—work from life, interest for the rendering of the light and the atmosphere, and the national landscape motif. For a long time, the pictorial modalities of the impressionists seemed too radical to them, leading to a feeling of the painting being unfinished and its content inconsistent. However, the experience of the Itinerants' contact with French art did not remain without consequences for them. Already in the paintings of the artists of the 1880s, Ilia Repin, Vasily Surikov, Victor Vasnetsov, Vasily Polenov and others, one can see infinitely more "light, colors and air" than in those of their predecessors, and all the while without any loss of "heart."

This new breath of fresh air revealed itself even more forcefully in the work of the artists who began their autonomous artistic lives at the end of the 1880s and early 1890s: Isaac Levitan (ill. 6), Valentin Serov, Michael Nesterov (ill. 7), Boris Kustodiev and others. While remaining faith-

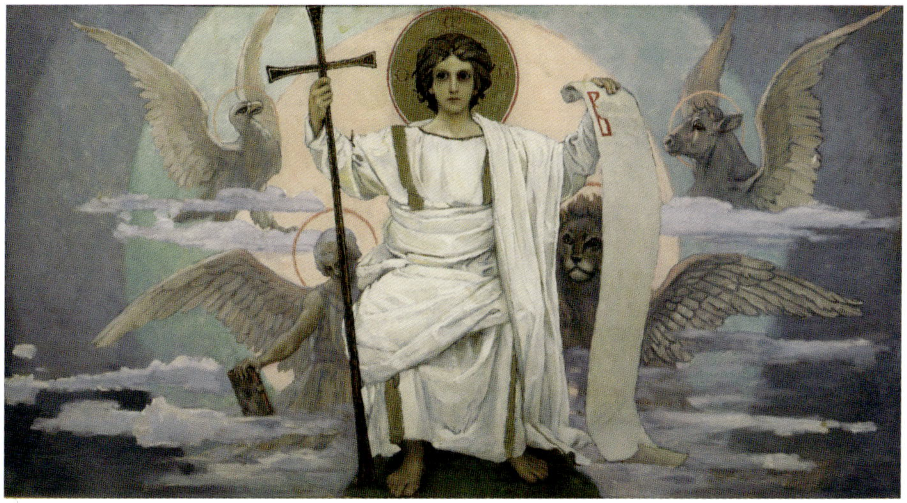

8. *V. M. Vasnetsov* “The only son” (cardboard of the plan of the central nave) *1885-1896 The State Tretyakov Gallery (Cat. 542)*

9. *V. M. Vasnetsov* “The joy of the Just Ones next to the Gods.” At the entrance of Paradise (Tympanum of the central dome). *1885-1896 Oil on canvas 205 × 1446 cm The State Tretyakov Gallery, inv. 1020*

ful to the fundamental postulates of realism, the Itinerants of the generation of the 1890s were far from always having the same interest as their masters for the expression in painting of almost exclusively social aspects of reality. The young painters were more attracted by the poetic and aesthetic elements of traditional subjects borrowed from real life, whether it was genre scenes, landscapes or portraits. Impressionist painting was infinitely more alluring for this group of artists (Isaac Levitan, Konstantin Korovin, and Valentin Serov, and others) than for their predecessors.

During this same time, the 1890s, there were the first signs of a movement leading the young artists toward symbolism. However strange it may seem, the leader of this movement was the “second generation” Itinerant painter Victor Vasnetsov (ill. 8). Particularly involved in religious painting from the end of the 1880s, he was led by force of circumstance to diverge from the usual realism, giving his figures the appropriate mystical nature (“The Joy of the Just Ones in front of the Lord. The anti-chamber of Paradise”; ill. 9) The first declared symbolist of Russian art of the 19th century, in other words the first to be conscious of being so, was Michael Vroubel. In his favorite images of “*Demons*”, “*Pans*” and others, he unceasingly seeks to incarnate a form of the Absolute, the Absolute of Good and of Evil, of God and of the Devil. Even a motif directly borrowed from life, the image of a luxuriant lilac bush (“*The Lilacs*”; cf. p. 30) is transformed by Vroubel into a sort of enchanted den for a Fairy of tales and legends or for the Soul of the lilac.

Victor Borisov-Mussatov was also a symbolist, although when compared to Vroubel, his symbolism as well as his painting itself is more lyrical, immaterial, and turned not toward myth or tale but toward the magical charm created by time past (“*Harmony*”; ill. 10).

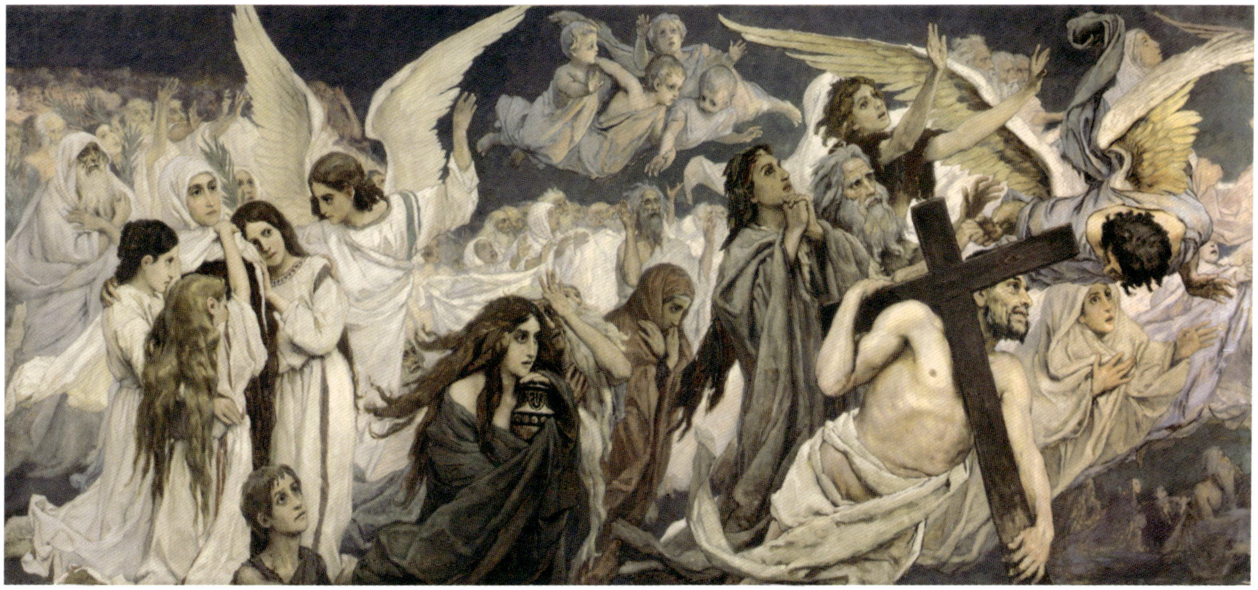

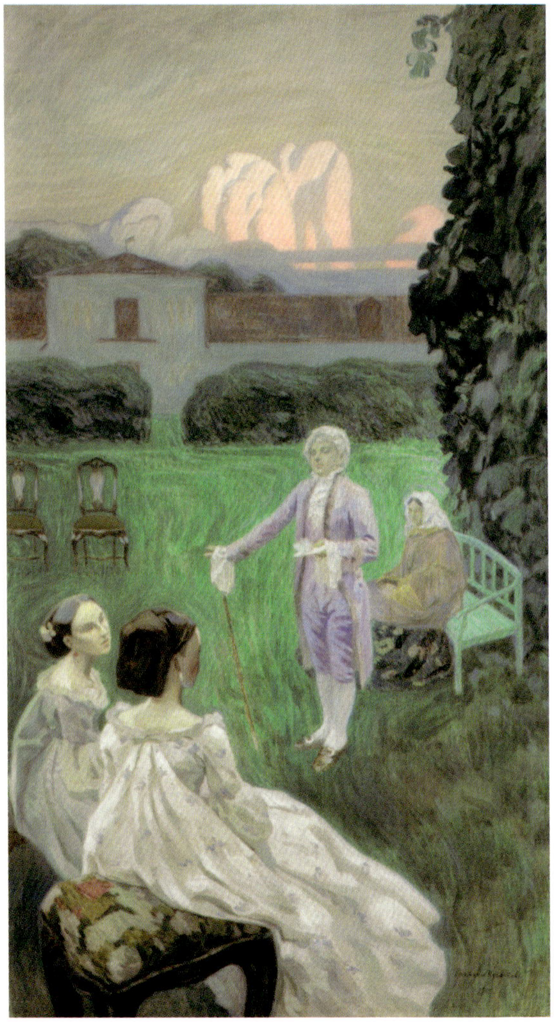

10. *V. E. Borrissov-Mussatov*
Harmony
1900
The State Tretyakov Gallery
(Cat. 636)

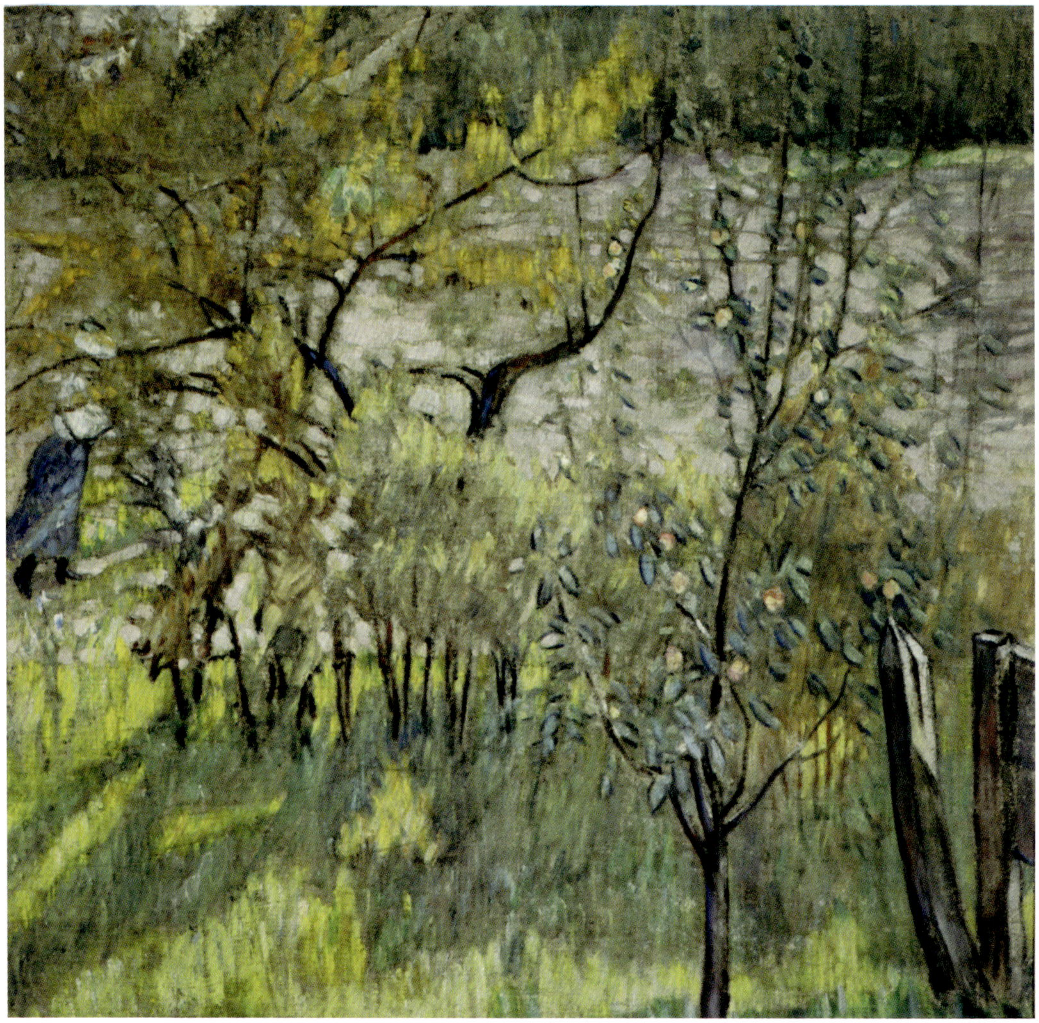

11. *M. F. Larionov*
Garden of peaches
1903-1904
The State Tretyakov Gallery
(Cat. 642)

Revolving around the powerful presence of Vroubel was a large group of young artists who gathered together around the St. Petersburg magazine *Mir iskusstva* (*The World of Art*, 1898-1903) founded by the famous Serge Diaghilev. Borisov-Mussatov was adored by the Moscow artists participating in the "*Scarlet Rose*" exhibition (1904), and the "*Blue Rose*" (1908), organized by Nicholas Riabuchinsky, the publisher of the Muscovite art review, *The Golden Fleece*.

At the turn of the century, these publications and exhibitions had become the "mentors" for the Russian youth, in actively influencing the emergence of a new aesthetic which was to be built now in opposition to the aesthetic of the Itinerants. All this encouraged the appearance in Russian art of a new style: the "modern" style which was none other than a variation of the French "Art Nouveau" but, as is often the case in Russia, with very basic and strong national features. At the beginning of the 20th century, the "modern" style penetrated into practically every aspect of Russian culture, as well as in literature, in painting and in music, but it expressed itself in a particularly flamboyant manner in the field of architecture and applied arts. However, the destiny of this "modern" art was of short duration. By the end of the 1900s, new voices were being heard in Russian art which were repudiating not only the 19th century realist but also the "modern" symbolism of the beginning of the 20th century. In Russia, a new movement emerged, the avant-garde, and its "idols" were not even the impressionists, but Henri Matisse, Paul Cézanne, Vincent Van Gogh, Paul Gauguin and others, in other words, the post-impressionists, many of whose works decorated the homes of the new Russian collectors and merchants, S. I. Shchukin and I. A. Morozov. The young avant-gardes (or, as they were then being called, the "futurists"), Michael Larionov (ill. 11), Natalia Gontcharova (cf. p. 31), Casimir Malevitch, Vladimir Tatlin (cf. p. 32), Olga Rozanova (ill. 12), Alexandra Exter (ill. 13), David Burliouk (ill. 14), Liubov Popova, the poets, Vladimir Mayakovsky, Velemir Khlebnikov, Alexeï Kroutchenykh and many others, even though they didn't form a unified group, nevertheless ended up radically changing the character of Russian art as a whole (and as one can see later, Russian art was not the only art concerned), renouncing practically everything which had existed before them, and wishing to start all over again in art, from

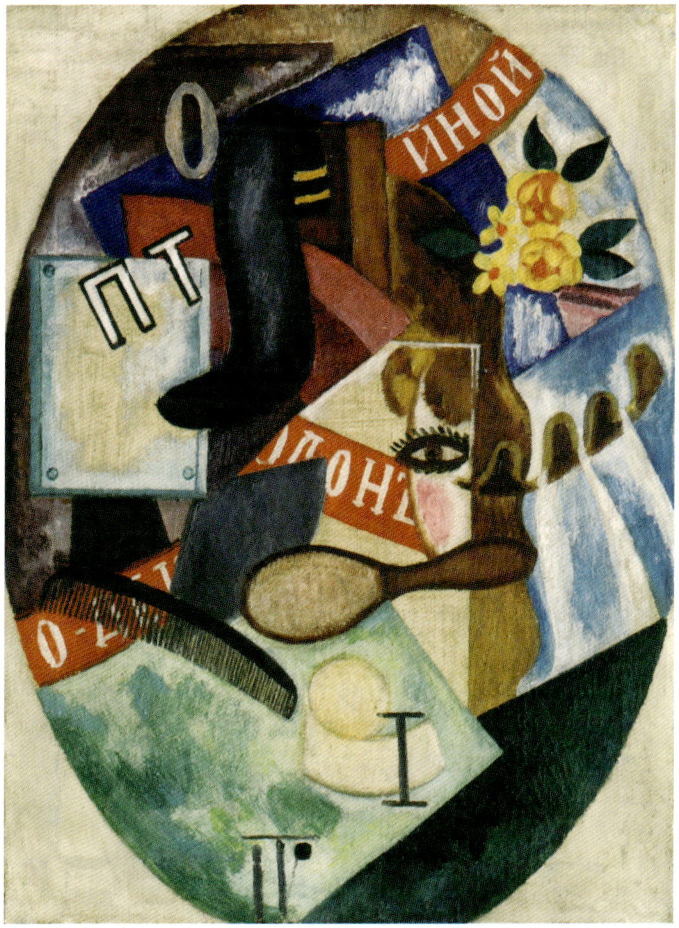

12. O. V. Rozanova
At the hairdresser's
1915
The State Tretyakov Gallery
(Cat. 648)

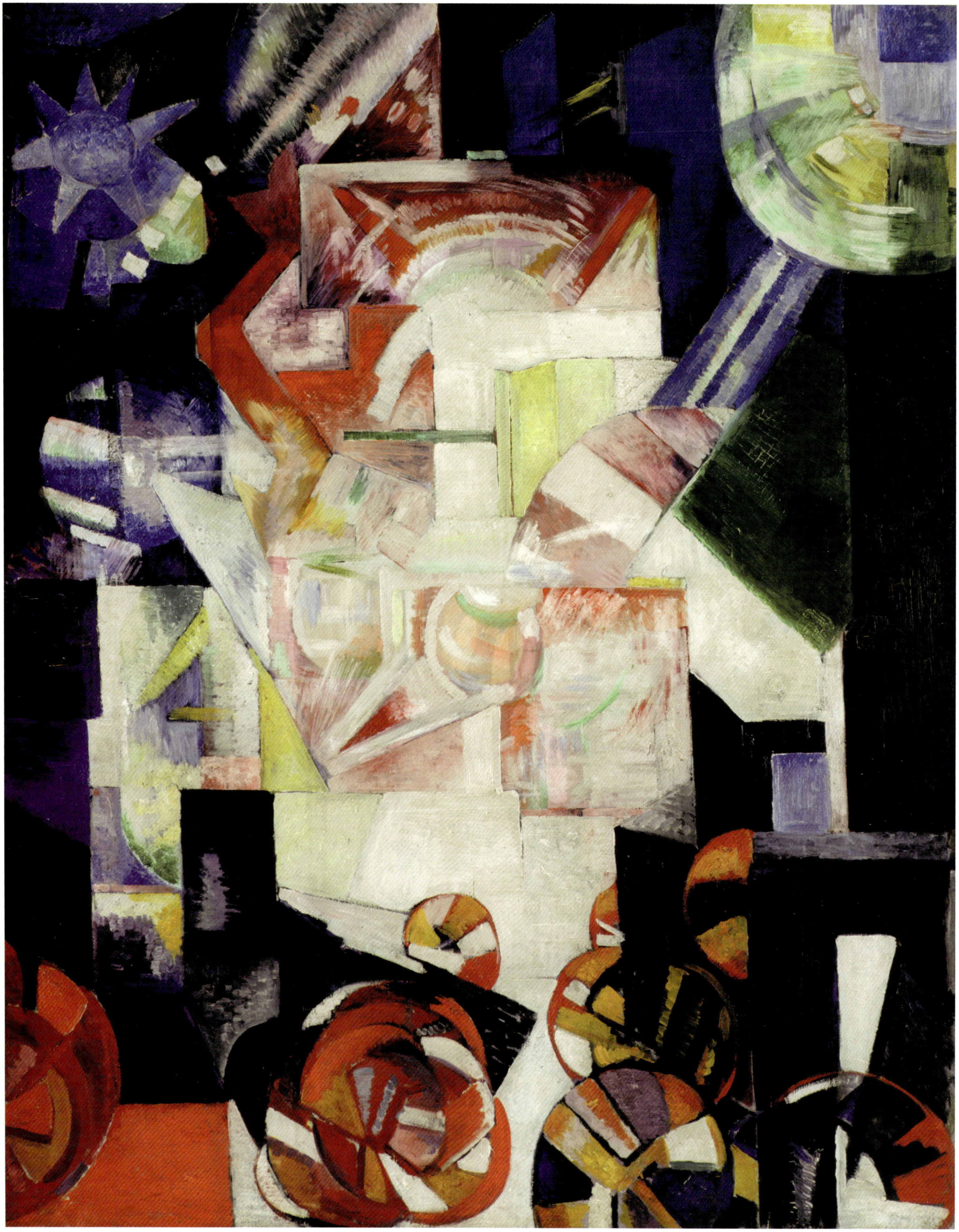

13. *A. A. Exter*
Composition
1914
The State Tretyakov Gallery
(Cat. 649)

Casimir Malevitch's "*Black Square*" which represented the end of everything upon which world art had been based since the time of the great Italian Renaissance. They succeeded to a large extent, but the Russian avant-garde as a movement or single trend was of relatively short duration: revolutionaries in art and undoubtedly reflecting the underground revolutionary fermentation which was stirring up Russian society during the reign of the three last Romanovs, these artists turned out to be absolutely of no use to the real "revolutionaries", those who came to power in October 1917. The "avant-garde" artists went on making noise for about a decade, thrilling the Russians, and then were forgotten: some of them emigrated, others died of hunger or were victims of repression, and only a few of them changed and adapted. The Russia of the Romanov dynasty was finished. Another history and another Russia was beginning. Whether we like it or not, thus decided History.

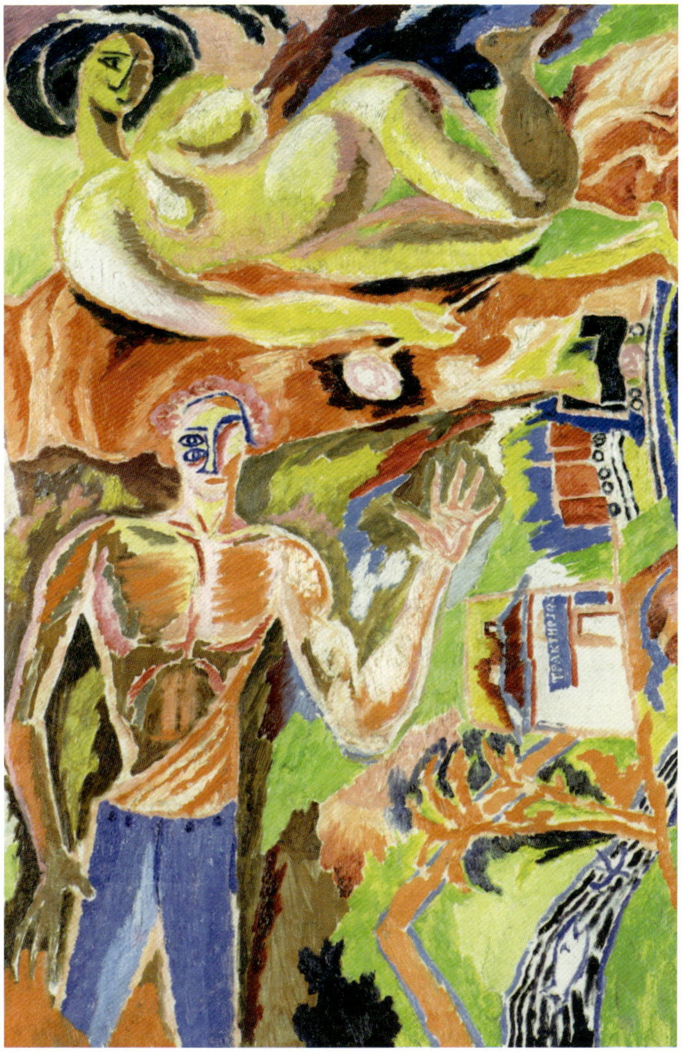

14. *D. Burliouk*
Portrait of a futurist fighter-singer
Vassily Kamensky
1916
The State Tretyakov Gallery
(Cat. 653)

[1] Taken from a letter by I. E. Repin dated June 3, 1872 addressed to the art critic V. V. Stassov, cf. I. E. Repin and V. V. Stassov, *Correspondence*, Moscow-Leningrad, ed. "Iskusstvo, 1948-1950", Volume I, p. 37 (in Russian).
[2] Taken from a letter by I. N. Kramskoy to I. E. Repin dated February 23, 1874, cf. I. N. Kramskoy, *Letters, articles*, 2 Vol., Ed. "Iskusstvo", Vol. I, Moscow, p. 233 (in Russian).

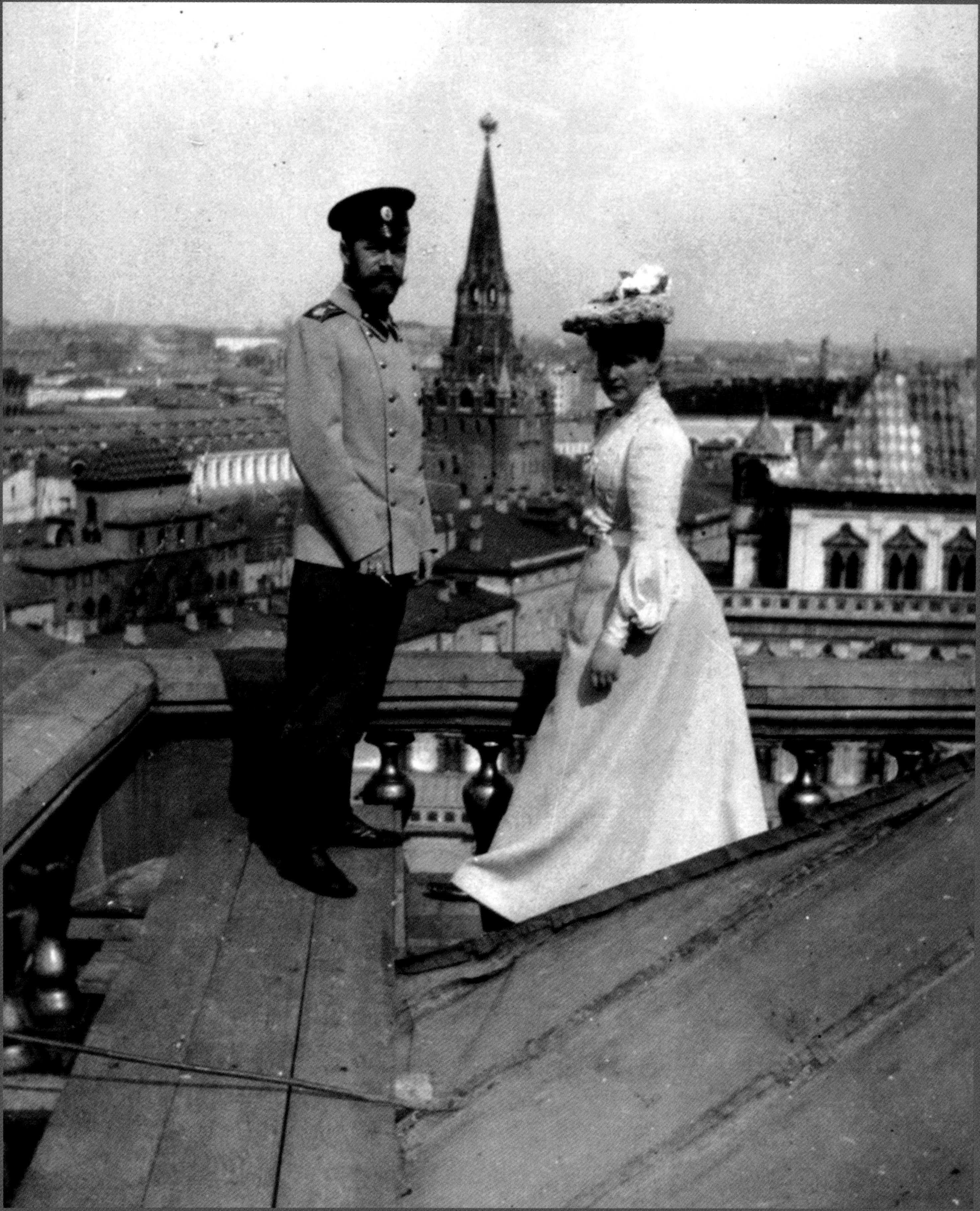

THE LAST ROMANOVS

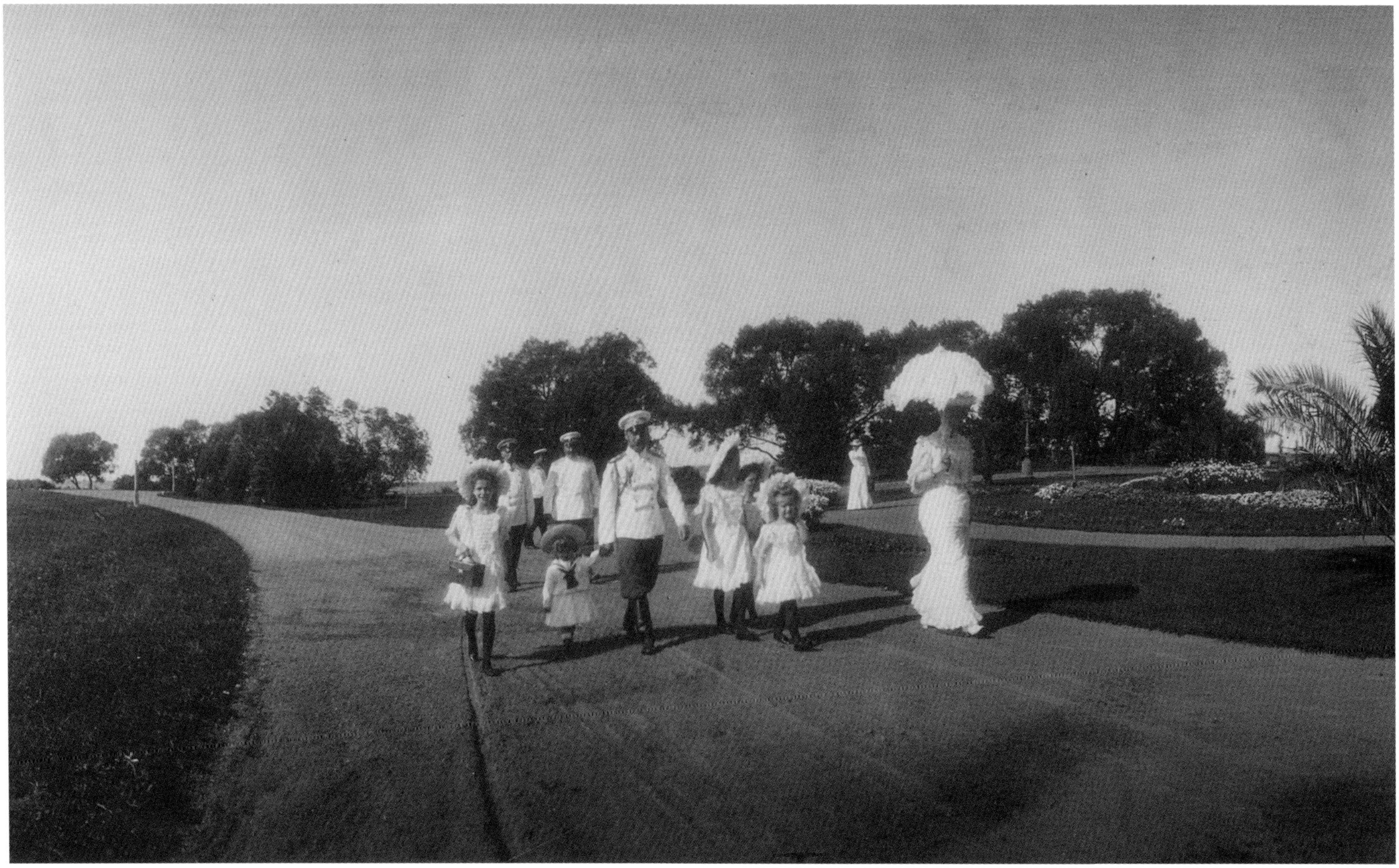

THE LAST ROMANOVS: INTIMACY OF A FAMILY

Iraïda Bott

Page 250
The Emperor Nicholas II and the Empress Alexandra Feodorovna during a visit to the Monastery of the Resurrection of the New Jerusalem
Province of Moscow, 1903
Russian State Cinematographic and Photographic Archives
(Cat. 584)

1. *C. E. de Hahn*
Promenade at Tsarskoye Selo
The State Historical Museum, Moscow
(Cat. 598)

The tragic end of the last Russian Emperor and of his family which shocked their contemporaries still moves us today. There are many biographical memories about Nicholas II and his family, stories have been written, films produced, and yet there have been few material traces of the life of the Czar and his family which have come down to us: part of the furniture from the imperial palaces and the personal belongings of the Romanovs were sold in the 1920s, part was destroyed during the Second World War but more than anything else, they were forgotten for long decades. This is why we give such close attention to what remains of the objects and traces of that époque: through them, we can try to discern the personality of Nicholas, Alexandra Feodorovna and their children.

The relationships within the imperial family were particularly close, there was nothing royal about daily life and it revealed bourgeois tastes which became the target of a great deal of criticism during the Soviet epoch. Through them, one discovers people who loved each other and who loved their house, people who enjoyed life and know how to share the sufferings of others. It wasn't Nicholas II's fault to have been born and raised to be the heir to the Russian throne but rather his misfortune. He was not ready to direct an immense country which, from the first years of his reign, was heading for catastrophe. Nicholas II was made for peaceful family life, to which he tried to return as often as possible. Behind the walls of the palace, in the ship cabins of his beloved *Standart*, politics was relegated to a back burner. In the family circle, with those he loved and who loved him, the Emperor, in spite of the cataclysms and upheavals of the epoch, found peace of mind, while being fully aware of its illusory nature. The beloved house, the Alexander Palace of Tsarskoye Selo, was suffused with this atmosphere of interior peace.

Nicholas II (1868-1918) was born in this palace.[1] He was particularly attached to Tsarskoye Selo and often repeated, "... here I feel completely at home."[2] This love for one of the most elegant and most agreeable residences to live in located in the outskirts of St. Petersburg, was also shared by the Empress Alexandra Feodorovna (1870-1918), as well as by the Emperor's whole family. For the young couple, everything had its first time at Tsarskoye Selo, and for that reason Nicholas and Alexandra cherished unforgettable memories: "their" first Christmas tree, on December 24, 1895, the first private apartments, decorated according to their taste, the first born of their children, the grand duchess Olga, who was born in the Alexander Palace in October 1895.

The imperial family which lived at Tsarskoye

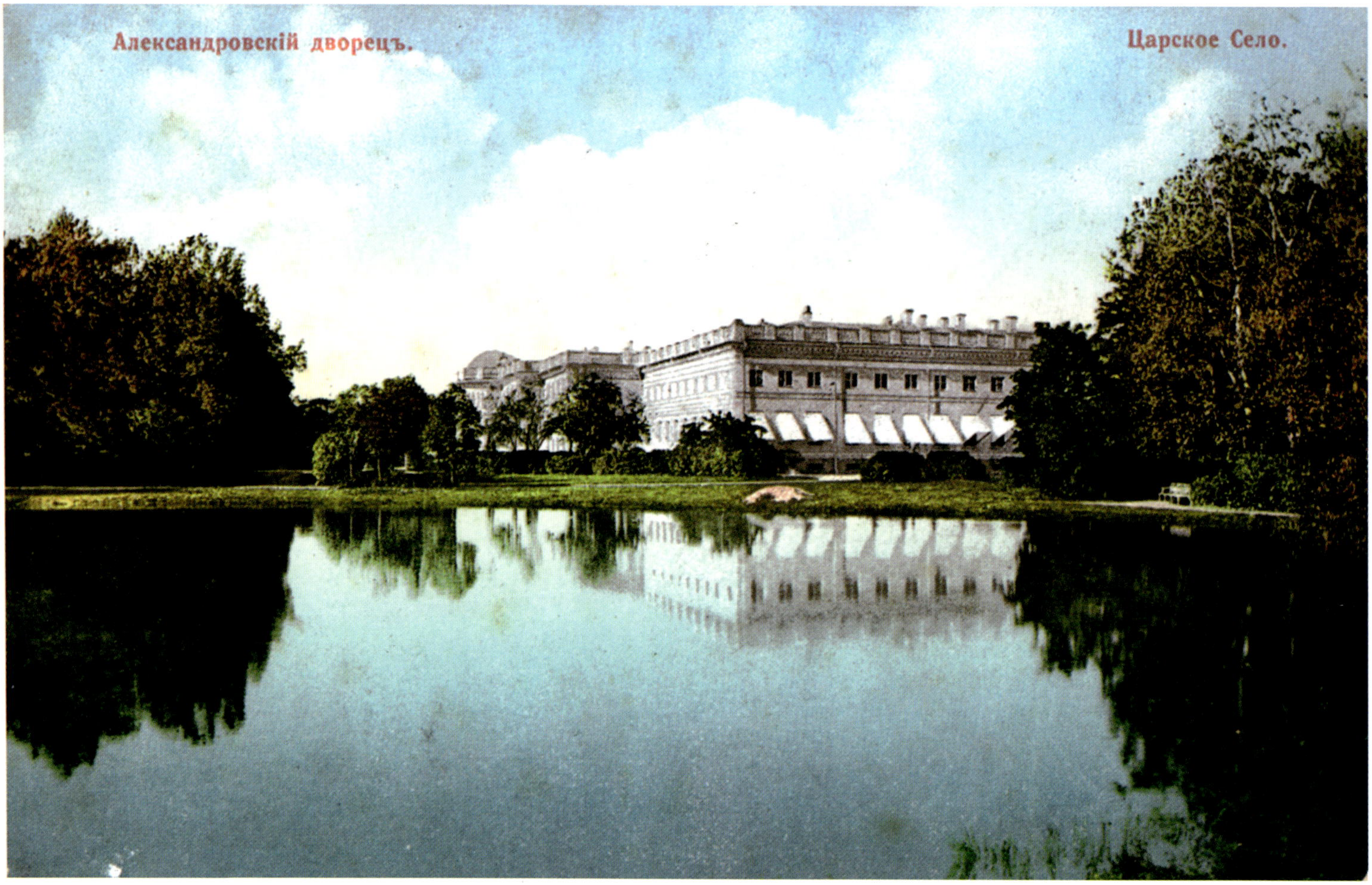

2. The Alexander Palace
Postcard from the beginning of the 20th century
The State Museum Preserve "Tsarskoye Selo"

Selo for long periods of time, definitively settled in the Alexander Palace in 1905, shortly after the birth of the imperial couple's fifth child, Alexis (1904-1918), the son so long hoped for. The place was chosen deliberately. Nicholas and Alexandra had long dreamed of getting away, at least geographically, from the effervescence of the capital and of a family world closed as much as possible to outsiders, an absolutely indispensable condition to their happiness. To live within a restricted circle of loved ones, especially after the birth of an heir suffering from hemophilia, was a necessity. The Alexander Palace, all the while spacious but with a completely "familial" atmosphere and surrounded by magnificent landscaped gardens, could not have corresponded better to this plan.[3]

For Nicholas and Alexandra, one's well-being and closeness to other people was more important than the life of the Court or then furnishing their palace in the latest fashion: the proof is that the interiors of the Winter Palace in St. Petersburg were re-arranged only once, for their marriage (1894-1896). As for the living quarters in the Alexander Palace, they were decorated in two periods, in the 1890s and in the 1900s, and for many years, were practically not changed.

Of all the rooms in the Alexander Palace, Alexandra Feodorovna preferred the "mauve" room, the Lilac Chamber, where the whole family gathered in the evening. Nicholas II came to take tea in the evening, the children came to play and to be with their parents. The master of the

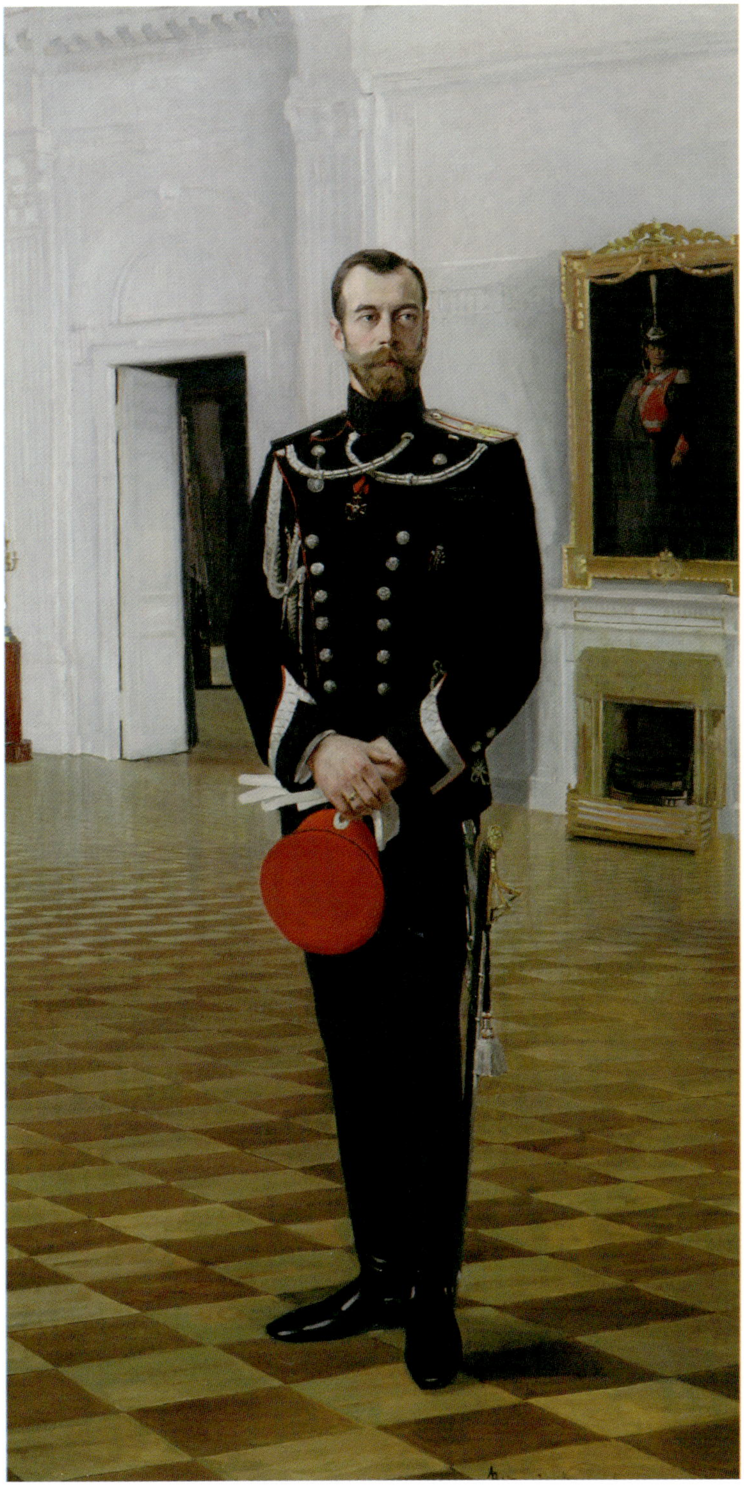

3. *V. A. Kuznetsov*
Portrait of Emperor Nicholas II
1914
The State Museum Preserve "Tsarskoye Selo"
(Cat. 562)

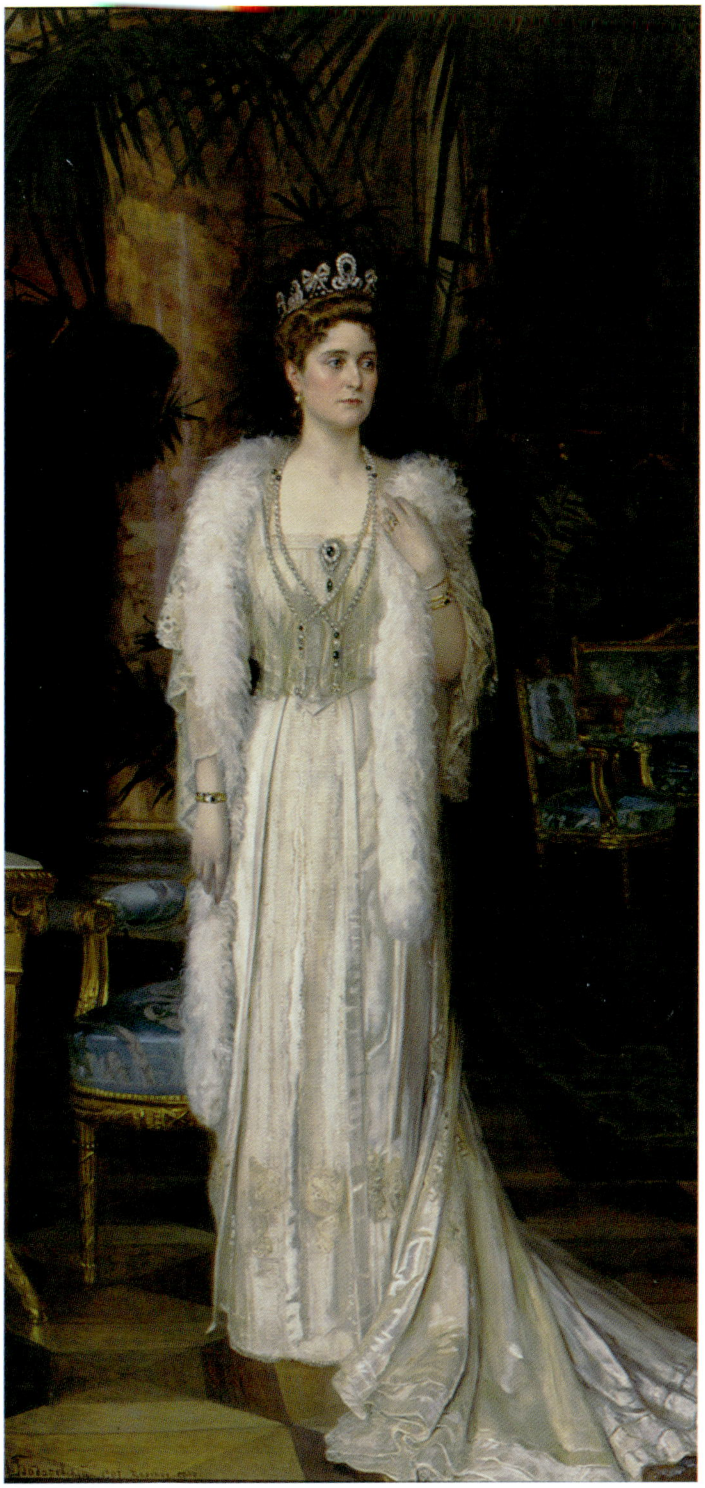

4. *N. K. Bodarevsky*
Portrait of the Empress Alexandra Feodorovna
1907
The State Museum Preserve "Tsarskoye Selo"
(Cat. 563)

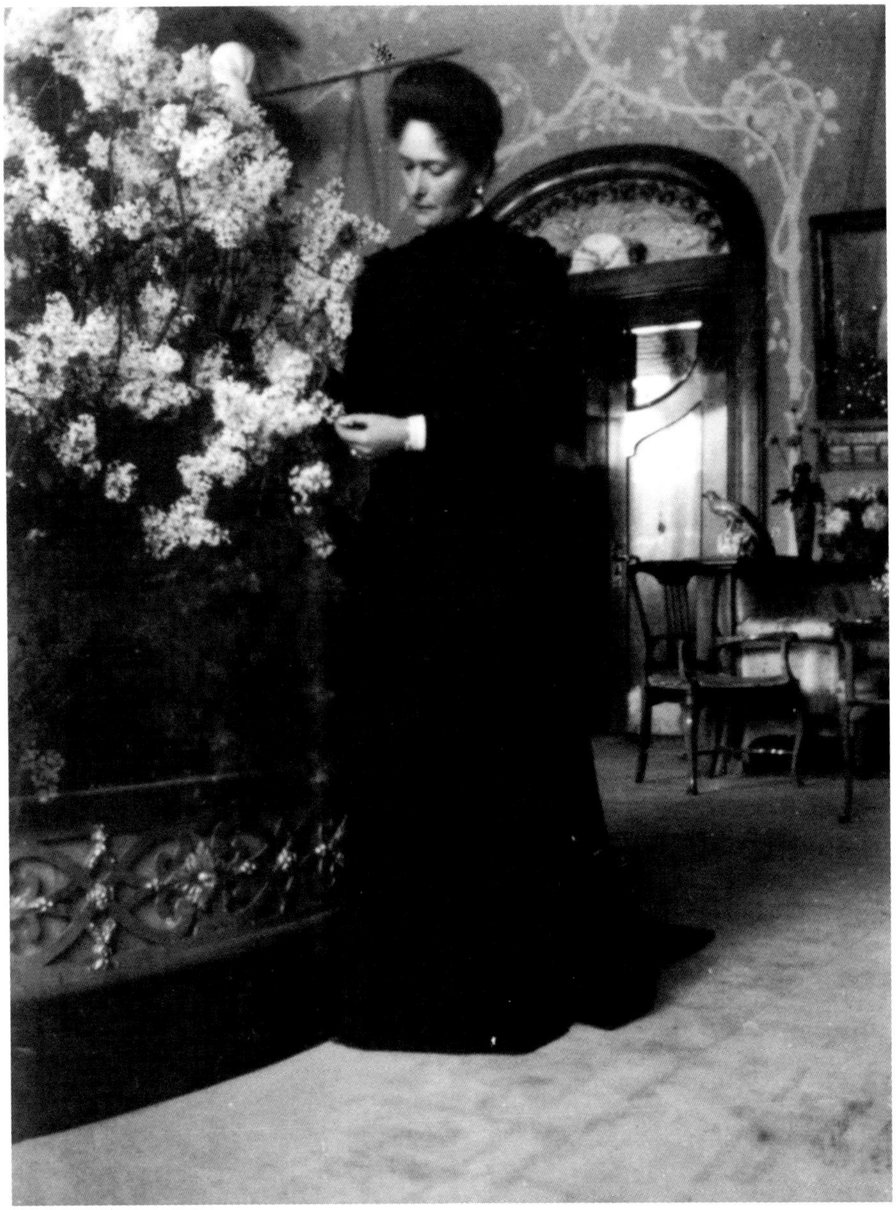

5. Alexandra Feodorovna near a lilac bush in the Maple Drawing-Room in the Alexander Palace
Photograph from the album by A. Vyrubova
Early 20th century
University of Yale library

house had his personal library in that room, a library which had several thousand volumes. Philosophical volumes but also religious and mystical ones made up a special part of the collection. The Empress's religiosity, reinforced by the terrible illness of the heir to the throne, found an echo in the living quarters at the Alexander Palace which had a great number of icons, pious images and crosses: offerings from communities, from army corps, and from private people. In the imperial bedroom alone, there were nearly seven hundred of them.

As for the decoration, the masters of the home preferred comfort over luxury. The Alexander Palace was equipped unlike any other with the latest technical innovations: elevator and telephone, but also a projection room where once a week there was movie night. The last palace commander recalled one of them, "I will never forget the last movie showing at the beginning of the month of February...Mme Du Barry was being shown, with all the horrors of the French revolution, the guillotine, the people's tribunal, the executions etc. After this film, I had such a heavy heart, and it's painful for me to remember it."[4]

Only a few years remained before the horrors of the Russian revolution, and Alexandra Feodorovna continued to lovingly furnish her house. To furnish the palace in her taste, she called upon the famous St. Petersburg firm F. F. Meltzer. Among its outstanding achievements which no longer exist were Nicholas II's ceremonial room, and the Maple Salon of the Empress where the table would be set up for evening tea. After the meal, the Em-

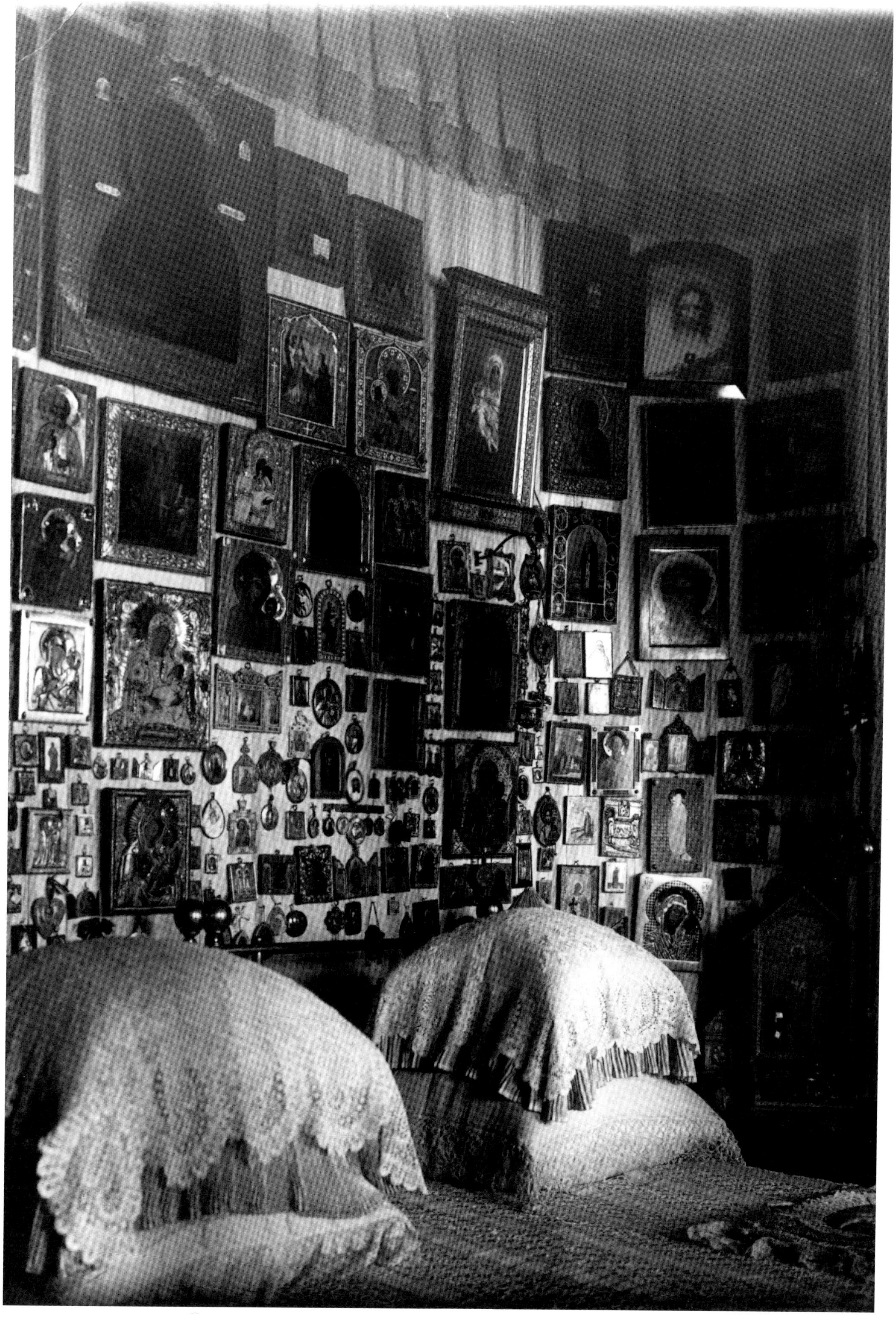

6. The bedroom. Alcove with icons
1930s
The State Museum Preserve "Tsarskoye Selo"

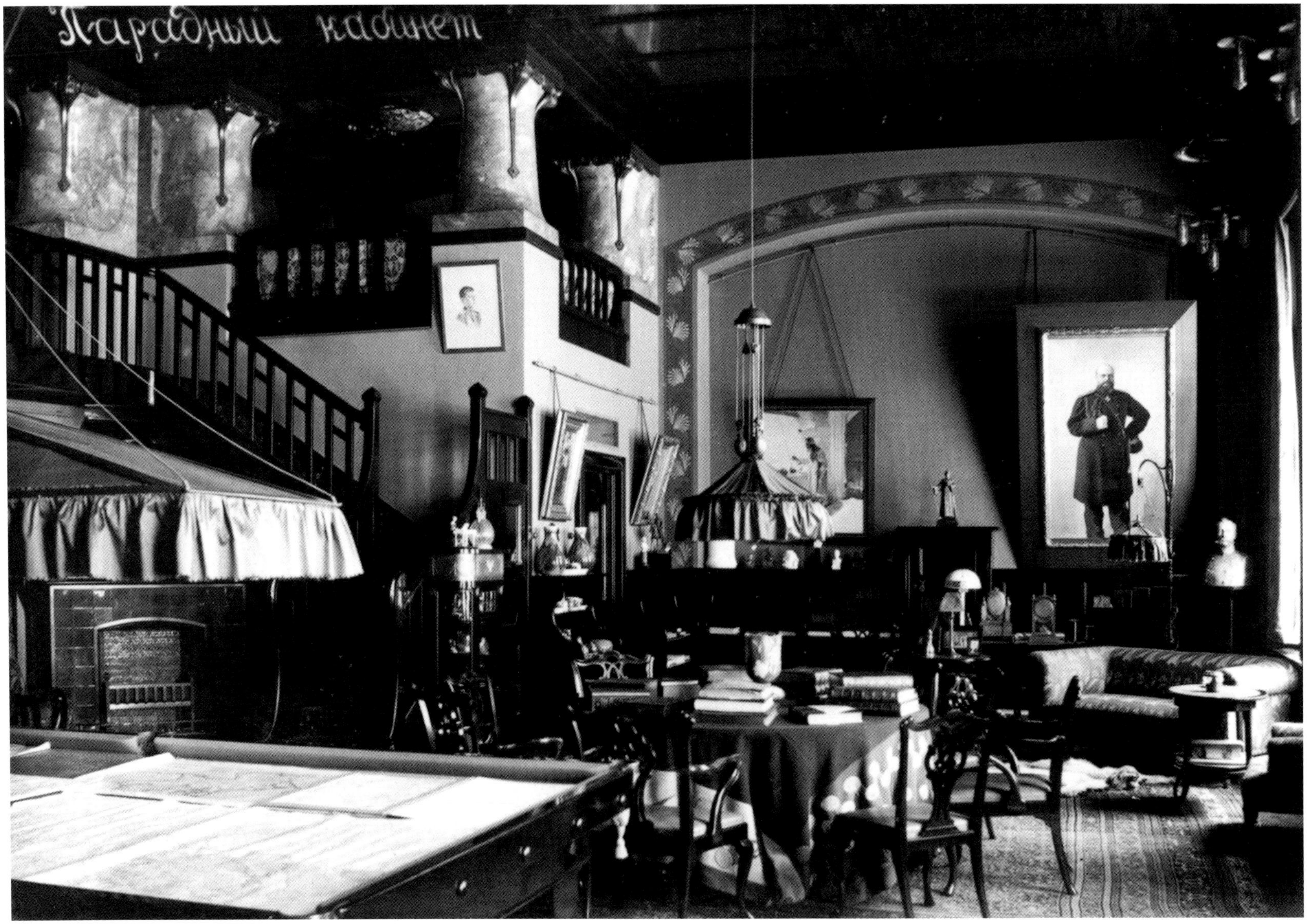

7. The State Study of Emperor
Nicholas II
1930s
The State Museum Preserve
"Tsarskoye Selo"

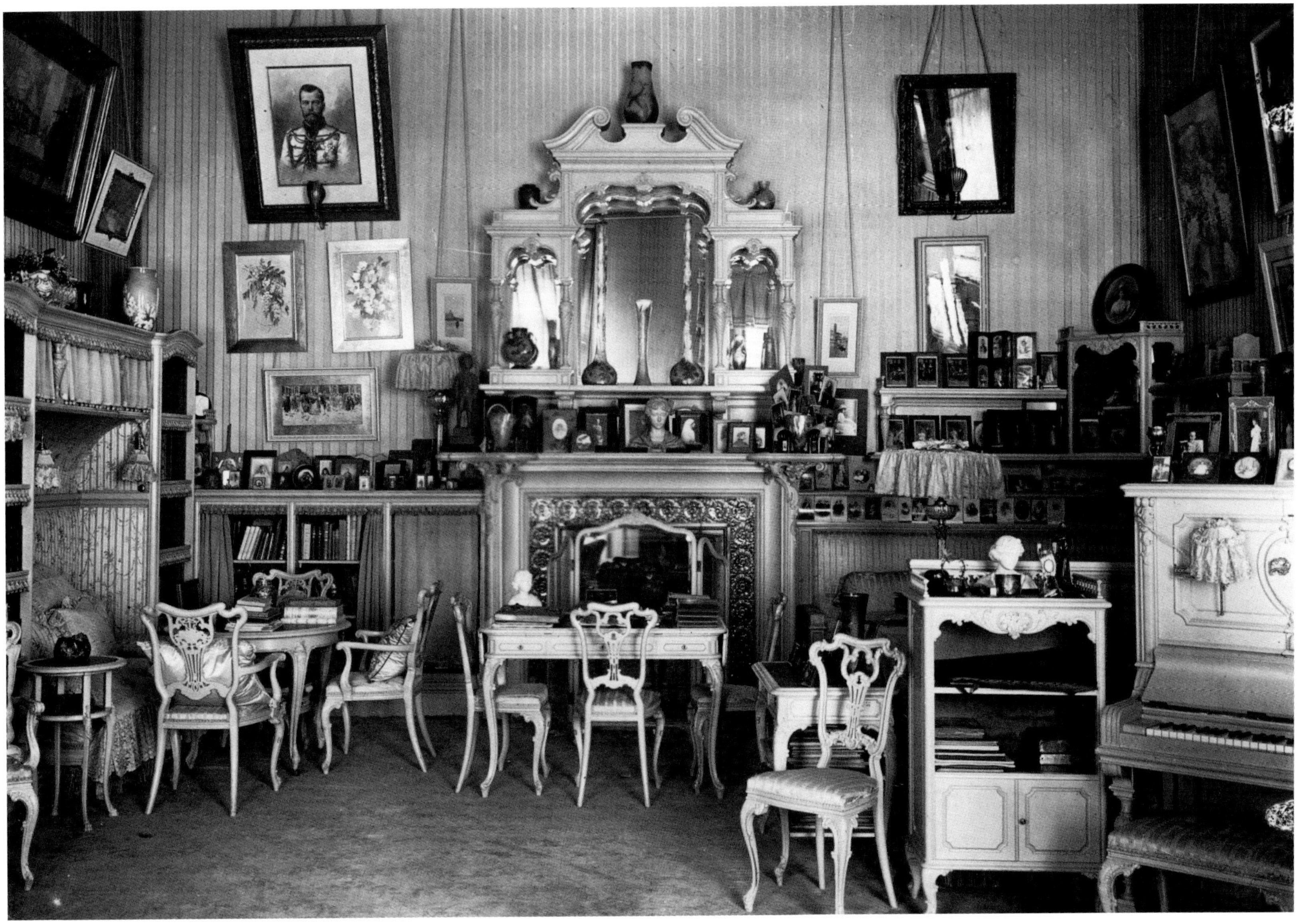

8. The Lilac or Mauve Study of
Empress Alexandra Feodorovna
1930s
The State Museum Preserve
"Tsarskoye Selo"

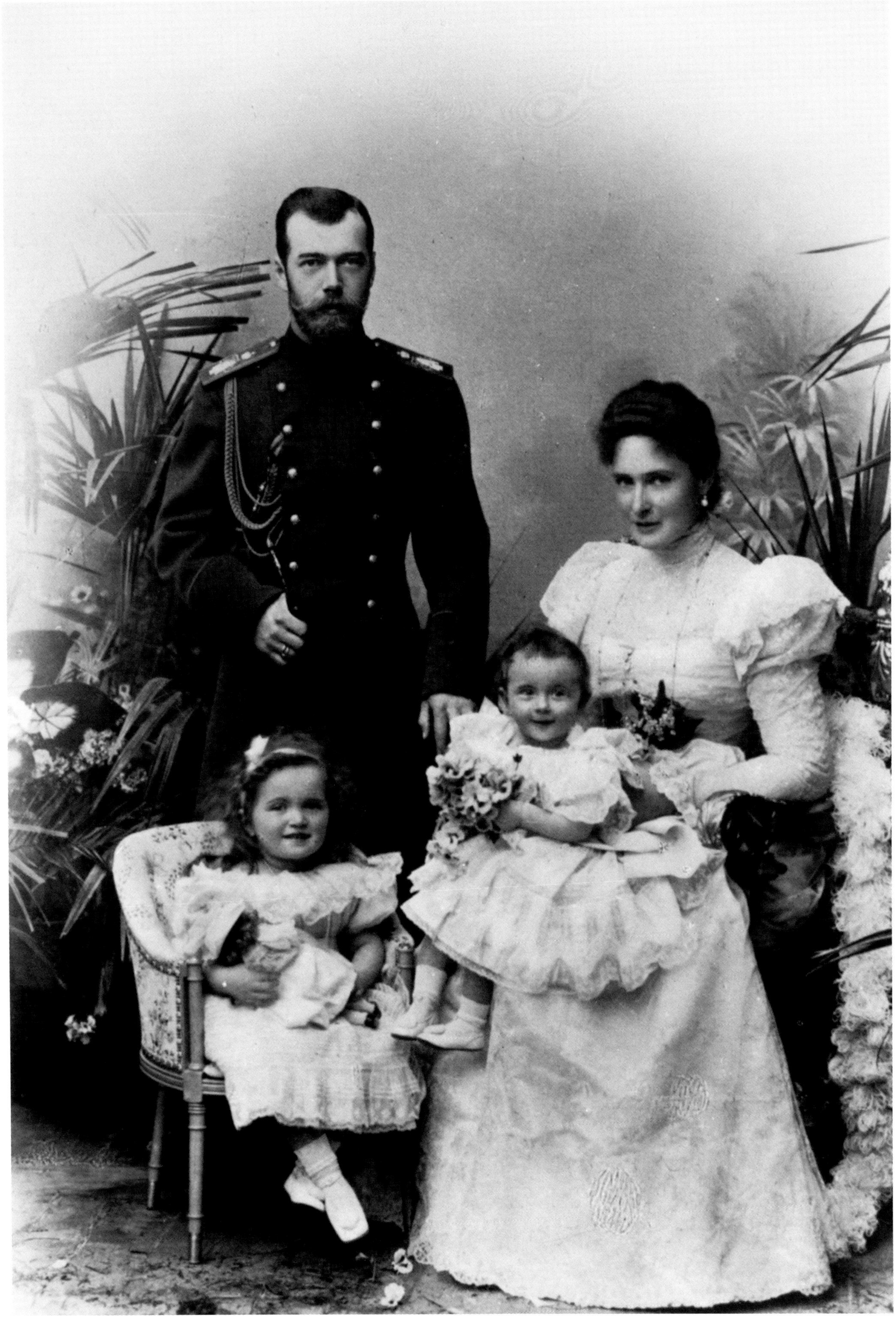

9. The Emperor Nicholas II and the Empress Alexandra Feodorovna with their daughters Olga and Tatiana
Tsarskoye Selo, June 1898
"C. E. de Hahn and Cie" Studio
Russian State Cinematographic and Photographic Archives, al. 299, SN 17

peror would read out loud, the youngest children playing, the bigger ones busy with needlework or drawing. So as to have communication with the rooms reserved for Nicholas II, a passage had been designed to unite the Maple Salon to the Emperor's Salon by a corridor. The Empress could therefore get to the part of the palace reserved for Nicholas II and to hear the Emperor's conversations with his ministers and entourage without being seen.

Nicholas received reports about current affairs and played billiards with the officers of his retinue in the ceremonial chamber during time of peace. This is also where the ex-Emperor held the last meeting with his brother, the grand duke Michael. In the spring of 1917, the imperial family, under arrest, did not have the right to receive letters or to greet guests or family members. This single and last encounter between close family members took place in the presence of the minister A. Kerensky who, conscious of living a his-

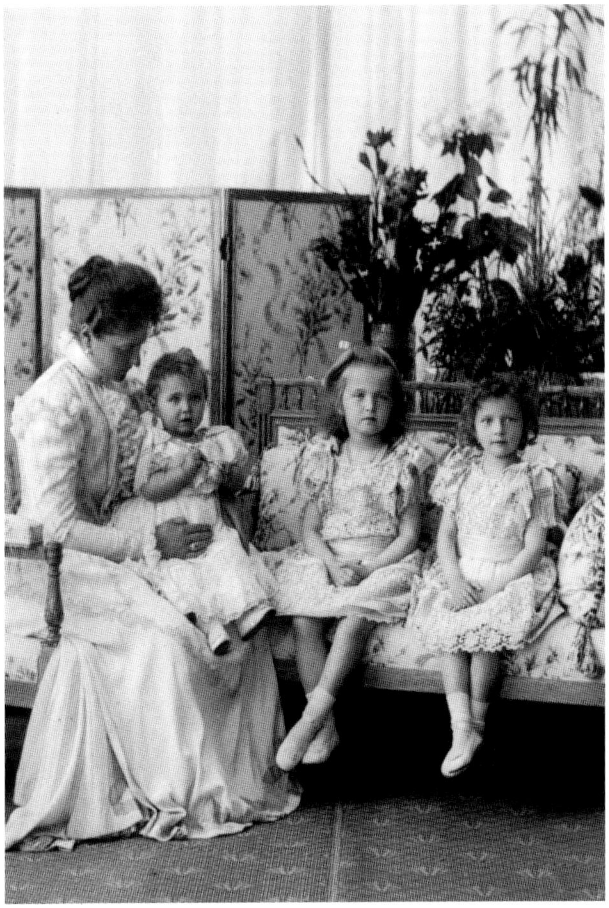

10. The Empress Alexandra Feodorovna with her daughters Maria, Olga, and Tatiana
1901
"V. Iasvoyn" Studio
Russian State Cinematographic and Photographic Archives, al. 299, SN 35

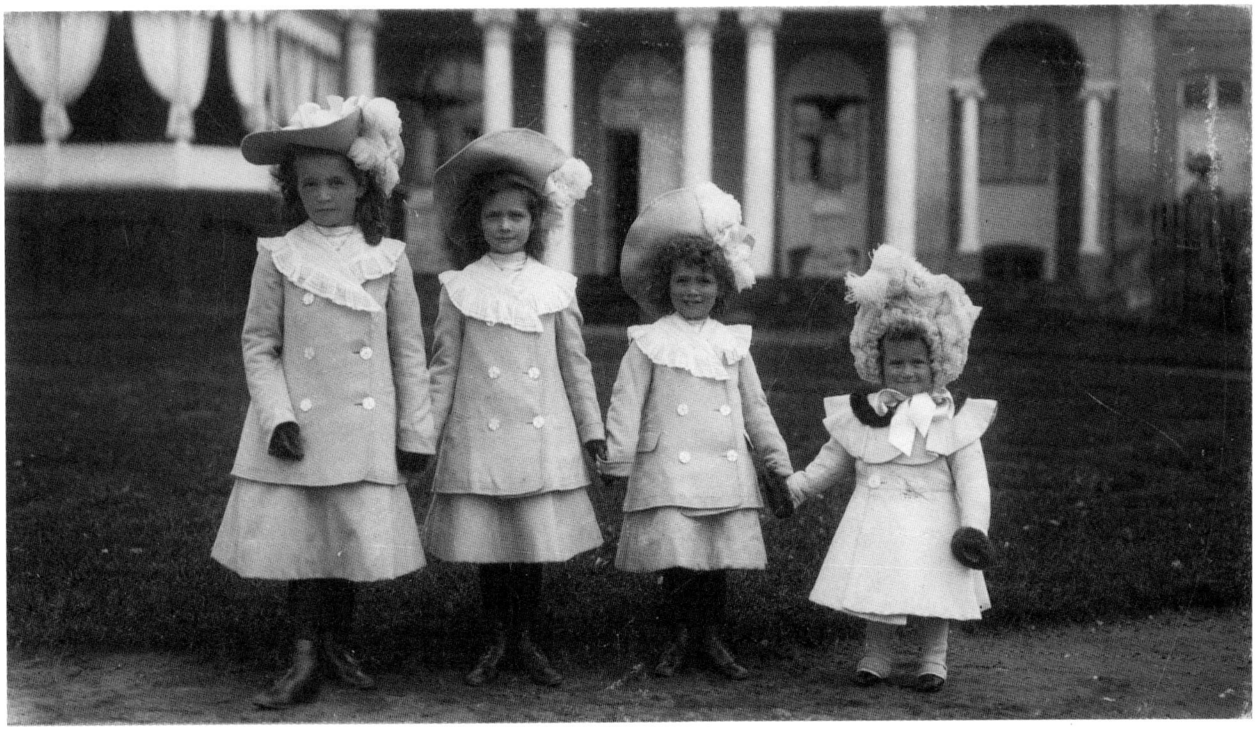

11. *C. E. de Hahn*
Olga, Tatiana, Maria and Anastasia
The State Historical Museum, Moscow
(Cat. 610)

toric moment, carefully observed and engraved in his memory all that was around him, fearful that an important element might escape him.

In the Alexander Palace, the imperial couple had the feeling of having been able to create a familial cocoon in which they were happy. The British ambassador expressed it thus, "In the solitude of Tsarskoye, the imperial family lived a simple domestic life which kept outsiders from interfering in the happiness of their family circle.[5] During the Revolution and during the war years, Tsarskoye Selo Palace became for Nicholas II and his family like an island. Behind the monumental walls, they were protected from the furors of the exterior world. Sheltered within those walls was the fragile and reclusive world of private life. The house in the Alexander Palace contained a quantity of objects which reminded their owners of the public and private events of their lives, a quantity of books and of photographs which were dear to them, it was fragrant with the perfume of the flowers that Alexandra Feodorovna loved so. A warm and agreeable place to live, it filled Nicholas II's family with joy, and, when they left it on August 1, 1917, in the early morning, they dreamed only of returning to Tsarskoye...

But destiny decided otherwise, and the history of the Palace[6] after the Romanovs was as trag-

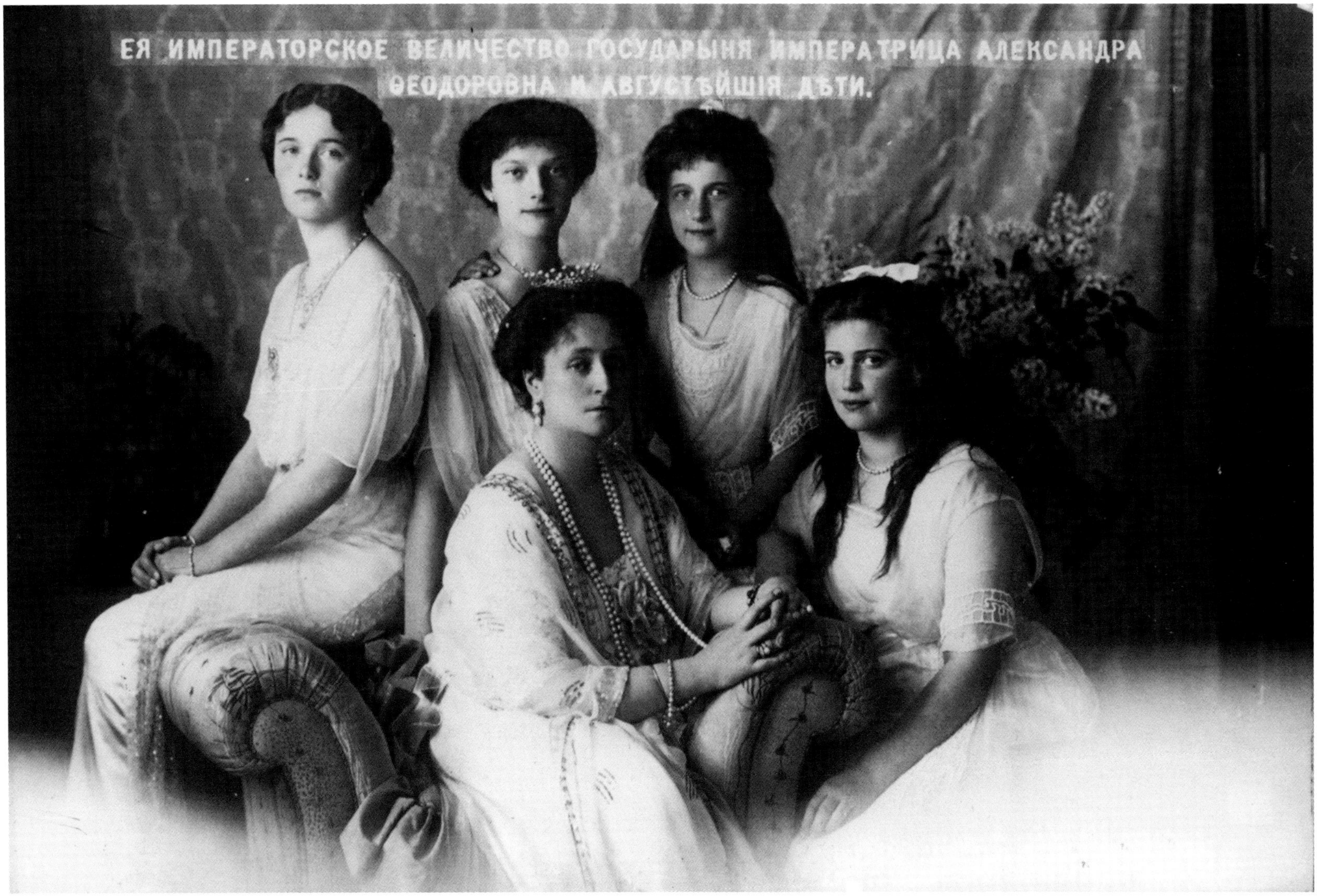

12. Portrait of the mother with her daughters
Postcard
The State Museum Preserve "Tsarskoye Selo"

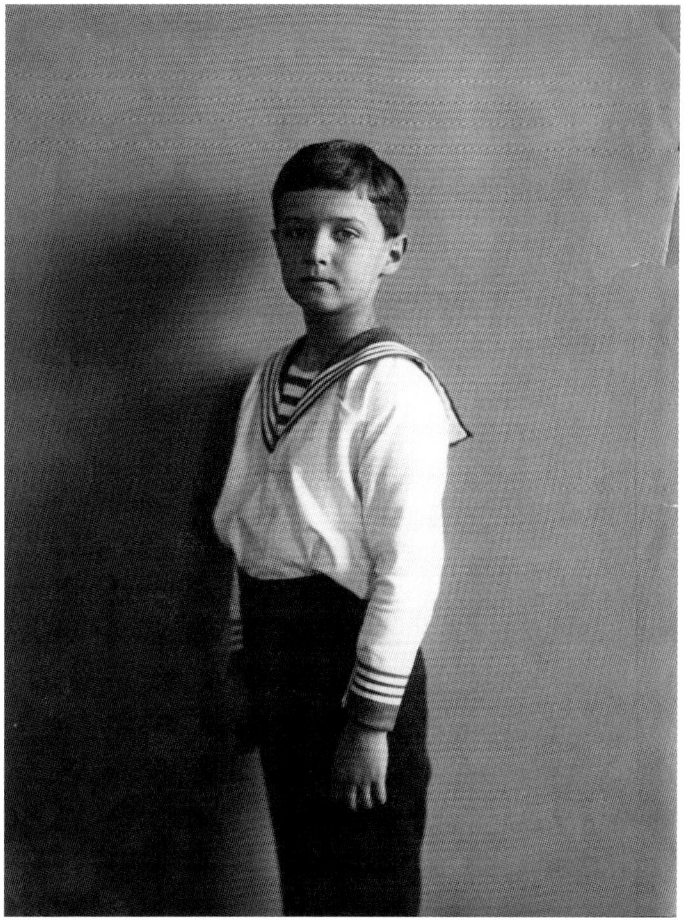

13. Alexis
The State Historical Museum, Moscow
(Cat. 595)

ic as the fate of its last occupants, shot in Ekaterinenburg a July night 1918.

The objects belonging to the members of the family of the last Russian Czar which were saved, some of which are presented in the exhibition, recreate the atmosphere of the private life which reigned in the Alexander Palace at Tsarskoye Selo, in the confused and tormented years of the beginning of the 20th century.

[1] On May 6, 1868, the heir to the throne Alexander Alexandrovich (1845-1894), future Emperor Alexander III, and his wife Maria Feodorovna (1847-1928) had a son, the grand duke Nicholas Alexandrovich.
[2] *Emperor Nicholas II's personal journals*, Moscow 1991, p. 81 (in Russian).
[3] Nicholas and his young wife went for the first time to Tsarskoye Selo in 1894, a week after their marriage. In his journal, the Emperor remembers that trip with deep emotion, which is not characteristic of his daily notes. "At three o'clock, Alix and I took the road for Tsarskoye," wrote Nicholas II on November 22. "It was a clear and happy day (...) At the Alexandrovka station, we were welcomed by the commanders of the army corps and by a crowd of inhabitants from Tsarskoye Selo. A fine light rain began to fall as we arrived at the Alexander Palace. I went to my former apartments, and my Alix, to Mama's room. It's more agreable than can be said to live peacefully without seeing anyone all day and all night, just the two of us!" Two days later, he exclaimed, "Words are powerless to describe the happiness of the two of us living in such a marvelous place as Tsarskoye."
[4] V. I. Voeikov, *With the Czar and without the Czar*, Moscow 1994, pp. 119-120 (in Russian).
[5] Quoted from M. Irochnikov, L. Protsay, Y. I. Cheaev, *Nicholas II. The last emperor of Russia*, St. Petersburg 1992, p. 162 (in Russian).
[6] The furnishings of the Alexander Palace were almost entirely destroyed during the Second World War. The museum which was located in the palace until the war was not restored after it. The unique commemorative objects which belonged to the sovereigns were preserved thanks to the evacuation.

THE GOSPEL

The book which opens and closes the history of a dynasty

Irina Zaïtseva

The relics of dynasties are usually preserved in precious chests, and their history studied in the last details. A whole different destiny was reserved for the holy book which belonged to the first reigning Romanov family. The history of this book reproduces, point by point, Russia's painful destiny.

In 2000, in the complex which has become the Tsarskoye Selo State Museum (GMZ), the former summer imperial residence, a whole group of books—about 4000 volumes—arrived, originating from the collection of the Tsarskoye Selo Imperial Memorial Library. Among other rarities, wrapped in German newspapers dated 1946,[1] one book among them attracted attention because of its dilapidated state—a 17th century binding on small boards covered with fabric, the upper part of which had figurative appliqués in engraved silver—it was a 1627 Gospel. Published by the Moscow printing press, this book alone is today an extremely rare edition. But it is not only rare and precious—in fact, the dedicatory inscription written in half-cursive Cyrillic on the first fourteen pages nearly four hundred years ago make it a truly unique book.

"In the year 7136, the 18th of the month of October, day of the commemoration of the Saint Apostle and Evangelist Luke, the very pious Sovereign and the venerable nun Marfa Ivanovna went to the sanctuary of the very Holy Mother of God and always the Virgin Mary, to the Church of the Glorious Annunciation and of the hierarch St. Basil the Great, bishop of Caesarea in Cappadocia located in the district of Kachin, in the heart of the Monastery of the Annunciation to make a gift of this book, a family Gospel of the four Evangelists destined for the altar, covered with black velvet, with the Evangelists in gilded silver. In presence of the hegumen Michee and all the fraternity. As to him who would carry this Gospel from the home of the Very Pure Mother of God to give it to a friend or to sell it, or to pawn it, or for any other evil action, God will judge that person during his Second Coming, during the Last Judgment and he will answer before God. The hegumen Michee has signed here in his own hand in 7136." (7136 corresponds to the year 1627 in the new calendar.)

"The Sovereign, the venerable nun Marfa Ivanova" who gave this book to the Kachin monastery is none other than the mother of Michael Feodorovich (1596-1645), first Czar of the Romanov family. Marfa Ivanova was the wife of one the richest notables of the state, the boyar Feodor Nikitich Romanov. Their only son, Michael, was elected Czar by the *Zemskii Sobor* in 1614 after the end of the Riourikide dynasty and the tormented years of the Time of Troubles. Michael, to justify that he was chosen, often repeated that "he had been entrusted to the great states by the benediction of his mother, the great sovereign, the venerable nun Marfa Ivanovna."[2] Marfa's direct influence on the affairs of state is clear in the acts of property concerning different monasteries which begin by these words, "By the grace of God, we, great sovereign...and our mother, the sovereign and venerable nun Marfa Ivanovna, have made a gift..." There are also acts of property written only in the name of the venerable nun herself.

1. Gospel
Moscow, 1627
The State Museum Preserve
"Tsarskoye Selo"
(Cat. 577)

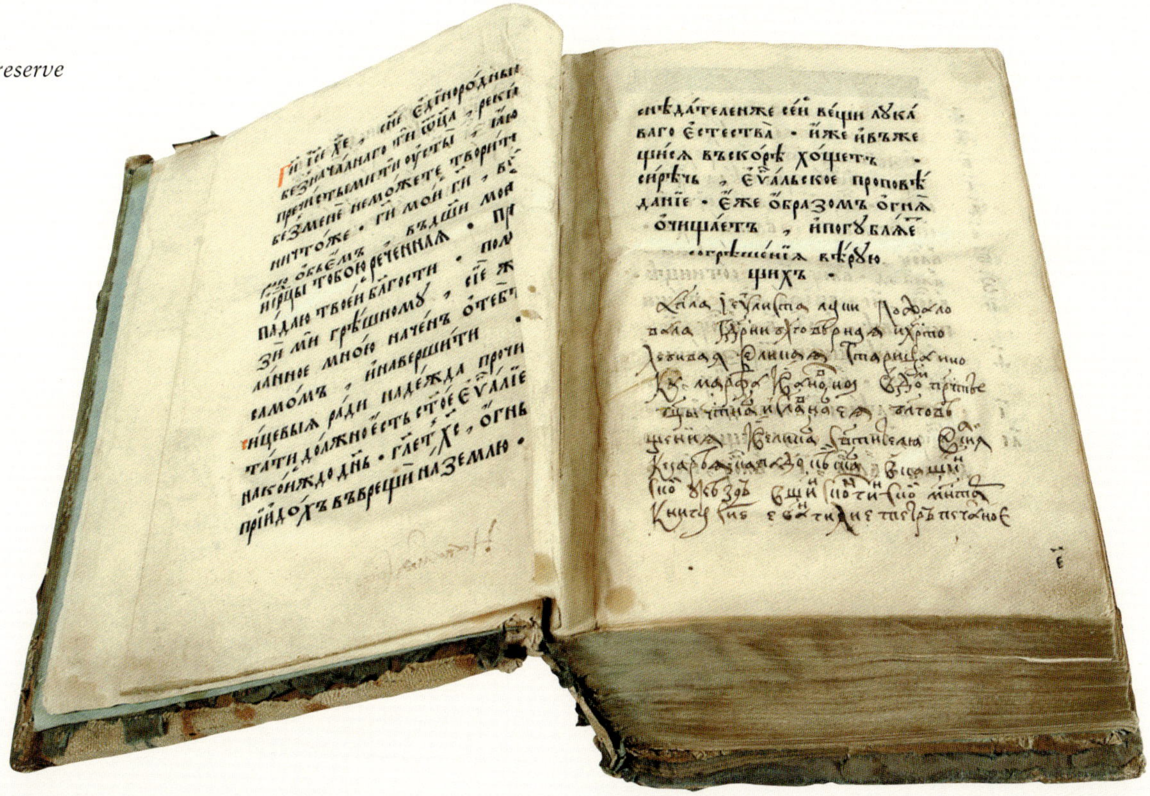

The many and difficult duties which awaited the young Czar put off the question of his marriage for a long time. But so that the dynasty would be continued, a heir was needed. The marriage was celebrated only in 1626, and in April 1627, finally a first child was born to the Czar's family, a girl, named Irina. For the birth of this granddaughter so long awaited, Marfa Ivanovna also made a gift to the Chirin Monastery of the Annunciation, in the district of Kachin in the province of Tver. The tradition of gifts goes back to the first years of Christianity. Men of all social classes were concerned about the salvation of their soul as of that of their relatives. The most generous donators were of course the sovereigns and members of their families. Beginning with Catherine II's reign, the situation of the monasteries within the State had considerably changed. The reform of the Church, determined by the enlightened sovereign, foresaw in particular the secularization of the Church's property: the transfer of much of the land and the possessions of the churches and the monasteries to the State, so as to use the revenues of the Church "in the interest of the homeland." In 1764, the Chirin monastery as many other monasteries was closed and transformed into a parish church. In the second half of the 19th century, on the same place, there remained only a simple chapel.[3] We don't know where the goods of the Chirin monastery were transferred to. Although it was a relic of the Romanov family, it is unlikely that this Gospel printed before the reform of the Patriarch Nikon would have been left in the church. The Patriarch Nikon's church reforms begun in the middle of the 17th century had the goal of unifying the Orthodox services, of correcting them and, in particular, of correcting the liturgical books, according to the Greek example. It was forbidden to the churches and to the faithful to use a book in the services which had been printed before the Nikon reforms. Starting at that time, the books published before 1652 were confiscated by the patriarchal church and replaced by "newly corrected" books. For the Old Believers, the books printed before the reforms were the very base which enabled them to preserve their points of view about the church and the dogma.[4] The adepts of the former faith actively tried to procure by any means the books published before the Nikon reform and very frequently exchanged them or bought them in the monasteries and in the churches.

At the beginning of the 20th century, after the publication of the 1905 *ukaze* "On the reinforcement of the principles of religious tolerance," the Old Believers, victims of persecution over almost two hundred and fifty years, finally saw their right to freely profess their faith recognized. They were now authorized to practice their Old Believer cult freely and publicly, and to use books which had been published in the past. For all that, the Old Believers who held a preeminent place among the merchant class in Russia at the beginning of the 20th century actively practiced business, and in particular, the business of liturgical objects, both recent as well as old.

So when and how did this Gospel finally end up in the hands of the Romanovs? Around 1917, the Imperial libraries contained more than 70,000 volumes, of which about 24,000 were in the Alexander Palace at Tsarskoye Selo. Most of the collections of books were inventoried.

But, there isn't a single of the preserved catalogues which mentions the 1627 Gospel. But examining the inventories of the furnishings of the Alexander Palace reveals that this Gospel, as a relic, was kept on the Emperor Nicholas II's desk in his ceremonial chambers and therefore was, in a way, his bedside book. Next to it had been placed a sculpture: a bust in bronze of the Czar Michael Feodorovich. Some time later, a lucky chance led to the discovery of the documents which shed full light upon the presence of this book in the Alexander Palace.[5]

In March 1916, the Empress Alexandra Feodorovna ordered the administrative head of the Tsarskoye Selo Palace, the prince M. Putiatin to look for some antiques which she could give to her husband for Easter. Among the objects which were presented to her, the Empress chose without hesitating the Gospel printed in 1627 with the sovereign Marfa Ivanovna's dedicatory inscription. In exchange for this book, the merchant of the Old Believers shop asked for five hundred rubles, a very high sum for the time. Perplexed, faced with such a sum but conscious of the historic significance of the object which had a direct link to the Imperial family, Putiatin consulted the professors at the Archeology Institute. These connoisseurs of ancient objects recognized the unique archeological qualities of the book—they also recognized that the dedicatory inscription on the first pages was authentic and that the sum for which the Gospel could be acquired corresponded to its historic value. In the family of the last Emperor, books were by far the gifts most frequently offered and the most appreciated at Christmas, Easter or on the occasion of other holidays. They were often religious works. Nicholas II and Alexander Feodorovna's great piety is well known. Their reciprocal love, of a rare strength and devotion, was astonishingly mixed up with their sincere love of God and their profound and unshakeable faith. There are touching accounts of the nobility of these feelings in the personal correspondence of the august spouses which was published.

Here are very typical notes by Alix addressed to her husband, "To my only one, to my little beloved soul, with my most tender prayers, may God in his generosity for you bless this coming year, may He accord you His benediction and give you the strength and the courage to bear your heavy load..."[6]

"My treasure....how difficult it is to let you leave alone...but I know that you are safely in the hands of God."[7] In the same way, in Nicholas II's letters, the love which he bears for his wife is inseparable from his faith,

"My little darling Bird, I am writing you only a few words because once again, I have little time, my ministers have brought me a mountain of paper—no doubt so that all will be done before Easter. I thank you tenderly for your dear letter and your eggs...This morning, I thought of you so much in our little church, there everything was so beautiful and peaceful. The pious image and the egg, I am going to put them in the church in front of the place where I sit...My prayers and my thoughts are with you, my little girl, my little Sun..."[8]

At the time of the Easter holiday 1916, when the famous Gospel was acquired, Nicholas II and Alexandra Feodorovna were not together. The Emperor was at the Moguilev military headquarters where he wrote sadly to his wife, "Last year, we were also separated this day...Being far from one another in the Holy Week and the day of Easter is a true ordeal. It goes without saying that I have not missed a single service...May God bless you, my precious treasure, and send you a happy and serene Easter."[9]

That was Nicholas II's last Easter celebration as Emperor. The following Easter, in 1917, he experienced it only as "citizen Romanov." After his abdication, on March 2 came his arrest, and then, for the Imperial family there were five months of "reclusion at Tsarskoye Selo." But until the last moment, the Emperor and the Empress, overcoming their grief, attempted to "find comfort in prayer and not doubt God's love and mercy."[10] When they left the Alexander Palace, they took with them into deportation a great number of religious books.[11] But as with many other precious personal affairs, the 1627 Gospel with Marfa Ivanovna's dedicatory inscription remained in their last home.

The book, having "survived" the antique sales during the Soviet era, the occupation, and a trip to Germany, was returned to Tsarskoye Selo.

Even as the Ipatiev house[12]where the Imperial family was killed closed the page on the history of Russia which had opened three hundred years earlier in the Ipatiev monastery,[13] so this unique Gospel closed the history of the dynasty. From the first reigning family of the Romanovs, it ended up some three hundred years later with the last reigning family. The last sovereign of the dynasty received it as a gift on the occasion of the last Easter that he and his family spent in their home at Tsarskoye Selo.

[1] In 1941 all the library collections of the Tsarskoye Selo palace (about 39,000 volumes) were taken to Germany by the Fascists. When a part of them were returned to Russia after the war (8476 volumes), the Catherine Palace was in ruins and the Alexander Palace had become the Academy of Science. The books of the Tsarskoye Selo library collections, abandoned and without a home, were divided among different institutions and preserved here and there, not even being unwrapped, for several decades.

[2] Quoted from I. P. Khruchtchov, *Xenia Ivanovna Romanova*, St. Petersburg 1882, p. 43.

[3] V. V. Zverinsky, *Material for the historic and topographical research on the Orthodox monasteries of the Russian empire*, Volumes 1 and 2, St. Petersburg 1890, Vol. 2, p. 68 (in Russian).

[4] I. V. Pozdeeva, Nikon/Kniga: Encyclopedia. Moscow 1999, p. 147.

[5] RGIA, F. 525; opis 3; delo 544; pp. 129-134.

[6] A. Meïlounas, S. Mironenko, *Nicolas and Alexandra, Love and life*, Moscow 1998, p. 305 (in Russian).

[7] *Ibid.*, p. 317.

[8] *Ibid.*, pp. 462-463.

[9] *Ibid.*, p. 462.

[10] *Letters from captivity of the Imperial saint martyrs*, St. Petersburg 1998, p. 382 (in Russian).

[11] *Ibid.*, p. 401.

[12] Near Ekaterinenburg. (Translator's note)

[13] This is the Ipatiev monastery, near Kostroma, where the young Michael Feodorovich spent several years of his youth and where his mother took the veil under the name of Marfa. (Translator's note)

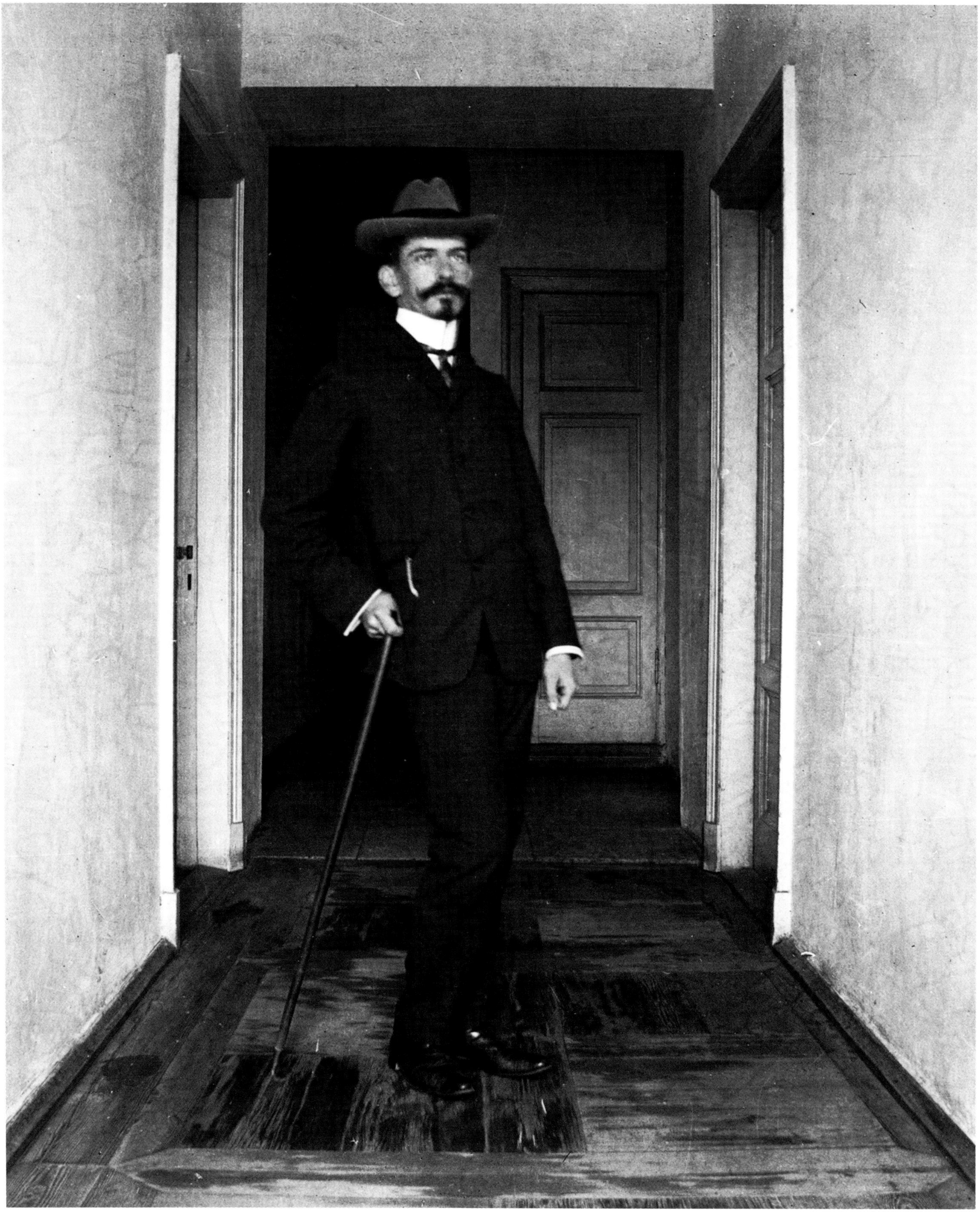

PIERRE GILLIARD, MEMORY OF RUSSIA

Daniel Girardin

Pierre Gilliard who was Swiss (1879-1962) lived closely with the imperial Russian family from 1905 to 1918. His exceptional destiny led him to become the humanistic and lucid eye-witness of the political and human events which led to the fall of Nicholas II, the most powerful monarch in Europe. Gilliard who was in charge of the education of the five Romanov children, and then private tutor to the Czarevich Alexis Nicholaevich. Gilliard lived in the corridors of power, from the splendors of Tsarskoye Selo, Peterhof and Livadia to the last places of captivity, Tobolsk and Ekaterinburg. That is where in the Ipatiev house the night of the 16th to the 17th of July 1918 the final destiny of the Romanov family was played out.

A democrat, in the service of autocracy

Tens of thousands of Swiss people—architects, engineers, wine-growers, bankers, jewelers, photographers, clockmakers, nurses and private tutors—emigrated to Russia in the 19th century. The private tutors, exclusively French-speaking Swiss, were particularly appreciated by the aristocratic families whose court language was French. Avoiding all contact with the public schools and universities which were considered too liberal, the Russian aristocrats generally relied on the private tutors for the education of their children. A tradition brilliantly illustrated by Frédéric-César de La Harpe from the canton of Vaud, Switzerland who was employed by Catherine II to oversee the education of her two grandsons, Constantine and his brother Alexander, the future Emperor Alexander I. His competencies and his prestige contributed to Swiss education becoming the current fashion. A century later Gilliard was to become the ultimate representative of this.

Gilliard arrived in St. Petersburg in 1904, right in the middle of the war between Russia and Japan. His first letters record his shock at discovering the poverty of the population, the illness, the hunger, the injustice, and later also, the anti-Semitism which was widespread in Russia. As a French professor in the service of Prince Serge Gueorguievich Romanovsky, Duke of Leuchtenberg, Gilliard soon made the acquaintance of the Emperor Nicholas II and of his wife, Alexandra Feodorovna. Soon after, in 1905, he went into their service to teach French to Olga, their oldest daughter, and then successively to Tatiana, Maria and Anastasia, before ultimately being in charge of their complete education. Then, in 1913, Gilliard was named private tutor to Alexis Nicholaevich, heir to the throne. As governor to His Imperial Highness the Grand Duke Heir, he acceded to one of the most prominent positions in Imperial Russia, and no doubt one of the best paid.

1. *P. Gilliard*
Self-portrait, Livadia Palace near Yalta, *Crimea, 1911*
22.5 × 22.5
Elysée Museum, Lausanne, call number 036243

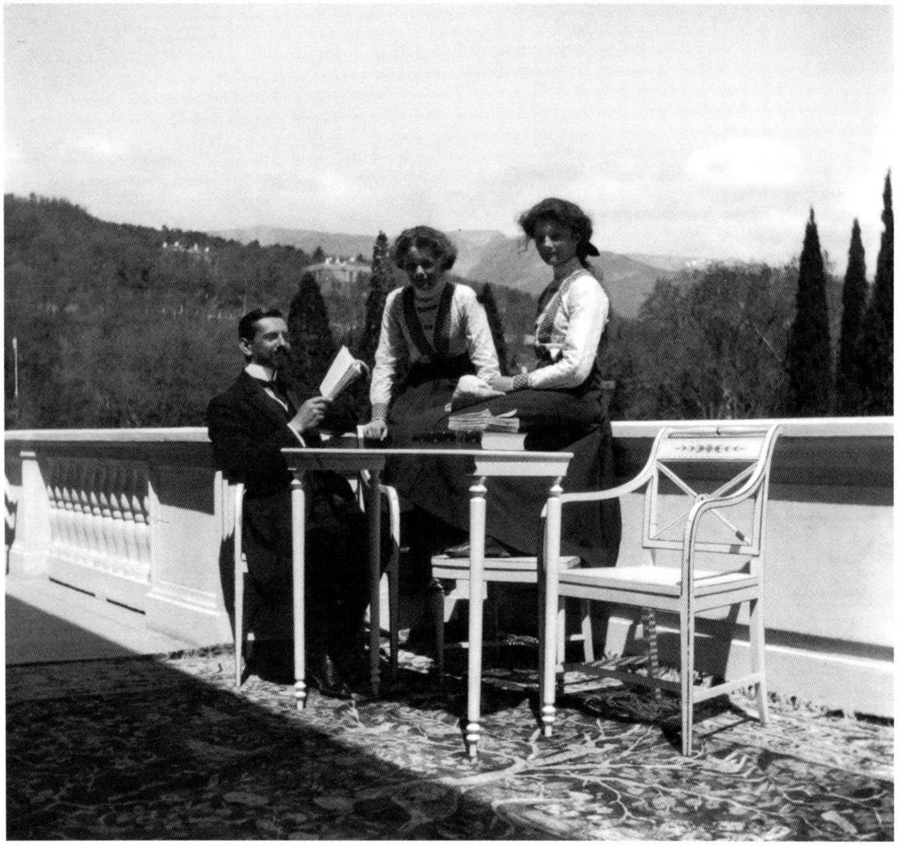

2. *P. Gilliard*
Pierre Gilliard with Grand Duchesses Olga Nicholaevna and Tatiana Nicholaevna
Livadia Palace, Crimea, 1911
Elysée Museum, Lausanne
(Cat. 624)

3. *P. Gilliard*
Olga, Tatiana, Maria and Anastasia, Biolevje forest
Russia, autumn 1913
Elysée Museum, Lausanne
(Cat. 612)

In his Memoirs published in 1921,[1] he voiced all the difficulties of being a democrat from a liberal federalist culture in a centralized and autocratic system.

A difficult childhood

A serious obstacle to the future of the Romanovs was the hemophilia which afflicted the Czarevich, a problem which remained a State secret until 1913. Incurable, particularly painful, the illness of the heir to a empire of more than 150 million inhabitants was a serious affair of State. The child was entrusted to Gilliard for whom the responsibility was overwhelming.

How could Gilliard, a critical, free, cultured spirit transmit to the child the values which in his eyes made up a just and honest man who knows how to use his intelligence and to show justice? He threw all his energy into the mission. He began by forbidding anyone to kneel in front of the child, banished the two body guards, found him some friends to play with, and sought above all to instill in him a personal discipline which the child completely lacked. For Gilliard, the problem of princes was primarily in their weak character, for nothing was refused them and they benefited even as children from privileges which discouraged all intellectual effort.

This was particularly the case for Alexis Nicholaevich. Often in agony, sometimes for whole months from the slightest blow on his joints, Alexis Nicholaevich was spoiled and protected by a desperate mother. Gilliard understood very quickly that the child needed to learn how to master his body and his gestures, it was his only hope of surviving the deadly illness from which he suffered. To the mastery of the body, Gilliard wished to associate knowledge, culture, and most subtly, spirit.

So it was the political future but also the personal future of the child which was played out in the long days Gilliard spent with him, and through the educational program taught the boy by a dozen professors who Gilliard managed and supervised. The young man could only hope to survive his illness and so govern if he acquired enough maturity to master his body and therefore be able to develop his knowledge and his intelligence.

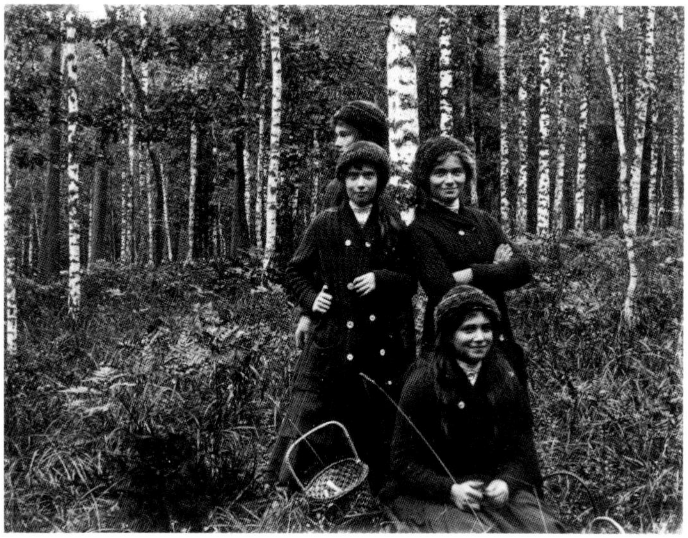

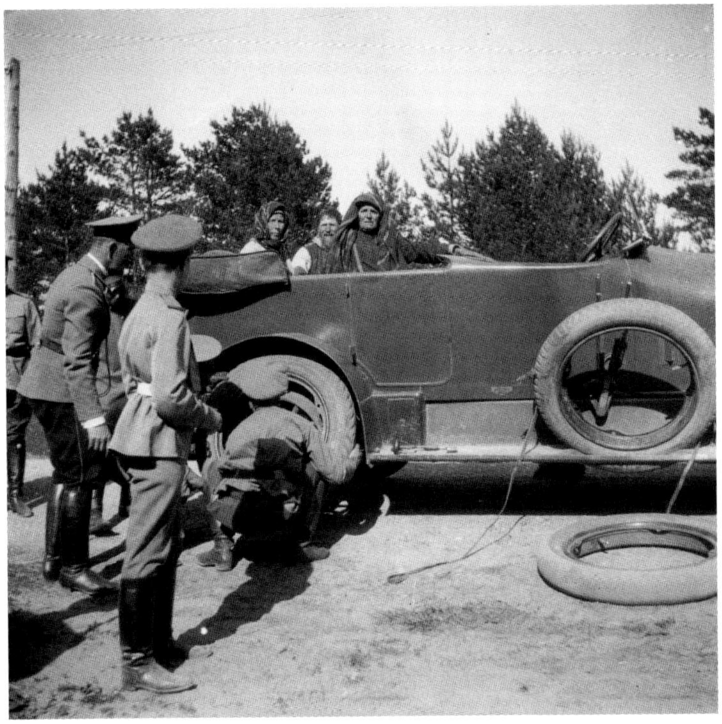
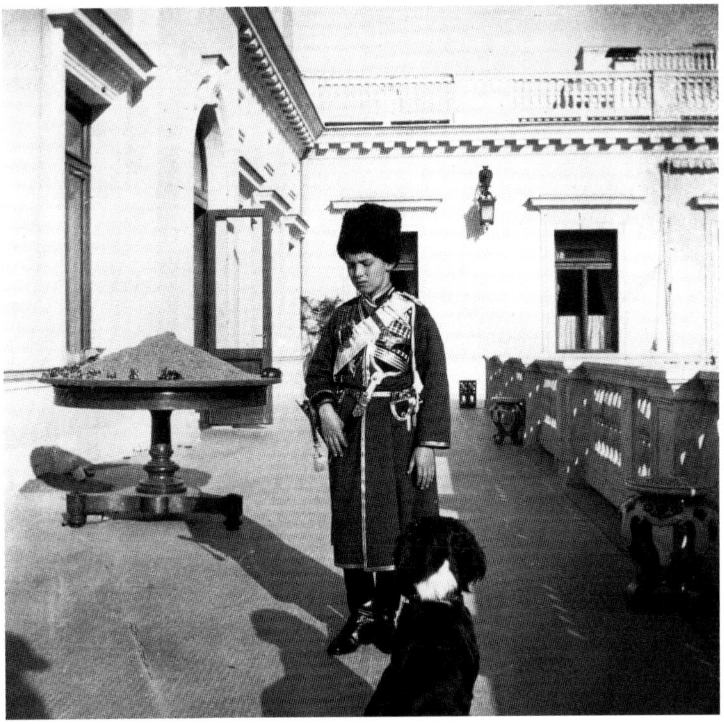
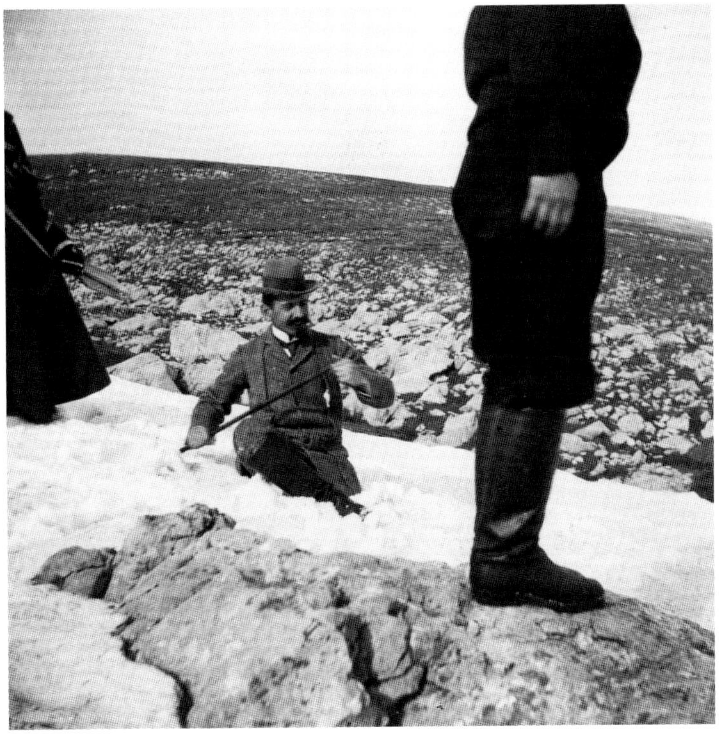
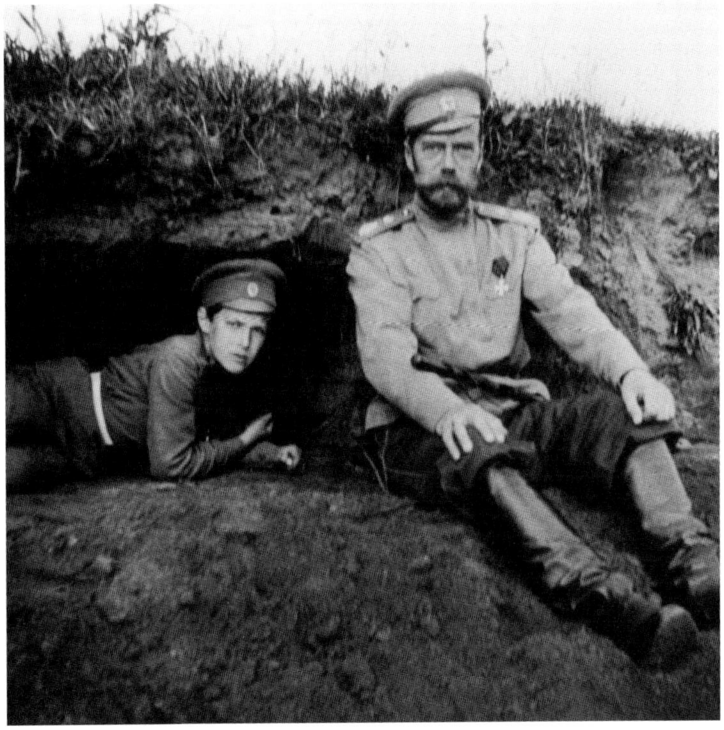

4. *P. Gilliard*
The Czarevich Alexis Nicholaevich with some Muzhiks being taken by Pierre Gilliard in the imperial automobile
Mohilev, Russia, 1915
22 × 22 cm
Elysée Museum, Lausanne, call number 027680

5. *P. Gilliard*
The Czarevich Alexis Nicholaevich with his spaniel Joy, Livadia Palace, near Yalta
Crimea, 1914
21.5 × 21.5 cm
Elysée Museum, Lausanne, call number 036212

6. *P. Gilliard*
With the Czarevich Alexis Nicholaevich on a excursion to the Red Stone
Jaila Mountains, Crimea, May 1914
22.5 × 22,5 cm
Elysée Museum, Lausanne, call number 036212

7. *P. Gilliard*
Alexis Nicholaevich and Nicholas II
Mohilev, Russia, 1915
Elysée Museum, Lausanne (Cat. 618)

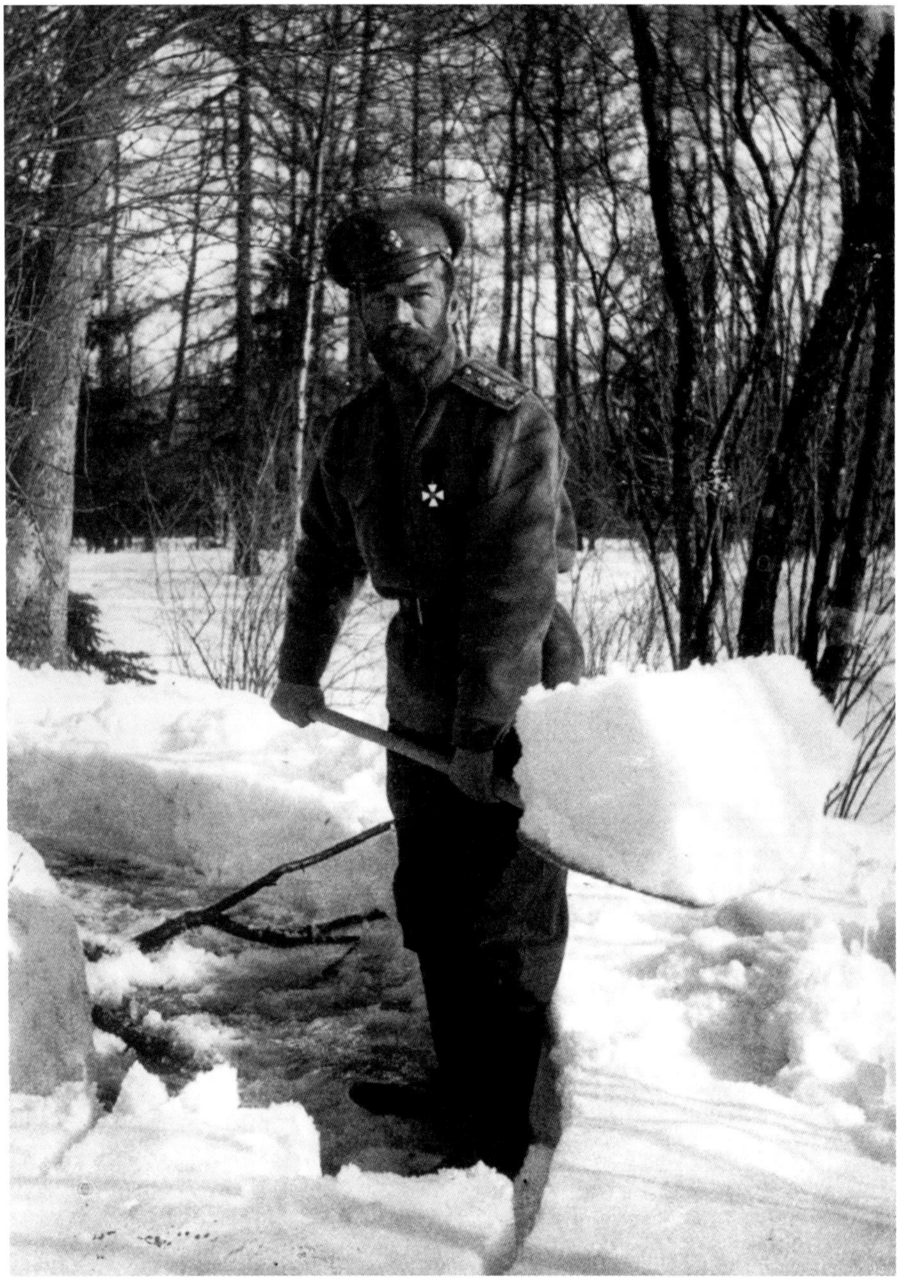

8. P. Gilliard
The Emperor Nicholas II in captivity, March 1917
Tsarskoye Selo, Russia, 1917
Elysée Museum, Lausanne
(Cat. 619)

For sheer enjoyment and also as an act of provocation, Gilliard often sneaked away in a car with his student, shaking off the security services, to have him visit farms, restaurants and cities to show a reality that the child could not even imagine, he who had never left the domains of Tsarskoye Selo, Peterhof, Livadia and Spala, who had never gotten off the *Standart*, the imperial yacht on which the family spent part of the summer, usually in the Gulf of Finland.

This education provided astounding results. It enabled Alexis Nicholaevich to go out, to play, to concentrate, to read, to learn. But the disaster of the war, the abdication, the February revolution and then captivity put an end to this original educational program. The heir's illness no doubt played a large role in the process which had led the imperial couple little by little into isolation and into secrecy.

Captivity without exile or hope

As soon as the family was arrested in the spring of 1917, Gilliard took full charge of the children and in great part of the daily organization of the royal family with whom he had become, by force of circumstance, very close. It was Gilliard himself who announced to Alexis Nicholaevich that his father had abdicated at the request of the provisory government and that he would never reign. Everyone believed however that they would find a place of exile, but no one wanted them, given how problematic the unpopularity of the imperial couple had become. King George V, even though a cousin of Nicholas II, refused to accept them in Great Britain. France, allied with Russia who against all odds faithfully assured its obligations confronted to Prussia, kept an ominous silence.

Finally, on the decision of the provisory government and Kerensky who feared for their lives, the family was exiled to Tobolsk in August 1917, then transferred to Ekaterinburg in Siberia in the spring of 1918 on the decision this time of the Bolshevik government. First a captive, and then in flight, Gilliard was able to return to Ekaterinburg a little while after the execution of the Romanov

9. P. Gilliard
Nicholas II and his children in captivity
Tobolsk, Russia, April 1918
Last known photograph of the Romanovs
22.5 × 22.5 cm
Elysée Museum, Lausanne, call number 27690

family when the city was retaken by Czechs and White Russians. At that time, the Bolshevik government officially admitted only the execution of the Emperor. But Gilliard had to accept the evidence in participating in Judge Sokolov's inquest: even if their bodies had not been found, the children too had been assassinated.

Evidence through images

Gilliard's many letters, his personal journal as well as the reports he wrote to the Swiss government show to what extent Gilliard was able to remain a critical political analyst of the situation, in spite of the deep attachment he felt for the children, and beyond his loyalty to the imperial family which he had supported even into its captivity, in courageously turning himself in as a voluntary prisoner.

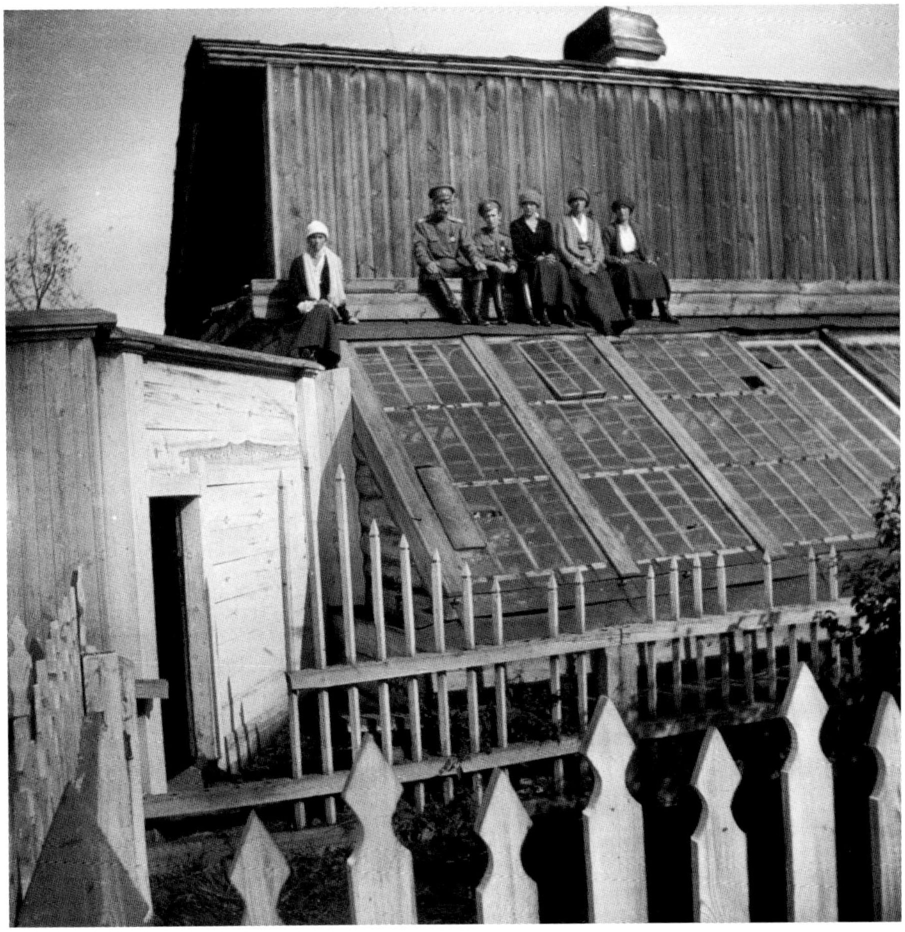

Gilliard showed how Nicholas II's systematic political errors, indecisions, incompetence and incapacity to govern and reform his country ended by bringing about his fall. Later he also explained that the policies of the Western states who backed corrupt and cruel dictators such as Koltchak or Wrangler to the detriment of the democratic government sprung from the February revolution had directly led to the take-over of power by the Bolsheviks in October 1917.[2]

Trapped by the civil war in Siberia, Gilliard remained two more years in the service of the French general Janin before being able to return to Switzerland in 1921, going through Vladivostok, then the Panama Canal with the Czech troops who were eventually evacuated. In Switzerland, he was finally able to marry Alexandra Tegleva who had also been in the service of the Romanovs and whom he had known for many years.

A passionate photographer, he was able to save several hundred of his photographs—no doubt the most precious ones—which are certainly the most interesting ones of the Romanovs. The photos are of their daily life, and then of their captivity, and are undoubtedly the most powerful account ever realized under such circumstances. Gilliard shows the many faces of power, from the happy days to the dark hours, bequeathing to us through his photos a subject for historical, political, philosophical and ethical reflection.

[1] Cf. P. Gilliard, *Le Tragique destin de Nicolas II et de sa famille*, Payot, Paris 1921.
[2] Cf. D. Girardin, *Précepteur des Romanov, le destin russe de Pierre Gilliard*, Actes sud, Paris 2005.

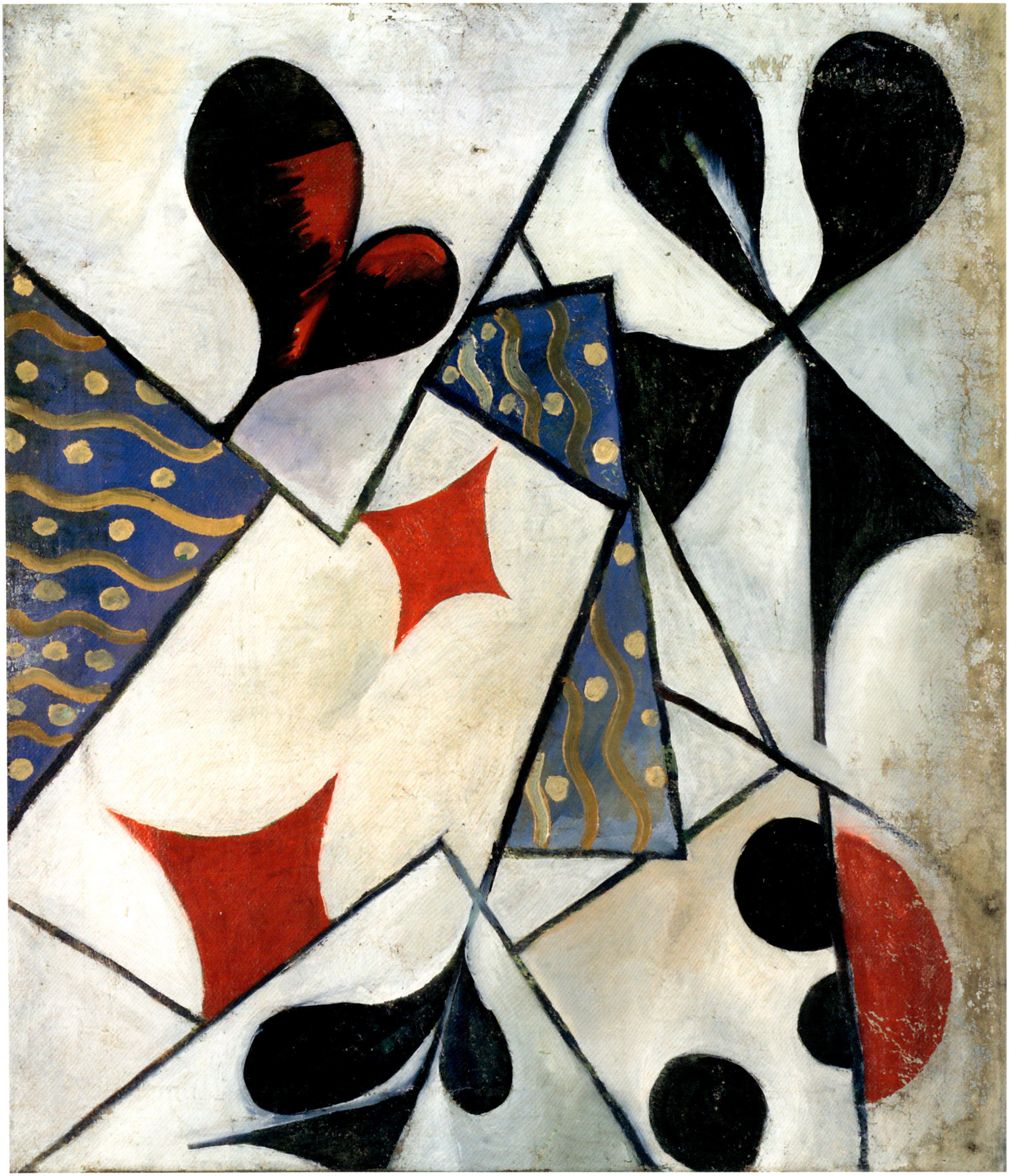

EPILOGUE

Brigitte de Montclos

And during that time, the great painting revolution was in preparation. The *Peredvijniki*, those painters who were called the Itinerants because they crisscrossed the country to show their work, painted Russia as it really was, with its undergrowth, its streams, its peasants, its snow, in other words, the reality of the land as well as its harshness. Their talent revealed a Russian truth. But this truth confronted new preoccupations: first of all, the movement which insisted on another way of painting to express the joy of light and line, and then the discovery of soberness which the icon had expressed since Andrei Rublev, a soberness which only suggested, which had no need for terrestrial details, and finally, the awareness that the Russian artists were not alone in seeking out another direction. The sensitive collectors Sergei Shchukin and Ivan Morozov opened their treasure chests to all the younger painters who wished to see them. The revelation of the works of Gauguin, Matisse or Picasso at Shchukin's, and those of Cezanne or Derain at Morozov's dazzled the young painters. Already the simplification of expression, linked to color which transmitted sensations, had appeared in the work of the symbolists such as Vroubel who purified the line to the point of making it unnecessary. From the beginning of the century, the movements of the *Blue Rose*, the *Jack of Diamonds*, the *Golden Fleece* or *The Donkey's Tail*, the journeys to Germany and France, made the artists aware of confrontation and in the same way, of creation. Matisse's visit, invited by Shchukin to install *Dance* and *Music* in his townhouse in 1911, was euphoric.

The avant-garde which accompanied the last years of the Russian autocracy appeared as the expression of a vitality which was never able to put into question the vacillating empires.

1. O. *Rozanova*
Playing cards
1915-1916
Ekaterina and Vladimir Semenikhin Collection
(Cat. 652)

Page 276
2. L. *Popova*
Painterly Architectonic
1916
Ekaterina and Vladimir Semenikhin Collection
(Cat. 650)

Page 277
3. L. *Popova*
Cubist portrait
1915
Ekaterina and Vladimir Semenikhin Collection
(Cat. 651)

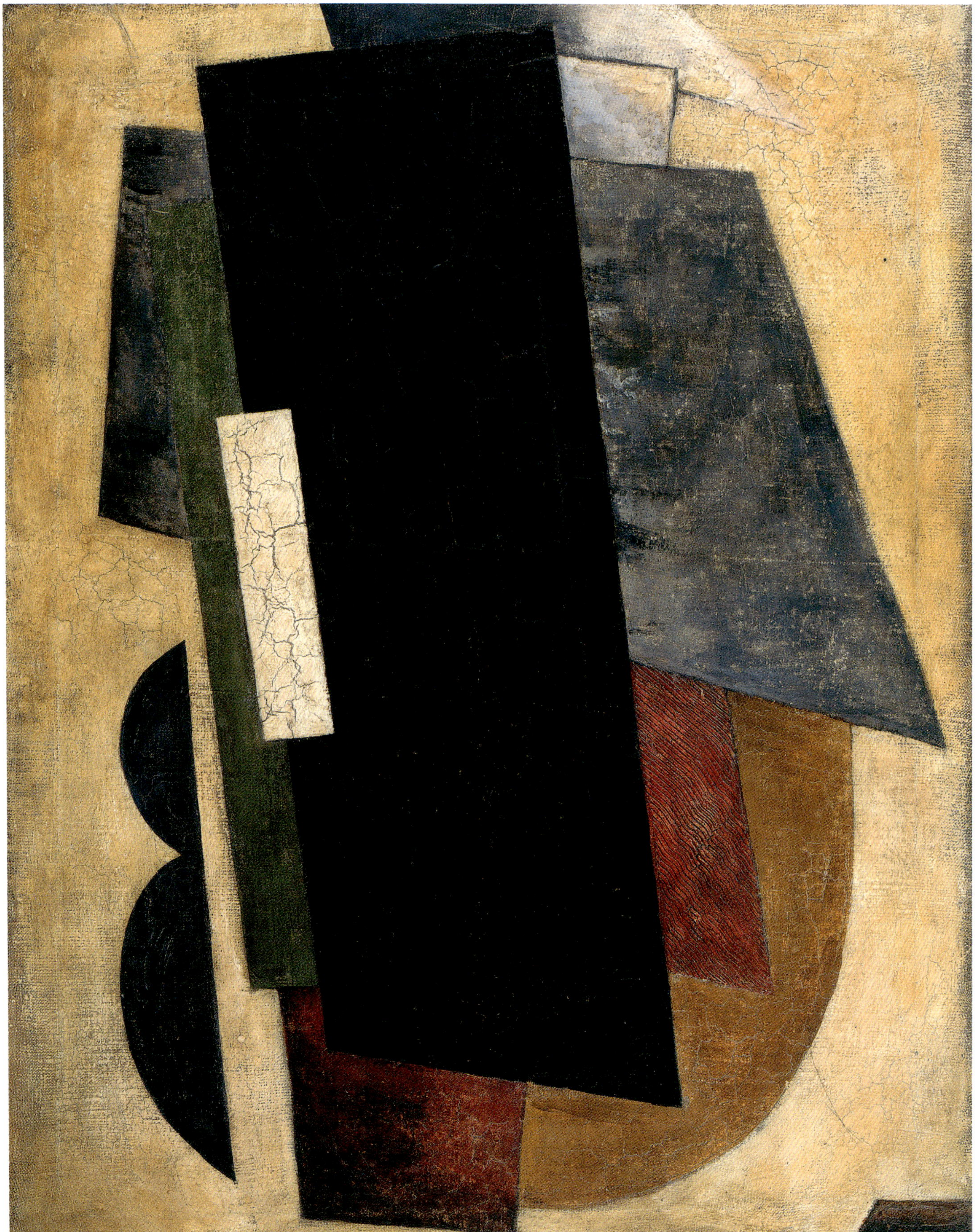

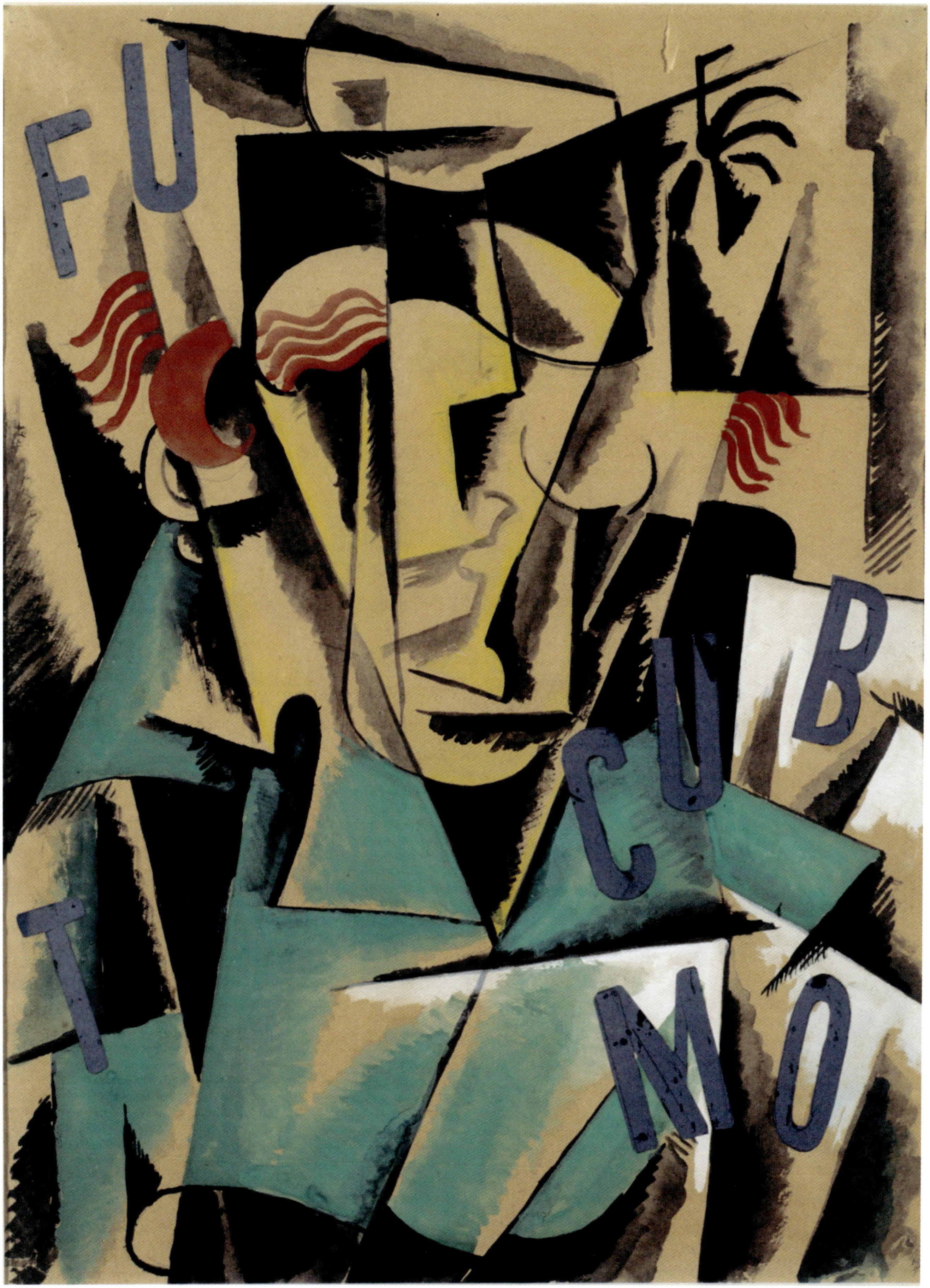
FU
T
CUB
C
MO

LIST OF WORKS

Cat. 1
Anonymous
Equestrian portrait of Czar Michael Feodorovich
Second half of the 1670s, first half of the 1680s (?)
Oil on canvas, gilded background
45 x 30 cm
The State Historical Museum, Moscow, GIM 32936/ I 1-3459
(Reproduced p. 16)

Cat. 2
Reliquary to hold the relics of the patriarch Hermongen
Russia, 1913
Copper, wood, glass, nacre, fabric, lacquer, tin
64 x 34 x 25 cm
The State Historical Museum, Moscow, GIM 92716 / 1-3

Cat. 3
Ceremonial mantle having belonged to the Empress Maria Alexandrovna, spouse of the Emperor Alexander II
Russia, St. Petersburg, Workshop for woven and gold-sewn articles I. P. Likhatchev, 1856
Glazed gold brocade, silk, ermine, gold thread, ribbon, tassels.
375 cm
Moscow, Kremlin Museums, Tk-2597
(Reproduced pp. 54 and 57)

Cat. 4
Album. Coronation of His Majesty the Emperor Alexander III
St. Petersburg, 1883
Binding: calico with stamps and gilded edges
67.5 x 53 x 3 cm (folded)
The State Historical Museum, Moscow, GIM 70156, A-28
(Reproduced p. 34)

Cat. 5
Tunic, shirt and hat of a coronation herald
Russia, 18th century
Velvet, taffeta, cotton, braid, fringe, ribbon, gold thread, silk thread, feathers, cotton wool, sash
84 cm
Moscow, Kremlin Museums, Tk-1616, Tk-1618, Tk-1557
(Reproduced pp. 60 and 61)

Cat. 6
Boots of a coronation herald
Russia, 18th century
Velvet, leather, glazed gold brocade, braid, ribbon, gold laces, silk ribbon
H. 40 cm
Moscow, Kremlin Museums, Tk-1399/1-2
(Reproduced p. 62)

Cat. 7
Emperor Nicholas I's coronation dress
Russia, 1826
Woolen cloth, cloth, gold thread, silver, metal
l. 87 cm
Moscow, Kremlin Museums, Tk-3022
(Reproduced p. 59)

Cat. 8
Doublet of the coronation dress of Emperor Peter II
France, 1727
Glazed brocade, silk, gold thread, purl
l. 95 cm
Moscow, Kremlin Museums, Tk-195
(Reproduced pp. 58 and 59)

Cat. 9
Cushion backing for the throne of Emperor Nicholas II
Moscow, Monastery of the Annunciation, 1896
Velvet, repp, satin, glazed brocade, gold thread, silk thread, metal plates, sequins, sash
Moscow, Kremlin Museums, Tk-1308
(Reproduced p. 63)

Cat. 10
V. S. Rozanov
Festivities by the population on Sophia Quay near the Kamenni Bridge
1883
Painting from the series, "Illuminations of the Coronation". Coronation of Emperor Alexander III
Oil on canvas
97.9 x 170.9 cm
The State Historical Museum, Moscow, GIM 39335, K-579

Cat. 11
G. Schwartz
Illumination of the Kremlin and Resurrection Gate during the celebrations given on the occasion of the coronation of the Emperor Alexander II
1856
Oil on canvas
67 x 107 cm
The State Historical Museum, Moscow, GIM 87869, K-46

Cat. 12
Alb (sticharion)
Russia, 19th century
Brocade, braid, cotton
l. 139 cm
The State Historical Museum, Moscow, GIM 80283/140 RB-2753

Cat. 13
Chasuble (phelonion)
Russia, third quarter of 18th century
Velvet, brocade, gilded glazed brocade, cloth, silver and gold wiredrawn thread, purl, metal
l. 141 cm
The State Historical Museum, Moscow, GIM 80283/205 RB-2759
(Reproduced pp. 66 and 77)

Cat. 14
Chasuble (phelonion)
Russia, 20th century
Brocade, damask silk fabric, braid, cotton fabric, silver and gold wiredrawn thread, purl, silver sequins, metal leaf
l. 143.5 cm
The State Historical Museum, Moscow, GIM 55258 RB-1381

Cat. 15
Chasuble (phelonion)
Russia, beginning of 20th century
Brocade, silk, cord, silver
l. 149 cm
The State Historical Museum, Moscow, GIM 78142/217 RB-3845 CB 1490

Cat. 16
Chasuble (phelonion)
First quarter of 19th century
Velvet, brocade, cotton fabric, taffeta, silver braid (ornamentation and border), gold and silver wiredrawn thread, gold and silver lamé, gold and silver whorls, purls of tinsel strips, gold and silver purls, sequins, metal plates with subject
l. 141.5 cm

The State Historical Museum,
Moscow, GIM 80283/47 RB-2739
(Reproduced p. 79)

Cat. 17
Chasuble (phelonion)
Russia, end 19th century
Gilded embossed velvet, gold wiredrawn thread, sequins, gold and silver purl, colored glass, metal
l. 149 cm
The State Historical Museum,
Moscow, GIM 61357 RB-2413

Cat. 18
Chasuble (phelonion)
Russia
Epaulette: end of 17th century;
Chasuble vestment: end of 18th-early 19th century;
Under-chasuble: second half of 19th century
Velvet, damask gilded silk, cloth, serge, silver and gold wiredrawn thread, gold and silver whorls, purls of tinsel strips, gold and silver purls, sequins, gold and silver braid
l. 140 cm
The State Historical Museum,
Moscow, GIM 55258 RB-1381
(Reproduced p. 75)

Cat. 19
Mitre
Russia, beginning of 19th century
Composite ornaments: 17th, 18th, 19th centuries
Gold, silver, emeralds, rubies, sapphires, beryl, quartz, leuco-sapphire, glass, spinel, diamonds, almandine garnet, tourmaline, enamel, velvet, silk, cannetille
H. 23.2 cm
The State Historical Museum,
Moscow, GIM 77319 OK 10821
(Reproduced p. 43)

Cat. 20
N. N. Karazin
Triumphal entrance through the Red Square
Russia, St. Petersburg, N. Brézé lithography, 1883
Paper, lithography in colors
66 × 55 cm
The State Museum Preserve
"Tsarskoye Selo,"
St. Petersburg, ED-684-XII

Cat. 21
V. I. Surikov
Procession around the Cathedral of Christ the Savior
Russia, St. Petersburg, A. Ilin Cartography Office, 1883
Paper, lithography in colors
65.5 × 50.5 cm
The State Museum Preserve
"Tsarskoye Selo,"
St. Petersburg, ED-867-XII

Cat. 22
V. D. Polenov
Their Majesties at the entrance of the Cathedral of the Assumption
Russia, St. Petersburg, A. Ilin Cartography Office, 1883
Paper, lithography in colors
65.5 × 50.5 cm
The State Museum Preserve
"Tsarskoye Selo,"
St. Petersburg, ED-871-XII
(Reproduced p. 36)

Cat. 23
N. E. Makovsky
Inauguration of the Cathedral of Christ the Savior
Russia, St. Petersburg, A. Ilin Cartography Office, 1883
Paper, lithography in colors
65.5 × 50.5 cm
The State Museum Preserve
"Tsarskoye Selo,"
St. Petersburg, ED-874-XII

Cat. 24
V. P. Verechaguin
Leaving the Cathedral of Christ the Savior
Russia, St. Petersburg,
N. Brézé lithography,
1883
Paper, lithography in colors
50.5 × 65 cm
The State Museum Preserve
"Tsarskoye Selo,"
St. Petersburg, ED-875-XII

Cat. 25
C. E. Makovsky
Blessing of the flags of the Preobrajensky and Semenovsky regiments
Russia, St. Petersburg, N. Brézé lithography, 1883
Paper, lithography
in colors
50 × 65.5 cm
The State Museum Preserve
"Tsarskoye Selo,"
St. Petersburg, ED-811-XII

Cat. 26
A. P. Sokolov
Portrait of the Empress Maria Feodorovna
Russia, St. Petersburg, A. Ilin Cartography Office, 1883
Paper, lithography in colors
57 × 51.5 cm
The State Museum Preserve
"Tsarskoye Selo,"
St. Petersburg, ED-882-XII
(Reproduced p. 45)

Cat. 27
Panagia of honor (bishop's pectoral medallion) with a portrait in miniature in enamel of Peter I on the reverse side
Russia, Moscow, first half of 18th century
Gold, silver, brilliants, diamonds, rubies, sapphires, zircon, aqua-marine, pyrope, enamel
15 × 7.7 cm
The State Historical Museum,
Moscow, GIM 81556/76 OK 13409
(Reproduced p. 99)

Cat. 28
Master A. Ovsov (painting on enamel). Based on a original by Tannauer
Panagia of honor (bishop's pectoral medallion) granted by Empress Catherine I to the archbishop Theophane Prokopoich in 1725 upon the occasion of her accession to the throne
Russia, St. Petersburg, 1725
Silver, diamonds, enamel
15.3 × 11 cm
The State Historical Museum,
Moscow, GIM 81557/77 shch OK 13408

Cat. 29
Panagia (pectoral image) "Virgin of the Sign" with a chain
Russia, Moscow, 1847
Gold, diamonds, brilliants, emeralds, cultured pearls, nacre
13.6 × 6.5 cm
The State Historical Museum,
Moscow, GIM 80052 OK 11628

Cat. 30
Three-winged icon with the "Virgin of Vladimir"
Russia, Moscow, 1691-1692
Silver, cultured pearls, enamel, wood, copper
15.2 × 10.7 × 3.2 cm
The State Historical Museum,
Moscow, GIM 1701 shch OK 4178/1-2

Cat. 31
Gospel book
Text: Russia, 1681
Covering: Russia, Moscow, 1683
Silver, wood, paper, velvet
47.5 × 32 cm
The State Historical Museum,
Moscow, GIM 95490 OK 14906

Cat. 32
Altar cross
Russia, 1637-1638
Silver
28.2 × 12.6 cm
The State Historical Museum,
Moscow, GIM 76282 OK 9481

Cat. 33
Chalice
Russia, Moscow, 1640
Silver
19.8 × 14.2 × 14.2 cm
The State Historical Museum,
Moscow, GIM 55231 OK 6492

Cat. 34
Mitre
Russia, Moscow,
P. I. Olovianichnikov firm, 1908-1917
Silver, emeralds, amethyst, aqua-marine, tourmaline, cultured pearls, enamel, fabric, nacre
H. 19.5 cm
The State Historical Museum,
Moscow, GIM 75691 OK 8787
(Reproduced p. 101)

Cat. 35
Tabernacle
Russia, Moscow,
F. Y. Michukov workshop, 1912-1917
Silver, enamel
37.5 × 9.5 × 9.5 cm
The State Historical Museum,
Moscow, GIM 109154/615 OK 23945

Cat. 36
Icon lamp
Russia, Moscow,

M. Semenovna workshop, end of 19th-early 20th century
Silver, enamel
14.5 × 9.7 × 9.7 cm
The State Historical Museum, Moscow, GIM 99085 OK 16054

Cat. 37
Chalice
Russia, Moscow, M. N. Ryndin workshop, 1894
Silver, enamel
H. 36.2 cm
The State Historical Museum, Moscow, GIM 99096 OK 16032

Cat. 38
Master M. Chein
Icon of the Virgin
Russia, Moscow, 1861
Silver, enamel, wood, velvet
31.4 × 25.5 cm
The State Historical Museum, Moscow, GIM 80090 OK 11848

Cat. 39
Altar cross
Russia, Moscow, P. I. Olovianichnikov firm, 1913
Silver, enamel
39.2 × 22 × 1.7 cm
The State Historical Museum, Moscow, GIM 99095 OK 16057

Cat. 40
Tabernacle with lid
Russia, St. Petersburg Glassworks Manufacture, second quarter of the 19th century
Clear crystal, milky white and blue cobalt, engraved, gold painting; top in gilded silver with strass of clear glass
H. 57 cm
The State Historical Museum, Moscow, GIM 89234/3610

Cat. 41
Master F. Studentsov
Discus (paten)
Russia, Moscow, 1873
Silver
12.5 × 28.8 × 28.8 cm
The State Historical Museum, Moscow, GIM 100425/54 OK 16661

Cat. 42
Master T. Ilin
Asterisk (backing for the veil protecting the paten)
Russia, Moscow, 1722
Silver
H. 8.5 cm
The State Historical Museum, Moscow, GIM 75497 OK 8772

Cat. 43
Element of a church chandelier
Russia, Moscow, 1703
Silver
l.17 cm
The State Historical Museum, Moscow, GIM 1554 shch OK 677

Cat. 44
Basin for holy water
Russia, 1672
Silver
H. 36.5 cm
The State Historical Museum, Moscow, GIM 55230 OK 8042
(Reproduced p. 87)

Cat. 45
Altar cross
Russia, Moscow, 1719
Gift from Czar Peter I to the Church of the Saints Thaumaturges Cosmas and Damian
Silver, wood
52.7 × 38.2 cm
The State Historical Museum, Moscow, GIM 77264 OK 9887

Cat. 46
Censor
Russia, Moscow, 1702
Silver
H. 29.7 cm
The State Historical Museum, Moscow, GIM 44640 OK 9644

Cat. 47
Censor
Russia, Moscow, 1698-1699
Silver
H. 27.3 cm
The State Historical Museum, Moscow, GIM 77193 OK 10560

Cat. 48
Icon lamp
Russia, Moscow, 1770s
Silver
12.9 × 9.5 cm
The State Historical Museum, Moscow, GIM 80100 OK 11853

Cat. 49
Master A. I. Ratkov
Gospel Book
Gospel: Russia, Moscow, 1749. Binding: Russia, Moscow, 1785
Silver, enamel, paper, wood
72.3 × 50 cm
The State Historical Museum, Moscow, GIM 77303 OK 10559
(Reproduced p. 96)

Cat. 50
Pectoral cross
Russia, Solvychegodsk, second half of 17th century
Silver, coral, enamel
6.5 × 7 cm
The State Historical Museum, Moscow, GIM 3427 shch OK 6918
(Reproduced p. 94)

Cat. 51
Small icon
Russia, end of 16th-early 17th century
Silver, wood, enamel, almandine garnet, quartz, turquoise, nacre
Diam. 4.7 cm
The State Historical Museum, Moscow, GIM 3282 shch OK 6914

Cat. 52
Small icon
Russia, end of 16th-early 17th century
Silver, wood, enamel, almandine garnet, nacre, quartz, turquoise, cultured pearls
Diam. 4.6 cm
The State Historical Museum, Moscow, GIM 3282 shch OK 6915

Cat. 53
Small icon
Russia, end of 16th-early 17th century
Silver, wood, enamel, turquoise, almandine garnet, quartz, nacre
Diam. 4.7 cm
The State Historical Museum, Moscow, GIM 3282 shch OK 6913

Cat. 54
S. Ushakov
The Savior "Archeiropoietos" (not done by the hand of man)
Moscow, Armory School, 1670
Wood, gesso, tempera
47.4 × 39.3 cm
The State Historical Museum, Moscow, GIM 68964, I-VIII 4421

Cat. 55
S. Ushakov
Christ on the Throne
Moscow, Armory School, 1672
Wood, gesso, tempera
140 × 101.5 cm
The State Historical Museum, Moscow, GIM 85738, I-VIII 1600

Cat. 56
The Nativity of Christ
Northern Russia, middle to the second half of the 17th century
Wood, gesso, tempera
152 × 122 cm
The State Historical Museum, Moscow, GIM 61847, I-VIII 5642

Cat. 57
Mother of God of Tolga
Kostroma, second half of the 17th century
Wood, gesso, tempera
114 × 98 cm
The State Historical Museum, Moscow, GIM 53054, I-VIII 5654

Cat. 58
N. Solomonov, P. Bilindin (?)
Enthroned Virgin
Moscow, Armory School, circa 1694
Wood, gesso, tempera
194 × 120 cm
The State Historical Museum, Moscow, GIM 80310, I-VIII 5643

Cat. 59
T. Filantyev
The Virgin Eleousa (Virgin of compassion or of mercy) of Kikkos
Moscow, late 17th century
Wood, gesso, tempera
118 × 78.6 cm
The State Historical Museum, Moscow, GIM 80310, I-VIII 3802

Cat. 60
Mother of God of the Sign
Kostroma, late 17th century
Wood, gesso, tempera
158.7 × 141.6 cm
The State Historical Museum, Moscow, GIM 108940, I-VIII 3420

Cat. 61
St. Nicolas
Moscow, 1737
62.5 × 27 cm
Wood, gesso, tempera
The State Historical Museum, Moscow, GIM 61847, I-VIII 2313

Cat. 62
Deacon I. Bessonov
Folding icons-basket
Middle: the Renewal of the Church in the name of Christ's Resurrection. Leaves: the Twelve Great Feasts
Moscow, 1741
Wood, gesso, tempera
84 × 122 cm (unfolded)
The State Historical Museum, Moscow, GIM 53054, I-VIII 3465

Cat. 63
Mother of God of Tolga
Kostroma, 1744
Wood, gesso, tempera
63 × 48.2 cm
The State Historical Museum, Moscow, GIM 53054, I-VIII 3741

Cat. 64
St. Basil the Blessed and Czarevich Dmitry in prayer
Moscow, early 19th century
Wood, gesso, tempera
142 × 97 cm
The State Historical Museum, Moscow, GIM 108818, I-VIII 5352

Cat. 65
Saints. Peter and Paul
Moscow, 1796
Wood, gesso, tempera
105 × 85 cm
The State Historical Museum, Moscow, GIM 108818, I-VIII 5353

Cat. 66
The Savior The Great Hierarch, on the Throne
Moscow, late 18th century to early 19th century
Wood, gesso, tempera
165 × 88 cm
The State Historical Museum, Moscow, GIM 99719, I-VIII 6092

Cat. 67
The Trinity of the Old Testament
Moscow, second half of the 19th century
Wood, gesso, tempera
158 × 89 cm
The State Historical Museum, Moscow, GIM 101285, I-VIII 6085

Cat. 68
St. Nicolas of Zaraisk with his hagiography
"Central Russia, seconde quarter of the 17th century" in regular typography
Wood, gesso, tempera
116 × 88 cm
The State Historical Museum, Moscow, GIM 54627, I-VIII 5303

Cat. 69
St. Alexius the Man of God
Moscow, circa 1650
Wood, gesso, tempera
138 × 101 cm
The State Historical Museum, Moscow, GIM 53054, I-VIII 5220
(Reproduced p. 52)

Cat. 70
Royal Gates
Russia, Yaroslav government, 18th century
Wood, sculpture, plaster coating, tempera, painting
165 × 45.5 × 12 cm;
165 × 40.6 × 5 cm
The State Historical Museum, Moscow, GIM 17166 shch/D.V – 1345/ 1, 2

Cat. 71 to 115
Iconostasis of the Trinity Church in Nikitniki
Coming from Saint Nikita Chapel in Moscow
circa 1634
Wood, gesso, tempera
(Reproduced p. 53)

Cat. 71
Patriarch Sabaoth, the Lord of Armies
Wood, gesso, tempera
98 × 55 cm
The State Historical Museum, Moscow, GIM 82848, I-VIII 3573

Cat. 72
Patriarch Noah
Wood, gesso, tempera
78.5 × 28 cm
The State Historical Museum, Moscow, GIM 82848, I-VIII 3575

Cat. 73
Patriarch Abraham
Wood, gesso, tempera
78.5 × 28 cm
The State Historical Museum, Moscow, GIM 82848, I-VIII 3886

Cat. 74
Patriarch Joseph
Wood, gesso, tempera
78.5 × 28 cm
The State Historical Museum, Moscow, GIM 82848, I-VIII 3887

Cat. 75
Patriarch Mahalalel
Wood, gesso, tempera
78.5 × 28 cm
The State Historical Museum, Moscow, GIM 82848, I-VIII 3890

Cat. 76
Patriarch Arphakshad
Wood, gesso, tempera
78.5 × 28 cm
The State Historical Museum, Moscow, GIM 82848, I-VIII 3574

Cat. 77
Patriarch Enos
Wood, gesso, tempera
78.5 × 28 cm
The State Historical Museum, Moscow, GIM 82848, I-VIII 3885

Cat. 78
Patriarch Methuselah
Wood, gesso, tempera
78.5 × 28 cm
The State Historical Museum, Moscow, GIM 82848, I-VIII 3888

Cat. 79
Patriarch Kenan
Wood, gesso, tempera
78.5 × 28 cm
The State Historical Museum, Moscow, GIM 82848, I-VIII 3889

Cat. 80
Patriarch Yared
Wood, gesso, tempera
78.5 × 28
The State Historical Museum, Moscow, GIM 82848, I-VIII 3892

Cat. 81
Patriarch Enoch
Wood, gesso, tempera
78.5 × 28 cm
The State Historical Museum, Moscow, GIM 82848, I-VIII 3891

Cat. 82
The Mother of God on the Throne
Wood, gesso, tempera
76 × 55 cm
The State Historical Museum, Moscow, GIM 82848, I-VIII 3898

Cat. 83
Prophet Habakkuk
Wood, gesso, tempera
76 × 28 cm
The State Historical Museum, Moscow, GIM 82848, I-VIII 3897

Cat. 84
Prophet Ezekiel
Wood, gesso, tempera
76 × 28 cm
The State Historical Museum, Moscow, GIM 82848, I-VIII 3902

Cat. 85
Prophet Elijah
Wood, gesso, tempera
76 × 27 cm
The State Historical Museum, Moscow, GIM 82848, I-VIII 3894

Cat. 86
St. Simeon the Receiver of God
Wood, gesso, tempera
76 × 28 cm
The State Historical Museum, Moscow, GIM 82848, I-VIII 3895

Cat. 87
Joachim
Wood, gesso, tempera

79 × 28 cm
The State Historical Museum, Moscow, GIM 82848, I-VIII 3893

Cat. 88
Saint Anne
Wood, gesso, tempera
76 × 28 cm
The State Historical Museum, Moscow, GIM 82848, I-VIII 3899

Cat. 89
Prophet Sophony
Wood, gesso, tempera
76 × 28 cm
The State Historical Museum, Moscow, GIM 82848, I-VIII 3896

Cat. 90
Prophet Zachary
Wood, gesso, tempera
76 × 28 cm
The State Historical Museum, Moscow, GIM 82848, I-VIII 3900

Cat. 91
Prophet Elisha
Wood, gesso, tempera
76 × 28 cm
The State Historical Museum, Moscow, GIM 82848, I-VIII 3901

Cat. 92
Prophet Nahum
Wood, gesso, tempera
76 × 28 cm
The State Historical Museum, Moscow, GIM 82848, I-VIII 3903

Cat. 93
The Savior among the Heavenly Powers
Wood, gesso, tempera
89.5 × 56.3 cm
The State Historical Museum, Moscow, GIM 82848, I-VIII 5268

Cat. 94
The Mother of God
Wood, gesso, tempera
89 × 28 cm
The State Historical Museum, Moscow, GIM 82848, I-VIII 3576

Cat. 95
John the Baptist
Wood, gesso, tempera
89.5 × 28 cm
The State Historical Museum, Moscow, GIM 82848, I-VIII 3577

Cat. 96
Apostle Peter
Wood, gesso, tempera
89 × 28 cm
The State Historical Museum, Moscow, GIM 82848, I-VIII 3918

Cat. 97
Apostle Paul
Wood, gesso, tempera
89 × 28 cm
The State Historical Museum, Moscow, GIM 82848, I-VIII 3921

Cat. 98
The Archangel Michael
Wood, gesso, tempera
90 × 28 cm
The State Historical Museum, Moscow, GIM 82848, I-VIII 3919

Cat. 99
The Archangel Gabriel
Wood, gesso, tempera
90 × 28 cm
The State Historical Museum, Moscow, GIM 82848, I-VIII 3920

Cat. 100
The Apostle Matthew
Wood, gesso, tempera
90 × 28 cm
The State Historical Museum, Moscow, GIM 82848, I-VIII 3917

Cat. 101
The Apostle John
Wood, gesso, tempera
89 × 28 cm
The State Historical Museum, Moscow, GIM 82848, I-VIII 3922

Cat. 102
The Apostle Mark
Wood, gesso, tempera
89 × 28 cm
The State Historical Museum, Moscow, GIM 82848, I-VIII 3916

Cat. 103
The Apostle Luke
Wood, gesso, tempera
90 × 28 cm
The State Historical Museum, Moscow, GIM 82848, I-VIII 3923

Cat. 104
The Crucifixion
Wood, gesso, tempera
45 × 27 cm
The State Historical Museum, Moscow, GIM 82848, I-VIII 3910

Cat. 105
The Resurrection – the Descent into Hell
Wood, gesso, tempera
45 × 27 cm
The State Historical Museum, Moscow, GIM 82848, I-VIII 3911

Cat. 106
Healing of the blind
Wood, gesso, tempera
45 × 27 cm
The State Historical Museum, Moscow, GIM 82848, I-VIII 3906

Cat. 107
Conversation with the Woman of Samaria
Wood, gesso, tempera
45 × 27 cm
The State Historical Museum, Moscow, GIM 82848, I-VIII 3905

Cat. 108
Healing of the paralytic
Wood, gesso, tempera
45 × 27 cm
The State Historical Museum, Moscow, GIM 82848, I-VIII 3907

Cat. 109
The Ascension
Wood, gesso, tempera
45 × 27 cm
The State Historical Museum, Moscow, GIM 82848, I-VIII 3914

Cat. 110
The Descent of the Holy Spirit
Wood, gesso, tempera
45 × 27 cm
The State Historical Museum, Moscow, GIM 82848, I-VIII 3915

Cat. 111
Halfway through Pentecost
Wood, gesso, tempera
45 × 27 cm
The State Historical Museum, Moscow, GIM 82848, I-VIII 3908

Cat. 112
The Women Myrrh Bearers
Wood, gesso, tempera
45 × 27 cm
The State Historical Museum, Moscow, GIM 82848, I-VIII 3912

Cat. 113
Entrance into Jerusalem
Wood, gesso, tempera
45 × 27 cm
The State Historical Museum, Moscow, GIM 82848, I-VIII 3909

Cat. 114
The Resurrection of Lazarus
Wood, gesso, tempera
45 × 27 cm
The State Historical Museum, Moscow, GIM 82848, I-VIII 3904

Cat. 115
Thomas's Conviction
Wood, gesso, tempera
45 × 27 cm
The State Historical Museum, Moscow, GIM 82848, I-VIII 3913

Cat. 116
Altar cross
Russia, Moscow, P. I. Olovianichnikov firm, 1917
Silver
29.2 × 14.8 cm
The State Historical Museum, Moscow, GIM 76286 OK 10138

Cat. 117
Tabernacle
Russia, Moscow, 1788
Silver, enamel
69 × 30 × 26 cm
The State Historical Museum, Moscow, GIM 76308 OK 9470
(Reproduced p. 95)

Cat. 118
Chalice
Russia. Moscow, 1752
Silver

H. 33.1 cm
The State Historical Museum, Moscow, GIM 68257/267 OK 6898
(Reproduced p. 97)

Cat. 119
Receptacle "for the evening service" (for the blessing of the bread, the wheat, the wine and the oil)
Russia, Moscow, 1789
Silver
66 × 40 × 40 cm
The State Historical Museum, Moscow, GIM 80121 OK 11872

Cat. 120
Master E. V. Ikornikov
Chalice
Russia, Moscow, 1795
Silver, enamel
40 × 15.3 cm
The State Historical Museum, Moscow, GIM 77169 OK 9859

Cat. 121
Master I. A. Ostrovsky
Discos (paten)
Russia, Veliky Ustyyug, end of 18th century
Silver
H. 12.8 cm
The State Historical Museum, Moscow, GIM 78726 OK 11236

Cat. 122
Wedding crown
Russia, Moscow, 1740
Gold, silver, diamonds, rubies, sapphires, emeralds, cultured pearls, spinel, quartz, enamel, small pearls, glass, copper
H. 26 cm
The State Historical Museum, Moscow, GIM 77681/1 OK 10985

Cat. 123
Wedding crown
Russia, Moscow, 1740
Gold, silver, diamonds, rubies, sapphires, emeralds, cultured pearls, spinel, quartz, enamel, small pearls
H. 26 cm
The State Historical Museum, Moscow, GIM 77681/2 OK 10986

Cat. 124
Icon "The Crucifixion with those who were present"
Russia, Moscow, second half of the 17th century
Silver, enamel, wood
25.4 × 21.5 cm
The State Historical Museum, Moscow, GIM 58383/91 OK 10069

Cat. 125
Icon of enamel miniatures with painted images
Russia, Moscow, 1805
Silver, enamel, wood, copper, fabric
32 × 26.3 cm
The State Historical Museum, Moscow, GIM 77364 OK 10630

Cat. 126
Icon "Saint Nicholas the Thaumaturge"
Russia, Moscow, 1807
Silver, wood
30.3 × 26.1 cm
The State Historical Museum, Moscow, GIM 77356 OK 10048

Cat. 127
Icon "St. Paphnutius of Borovsk"
Russia, Moscow, 1780
Silver, enamel, wood
30 × 27.7 cm
The State Historical Museum, Moscow, GIM 58383/93 OK 8130

Cat. 128
Icon "Saint Nicholas the Thaumaturge"
Russia, Moscow, second half of the 17th century
Silver, wood
26.1 × 21.7 cm
The State Historical Museum, Moscow, GIM 6123 shch OK 10087

Cat. 129
Icon Diesis "in bust"
Russia, Moscow, beginning of the 18th century
Silver, wood, fabric, gild
16 × 28.7 cm
The State Historical Museum, Moscow, GIM 2067 shch OK 10076

Cat. 130
Icon "The Virgin of Bogolubovo"
Russia, 1772
Silver, wood, gild
36 × 29.2 cm
The State Historical Museum, Moscow, GIM 16147 shch OK 9463

Cat. 131
Image of the "Nine Martyrs and Saint Mamont"
Russia, Moscow, 1779
Silver, rubies, goshenit, wood, paint
43 × 36 cm
The State Historical Museum, Moscow, GIM 95475 OK 14901

Cat. 132
Liturgical linen representing Saints Zosima and Savvatii of Solovky
Russia, Solvytchegodsk, workmanship by D. A. Stroganov's wife, 1670s
Satin, taffeta, silver and gold wiredrawn thread, twisted thread, colored silk thread
33.5 × 26.5 cm
The State Historical Museum, Moscow, GIM 15657 shch RB-10
(Reproduced p. 69)

Cat. 133
Liturgical cuff (Annunciation: The Archangel)
Russia, first quarter of 18th century
Velvet, cloth, paper, silver and gold wiredrawn thread
19.3 × 28.5 cm
The State Historical Museum, Moscow, GIM 18971 shch RB-1096/1

Cat. 134
Liturgical cuff (Annunciation: the Virgin Mary)
Russia, first quarter of 18th century
Velvet, cloth, paper, silver and gold wiredrawn thread
19.1 × 29 cm
The State Historical Museum, Moscow, GIM 15971 shch RB-1096/2

Cat. 135
Liturgical linen representing the Very Orthodox Princes Feodor, David and Constantine
Russia, second half of the 17th century
Damask, gold and silver wiredrawn thread, colored silk thread
63.5 × 54.5 cm
The State Historical Museum, Moscow, GIM 15116 RB-116
(Reproduced p. 71)

Cat. 136
Stole (epitrakhelion)
Southern Russia (?), 18th century
Satin, cotton, silver and gold wiredrawn thread, silver lamé, silk colored thread
144.5 × 30.5 cm
The State Historical Museum, Moscow, GIM 78142/ 92 RB-3732
(Reproduced p. 74)

Cat. 137
Paten veil or chalice, "Transfiguration"
Russia, second half of 19th century
Velvet, taffeta, chenille, silver and gold wiredrawn thread, whorls of gold and silver, silver and gold thread lamé, gold purl, sequins, small gold plates with subject, in form of rosettes
56 × 55 cm
The State Historical Museum, Moscow, GIM 85179 RB-4782

Cat. 138
Chalice veil: "Christ carrying the Cross"
Russia, second half of 19th century
Velvet, taffeta, silver and gold wiredrawn thread, whorls of gold and silver, silver and gold thread lamé, gold purl, sequins, small gold plates with subject, in form of rosettes
56.5 × 56 cm
The State Historical Museum, Moscow, GIM 85263 RB-4781

Cat. 139
Altar curtain
Russia, beginning of 20th century
Velvet, brocade, taffeta, braid, gold wiredrawn thread, silk threads, metal
228 × 91.5 cm
The State Historical Museum, Moscow, GIM 56740 RB-1935
(Reproduced p. 81)

Cat. 140
Veil covering the paten and the chalice (aer), "The Last Supper"
Russia, middle to second half of the 19th century
Velvet, taffeta, silver and gold wiredrawn thread, whorls of gold and silver, silver and gold thread lamé, gold purl, sequins, small gold plates with subject in form of rosettes
56 × 78 cm
The State Historical Museum, Moscow, GIM 85233 RB-4733

Cat. 141
Chalice veil
Southern Russia (?), 18th century
Satin, silk cloth, silver and gold wiredrawn thread, silver lamé, silk colored thread
43 × 43 cm
The State Historical Museum, Moscow, GIM 78142/ 291 RB-3724

Cat. 142
Chalice veil "The Virgin of the Sign"
Southern Russia (?), 18th century
Satin, silk cloth, gold and silver wiredrawn threads, silver lamé, colored silk thread
43.5 x 41.5 cm
The State Historical Museum, Moscow, GIM 78142/ 292 RB-3725

Cat. 143
Veil covering the paten and the chalice (aer) "The Last Supper"
Russia, second half of 18th century
Damask silk fabric, cotton, silver and gold wiredrawn thread
55 × 57.5 cm
The State Historical Museum, Moscow, GIM 23991 RB-481/1

Cat. 144
Paten veil (The Lamb of God)
Russia, second half of the 18th century
Damask silk fabric, cotton, silver and gold wiredrawn thread
42 × 44.5 cm
The State Historical Museum, Moscow, GIM 23992 RB-481/2
(Reproduced p. 73)

Cat. 145
Chalice veil
Russia, second half of 18th century
Damask silk fabric, cotton, silver and gold wiredrawn thread
48 × 49.5 cm
The State Historical Museum, Moscow, GIM 23989 RB-482

Cat. 146
Paten or chalice veil (Lamb of God)
Russia, first half of the 17th century
Damask, silk twisted thread, gold and silver wire-drawn thread, metal
46.5 × 47.5 cm
The State Historical Museum, Moscow, GIM 15815 shch RB-53
(Reproduced p. 70)

Cat. 147
Paten or chalice veil (The Virgin of the Sign)
Russia, first half of the 17th century
Damask, cloth, twisted silk thread, silver and gold wire-drawn threads, metal
46.5 × 47.5 cm
The State Historical Museum, Moscow, GIM 15816 shch RB-54
(Reproduced p. 70)

Cat. 148
Anonymous
Portrait of Czar Alex Mikhailovich
Middle of 18th century
Oil on canvas
91 × 72 cm
The State Historical Museum, Moscow, GIM 90536/I 1-5618

Cat. 149
Anonymous
Portrait of the Czar Michael Feodorovich and its frame
18th century
Oil on canvas
83 × 69 cm
Rectangular frame in sculpted wood: second half of 18th century (94.5 × 78.8 cm)
State Ceramics Museum and 18th century Kuskovo estate, J-13 KP 13528, R-114 KP 14396

Cat. 150
Anonymous
Portrait of Emperor Peter I
1697
Oil on canvas
74 × 54 cm
The State Historical Museum, Moscow, GIM 15999 shch/ I 1-288

Cat. 151
Anonymous
Equestrian portrait of Empress Elizabeth Petrovna
Middle of the 18th century
Oil on canvas
51 × 43 cm
The State Historical Museum, Moscow, GIM 16744 shch/ I 1-1854

Cat. 152
Anonymous. Based on an original by G. H. Grooth
Portrait of Emperor Peter III
1750s
Oil on canvas
89 × 71 cm
The State Historical Museum, Moscow, GIM 92455/ I 1-4184

Cat. 153
Anonymous. Based on a original by G. H. Grooth
Portrait of Empress Catherine II
1750s
Oil on canvas
90 × 71 cm
The State Historical Museum, Moscow, GIM 16842 shch/ I 1-1834

Cat. 154
Jean-Louis Voille
Portrait of Emperor Paul I
Years 1797-1798
Oil on canvas
74 × 57.5 cm
The State Historical Museum, Moscow, GIM 77716/ I 1-2831

Cat. 155
Anonymous. Based on an original by A. Roslin, 1777
Portrait of Grand Duchess Maria Feodorovna
D. G. Devitsky's studio, 1780s
Oil on canvas
85 × 66 cm
The State Historical Museum, Moscow, GIM 16845 shch/ I 1-2474

Cat. 156
Anonymous
Portrait of Emperor Alexander I (1777-1825)
Middle of the 19th century
Oil on canvas
98 × 74 cm
The State Historical Museum, Moscow, GIM 13597 shch/I 1-3391

Cat. 157
Anonymous. Based on a original by G. von Kügelgen
Portrait of Elizabeth Alexeivna
1802
Oil on canvas
55 × 46 cm (oval)
The State Historical Museum, Moscow, GIM 13584 shch/ I 1-2152

Cat. 158
A. P. Schwabe
Equestrian portrait of Emperor Nicholas I (1796-1855)
1843
Canvas on oil
139 × 100 cm
The State Historical Museum, Moscow, GIM 68257/ I 1-4144

Cat. 159
F. Krüger
Portrait of Empress Alexandra Feodorovna (1798-1860)
Russia, St. Petersburg, post 1836
Oil on canvas
135 × 92 cm
The State Historical Museum, Moscow, GIM 91989/ I 1-3556
(Reproduced p. 148)

Cat. 160
N. E. Svertchkov
Portrait of Emperor Alexander II (1818-1881)
1871
Oil on canvas
74 × 98 cm
The State Historical Museum, Moscow, GIM 72318/ I 1-2139

Cat. 161
Anonymous
Portrait of Emperor Alexander II
Russia, 1870s
Oil on canvas
77 × 91 cm (oval)
The State Museum Preserve "Tsarskoye Selo," St. Petersburg, ED-348-X
(Reproduced p. 21)

Cat. 162
N. D. Dmitriev-Orenburgsky
Portrait of Emperor Alexander III (1845-1894)
posthumous portrait 1896
Oil on canvas
310 × 139.5 cm
The State Historical Museum, Moscow, GIM 68257/13812/ I 1-5964
(Reproduced p. 21)

Cat. 163
N. F. Yash
Portrait of Emperor Nicholas II (1868-1918)
1896
Oil on canvas
240 × 175 cm
The State Historical Museum, Moscow, GIM 68257/ I 1-4991

Cat. 164
A. V. Makovsky
Portrait of Empress Alexandra Feodorovna (1872-1918)
1914
Oil on canvas
115 × 76 cm
The State Historical Museum, Moscow, GIM 65858/ I 1-3962
(Reproduced p. 190)

Cat. 165
Vase on the stem of which figures a young peasant
Guriev table service pieces, Imperial Porcelain Manufacture, 1809-1816
Porcelain, underglaze and polychrome overglaze design, gilding, guilloche
H. 44.7 cm
State Ceramics Museum and 18th century Kuskovo estate, FR 8989 KP 15452

Cat. 166
Vase on the stem of which figures a young peasant
Guriev table service pieces, Imperial Porcelain Manufacture, 1809-1816
Porcelain, underglaze and polychrome overglaze design, gilding, guilloche
H. 33.8 cm
State Ceramics Museum and 18th century Kuskovo estate, FR 10502 KP 15460

Cat. 167
Vase on the stem of which figures a young woman peasant
Guriev table service pieces, Imperial Porcelain Manufacture, 1809-1816
Porcelain, underglaze and polychrome overglaze design, gilding, guilloche
H. 34.5 cm
State Ceramics Museum and 18th century Kuskovo estate, FR 10676KP 15461
(Reproduced p. 124)

Cat. 168
Vase in the form of an eagle, on small pedestal
Guriev table service pieces, Imperial Porcelain Manufacture, 1809-1816
Porcelain, underglaze and polychrome overglaze design, gilding, guilloche
H. 16.6 cm
State Ceramics Museum and 18th century Kuskovo estate, FR 4190/1-2 KP 15450/1-2

Cat. 169
Vase in the form of an eagle, on small pedestal
Guriev table service pieces, Imperial Porcelain Manufacture, 1809-1816
Porcelain, underglaze and polychrome overglaze design, gilding, guilloche
H. 16.6 cm
State Ceramics Museum and 18th century Kuskovo estate, FR 10559/1-2 KP 15463/1-2

Cat. 170
Vase with stem representing a young girl
Guriev table service pieces, Imperial Porcelain Manufacture, 1809-1816
Porcelain, underglaze and polychrome overglaze design, gilding, guilloche
H. 20.2 cm
State Ceramics Museum and 18th century Kuskovo estate, FR 10558/1-3 KP 15462/1-3

Cat. 171
Plate "Child's game in the spring"
Guriev table service pieces, Imperial Porcelain Manufacture, 1809-1816
Porcelain, underglaze and polychrome overglaze design, gilding, guilloche
Diam. 25 cm
State Ceramics Museum and 18th century Kuskovo estate, FR 8724 KP 15451

Cat. 172
Small plate "Young Countrywoman"
Guriev table service pieces, Imperial Porcelain Manufacture, 1809-1816
Porcelain, underglaze and polychrome overglaze design, gilding, guilloche
Diam. 25 cm
State Ceramics Museum and 18th century Kuskovo estate, FR 10097 KP 15453
(Reproduced p. 130)

Cat. 173
Small plate "Easter custom"
Guriev table service pieces, Imperial Porcelain Manufacture, 1809-1816
Porcelain, underglaze and polychrome overglaze design, gilding, guilloche
Diam. 25 cm
State Ceramics Museum and 18th century Kuskovo estate, FR 10098 KP 15454
(Reproduced p. 130)

Cat. 174
Small plate "Itinerant merchant of icons and icon coverings"
Guriev table service pieces, Imperial Porcelain Manufacture, 1809-1816
Porcelain, underglaze and polychrome overglaze design, gilding, guilloche
Diam. 25 cm
State Ceramics Museum and 18th century Kuskovo estate, FR 10099 KP 15455

Cat. 175
Plate "Nurse and milk seller from Okhta"
Guriev table service pieces, Imperial Porcelain Manufacture, 1809-1816
Porcelain, underglaze and polychrome overglaze design, gilding, guilloche
Diam. 25 cm
State Ceramics Museum and 18th century Kuskovo estate, FR 10100 KP 15456

Cat. 176
Small plate "Itinerant flower seller"
Guriev table service pieces, Imperial Porcelain Manufacture, 1809-1816
Porcelain, underglaze and polychrome overglaze design, gilding, guilloche
Diam. 25 cm
State Ceramics Museum and 18th century Kuskovo estate, FR 10101 KP 15457

Cat. 177
Plate "The Cossack Alexander Zemlianukhin"
Guriev table service pieces, Imperial Porcelain Manufacture, 1809-1816
Porcelain, underglaze and polychrome overglaze design, gilding, guilloche
Diam. 25 cm
State Ceramics Museum and 18th century Kuskovo estate, FR 10102 KP 15458
(Reproduced p. 131)

Cat. 178
Small plate "Tula woman peasant"
Guriev table service pieces, Imperial Porcelain Manufacture, 1809-1816
Porcelain, underglaze and polychrome overglaze design, gilding, guilloche
Diam. 24.5 cm
State Ceramics Museum and 18th century Kuskovo estate, FR 11299 KP 15464

Cat. 179
Small plate "Young girl from Valdai"
Guriev table service pieces, Imperial Porcelain Manufacture, 1809-1816
Porcelain, underglaze and polychrome overglaze design, gilding, guilloche
Diam. 24.7 cm
State Ceramics Museum and 18th century Kuskovo estate, FR 12336 KP 2287

Cat. 180
Small plate "A woman cook and a fisherman"
Guriev table service pieces, Imperial Porcelain Manufacture, 1809-1816

Porcelain, underglaze and polychrome overglaze design, gilding, guilloche
Diam. 24.5 cm
State Ceramics Museum and 18th century Kuskovo estate, FR 12337 KP 2288

Cat. 181
Small plate "Fruit and vegetable seller"
Guriev table service pieces, Imperial Porcelain Manufacture, 1809-1816
Porcelain, underglaze and polychrome overglaze design, gilding, guilloche
Diam. 24 cm
State Ceramics Museum and 18th century Kuskovo estate, FR 12338 KP 2289
(Reproduced p. 130)

Cat. 182
Small plate "Itinerant seller of diverse objects"
Guriev table service pieces, Imperial Porcelain Manufacture, 1809-1816
Porcelain, underglaze and polychrome overglaze design, gilding, guilloche
Diam. 24.6 cm
State Ceramics Museum and 18th century Kuskovo estate, FR 12339 KP 2290

Cat. 183
Round white plate with gilding decoration along the red-brown edge
Guriev table service pieces, Imperial Porcelain Manufacture, 1809-1816
Porcelain, underglaze and polychrome overglaze design, gilding, guilloche
Diam. 36.8 cm
State Ceramics Museum and 18th century Kuskovo estate, FR 58 KP 15449

Cat. 184
Round white plate with gilding decoration along the red-brown edge
Guriev table service pieces, Imperial Porcelain Manufacture, 1809-1816
Porcelain, underglaze and polychrome overglaze design, gilding, guilloche
Diam. 36.8 cm
State Ceramics Museum and 18th century Kuskovo estate, FR 1570 KP 15448

Cat. 185
Large cylindrical glass with representation of architectural views within medallions
Russia, 1st third of the 19th century
Clear glass, cut, gold and silver design
H. 15.1 cm
State Ceramics Museum and 18th century Kuskovo estate, ST-1062 KP-23565

Cat. 186
Large conical glass with male figures on a landscape background
Russia, 1st third of 19th century
Clear glass, cut, gold and silver design
H. 16 cm
State Ceramics Museum and 18th century Kuskovo estate, ST-1073 KP-23576

Cat. 187
Large cylindrical glass with initials in a medallion
Russia, 1st third of 19th century
Clear glass, cut, gold and silver design
H. 16 cm
State Ceramics Museum and 18th century Kuskovo estate, ST-1074 KP-23577

Cat. 188
Large cylindrical glass with flowers, birds and foliated pattern
Russia, 1st third of 19th century
Clear glass, cut, gold and silver design
H. 16.2 cm
State Ceramics Museum and 18th century Kuskovo estate, ST-1076 KP-23579

Cat. 189
Large cylindrical glass with flowers and butterflies
Russia, 1st third of 19th century
Clear glass, cut, polished, gold and silver design
H. 15.7 cm
State Ceramics Museum and 18th century Kuskovo estate, ST-1445 KP-26381

Cat. 190
Small cylindrical glass with landscape of ruins
Russia, 1st third of 19th century
Clear glass, cut, gold and silver design
H. 16.3 cm
State Ceramics Museum and 18th century Kuskovo estate, ST-2511 KP-4980

Cat. 191
Large tapered glass decorated with gilded stars and a stylized vegetal design
Russia, 1st quarter of 19th century
Clear glass, cut, gold design
H. 16.2 cm
State Ceramics Museum and 18th century Kuskovo estate, ST-1604 KP-26519

Cat. 192
Large tapered glass decorated with gilded stars and a stylized vegetal design
Russia, 1st quarter of 19th century
Clear glass, cut, gold design
H. 16.2 cm
State Ceramics Museum and 18th century Kuskovo estate, ST-1605 KP-26520

Cat. 193
Large tapered glass decorated with gilded stars and a stylized vegetal design
Russia, 1st quarter of 19th century
Clear glass, cut, gold design
H. 16 cm
State Ceramics Museum and 18th century Kuskovo estate, ST-1606 KP-26521

Cat. 194
Large tapered glass decorated with gilded stars and a stylized vegetal design
Russia, 1st quarter of 19th century
Clear glass, cut, gold design
H. 16.1 cm
State Ceramics Museum and 18th century Kuskovo estate, ST-1607 KP-26522

Cat. 195
Large tapered glass decorated with gilded stars and a stylized vegetal design
Russia, 1st quarter of 19th century
Clear glass, cut, gold design
H. 16 cm
State Ceramics Museum and 18th century Kuskovo estate, ST-1610 KP-26524

Cat. 196
Large tapered glass decorated with gilded stars and a stylized vegetal design
Russia, 1st quarter of 19th century
Clear glass, cut, gold design
H. 16.1 cm
State Ceramics Museum and 18th century Kuskovo estate, ST-1611 KP-26525

Cat. 197
Corked decanter in cylindrical form, with a cupid near a rectangular altar with a fire
Russia, 1st half of 19th century
Clear glass, cut, engraving
H. 28.6 cm
State Ceramics Museum and 18th century Kuskovo estate, ST-642/1-2 KP-18379/1-2

Cat. 198
Corked decanter with cupids
Russia, 1st third of 19th century
Clear class, cut, mat engraving
H. 28.6 cm
State Ceramics Museum and 18th century Kuskovo estate, ST-4090/1-2 KP-9710/1-2

Cat. 199
Bronze candelabra with three arms in the form of a winged woman dressed in antique clothing
Russia, 1st quarter of the 18th century
Bronze, copper, metal, casting, engraving, gilding, patina, assemblage
90.1 × 26.5 cm
State Ceramics Museum and 18th century Kuskovo estate, OS -72 KP 14673

Cat. 200
Bronze candelabra with three arms in the form of a winged woman dressed in antique clothing
Russia, 1st quarter of the 18th century

Metal, casting, engraving, gilding, patina, assemblage
91.5 × 26.5 cm
State Ceramics Museum and 18th century Kuskovo estate, OS -73 KP 24073

Cat. 201
Chain and insignia of the order of Saint Andrew the First Called with 17 rings (for a child). Belonged to the Imperial family.
1856
Gold, enamel
l. 71 cm
The State Historical Museum, Moscow, GIM 93355/ KP ON 786981

Cat. 202
Star of the order of Saint Andrew the First Called (for child). Belonged to the Imperial family
1856
Silver, enamel
7.5 × 7.5 cm
The State Historical Museum, Moscow, GIM 93355/ KP ON 786982

Cat. 203
Insignia of the order of Saint Anne second class with crown
1855-1874
Gold, enamel
4.3 × 6.6 cm
The State Historical Museum, Moscow, GIM 93355/ KP ON 787021

Cat. 204
Insignia of the order of Saint Anne second class with brilliants
Second quarter of 19th century
Gold, silver, enamel, glass
3.7 × 4.2 cm
The State Historical Museum, Moscow, GIM 93355/ KP ON 787020

Cat. 205
Star of the order of Saint Alexander Nevsky with brilliants
Middle of 19th century
Gold, silver, enamel, strass
8.5 × 8.5 cm
The State Historical Museum, Moscow, GIM 93355/ KP ON 787429

Cat. 206
Initials of a lady-in-waiting with the monogram "A" of the Empress Alexandra Feodorovna (1828-1855)
Gold, silver, glass
The State Historical Museum, Moscow, GIM 93356/ KP ON 800790

Cat. 207
Insignia of the Order of St. Andrew the First Called. Belonged to Napoleon I
Beginning of 19th century
Gold, enamel
6 × 10 cm
The State Historical Museum, Moscow, GIM 82005/ KP ON 917369

Cat. 208
Insignia of the order of Saint Stanislaw second class with crown
Third quarter of 19th century
Gold, enamel
4.6 × 7.7 cm
The State Historical Museum, Moscow, GIM 95591/ KP ON 996024

Cat. 209
Star of the order of Saint Andrew the First Called with brilliants. Belonged to the General Field Marshal A. I. Bariatinsky
1862
Gold, silver, enamel, brilliants, glass
11.4 × 11.4 cm
The State Historical Museum, Moscow, GIM 93375/ KP ON 913493

Cat. 210
Insignia of the Order of St. Andrew the First Called with brilliants. Belonged to General Field Marshal A. I. Bariatinsky
1862
Gold, silver, enamel, brilliants, garnets, glass
7 × 10.6 cm
The State Historical Museum, Moscow, GIM 93375/ KP ON 913492

Cat. 211
Emperor Alexander I's throne
Russia, first quarter of the 19th century
Made from a project designed by A. de Montferrand
Oak, limewood, sculpture, wheel work, plaster coating, gilding, velvet
135 × 96 × 63 cm
The State Historical Museum, Moscow, GIM 47744/D II – 1502

Cat. 212 and 213
Pair of candelabras with nine branches
Moscow, 1930s
Bronze, glass
99 × 52 × 20 cm
The State Historical Museum, Moscow, GIM 62182 BR 830/1-2

Cat. 214
Drawing Room Armchair
Russia, Tula government, second third of 19th century
Walnut, sculpture, matte varnish, bronze, velvet, wool, embroidery
97.4 × 50 × 56 cm
The State Historical Museum, Moscow, GIM 83864/D II – 2131
(Reproduced p. 138)

Cat. 215
Torch Holder
Russia, St. Petersburg, Hambs Brothers workshop, middle of 19th century
Walnut, sculpture, wheel work, varnish
184 × 41 × 41 cm
The State Historical Museum, Moscow, GIM 70488/ D II – 1176
(Reproduced p. 139)

Cat. 216
Small vase with lid with the portraits of Emperor Alexander I, and Empress Elisabeth Alexeievna
Imperial Porcelain Manufacture, 1st quarter of the 19th century
Porcelain, moulding, polychrome overglaze, gilding, guilloche
H. 16.9 cm
State Ceramics Museum and 18th century Kuskovo estate, FR 7213/1-2 KP 16280/1-2
(Reproduced p. 133)

Cat. 217
Cup and saucer with the portrait of Empress Elisabeth Alexeievna
Imperial Porcelain Manufacture, 1810.
Porcelain, relief, mat underglaze, gilding
H. 11.2 cm
State Ceramics Museum and 18th century Kuskovo estate, FR 5825/1-2 KP 28781/1-2

Cat. 218
Cup with the portrait of Emperor Alexander I
Gardner Manufacture, 1810
Porcelain, polychrome overglaze, gilding, guilloche
H. 10 cm
State Ceramics Museum and 18th century Kuskovo estate, FR 6422/1-2 KP 27789/1-2
(Reproduced pp. 127 and 133)

Cat. 219
Cup and saucer with the portrait of Grand Duke Constantine Pavlovich
Brothers Novy Manufacture, years 1820-1830
Porcelain, polychrome overglaze, gilding, silvering
H. 13.7 cm
State Ceramics Museum and 18th century Kuskovo estate, FR 4352/1-2 KP 21055/1-2

Cat. 220
Cup and saucer with the portrait of Emperor Nicholas I
Batenin Manufacture, end of the 1820s
Porcelain, polychrome overglaze, gilding
H. 17.8 cm
State Ceramics Museum and 18th century Kuskovo estate, FR 6948/1-2 KP 29585/1-2

Cat. 221
Cup and saucer with the portrait of Empress Alexandra Feodorovna
Batenin Manufacture, end of the 1820s
Porcelain, polychrome overglaze, gilding, guilloche
H. 10.1 cm
State Ceramics Museum and 18th century Kuskovo estate, FR 7061/1-2 KP 19162/1-2

Cat. 222
Gilded cup with the portrait of the Grand Duke Alexander

Nicholaevich as a child
Batenin Manufacture, end of the 1820s
Porcelain, polychrome overglaze, gilding, guilloche
H. 9.8 cm
State Ceramics Museum and 18th century Kuskovo estate, FR 7295/1-2 KP 28998/1-2

Cat. 223
Dark blue glass with saucer decorated with the portraits of Grand Duke Alexander Nicholaevich and Maria Alexandrovna
Safronov Manufacture, beginning of the 1840s
Porcelain, underglaze and glaze design, gilding
H. 11.1 cm
State Ceramics Museum and 18th century Kuskovo estate, FR 6603/1-2 KP 27270/1-2

Cat. 224
Tumbler with lid with the portrait of Empress Elizabeth Petrovna and her monogram within the State coat of arms
Russia, St. Petersburg Glassworks Manufacture, 1750s
Clear glass, cut, engraved, gilded
H. 32.7 cm
The State Historical Museum, Moscow, GIM 88487/1690 cm

Cat. 225
Tumbler with lid representing the State Coat of Arms with the monogram of Empress Elizabeth Petrovna
Russia, St. Petersburg Glassworks Manufacture, 1750s
Clear glass, cut, engraved
H. 23.7 cm
The State Historical Museum, Moscow, GIM 62538/1522 cm

Cat. 226
Tumbler with lid with the portrait of Empress Catherine II and her monogram within the State Coat of Arms
Russia, St. Petersburg Glassworks Manufacture, 1770s
Clear glass, cut, engraved
H. 35.6 cm
The State Historical Museum, Moscow, GIM 17587/1628 cm

Cat. 227
Tall glass with the portrait of M. I. Kutuzov and the inscription, "He is living! He is immortal! He who saved the Homeland."
Russia, St. Petersburg Glassworks Manufacture, 1810s
Clear crystal, milky white glass, cut in facets, painting in grisaille
H. 18.1 cm
The State Historical Museum, Moscow, GIM 13715 shch/1778 cm

Cat. 228
Tall glass with the image of the map of Europe and the goddess of Victory flying above it
Russia, St. Petersburg Glassworks Manufacture, 1810s
Clear crystal, milky white glass, cut in facets, painting, gilding
H. 13.5 cm
The State Historical Museum, Moscow, GIM 13708 shch/3885 cm

Cat. 229
Tumbler with lid with the portrait of Emperor Alexander I and the inscription "Long Live Alexander I"
Russia, St. Petersburg Glassworks Manufacture, first quarter of the 19th century
Clear crystal, milky white glass, cut in facets, painted in grisaille, gilded
H. 14.5 cm
The State Historical Museum, Moscow, GIM 13722-shch/3873 cm

Cat. 230
Tall glass with the monogram of Emperor Alexander I and the inscription, "November 8, 1815 World Peace."
Russia, St. Petersburg Glassworks Manufacture, 1810s
Clear crystal, milky white glass, diamond-cut, gold painting
H. 12.2 cm
The State Historical Museum, Moscow, GIM 13719 shch/3874 cm

Cat. 231
"Russian" court dress
Russia, end of 19th century-beginning of 20th
Watered fabric, silk, velvet, gauze, gold thread, feathers, cloth, lace, sequins
Length of the skirt: 121 cm; length of the train: 258 cm
Moscow, Kremlin Museums, Tk-3494/1-3

Cat. 232
"Russian" Court dress
Germany, Frankfurt-on-Main, 1898-1914 (?)
Velvet, satin, satin ribbon, silk, silver lace, fringe, sequins, silver thread, lace, gauze, satin ribbon, silk fringe
Length of the skirt: 175 cm; length of the train: 315 cm
Moscow, Kremlin Museums, Tk-3493/1/3

Cat. 233
Bowl
Russia, Solvychegodsk, late 17th century
Silver, enamel
3.9 × 15.2 × 15.2 cm
The State Historical Museum, Moscow, GIM 80868 OK 14072

Cat. 234
Little chest
Russia, Solvytchegodsk, last quarter of 17th century.
Enamel, wood, copper, paper, mica, wax; gilding, filigree, drawing, painting
8.5 × 11.2 × 8.5 cm
The State Historical Museum, Moscow, GIM 18249shch OK 728

Cat. 235
Tankard with lid
Russia, Moscow, end of 17th-early 18th century
Silver
H. 17 cm
The State Historical Museum, Moscow, GIM 41515 OK 3704
(Reproduced p. 19)

Cat. 236
Plate
Russia, Moscow, Kremlin Workshops, end of 17th century
Silver
Diam. 21.1 cm
The State Historical Museum, Moscow, GIM 428 shch OK 888
(Reproduced pp. 84 and 93)

Cat. 237
Tumbler (stopa)
Russia, Moscow, 1690-1691
Silver
H. 21.8 cm
The State Historical Museum, Moscow, GIM 50146 OK 1021
(Reproduced p. 89)

Cat. 238
Ladle (kovch) of the Grand Duke Vasily Vasilyevich Golitsyn
Russia, Moscow, end of the 16th-early 17th century
Silver
6 × 22 × 14.5 cm
The State Historical Museum, Moscow, GIM 80868 OK 14077

Cat. 239
Ladle of honor (kovch) given to the voivod Tomila Yudich Lugovskoy by the etropolitan of Kazan and of Sviaj, Matthew
Russia, end of the 16th-early 17th century
Silver, turquoise
9.1 × 25 × 15 cm
The State Historical Museum, Moscow, GIM 81663 OK 13456
(Reproduced p. 90)

Cat. 240
Ladle of honor (Kovch) given by the Czars Ivan Alexeievich and Peter Alexeievich to the elected chief Michael Popov (tax collector)
Russia, Moscow, 1693
Silver
11.2 × 24.6 × 16.7 cm
The State Historical Museum, Moscow, GIM 41962 OK 914
(Reproduced p. 91)

Cat. 241
Chair
Russia, second half of 19th century
Oak, sculpture, wheel work, varnish, bronze, gilding, wool tapestry
126 × 51.5 × 61 cm

The State Historical Museum, Moscow, GIM 68042/D II – 761
(Reproduced p. 147)

Cat. 242 and 243
Pair of vases
Russia, middle of 19th century
Malachite, bronze
36 x 32 x 32 cm
The State Historical Museum, Moscow, GIM 60258/163 BR 2109/1-2

Cat. 244
Master P. Petrov
A drinking set with two faceted crystal decanters with lids and four glasses on a tray
Moscow, 1830s
Bronze, crystal
26 x 44 x 26 cm
The State Historical Museum, Moscow, GIM 74872 BR 1164/1-7

Cat. 245
Writing set with inkwell, hourglass, and small bell
Moscow, P. Petrov's workshop, 1840s
Bronze, glass
12 x 34 x 15 cm
The State Historical Museum, Moscow, GIM 66277 BR 416/1-4

Cat. 246 and 247
Pair of chandeliers
Moscow, P. Petrov's workshop, 1840s
Bronze, glass
24 x 12 x 12 cm
The State Historical Museum, Moscow, GIM 66754 BR 350/1-2

Cat. 248
Candelabrum known as "the Czarina's candelabrum"
1867
Mould-blown and cut clear crystal
215 x 85 cm
Heritage collection, Baccarat
(Reproduced p. 214)

Cat. 249-252
"Czar's stemware"
1909
Mould-blown and cut clear crystal
Champagne glass: 27.7 cm; water glass: 36 cm; wine glass: 27 cm; vodka glass: 20 cm
Heritage collection, Baccarat
(Reproduced p. 218)

Cat. 253
Design for the "Czar's stemware" (Blessed for the Colonel of Tchemerzine at St. Petersburg, order 31845, August 20, 1909)
Beginning of the 20th century
Ink and water-color on tracing paper glued into a volume
Volume titled "Special orders No. 20", Baccarat Archives
65 x 102 cm (unfolded)
Heritage collection, Baccarat
(Reproduced p. 219)

Cat. 254
Ruby "czarina" pitcher
1907
Clear crystal doubled with red crystal, mould-blown, cut
46.5 x 16 cm
Heritage collection, Baccarat

Cat. 255
Glass for Grand Duke Vladimir Alexandrovich
1870
Mould-blown clear crystal, initials topped by a wheel-engraved and gilded crown
20.1 x 10.3 cm
Heritage collection, Baccarat
(Reproduced p. 220)

Cat. 256
Glass from the G Service intended for Mr. Morozoff
1878
Mould-blown clear crystal, wheel-engraved and gilded
14.6 x 8.1 cm
Heritage collection, Baccarat
(Reproduced p. 220)

Cat. 257
Glass for Prince Demidoff
1878
Mould-blown clear crystal, cut, engraved and gilded
15.6 x 8.1 cm
Heritage collection, Baccarat

Cat. 258
Volume "Candelabra No. 10" (including the drawings of the candelabrums known as "the Czar's candelabrum" and "Czarina's candelabrum")
Beginning of the 20th century
Pencil, watercolor and gouache highlights on beige paper, ink inscriptions
65 x 102 cm (unfolded)
Heritage collection, Baccarat
(Reproduced pp. 216-217)

Cat. 259
F. I. Alekseev
Parade of troops on the Kremlin Cathedral Square (view from the side of the Cathedral of the Dormition)
1800s
Oil on canvas
82 x 113 cm
The State Historical Museum, Moscow, GIM 70156, K-259

Cat. 260
F. I. Alekseev
Moscow. View of the Square of the Cathedrals in the Kremlin
1800s
Oil on canvas
80 x 106 cm
The State Historical Museum, Moscow, GIM 701576, K-328
(Reproduced p. 18)

Cat. 261
F. I. Alekseev
View of the Kremlin near the Spasskaya Gate
1800s
Oil on canvas
82 x 112 cm
The State Historical Museum, Moscow, GIM 70156, K-347

Cat. 262
F. I. Alekseev
Moscow. View of the Kremlin and the Kamenni Bridge
1815
Oil on canvas
80 x 106 cm
The State Historical Museum, Moscow, GIM 70156, K-260
(Reproduced p. 109)

Cat. 263
F. I. Alekseev
View of the Kremlin from Boyars Square (west side)
1800s
Paper on paper, watercolor, Indian ink, black lead, inks, brush, feather
49.3 x 65.5 cm
The State Historical Museum, Moscow, GIM 86892, R-8645
(Reproduced pp. 104 and 117)

Cat. 264
F. I. Alekseev
View of the Kremlin: the Borovitskaya Gate, the Court Stables and the Church of the Nativity of St. John the Precursor
1800s
Paper on paper, watercolor, Indian ink, black lead, inks, brush, feather
41.5 x 55.5 cm
The State Historical Museum, Moscow, GIM 105887, R-9814
(Reproduced p. 113)

Cat. 265
F. I. Alekseev
View in the Kremlin on the Kremlin Palace from the Podol (north side)
1800s
Paper on paper, watercolor, Indian ink, black lead, inks, brush, feather
43.8 x 64.3 cm
The State Historical Museum, Moscow, GIM 105887, R-9821
(Reproduced p. 117)

Cat. 266
F. I. Alekseev and his students
View of the Kremlin on the Kremlin Grande Palace Office, the Court Stables and the Gate of the Armories
1800s
Paper on paper, watercolor, Indian ink, black lead, inks, brush, feather
33.2 x 47.2 cm
The State Historical Museum, Moscow, GIM 105887, R-9820
(Reproduced p. 115)

Cat. 267
F. I. Alekseev and his students
View of the Kremlin on the Little Pleasures Palace from the side of the inside courtyard
1800s
Paper on paper, watercolor, Indian ink, black lead, inks, brush, feather
35.7 x 48.5 cm
The State Historical Museum, Moscow, GIM 105887, R-9819
(Reproduced p. 116)

Cat. 268
F. I. Alekseev and his students
View of the Cathedral of Basil the Blessed, of the Spasskaya

Tower and of the Café
1800s
Paper on paper, watercolor, Indian ink, black lead, inks, brush, feather
44.7 × 54.3 cm
The State Historical Museum, Moscow, GIM 86892, R-9812

Cat. 269
F. I. Alekseev
View of Resurrection Gate, the Grand Pharmacy, the Neglimennii Bridge and Peter's bastions
1800s
Paper on paper, watercolor, Indian ink, black lead, inks, brush, feather
48.2 × 63 cm
The State Historical Museum, Moscow, GIM 105887, R-9815
(Reproduced p. 113)

Cat. 270
F. I. Alekseev and his students
View of Resurrection Gate, the Grand Pharmacy, the Mint, and Kazan Cathedral next to the Red Square
1800s
Paper on paper, watercolor, Indian ink, black lead, inks, brush, feather
49.2 × 65.5 cm
The State Historical Museum, Moscow, GIM 105887, R-9813

Cat. 271
F. I. Alekseev and his students
Near the Troiyskaya Gate of the Kremlin and the Church of St. Nicholas of the Cobblers
1800s
Paper on paper, watercolor, Indian ink, black lead, inks, brush, feather
48.5 × 62 cm
The State Historical Museum, Moscow, GIM 105887, R-9818

Cat. 272
F. I. Alekseev and his students
View of the Outer Muscovy district (Zamoskvorietchy) on the Kadachevsky Khamovny Dvor and the steeple of the Church of Cosmas and Damian
1800s
Paper on paper, watercolor, Indian ink, black lead, inks, brush, feather
49 × 59 cm
The State Historical Museum, Moscow, GIM 105887, R-9816
(Reproduced p. 110)

Cat. 273
F. I. Alekseev studio
View of Resurrection Gate, the Grand Pharmacy and Tver street Neglimennii Bridge 1880s.
Paper, watercolor, white lead, brush
50 × 68 cm
The State Historical Museum, Moscow, GIM 23495 shch, R-2225

Cat. 274
F. I. Alekseev studio
General view of the Red Square and the Cathedral of Basil the Blessed
1880s
Paper, watercolor, white lead, brush
51 × 69 cm
The State Historical Museum, Moscow, GIM 86892, R-5435
(Reproduced p. 26)

Cat. 275
J. B. Arnout. Based on an original by an anonymous artist
View on the Kremlin cathedrals
From I. H. Datsiaro series "Moscow"
End of the 1840s
Paper, colored lithograph, watercolor, varnish
38.5 × 54.4 cm
The State Historical Museum, Moscow, GIM 70156, L-2637

Cat. 276
Ch. K. Bachelier, J. Jacottet. Based on an original by I. I. Charlemagne
The Red Square. View on the monument of Minin and Pojarsky, the Savior Gate and the Cathedral of Basil the Blessed
From I. H. Datsiaro series "Moscow"
Moscow, 1850s
Paper, colored lithograph
40 × 57.1 cm
The State Historical Museum, Moscow, GIM 42949, L-1057

Cat. 277
Müller. Based on an original by I. E. Vivien
The Kitai-gorod Resurrection Gates and the Chapel of the Virgin of Iberia
1840s
From I. H. Datsiaro series "Moscow"
Paper, colored lithograph, watercolor, varnish
39.9 × 57.2 cm
The State Historical Museum, Moscow, GIM 70156, L-6854
(Reproduced p. 118)

Cat. 278
Ch. K. Bachelier, J. Jacottet. Based on an original by I. I. Charlemagne
The Alexander Garden. View from the Troitsky bridge toward the Church of Christ the Savior
From I. H. Datsiaro series "Moscow"
1850s
Paper, colored lithograph
39.9 × 57.2 cm
The State Historical Museum, Moscow, GIM 71880, L-1715
(Reproduced. p. 27)

Cat. 279
Ch. K. Bachelier, J. Jacottet. Based on an original by I. I. Charlemagne. Figures executed by J. A. Duruy
Strastnaya Square (Passion Square)
From I. H. Datsiaro series "Moscow"
Moscow, 1850s
Paper, colored lithograph, watercolor, varnish
38.2 × 54 cm
The State Historical Museum, Moscow, GIM 42949, L-1339
(Reproduced p. 120)

Cat. 280
L. Ph. Bichebois. Based on an original by S. Ph. Dits. Figures executed by P. M. Roussel
Lubianka Square
From I. H. Datsiaro series "Moscow"
Moscow, end of the 1840s
Paper, colored lithograph, watercolor
38.1 × 50 cm
The State Historical Museum, Moscow, GIM 70156, L-15543

Cat. 281
Ch. K. Bachelier, J. Jacottet. Based on an original by Bronin. Figures executed by A. Duruy
Theater Square. View toward Kitai-gorod
From I. H. Datsiaro series "Moscow"
Moscow, end of 1840s
Paper, colored lithograph
39.6 × 52.8 cm
The State Historical Museum, Moscow, GIM 76712, L-1308

Cat. 282
Anonymous lithograph. Based on an original by an anonymous artist
View of the Synod Printing Press on Nikolskaya street in Kitai-gorod
From I. H. Datsiaro series "Moscow"
Moscow, end of the 1840s
Paper, colored lithograph, watercolor, varnish
38.5 × 53 cm
The State Historical Museum, Moscow, GIM 70156, L-1105

Cat. 283
A. Gedon. Based on an original by S. Ph. Dits. Figures executed by P. M. Roussel
Club of the Union of Nobility on Okhotny riad with the Church of St. Paraskevia-Piatnitsa
From I. H. Datsiaro series "Moscow"
Moscow, end of 1840s
Paper, colored lithograph, watercolor, varnish
48 × 54.8 cm
The State Historical Museum, Moscow, GIM 76712, L-1290

Cat. 284
L. P. Bichebois, Ch. Fichot. Based on an original by G. F. Baranovsky. Figures executed by A. Bayot
The Institute of Nobility on Mokhovaya Street
From I. H. Datsiaro series "Moscow"
End of the 1840s
Paper, colored lithograph, watercolor, varnish
36.2 × 45.5 cm
The State Historical Museum, Moscow, GIM 70156, L-14102
(Reproduced p. 119)

Cat. 285
Müller. Based on an original by S. Ph. Dits
Moscow Post Office on Miasnikskaya street (street of Butchers)
From I. H. Datsiaro series "Moscow"
End of the 1840s
Paper, colored lithograph, watercolor, varnish
37.1 × 54 cm
The State Historical Museum, Moscow, GIM 42949, L-1281
(Reproduced. p. 120)

Cat. 286
L. P. Bichebois. Based on an original by S. Ph. Dits. Figures executed by P. M. Roussel
Building of the Tutelary Council on Solianka Street
From I. H. Datsiaro series "Moscow"
Moscow, end of the 1840s
Paper, colored lithograph, watercolor, varnish
38.5 × 54.9 cm
The State Historical Museum, Moscow, GIM 70156, L-6910

Cat. 287
A. A. Afanassiev (?).
Publishers: I. Syroiejin, N. Trukhatchov
Plan of Moscow illustrated with 14 views
1825
Paper, stippled engraving, watercolor
76.1 × 88 cm
The State Historical Museum, Moscow, GIM 42949, L-228
(Reproduced p. 106)

Cat. 288
Anonymous
Plan of Moscow in the 1630s
Title of the book, "Adam Olearius's Travels"
Leyde, 1719
Paper, etching
30.7 × 40 cm
The State Historical Museum, Moscow, GIM 42949, L-77

Cat. 289
F. L. Florov. Based on a original by I. Martchenkov
Plan of Moscow
1789
N. Koltchuguin Edition
Paper, engraving, watercolor
80.2 × 50.5 cm
The State Historical Museum, Moscow, GIM 70156, L-176

Cat. 290
P. Picart
Moscow, capital of Russia
Beginning of the 18th century
Paper, etching
105.6 × 256.9 cm
State Ceramics Museum and 18th century Kuskovo estate, GR-155 KP 816
(Reproduced pp. 24-25)

Cat. 291
Prince A. A. Golitsyn
Sleigh race on the St. Petersburg roadway near the Petrovsky Palace
1848
Oil on canvas
50 × 68 cm
The State Historical Museum, Moscow, GIM 42567, K-258
(Reproduced p. 228)

Cat. 292
P. Ovtchinnikov
Jewel chest having belonged to Grand Duchess Xenia Alexandrovna and Grand Duke Alexander Mikhailovich
Russia, Moscow, 1894
Gold, silver, brilliants, diamonds, rubies, spinel, garnet, almandine, amethyst, pyrope, citrine
13.2 × 37.7 × 24.3 cm
The State Historical Museum, Moscow, GIM 62743 OK 1834

Cat. 293
Carl Fabergé. Master goldsmith: Albert Holström
Brooch
Russia, St. Petersburg, 1908-1917
Gold, silver, diamonds, aquamarine, topazes
3.7 × 3.2 cm
The State Historical Museum, Moscow, GIM 102157/7 OK 17233
(Reproduced p. 156)

Cat. 294
Bolin (?)
Mary of Serbia's diadem
Circa 1880
Gold, silver, diamonds, green paste
5.6 × 19.5 × 15.8 cm
Van Cleef & Arpels Collection, NY 48518
(Reproduced p. 189)

Cat. 295
Pendant brooch
Russia, second half of the 18th century
Silver, diamonds
23.7 × 8.5 cm
The State Historical Museum, Moscow, GIM 14780 shch OK 2016
(Reproduced p. 152)

Cat. 296
Bracelet
Russia, middle of the 19th century
Silver, emeralds, rubies, zircon, spinel, garnet, almandine garnet, chalcedony, glass, lining, enamel
6.8 × 7 × 6.5 cm
The State Historical Museum, Moscow, GIM 53030/310 OK 1927
(Reproduced p. 154)

Cat. 297
Pair of earrings
Russia, 18th century
Gold, silver, diamonds, rubies, emeralds, cultured pearls; setting
l. 6 cm
The State Historical Museum, Moscow, GIM 14593 shch OK 6508/1-2
(Reproduced p. 153)

Cat. 298
Pair of earrings
Russia, beginning of 20th century
Gold, silver, brilliants, diamonds, emeralds
l. 52 cm
The State Historical Museum, Moscow, GIM 107080/138 OK 23186/1-2

Cat. 299
Comb
France, Paris, 1798-1809
Gold, silver, cultured pearls, enamel, glass, steel
12.3 × 10.6 cm
The State Historical Museum, Moscow, GIM 11641 shch OK 15518
(Reproduced p. 153)

Cat. 300
Master goldsmith Henri Lassas
"Scarab" brooch
Russia, St. Petersburg, last quarter of 19th century
Gold, brilliants, diamonds, sapphires, glass
6 × 2.7 cm
The State Historical Museum, Moscow, GIM 107001 OK 23092
(Reproduced p. 156)

Cat. 301
I. D. Tchitchelev (?)
Cuff bracelet
Russia, Moscow, 1860s
Gold, rubies, cultured pearls, enamels
5.6 × 7.4 × 6.8 cm
The State Historical Museum, Moscow, GIM 74142 OK 7140
(Reproduced p. 155)

Cat. 302
"Dragonfly" brooch
Russia, Moscow, 1899-1908
Vasily Semenovich Agafonov workshop
Gold silver, diamonds, brilliants, emeralds, rubies, spinel, phenacite, cultured pearls
1.3 × 6.2 × 6.8 cm
The State Historical Museum, Moscow, GIM 106599 OK 23072
(Reproduced p. 157)

Cat. 303
Pectoral insignia with the photographic portraits of the Russian Emperors Alexander II and Alexander III
Russia, second half of the 19th century
Gold, silver, diamonds, phenacite, quartz, glass, paper
8.4 × 5 cm
The State Historical Museum, Moscow, GIM 10525 shch OK 22560

Cat. 304
Brooch
Middle of 19th century
Gold, silver, brilliants, diamonds, turquoise, glass
5.6 × 8.3 cm
The State Historical Museum, Moscow, GIM 14827 shch OK 1980
(Reproduced pp.150 and 154)

Cat. 305
Pair of earrings
Western Europe, end of 18th-first quarter of 19th centuries
Gold, silver, cultured pearls, diamonds, enamel
4.7 × 1.5 cm
The State Historical Museum, Moscow, GIM 14568 shch
OK 2121/1-2
(Reproduced p. 153)

Cat. 306
Purchase by Prince Yussupov in 1856
Folio of a client book, 1856
32 × 29.5 cm
Mellerio *dits* Meller collection

Cat. 307
Plaster cast of the diadem in rock crystal and diamonds
Paris, Lavabre workshop, 1911
15.7 × 4.6 × 2.2 cm
The Cartier Archives, Paris, DIA68

Cat. 308
Diadem in platinum, rock crystal and diamonds
Creation for the collection, Paris, 1911
Sold to Prince Yussupov
January 31, 1914
Photographic print from the original silver gelatine-bromide negative glass plate
The Cartier Archives, Paris, (negative 2525)

Cat. 309
Purchases by Princess Yussupov in 1857
Folio of a client book, 1857
32 × 29.5 cm
Mellerio *dits* Meller collection

Cat. 310
Drawing of a bracelet of Egyptian inspiration, scarab centre
Circa 1856
Pencil, ink on paper (facsimile)
4.5 × 11.5 cm
Mellerio *dits* Meller collection

Cat. 311-314
Collection of drawings for jewelry for Princess Felix Yussupov's wedding presents
-Drawing for a bodice front knot in rubies and diamonds
-Drawing for a bodice front in rubies and diamonds, in a motif of knots of cascading ribbons and pompons
-Drawing for a bodice front in rubies and diamonds
-Drawing for a bodice front in garlands of emeralds and diamonds (reproduced p. 26)
Watercolor and gouache on paper
Joseph Chaumet, 1914
Chaumet collection, Paris

Cat. 315
Portrait of Princess Felix Yussupov
Chaumet collection, Paris
(Reproduced p. 204)

Cat. 316
Acanthus-pattern wristwatch
Cartier Paris, 1912
Platinum, yellow gold, pink gold, rose-cut diamonds, pearls, onyx beads
Sold to Princess Orlov
2.25 × 2.25 cm (case)
The Cartier Collection, WWL02A12
(Reproduced p. 195)

Cat. 317
Attributed to Mellerio *dits* Meller
Jointed feather
Silver on gold, diamonds
Circa 1870
16.5 × 9.5 × 3 cm
Mellerio *dits* Meller collection
(Reproduced p. 194)

Cat. 318
Diamond diadem on platinum decorated with seven pear diamonds
Kelch order, 1912
Photograph
Boucheron archives

Cat. 319
Necklace made of 20 emeralds, of diamonds and rose-cut diamonds
Kelch order, 1906
Photograph
Boucheron archives

Cat. 320
Necklace made of 26 rubies and of diamonds, forming two large pompons.
Kelch order, 1907
Photograph
Boucheron archives

Cat. 321
Diamond rivière necklace decorated with diamond flowerets
Kelch order, 1906
Photograph
Boucheron archives

Cat. 322
Large diadem made of three diamond knots, rose-cut diamonds and fourteen rubies, the knots can be taken apart
Polovtsov order, 1887
Photograph
Boucheron archives

Cat. 323
Outside façade of the Boucheron store in Moscow (opened in 1897)
Photograph
Boucheron archives
(Reproduced p. 174)

Cat. 324
Inside of the Boucheron store in Moscow (opened in 1897)
Photograph
Boucheron archives
(Reproduced p. 178)

Cat. 325
Boucheron
Toiletry bottles
Russian importation stamps, around 1910
Silver and glass
9.8 × 6 × 3.9 cm;
16.5 × 6.7 × 4.6 cm
Boucheron collection
P618 et P619

Cat. 326
Boucheron, Menu
Round watch and knot brooch
Russian importation stamps, 1898
Gold, silver, round and rose-cut diamonds, enamel
7 × 2.8 × 1.2 cm
Boucheron collection, P315
(Reproduced p. 179)

Cat. 327
Boucheron
Waistcoat pocket watch
Sold to Mr. Zubaloff in 1908
Gold, enamel
Diam. 4,7 cm
Boucheron collection, P631
(Reproduced p. 195)

Cat. 328
Boucheron, J. A. Martel
Large vase with irises
"Boucheron Paris Moscow"
Russian importation stamps, circa 1905
Crystal, vermeil
H. 53 cm
Boucheron collection, P644

Cat. 329
Boucheron, J. A. Martel
Large vase with chrysanthemums
"Boucheron Paris Moscow"
Crystal, vermeil
Russian importation stamps, circa 1905
H. 53 cm
Boucheron collection, P645
(Reproduced p. 181)

Cat. 330
General view of the French exhibition in Moscow, 1891
Reproduction taken from the *Memorial of the French exhibition, in Moscow 1891*, a work presented to His Majesty the Emperor Alexander III by the major French firms, Paris, Administration of the Grand Factories (The Turgan Grand Factories)
L. Berger & Cie Editor, no date.
French National Library
(Reproduced p. 176)

Cat. 331
L. O. Roty
Commemorative medal from the French exhibition, 1891, in Moscow
1891
Bronze
Diam. 6.3 cm
Boucheron collection, P748

Cat. 332-337
Diverse reproductions from the *Memorial of the French exhibition in Moscow 1891*, an event presented to His Majesty the Emperor Alexander III by the major French firms, Paris, Administration of the Grand Factories (The Turgan Grand Factories)
L. Berger and Cie Editor, no date.
-L. Coulon & Cie, headdress forming two wings in diamonds
-L. Coulon & Cie, diadem
-Th. Bourdier, Imperial egg

offered to Maria Feodorovna during the French exhibition in Moscow in 1891
(Reproduced p. 177)
-Th. Bourdier, Imperial egg offered to Maria Feodorovna during the French exhibition in Moscow in 1891 (general view with the surprise that it contains)
-Vever jewelry making stand at the French exhibition in Moscow in 1891

Cat. 338
Purchases of Emperor Alexander II at the Universal Exhibition of 1867
Folio of a client book, 1867 (facsimile)
32 x 29.5 cm
Mellerio *dits* Meller collection

Cat. 339
"Rosaline" chatelaine and watch in rose-cut diamonds, the watch decorated with a monogram and a crown, No. 4770
Purchased by the future Alexander III in 1876
Photograph
Boucheron archives

Cat. 340
Small crown decorated with eighteen pearls, diamonds and rose-cut diamonds, No. 12286
Purchased by the future Nicholas II in 1894
Photograph
Boucheron archives
(Reproduced p. 196)

Cat. 341
Czar Nicholas II and his family
Circa 1910
Photograph
(Reproduced p. 197)

Cat. 342
The Emperor Nicholas II and the Empress Alexandra Feodorovna wearing costumes of Russian Czars of the 17th century
St. Petersburg, 1903
Photograph, "S. Levitsky" studio
Russian State Cinematographic and Photographic Archives, al. 299, sn.45
(Reproduced p. 23)

Cat. 343
Hugues
Portrait of Princess Alix of Hesse
1894
Photograph
Russian State Cinematographic and Photographic Archives, al. 1054, sn.265

Cat. 344
Drawing for lily of the valley bracelet
Circa 1867
Pencil, gouache on paper (facsimile)
3.3 x 16.3 cm
Mellerio *dits* Meller collection

Cat. 345
Drawing for lily of the valley bracelet
Circa 1867
Pencil, gouache on paper (facsimile)
3.3 x 16.3 cm
Mellerio *dits* Meller collection

Cat. 346
Drawing for lily of the valley bracelet decorated with enamel
Circa 1865
Pencil, gouache on paper (facsimile)
7.3 x 15.7 cm
Mellerio *dits* Meller collection

Cat. 347
Spring-loaded peacock feather necklace in diamonds and rose-cut diamonds. The motif is decorated with a 5-carat sapphire, diamonds and emeralds, No. 11752
Purchased by Grand Duke Alexis in 1883
Photograph
Boucheron archives

Cat. 348
Photograph of a frame done for the Grand Duchess Serge (Elizabeth Feodorovna)
"L'Art Décoratif," 1905, p. 223
Bibliothèque des Arts Décoratifs, Paris

Cat. 349
Bodice front
Paris, 1910
Pencils on transparent beige paper
Drawing to scale for the creation in platinum and diamonds, order by Grand Duchess Wladimir
20 x 15 cm
The Cartier Archives, Paris, GII/18a

Cat. 350
Bodice front in sapphires and diamonds
Ordered by Grand Duchess Wladimir, Paris, 1910
Gold and silver setting, brilliant-cut, rose-cut and briolette diamonds, sapphires
Photographic print from the original silver gelatin-bromide negative glass plate
The Cartier Archives, Paris, (negative 1960)

Cat. 351
Dog collar in pearls and diamonds with two plates on which figures the motif of the imperial eagle
Order by Grand Duchess Wladimir, Paris, 1900
Pearls, rose-cut and brilliant-cut diamonds
Photographic print from the original silver gelatin-bromide negative glass plate
Cartier archives, Paris (negative 543)
(Reproduced p. 199)

Cat. 352
Kokoshnik diadem in sapphires and diamonds on silver and gold setting
Ordered by Grand Duchess Wladimir, Paris, 1909
Brilliants, sapphires
Photographic print from the original silver gelatin-bromide negative glass plate
Cartier archives, Paris (negative 1694)

Cat. 353
"The Grand Duchesses of Russia"
Fémina, March 15, 1905, No. 100

Cat. 354
C. Bergamasco
The Grand Duchess Maria Pavlovna
St. Petersburg, 1883
Photograph
Russian State Cinematographic and Photographic Archives, al. 946, sn.22
(Reproduced p. 198)

Cat. 355
Plaster cast of the Regency with the Order of Saint Andrew (cfr. cat. 358)
Paris, Lavabre workshop, 1913
15.5 x 4 x 1.6 cm
Cartier archives, Paris, PE415

Cat. 356
Plaster cast of the pendant with briolette diamonds (see cat. 363)
Paris, Lavabre workshop, 1913
9.6 x 4.8 x 2 cm
Cartier archives, Paris, BRO302

Cat. 357
Diadem called "the waterfall" which belonged to Grand Duchess Wladimir
1899
Original silver-gelatine print on mat paper
Chaumet collection, Paris
(Reproduced p. 199)

Cat. 358
Order of Saint Andrew
Ordered by Grand Duchess Wladimir, Paris, 1908
Black moiré and diamonds on platinum setting
Photographic print from the original silver gelatin-bromide negative glass plate
Cartier archives, Paris (negative 1245)

Cat. 359
Pendant in platinum and diamonds
Ordered by Grand Duchess Wladimir, Paris, 1913
Platinum setting, briolette and pear diamonds
Photographic print from the original silver gelatin-bromide negative glass plate
Cartier archives, Paris (negative 3750)

Cat. 360
Plaster cast of headband with starry motifs, order by Grand Duke Paul (see cat. 368)
Paris, Lavabre workshop, 1910

27 × 6 × 1.4 cm
Cartier archives, Paris, COL112

Cat. 361
Plaster cast of the pendant in turquoises and diamonds, ordered by Grand Duke Paul (see cat. 369)
Paris, Lavabre workshop, 1909
10.1 × 9 × 2.1 cm
Archives Cartier, Paris, PE54

Cat. 362
Plaster cast of the bodice front for Countess Hohenfelsen (see cat. 363)
Paris, Lavabre workshop, 1908
10.6 × 9.9 × 3.2 cm
Cartier archives, Paris, DC62

Cat. 363
Bodice front in pearls and diamonds
Ordered by Countess Hohenfelsen, Paris, 1908
Setting in platinum, pear pearls and buttons, brilliant-cut and rose-cut diamonds
Photographic print from the original silver gelatin-bromide negative glass plate
Cartier archives, Paris (negative 1079)
(Reproduced p. 202)

Cat. 364
Diadem in diamonds with a motif of entwined rings
Ordered by Countess Hohenfelsen, Paris, 1911
Setting in platinum, pear pearls
Photographic print from the original silver gelatin-bromide negative glass plate
Cartier archives, Paris (negative 2506)
(Reproduced p. 201)

Cat. 365
Boissonas and Taponnier
The Princess Olga Paley, Countess Hohenfelsen, and wife of the Grand Duke Paul, wearing a bodice ornament in diamonds and pearls by way of a hat brooch, and a diadem of pear diamonds (created in 1911) as bodice ornament. Her robe was made by Worth.
1912
Photograph
Cartier archives, Paris
(Reproduced p. 192)

Cat. 366
Brooch
Cartier Paris, 1913
Sold to the Countess of Hohenfelsen
Gold, platinum, sapphire cabochons, white and green enamel
5.5 × 2 × 0.5 cm
The Cartier collection, CL121A13
(Reproduced p. 200)

Cat. 367
Partial plaster cast of the diadem which belonged to the Countess Hohenfelsen (see cat. 364)
Paris, Picq workshop, 1911
21.1 × 7.6 × 1.8 cm
Cartier archives, Paris, DIA112
(Reproduced p. 201)

Cat. 368
Headband in diamonds with starry motif
Ordered by the Grand Duke Paul, Paris, 1910
Platinum setting, centre in cames
Photographic print from the original silver gelatin-bromide negative glass plate
Cartier archives, Paris (negative 1898)

Cat. 369
Pendant in turquoises and diamonds
Ordered by the Grand Duke Paul, Paris, 1909
Platinum setting, turquoises
Photographic print from the original silver gelatin-bromide negative glass plate
Cartier archives, Paris (negative 1519)

Cat. 370
Diadem with motifs of laurel crowns in sapphires and diamonds
Platinum setting, brilliant-cut and rose-cut sapphires and diamonds
Photographic print from the original silver gelatin-bromide negative glass plate
Cartier archives, Paris (negative 1083)

Cat. 371
Partial plaster cast of a diadem in sapphire and diamonds which belonged to the Countess Hohenfelsen (see cat. 360)
Lavabre workshop, Paris, 1908
2.5 × 9.1 × 1.9 cm
Cartier archives, Paris, DIA57

Cat. 372
Calendar Clock with Phases of the Moon
Cartier Paris, 1912
Silver, gilded metal, silver-gilt, platinum, translucent royal blue enamel over guilloche ground, white enamel, rose-cut diamonds
10 × 10 × 1 cm
The Cartier collection, CDS51A12

Cat. 373
Watch on Necklace
Cartier Paris, 1910
Platinum, gold, translucent royal blue enamel over guilloche ground, white enamel, pearls, rose-cut diamonds
2.48 cm (diameter of the watch); 40 cm (length of the chain)
The Cartier collection, WN05A10

Cat. 374
Cigarette case
Cartier Paris, 1907
Gold, translucent royal blue enamel over guilloche ground, white and green enamel, rose-cut diamonds (thumbpieces)
1.3 × 9.8 × 5.9 cm
The Cartier collection, CC41A07
(Reproduced p. 186)

Cat. 375
Perfume bottle with spray
Cartier Paris, 1912
Silver, yellow gold, pink gold, platinum, translucent royal blue enamel over guilloche ground, button pearls, rose-cut diamonds
7.45 × 2.54 cm
The Cartier collection, FK09A12

Cat. 376
Cube Clock with Minute Repeater
Cartier Paris, 1910
Platinum, gold, silver, agate (base), moonstone (repeater button), translucent pink enamel over guilloche ground, white enamel, rose-cut diamonds
10 × 6.2 × 7.7 cm
The Cartier collection, CR01A10

Cat. 377
Watch on Necklace
Cartier Paris, 1907
Platinum, gold, translucent pink enamel over guilloche ground, white enamel, pearls, rose-cut diamonds
3.05 cm (diameter of the watch); 43 cm (length of the necklace)
The Cartier collection, WN14A07

Cat. 378
Telescopic reading lamp propelling pencil
Cartier Paris, 1906
Gold, translucent pink and green enamel over guilloche ground, white enamel, one rose-cut diamond
Sold to a member of the Rothschild Family
l. 11 cm
The Cartier collection, WI 46 A06

Cat. 379
Dress set
Cartier Paris, 1906
Gold, platinum, translucent pink enamel over guilloche ground, rose-cut diamonds, millegrain setting
1.24 × 0.9 cm
The Cartier collection, BC 17 A06

Cat. 380
Model A Mystery Clock
Cartier Paris, 1921
Gold, platinum, onyx (base), rock crystal, rose-cut diamonds, white enamel
Sold to Sir Bhupindra Singh, Maharajah of Patiala
H. 13.35 cm
The Cartier collection, CM 18A21

Cat. 381
Comet Clock
Cartier Paris, 1918
Platinum, gold, gilded metal, onyx, translucent sky-blue enamel over guilloche ground,

white enamel, rose-cut diamonds
Diam. 7.8 cm
The Cartier collection, CS03A18
(Reproduced p. 182)

Cat. 382
Borne Desk Clock with Strut
Cartier Paris, 1924
Gold, platinum, silver-plated metal, rock crystal, translucent pale blue enamel over guilloche ground, white enamel, rose-cut diamonds
7.5 × 6.8 × 1.5 cm
The Cartier collection, CDS27A24

Cat. 383
Desk Clock with Strut
Cartier Paris, 1912
Platinum, silver, gilded copper, translucent purple enamel over guilloche ground, white enamel, rose-cut diamonds
Diam. 6.5 cm
The Cartier collection, CDS41A12

Cat. 384
Desk Clock with Strut
Cartier Paris, 1913
Platinum, silver, gilded metal, translucent periwinkle-blue enamel over guilloche ground, white enamel, rose-cut diamonds
Diam. 6.63 cm
The Cartier Collection, CDS 82A13

Cat. 385
Desk Clock with Strut
Cartier Paris, 1914
Sold to Mrs. J.J. Astor
Platinum, silver, gilded metal, translucent yellow enamel over guilloche ground, white enamel, rose-cut diamonds
Diam. 7.9 cm
The Cartier collection, CDS 62 A14
(Reproduced p. 184)

Cat. 386
Carl Fabergé; M. Perkhin
Case
St. Petersburg 1899-1908
Guilloching of two types of gold
9 cm
Joseph Maouad, private collector
(Reproduced p. 185)

Cat. 387
Invitation for an exhibition organized in the Moscow National Hotel salons for the winter season
1907
Cartier archives, Paris, INS10

Cat. 388
Boucheron
Gilded silver frame
Circa 1895
Vermeil
H. 23 cm
Boucheron collection, P425

Cat. 389
Boucheron
Cames comb, diamonds and pearls
Circa 1880
Gold, silver, 24 diamonds, 11 cultured pearls
14.5 × 5 cm
Boucheron collection, P579

Cat. 390
Boucheron, Menu
Pocket mirror
1906
Gold, enamel
Stamp by the master A. Menu
8 × 5.05 × 0.8 cm
Boucheron collection, P359

Cat. 391
Boucheron
Canive copied from Hirtz; Vicker
Paper knife and page marker
1911
Gilded silver and green nephrite
Paper knife: 38 × 5 cm; page marker: 20 × 2.3 cm
Boucheron collection, P489
(Reproduced p. 188)

Cat. 392
Cigarette case with propelling pencil
Cartier Paris, 1928
Gold, nephrite, buff-top and caliber-cut sapphires, one flat sapphire to be engraved, blue enamel
9 × 6.7 × 1.8 cm
The Cartier collection, CC69A28

Cat. 393
Trump marker
Cartier Paris, 1907
Silver-gilt, silver, rose quartz (base), one moonstone, translucent gray-blue enamel over guilloche ground, opaque white enamel, red and black enamel
H. 13.04 cm
The Cartier collection, IO 68A07

Cat. 394
Powder box
Cartier Paris, 1911
Gold, platinum, translucent pale pink opaline enamel over guilloche ground, white enamel, rose-cut diamonds
Diam. 4.02 cm
The Cartier collection, BS04A11
(Reproduced p. 183)

Cat. 395
Russian cigarette case
Cartier Paris, 1913
Gold, sapphire cabochons (push-pieces), white enamel
9.6 × 5.5 × 1.38 cm
The Cartier collection, CC58A13

Cat. 396
Cigarette case
Cartier Paris, 1912
Yellow gold, pink gold, one sapphire cabochon (push-piece)
8.33 × 6.32 × 1.12 cm
The Cartier collection, CC03A12
(Reproduced p. 196)

Cat. 397-400
J. Chaumet
Examples of Kokoshnik-shaped diadems
Painted German silver
Paris, circa 1900-1915
Chaumet collection, Paris

Cat. 401
J. Chaumet
Chain with small bell pendant
Gold, emerald, engraved rock crystal, enamel
Paris, circa 1911
Chaumet collection, Paris
(Reproduced p. 185)

Cat. 402
G. Lafitte
"Butterfly" pendant
France, Paris, 1904
Gold, silver, brilliants, phenacite, enamel; Case: velvet, silk, cardboard, vellum, iron
Pendant: 6.5 × 8.4 cm; Chain: 59.5 cm
The State Historical Museum, Moscow, GIM 104464 OK 22733/1-2
(Reproduced p. 158)

Cat. 403
Carl Fabergé; Workmaster: M. Perkhin
Small blue snake clock
1887
Gift from the Emperor Alexander III to his wife Maria Feodorovna
Gold, precious stones, enamel
H. 18.4 cm
Prince's Palace, Monaco
(Reproduced p. 187)

Cat. 404
Fossin and Son
Posy holder and its case
France, Paris, 1819-1838
Stamped gold, engraved, turquoise, wood, brown red leather, velvet, silk, metal
H. 12.4 cm
Kenber collection, Paris, MFM 8

Cat. 405
Posy holder
Northern Europe (?), 1820-1830
Stamped gold, incised, engraved, hallmarked
H. 8.6 cm; diam. 2.5 cm
Kenber collection, Paris, MFM 1

Cat. 406
Posy holder and its case
Russia (?), 1850-1856
Stamped gold, engraved
H. 12.3 cm
Kenber collection, Paris, MFM 58
(Reproduced p. 209)

Cat. 407
Three-branched posy holder
Russia (?), 1870-1880
Gilded silver (vermeil), filigree
H. 14.1 cm
Kenber collection, Paris, MFM 78

Cat. 408
Three-branched posy holder
Russia (?), 1870-1880
Silver, filigree

H. 15.8 cm
Kenber collection, Paris,
MFM 79
(Reproduced p. 210)

Cat. 409
Posy holder
Russia (?), 1870-1880
Silver, filigree
H. 11.2 cm
Collection Kenber, Paris,
MFM 80

Cat. 410
I. Z. Manilov
Posy holder
Russia, Kostroma, Aleevo,
1899-1905
Silver, gilded silver (vermeil)
engraved ivory
H. 19.5 cm
Kenber collection, Paris,
MFM 118
(Reproduced p. 212)

Cat. 411
Fabergé firm stamp
Three-branched posy holder
Russia, 1900-1910
Gold, twisted filigree,
diamonds, turquoise
H. 11.5 cm
Kenber collection, Paris,
MFM 120
(Reproduced p. 211)

Cat. 412
Carl Fabergé. Workmaster:
Michael Perkhin
Lily of the Valley Egg
St. Petersburg, 1898
Gift from the Emperor
Nicholas II to his wife
Alexandra Feodorovna
Enamel, diamonds, rubies,
gold, pearls
H. 20 cm
The Link of Times Foundation
(Reproduced p. 170)

Cat. 413
Carl Fabergé. Workmaster:
Henrik Wigström
*Fifteenth Anniversary Egg,
with stand*
St. Petersburg, 1911
Gift from the Emperor
Nicholas II to his wife
Alexandra Feodorovna
Enamel, diamonds, gold
H. 13 cm
The Link of Times Foundation
(Reproduced p. 171)

Cat. 414
Carl Fabergé. Workmaster:
Michael Perkhin
Renaissance Egg
St. Petersburg, 1894
Gift from the Emperor
Alexander III to his wife
Maria Feodorovna
Agate, gold, enamel,
diamonds, rubies
13.3 cm
The Link of Times Foundation
(Reproduced p. 172)

Cat. 415
Carl Fabergé
*Cross of St. George Egg, with
stand*
St. Petersburg, 1916
Gift from the Emperor
Nicholas II to his mother
Maria Feodorovna
Enamel, silver, gold
H. 8.4 cm
The Link of Times Foundation
(Reproduced p. 173)

Cat. 416
Carl Fabergé
Scythian-style bracelet
St. Petersburg, before 1899
Gold
7.3 cm
The Link of Times Foundation
(Reproduced p. 162)

Cat. 417
Carl Fabergé. Workmaster:
Erik Kollin (?)
Hen Egg (First Imperial Egg)
St. Petersburg, 1885
Gift from the Emperor
Alexander III to his wife
Maria Feodorovna
Enamel, gold, rubies
H. 6.4 cm
The Link of Times Foundation
(Reproduced p. 160)

Cat. 418
Carl Fabergé
*Elizabeth Feodorovna
Miniature*
8 × 4.3 cm
The Link of Times Foundation

Cat. 419
Carl Fabergé
Miniature Moss Agate Egg
St. Petersburg, 1899-1908
Gold, enamel, diamonds
2.1 × 1.4 cm
The Link of Times Foundation

Cat. 420
Carl Fabergé
*Miniature Mushroom Basket
Egg*
Gold, enamel
2.2 cm
The Link of Times Foundation

Cat. 421
Carl Fabergé. Workmaster:
Michael Perkhin
Miniature Ribbon Egg
St. Petersburg
Gold, silver, enamel, diamonds
2.2 × 1.1 cm
The Link of Times Foundation

Cat. 422
Carl Fabergé. Workmaster:
Henrik Wigström
*Miniature Banded Nephrite
Egg*
St. Petersburg
Nephrite, gold, diamonds
2.9 × 2.4 cm
The Link of Times Foundation

Cat. 423
Carl Fabergé. Workmaster:
Michael Perkhin
Miniature Ducal Coronet Egg
St. Petersburg, 1899-1908
Gold, enamel, diamonds
1.7 × 1.1 cm
The Link of Times Foundation

Cat. 424
Carl Fabergé. Workmaster:
Erik Kollin
Miniature Anchors Egg
St. Petersburg
Gold, enamel
2 × 1.3 cm
The Link of Times Foundation

Cat. 425
Carl Fabergé. Master
goldsmith: Auguste Hollming
Miniature Rococo Trellis Egg
St. Petersburg
Gold, crystal
1.7 × 1.3 cm
The Link of Times Foundation

Cat. 426
Carl Fabergé. Workmaster:
Alfred Thielemann
*Miniature Trelliswork Frame
Egg*
Platinum, gold, diamonds,
sapphires
2 × 1.3 cm
The Link of Times Foundation

Cat. 427
Carl Fabergé
Miniature Zig-Zag Egg
2 × 1.4 cm
The Link of Times Foundation

Cat. 428
Carl Fabergé
Miniature Geometric Egg
1.7 × 1.1 cm
The Link of Times Foundation

Cat. 429
Carl Fabergé. Workmaster:
Alfred Thielemann
*Miniature Castellated Egg
Pendant*
1.7 × 1.1 cm
Gold, enamel, diamonds
The Link of Times Foundation

Cat. 430
Carl Fabergé
*Miniature Castellated White
and Blue Egg Pendant*
1.7 × 1.3 cm
The Link of Times Foundation

Cat. 431
Carl Fabergé
Miniature Blue Stripe Egg
1.9 × 1.2 cm
The Link of Times Foundation

Cat. 432
Carl Fabergé
*Czarina Alexandra Egg-shaped
charm*
2 × 1.2 cm
The Link of Times Foundation

Cat. 433
Carl Fabergé
Miniature Primrose Egg
Gold, enamel
1.8 × 1.2 cm
The Link of Times Foundation

Cat. 434
Carl Fabergé
*Miniature White Egg with
Square-cut Ruby*
Gold, enamel, rubies
1.8 × 1.3 cm
The Link of Times Foundation

Cat. 435
Carl Fabergé
*Miniature Gunmetal Blue
Egg*
Gold, enamel
1.9 × 1.2 cm
The Link of Times Foundation

Cat. 436
Carl Fabergé
Miniature Royal Blue Egg
1.7 × 1.3 cm
The Link of Times Foundation

Cat. 437
Carl Fabergé
Miniature Stars Egg
1.7 × 1.1 cm
The Link of Times Foundation

Cat. 438
Carl Fabergé. Workmaster:
Auguste Holmström
Coronation Box, in case
St. Petersburg, 1896
Gold, enamel, diamonds
9.5 cm
The Link of Times Foundation
(Reproduced p. 167)

Cat. 439
Carl Fabergé. Workmaster:
Michael Perkhin
Rocaille Box
St. Petersburg, before 1899
Gold, enamel, diamonds
9.5 cm
The Link of Times Foundation

Cat. 440
Carl Fabergé. Workmaster:
Michael Perkhin
Louis XVI-style Ladies' Cigarette Case
St. Petersburg, 1899-1903
Gold, enamel, diamonds, pearls
8.2 cm
The Link of Times Foundation

Cat. 441
Carl Fabergé
Smoke-quartz Bust of Alexander III, in case
The Link of Times Foundation

Cat. 442
Carl Fabergé
Pipe Cigarette Holder
Nephrite, diamonds
The Link of Times Foundation
(Reproduced p. 164)

Cat. 443
Carl Fabergé. Workmaster:
Michael Perkhin
Serpent Pen
St. Petersburg, 1886-1899
Nephrite, gold, diamonds
17.7 cm
The Link of Times Foundation

Cat. 444
Carl Fabergé. Workmaster:
Auguste Holmström
Prince Waldemar Paper Knife
St. Petersburg, 1899-1908
Nephrite, gold, garnet
The Link of Times Foundation

Cat. 445
Carl Fabergé
Grand Duchess Olga's Paper Knife
St. Petersburg, 1899-1908
Nephrite, gold, enamel, diamonds
22.8 cm
The Link of Times Foundation
(Reproduced p. 164)

Cat. 446
Carl Fabergé. Workmaster:
Henrik Wigström
Globe Clock, with key
St. Petersburg, 1908-1917
Gold, rock crystal, nephrite, enamel
H. 21 cm
The Link of Times Foundation

Cat. 447
Carl Fabergé
Nobel Necklace/Bracelet
1912
Platinum, silver, diamonds, rock crystal
L. 33.3 cm
The Link of Times Foundation
(Reproduced p. 166)

Cat. 448
Carl Fabergé. Workmaster:
Michael Perkhin
A pair of opera glasses
St. Petersburg, 1899-1903
Gold, enamel, diamonds
10.5 cm
The Link of Times Foundation
(Reproduced p. 166)

Cat. 449
Carl Fabergé
Imperial Parasol Handle with Empress Alexandra's monogram
St. Petersburg, 1896-1917
Bowenite, gold, enamel, diamonds
6.5 cm
The Link of Times Foundation

Cat. 450
Carl Fabergé. Workmaster:
Michael Perkhin
Swirl Egg with Jeweled and Enameled Chain
St. Petersburg, 1886-1899
Gold, enamel, diamonds, pearls
2 cm (egg); 60 cm (chain)
The Link of Times Foundation

Cat. 451
Carl Fabergé
Miniature candy box in the form of a Louis XVI-style armchair, in case
The Link of Times Foundation
(Reproduced p. 165)

Cat. 452
Carl Fabergé
Miniature Pedestal Scent Flacon
The Link of Times Foundation

Cat. 453
Carl Fabergé
A miniature watering can, in fitted case
Nephrite, gold, enamel, diamonds
10.5 cm
The Link of Times Foundation
(Reproduced p. 164)

Cat. 454
Carl Fabergé. Workmaster:
Henrik Wigström
Wild Pansy Sprig
Nephrite, gold, enamel, diamonds
10.5 cm
The Link of Times Foundation
(Reproduced p. 163)

Cat. 455
Carl Fabergé. Master goldsmith: Michael Perkhin
Imperial Presentation Frame, in case
St. Petersburg, 1899-1903
Presented by the Emperor Alexander III to his wife Maria Feodorovna whose monogram decorates the frame
Gold, rock crystal, diamonds, gilded silver, wood
37.2 cm
The Link of Times Foundation

Cat. 456
Carl Fabergé
Queen Alexandra Seal
The Link of Times Foundation

Cat. 457
Carl Fabergé
George V Presentation Seal
The Link of Times Foundation

Cat. 458
Carl Fabergé
Ivan Kalita Bowl
Moscow, 1899-1908
Silver, gilding, emeralds, rubies
15.8 cm
The Link of Times Foundation

Cat. 459
A. Pasetti
Portrait of the Grand Duchess Maria Pavlovna (Wladimir)
St. Petersburg, 1898
Photograph, collodion technique, cabinet card
The Link of Times Foundation

Cat. 460
Photograph of Czar Alexander III with his family
Photograph
The Link of Times Foundation

Cat. 461
Photograph of Czar Alexander III
Photograph
The Link of Times Foundation

Cat. 462
Ch. Bergamasko
Photograph of the Empress Maria Feodorovna
St. Petersburg
Photograph
The Link of Times Foundation

Cat. 463
Photograph of the Empress Maria Feodorovna
Photograph
The Link of Times Foundation

Cat. 464
Photograph of Czar Alexander III
Photograph
The Link of Times Foundation

Cat. 465
Photograph of Czar Nicholas II and Czarevich Aleksey
Photograph
The Link of Times Foundation

Cat. 466
Photograph of Czar Nicholas II
Photograph
The Link of Times Foundation

Cat. 467
Portrait of Grand Duchess Elizabeth Feodorovna
Photograph, cabinet card
The Link of Times Foundation

Cat. 468
Photograph of the Empress Alexandra Feodorovna with her eldest daughters in a garden
Photograph
The Link of Times Foundation

Cat. 469
Gan et Co
Photograph of the Empress Alexandra Feodorovna holding a baby
Tsarskoye Selo
Photograph
The Link of Times Foundation

Cat. 470
Carl Fabergé. Workmaster: Michael Perkhin
Coronation Egg with a surprise inside
St. Petersburg, 1897
Gift from Emperor Nicholas II to his wife Alexandra Feodorovna
Enamel, gold, diamonds, rubies, platinum, rock crystal
H. 12.7 cm
The Link of Times Foundation
(Reproduced p. 169)

Cat. 471
Drawing room chair
Russia, St. Petersburg (?), end of 19th- beginning of 20th centuries
Walnut, sculpture, plaster coating, silver coating, damask taffetas
102 x 49 x 44 cm
The State Historical Museum, Moscow, GIM 74319/D II – 566

Cat. 472-483
Traveling tea set which belonged to the Grand Duke Sergei Alexandrovich Romanov
Russia, St. Petersburg, Carl Boyanovsky's workshop, 1839
Silver, bone, metal, nacre
Samovar with lid on a base (H. 52 cm)
Serving plate for the samovar (H. 2.1 cm)
Cover for the samovar pipe (Diam. 6.2 cm)
Samovar tray (81 x 52 cm)
Tray: Sazikov firm, 1838 (3.2 x 39.3 x 21.9 cm)
Cake plate (35 x 33.4 cm)
Case: 1860s, wood, copper, leather (39 x 60 x 91 cm)
The State Historical Museum, Moscow, GIM 68257/407-408
OK 8308, GIM 68257/409
OK 8309, GIM 68257/410
OK 8310, GIM 68257/411
OK 8311, GIM 68257/412
OK 8312, GIM 68257/413
OK 8313, GIM 68257/407-418 OK 8308-8318

Cat. 484
A wine set made up of a loving cup, a wine ladle, a tray and eight wine tasting cups.
Russia, Moscow, Pavel Ovchinnikov firm, 1889
Silver
Loving cup (H. 22 cm)
Wine ladle (5 x 9.7 x 6.6 cm)
Tray (6.5 x 42.8 x 42,8 cm)
Cups (5 x 9.6 x 6.6 cm)
The State Historical Museum, Moscow, GIM 97845/1 OK 15535/1

Cat. 485
M. V. Folomin
Decorative ladle (kovch)
Russia, Kiev, beginning of 20th century
Silver, glass
25.5 x 30 x 18.5 cm
The State Historical Museum, Moscow, GIM 82280/2 OK 13975

Cat. 486
Tankard
Russia, Moscow, Pavel Ovchinnikov firm, 1873
Silver, gilding
H. 47 cm
The State Historical Museum, Moscow, GIM 53054/225 OK 3768
(Reproduced p.102)

Cat. 487
Vase
Russia, Moscow, 1908-1917
Silver, crystal
45 x 18.5 x 24 cm
The State Historical Museum, Moscow, GIM 107098 OK 23188

Cat. 488
Writing set
Russia, Moscow, 1899-1907
Silver
13.3 x 25.5 x 21.5 cm
The State Historical Museum, Moscow, GIM 109154/25 OK 23573
(Reproduced p. 233)

Cat. 489
Paper Cutter
Russia, Moscow, 1908-1917
Silver
38.5 cm
The State Historical Museum, Moscow, GIM 103173/14 OK 21112

Cat. 490
Decorative plate
Gift of the Nijni Novgorod nobility to "Their Imperial Highnesses" on the occasion of the 300th anniversary of the Romanov House
Russia, Moscow, I Khlebnikov firm, 1913
Silver, wood, enamel, amethyst, chalcedony, glass
Diam. 64.5 cm
The State Historical Museum, Moscow, GIM 90889 OK 14594
(Reproduced p. 103)

Cat. 491
Table centrepiece based on the model of the Minin and Pojarsky monument in the Red Square, Moscow
Moscow, G. Schmidt factory, middle of the 1850s
Bronze, wood
28 x 14.5 x 8.5 cm
The State Historical Museum, Moscow, GIM 42567 BR 2998

Cat. 492
Paperweight made based on the model of the "Unicorn" cannon
Moscow, G. Schmidt workshop, middle of the 1850s
Bronze, marble
12 x 17 x 11 cm
The State Historical Museum, Moscow, GIM 79839 BR 1497

Cat. 493
Paperweight made based on the model of the "King of Cannons" monument
Moscow, 1880s
Bronze, white metal, marble
10.5 x 22 x 10.5 cm
The State Historical Museum, Moscow, GIM 105426 BR 2492

Cat. 494
Table centrepiece based on the model of the Chapel-Monument of the Borodino plain
Moscow, G. Schmidt factory, middle of the 1850s
Bronze
31.5 x. 13 x 13 cm
The State Historical Museum, Moscow, GIM 74176/1 BR 1823

Cat. 495
Table centrepiece based on the model of the "Queen of Bells"
Moscow, G. Schmidt workshop, middle of the 1850s
Bronze, alloy of zinc
21.5 x 17 x 15 cm
The State Historical Museum, Moscow, GIM 42567 BR 921/1-2

Cat. 496
Round plate with green edging and with a view of the Kremlin from the other side of the Moskva river
Gardner Manufacture, second half of 19th century
Porcelain, underglaze and glaze design, gilding
Diam. 38.2 cm
State Ceramics Museum and 18th century Kuskovo estate, FR 1572 KP 15610
(Reproduced p. 229)

Cat. 497
Round plate with green edging and with view of St. Basil the Blessed Church in Moscow
Gardner Manufacture, 1850s-1860s
Porcelain, glaze, gilding
Diam. 37.8 cm
State Ceramics Museum and 18th century Kuskovo estate, FR 1571 KP 15609
(Reproduced p. 224)

Cat. 498
Dish with the Ivan Vekily bell tower in the Kremlin
Popov Manufacture, 1860s
Porcelain, glaze, gilding
Diam. 52 cm
State Ceramics Museum and 18th century Kuskovo estate, FR 467 KP 15534
(Reproduced p. 132)

Cat. 499
Round dish with view of the Red Square, Moscow
Gardner Manufacture, 1850s

Porcelain, glaze, gilding, guilloche
Diam. 40 cm
State Ceramics Museum and
18th century Kuskovo estate,
FR 477 KP 15540

Cat. 500
Plate belonging the Babigon service with a view of the Pachkov house in Moscow
Imperial Porcelain
Manufacture, 1820s
Porcelain, glaze,
gilding, guilloche
Diam. 21.8 cm
State Ceramics Museum and
18th century Kuskovo estate,
FR 10952 KP 15480

Cat. 501
Plate belonging to the Babigon service with views of the gates of Saint Nicolas of Kitai-Gorod in Moscow
Imperial Porcelain
Manufacture, 1840s
Porcelain, glaze, gilding
Diam. 21.8 cm
State Ceramics Museum and
18th century Kuskovo estate,
FR 10953 KP 15481

Cat. 502
Small plate belonging to the Babigon service, decorated with a leaf ornament gilded onto on a grey background with view of the Sparrow Hills
Imperial Porcelain
Manufacture, 1824
Porcelain, glaze, gilding
Diam. 22 cm
State Ceramics Museum and
18th century Kuskovo estate,
FR 4751 KP 15471

Cat. 503
Little plate with a view of the Boarding School
Safronov Manufacture, 1820s-1830s
Porcelain, design in overglaze,
gilding
Diam. 21.6 cm
State Ceramics Museum and
18th century Kuskovo estate,
FR 4725 KP 17599

Cat. 504
Small white plate with a monochrome image of the Sukharev Tower
Safronov Manufacture, 1820s-1830s
Porcelain, glaze, gilding
Diam. 21.6 cm
State Ceramics Museum and
18th century Kuskovo estate,
FR 4764 KP 17630

Cat. 505 to 517
Pieces belonging to Grand Duke Constantine Nicholaevich's porcelain service
St. Petersburg, Imperial
Porcelain Manufacture,
1848-1852, (Project of the
painter F. G. Solntsev,
1847-1848)
Porcelain, underglaze,
painting, gilding, guilloche,
bronze.
(Reproduced pp. 226 and 232)

Soup dish
The State Historical Museum,
Moscow, GIM 62549/3339 FF
(H. 4.7 cm; diam. 24 cm),
GIM 62549/3343 FF
(H. 5.1 cm; diam. 23.6 cm),
GIM 62549/3347 FF
(H. 4.8 cm; diam. 23.9 cm),
GIM 62549/3350 FF (H. 5
cm; diam. 23.6 cm)

Small plates
The State Historical Museum,
Moscow, GIM 62549/3351 FF
(H. 3.7 cm; diam. 23.6 cm),
GIM 62549/3355 FF (H. 3.3
cm ; diam. 23.6 cm), GIM
62549/3359 FF (H. 3.5 cm;
diam. 24 cm), GIM
62549/3361 FF (H. 3.3 cm;
diam. 23.6 cm)

Oval dish
The State Historical Museum,
Moscow, GIM 62549/3363/1 FF
(30.8 × 20.8 cm)

Small oval dish
The State Historical Museum,
Moscow, GIM 62549/3363/2
FF (37.5 × 24.4 cm)

Large oval dish
The State Historical Museum,
Moscow, GIM 62549/3364 FF
(45.5 × 29.8 cm)

Sauce boat
The State Historical Museum,
Moscow, GIM 62549/3321 FF
(H. 29 cm)

Display stand with three shelves (made of 7 elements in porcelain and 6 in bronze)
The State Historical Museum,
Moscow, GIM 62549/3383 FF
(H. 52.5 cm)
(Reproduced p. 230)

Cat. 518
Serving dish (without lid)
Pieces of Great Duke
Constantine Nicholaevich's
ceremonial service. Based on
F. G. Solntsev's project.
Imperial Porcelain
Manufacture, 1848
Porcelain, polychrome glaze,
gilding
13.8 × 16.5 cm
State Ceramics Museum and
18th century Kuskovo estate,
ST 16372 KP 10405/1

Cat. 519
Sauce boat on small pedestal
Pieces of Great Duke
Constantine Nicholaevich's
ceremonial service. Based on
F. G. Solntsev's project.
Imperial Porcelain
Manufacture, 1848
Porcelain, polychrome glaze,
gilding
H. 15.2 cm
State Ceramics Museum and
18th century Kuskovo estate,
FR 16373 KP 10405/2

Cat. 520
Tall-stemmed cup belonging to a dessert service
Pieces of Great Duke
Constantine Nicholaevich's
ceremonial service. Based on
F. G. Solntsev's project.
Imperial Porcelain
Manufacture, 1848
Porcelain, polychrome glaze,
gilding
H. 36.5 cm
State Ceramics Museum and
18th century Kuskovo estate,
FR 16374 KP 10405/3

Cat. 521
Small fruit bowl on stem, belonging to a dessert service
Pieces of Great Duke
Constantine Nicholaevich's
ceremonial service. Based on
F. G. Solntsev's project.
Imperial Porcelain
Manufacture, 1848
Porcelain, polychrome glaze,
gilding
H. 12 cm
State Ceramics Museum and
18th century Kuskovo estate,
FR 4007 KP 20883

Cat. 522 and 523
Round dish
Pieces of Great Duke
Constantine Nicholaevich's
ceremonial service. Based on
F. G. Solntsev's project.
Imperial Porcelain
Manufacture, 1848
Porcelain, polychrome glaze,
gilding
Diam. 32.3 cm
State Ceramics Museum and
18th century Kuskovo estate,
FR 16375 KP 10405/4, FR
16376 KP 10405/5

Cat. 524 and 525
Oval dish
Pieces of Great Duke
Constantine Nicholaevich's
ceremonial service. Based on
F. G. Solntsev's project.
Imperial Porcelain
Manufacture, 1848
Porcelain, polychrome glaze,
gilding
State Ceramics Museum and
18th century Kuskovo estate,
FR 16377 KP 10405/6
(37.4 × 24.3 cm), FR 16378
KP 10405/7 (40.6 × 27.1 cm)

Cat. 526 to 531
Small plate
Pieces of Great Duke
Constantine Nicholaevich's
ceremonial service. Based on
F. G. Solntsev's project.
Imperial Porcelain
Manufacture, 1848
Porcelain, polychrome glaze,
gilding
State Ceramics Museum and
18th century Kuskovo estate,
FR 1346 KP 23150, FR 16381
KP 10405/10, FR 16382 KP
10405/11, FR 16383 KP
10405/12, FR 16385 KP
10405/14, FR 16386 KP
10405/15 (diam. 23.5 cm)

Cat. 532 to 537
Soup dish
Pieces of Great Duke
Constantine Nicholaevich's
ceremonial service. Based on
F. G. Solntsev's project.
Imperial Porcelain
Manufacture, 1848

Porcelain, polychrome glaze, gilding
Diam. 23.3 cm
State Ceramics Museum and 18th century Kuskovo estate, FR 16387 KP 10405/16, FR 16388 KP 10405/17, FR 16389 KP 10405/18, FR 16390 KP 10405/19, FR 16391 KP 10405/20, FR 16392 KP 10405/21

Cat. 538
Serving dish on stem
Added to Great Duke Constantine Nicholaevich's service
Kornilov Manufacture, 1860s
Porcelain, polychrome glaze, gilding
32 × 21 cm
State Ceramics Museum and 18th century Kuskovo estate, FR 16393 KP 10406

Cat. 539
K. A. Korovin
Moskva bridge (Moskovorietsky)
1914
Oil on canvas
104 × 134 cm
The State Historical Museum, Moscow, GIM 70156, K-322

Cat. 540
V. V. Vereschagin
View of the Kremlin
1860
Oil on canvas
33 × 40.5 cm
Ekaterina and Vladimir Semenikhin Collection

Cat. 541
Chichkin
Stream in the forest
1883
Oil on canvas
76 × 120.5 cm
Ekaterina and Vladimir Semenikhin Collection
(Reproduced p. 28)

Cat. 542
V. M. Vasnetsov
"The only son" (model of the plan of the central nave)
1885-1896
Oil on canvas
70 × 138 cm
The State Tretyakov Gallery, inv. 1022
(Reproduced p. 245)

Cat. 543
I. N. Kramskoy
Portrait of the painter Alexander Dmitrievich Litovtchenko
1878
Oil on canvas
134 × 108.2 cm
The State Tretyakov Gallery, inv. 671
(Reproduced p. 240)

Cat. 544
A. I. Kuindji
In the North
1879
Oil on canvas
178 × 146.5 cm
The State Tretyakov Gallery, inv. 881
(Reproduced p. 242)

Cat. 545
I. I. Levitan
A summer evening
1900
Oil on canvas
49 × 73 cm
The State Tretyakov Gallery, inv. 1498
(Reproduced p. 243)

Cat. 546
V. E. Makovsky
Barrel organ player
1879
Oil on canvas
116 × 133 cm
The State Tretyakov Gallery, inv. 603
(Reproduced p. 241)

Cat. 547
G. G. Miassoedov
Regulation of February 19, 1861
1873
Oil on canvas
138.2 × 209 cm
The State Tretyakov Gallery, inv. 640

Cat. 548
I. E. Repin
Leon Tolstoy resting in a forest
1891
Oil on canvas
77.5 × 66 cm
The State Tretyakov Gallery, inv. 6313
(Reproduced p. 239)

Cat. 549
V. I. Surikov
A czarina's visit to a monastery
1912
Oil on canvas
174 × 232 cm
The State Tretyakov Gallery, J-158
(Reproduced p. 29)

Cat. 550
A. A. Vassiliev
Landscape with pine trees
1860
Oil on canvas
22.5 × 16 cm
Ekaterina and Vladimir Semenikhin Collection

Cat. 551
A. K. Savrassov
Pietchersky Monastery
1870
Oil on canvas
22.9 × 33.5 cm
Ekaterina and Vladimir Semenikhin Collection

Cat. 552
Makovsky
Ukrainian woman
1880
Oil on cardboard
260 × 135 cm
Musées de la Citadelle, dépôt de l'Observatoire Océanologique Villefranche s/ mer, inv. 84.1.14

Cat. 553
Polenov
Winter
Oil on cardboard
260 × 135 cm
Musées de la Citadelle, dépôt de l'Observatoire Océanologique Villefranche s/ mer, inv. 84.1.15

Cat. 554
N. I. Podkliutchnikov
The interior of the artist's apartment on Tverskaya street (Tver street) in Moscow
Second half of the 1850s
Oil on canvas
96 × 143 cm
The State Historical Museum, Moscow, GIM 42572/I 1-2176

Cat. 555
C. A. Ton
Project for the Cathedral of Christ the Savior. Main façade. Final version of the exterior of the cathedral.
Early 1850s
Paper, watercolor, Indian ink, brush, feather
53.6 × 68.9 cm
The State Historical Museum, Moscow, GIM 68558, R-1874

Cat. 556
Plates from the album "Views of the church, living quarters and reception rooms of the house of the Moscow governor general."
Paper, passe-partout, watercolor, white lead
63.8 × 82.6 cm

I. I. Nivinsky
Private church dedicated to St. Serge of Radonege and St. Alexander Nevsky. View of the iconostasis
1904
The State Historical Museum, Moscow, GIM 47542, A-105/m

I. I. Nivinsky
Boudoir having belonged to Grand Duchess Elizabeth Feodorovna
1905
The State Historical Museum, Moscow, GIM 47542, A-105/v

A. P. Barychnikov
Inside view of the chamber of Grand Duke Sergei Alexandrovich
Moscow, 1902
The State Historical Museum, Moscow, GIM 47542, A-105/o
(Reproduced p. 137)

V. P. Trofimov
White salon with portrait of Emperor Nicholas II
Moscow, 1900s
The State Historical Museum, Moscow, GIM 47542, A-105/n

I. I. Nivinsky
The Grand Duchess Elizabeth Feodorovna's salon
Moscow, 1909
The State Historical Museum, Moscow, GIM 47542, A-105/d

A. P. Barychnikov
Red Salon with portraits of Emperor Alexander III and Empress Maria Feodorovna
1902
The State Historical Museum, Moscow, GIM 47542, A-105/k
(Reproduced p. 122)

Cat. 562
V. A. Kuznetsov
Portrait of Emperor Nicholas II
1914
Oil on canvas
260 × 142 cm
The State Museum Preserve
"Tsarskoye Selo,"
St. Petersburg, ED-634-X
(Reproduced p. 255)

Cat. 563
N. K. Bodarevsky
Portrait of the Empress Alexandra Feodorovna
1907
Oil on canvas
268 × 135 cm
The State Museum Preserve
"Tsarskoye Selo,"
St. Petersburg, ED-635-X
(Reproduced p. 255)

Cat. 564
Master I. Sazikov
Plaque with the portraits of Emperor Alexander II's grandchildren
Russia, St. Petersburg, 1879
Silver, enamel, velvet, leather, non precious metal
39.6 × 26.9 cm
The State Museum Preserve
"Tsarskoye Selo,"
St. Petersburg, ED-723-IV

Cat. 565
Woman's clothing (bodice, skirt)
Moscow, Russia, N.P. Lamanova workshop, 1902-1905
Woolen cloth, filmy fabric, silk, satin, machine lace, metal
l. of skirt: 109 cm/145 cm
The State Historical Museum, Moscow, GIM 82820 B-1237/1-2

Cat. 566
Colonel's Hungarian Hussar uniform, Life Guard Grodno Hussar Regiment
Russia, early 20th century
Cloth, metal, silvered cord, silvered lace, silk, cashmere
l. 67 cm
The State Museum Preserve
"Tsarskoye Selo,"
St. Petersburg, ED-579-II KP-6673, ED-581-II KP-6675, ED-580-II KP-6674

Cat. 567
Officer's uniform from His Imperial Majesty Czar Alexis Nicholaevich's 12th Siberian Orient Infantry
Russia, St. Petersburg, 1910s
Tunic: woolen cloth, metal, golden thread, silk serge, atlas silk, golden embroidery, gilding (l. 55 cm)
The State Museum Preserve
"Tsarskoye Selo,"
St. Petersburg, ED-828-II KP-6904/6915

Cat. 568
Small table from the "Silver Drawing Room" set
Moscow, Schmitt fabrication, last quarter of the 19th century
Limewood, sculpture, plaster coating, silver coating, damask satin
73 × 46 cm
The State Historical Museum, Moscow, GIM 74124/D II – 514
(Reproduced p. 143)

Cat. 569
Chair from the "Silver Drawing Room" set
Moscow, Schmitt factory, last quarter of 19th century
Limewood, sculpture, plaster coating, silver coating, damask satin
105 × 45 × 47 cm
The State Historical Museum, Moscow, GIM 74124/D II – 516
(Reproduced p. 143)

Cat. 570 to 576
Pieces belonging to the Purple Service
Russia, St. Petersburg, Imperial Porcelain Manufacture, 1905-1906, 1908
Based on a sketch by E. I. Kremer
Porcelain: monochrome painting on over-glaze, gilding on the paste, guilloche
Soup dish (H. 3.7 cm; diam. 24.7 cm) ED-1656-I
Dinner plate (H. 1.7 cm; diam. 24.7 cm) ED-1690-I
Dessert plate (H. 1.2 cm; diam. 22.7 cm) ED-1736-I
Cake plate (H. 1.2 cm; diam. 18 cm) ED-1798-I
Cup (4.1 × 11.6 × 7.7 cm) ED-1858/1-I
Saucer (1.5 × 14.5 × 12.9 cm) ED-1858/2-I
The State Museum Preserve
"Tsarskoye Selo," St. Petersburg

Cat. 577
Gospel
Moscow, Moscow printers, 1627
Paper, wood, leather, fabric, metal
31 × 20 × 9 cm
The State Museum Preserve
"Tsarskoye Selo,"
St. Petersburg, ED-1994-XIV

Cat. 578
L. Bernstamm
Bust of Czar Nicholas II
Sevres bisque
47 × 33 × 18 cm
City of Menton, inv. 87.1662

Cat. 579
L. Bernstamm
Bust of Grand Duchess Alexandra
1905
Sevres bisque
47 × 33 × 16 cm
City of Menton, inv. 87.1661

Cat. 580
Emperor Nicholas II, Empress Alexandra Feodorovna, Grand Duchess Olga Nicholaevna, Grand Duke Sergei Alexandrovich, Grand Duchess Elizabeth Feodorovna at the moment of their solemn appearance on the Red Porch (Great Stairway of Honor) during the Emperor's stay in Moscow
Moscow, 1903
"C.E. de Hahn and Cie" studio
Photograph
Russian State Cinematographic and Photographic Archives, al. 215, sn.7

Cat. 581
Imperial outing for the Cathedral of the Dormition
Moscow, 1903
"C.E. de Hahn and Cie" studio
Photograph
Russian State Cinematographic and Photographic Archives, al. 215, sn.9

Cat. 582
Departure of Empress Alexandra Feodorovna and Grand Duchess Olga Nicholayevna in a barouche
Moscow, 1903
"C.E. de Hahn and Cie" studio
Photograph
Russian State Cinematographic and Photographic Archives, al. 215, sn.11

Cat. 583
Banquet in the Room of Columns of the Assembly of Nobles during the Emperor's stay in Moscow
Moscow, 1903
"C.E. de Hahn and Cie" studio
Photograph
Russian State Cinematographic and Photographic Archives, al. 215, sn.14

Cat. 584
Emperor Nicholas II and Empress Alexandra Feodorovna during a visit to the Monastery of the Resurrection of the New Jerusalem
Province of Moscow, 1903
"C.E. de Hahn and Cie" studio
Photograph
Russian State Cinematographic and Photographic Archives, al. 215, sn.40
(Reproduced p. 250)

Cat. 585
Emperor Nicholas II reviews the students of the Cadet Corps during the festivities on the occasion of the centennial of the Patriotic War of 1812
Moscow, August 27-29, 1912
"C. E. de Hahn and Cie" Studio
Photograph
Russian State Cinematographic and Photographic Archives, al. 243, sn.29

Cat. 586
Emperor Nicholas II and his daughters Olga, Tatiana, Maria entering the Church of Christ the Savior
Moscow, August 27-29, 1912
"C. E. de Hahn and Cie" Studio
Photograph
Russian State Cinematographic and Photographic Archives, al. 243, sn.91

Cat. 587
Departure of Emperor Nicholas II and his daughters after visiting the Church of Christ the Savior
Moscow, August 27-29, 1912
"C. E. de Hahn and Cie" Studio
Photograph

Russian State Cinematographic and Photographic Archives, al. 243, sn.94

Cat. 588
Emperor Nicholas II and Empress Maria Feodorovna going toward the Alexander III monument near the Church of Christ the Savior
Moscow, August 27-29, 1912
"C. E. de Hahn and Cie" Studio
Photograph
Russian State Cinematographic and Photographic Archives, al. 244, sn.36

Cat. 589
Emperor Nicholas II and Empress Maria Feodorovna going toward the Alexander III monument near the Church of Christ the Savior
Moscow, August 27-29, 1912
"C. E. de Hahn and Cie" Studio
Photograph
Russian State Cinematographic and Photographic Archives, al. 244, sn.37

Cat. 590
Ladies from the Court on the stairway near the Church of Christ the Savior during the inaugural ceremony of the Alexander III monument.
Moscow, August 27-29, 1912
"C. E. de Hahn and Cie" Studio
Photograph
Russian State Cinematographic and Photographic Archives, al. 244, sn.55

Cat. 591
The public near the monument to Alexander III the day of its solemn inauguration
Moscow, August 27-29, 1912
"C. E. de Hahn and Cie" Studio
Photograph
Russian State Cinematographic and Photographic Archives, al. 244, sn.61

Cat. 592
Emperor Nicholas II and Empress Alexandra Feodorovna at the Saint Serge Trinity Lavra
Province of Moscow, August 27-29, 1912
"C. E. de Hahn and Cie" Studio
Photograph
Russian State Cinematographic and Photographic Archives, al. 244, sn.69

Cat. 593
Anonymous
Anastasia (?), Alexis and Maria Vichniakova
Photograph
The State Historical Museum, Moscow, GIM 95171, I-VI 31276

Cat. 594
C. E. de Hahn
Olga and Tatiana
Photograph
The State Historical Museum, Moscow, GIM 95171, I-VI 5135

Cat. 595
Anonymous
Alexis
Photograph
The State Historical Museum, Moscow, GIM 98221, I-VII 31192/196
(Reproduced p. 263)

Cat. 596
C. E. de Hahn
No title (Czarevich Alexis on the bridge, 1910-?)
Photograph
The State Historical Museum, Moscow, GIM 95171, I-VII 37828

Cat. 597
Anonymous
No title (Czarevich Alexis on the bridge next to a sailboat model)
Photograph
The State Historical Museum, Moscow, GIM 98221, I-VI 37841/158

Cat. 598
C. E. de Hahn
Promenade at Tsarskoye Selo
Photograph
The State Historical Museum, Moscow, GIM 70056, I-VI 5166
(Reproduced p. 252)

Cat. 599
Anonymous
Alexis
Photograph
The State Historical Museum, Moscow, GIM 95171, I-VI 5303

Cat. 600
Anonymous
Alexis
Photograph
The State Historical Museum, Moscow, GIM 70156, I-VI 7524

Cat. 601
Grand Duchesses Olga and Tatiana Nicholayevna.
Photograph
The State Historical Museum, Moscow, I-III chrom. 18823

Cat. 602
Anonymous
No title. The Czarevich Alexis, Maria Vichniakova and the sailor Derevenko
Photograph
The State Historical Museum, Moscow, GIM 95171, I-VI 31264

Cat. 603
C. E. de Hahn
On the jetty
October 8, 1931
Photograph
The State Historical Museum, Moscow, GIM 95171. 21_02028-95171

Cat. 604
F. Boissonas and F. Eggler
Maria
1910
Photograph
The State Historical Museum, Moscow, GIM 98221, I-VI 31207

Cat. 605
C. E. de Hahn
Olga
Livadia, 1900
Photograph
The State Historical Museum, Moscow, GIM 95171, I-VI 31221

Cat. 606
F. Boissonas and F. Eggler
Olga
Photograph
The State Historical Museum, Moscow, GIM 70156, I-VI 5131

Cat. 607
C. E. de Hahn
Olga
Photograph
The State Historical Museum, Moscow, GIM 95171, I-VI 5285

Cat. 608
C. E. de Hahn
Tatiana
1911 (?)
Photograph
The State Historical Museum, Moscow, GIM 98221, I-VI 37824/103

Cat. 609
F. Boissonas and F. Eggler
Olga and Tatiana
Photograph
The State Historical Museum, Moscow, GIM 95171, I-VI 51265

Cat. 610
C. E. de Hahn
Olga, Tatiana, Maria and Anastasia Nicholayevna
Photograph
The State Historical Museum, Moscow, GIM 70156, I-VI 7758
(Reproduced p. 261)

Cat. 611
Grand Duchess Anastasia Nicholaevna. Open letter
Photograph
The State Historical Museum, Moscow, I-III chrom. 18826

Cat. 612
P. Gilliard
Olga, Tatiana, Maria and Anastasia, Biolevje forest Russia, autumn 1913
20 x 27 cm
Photograph
Elysée Museum, Lausanne, call number 036249
(Reproduced p. 270)

Cat. 613
P. Gilliard
The Czarevich Alexis Nicholaevich and Pierre Gilliard going fishing on the Dniepr
Mohilev, Russia, around 1916
20 x 20.5 cm
Photograph
Elysée Museum, Lausanne, call number 036211

Cat. 614
P. Gilliard
Alexandra Alexandrovna Tegleva in a canoe with the Czarevich Alexis Nicholaevich
Crimea, 1911
22.5 x 22.5 cm

Photograph
Elysée Museum, Lausanne,
call number 036211

Cat. 615
P. Gilliard
Pierre Gilliard and Alexis Nicholaevich
Tsarskoye Selo, Russia, 1916
22.5 × 22.5 cm
Photograph
Elysée Museum, Lausanne,
call number 0285081

Cat. 616
P. Gilliard
Alexis Nicholaevich
Tsarskoye Selo, Russia, 1913
22.5 × 26 cm
Photograph
Elysée Museum, Lausanne,
call number 027650

Cat. 617
P. Gilliard
Alexis Nicholaevich with the Emperor at the Russian army headquarters
Mohilev, Russia, 1915
22.5 × 22.5 cm
Photograph
Elysée Museum, Lausanne,
call number 028518

Cat. 618
P. Gilliard
Alexis Nicholaevich and Nicholas II
Mohilev, Russia, 1915
20.5 × 21 cm
Photograph
Elysée Museum, Lausanne,
call number 036221
(Reproduced p. 271)

Cat. 619
P. Gilliard
The Emperor Nicholas II in captivity, March 1917
Tsarskoye Selo, Russia, 1917
22.5 × 22.5 cm
Photograph
Elysée Museum, Lausanne,
call number 027645
(Reproduced p. 272)

Cat. 620
P. Gilliard
Alexis Nicholaevich in his toy car
Tsarskoye Selo, Russia, 1913
22.5 × 22.5 cm
Photograph
Elysée Museum, Lausanne,
call number 027652

Cat. 621
P. Gilliard
Alexandra Feodorovna and her son
Livadia Palace, Crimea, 1911
22.5 × 22.5 cm
Photograph
Elysée Museum, Lausanne,
call number 027653

Cat. 622
P. Gilliard
Alexis Nicholaevich standing up in a boat
Peterhof, Russia, 1914
22.5 × 22.5 cm
Photograph
Elysée Museum, Lausanne,
call number 027669

Cat. 623
P. Gilliard
Grand Duchess Maria Nicholaevna working in the classroom
Livadia Palace, Crimea, 1911
22.5 × 22.5 cm
Photograph
Elysée Museum, Lausanne,
call number 027688

Cat. 624
P. Gilliard
Pierre Gilliard with Grand Duchesses Olga, Tatiana
Livadia Palace, Crimea, 1911
22.5 × 22.5 cm
Photograph
Elysée Museum, Lausanne,
call number 027962
(Reproduced p. 270)

Cat. 625
P. Gilliard
Alexis Nicholaevich on his pony
Tsarskoye Selo, Russia, 1913
22.5 × 22.5 cm
Photograph
Elysée Museum, Lausanne,
call number 027966

Cat. 626
P. Gilliard
Tatiana and Anastasia Nicholaevna
Tsarskoye Selo, Russia, 1917
22.5 × 22.5 cm
Photograph
Elysée Museum, Lausanne,
call number 027968

Cat. 627
Anonymous
Portrait of Grand Duchess Tatiana Nicholaevna on horseback in the uniform of the Lancers Wossnessensky No. 8 regiment "Grand Duchess Tatiana."
Peterhof, Russia, August 1913
22.5 × 22.5 cm
Photograph
Elysée Museum, Lausanne,
call number 028515

Cat. 628
P. Gilliard
Alexis Nicholaevich with his spaniel Joy
Livadia Palace, Crimea, 1914
22.5 × 22.5 cm
Photograph
Elysée Museum, Lausanne,
call number 028517

Cat. 629
P. Gilliard
Nicholas II, Alexandra Feodorovna and Alexis Nicholaevich
Mohilev, Russia, 1915
20 × 20.5 cm
Photograph
Elysée Museum, Lausanne,
call number 036213

Cat. 630
P. Gilliard
Alexandra Alexandrovna Tegleva
Livadia Palace, Crimea, 1911
17.5 × 27 cm
Photograph
Elysée Museum, Lausanne,
call number 036220

Cat. 631
P. Gilliard
Self-portrait in his office
Livadia Palace, Crimea, 1911
20.5 × 20.5 cm
Photograph
Elysée Museum, Lausanne,
call number 036224

Cat. 632
P. Gilliard
Olga and Tatiana on the Standart, imperial yacht
Gulf of Finland, June 1914
19.5 × 20.5 cm
Photograph
Elysée Museum, Lausanne,
call number 036232

Cat. 633
P. Gilliard
The Czarevich Alexis Nicholaevich in a canoe
Peterhof, Russia, around 1914
22.5 × 22.5 cm
Photograph
Elysée Museum, Lausanne,
call number 027675

Cat. 634
P. Gilliard
Pierre Gilliard with Olga Nicholaevna
Livadia Palace, Crimea, 1911
22.5 × 22.5 cm
Photograph
Elysée Museum, Lausanne,
call number 027649

Cat. 635
V. A. Serov
Portrait of Prince V. M. Golitsyn (1847-1932)
1906
Oil on canvas
114 × 94 cm
The State Historical Museum,
Moscow, GIM 72304/ I 1-2114

Cat. 636
V. E. Borrissov-Mussatov
Harmony
1900
Tempera on canvas
175.5 × 103.5 cm
The State Tretyakov Gallery,
J – 867
(Reproduced p. 246)

Cat. 637
M. A. Vroubel
Lilacs
1900
Oil on canvas
160.5 × 177 cm
The State Tretyakov Gallery,
inv. 11054
(Reproduced p. 30)

Cat. 638
K. A. Somov
Confidence
1897
Oil on cardboard
53 × 72.2 cm
The State Tretyakov Gallery,
inv. 9178

Cat. 639
M. V. Nesterov
Portrait of Ekaterina Petrovna Nesterova embroidering
1909
Oil on cardboard
43 × 60 cm
The State Tretyakov Gallery,

J-1458
(Reproduced p. 244)

Cat. 640
N. S. Gontcharova
Thistle
1908-1910
Oil on canvas
103 × 73 cm
The State Tretyakov Gallery,
J-1631
(Reproduced p. 31)

Cat. 641
V. E. Tatlin
Still life. Bouquet
1911-1912
Oil on canvas
93 × 48 cm
The State Tretyakov Gallery,
inv. 4319
(Reproduced p. 32)

Cat. 642
M. F. Larionov
Garden of peaches
1903-1904
Oil on canvas
108 × 103 cm
The State Tretyakov Gallery,
J-1689
(Reproduced p. 246)

Cat. 643
M. P. Konchalovsky
Portrait of the sculptor Galouzi
1908
Oil on canvas
40 × 38 cm
Ekaterina and Vladimir
Semenikhin Collection
(Reproduced p. 31)

Cat. 644
B. M. Kustodiev
A Moscow cabaret
1916
Oil on canvas
99.3 × 129.3 cm
The State Tretyakov Gallery,
inv. 25452

Cat. 645
A. V. Kuprin
Landscape. Crimea
1912
Oil on canvas
70.5 × 88 cm
Ekaterina and Vladimir
Semenikhin Collection

Cat. 646
A. V. Lentulov
Church
1916
Oil on canvas
100 × 73 cm
Ekaterina and Vladimir
Semenikhin Collection
(Reproduced p. 33)

Cat. 647
L. S. Popova
Pictorial architectonic with a yellow board
1916
Oil on canvas
92 × 74.5 cm
The State Tretyakov Gallery,
J-1309

Cat. 648
O. V. Rozanova
At the hair-dresser's
1915
Oil on canvas
71.3 × 53.5 cm
The State Tretyakov Gallery,
J-1293
(Reproduced p. 247)

Cat. 649
A. A. Exter
Composition
1914
Oil on canvas
90.7 × 72.5 cm
The State Tretyakov Gallery,
J-1303
(Reproduced p. 248)

Cat. 650
L. Popova
Painterly Architectonic with black board
1916
Oil on canvas
98.5 × 77 cm
Ekaterina and Vladimir
Semenikhin Collection
(Reproduced p. 276)

Cat. 651
L. Popova
Cubist portrait
1915
Oil on canvas
Ekaterina and Vladimir
Semenikhin Collection
(Reproduced p. 277)

Cat. 652
O. Rozanova
Playing cards
1915-1916
Oil on canvas
70 × 62 cm
Ekaterina and Vladimir
Semenikhin Collection
(Reproduced p. 274)

Cat. 653
D. Burliouk
Portrait of a futurist fighter-singer Vassily Kamensky
1916
Oil on canvas
97.2 × 66 cm
The State Tretyakov Gallery,
inv. 9371
(Reproduced p. 249)